The
Life of
Jean Jaurès

Même si les socialistes éteignent un moment toutes les étoiles
du ciel, je veux marcher avec eux dans le chemin sombre
qui mène à la justice, étincelle divine, qui suffira à rallumer
tous les soleils dans toutes les hauteurs de l'espace.

Jean Jaurès

Il a disparu. Mais comme les splendides lueurs qui suivent le
coucher du soleil rayonnent au-dessus de l'Europe sanglante
d'où monte le crépuscule, les reflets de son lumineux
génie, sa bonté dans l'âpre lutte, son optimisme indestructible
dans les désastres mêmes.

Romain Rolland

Jaurès speaking at the Congress of Saint-Quentin, 1911, with
Groussier presiding. Sketch by H. P. Gassier. Caption:
"On aborde, enfin, les rapports de l'*Humanité* et du Patri."

The Life of
JEAN
JAURÈS

HARVEY GOLDBERG

MADISON, MILWAUKEE, AND LONDON 1968
THE UNIVERSITY OF WISCONSIN PRESS

FOR

ALEXANDER WERTH

AND

MICHEL LAUNAY

WISE AND COURAGEOUS MEN

Published by
The University of Wisconsin Press
Box 1379, Madison, Wisconsin 53701

The University of Wisconsin Press, Ltd.
27–29 Whitfield Street, London, W.1

Second printing, 1968

Printed in the United States of America
Library of Congress Catalog Card Number 62–7216

Acknowledgments

I wish to express my deep appreciation to the following professional associates, friends, and institutions for their assistance and service:

M. Gaston Poulain, Conservateur of the Musée Jaurès (Castres), who replied courteously to my many questions and permitted me to use several pictures from the museum's collection as illustrations for this book; Dr. Kool, Miss Hunink, and Mr. van Tijn of the International Institute for Social History (Amsterdam), who granted me full use of the Institute's important archives; the American Philosophical Society, which awarded me a research grant in 1955; Dean Osborn Fuller, Professor Harold Grimm, and Dean Everett Walters of Ohio State University, who unfailingly encouraged and supported my research; Professors Joel Colton of Duke University, Henry Hill of the University of Wisconsin, Aaron Noland of the City College of New York, and John Sperling of Northern Illinois University, who read the manuscript critically and suggested many useful changes; Dr. James Butler, Mr. James Graham, and Mr. Merle Rife, formerly my graduate students at Ohio State University, who willingly exchanged views with me on the history of the Third Republic; and Miss Joan Liftin, who cheerfully typed much of the manuscript from almost illegible copy.

HARVEY GOLDBERG

60, rue de Seine
Paris 6, France
May 1, 1961

Contents

PART IV
YEARS OF PASSION, 1906–1914

Illustrations

PART I

Years
of Growth
1859-1892

Oui, en haut comme en bas, l'ordre social actuel ne fait que des esclaves, car ceux-là ne sont pas des hommes libres qui n'ont ni le temps ni la force de vivre par les parties les plus nobles de leur esprit et de leur âme.

1890

Que le monde sera beau lorsque, en regardant à l'extrémité de la prairie le soleil mourir, l'homme sentira soudain, à un attendrissement étrange de son coeur et de ses yeux, qu'un reflet de la douce lampe de Jésus est mêlé à la lumière apaisée du soir!

1891

1

The Early Years

1859-1885

Late in the evening of July 31, 1914, Jean Jaurès, Socialist deputy, philosopher, and journalist, was killed by an assassin's bullet. An outpouring of emotion, intense and almost uncontrolled, followed the act. Years later, Roger Martin du Gard recovered the high drama of the event, recording the response of the shocked Parisians who watched as the body of Jaurès was carried from the Café du Croissant.

Slowly, in a silence so deep that the footfalls of the bearers were clearly audible, the white-hung stretcher crossed the sidewalk, swayed for a moment in mid-air, then abruptly slid forward into the darkness of the van. Two men sprang in after it. A police officer climbed onto the seat beside the driver. The door was slammed to. Then, as the horse broke into a trot and, escorted by police-men on bicycles, the ambulance started clanging its way toward the Bourse, there rose a sudden clamor, like the roar of an angry sea that drowned the jangling of the bell; it was as though at last flood-gates had fallen, releasing the pent-up emotions of the crowd. "Jaurès! Jaurès! Jaurès! Jaurès forever."[1]

The reaction of the Paris poor, who had so suddenly experienced the loss of their great defender, was collective and general. But at Carmaux, deep in the Tarn, the feeling was different, more intimate, almost famil-ial. Their friend was dead, the deputy who had walked among them

3

for three turbulent decades, so clearly their superior while somehow remaining their equal. Here the word of his death spread rapidly among a near-hysterical people. "The dawn of August 1 broke in upon this stunned workers' city. The miners who were off to the morning shift at 4 A.M., their pouches across their shoulders, heard en route that 'Jaurès had been killed!' They returned home and remained there motionless and speechless. One man said simply: 'They have cut down a mighty oak.' Those who learned the news when they reached the mine gave back their lamps without a word and turned away, staring vacantly, full of feverish tears that would not flow."[2]

The death of any man breaks continuity in the lives of others and leaves a feeling of loss and bewilderment. But the reaction to the death of Jaurès went beyond sorrow and regret. Why did Socialists in Piacenza weep and workers in Liverpool stand thunderstruck? Why was there such grief in London, in Rome, in Milan? The novelist Anatole France wrote of Jaurès' "goodness and gentleness," the philosopher Gabriel Séailles of his "generosity." Speaking for the organized workers of France, Léon Jouhaux said: "Jaurès embodied our thought, our doctrine; in his spirit, we will face the future." Sensitive judgments no doubt, but there was something more. A popular instinct, perhaps, that leaders of courage and integrity such as his are hard to find; a feeling that the future would be emptier, more difficult without him; an appreciation that life would be different because of him.

What one man meant to many others must always remain uncertain and elusive. But to approach the meaning of Jaurès at all, to grasp his significance in the France of the Third Republic and the Europe before 1914, one must first retrace the steps of his crowded and complex career.

I

At noon on September 3, 1859, in a modest house on the rue Reclusane, city of Castres, department of the Tarn, a son was born to Jean-Henri Jules Jaurès and his wife Marie-Adélaïde Barbaza. The event, recorded in the city hall on September 4 and in the record of baptism on September 6, must surely have been a momentous one for parents whose marriage had been childless for over six years. The baby, elaborately christened August-Marie-Joseph-Jean, came to be known simply as Jean Jaurès.[3]

The family into which Jaurès was born was bourgeois, though certainly not prosperous. The Jaurès and Barbaza clans had settled in the Tarn over a century before; Jean's maternal great-grandfather, according to the earliest records, had established himself in Castres in 1758 as a cloth merchant; and both his father and mother were natives of the city, born there in 1819 and 1822 respectively. In the rather sketchy history of the Jaurèses and Barbazas, one encounters a few members of both families whose achievements were far from negligible. The Barbazas especially, moderately successful in the textile trade, could point pridefully to Joseph Salvayre, Adélaïde's grandfather, who was once mayor of Castres and then, for a considerable time, professor of philosophy in the Institut Bonhomme, which in 1840 became the Collège de Castres. His was reputedly a free-thinking "Voltairian,"[4] learned and enlightened.

The Jaurèses were neither substantial economically nor prominent socially. In fact, the Barbazas viewed with considerable apprehension Adélaïde's marriage to Jules Jaurès in 1852. As far back at least as the start of the eighteenth century the Jaurèses were respectable but menial artisans, weavers of woolens and merchants of textiles. But in their slow evolution toward bourgeois respectability they also included within their ranks a few men of real professional standing: two of Jules' second cousins became admirals (one was Benjamin-Constant Jaurès, who served at various times as Senator, Ambassador to Spain and Russia, and Minister of the Navy); one brother-in-law of Jules became a doctor and another a professor, while an uncle attained some local fame as a lawyer.

All of this seems quite impressive for a provincial family. But Jules Jaurès was neither successful nor eminent. Of an unstable temperament, he shifted from one occupation to another. As a petty merchant he traveled to the fair of Beaucaire where he bought merchandise which he later peddled in and around Castres; as a small landowner, he had, some three kilometers from Castres, six hectares of farmland called La Fédial Haute, where young Jean passed much of his childhood.[5] But he was never really successful, and throughout Jaurès' boyhood the family was always financially insecure. With such a background of local bourgeois eminence and serious economic difficulties, young Jean Jaurès might hope for an education and even a career; but he had no feeling of superiority over the peasants and artisans of the area.[6]

The Jaurès family was apparently a close-knit unit, harmonious and mutually devoted. Jean's relations with his brother Louis, who was less than a year younger, were characterized by affection and comradeship. Jules' impact on his sons was slight at best, and it is certain that his monarchist political sentiments never rubbed off on them. Yet, though unsuccessful and subject to streaks of obvious impracticality, he obviously enjoyed the respect of both boys, if one can judge by their deep sorrow at the time of his death in 1882. Certainly it was Adélaïde who dominated the family, made it strong, and helped so decisively to shape Jean's personality. The insecurities that might have attended his early years dissolved before his mother's love and encouragement.

Two of Adélaïde's qualities in particular, a selfless devotion and a deep tolerance, may have touched the inner consciousness of the future socialist leader. The sacrifices she made to provide the boys with a pleasant life and a good education can be appreciated only against the background of the family's chronic economic difficulties. She "redoubled her efforts to increase the yield of La Fédial, but that was not sufficient, and her modest jewels, which the children always admired on special occasions, disappeared one by one. But they were deeply conscious of their mother's sacrifices; she would find in their pockets on Monday the small change she had put there for spending money on Sunday."[7]

Though Adélaïde was a practicing Catholic, she showed not the slightest trace of intolerance. She was the model of those French mothers whom Jaurès affectionately described some years later: "They dislike bigotry and recoil from intolerance." Religion for them was the connecting link for "the great events of life: marriage, the birth of children, death. And in raising their children, they do not believe it right to break with the tradition which they themselves have accepted." So Jaurès grew up in the household religion which was then characteristic of the petty bourgeoisie. But when he eventually broke with it, Adélaïde made no attempt to force him back into the Church. "And if their children are raised in a free atmosphere," he wrote of the reactions of typical French mothers, "in contact with other children of every religion or no religion at all, with teachers who guide their thinking and expose them to the great works of the human mind, the conquests and the hypotheses of science — then life and liberty, those great educators, will have the last word. The child, little by little accustomed to governing himself in matters of conscience, will continue or will abandon the religious tradition. But they, the mothers, do not believe they have the right to interfere."[8] As a boy, Jaurès was "alert, rather buoyant and outgoing, yet serious and reflective, always good-tempered and kind."[9] Such a nature reflected his mother's influence.

Yet in Jaurès' personality, formed in these earliest years, certain traits probably reveal the unequal influence of his parents. The painful hesitation before difficult issues and the persistent edge of an inferiority complex, both of which cropped to the surface occasionally;[10] the nervous tic in one eye and the recurrent headaches; the search for approval and the momentary reeling under defeats — all of these, taken together and magnified, should perhaps be linked to the absence of strong paternal authority and affirmation. Adélaïde's influence is more evident, however. For her love encouraged his faith in life and in the goodness of man, a belief so deep that it led Jules Romains to the mistaken supposition that there was in him "no sense of the essential absurdity which is the very warp and woof of life."[11]

The influences of both region and town also leave their imprint on the young, and Jaurès' biographers have indeed claimed such influence for the Languedoc, that ancient region so full of violent and dramatic history.[12] In the Middle Ages a flourishing culture capitulated there before the sword of the Albigensian crusaders, and a land that in song and poem had celebrated love and beauty submitted to the force of Christian discipline. In such a region a sensitive and inquisitive boy could well become conscious of the movements and convulsions of history, its heroes and villains, its glories and disasters. How early may Jaurès have sensed something of the struggle for freedom of the mind? It was with some evident pride in region that he spoke in the Chamber of Deputies, many years later, of "the twelfth and thirteenth centuries when our intrepid and fervent Southern France rose against the despotism of the Church."[13]

Jaurès was probably influenced more directly by the Tarn, and particularly Castres. The Tarn, formed in 1789 by uniting three dioceses, sprawls across the fertile basin of the Garonne. At the time of his boyhood the area was predominantly agricultural, though both mining and manufacturing had begun to give the towns an industrial complexion. The peasants were the people the boy knew best, for, despite some drift to the city, most of the *tarnais* continued to live by the land.[14] Their condition was not an easy one, though three quarters of them owned their own land by the end of the Second Empire. Life was a constant struggle with inadequate tenures and natural catastrophes as destructive as the vine phylloxera.

But the wonders of the rural landscape were a constant enchantment to Jaurès. The infinite variety in nature, the sounds and silence of the farms, the timeless rhythm of rural life filled his childhood with an indelible joy. Even as a schoolboy absorbed with his studies, he could never resist the outdoors; at La Fédial he and his brother often learned their lessons while sitting on top of an old covered well.[15] Though there was scarcely a trace in his intellectual or political development of peasant traditionalism, Jaurès felt spontaneously comfortable in the countryside, and, more than most militants of the socialist movement, he could appreciate the round of village life and sympathize with the peasant's struggle for existence.

But like the rest of France the Tarn was changing. The small industries which had nestled in the valleys and hills, turning out leather goods, hats, furniture, and cloth, had produced only a limited effect on either the landscape or the mode of life. Now new economic phenomena were appearing, which were destined to work real changes. By the last third of the century the Tarn had been penetrated by branches of the large Parisian banks, anonymous but powerful institutions, ready to extend

credit to businesses and mortgages to the peasants.[16] Of greater significance was the intrusion of two large-scale industries, one a mining and
metallurgical enterprise, the other a glass factory, both introducing large-
scale capitalism into the province.[17] At the center of the development
stood the powerful clan of the Solages, who came to control the coal
and iron resources of the Carmaux region.

Years before the French Revolution a resourceful nobleman, Gabriel
de Solages, had become master of the coal mines at Carmaux, then the
iron works, and finally even factories for the manufacture of bottles and
shipbuilding materials.[18] Surviving the Revolution of 1789, the Solages
expanded their power in the nineteenth century, and, in so doing, altered
the customary economic life of the Tarn. It was their capitalism which
eventually supplied Jaurès with his labor support, just as their power
provided him with his political opposition.

As Jaurès passed through childhood to young manhood, therefore, his
native region was slowly but surely caught up in the net of modern
institutions. Albi, Castres, and Carmaux all became, for the Midi, cities
of some importance, though none by 1900 had achieved a population
of twenty thousand.[19] Castres, where the Jaurès family spent the winter
months, was not an inferno of "satanic mills," but it nonetheless became
a bleak counterpoint to the surrounding countryside. The dull grey
stone of its buildings created a cheerless atmosphere, and may have
stimulated the furtive streak of melancholy in Jaurès' nature. "Those
who knew him best," wrote his friend Lévy-Bruhl, "realized that in this
optimist, in this man of action, there was always a note of sadness."[20]

This, then, was the world of Jaurès' boyhood. It was bourgeois —
not the universe of the wealthy middle class, where the rules of behavior
were strictly set, but rather the less pretentious, more tolerant world of
the lesser middle class, where he could easily mix with the laboring
classes and freely develop his values. It was the milieu of those *nouvelles
couches provinciales*, ambitious and mildly liberal, which, as Gambetta
predicted, would rally to the Republic. Like other sons of this provincial
bourgeoisie, Jaurès would become a republican and a friend of the
Opportunists; it was the way of his world. It was not his milieu, however, which prepared him for socialism, but rather his learning, his
philosophy, and his incomparable integrity.

II

Jaurès began his education at the pension Séjal, a tiny private establish-
ment run by a priest, Abbé Rémy Séjal, and his two sisters, Claudine and
Lisotte. Walking each morning with Louis through the hills of the Tarn,
Jaurès never dallied along the way; "this little boy of nine, fair, plump,

lively, and bright had a passion for school; he loved to learn as much as to eat, and he digested the fundamentals of Latin as easily as roast goose."[21] The opportunity for education under the Second Empire was limited. The laws of the Third Republic, providing free, secular education for all, were still in the future, and only the sacrifice of his family gave Jaurès the chance to indulge his zest for learning.

He never wasted his opportunity. Among the few students at the pension Séjal he was easily the best, mastering Latin and French despite the dull pedagogy of the priest and his sisters. So impressive was his performance that even the stiff and unbending Abbé Séjal was willing to predict for Jaurès the fulfillment of his early ambition to be a post-master.[22]

In October, 1869, opportunity knocked more authoritatively when Jaurès was able to enter the Collège de Castres with the aid of a scholar-ship. Adélaïde wished, of course, to secure the best possible training for both her boys, and through the influence of her distant cousin, Admiral Jaurès, she was able to have the scholarship divided between Jean and Louis; the rest of the necessary money she scraped together, but only with conspicuous difficulty.

During his seven years at the Collège, Jaurès performed so well that he caught the attention of fellow students and teachers who, years later, still retained their impressions. When Louis Soulé, around 1920, was compiling his book on the early life of Jaurès, he consulted those teachers, still alive, who had been at the school half a century before. From their recollections Jean emerges as a boy athirst for all of learning, though most deeply absorbed in the humanities. Auguste Delpech, then assistant principal, and later a vigorously anticlerical Senator from the Ariège, frequently chatted with him during the brief recess periods; and "each time I came away from these conversations with a growing admiration for that extraordinary nature in which mature judgment, profound thought, fluent expression, and an amazing range of information were accentuated by an ingenuous modesty. History, philosophy, and litera-ture were the subjects of our conversations."[23] Yet Surre, his physics teacher, was certain that Jaurès could have had a significant career in science, while Dor, the mathematician, discovered in him a remarkable aptitude for logical abstraction.[24]

A few of his teachers, delighted to discover such a student, took a personal interest in his education. Brinon, his philosophy teacher, intro-duced him to the great problems of the universe during their long walks together; the historian Imart stimulated him with a detailed record of the local past; but no one was closer to him than Germa, the professor of ancient literature; in Jaurès he had found a student who devoured the

Greek and Latin classics, and committed to memory long passages of both prose and poetry.[25]

It was to Jaurès that Germa turned one hectic day when the new Prefect of the Tarn paid an unexpected visit to the school. An impressive reception should have been prepared, but how could any student on such short notice compose a brilliant welcoming address? Only Germa seemed calm under the pressure, and he suggested Jaurès for the speech. He had in mind many past classroom performances by the boy, especially the one when Jaurès had improvised in class the reply, unknown to history, which Vercingetorix might have given to the victorious Caesar. Thus, "while the pride of the school prepared his speech in the principal's office, the high authorities tried to brighten up his shabby attire."[26]

Before the honored guest and the school's 150 students Jaurès began to speak, and as he did the amused Prefect grew serious. "The speaker," one of the boys in the audience recalled years later, "unfolded his paper without reading it. He already knew it by heart. . . . The Prefect stopped smiling; the eloquence of the speaker, who used Latin references while avoiding clichés, surprised him."[27] So pleased, indeed, was the Prefect that he persuaded the principal to grant the students a full day off!

If the scattered testimony of these years provides striking evidence of his devotion to the world of books and nature, it tells little of the values and attitudes that Jaurès formed as he passed through adolescence. Certain political events and intellectual currents may well have affected him. It has been said that the Franco-Prussian War, fought when he was only eleven, stirred his nascent patriotism.[28] In a boy's mind the issues of battle become personified; so to Jean, Bazaine came to represent treason and Gambetta, whom Benjamin Jaurès served with distinction, heroism. Much later, as socialist and historian, Jaurès analyzed the Franco-Prussian War and blamed the Second Empire for its refusal to recognize the German claim to unity.[29] But now, in his youth, he could only weep for his country and thrill to Gambetta's call for national resistance.[30] The grand passion of Paris, the lower-class uprising in the Commune in 1871, apparently had no impact on the boy, a fact that would long separate him from those later comrades who were then in the thick of the fight.

Though Jaurès probably already had republican sentiments at this time, neither he nor his friends have left documentary evidence of them. Even as late as 1878, in fact, when Jaurès was already approaching nineteen, an incident occurred in Castres, at a celebration of his success in the *concours général*, which showed his political reticence. The sub-Prefect had given a speech praising the French nation but conspicuously omitting mention of the Republic. Concluding with "Vive la France!" he was startled to hear the cry "Vive la République!" which came boldly from Louis Jaurès. Sharply castigated by a Bonapartist colonel, Louis protested that France was, after all, a republic. Jules, a convinced Orleanist, gave his son no support. But Jean too remained silent.[31] It is probable, even at that date, that he considered political questions too discordant and time-consuming for the scholar. Thus, when M. Jean Julien, a neighbor and friend of the family, once approached Jaurès to congratulate him on his scholastic triumphs, the future socialist leader asked after Julien's little boy, adding reflectively: "He has no worry except learning to walk. . . . He is not concerned with politics, and he is all the happier for it."[32]

Yet one may assume that he was subject to certain political influences. In and around Castres, among bourgeois families like his own and even among his own relatives, he met republicans, whose sentiments he rather naturally absorbed. And at the lycée he was exposed by some of his teachers to progressive ideas — rationalism, the belief in progress, and republicanism. By 1876, he had come to know such masterpieces of critical reason as Renan's *Origines du Christianisme* and Fustel de Coulanges' *Institutions de l'ancienne France*;[33] he had developed his belief in progress, the conviction, as Kingsley Martin once put it, that "man was born rational and could construct his own destiny, instead of accepting the dogma that he was born in sin and owed his allegiance to Divine intervention."[34] And he had heard, from masters like Delpech, the strongest of republican views. From his petty bourgeois world he thus drew a sense of tolerance, a faith in reason, and a belief in the Republic.

Nor can it be overlooked that the literature and philosophy of the ancients, which occupied so large a part of Jaurès' studies, helped to shape his values. Read the bulk of his writings and speeches, and you find his great debt to classical learning. So much that was later turned to the service of democracy and socialism began with his contemplation and repetition of Greek and Latin texts. The respect for reason he surely found in Aristotle. The ideal of democracy he encountered in the famous funeral oration of Pericles, reported by Thucydides, which he never tired of quoting: "We differ from other states in regarding the man who holds aloof from public life as useless, yet we yield to none in independence of spirit and complete self-reliance." When Jaurès mastered the ancients, as a growing schoolboy, he built the foundations for his mature philosophy. It can hardly be surprising, therefore, that when Anatole France called on him in his modest apartment in the rue de la Tour, just a few weeks before Jaurès was assassinated and in the midst of his frenzied campaign for European peace, the novelist found the deputy absorbed in a tragedy of Euripides.[35] How close he must have felt, all through his life, to that Greek, whom Aristophanes satirized in the *Frogs* because he had taught Athenians "to think, see, understand, suspect, question, everything!"

As for his personal values, Jaurès placed all his emphasis on learning and none at all on wealth. He wanted to know, to understand, to probe the universe. Money or the lack of it concerned him not at all: "he lived as happily as a king without a cent in his pocket."[36] His devotion to learning, however, brought him rewards of another kind; his record of scholastic achievement at the Collège de Castres, from 1869 to 1876, was unmatched in the history of the school. Each year at the annual distribution of prizes he won highest honors in a range of subjects that included Latin, Greek, French, history, geography, science, mathematics, rhetoric, German, philosophy, and even religion. In spite of family poverty Jean Jaurès seemed headed for the highest reaches of intellectual life. And at a crucial moment his destiny was taken in hand by the distinguished scholar, Félix Deltour.

III

Nicolas-Félix Deltour, formerly a professor at the famous Lycée Louis-le-Grand, author of histories of ancient literature and a renowned thesis on *Les Ennemis de Racine au XVIII*e *siècle*, had been named by Wallon, Minister of Education in the Buffet ministry of 1875, to the post of Inspector-General of schools. In his devoted effort to maintain and improve the quality of the French educational system, Deltour visited the many secondary schools of France, seeking to recruit, especially for the famed École Normale Supérieure, those young men who would eventually fill the highest posts of teaching and scholarship. Thus a day arrived in 1875 when the principal of the Collège de Castres introduced to Germa's rhetoric class "a small, withered old man, with a birdlike neck, a squeaky voice, and precise, sharp gestures."[37] Ostensibly using the visit to deliver a lecture on Racine, Deltour was actually on his recruiting mission.

As he examined the class on the texts they had been studying, the Inspector discovered, in the book from which he had been conducting the lesson, a sheet of paper filled with Latin verses. Both the book and the verses belonged to Jaurès, as Deltour learned after having read the sheet with scarcely veiled delight. He was on the way to a discovery. Deltour questioned the principal and several teachers, examined Jaurès' notebooks, put the boy through an exacting discussion of literature, and determined then and there that Jaurès, whatever his economic difficulties, would be in the École Normale within two years. Telling the principal that he had "never met a young student with such an array of intellectual qualities,"[38] Deltour went at once to the Jaurèses' home to discuss the future with the boy's parents.

Jules and Adélaïde were both excited and apprehensive over the prospect of sending Jean to a great Parisian lycée in preparation for the École Normale. Deltour, conscious of their fears, spoke reassuringly about matters of money, distance, and politics. A scholarship would be obtained, he promised, so that the boy could receive the best training. As to the dangers of exposing Jaurès to the temptations of Parisian social and political life, Deltour offered to keep a protective eye on him. The issue was then settled; the parents consented, and Deltour left, prepared to have Jean's scholarship transferred from the Collège de Castres to the Parisian Lycée Sainte-Barbe. That arrangement was not easily made, but the persistence of the Inspector-General finally brought results. As late as October 5, 1876, with one of the precious places at Sainte-Barbe still eluding Jaurès, Deltour wrote to his friend Dubief, director of the school, urging him to arrange the transfer. That final pressure worked, and in the fall Jaurès entered Sainte-Barbe.[39] Thus began a friendship between the man and the boy which was devoted and, surprisingly enough, enduring. Between the conservative Catholic scholar and the anticlerical socialist tribune there was never any common political ground. But their alliance, based as it was on strong human feelings and a mutual love of learning, survived all ideological differences. Jaurès' friendship with Deltour reveals, in fact, his essential tolerance, his unwillingness to impose his point of view or to destroy those who dissented from it. "His human sympathy was so universal," Romain Rolland once wrote of Jaurès, "that he could be neither nihilistic nor fanatical. Every act of intolerance repelled him."[40]

Jaurès spent two years at Sainte-Barbe, from 1876 to 1878, preparing for the École Normale. One of the fine lycées of France, it offered him the most rigorous training in the humanities; the students were considered the future generation of scholars and statesmen, and the professors expected of them a diligence and understanding well beyond the ordinary. The wide learning of his teachers, the variety of interests among his fellow students, all the marvels of this new universe of scholarship exhilarated Jaurès. Yet his adjustment to the life and learning at Sainte-Barbe was not always easy. Competing with such excellent students, he drove himself hard, and it was during those years that he began his lifelong battle with migraine headaches. Confined for long periods within the school, the young provincial desperately missed the outdoors, and his craving was only partly satisfied by walks around Paris.

This was a difficult time for Jaurès in a more significant way, however, for in this period he finally abandoned, under the pressure of his rationalistic critique, his traditional Christian faith. Over a decade later, in his philosophical thesis, *De la Réalité du monde sensible*, he traced the course of this great change. It was his transition, he wrote poetically, from Bossuet's confident contemplation of the vast, silent universe, in which man was fixed in God's order, to Pascal's profound fear: "The eternal silence of the infinite universe frightens me." Stripped of his Catholic security after serious reflection, Jaurès now confronted a vast universe in which man had a wonderful but terrifying freedom.[41] It could have been a crushing blow, an unbearable burden. Catholicism provides a guide, like Vergil to Dante, for man's painful journey through life. Once reject the faith and what moral anarchy might not result! But for Jaurès, in youth as in maturity, the converse of Catholicism was not nihilism, but a self-conscious application of the human will to large and noble ideals. Some years later, he contrasted a nihilistic individualism, "each one living only for himself," and a genuine freedom, "when one lives for the good of all."[42] Yet the journey from a comfortable theology to a demanding philosophy, however exhilarating or liberating, created some uneasiness in his personal relationships. To his friend and fellow student, the future Monseigneur Baudrillart, he confessed his loss of Catholic faith; but to his benefactor Deltour he tactfully said nothing and continued to accompany him to Mass.[43]

As his training at Sainte-Barbe neared its end, Jaurès concentrated on the *concours général* of 1878 for the secondary schools of Paris and Versailles. Casting about for a subject for his competitive speech, he finally selected a little-known but fascinating episode from the reign of Francis I, which centered about Jacques Amyot and Pierre Duchâtel. Amyot, professor of Greek and Latin at Bourges, who had undertaken to translate Plutarch into French, was rewarded by King Francis around 1546 with a substantial subsidy. Jaurès ingeniously speculated about the role that might have been played by Duchâtel, the Bishop of Tulle and a zealous Greek scholar, in calling the attention of the King to the plight of the poverty-stricken Amyot. Appealing to Francis by stressing the value of French translations of the classics, Duchâtel, according to Jaurès, might have made an effective plea, and it was that plea which he recreated.

The theme of assistance to a worthy scholar was quite obviously close to the heart of a young man who had received crucial help from Deltour. Duchâtel stressed, in Jaurès' composition, Amyot's devotion to letters and his plaguing poverty. The work he could do if he were given a grant would serve the nation well; for the lessons in Plutarch "will show the French that you can join courage to prudence, generosity to moderation,

freedom to order, and that good actions do not lose their value by eliminating excess."[44] The speech was a clear reflection of Jaurès — the sensitivity to poverty, the appreciation of the disinterested patron, and the
stress on the classical virtues. Underneath it all, there lay his growing
identification with the Republic which could guarantee *la carrière ou-
verte aux talents*. Not yet twenty, he had displayed a rare wisdom which
brought him the first prize in the *concours général*. It was 1878, and he
now entered the École Normale Supérieure.

IV

Being no ordinary institution, the École Normale had extraordinary
standards. "For students," wrote one historian of the school, "the École
Normale has taken the choicest and keenest young men of the entire
land, already well-equipped academically for honorable positions in
life. It has provided for these the most learned masters and best teachers
to be found. It has placed at their disposal the best equipment in library
and laboratory facilities that money could buy. . . . As students it has
made them free spirits roaming at will under wise and efficient
guidance."[45]

Jaurès swept past the obstacle of stiff qualifying examinations and
entered at the height of his youthful powers. Again, as at Sainte-Barbe, he
cut no figure of elegance, showing his usual lack of interest in fashionable
dress and elegant taste. Even more than a quarter of a century later, as
a famed figure at the Stuttgart Congress of the Second International in
1907, Jaurès appeared to the English Socialist Ramsay McDonald as "a
strange creature. . . . Jauntily set upon its head was a straw hat, somewhat the worse for wear, its clothes were baggy and pitch-forked on its
back, below its trouser legs were folds of collapsed white stockings, under
its arms it carried, or rather dragged an overcoat. It sauntered along
looking at the shops and houses as it went, unconscious of everything
except its own interest, like a youth upon a new world, or a strolling
player who had mastered fate and discovered how to fill the moments
with happy unconcern."[46]

Just as his absorption with events and ideas endeared him to most
of his socialist colleagues later, so his simplicity and love of learning
gave him a special place among his fellow students at the École Normale.
Strongly in need of community, he throve on close companionship at the
school. During those years, and for some time afterwards, his closest
friend was Charles Salomon, with whom he shared a library cubicle in
the famous school on the rue d'Ulm. Baudrillart found in him a tutor
as well as a friend; for who else could have been so helpful with the
intricacies of Greek literature? By one of those strange twists of fate, it

was help of this sort that enabled Baudrillart to become years later rector of the Catholic Institute and a noted apologist for the Church. A year behind Jaurès, in the class that entered in 1879, was the future giant of French sociology, Émile Durkheim. The two boys struck up a lasting friendship which proved especially fruitful in these formative years when Durkheim tended to nudge Jaurès toward a greater preoccupation with social problems.

Among the twenty-five students concentrating on the humanities rather than the sciences, only one stood out as a rival. This was the future leader of French philosophy, Henri Bergson, who had been born in Paris only a few months after Jaurès was born in Castres. No two boys could have had more different origins and personalities.[47] The young Parisian Jew, son of a talented musician-composer and a gifted English mother, was mannered and somewhat supercilious. Seldom mixing with his fellow students, he found his home among books in the school library. But if he stood aside from the boys, he made fruitful contacts with his masters, especially antipositivist philosophers like Léon Ollé-Laprune and Émile Boutroux.[48]

The genius of Bergson, whose solution to a difficult mathematical problem had been published in the *Annales des Mathématiques* even before he had entered the École Normale, can hardly be questioned. When he became interested, as did Jaurès, in philosophy, literature, and history, rivalry between them seemed as certain as the law of gravity. So it appeared, at any rate, to Ernest Desjardins, professor of history, who was once inspired to arrange a contest between the two. Choosing as a subject the alleged corruption of Fonteius, the Roman provincial governor whom Cicero had successfully defended, Desjardins set up a debate, assigning to Jaurès the role of prosecutor and to Bergson that of defender of Fonteius. No verdict has been recorded, though some felt that Jaurès' oratorical fervor was bested by Bergson's logic.[49]

Because of his wide range of interests, Jaurès had real difficulty in deciding on a field of specialization. He thought first of Greek literature, for which he had so great an affinity that he could undoubtedly have carved out a distinguished career as a classicist. But through his studies at the École Normale he was powerfully attracted to history, whether the imposing scientific efforts of Fustel de Coulanges or the moving idealistic epic of Michelet. In Fustel de Coulanges, who was the towering intellectual of the École Normale, he came to admire the rigorous critical standards and the indefatigable pursuit of evidence which characterize the great modern historian; he was, Jaurès was later to write, "fearless beneath an outward reserve and discretion, repelled by anything that might shackle freedom of the mind and scientific inquiry."[50]

In Michelet he found a moral idealism which both moved and inspired him. "With the world," wrote Michelet in his *Introduction to Universal History*, "began a war which will end only with the world: the war of man against nature, of spirit against matter, of liberty against fatality. History is nothing other than the record of this interminable struggle."[51] Jaurès absorbed the heady wine of history as the story of liberty. It was partial inspiration for his own historical studies, and one of the starting points for his socialism. As he would many times note, true freedom is universal freedom and that universality requires socialism.[52] But despite the attraction of both literature and history, philosophy, the synthesis of all other studies, finally claimed Jaurès. His choice was no surprise to Émile Boutroux, distinguished professor of philosophy, who had marveled when Jaurès once held forth on Kant's *Critique of Pure Reason* during three entire classroom sessions.

The intense intellectual life of those years was fortunately punctuated by long summer holidays when Jaurès was able to return not only to his family but also to the hills and fields of the Tarn. In frequent vacation letters to Charles Salomon he told of the therapeutic effect of his life at home. Rising at seven each morning, he once wrote, "I drink in the fresh air; I take a long walk and at nine I sit at a table outside the house in the shadow of two acacia trees. . . . In this semi-solitude you can overcome almost all of those petty, self-centered concerns; you have no one with whom to compete. You dream of living, thinking, and behaving nobly. . . ."[53]

On the record, one could only assume that Jaurès was destined for a life of scholarship, and that he was especially well qualified for it; very little pointed to politics, particularly socialism. But however cloistered he was within the École Normale, Jaurès was in Paris, and under its influence he developed his political and social ideas. Years later, he recalled his shocked, depressed reaction when, as a young student in Paris, he first sensed the utter loneliness of men and women thrown together in that vast city: "I saw thousands upon thousands of people, passing each other without the slightest sign of recognition, each one completely isolated from all the rest. And I asked myself how they could accept it, how such an unjust social order could endure." Why, he wondered, why were the masses so impassive? Only later, he confessed, did he understand: "They were products of the social system as well as its victims; it was ingrained in them, and they would not revolt against it because they had identified themselves with it."[54]

Though discouraged by the aimless wandering of the big city crowds, Jaurès was also stimulated by one of his first contacts with a group of class-conscious workers. On his trip to Paris in 1878 he met on the train a group of workmen from the Haute-Garonne, who were headed for the Exposition Universelle. Writing to his neighbor, M. Julien, he revealed how fascinating it was to hear the workers speak warmly of the French revolutionary tradition, a view very different from the one he had generally heard among the peasants of the Midi.[55] In learning that the workers considered as heroes those who had fallen in defense of the Commune, he grasped, perhaps for the first time, something of the nature of labor's struggle against authority.

As for his political views, he certainly opted for the Republic, and this at a time when the issue of monarchism was far from dead; he greatly admired its early heroes, Léon Gambetta and Jules Ferry, who were defending a regime still heavily under attack. After all, the Third Republic, born in 1870 out of the collapse of Napoleon III's Second Empire, had survived, until it was formalized by the adoption of its scanty constitution in 1875, only because the conservatives at its helm, Orleanists and Bourbonists, were divided on the question of the next monarchy. The Republic was, for its rulers, until 1876, a bad second choice. It bore none of the marks of grandeur of the First Republic, proclaimed after the Paris mob had seized and imprisoned Louis XVI on August 10, 1792. It represented none of the great hope of the Second Republic, created when the people of Paris had again intervened on February 24, 1848, to direct the departure of the Orleanists. Only in the actions of Gambetta did the early Third Republic show signs of fervor and militancy.

As a young lawyer of Italian descent and an active republican critic of the Second Empire in its later years, Gambetta had competed for a place in the Corps législatif in 1869, when he was only thirty-one, on his renowned Belleville program, so named for the Paris district from which he ran. It was a radical program, calling for separation of Church and State and the suppression of permanent armies, thus striking at the clerical and military props of the Empire. Elected, he had made his first speech in Parliament on January 10, 1870, and boldy enunciated this objective: "What we want is to be done with monarchy, to organize a complex of institutions based on universal suffrage and national sovereignty."[56]

When France declared war on Prussia on July 19, 1870, the Empire suffered a short agony and an even swifter death. By September 2, MacMahon's army, accompanied by the emperor himself, capitulated to the Prussians at Sedan. But if the Bonapartist regime was over, the war was not, for it was carried on during the next few months by a Government of National Defense, in which Gambetta alone, as Minister of the Interior, displayed hope and daring. When he left besieged Paris in a balloon in order to reach Tours on October 9 and to rouse the country to resistance, he performed an act, however futile, of real courage. It was in vain, however, and on January 26, 1871, the Government of National Defense accepted Bismarck's armistice.

The National Assembly elected by the French in 1871 was monarchist and Catholic, and in the early uncertain years of the new regime the conservative Thiers, who had lived long enough to have crushed the Lyon strikers in 1834 and the Paris workers in 1871, played the crucial role as chief executive. But there was always Gambetta to inspirit the republicans of Paris. During the election campaign of 1876, the first held under the Constitution of 1875, it had been the orator of Belleville who had led the republican forces to victory.

But the Republic was still in danger of attack by those with vested interest in king, Church, and property. The monarchist President, Marshal MacMahon, resorted to the *coup de Seize-mai*, when he dismissed the moderate republican Premier, Jules Simon, and called in the monarchist Duc de Broglie to replace him. Though not actually unconstitutional, this action of May 16, 1877, was aimed at a ministry that had majority support in the Parliament. The next step was obvious, the dissolution of the Chamber of Deputies, and, as the Constitution prescribed, the President on June 16 requested the Senate to take that action. It was Broglie who frightened the Senators into compliance by offering them the choice of the stable MacMahon or the Jacobin Gambetta. Then it was that Gambetta galvanized the republicans into action, creating a temporary unity, in order to win the elections, among men as far to the Right as Thiers and as far to the Left as Louis Blanc. He gave the movement passionate words and a whirlwind campaign, so that, despite the violent tactics of the regime, the elections of October brought into the Chamber 326 republicans against 207 deputies of the Right.

Jaurès, still cloistered in his academic world, was moved by his strong, book-bred idealism to equate pure republicanism with personal freedom and public virtue. Gambetta, for whom his admiration never fully waned, appeared to him as the heroic defender of the good society, who worked for justice at home and peace abroad.[57] Recalling later the impact of Gambetta on the young republicans of the École Normale, Jaurès admitted their lack of sophistication. They embraced him, not as the builder of a program, but as the spiritual embodiment of the Republic. The vague and rhetorical quality of his message escaped them, but his style and manner, his apparent vigor left an indelible impression.[58] Since 1792 a strong tradition had developed in France, which associated the Republic with a just social order.[59] It is not surprising, therefore, that a young idealist like Jaurès should have expressed uncritical admiration for its most heroic tribune. His appreciation, though not his devotion, was as great for Jules Ferry, whose importance in the Third Republic waxed during the last half of Jaurès' apprenticeship at the École Normale. If, as D. W. Brogan once pointed out, Louis de Freycinet, a flexible *polytechnicien*, unencumbered by strong commitments, was the characteristic politician of the newly strengthened Republic after 1877, it was Ferry who gave it a vigorous turn with his program of expansion, both against Catholic pretensions at home and into backward areas abroad.

Born in 1830 in Lorraine, Ferry was a tenacious and tireless politician, whose republicanism could never be questioned. As lawyer and journalist, he had fought the Second Empire, and in 1869, elected to the Corps législatif, he had stood at the side of Gambetta. And he would be there again in the Government of National Defense and in the campaign against *Seize-mai*. As an ardent positivist, Ferry's chief preoccupation was secular control of education, which he considered the foundation stone of a free republic. On this explosive issue Jaurès warmly defended the man who had first become Minister of Education in the Waddington ministry of 1880. Among Ferry's anticlerical reforms was the provision, embodied in the famous Article 7 of one of his proposals, which sought to forbid the administration of schools by unauthorized religious orders.[60] This blow to Catholic education sharply divided the students at the École Normale. Most of the boys ardently supported the measure, which they considered a valid weapon against reaction and superstition; but a minority, known as the Talas (those *qui vonT À LA messe*), bitterly opposed it; and some were simply indifferent. Jaurès held a position apart from all three groups, the position of a nonbeliever in formal church ritual who was nonetheless respectful of the beliefs of others.[61]

Thus, though he supported Ferry's proposals, he felt strongly about both freedom of conscience and the right of criticism. The case of Ollé-Laprune, professor of philosophy and ardent Catholic, suspended in 1881 over his vehement opposition to Article 7, brought out this concern of Jaurès. "It was at the time of the decrees," he wrote later, "that I wrote my first lines in a newspaper — a letter of protest to Edmond About over his assertion that the students at the École Normale had no sympathy for Ollé-Laprune. My letter was published and caused a lively reaction. I thought that professors . . . were entitled to their freedom."[62]

Aside from his republicanism, Jaurès had no views on the political and social history of the period. Of economic developments and of the socialist movement, he had, as yet, nothing to say. Yet it was a time of growth, however slow, for both capitalism and socialism. France was still a nation primarily of peasants, artisans, and shopkeepers, but important changes were already taking place. Thus, the number of power-driven machines in France increased some 84 per cent between 1871 and 1883; annual steel production rose from 110,000 tons in 1869 to

512,000 in 1881; industrial combines, like the Comptoir métallurgique de Longwy in metals and the Compagnie Saint-Gobain in chemicals, introduced trusts into France. Developments like these were destined to change the character of capitalism.

As for socialism, it was emerging by 1880 from a decade of repression and silence. New life was pumped into the working-class movement by the return of the exiled Communards and the coming of Marxism. Back in France were Paul Brousse, Benoît Malon, and especially Jules Guesde, the head and heart of the Marxist movement.[63] A republican journalist at Montpellier toward the end of the Second Empire, Guesde had sympathized with the Commune in 1871; to escape imprisonment, he had chosen exile, and for five years, he wandered — first to Geneva, then Rome, finally Milan. Living among Communard exiles and foreign radicals, Guesde switched his allegiance from Gambetta to Bakunin; but in Milan, under the influence of Italian workers as well as his own reading, he finally abandoned his anarchism for a rather utopian brand of socialism. By 1876, Guesde had returned to Paris, and there, among the young Marxist intellectuals who gathered at the Café Soufflet on the Boulevard Saint-Michel, he discussed, studied, and finally embraced Marxism. Once he had read and virtually memorized *Capital*, recently translated into French by Jules Roy, Guesde had a text, a gospel, a faith. Never an original thinker, he became, out of his heroic devotion to a cause, a great organizer and an even greater propagandist.

Convinced that the workers needed a party of their own, revolutionary and collectivist, Guesde worked passionately for that objective until, in November, 1880, the first Marxist party was organized at Le Havre. By 1882, however, that party had split into two separate groups, the Possibilists, who followed Brousse into the reformist Fédération des travailleurs socialistes de France, and the Guesdists, who upheld revolutionary Marxism in the Parti ouvrier français. Neither party was strong in the 1880's. But the Guesdists, through organizing efforts that must have been as discouraging as they were dangerous, finally established some strongholds among the textile and steel workers of the Nord (Lille, Roubaix, Calais, Saint-Quentin) and the Centre (Lyon, Roanne, Montluçon, and Commentry). The Possibilists, appealing more effectively to the craft workers of the clothing and building trades, had their greatest influence in and around Paris, in the Ardennes, and in the Ouest (Brest, Tours, and Châtellerault). At about the same time, the Blanquists organized their Comité révolutionnaire central, dedicated to the overthrow of capitalism.[64]

None of that activity made any impression on Jaurès. As his classmate, Paul Morillet, later Dean of the Faculty of Letters at Grenoble, once wrote to Lévy-Bruhl: "His opinions were purely republican. There were no signs of his future socialist orientation."[65] It is hardly surprising that the early history of these tiny socialist groups went on unnoticed by Jaurès. He was, after all, a student, a provincial, a petty bourgeois. Still, he was much more sheltered in his youth than certain others, Édouard Vaillant, for example, who came out of Sainte-Barbe in the 1860's and plunged at once into a career as a revolutionary.[66] Vaillant's early identification with the cause gave him the best credentials in the socialist movement; Jaurès, on the other hand, had to live down the distrust of those who could never forget his youthful ignorance of socialism.

By 1881 Jaurès, almost twenty-two, prepared for the aggregation. Aggregation, from its origin in 1766, was "the gateway to desirable teaching positions."[67] On the basis of a series of written and oral examinations, the state chose the handful who would occupy the best teaching posts in the nation's lycées and collèges. For the *normaliens* of 1881 it was an exciting competition, one which promised to bring highest honors to either Bergson or Jaurès. At the oral examination, held in an amphitheatre before a jury of professors, the interest ran high. When Jaurès appeared, the large hall was jammed to capacity. Speaking on the True, the Beautiful, and the Good, he was in brilliant form, drawing at his conclusion a great ovation. The public demonstration may, in fact, have disturbed the jury; for when the decision was announced, the examiners judged the obscure Lesbazeille first, Bergson second, and Jaurès third.

But Jaurès was now *agrégé*, and a teaching career lay before him. To be near his parents, he asked for and received a post in philosophy at the lycée of Albi. He now prepared to leave Paris after five momentous years there, and to devote himself to his students and to the preparation of his doctoral dissertations. Parting with his good friend Charles Salomon was not easy. So much that they had shared was now at an end. They walked together down the rue Jacob on the Left Bank, and they promised each other long letters. A quick handshake sealed the friendship, and Jaurès went sadly down the rue Bonaparte. He walked the crooked, narrow, enchanting streets of the Latin Quarter before taking his train, his mind full of the most exciting memories of his life. He would be back in Paris, and the real excitement was still to come. But for now, it was the world of teaching and the life of the provinces that claimed him.

V

The summer of 1881 marked a watershed in his early life. The provincial had been to Paris, the student had become a scholar, and the *agrégé* had emerged a teacher. The development of his mind had been impressive, and his petty bourgeois values — republicanism, tolerance, belief in progress — had been confirmed in Paris as in Castres.

It was during this particular summer that Jaurès' thoughts turned to a girl, Marie-Paule Prat, "so charming and full of life," as he wrote to Salomon.[68] A childhood friend living only a short distance from La Fédial, she proved to be a wonderful companion. Jaurès told her stories of Paris and its exciting life, and he was as attentive to her as his sense of propriety permitted. She listened to him, obviously impressed by his philosophical turn of mind. Though his rejection of Catholicism and his devotion to secular letters disturbed her, each seemed to respect the sincerity of the other.

So began a fine friendship, which in the end disappointed and perplexed Jaurès. For despite his obvious talent and prospects, his present circumstances were too precarious to suit the solidly bourgeois Prat family. Her parents, therefore, stepped in and ended the two-year friendship by arranging Marie's marriage to M. Fournes, a local lawyer. Fournes' career was to bog down in a provincial marsh, far from the heights eventually achieved by Jaurès, but in 1883 the lawyer seemed a better risk than the schoolteacher. Jaurès poured out his confusion to Salomon in a letter of March 11, 1883. "My confidence is gone; girls now affect me strangely; the simplest ones appear so very complicated. It used to seem that an evening was enough to understand them; now it appears that an entire lifetime would not be too much, and that one always risks something of himself in love." And then, in a remark well tinged with a Balzacian contempt for the corrosive power of money over human sentiments, he added: "One in the hand is worth two in the bush."[69]

In October, 1881, he assumed his teaching post at Albi, an almost ideal position requiring only eleven hours of teaching a week to a handful of students. His success as a teacher was as great as had been expected. Lecturing without notes, he ranged widely over the fields of philosophy and literature, bringing into play not only the fruits of his own reading and thinking but also the views of experts on Vergil, Villon, Pascal, or Rabelais. His students admired his learning; and more than that, they warmed up to the young teacher who treated them as equals and engaged them in long, informal conversations. What did Jaurès teach, what philosophical principles emerged in his lectures? One can follow them in the outline of the course he gave between November, 1882, and July, 1883.[70] It was a course that reflected Jaurès' wide reading in the history of philosophy and especially his understanding of the eighteenth century *philosophes*. Like the men of the Enlightenment, he found neither formal Christianity nor mysticism acceptable in explaining the origin and development of the universe. In his thirty-fourth lesson, he posed the question of life and in his explanation revealed his debt to materialism: "If life were, as the vitalists or the animists claim, the result of some immaterial force appearing in Nature one fine day, then it would be sudden, unprepared by any previous development. The mechanistic doctrine, which views life as the result of matter and its various chemical, physical, and material properties, all of which are reducible to their final elements, has on its side both logic and science." Yet the materialist in Jaurès continued to meet with the idealist, the scientist with the moralist. Science could not explain the evolution of living consciousness, and for this he accepted the existence of mind or spirit. As early as the second lesson he wove together these strands of his position: "It is true that above all there is matter. Matter is both eternal and essential, since not a single one of its particles is either created or destroyed. It is also true that, above all, movement is present, nothing is without movement, and also through all these transformations the quantity of movement is constant in the universe. But, nonetheless, with brute matter and its movement you cannot explain the smallest fact of animal or human consciousness, the slightest sensation. . . . Indeed, between the movement of the acoustic nerve and a sound, between a vibration of the optic nerve and the color blue, between the tearing of a tissue and a sensation of acute pain, there is no comprehensible connection. So science cannot by itself explain the bases of the universe." Few of his students realized it, no doubt, but they were the first to hear in outline that system of materialism and idealism which underlay so large a part of his socialist experience.

Into his schedule of teaching and study, politics persistently intruded. The general elections of August, 1881, in which the central public issue continued to be the struggle between monarchists and republicans, roused the interest of Jaurès, who sided strongly with republicanism. His philosophical speculations, he revealed in his letter to Salomon on August 10, 1882, led him towards, not away from, politics: "When I shall have fathomed the depths of the universe, I will have to come back to the surface. . . . I tell you, my dear friend, that instead of taking me away from politics, my studies push me into it. I understand my shortcomings, but frankly I think I am capable of showing less petty ambition than many others."[71] The text of the letter is doubly revealing, first because of the connection it established between understanding life and participating in it, and then because of its allusion, already, to mediocrity and careerism in the Republic.

The more challenging public life seemed, the more it attracted him.

In talks with friends and neighbors, in discussions at the local salon of one Madame de Lastour who gathered to her home some of the best conversationalists of Albi, Jaurès heard many a story of political chicanery. But he, at least, might serve the common good, and he poured out these inner thoughts to Salomon: "It would not make our poor country the laughing stock of the world if I were named secretary of some group; I would at least have the courage of my convictions in the face of those café politicians who frighten even our political bigwigs. But then what? I would have to make a big decision in four years if Frédéric Thomas were to retire."[72]

Jaurès was thinking aloud, thinking that he might one day run for the Chamber seat now held by the republican Thomas. His growing interest in politics, however, disturbed his mother, who hoped to shield him from the dangers and vicissitudes of public life. Adélaïde even sought to enlist the help of Admiral Benjamin-Constant Jaurès in dissuading her son from contemplating politics as a career. But the admiral perceptively replied to her: "Let him alone. Don't worry. Jean takes to politics like a duck to water."

On May 27, 1882, his father Jules, then sixty-three, died after several months of great suffering, an event which greatly saddened Jaurès.[73] Out of respect and in spite of his own religious views, he stood by while a priest administered extreme unction, repeating from memory the customary Latin phrases. But by increasing his responsibilities toward his mother, his father's death served to stimulate Jaurès' ambition, to intensify his desire for a significant career.

Thus, he could write to Salomon soon after his father's death: "I had good reason to go to Albi (to teach); but there is no longer any reason to stay since Mama is coming to live with me. I will either look for a post in the Faculty of Toulouse or in a more important lycée in the Midi. The thesis is already outlined in my mind, and I will soon begin work on it."[74] Unlike Marcel Proust, for whom the death of a vigorous father meant increasing dependence on a doting mother, Jaurès contemplated a more independent life after Jules died, one in which politics would play an important part.

The possibility of a good university career seemed assured when Jaurès, after two years at the lycée of Albi, moved to Toulouse in November, 1883, where he became *maître des conférences* in philosophy in the Faculty of Letters.[75] Behind the promotion stood Claude-Marie Perroud, another of that handful of devoted men who helped to promote Jaurès' career. A republican educator in the new era of secular instruction ushered in by Ferry's reforms, Perroud, rector of the Academy of Toulouse, had "a deep commitment to reason and liberty."[76] His affection for Jaurès, who considered education essential to man's development, is not difficult to understand.

Their first meeting resulted from Perroud's visit to the lycée of Albi in search of new teaching talent. He later recorded his immediate impressions of Jaurès during that important visit: "He spoke fluently during his entire class, and I was careful not to interrupt. . . . After class I presided over a meeting of the faculty, and there also he spoke often, with a remarkable acuteness, about matters of school administration. . . . He was positively dazzling."[77] From that brief encounter came first an offer of a teaching post at Toulouse, and then a deep friendship between the two men. Jaurès' sense of gratitude toward the republicans of the Midi, men like Perroud, certainly helped to confirm his faith in the future of the bourgeois Republic.

As *maître des conférences*, Jaurès enjoyed a relatively satisfying academic life. The friendship of Perroud and his wife gave him confidence and assurance; among his students he found half a dozen very promising candidates for the *licence* in philosophy; and all the while he was at work on the doctoral thesis he expected to submit to the Sorbonne. It would be a philosophical work on the nature of the universe, in which he would demonstrate, contrary to the absolute idealists, that "the external world, however transformed by the human brain, has its own independent existence outside ourselves."[78]

But other events and other people, outside his academic world, persistently claimed his attention. Into his life by 1885 came Louise Bois, who would eventually, in 1886, become his wife. The daughter of a wholesale cheese merchant, Louise was fairly attractive, in the buxom rather than the delicate style. Though lacking in intellectual interests, she attracted Jaurès because of an ingenuous sincerity. Always rather self-centered, Louise was less impressed with her suitor; but her parents, prosperous enough to offer as a dowry their property of Bessoulet, would decide in favor of Jaurès if they felt he showed real prospects for success. Always it was money that seemed to concern the successful bourgeoisie, and this disturbed Jaurès deeply.

But it was political activity, rather than marriage, that impinged directly on his academic life. Under the stimulating influence of its great daily newspaper, *La Dépêche de Toulouse*, Toulouse was a city where strong republican attitudes could develop and flourish, and it was in this newspaper that Jaurès published his first articles. The attraction of politics proved increasingly magnetic, and by August, 1883, he wrote to Delpech, by then the principal of the Collège de Castres, stating candidly the conflict he felt between pure philosophy and practical politics: "I cannot deny that from time to time I turn my ear to the noise of politics, and then I think I could move into that world; yet I'm not really sure, for I feel an inner resistance which tells me that I am made for a more tranquil life. But I don't pretend to regulate and circumscribe the future."[79]

Eager to participate, to turn thought into action, Jaurès overcame his caution and indecision. Thus, after his philosophy class one afternoon, while engaged, as usual, in informal discussion with his students, he heard the sound of a crowd in the large amphitheatre in Toulouse. Out of curiosity he went there and found one Estacelin, once a deputy under the Second Empire, making a vigorous antirepublican speech. Jaurès stood up in the audience and interrupted the speaker with an eloquent defense of the Republic. "It was a spectacular success," Gheusi recalled years later. "Jaurès thawed his audience, so cold at first, and at the end of his wonderful improvisation, there was a tremendous ovation."[80]

As the elections of 1885 approached, Jaurès drew closer to a vital decision. He sought advice and counsel. Once, in 1884, he went to see Surre, his old physics teacher, who had become director of the Municipal Laboratory of Toulouse. After talking for some time about matters of science, Surre urged Jaurès to run for the Chamber. And when the younger man replied that he had no money, the older man declared wisely: "Your eloquence will suffice."[81] It was a major step, to abandon scholarship for politics. But once Jaurès made the decision he never turned back. He agreed to submit his name to the congress of republican notables of the Tarn, meeting at Albi on August 16, 1885, to designate six candidates for the republican ticket in the department. When the meeting was held, his candidacy was enthusiastically accepted by most of the delegates, headed by the moderate Senator Barbey. Once again, as at home and at the university, those who sponsored his career were good bourgeois republicans. A corner had been turned, and Jaurès took his first step into politics.

VI

He was not well prepared in 1885 to understand the political process, the parties and the interests they represented. Almost twenty years later he would complain about the rather remote, abstract training of French higher education. "When I first went into Parliament at the age of twenty-six, I can say that I was really only just out of college. For in our country there is nothing comparable to that English aristocracy which propagates political culture in every circle in which its sons move."[82] The French system, the university, had become the "training school of the liberal bourgeoisie, not the seedbed of democracy." As such, Jaurès noted critically, it had long "remained a closed corporation, where the idea of freedom in Cicero and Tacitus was honored, while popular protest was scornfully treated as intemperate brawling."[83] It was criticism of the kind made earlier and more vociferously by Durkheim, who attacked the École Normale, rather too harshly, for dilettantism and superficiality.[84]

Not that Jaurès' experience and education were unimportant. Far from it. In the Tarn, he had lived among humble men and women, observed their days of work, sympathized with their insecurity. If he had not yet probed to the root of the social problem, he at least knew that it existed; and if he knew little of working-class organizations, he felt a kind of kinship with the poor. At the École Normale, his own curiosity had led him where the curriculum did not. He had dipped liberally into the writings of nineteenth-century French socialists, learning from St. Simon, Fourier, and Proudhon what he never heard from his professors. Furthermore, from the community life at school, he had grown receptive to new ideas and tolerant of opposition. In 1881, he had delivered on behalf of his class an address of appreciation to Fustel de Coulanges, then head of the school. In this, his first public oration, he had praised the École Normale for discouraging that narrow specialization which could only limit the student and encourage his dogmatism: "The great remedy here is the common life we live. Constantly, we are forced to understand our many fellow students, whose ideas and investigations may be very different from our own. . . . In our daily contacts, in the competition of our ideas, . . . there is a continuous process of conversion and conquest. Yet there are neither victors nor vanquished; instead, we all emerge with better minds and expanded horizons."[85] Thus, when Jaurès entered politics, he went with a receptive mind and a spirit of tolerance. It was not human sympathy he lacked or the courage of his convictions, but rather direct contact with the social struggle and a deep understanding of power. His horizon, for the time being, was bounded on all four sides by his good republicanism.

Despite an array of crucial problems, like imperialism abroad and depression at home, the election campaign centered on the endlessly debated question of Republic versus Monarchy. The republicans were split into Opportunists, Radicals, and socialists, but the monarchists and Bonapartists joined forces in the Union conservatrice. Against that coalition Jaurès conducted his first campaign in the summer and fall of 1885.

The electioneering was marked the country over by considerable bitterness. In the Tarn, most of the priests denounced the republicans as wanton Freemasons, aiming to destroy organized religion, while the liberal minority among the clerics was silenced by the Archbishop of Albi's threat of severe discipline. Despite the asperity of the charges and accusations, Jaurès often lectured in eloquent but rather abstract terms. Thus, appearing one day at the fair of Lacaune, he talked to the peasants, not about the concrete issues of the election, but rather about the benefits of republican government. In the audience that day, as on later days at Dourgnes, Saix, Pampelonne, and Carmaux, were many who, as one critic has noted, became his devoted followers for the rest of his political life.[86]

But general themes were only the basis for a specific program, and Jaurès was instrumental in drawing up for the republican candidates an election proclamation which was a defense against both the extreme Right and Left and an answer to charges of financial waste, high taxes, economic crises, and religious persecution. It was stated in the proclamation that the Second Empire, not the Third Republic, had created financial deficits, thrown France into useless wars in the Crimea, China, Italy, and Mexico, and finally lost Alsace and Lorraine. The record of the Republic, on the other hand, was one of accomplishment; it had built schools and railroads, safeguarded freedom of conscience, added great colonies in Tunisia and Indo-China. Such was the unquestioning approval Jaurès then gave the Republic whose imperialism and unequal distribution of wealth he would later attack so furiously. But now he shared the outlook of the republicans of the Tarn, who held that the Republic was the font of progress. It was a point of view he had expounded one day in 1884 when, as *maître des conférences* from Toulouse, he had delivered a lecture in Albi praising imperialism as a means of spreading French culture to backward lands.[87]

In his own campaign speeches Jaurès reiterated the major themes of the proclamation. At Graulhet on September 18 he attacked the spirit of *Seize-mai*; he charged that the constant campaign against the Republic by reactionaries like Baron Reille, head of the antirepublican forces in the Tarn, had deflected the government from its proper concern with social justice. At Saint-Amans two days later, praising actions of the Republic which would never have passed any socialist test, he stood behind the tariff system for agriculture, the building of the railroad system with private capital, and the acquisition of two colonies. But occasionally Jaurès pointed to the direction he would eventually take. In his speech at Castres on September 5, he proposed that the Republic sponsor social reforms to improve the lot of the poor. And at the conclusion of the Graulhet speech of September 18, he made a promise that was more than campaign rhetoric. Where, he asked, would he stand in the Chamber? "I will not be part of any group, any clique, and, as a son of the people, I will vote for all reforms that will improve the lot of the suffering."[88]

Violence and crime marked the voting of October 4. The Prefect of the Tarn complained to the Minister of the Interior that the principle of the secret ballot was frequently violated by unfair tactics; employers were trying to control the votes of those who were in any way dependent upon them.[89] But for Jaurès the results were completely successful. Five republicans were elected for the Tarn, leaving Baron René Reille as the only victor for the conservatives; and among the six the young philosopher headed the list of victors with 48,040 votes. It was a time for elation, and excitedly he raced to La Fédial to his mother's side. Their personal celebration was short, for soon his admirers, shouting "Jaurès! Vive Jaurès!" carried him off, and Adélaïde learned her first lesson in the loneliness imposed by politics.

But the work of the campaign was not yet over. Though the first ballot had resulted in a republican success in the Tarn, it had produced over the whole nation a surprising show of conservative strength. The parties of the Right won 177 seats outright, while the combined republicans were sure of only 129. The split in republican ranks and the unity of the conservatives were partially responsible for the unexpected result. But the conservatives also had some strong issues in the economic crisis, the imperialism, and the political corruption that were conspicuous features of the Republic.

The challenge galvanized the republicans into action before the second ballot. Despite differences they joined in an electoral alliance, supported even by Guesde and the Marxists. The tactics produced strange lists, such as the one in the department of the Seine, where the economic liberal Frédéric Passy ran beside the radical Henri Rochefort and the socialist Émile Basly. Jaurès, already known for his oratory, was pressed into service by the republicans of the Haute-Garonne. Before a mass meeting at Revel on October 15 he spoke on behalf of Paul Constans and Armand Duportal, and defined some of the chief principles of his political faith. The Republic had made mistakes, he admitted, but that was hardly sufficient reason to abandon it:

No, a hundred times no, because the Republic alone can correct them. Under a king, mistakes are made, and then only two courses are open to us: either to lower our heads and continue to live under a capricious regime, or to turn against it fiercely and, in a civil war, to man the barricades and spill French blood. With the Republic a mistake can be corrected because every man can make his criticisms known and help to reshape national policy. The only form of government which can err without irreparable harm . . . is the Republic, the regime of popular control, discussion, and freedom.[90]

His efforts and those of other republicans were rewarded in the balloting of October 18. In the final tally their party controlled 383 seats against 201 for the conservatives. Jean Jaurès was now a deputy in a republican majority. Learned, idealistic, youthfully naïve, he brought rare qualities to politics. And at the core of his personality, observed one who watched him closely, was neither ambition nor a sense of superiority, but "one of the most sincere consciences of our age."[91]

Campaigning essentially on Ferry's Opportunist program, Jaurès had undoubtedly won the confidence and the support of the liberal bourgeoisie. But it appears equally certain, and rather more significant, that he had also impressed some workers in the Tarn. For on October 5, 1885, the republican *Courrier du Tarn* carried an open letter to their "Cher député" from a group of industrial workers in Castres. "Yesterday," they wrote, "the republican workers voted for you because they knew that the goals of your program — the defense and the evolution of republican democracy — are their goals. You have never failed us; for several months you have fought for our cause in the party we ardently support. As for us, we will never fail you." These were prescient words. For though they did not yet share a common socialism, some workers already sensed that Jaurès would defend them against the authority of priests and employers.

2

The Loyal Republican
1885-1889

I

The Second Empire, Jaurès once wrote scornfully, was "a horrible Caesarean travesty on popular sovereignty."[1] And the Republic under Thiers, the ex-Minister of Louis Philippe who became its president from 1871 to 1873, sagged under "an antiquated European conservatism, obstinate and presumptuous."[2] In contrast to Napoleonic treachery and pseudorepublicanism, the democratic Republic was the great hope of France and the key to unprecedented happiness. The newly elected deputy from the Tarn felt that it was just such a regime that he was about to serve.

The fate of the Republic had been for half a decade uncertain at best, but had not the events of 1877 confirmed its existence and strengthened its foundations? Onlookers as interested as the young Jaurès could easily have been persuaded by the aftermath of *Seize-mai* that, as historians are wont to say, "the republicans took over the Republic." By January 30, 1879, MacMahon was replaced as President by a stalwart of 1848, the respectable, seventy-one-year-old bourgeois republican, Jules Grévy. No portent of the future could have engendered more hope among republicans than Grévy's declaration on February 7, 1879, that he would "never enter into the struggle against the national will as expressed by its constitutional organs."[3]

But mere confirmation of a republican constitution was no guarantee of progress. In the prefectures, courts, police, and army, not to mention the pulpit and the Bourse, the conservative influence flourished. To the Right in the Parliament sat the strong monarchist minority. To the Left and in the Center sat a republican majority, which, badly divided in its approach to social reform and colonial expansion, compiled a record marred by hesitancy and chicanery. The political order which emerged by the end of the first decade of the Third Republic's history could only discourage impassioned radicals like the young Georges Clemenceau.

In the first half dozen years there had been four identifiable groups in the National Assembly contesting for power — the Legitimists, supporters of the Comte de Chambord and a Bourbon restoration; the Orleanists, followers of the Comte de Paris, grandson and heir of Louis Philippe; the Bonapartist remnants, bloodied after the debacle of the Second Empire but still unbowed; and the minority of genuine republicans, who burned with varying degrees of fervor. In that Assembly, which sat between 1871 and 1876, the Orleanists, occupying the Center as befits monarchists who drew their inspiration from the postrevolutionary regime of 1830 rather than from the order before 1789, underwent a crucial transformation. At the top levels of command among the liberal monarchists were certain capitalist families whose powers had derived in part from the favoritism of Orleanism, which bestowed upon them the direction of mines, railroads, and banks. Since their basic concern was less with the mechanics of the political order than the protection of their valuable privileges, many Orleanist leaders came, in that uncertain decade when Legitimist orthodoxy threatened to spawn an opposing radicalism, to look favorably upon a conservative Republic, dominated by men of their own. Thus the Center, self-interested and fissionable, split into a Right and a Left, the Centre droit under the Duc de Broglie standing firm for the monarchy, and the Centre gauche, led by powerful figures like Jean Casimir-Périer, grandson of Louis Philippe's repressive First Minister and head of the Anzin Mining Company, and Léon Say of the Rothschild Bank, who hoped, by dominating republican politics, to control democracy.

When the Republic was then firmly installed by the elections of 1877 and the Presidency of Grévy in 1879, it was this Centre gauche, replete with experienced politicians, which supplied much of the early leadership. The Republic was still, in part, dominated by men without a shred of democratic idealism; like so many later ralliés in the history of the Third Republic, they accepted the regime with cool cynicism and careful calculation. Their position was assured when Grévy, at the very start of his administration, passed over men of vigor and commitment like Gambetta, to entrust the formation of a ministry to the wealthy and conservative William Waddington. No better assurance could have been given to the Centre gauche that the Republic would not endanger its interests than such a ministry, which included in its ranks ex-Orleanists like Cochery and Léon Say.[4]

Yet, in large part, the republican majority in the Chamber of Deputies was composed of new men, dedicated to a program of political reform, who, with a show of energy and determination, might have carried the day against both devout monarchists and Orleanist ralliés. "It is not enough that republicans make their way into good jobs," cried Charles Floquet, a devoted follower of Gambetta and frequent contributor to that leader's influential newspaper La République française. "Great principles must underlie our laws."[5] Those principles, as Gambetta had often enunciated them, were freedom of speech, press, and association; democratization of the army and bureaucracy; the establishment of free, secular education; and even the imposition of an income tax.

But the mass of republicans in the Chamber, perhaps contented merely to be in office, perhaps confused now that the inspiring mystique of the Republic gave way to the business of legislation, moved slowly at best to the accomplishment of their program. Gambetta himself, displaying a recently acquired caution, insisted that republicans had to be prudent, pressing for reforms only at the opportune moment. So it was that the dominant republican group, enjoying power while awaiting the moment, came to be known as the Opportunists, a derisive label originally hung on them by the Radical pamphleteer Rochefort.

This hesitancy, akin to the Girondism of 1793 and to the moderate republicanism of 1848, seemed a betrayal of freedom and justice to the most militant among the republicans. By the time of the election campaign of 1881, the Opportunists ran into the determined opposition of extremists, who were now identified as Radicals. Their program, a chapter in the Jacobin tradition of France, was the handiwork of Georges Clemenceau, a brilliant politician and journalist, the ex-physician from the Vendée who at twenty-eight had been mayor of the Montmartre under the Government of National Defense.

There was a streak of wildness about Clemenceau in those days. "He was not really a parliamentary leader," complained Maurice Reclus, the devoted biographer of Ferry, "but a lone wolf, a man without a party, following no law except that of his own pride and fantasy. . . . The Clemenceau of those years of intense political activity seemed to exist only for and by his passions."[6] Despite his irresponsibility, or perhaps because of it, Clemenceau put the Opportunists on the spot with a Radical platform, hammered out in his own constituency in the Montmartre, which called not only for the political reforms of his republican opponents but also for solution of the increasingly pressing social problem. Against Opportunist inactivity, he demanded the shortening of the working day, a system of social security, the legalization of trade unions, and even nationalization of mines and railroads.[7] Here at least was some recognition of the fact that the development of capitalism in France involved the needs of the workers.

But the Opportunists carried the elections of 1881, while the monarchist Right was reduced to only eighty places in the Chamber of Deputies. And if among the republicans the Centre gauche won thirty-nine seats and the extreme Left forty-six, the moderates controlled over 372 seats, a total divided between the somewhat larger Union républicaine of Gambetta and the Gauche républicaine of Ferry. These were then the glorious years for the Opportunists, and their version of the Republic was now most clearly developed. "One essential thought will dominate us," declared the technician Freycinet in his ministerial statement of January 31, 1882, "to make peace reign in the country, spiritual as well as social peace, peace both inside and outside France."[8] What, then, were the accomplishments during this reign of peace?

At first glance, the pace of legislation from 1881 to 1885 was rapid and dramatic enough to suggest an energetic program of reform. The influential Opportunist deputy Joseph Reinach, reviewing the performance of those years, could sum it all up in these glowing terms: "One can attack the Republic; one can defame the republican majority of the two Houses; but after reviewing the record, how can one question the fruitfulness of parliamentary activity over the past four years? . . . This legislature, whatever may be its faults, and they are many, has been hard-working, enthusiastic, animated by the desire to do well, sincerely devoted to democracy and progress."[9] Reinach's summation was a piece of special party pleading, but some of the foundation stones of the Republic were undeniably laid in that period.

When the Waddington ministry fell in December, 1879, victim of Radical attacks on its irresolution, Grévy again ignored Gambetta and called upon Freycinet to form a government. Described by its critics as a *replâtrage d'un replâtrage*, the Freycinet ministry nonetheless included Jules Ferry as Minister of Education and the era of secular education began in earnest. Ferry's Article 7, which aimed a mortal blow at the numerous Catholic schools, was the cause of a bitter debate. Though Article 7 was voted down by the Senate on February 23, 1880, by the narrow margin of 148 to 127, the Freycinet ministry was sufficiently committed to the anticlerical program to enforce it on the basis of older, unrepealed laws, which dated back to the First Empire. Three times between 1879 and 1883 Ferry held office as Minister of Education,[10] working relentlessly to reverse the Catholic trend launched by the Falloux Law of 1850. "Against the theocratic absolutism of the Syllabus of Errors," Reclus noted in explanation of Ferry's tenacity, "he meant to defend the democratic individualism of the Declaration of the Rights of Man."[11] Jaurès, always the student and teacher at heart, no doubt saw a confirmation of his republican faith in a program which met the needs of the 624,000 French children who were without formal education in 1880, while reducing Catholic influence in the schools.

Yet despite universal suffrage and certain republican achievements (all of them noneconomic), there was scarcely any concern for social reforms. The Opportunist Republic, which supported the conquest of Tunisia and Indo-China and founded a new system of schools, evinced little concern over the structure of unequal economic power. If an oligarchy had emerged in the first half of the century through the extension of economic privileges to the upper bourgeois families with political influence,[12] it been accentuated in the second half by the progress of industry and commerce. Yet none were to be found in the ministries of the time who proposed to limit the power of the wealthy in the interest of the poor.

What had happened to the militants of the early Republic, the most impassioned *gambettistes*, committed to social as well as political democracy? They were, in the final analysis, united behind a leader, not a program. For if Gambetta had a great voice and an athletic energy, he had little wisdom for a time of social problems. "Not only did he know nothing of economic questions, but he lacked understanding of the Centre gauche which had rallied to the Republic."[13] Had he not observed that "there is no social solution because there is no social question?"[14] Those who walked in his shadow, therefore, were left without a program beyond the themes of pure republicanism. They went the way of Maurice Rouvier, frequently Minister of Finance, whose early advocacy of the income tax was forgotten when he moved among the leading bankers of the time, or of Émile Loubet, who made his way to the Presidency in 1899 by consistently avoiding the strong stand.[15]

Now, in 1885, a real time of testing for the Republic had arrived. If it did not go forward, it might well go down. The rule of the moderate republicans had been seriously challenged in the election by the surprising strength of royalists and Bonapartists, who won 201 seats. And the Radicals, now 110 in the Chamber, had been led by the fiery Clemenceau to their first significant victory. The elections had even brought into the Chamber, for the first time since 1848, six genuine socialists. Jaurès was thus destined to meet men of a milieu very different from his own academic world: Basly, the ex-miner of Anzin; Numa Gilly, the cooper from Nîmes; Camélinat, the old Communard.

But along with the majority of Opportunists, the men of the Centre gauche, the great *affairistes* of the Republic, were still in the corridors, imposing their views on the majority of Opportunists. Virtually none of this, however, was evident to Jaurès, just turned twenty-six, when he first participated in the politics of the Third Republic.

II

He entered the Chamber in 1885 as its youngest member. Photographs of the period show him as short and stocky, neither elegant nor graceful. But they also show a large and impressive head, a deeply sensitive face, restless eyes, and a determined, bearded chin. If the body of Jaurès suggested the provincial bourgeois, the head suggested the scholar-philosopher.[16]

For the new deputy, the immediate problem was one of political identification. Where would he sit in the Chamber and with whom would he ally himself? The answers, of course, hinged on his grasp of French politics, his view of the most pressing problems of the day. Jaurès himself revealed, almost a decade later, how rather simple and categorical his political outlook then was. "When I entered politics in 1885, I knew only two things—the Republic on one side and the royalist-clerical reaction on the other."[17] For almost a century, he felt, the promise of the Great Revolution of 1789 had been frustrated by "divine right monarchy, pseudodemocratic Caesarism, or bourgeois oligarchy."[18] Even now, as the recent elections had proved, conservative forces, the traditional Right of monarchist and clericals, were strong enough to threaten the Republic. What seemed to him paramount, therefore, was republican defense, the alliance, temporary at least, of Opportunists and Radicals, to end once and for all the lingering influence of Old Regime conservatives, while enacting those laws which would strengthen and perfect the Republic.

In the legislative session just past, the Radicals had consistently attacked the Opportunists, and it was this split in republican ranks which had given the monarchists their influence. Indeed, at the outset of the new session, Jaurès, listening in the corridors of the Palais Bourbon, had heard a conversation which seemed to confirm this view. The monarchist Gustave de Lamarzelle said to Clemenceau, who had brought down Ferry's second ministry on March 30, 1885, with a savage attack on French imperialism in Indo-China: "What a vote of gratitude we owe you! In our electoral campaigns we needed only to read your speech on Tonkin." Clemenceau testily replied that the monarchists had not read as far as his conclusions, which called for a Radical Republic. But despite Clemenceau's retort, Jaurès felt, the fact remained that the conservatives, exploiting Radical attacks on the Opportunists, emerged much stronger in 1885 than in 1881.[19]

So Jaurès hoped for a republican party, broad and unified. The attraction of unity out of diversity was always a powerful one for Jaurès, whether as republican or socialist, as philosopher or politician. Since the Opportunists were the larger of the two groups and had led in the struggle to establish the Republic, he felt that they must spearhead the republican movement, and he sat, somewhat Left-of-Center, in their midst. But he called himself a republican-at-large, essentially uncommitted to any partisan faction.

Over the next four years, he occupied the same geographical position in the Chamber, working in his own way for what he considered democratic goals; but it was an experience which, if it pulled him to political maturity, also pushed him into spells of confusion and disillusion. "I fluctuated from gnawing discontent to frivolous optimism," he wrote later. "Stimulated by this completely new and absorbing spectacle, I enjoyed my experience. Yet I felt a sadness because we had entered a period of decadence."[20] By decadence he meant the failure of both will and nerve, the inability or unwillingness of the republican parties to combine on a progressive program. And by sadness, he referred to his feeling that the groups which composed the majority were in one way or another deficient.

Two decades later, in 1904, when Edmond Claris, one of his socialist followers, collected his early parliamentary speeches into a volume, Jaurès wrote a long and revealing introduction, recording his first impressions of the parties and their leaders. Though some of his insights reflected his later judgments, the document remains a valuable guide to his earlier attitudes. To those who argued that the experienced socialist of 1904 could not reproduce the thought of the inexperienced republican of 1885, Jaurès replied that he had, throughout his public life, judged events by the same standard. "I have always been republican and socialist," he wrote.[21] That statement justifiably produced a sarcastic reaction from his critics, who were well aware of his early association with Opportunism; they accused him of trying to cover up his early record and to endear himself to old socialist militants.[22] In a strict sense, the statement cannot be justified, since in 1885 Jaurès did not stand for collectivization of property. Only in the vaguest sense is it acceptable, for as a young deputy he did concern himself most with welfare legislation. Yet there is no evidence that in 1904 he did not accurately describe his views in 1885. How, then, did he view the republicans and their critics?

Impressed by the past accomplishments of the Opportunists — especially Gambetta and Ferry — in solidifying the Republic, Jaurès was now hopeful that they would work to perfect its institutions. His disenchantment was slow but steady over the next four years. Men who had done battle with royalists and clericals now showed little interest in, and in fact outright opposition to, reform of the social order. Gambetta was dead, but Jaurès followed Ferry very closely during the parliamentary session, and he found that the spirited *vosgien,* who had fought for schools and colonies, led no campaigns for social reforms.

Cornering Ferry one day in the corridors of the Chamber, he asked him to formulate his political ideals. Reflecting for a time, the ex-Premier replied: "My goal is a society without a God and without a king."[23] He did not, Jaurès mused, think also of a society without bosses. Considering the rights of property virtually inviolable, Ferry contemplated no real changes in the social system, while Jaurès looked upon universal suffrage as "the decisive instrument for the transformation of property."[24] For one of his talents the doors to the world of success and material comfort were seductively ajar, and the leaders of Opportunism urged him in. But though others of the parliamentary class of 1885 entered eagerly, Jaurès, loyal to the "laboring bourgeoisie," began to look elsewhere.

When he looked to the Left, to the Radicals, among whom he might conceivably have found a home, he became even more critical. Jaurès suspected their sincerity and questioned their program, not only because their attacks on Opportunism seemed to him reckless and vague, but also because they were sectarian and self-interested, unwilling to unite with the moderates in a solid republican movement. Their stand on Ferry's Indo-China campaign in 1885, for example, struck him as a good illustration of their irresponsibility. The sustained and brilliant attack which brought down Ferry's ministry he called "the greatest error of Clemenceau's life."[25] With the expedition almost completed, the only possible result of the Radical assault was a split in republican ranks, a division which cost heavily in the general elections of that year. And then, Jaurès charged, imperialism continued anyway, and the Radicals, once Ferry was out of the way, accepted the new Indo-Chinese colony. In fact, he had overheard a revealing conversation between Clemenceau and the Radical deputy Georges Périn. When the latter said he favored withdrawal from the Far East, Clemenceau replied firmly: "No, that is impossible."[26] From that time on, Jaurès noted, the Radicals remained reconciled to colonial expansion. In 1904, he accused the Radicals of being, like the Opportunists, "the representatives of capitalist privilege."[27] Two decades earlier he at least suspected the purity of their motives and the caliber of their program. Nothing is more important in Jaurès' development than his refusal, once his illusions about the Opportunists were lost, to take the main road to Radicalism. It was something more, something different for which he was searching.

To the Left of the Radicals in the Chamber he met the handful of socialists whose passion for a new social order was plainly evident. And beyond the Chamber, in hundreds of French communities, were the groups, factions, and parties in whose organizations the socialist movement was, slowly and heroically, being built. Yet Jaurès, who claimed that even in 1885 he was a "socialist," remained a stranger to the movement. In the Chamber the few militants, men like Antide Boyer, Camélinat, Basly, and Clovis Hugues, impressed him with their obvious sincerity, but also repelled him with a spirit that seemed vindictive and doctrinaire. Jaurès, humanistic, democratic, and still essentially untutored in the power of class in state and society, was startled by their militancy against capitalism. If there was ever a chance that the young deputy might gradually slide over into their ranks, it disappeared after the long debate on the Decazeville strike. This historic miners' strike, which began on January 26, 1886, grew out of deep and genuine misery. The harsh policies of management provoked violence by the workers, which reached a high pitch when the unpopular negotiator, the engineer Watrin, was killed by a mob. Basly, having made an investigation on the spot, interpellated the government on February 11 in a speech which Jaurès followed intently. When Basly evoked sympathy for the miners, Jaurès was with him. But they parted company when the ex-miner excused the murder because of the barbarism of the company.[28]

Whatever the provocation, Jaurès considered the murder a "shocking and useless piece of violence." When he voted, therefore, it was with Catholics like Albert de Mun and conservatives like Jacques Piou, against Basly's proposed censure of the government on March 10. Camélinat, proposing censure again some four days later, charged the deputies with "burying the social question." Jaurès felt otherwise. It was, he thought, the extremism of the tiny socialist group "which frustrated a real debate on Decazeville and discredited socialist thought."[29] Yet, the young deputy talked to these militants, questioning them about the realities of working-class life and pressing them about the program of socialism. Speaking one day to Duc-Quercy, like Guesde and Lafargue a founder of the Parti ouvrier français, he put the big question: What, asked Jaurès, would the socialists do when capitalism had crumbled and a new society was yet to be built? The Marxist, little realizing that the good bourgeois could be seriously interested, rattled off a stock reply.

"It will depend on the level of economic evolution that society will have reached by the time we take power." It was, strictly speaking, a doctrinally proper response. "But," reflected Jaurès, thinking later how mechanical the words had seemed, "I would have wanted some more detailed explanation; the formula appeared a little futile."[30]

The small, organized parties, operating mainly in Paris and some of the other industrial centers, likewise espoused doctrines too rigid for him or too glib. The Blanquists, for example, thinking to emulate the great insurrectionist in whose name they operated, "believed that the conquest of the bourgeois state and the subsequent overthrow of capitalism would ultimately be achieved through revolutionary action."[31] Much the same position was held by the Marxist chieftain Guesde and his Parti ouvrier français. This did leave one group, the Possibilists, who advocated a peaceful evolution toward socialism. But for Jaurès, the difficulty of establishing contact with the socialist movement was not only doctrinal; it was also a matter of ignorance about how to contact these groups. "In spite of my intense interest in the social problem and my full intellectual commitment to socialism," he later wrote, "I simply didn't know how to join an organized party or to get involved in the working-class movement."[32]

On only one occasion did Jaurès try to make contact with the socialist movement. He sought out those socialists, who clustered around *La Revue socialiste*, which Jaurès read regularly, and its founder, Benoît Malon. In their so-called *socialisme intégral*, Malon and his disciples sought to unite the moralism of French socialism and the materialism of Marxism; they advocated an evolutionary socialism, based on municipal ownership of natural monopolies, social and fiscal reforms, and an active program of public works. Both the theory of the Malon group and the program they proposed attracted Jaurès, and they strongly influenced him in his own socialism. Increasingly isolated in the Chamber, he decided to meet these socialists.

It all started when Gustave Rouanet wrote an article for the March 8, 1887, issue of *La Revue socialiste*, in which he praised a recent speech by Jaurès on the tariff question; he concluded the article by calling the young deputy "one of us." Shortly afterward, Jaurès, excited but a little shy, made his way up a narrow staircase to the offices of *La Revue socialiste* in the rue des Martyrs. "A little frightened by this completely unfamiliar world," he later recalled, "I blurted out: Is *Monsieur* Benoît Malon in? He was not, or so they told me. Without another word, I turned round and went down the stairs. Halfway down, I heard loud laughter from upstairs, and I didn't dare to undertake again a pilgrimage from the Left of Center to integral socialism."[33]

So it was that Jaurès remained in his first parliamentary experience a republican-at-large, seated to the Left of Center and rubbing elbows with the Opportunist rank and file. From this position he worked for two main objectives, social reforms to help the poor and effective unity to protect the Republic. And though he experienced those moments of despair — when he met with political chicanery, or when he witnessed attacks upon the Republic, or when he discovered unreasonable obstacles to reasonable progress — he was, on the whole, an optimist. For he believed in the destiny of mankind, and if one political movement did not forward it, another would.

III

Jaurès did not face his parliamentary career alone, however. Now entrenched in French political life, he was considerably more attractive than before to the Bois family as a husband for eighteen-year-old Louise. The formal arrangements were quickly made, and the wedding took place on July 29, 1886. In addition to a wife Jaurès gained also a modest house and property, some thirty-seven hectares in all, located in Villefranche-les-Albigeois and known as Bessoulet. Comfortable and ample, the summer house, set in the midst of roses and trees, became a source of joy and repose to him throughout his life.

Back in Paris after the elaborate wedding, the couple settled into an apartment at 19, avenue de la Motte-Picquet, where Louise, served by a maid, accustomed herself to a life of banality and indolence. But Jaurès never complained; in fact he seemed to appreciate home as a refuge from the tensions of politics. For from the first, he took his parliamentary responsibilities with the greatest seriousness. Sitting through sessions from start to finish, reading extensively on the issues under discussion, following detailed technical debates as well as the few major ones, he demonstrated his deep respect for politics. Especially impressive were the scope and scale of his daily research. "In the time it might take someone else to cut the pages of a book, Jaurès had actually read and digested it."[34] He talked a great deal with colleagues, listened to waiters at the cafés, everywhere asking questions, studying answers. It was his habit, even years later when his authority was widely respected, to learn from the humblest of men "instead of crushing others with the weight of his immense knowledge."[35]

His guiding principle was his ideal of justice, but without a dynamic political movement behind him and a solid sociological base under him, Jaurès was often insecure and uncertain of his way. Camille Sabatier, Radical deputy from Oran and a colleague in those early days, recalled later that Jaurès was quite incoherent at times, "oscillating from one position to another."[36] He ended up following the Opportunist party line on most issues; and some of his recorded votes, however much they helped to support the republican majority, were in no way linked to the Left, as later critics on both wings never tired of pointing out.[37]

Thus, on December 13, 1885, he approved the appropriation of eighty million francs for the Indo-China expedition, and five days later voted in favor of the religious budget. In the weeks that followed he opposed Rochefort's proposed amnesty for political prisoners and the Basly-Camélinat censures on Decazeville. In 1887 he recorded votes for the Church budget when Radicals like Camille Pelletan were fighting it, and he opposed both Georges Périn's income tax proposal and Jean-Marie Labordère's project for direct election of Senators. At no time did he express any of the doubts about colonialism that made him the great conscience of France during the conquest of Morocco. In fact, when Sabatier expressed his opposition to the funds for the Tonkin campaign, Jaurès argued with him, even resorting to logic which would later be used against him: "You really don't see," he warned Sabatier, "that you're playing the game of the revolutionaries."[38]

At the start of the session he expected enlightened bourgeois leadership from the Opportunists; then he hoped for it; and finally he pleaded for it. He thought it possible, if not inevitable, that good bourgeois deputies, heirs of the Enlightenment and the French Revolution, would, despite occasional setbacks, lead society up the road of progress. The Republic was man's hope, and Jaurès loudly sang its praises. As young as it is, he wrote in *La Dépêche de Toulouse*, "it has been able to bounce back from every new assault with renewed vigor and fresh triumphs."[39] But he felt that the Republic was like an idle machine, impressive but unproductive, without a progressive leadership which would take in hand those pressing problems — depressed agricultural prices and stagnant real wages, for example — that plagued French society. And when Jaurès spoke of reform, he was thinking not of this palliative or that, but of comprehensive change. "If only one organ is diseased, it can be cured by localized and appropriate treatment; but when all the organs are suffering, it must be recognized that the entire body politic rests on a bad principle."[40] His spirit here was socialist, and he expected the majority to establish those strong controls over the free market, which would ensure basic security for the mass of Frenchmen.

Thus, whenever Jaurès took to the forum to make his own lengthy speeches, he appeared consistently on behalf of reform. For almost a year he recorded votes without making a genuine maiden speech. When he finally broke the ice on October 22, 1886, in a speech defending the right of local towns to control primary education, his oratory was praised in several sectors of the press. Clemenceau's *La Justice* and the conservative *Le Figaro* both applauded his eloquence. And *Le Temps* said of his effort, "a real orator has entered the Chamber."[41]

But his message, like those that followed, made considerably less impression where it really counted. Among both Opportunists and Radicals there was so casual a reception of the newcomer that Jacques Piou could later remark, with little understanding of Jaurès: "They [the moderate republicans] made a gift to French socialism of a great leader and orator."[42] Even at home he received scant encouragement from Louise, who remained apathetic to his political efforts. Unlike Steinbeck's Marie Héristal, who "admired her husband without trying to understand him," Louise seemed neither to admire nor to understand. But what was more disturbing to Jaurès was the feeling that his fight for improvements in the lives of the poor did not much stir his own poor constituents, whose muteness he considered a defeat for democracy. What sustained his optimism was a deep conviction that his social ideals should, and ultimately could, be turned into concrete reforms.

Over the four-year session he concentrated mainly on proposals for labor legislation, tariff revision, and fiscal reform. He pressed hardest perhaps for protection of the miners, who, among the workers of industrial France, endured the most hazardous conditions. For them the insecurity that comes from low wages, long hours, and irregular employment was compounded and intensified by the ever-present threat of mine disasters. It was for the law on miners' delegates that Jaurès expended a good deal of his energy.

If the proposal for miners' delegates, which was discussed again and again in the Chamber, were accepted, it would mean that the inspection of mines would be the work not only of government and company representatives but also of delegates chosen by the workers. They would serve for three years and would be able, Jaurès felt, to prevent any attempted whitewash of unsafe conditions.[43] The defenders of the companies in the Chamber fought the measure vigorously and Jacques Piou, speaking on their behalf in the debate of June 17, 1887, made the sweeping claim that the mines were actually well run and safe.[44]

Acting as spokesman for the proposal, Jaurès led the discussion of July 1, 1887. After he had answered certain concrete objections, he confronted the Chamber with this direct challenge: "The law on miners' delegates is the first piece of social legislation which this body has brought to a vote in this session. I implore you not to begin consideration of social reforms by deceiving the workers."[45] A week later, after some modifications, the Chamber passed the measure. But as late as May 24, 1889, the proposal, now modified by the Senate, was still being debated in the Lower House. Again Jaurès lectured his colleagues on their social responsibility, and urged them to proceed "with the emancipation of the workers. . . . If we have the courage, without hesitation, weakness, and fear, to turn toward the future and to collaborate resolutely with the people in moving forward toward justice; if we so understand our goal and define our principles, we can confidently submit them to the judgment of the people."[46] Yet, by the time the parliamentary term ended in 1889, the proposal for miners' delegates had still not been enacted into law. It was tough old Basly, who had come out of the pits of the Nord as the socialist representative of the workers, who once observed before a meeting of miners: "When a measure which is pleasing to the Government is suggested, it is voted into law in four days. But all those proposals which we make that touch upon capitalistic interests are violently opposed."[47] It would not be long before Jaurès, witness to so many dilatory tactics, came to share that judgment.

But he fought just as hard for workers' insurance schemes, proposals to alleviate the insecurity which surrounded most lives. As early in his career as April 8, 1886, he introduced a measure to establish pension funds by the compulsory contributions of both management and labor; these funds were then to serve workers in time of need or at the end of their working days. The proposal was unsuccessful, but two years later Jaurès was in the thick of the fight to establish accident, sickness, and old-age insurance for miners. During the long debate on miners' delegates he had, from his knowledge of the Tarn, described conditions in the mines, where lives ebbed away without freedom or security.[48] Now again, he was trying to apply a measure of conscience to the capitalist economy. In the debate of March 24, 1888, he urged comprehensive social insurance, and this time the Chamber approved the principle.[49]

The politicians who dominated the legislature moved with little enthusiasm or speed in constructing the outworks of a genuine social security. But if a project was forced before the assembly, it usually meant another appearance by Jaurès. Twice he spoke on the question of compensation for victims of industrial accidents; very moderate in his approach in order to win votes for the measure, he supported a proposal which differentiated between injuries attributable to the carelessness of the workers and those resulting from lack of necessary safety measures.[50] Though the coverage in the law was woefully limited, it at least passed the Chamber on June 26, 1888. By the slow route that social legislation then took, it became law on March 9, 1898.

Neither Jaurès' efforts nor his colleagues' program coped adequately with the needs of the poor. By the last decade of the century, as one critic has recently pointed out, the business of living was desperately hard for most Frenchmen. "Wages, especially among working women were often insufficient for subsistence; the work day remained dreadfully long (ten to twelve hours, and even more for the men of the Nord); the six-day week was not yet the general rule . . . there were no paid holidays; unemployment, total or partial, remained chronic, and in 1893 12% of the working force were totally unemployed; finally, except in public service or in a few large enterprises where employers had taken the initiative, there was no insurance to cover sickness, accidents, unemployment, or old age."[51]

The failure of the republican majority to cope with those conditions disturbed Jaurès, and as he pondered the dilemma of democracy, he concluded that it resulted not from republican ideas and institutions but from the "hesitancy and lethargy"[52] of the once-enlightened bourgeoisie. By 1888, he was uttering aloud his serious doubts about bourgeois leaders. "Will they turn, out of lassitude and contempt, to conservatism," he asked, "or will they function as the torch-bearers of democracy?"[53]

The more he saw and reflected, the more his hope for a progressive republican party, led by the Opportunists, evaporated. Years later, in 1910, in the midst of a debate before a Socialist Congress, he praised what he felt gave his party its strength: "There is one thing at least, which establishes the greatness of the Socialist Party in the midst of our political confusion; it is that it does not yield before insults and attacks, that it has a philosophy, a will, a program, a perseverance, a method, that it moves toward its highest goals and its star."[54] In the Left-of-Center where he now sat, he found no such will or direction.

But the Republic, however badly served, was still man's best hope, and at whatever sacrifice it had to be defended. So he felt throughout the stormy season when antirepublican movements, whirling around the explosive words Boulanger and Panama, swept through the country.

IV

Boulangism was not without precedent in a country that had experienced two Napoleons. Yet, in the support it received and the appeals it made, Boulangism was more of the twentieth century than of the nineteenth. At the height of the movement Maurice Barrès, novelist, nationalist, and self-appointed spokesman of French greatness, stated plainly his reasons for supporting Georges Boulanger. "It is because the general is the only one in France capable of expelling the talkers and scoundrels from the Palais Bourbon."[55] Such distrust of Parliament is now familiar as the preface to dictatorship.

The movement was a denial of rational politics and democratic practice. Winning support among the disillusioned masses, the ultrapatriotic chauvinists, and the disgruntled monarchists, Boulangism ultimately rested, like every new wave of Bonapartism, on an emotional and incoherent program that seemed to offer something to everyone. Intellectuals like Paul Adam and Barrès found in the movement the promise of an authoritarian republic; financiers like the spurious "Count" Dillon exploited it as a potentially profitable economic venture; and the general himself, who seemed hardly sure of his ambition, looked to it for high office and fame.[56]

But Boulangism became significant, not because of the prodding of a handful of adventurers, but because the general became, in turn, the hero of whole sections of the radical Left and then of the antirepublican Right. The Left was seduced by the record of a general, not only committed to the Republic but also capable, as most of the deputies were not, of effecting reforms in French society. In reality, Boulanger's republicanism was a bit dubious, since he had had close relations with monarchists as late as 1880, when he was thanking the Duc d'Aumale for facilitating his promotion to brigadier general. But he had more recently found friends in important republican circles. In Tunisia, where he was sent in 1884 as commander of the occupation troups, he cultivated Paul Cambon, intimate of leaders like Léon Say and Casimir-Périer. Once back in Paris, Boulanger resumed an old friendship with Clemenceau, which dated back to their schooldays in Nantes. And through Clemenceau Boulanger got his political start, for it was the Radical chief who helped to procure for the general his appointment as Minister of War in the Freycinet ministry of 1886.

It was not long before the dashing attractive Boulanger had taken steps enough to convince the public that he was an energetic reformer. Only a few months after assuming office he had removed or transferred a few proroyalist officers, while instituting minor reforms to improve the life of the ordinary soldier.[57] His blue eyes and blond beard were becoming the trademark of a hero. Newspapers like *La Lanterne* and particularly *L'Intransigeant*, organ of Henri Rochefort, an implacable ex-Communard,[58] followed enthusiastically the day-by-day exploits of this unusual republican soldier.

Boulanger's popularity finally disturbed the Opportunists for the same reason that it appealed to the Radicals. Political power was at stake, and it was not surprising that Joseph Reinach should have opened a strong campaign in *La République Française* against the general, who, by his vigor, was putting Opportunist rule to shame.

But if men of the Left thought Boulanger would sweep them into power, they were quickly disillusioned. The "man on horseback" is never easily controlled by his original supporters, and Boulanger was no exception. Soon the ultrapatriots, who had long dreamed of a war of revenge against Germany, pinned their own chauvinistic hopes on him, and through the efforts of Paul Déroulède, guiding genius of the League of Patriots, they made their way into the general's camp. This tie to the *revanchards* did not escape astute old Bismarck. Anticipating war, he presented to the Reichstag a proposal for extending German army service to seven years and for raising by 70,000 the number of active troops. Only after an alarmist speech before the deputies on January 11, 1887, and the election of a new Reichstag in February was the German Chancellor able to push his proposals through the Parliament. In the course of expressing public concern over Boulanger, Bismarck managed to enhance the general's prestige among French patriots.

Franco-German tension mounted in 1887, and in that surcharged atmosphere the so-called Schnaebelé affair sent the General's stock soaring. On April 20 the Germans arrested one Schnaebelé, the police commissioner of the French frontier town of Pagny-sur-Moselle. Though the Germans claimed that the arrest took place on German soil, to which the victim had been enticed, the rumor circulated that he had actually been seized in French territory, and indignation mounted in Paris. Boulanger drew up for President Grévy an order for rapid mobilization, but the cautious President insisted on an investigation and thus discovered that, just as the Germans had charged, the French Minister of War was using the frontier police as spies. War was avoided by the calm of Grévy and the release of Schnaebelé by Bismarck on April 30. But the affair was important in the history of Boulangism, for it made the general seem to many the only real guardian of national honor.[59]

It was now obvious to the moderate republicans that Boulanger, who was rocking the boat, had to go. The fall of the ministry over a budget question on May 8, 1887, meant a new Cabinet, one from which he could be dropped. The Rouvier ministry was formed after a behind-the-scenes deal between the Union of the Right, headed by the Legitimist Baron de Mackau, and the Opportunists, which safeguarded the former from anticlericalism and the latter from the popular general.[60] At this stage, with Boulanger still considered radical and with chauvinism absent from the thought of monarchists and Catholics, the traditional Right could oppose the general, and he was now swept out of office.

Whatever defenses were thrown up against Boulangism, however, proved only cardboard outworks. Though out of office the general continued to gain popularity, and in a desperate move the ministry exiled him from Paris by sending him off to Clermont-Ferrand as commander of the thirteenth army corps. Even that move seemed to backfire; on the night of July 8, 1887, as he prepared to depart from the Gare de Lyon a great crowd gathered to cheer him, exhorting him to strong action. A *coup d'état* was in the making, but the general did not rise to the occasion, and only by climbing onto the locomotive did he manage to escape his following.

All of this rolled into a mounting threat to the Republic; yet it was not until May 28, 1887, that Jaurès first spoke out on Boulangism, a strange delay in the light of his deep republican convictions. But then, the general in his first year as Minister of War had displayed what the deputy from the Tarn called "a liberal and patriotic ardor for reform."[61] Finally, however, Jaurès recognized that the popular man on horseback posed a threat to democracy; and he urged that the answer to Boulanger lay not in devious political tactics but rather in the success and strength of the Republic. "The deviations in Boulanger's conduct and attitude," he wrote, badly underestimating the general's strength, "will be easily contained by a Premier with some real prestige and supported by a steady majority."[62]

The Rouvier ministry, formed with the aid of the Right, hardly qualified as a strong democratic government.[63] Indeed, Jaurès saw in Opportunist tactics, not a solution, but a new springboard for the traditional Right in its "resistance to democracy and human progress."[64] The tactics were to prove futile anyway, for Boulangism won new support when the Wilson scandal broke. The unsavory activities of Daniel Wilson, a deputy but also Grévy's son-in-law, culminated in the damaging revelation in the fall of 1887 that he was carrying on a lively traffic in various favors, including honorary decorations. Despite proof that Wilson had used Grévy's influence to conduct his shady business affairs, the President took no action against him, and Boulangist and Radical newspapers had a field day at the expense of the Republic. Even after the Rouvier ministry fell on November 19, stubborn old Grévy, jealous of his position, refused to resign. But when the President could find no politician willing to form a new government, he finally left office on December 2, 1887. Disillusion with the Republic mounted, as cynicism and corruption again helped the general, waiting patiently in the wings.

The shape of Boulangism now began to change drastically. The majority of Radicals, led by Clemenceau, dropped the general as too dangerous and unreliable, and made common cause with the Opportunists to block him. The alliance was reflected in the Tirard ministry, installed on December 12, which included, not Boulanger, but some reform-minded Opportunists. All of this led to the murkiest, shadiest phase of Boulangism, for in search of new allies, the general and his closest supporters grew dangerously reckless and joined their movement to Mackau's Union of the Right, which no longer feared the radicalism of Boulangism, while publicly exploiting the insecurity of workers, artisans, shopkeepers, and intellectuals.

By March 12, 1888, a new and noisy Boulangist newspaper, *La Cocarde*, was launched, espousing the seductive if meaningless program of "dissolution, revision, and constituent assembly." The Napoleonic technique of the plebiscite became the operating procedure for the movement, and Boulanger's name was entered, very successfully, in a series of special by-elections in 1888. A band of reckless men spearheaded the drive to power — Mackau the monarchist; Déroulède the ultrapatriot; Rochefort the radical journalist; the "Count" Dillon, financier extraordinary; and Leftist deputies Georges Laguerre, Charles Laisant, and Francis Laur. Their attacks helped to bring down the Tirard ministry on March 30, 1888, but that brought into office the tough republican, Charles Floquet, whose conservative views were often wrapped in radical rhetoric.

Though unaware of the full measure of republican corruption on the one hand and Boulangist maneuvers on the other, Jaurès watched the events that swirled around the general with growing comprehension. By the spring of 1888 he had formulated his understanding of Boulangism, finding in it most of those ingredients that a later age found in Fascism. A movement exploiting ultrapatriotism, accepting support from all the discontented, espousing a program vague enough to mean anything to anyone, such a movement, Jaurès charged now, was a threat to freedom.[65] The danger was despotism and, as he was to warn again during the Dreyfus crisis a decade later, "despotism is the most monstrous of inequalities, since there are millions of men who can do nothing while one man can do anything."[66]

Still, Boulanger's success continued to mount, and, as the summer of 1888 wore on, he won handily in three by-elections. Jaurès stepped up his attacks on the general, exposing in the press the close ties between Boulanger and the Right, which, he charged, made of the man on horseback not a reformer, but a front for conservatism.[67] While others were willing to resort to artificial devices in their fight against the movement, however, Jaurès consistently opposed expedients. Why, as the Opportunists were demanding, replace the *scrutin de liste*, the voting system adopted in 1885, with the old *scrutin d'arrondissement*? *Scrutin de liste*, Jaurès pointed out, had been devised as the best system of democratic politics, for the electors, in selecting a department-wide list of candidates, voted more for issues than personalities. Yet the restoration of *scrutin d'arrondissement*, voting for a single candidate in an electoral district, was being proposed as a means of defeating Boulangist candidates, on the theory that the influence of local notables might overcome the appeal of the general's rhetoric. "If our country, after eighteen years of freedom, wants slavery," Jaurès wrote, "then everything is lost and no political expedient will save us."[68]

Despite Jaurès' confidence, the attacks against the Republic grew stronger. Out of the backwash of Boulangism emerged charges against the regime, sensational to be sure, but credible in the atmosphere of the time. There was the strange case of Numa Gilly, self-styled socialist, who sought to discredit completely the probity of the government. It all began on September 3, 1888, when the mayor of Nîmes, the deputy Numa Gilly, spoke and accused virtually the entire Budget Committee of the Chamber of corruption. He eventually published his "proof" in a book entitled *Mes Dossiers*, which proved to be only a collection of assorted scraps of hearsay. Though he lacked solid evidence, Numa Gilly won the limelight for himself by denouncing "so many favors for the rich" in the budget.[69] Supported to the hilt by publicists like Rochefort,[70] he became a minor celebrity. Watching the case carefully, Jaurès, in two long essays, sought to respond to the charges, not by defending or denying corruption, but by analyzing it. Writing in the first place that Gilly's book was the product of ambition rather than observation, he went on to discuss the real reason for political corruption. "The evil is not there," Jaurès insisted, in referring to public officials themselves, "but in the economic immorality of an irresponsible capitalism."[71] So long as the society rested on the ethics of private gain and selfishness, public and private life would continue to reflect that morality. The answer to corruption lay, not in abandoning the Republic or exposing a few evil politicians but in the transformation of the social system. The long fight to help save the regime was pushing him to a new position — that democracy could flourish only in a new moral climate.

Boulanger meanwhile continued his ascent to power. The general finally invaded Paris standing as a candidate there in the by-election of January 27, 1889. The republicans united, as Jaurès had hoped, to back a common candidate, Jacques, the president of the Conseil général of the Seine. The Boulangist campaign was at its height, however, and the election resulted in a smashing victory for the general; cries were now heard in the streets of Paris urging him to seize power. At the crucial moment, when 100,000 Parisians were ready to follow him, the general decided to wait for the national elections that fall, and thus obtain a legal grant of power. The decisive moment for Boulanger, though he hardly knew it then, had passed.

On the morrow of the general's victory Jaurès, writing especially for his audience in the Midi, sought to rally support for the Republic. How had the general achieved his victories? Not, charged Jaurès, by presenting

a clear program or argument; the sources of his victories were clear —
the exploitation of every discontent, the use of emotional appeals, and
money. Presaging a later day when money would be so essential a part
of political campaigning, he deplored "the intrusion of big capitalism
into the business of elections."[72]

The republican majority, now thoroughly frightened, sought some
viable instrument for stopping a dangerous political rival. They revived
the much-discussed proposal for the *scrutin d'arrondissement*, and Premier Floquet urged the change in the Chamber debate of February 11.
Despite strong majority pressure, Jaurès again opposed these tactics. Was
it right to defend the Republic so surreptitiously? No, he insisted, let
the Republic take the offensive and win on the plane of ideas.[73] His
colleagues, less convinced that right makes might, voted the change by
a firm majority.

Floquet gave way to Pierre Tirard as Premier on February 22, 1889, and
the change raised the curtain on the last act of Boulangism. For it brought
into public office as Minister of the Interior Jean Constans, who was
now charged with conducting the all-important general elections that
fall. Immoral, vain, and venal, Constans approached the job of finishing
off Boulanger in the fashion of a prizefighter disposing of an opponent.
He moved at once, arresting the leaders of the League of Patriots and
spreading the rumor of the impending arrest of Boulanger. The effect
was better than even Constans anticipated. On April 1 the general and
his mistress, in a classic failure of nerve, fled to Brussels. Constans was
elated. "The arrest of that mediocrity might have provoked a street
riot; but his flight discredited him in the eyes of many of his followers,
and Laguerre, one of the most spirited, groaned: 'What can you do with
a coward?'"[74]

Now, especially, Jaurès urged a clean and open fight against Boulangism. Thus, when the Chamber was considering, on July 13, François
Viette's proposal to outlaw multiple candidacies in the coming elections,
Jaurès opposed the move as an insult to popular suffrage. "In the public
conscience there is a mixture of good and bad. But in the spirit of the
people there are not only base instincts but also a sense of justice and a
great desire for liberty."[75] Living in the age before massive propaganda,
Jaurès still believed, in the fashion of Mill, that truth would prevail in
any free and open encounter.

Henri Brisson, a sincere republican of Radical tendency and a former
Premier, answered Jaurès. While praising his idealism, he reminded
his young colleague that Lamartine in 1848 had likewise placed his trust
in the people in advocating popular election of the President of the Second Republic. "And we all know," Brisson concluded, thinking of Louis

Napoleon, "what that vote meant for freedom and national integrity."[76] Multiple candidacies were outlawed, the election campaign was taken well in hand by Constans and his Prefects, and Frenchmen voted on September 22 and again on October 6. The results crushed Boulangism. Only thirty-eight avowed supporters of the general were elected against 366 "true" republicans. Boulangism groaned a few death gasps and soon perished. The burial was performed by the general himself, who first watched his beloved mistress, Marguerite de Bonnemains, die in Brussels, and then, on September 30, 1891, shot himself on her grave.

How was it all to be evaluated? A great victory, some insisted, had been scored by the Republic. But, as happens in the imperfect world of politics, the result was no clearcut triumph of good over evil or justice over injustice. The whole affair, in fact, meant a new conservative turn for the Republic. The Opportunists, jolted by the threat of losing control and uneasy in an alliance with Radicals, came to terms with the conservatives of the Right. The bargaining point was the clerical issue, and anticlericalism was to be put aside along with the hope for a royalist restoration. "The Union of the Left was replaced by accord on the Right to maintain social order — an already classic alliance."[77] The effect on the working class was also decisive. For those who had been tricked by Boulangist rhetoric the results were disillusioning enough to turn them away from any political party but their own. Out of the ashes of Boulangism rose a stronger socialism.[78]

These new directions could not help but influence Jaurès deeply. The rallying of conservatives to the moderate Republic and the growing adherence of labor to socialism sharpened the split between order and progress and pushed him toward a firmer commitment. The lassitude of the Opportunists, which was a stimulus to Boulangism, and their ultimate resort to trickery and coercion encouraged his disenchantment with "pure republicanism." But Jaurès was too much the moralist to draw only political lessons from the recent drama. The whole affair revealed to him the debasement of modern society, where men were systematically depersonalized by the industrial system. "The worker must have mastery over the machine," he reflected. "Only when a man has acquired the feeling of his own worth in his daily life can he act nobly in society."[79]

In his opposition to Boulangism, Jaurès again demonstrated his fundamental differences from those Opportunists among whom he still sat. They fought it primarily because it threatened their hegemony and exposed their failures; he fought it because it was demagogic and deceptive. But in its widespread appeal, he realized, Boulangism reflected a profound disillusion with the Opportunists and a protest against the social system. Thus, though Jaurès defended the Republic as the best hope of man, he broke with those Opportunists who, by their chicanery and self-interest, had debased its value.

Nor did Jaurès follow the course of those socialists and pseudo-socialists, who supported Boulangism out of conviction or gross miscalculation. Though the Possibilists had rallied to the defense of the Republic, an indispensable instrument in their view for the slow evolution to socialism, others, either less coherent or more revolutionary, boarded the Boulangist bandwagon. Among them were some who were socialists only in the vaguest sense, men without a precise socialistic philosophy or program, who reacted emotionally to corruption and misery. They might be antisemitic, persuaded that the Jews were the manipulators of an exploitative capitalism; Numa Gilly's *Mes Dossiers*, for example, carried a preface by Auguste Chirac, a notorious antisemite who himself contributed frequently to Malon's *Revue Socialiste*. Or, in the fashion of Maurice Barrès, they might be patriots and Catholics, whose "socialism" smacked of a medieval corporatism; his socialism, Barrès declared in *Le Figaro* on February 22, 1890, was a return to Christianity and a repudiation of the Jewish influence. For such self-styled socialists, national socialists as a later day would label them, Boulangism promised to regenerate the nation, restore its traditions, and extirpate its enemies. They were neither responsible thinkers nor organized socialists; they misled the masses and eventually went the way of pure nationalism or reactionary politics.

But on the organized revolutionaries, especially the Blanquists but even some of the Marxists, Boulangism also exercised an influence. And why? Because it *was* a mass movement, winning wide support from the working classes and thus persuading the revolutionaries that it might overthrow a corrupt Republic and an exploitative society. In his important unpublished dissertation at the University of Paris, "La Crise économique et sociale de 1882 et le mouvement boulangiste," Jacques Néré recently demonstrated how closely linked were the effects of the economic crisis in the 1880's and the growth of Boulangism. Subjected to periodic unemployment and low wages, the workers, especially the most highly industrialized among them, more readily expressed their protest through Boulangism than through the underdeveloped socialist parties. Thus, when the general swept to victory in the Seine in January, 1889, he scored most impressively in those districts populated mainly by industrial workers. If artisans, less directly affected by economic slump, more easily resisted Boulangism, others, like the dockers, responded to its frenetic attacks on the "system."

The Blanquists, put off neither by the reactionary ties of the movement nor its authoritarian appeals, were most seriously infected by

Boulangism; if Vaillant managed to keep his head, leaders like Ernest Roche, chauvinistic and insurrectionary, became willing instruments of the general's revolution. The Marxists were generally more realistic and less sanguine about Boulangism, but some of their chiefs at least, notably Paul Lafargue, toyed with the idea of a Boulangist-Marxist alliance; that astonishing fact emerges clearly in the second volume of the recently published *Correspondance* (Paris, 1956) between Engels and Lafargue.

As late as 1888, Lafargue, though he recognized the dangers of chauvinism, tended to write Boulanger off as a political buffoon.[80] Engels, on the other hand, reflecting views similar to those of Jaurès and prevalent among the German Social Democrats, scored Boulangism as a serious threat to the peace between France and Germany. By the end of 1888, however, Lafargue had been so impressed by its mass support that he could view Boulangism as a serious protest movement and one that would ultimately benefit the Parti ouvrier français. For Boulangism, he argued, reflected the contempt of the working classes not only for the bourgeois Republic and its powerful masters, but also for the reformist Possibilists. Underestimating the grave danger of confusion among the workers and of their infection with a spirit at once nationalistic and authoritarian, Lafargue suggested for the Guesdists a temporary game of collaboration. In cities like Marseille and Bordeaux, in fact, Marxists made common cause with Boulangists in the general elections of 1889; so important a Guesdist as Raymond Lavigne wrote articles for the antisemitic *Petit Boulanger*; and workers who had been taught the meaning of class struggle and internationalism now exalted the nation over class.

Exasperated and critical, Engels warned the French Marxists that they must work to destroy Boulangism. Lafargue's policy not only gave head to a virulent brand of chauvinism, but it also undermined the international solidarity of French and German socialists. Writing to Lafargue on August 27, 1889, he insisted that the future of French socialism depended not on the success but on the defeat of Boulangism:

If Boulanger got well thrashed, and his following reduced more or less to the Bonapartists, it would prove that this Bonapartist vein in the French character — explicable by the inheritance from the great Revolution — is gradually dying out. And with the elimination of this incident the regular development of French republican revolution would *reprendre son cours*; the Radicals would, in their new incarnation Millerand, gradually discredit themselves as much as in the incarnation Clemenceau, and the better elements among them pass over to us; the Opportunists would lose their last pretext for political existence, that of being at least defenders of the republic against pretenders;

the liberties conquered by the socialists would not only be maintained but gradually extended, so that our party would be in a better position for fighting its way than elsewhere on the Continent; and the greatest danger of war would be removed.[81]

By 1890 the Marxist flirtation with Boulangism was over, and even the best of the Blanquists, like Vaillant, fully understood the danger of the movement.[82] But in their dangerous interlude, these experienced socialists had been less wise and more opportunistic than Jaurès, not yet officially enrolled in the ranks of socialism. He sensed that the working classes, out of a genuine social protest, had fallen prey to Boulangism; but in a movement based upon the wild, irrational politics of chauvinism and dictatorship, he realized, they could never find their way to a better future.

V

French democracy suffered not only from its open enemies but also from its professed friends. This became apparent when the word "Panama," at first whispered only in high political circles, began to be shouted in the public forum. That shout also turned into a roar against the Republic.

The Panama episode began as the exciting dream of Ferdinand de Lesseps, hero of Suez, who hoped to build a canal across the Isthmus of Panama. By March, 1881, a company was founded for that purpose and easily found investors, beguiled by de Lesseps' fame. Instead of completing its work in two years as it had promised, the company soon ran out of both time and money. The lavish salaries of the directors, the unexpected challenge of an inhospitable climate and a mosquito-infested terrain, and the unbelievably poor planning led to near-collapse of the enterprise by 1885.[83]

The company turned to the public for help, hoping to salvage the enterprise by calling in more money through a government-approved lottery. When de Lesseps appealed to the Brisson ministry for authorization on May 27, 1885, he supplied misleading and overoptimistic information. But the Premier commissioned Armand Rousseau, chief engineer in the Department of Bridges and Roads, to investigate the condition of the project. Rousseau's report, rendered on April 30, 1886, to Charles Baïhaut, the Minister of Public Works in the Freycinet ministry, was unfavorable and seemed to dash the company's hopes.

At this point the entrepreneurs of the company, playing for high stakes, began the endless process of bribery. Baïhaut, bribed with a million francs to be paid in three installments, placed the lottery proposal before the appropriate parliamentary committee. But when the committee demanded to see the company's records, the request for the lottery was withdrawn. In the face of almost certain disaster, the administration of the Panama Company resorted to even more widespread bibery. By March 1, 1888, the Radical deputy Alfred Michel again proposed the lottery in the Chamber, while a small group of men in the employ of the Panama Company — Baron Jacques de Reinach, Aaron Arton, and Cornélius Herz — controlled the distribution of favors among officials and the spread of favorable publicity in the press. "The Baron de Reinach, through his nephew and son-in-law Joseph Reinach, was well qualified to operate in the Opportunist world; Cornélius Herz, proud of his role as silent partner of *La Justice* and of his personal relations with Clemenceau, was assigned the task of influencing the Radicals."[84]

The stock lottery was approved by the Chamber on June 9. The complex, behind-the-scenes negotiations, the fraud and bribery, were, of course, hidden from Jaurès. But he was learning the facts of political and financial life rapidly. Speaking in 1888 with the editor of a provincial republican newspaper, he discovered that agents of the company had offered to pay for favorable editorials about Panama. And if the deputies of his department voted for the stock lottery, the editor was promised a good bonus. Jaurès felt the weight of the company's propaganda even more directly, for when he voted against the lottery, he was bombarded with hostile mail from his own constituents hoping for quick profits through investment.[85]

The stock lottery proved a failure, and by the end of 1888 the Floquet ministry, trying to avoid a financial panic, urged the Chamber to comply with the company's request for a three-month moratorium on its debts. The spirited debate of December 14, 1888, brought Jaurès to the forum again as defender of the Republic against the barbed attack of the Catholic Bonapartist, Paul de Cassagnac, editor of the antirepublican *L'Autorité*. Cassagnac used the growing scandal of Panama to discredit the Republic, but Jaurès turned on him sharply recalling that wary republicans had voted against the stock lottery while the Right had overwhelmingly supported it.[86] In establishing the complicity of the Right in financial schemes, Jaurès was, in effect, placing the blame for scandals not on the Republic or republicans but rather on the unholy lure of profit.

Panama was beyond salvation, and early in 1889, on February 4, the Civil Court of the Seine ordered dissolution of the company. The dam of protest now broke, and embittered shareholders demanded a government investigation. By 1892 the lid had been completely blown off this fantastic Pandora's box, and the roster of implicated politicians and journalists grew dangerously long. The Chamber debate of November

21, 1892, savage and recriminatory in tone, was another field day for the antirepublicans, though the truism that emerged was the quite obvious one that money often corrupts the morals of men.

Out of the Chamber after his defeat of 1889, Jaurès, who followed the revelations closely, found in the scandal a powerful argument for a socialist republic. Only a system that placed public welfare above private gain could cope with the evil of corruption. Socialism would save the Republic from destruction; and, as he thundered in the Chamber in 1897, "with the revelation of the corruption embedded in all the cells of the society, we will soon see the triumph of our ideas and our cause."[87]

VI

By the end of the Chamber session of 1889 Jean Jaurès was not quite thirty. But his world of experience had burst at the seams in the past four years. Gone was the peaceful life of the provinces; gone was the reflective life of scholarship. Thrown into the swirl of politics and Parisian life, he suffered hours of doubt and unhappiness. Disillusion is the price of walking knee-deep in the world of reality, and it offered a challenge to his youthful idealism.

The assessment which a man should make of himself and his career comes often too late or not at all. But Jaurès was too honest for evasion. Was he to become another self-seeking politician, or should he leave the public arena completely? Questions of this order troubled him, but he indicated his answer one July day in 1888 in addressing students at his old lycée of Albi. "The artist, the orator, the painter, the musician are often forced, if they are to live and survive, to waste or debase their talents; but there comes a time when they have to pull themselves together, to fulfill themselves totally by some noble contribution."[88]

Sensitive though he was to the deep sorrows of life, Jaurès welcomed the challenge of living. So, if the world of public affairs was often discouraging, it was also the world of good and noble actions. Another *normalien*, somewhat younger, Édouard Herriot, once wrote that Jaurès was sufficiently depressed by politics in 1889 to move permanently from public to academic life.[89] The erstwhile mayor of Lyon really misunderstood Jaurès. It was the year of the great Paris Exposition, commemorating the centenary of the French Revolution, an international fair showing the progress of the arts, sciences, and industry. From the Invalides to the Champs de Mars the Exposition bespoke achievement and promise; Jaurès wanted to work for a brighter, fuller future, and he decided to stand for reëlection on the republican ticket.

His second election campaign, however, was plagued from the start. In the first place, he was greatly concerned about the health of Louise, who was then expecting a child. Though her health was good she now demanded very special attention, and when Jaurès moved her to Bessoulet, their cottage in the south, he had to attend her far more than a vigorous campaign schedule would have permitted.[90] Then, he faced the strong opposition of the antirepublican clergy. So bitter, in fact, were some of the clerical attacks in the electoral districts of the Tarn that one of the republican candidates, Émile Level, registered a formal protest with the Prefect.[91]

But most damaging to his cause, by far, was the determined drive against Jaurès of the Reille-Solages group, so long the decisive political as well as economic force of the Tarn. Connected by ties of marriage and class interest, these families had great wealth, concentrated mainly though not solely in mines, and prestige, compounded of aristocratic title and long local leadership. The nominal head of the clan, Baron René Reille, was direct heir of a family that had reaped profits from continuous political influence dating back to the first Napoleon. As one of the founders of the Comité des forges, a member of the Comité des houillères, and president of the board of directors of the Carmaux mining company, Reille was a gigantic figure in the capitalism of the Midi. He had brought his Bonapartist loyalties into the Chamber of Deputies in 1876, and, virtually unbeatable in his own political fief, the second electoral district of Castres, had been victor in the three general elections that followed. But it was Reille's son-in-law, the Marquis Jérome-Ludovic-Marie de Solages, who was, in a real and practical sense, the director of clan interests, both economic and political. Though a staunch Legitimist and Catholic, he found difficulty neither in uniting with his Bonapartist father-in-law nor in lining up with any republicans conservative enough to do battle with the Left.

The results in 1885 had not been happy for the clan. *Scrutin de liste* had meant department-wide elections, and though Baron Reille survived, the other seats from the Tarn had gone to republicans, on the basis, especially, of the Carmaux vote. In addition, one of those republicans, the unknown young professor Jean Jaurès, had turned out to be an orator, a reformer, and, worst of all, a socialist at heart. Now, in 1889, *scrutin d'arrondissement* had been restored, and the Reille-Solages group was determined to swing its weight in several of the electoral districts, especially the first district of Castres, where victory would mean the defeat of Jaurès. The Baron would run, of course, from the second district of Castres; the Marquis chose the second district of Albi as his fief. (The Baron's son, Xavier Reille, was only nineteen, and still nine years away from his Chamber seat.) The task of defeating Jaurès fell, therefore, to a henchman of the clan, Jean-Léon Abrial, and once the choice was made, everything but the Montagne Noire itself was thrown into the battle to assure victory.

Jaurès was unintimidated. At the outset, speaking in Castres on August 22, he sounded the keynote of his campaign. "I carry within me a dream of fraternity and justice, and toward those goals I wish to work."[92] In the following weeks he formulated his specific program, still reformist but more extreme than in 1885. He stood now for strong state surveillance over capitalist enterprise in transportation, banking, and insurance. Pointing out the incongruity of political independence and economic insubordination, he urged strong, independent unions and extensive social security to correct the imbalance.[93]

But even as he spoke, the opposition organized an unscrupulous campaign against him. To assure the victory of Abrial, Reille and Solages counted heavily on their control over the workers, whose very jobs depended on their pleasure. Jaurès had plenty of evidence that the miners were being cajoled and intimidated; some weeks before the elections, he denounced this cruel game and called upon the workers to resist the threats of their employers, who "have said to you: 'Vote right and you will keep your jobs.' "[94] Several days later, he wrote of another form of pressure, the sudden generosity of the marquis toward the workers, which was little more than open bribery: "In recent days, workers, who had always been kept out of the great chateau, have been invited in; there have been celebrations, a warm welcome, beer and tobacco, a new familiarity."[95]

Going to the voters on the issues alone, and hampered by a lack of campaign funds,[96] Jaurès compelled attention by his warm sincerity and the power of his oratory. But though he won applause, he did not always win votes from men frightened or seduced by the opposition. Thus, when the voters had their day on September 22, they supported Abrial over Jaurès, 9632 to 8776. The next morning, the incumbent, now retired to private life, issued a statement to his supporters. He had been defeated, he pointed out, by "the combination of clerical and monied interests, which has come to dominate both districts of our arrondissement. . . . I leave public life, not with discouragement or bitterness, but with strong heart and upraised head. A man can serve the Republic well in private life by his thoughts, his work, and especially his integrity."[97]

Others, better known, were also beaten in 1889. Ferry and Goblet were on their way out. At the same time certain newcomers, the future pillars of moderate republicanism, Delcassé, Jonnart, Reinach, and Barthou, were returned. For Jaurès the immediate future would be a time of study and writing, teaching and local politics, speculation and socialism.

3

Preparation for
Socialism, 1889-1892

I

On July 12, 1890, when Jaurès, now back in the Tarn, took
the platform at the Théâtre des Nouveautés to accept the nomination of
Radicals and socialists for a seat on the municipal council of Toulouse,
he alluded to his defeat in the recent general elections. Did the defeat
embitter him? Was he frustrated by the vagaries of politics? "Yes, I was
a defeated man on the night of September 22; but the next day, when I
read in the newspapers the final results of the election, I saw that the
Republic had laid its enemies low; I saw that the Republic was victorious;
I was no longer a loser but a winner."[1]

If Jaurès was a disappointed office-seeker, he didn't show it. Nor did
his return to private life appear as a bleak exile. Cheered by the birth of
Madeleine, his first child, on September 19, 1889, he could look forward
to a fuller family life, and vitally interested, as always, in scholarship,
he could resume once again his teaching career.

With the help of Perroud, Jaurès took up a position as professor of
philosophy at Toulouse. Yet he was prodded by his strong political and
social consciousness, and he could hardly seclude himself in an ivory
tower. Thus, when he received a letter from the editor of *La Dépêche de*

Toulouse asking him to continue his connection with the paper, he eagerly sought permission from the rector to devote some time to journalism. Perroud informed him that there was objection by some members of the faculty to mixing professional and political activity, and that occasioned a spirited defense of his request by Jaurès. "Professors enter both municipal and departmental councils," he argued. "They consequently become involved in partisan debates. Why shouldn't they also argue with the pen, especially when they refrain, as I do, from dealing in personalities and generally give their articles a theoretical turn?"[2] Perroud supported the request, and Jaurès was able to retain a significant forum for political expression.

Settled in a modest apartment at 20, rue Saint-Pantaléon, and enjoying easy access to both the university and the municipal libraries, he lived an intellectual life considerably more vibrant than usual in provincial France. In Toulouse at the time there were several young scholars who gathered in the evenings at the Café de la Paix for spirited discussions.[3] One of them, Georges Dumesnil, later a professor at Grenoble, recalled the unaffected brilliance of Jaurès, who "spoke so well on the subject of the conversation, whatever it might be."[4]

The year that had stretched from the summer of 1889 to July of 1890 was a time when Jaurès began to set his thoughts in order, to organize his social theories systematically. His petty bourgeois republicanism had succumbed to disappointment, and he was ready for socialism. In a crucial interlude in 1889, he struck up a friendship with the erudite librarian of the École Normale Supérieure, Lucien Herr, who guided him toward a new affirmation. Five years younger than Jaurès, Herr had begun his thirty-eight-year directorship at the library of the École Normale in 1888. Equipped with a staggering mastery of sources and endowed with great personal warmth, Herr, who had become socialist by 1889, directed successive generations of *normaliens* to the important treatises on socialist theory. "Here was the man, whom the public did not know," Léon Blum once exclaimed, "yet under whom the socialist *universitaires* were formed, from Jaurès to Déat, including my generation and that of Albert Thomas."[5]

Herr knew the works of the French socialists, but he had especially studied Marx; and if he chose to range himself, not with the Parti ouvrier français but with the Allemanist wing of Possibilism, it was out of opposition to what he considered the doctrinaire attitude of Guesde and Lafargue. Jaurès, who so frequently used the library of his old school, met Herr and what followed was a fruitful dialectic that lasted as long as the two were alive. Now, in 1889, Jaurès was persuaded to study Marx particularly and socialist thinkers generally. On one crucial occasion, the two men bared their ideas in a discussion that "lasted almost all the night." The prodding of the librarian and the subtlety of his argument had their effect, and Jaurès soon stepped through the door to collectivist socialism. "He took that crucial step," remarked the socialist philosopher Charles Andler, "because Herr knew how to convince him."[6]

On February 25, 1890, Jaurès published in the columns of *La Dépêche* an article on German socialism, which is significant in his development. For he therein decisively identified himself as a socialist and first mentioned Marx in public print. What he admired in "our German socialist comrades," he explained, was their devotion to theory; "they are equipped with the thought of Marx and Lassalle . . . German socialism is not a random collection of discontents and petty aspirations; it is rooted in a doctrine, an idea, and that idea reaches the masses."[7] By his interest in doctrine, in a theory of social and economic evolution, Jaurès indicated that his socialism would rest on a more solid foundation than a vague moral yearning.

The coincidence of his socialist profession and his reading of Marx was significant. He was, as one critic has recently written, "one of the few Frenchmen in the last decade of the nineteenth century to study it [Marxism] with the greatest attention and intelligence. Jaurès had written marginal notes throughout a copy of *Capital*, and his skill in German enabled him to read Marxist works not yet translated into French."[8] What he derived from Marx was significant though limited; it centered largely around the critique of capitalist production. What remained conspicuously absent from Jaurès' references was any mention of the *Communist Manifesto* and its sharply etched tableau of class struggle; for this implied a determinism in history, which neither his philosophy nor his experience to date could justify. In the eclectic socialism of Herr and *La Revue socialiste*, in their emphasis on the traditions of the French Revolution and earlier utopian socialism, he drew inspiration for the idealism and democratic faith which always modified his commitment to Marxism. So he indicated sometime later when he answered the letter of a schoolteacher who had asked Jaurès for a socialist reading list. He was delighted by the interest and he responded warmly. Consult many good works, he advised; and in compiling a list of suggested readings, he reflected his own investigations of the time: Marx's *Capital*, especially the chapters on the labor theory of value, the brochures of Guesde and Lafargue, and, very prominently, works of St. Simon, Fourier, Louis Blanc, Proudhon, Lassalle, and Malon.[9]

Despite his teaching and newspaper work, Jaurès found this life not absorbing enough. Less than a year after his defeat at the polls, he announced his candidacy for the seat on the municipal council which was to be filled in a special election on July 27, 1890. Toulouse, where Radicals and socialists worked together against conservatives and moderates, was an excellent laboratory for his socialism. In his campaign for the office Jaurès burst the limits of local questions and sketched the main outlines of his political creed. Speaking on July 19 to a large audience in the workers' district of Saint-Cyprian, he placed himself squarely in the socialist camp: "I say that there will be no real accomplishments until we resolve the social questions. And it is that effort which I am asking the Radicals to make. But they ought not imagine that they can resolve it with the simple formulas of the French Revolution. Since 1789 other questions have been posed that must be solved by a program which is, in essence, socialism."[10]

The eloquent professor scored an easy victory in the election, and became not only a municipal councilor but also, by designation of his new colleagues, one of the several deputy mayors. The municipal council was dominated by Radicals, though the presence of four socialist workers, led by Charles de Fitte, demonstrated the sharp turn to the Left. Substantially the same group was reëlected, along with Jaurès, on May 1, 1892.

An active and conscientious councilor, he intervened frequently in the debates of the council. Often when he spoke, he found citizen De Fitte, who scoffed at his idealistic version of socialism, glaring across the table. De Fitte was a Marxist firebrand, speaking at council meetings "as I would if I were in the street,"[11] and hewing to an inflexible line. Jaurès locked horns with him on November 3, 1891, when he opposed De Fitte's proposal to rid the civic welfare homes at once of all religious personnel. The principle of secularization, however crucial, appeared to Jaurès less important than the relief of the needy. "Yes, when the Republic will have done its duty on social questions by assuring security," he argued, "then secularization will work. . . . But today, faced with terrible suffering and with a widespread selfishness which frustrates plans for social improvement, you cannot raise that disrupting question."[12] His eye was fixed much more steadily on relief than on dogma, and one can easily imagine how unreliable he must have seemed to the doctrinaires.

The two men clashed again on June 25, 1892, when De Fitte proposed an end to the subsidy for the Théâtre du Capitole, a municipal enterprise, as a needless expense. But Jaurès, for whom socialism was to serve the cultural as well as the economic needs of men and women, successfully opposed the suggestion. In the tradition of Danton, who had coupled enlightenment with bread as the chief needs of the people, Jaurès set for socialism the broadest goal of enabling humble men and women "to savor all the joys of life which are now reserved for the privileged."[13] Through the theatre, as through all the arts, people could penetrate beneath the surface of life to its underlying truth, understand its ebb and flow, appreciate its beauty and tragedy. It was the view of an intellectual and a humanist, not yet in intimate contact with the working class, but deeply sensitive to the requirements of a full life. The clashes with Charles de Fitte were significant, for in the face of attacks Jaurès was forced to question his socialism and to give it more thought.

In the discharge of his duties as deputy mayor, Jaurès appeared frequently at educational ceremonies. When he addressed the students of the Grand Lycée on July 31, 1892, he offered them a creed derived from his evolving philosophy:

To live for others while developing the self — that is what I consider our double law, and with the increasing pressures of civilization, it is worthwhile to recall it. . . . You must learn to say "I," not out of violence or pride but out of awareness of your inner existence. . . . When you read the most beautiful pages of the great writers, the most beautiful verses of the great poets, you must understand them deeply both in their purpose and their style; you must absorb their beauty through all your senses and in all your faculties. . . . Then, young people, you will have developed within you the only power which will never die, the power of the spirit.[14]

Such sentiments revealed what an idealistic poet had come to socialism. Translated into more prosaic terms, this plea for the wholeness of man suggested the critique of human alienation in Marx's *Capital*. In *La Dépêche de Toulouse*, however, Jaurès could address himself to issues of national rather than local interest, and, against the backdrop of French politics, construct a concrete political position.

II

The collapse of Boulangism had led the monarchists, whose alliance with the general had been so futile, to change their course. Since the preservation of a ruling élite and defense against lower-class aspirations were considerably more significant to conservatives than the restoration of a decorative king, the new direction of the Right was perfectly logical. It was nothing less than a rallying to the Republilc by men who had fought it for two decades.[15]

By 1889 the deputy Jacques Piou, erstwhile monarchist, was proposing a Constitutional Right to support a safe and sane Republic. Despite the opposition of some diehards like Cassagnac, the idea had real possibilities for the ex-monarchists if the Opportunists were willing to accept their former antagonists as friends. Alexandre Ribot, a leader among the moderates, openly indicated such willingness in a series of Chamber speeches in February, 1890.[16] The new fusion that was in the making was an enormous challenge to those who thought of the Republic as the font of social reform.

Jaurès watched, recorded, and reflected on these moves. They seemed especially distressing to him as he studied the course of capitalist development and found, in the growing concentration of capital and enterprise, "the continuous crushing of the proletariat and the petty bourgeoisie." How, he asked rhetorically, could small shopkeepers compete against department stores like the Bon-Marché? How, in the villages, could the traditional lower middle class survive?[17] An age was closing, he felt, and with it its frontier of opportunity. Those who had always believed that by dint of hard work they could nurse small businesses into large ones were doomed to frustration. There was only one viable answer to this relentless trend, and it was socialism. He thought thus of a socialist movement which should embrace the petty bourgeoisie as well as the workers, and a socialist government that would be a coalition of the distressed classes rather than proletarian dictatorship. "If that were so," he wrote, "it would simply mean the replacement of one tyranny by another, one oppression by another."[18] Socialism was to be a "truly human" movement, a source of aid and comfort for all who suffered and were threatened with extinction.

Devoted to the democratic method, Jaurès believed that socialism could grow out of free elections and gradual reforms. But as he watched the antics of Parliament, he realized that the Republic was becoming ever more conservative. What most disturbed him now was the *ralliement*, a startling reversal of Church policy, which led staunch Catholics to abandon their monarchism and to support the Republic.

It had not escaped the highly intelligent Leo XIII, Pope since 1878, that the debris of royalism lay scattered amid the ruins of Boulangism. The Pope reckoned that French Catholicism could scarcely profit from support of a bankrupt cause, and that it would continue to incur the hostility of the State so long as it remained isolated from the Republic. These were views he shared with certain French Catholics who were ready to gamble on a sympathetic Republic. The most important of them was the energetic Archbishop of Algiers and Carthage, Cardinal Lavigerie, who, after the elections of 1885, was seriously proposing a *rapprochement*. His point of view was strikingly similar to that expressed by Pope Leo in his encyclical of 1884, *Nobilissima Gallorum Gens*, in which Catholics, while urged to defend the faith vigorously, were encouraged to support the existing state, even if it were a republic.

The elections of 1889 demonstrated better than arguments the durability of the Republic, and Pope Leo was more fully convinced than ever that Catholics could influence it only by joining it. Never had the time for a *ralliement* seemed more propitious. Had not Freycinet announced at the start of his fourth ministry in March, 1890, that he would follow a "broad and tolerant policy"?[19] In October, 1890, the Cardinal traveled to Rome, after important talks with Piou, Freycinet, Ribot, and Constans. Convinced that the moderate republicans would drop anticlericalism as an issue, he reported his findings to the Pope. Reluctant to intervene directly in French affairs, Leo authorized Lavigerie to find the right public occasion for stating a pro-republican position.[20]

The Cardinal waited less than a month. On November 12, 1890, at a banquet in Algiers for the officers of the French Mediterranean fleet, he offered his famous "toast" in which he insisted on the duty of citizens, regardless of personal preferences, to support the prevailing form of government. Though he ended with the assurance that his position would not be opposed by any high authority of the Church, the *toast de'Alger* created consternation in French Catholic circles. Cassagnac attacked the Cardinal's stand, while of the French high clergy only the Bishops of Réunion and Annecy supported Lavigerie at once.

For a time the Pope skirted the issue of French politics, concentrating his efforts on constructing a more effective social policy for Catholicism. On May 15, 1891, he promulgated his immensely important encyclical *De Rerum Novarum*, in which Catholic labor policy was refurbished. In an attempt to wean the Catholic working masses away from the secular radical movements, the Pope attacked economic liberalism and restated the Church's preference for the regulated market.

This move to win the workers was soon followed, however, by the Pope's action to prevent the complete political isolation of French Catholics. With the rumblings about separation of church and state growing louder, Leo XIII acted. On February 17, 1892, he granted an interview to Ernest Judet of *Le petit Journal* in which he declared that "the Republic is a legitimate form of government. . . ."[21] This sensational statement was followed at once by the encyclical *Inter Multiplices Sollicitudines*, published in the religious press of Paris on February 20, which codified the *ralliement*.

Old Opportunists welcomed the adherence to republicanism of Catholics like De Mun, Cochin, and Mackau; not only did it presage the end of the monarchist threat, but it brought to their side a group of social conservatives. Ferry, that great crusader for secularism, expressed especially well the significance of the *ralliement* for those who were deeply disturbed by social radicalism. "The conservatives who have rallied to the Republic," he declared with satisfaction, "will bring over others. This is natural and not at all disturbing."[22] But if the Republic was for the time being safe, now that the Church had tempered its hostility, the question that remained was what kind of a republic it would be. This, indeed, was the question that Jaurès posed during the entire sequence of events. And in giving his own answer he was directed by his understanding of the philosophy and politics of the Catholic Church.

Jaurès minced no words; toward orthodox theology and powerful churches he was hostile and critical. Yet, it was a position that grew neither from ignorance nor prejudice. In religion he found a subject for perpetual study, and his own library contained a wide range of theological works, their margins filled with his own running debates with Bossuet, Augustine, or Thomas. But more than that, religion seemed to him a vital manifestation of man's spiritual quest, that perpetual search for ideals and purpose in an otherwise aimless world. "At the outset, it is very difficult for man not to raise certain questions," he wrote of the religious revival of the early 1890's. "The little episodes of parliamentary politics are not the full answer to human curiosity, and faced with the immense and external universe, man cannot concern himself only with the future of the Constitutional Right."[23]

But what Jaurès accepted as the religious quest had little to do with the teaching and ambition of organized churches. It was linked rather to the idealistic side of his philosophy, which tied man to a whole universe by his pursuit of ideals like justice. He had, in this light, professed sympathy for the ethics of Jesus; yet he found that creed denatured in organized Christianity. "All those who believe themselves Christians, but who do not work to kindle the dignity within man, to dissipate his ignorance, to alter his egotism by the example of altruism, to realize in human societies that perfect equality which is the genuine recognition of human worth, all those take the shadow for the substance and delude themselves."[24]

That was 1887. Five years later, as an avowed socialist, he was equally absorbed with religious questions but firmly opposed to the organized creeds. The new religiosity of certain intellectuals, his old acquaintances Bergson and Paul Desjardins among them, was totally unacceptable to him. "There are certain fastidious spirits," he wrote, with scarcely veiled sarcasm, "who, without being Christians, love to entwine themselves in Christian formulae. . . . To escape anticlericalism, which seems to them mundane and coarse, they take on little airs of orthodoxy. . . . Are they in the Church or out? One doesn't know; their work is the essence of equivocation; it exudes both an odor of incense and the perfume of refined nonbelief." No, he insisted, the search for ideals belonged outside established churches. "The real problem is not how to restore and rejuvenate Christian dogmatism. It is whether, outside of an out-moded Christianity, we can develop a religion in harmony with science and history." The thinking of the French Marxists, on the one hand, was too deterministic to confine Jaurès. But he remained equally tough-minded in saying 'no' to a Christianity which found expression in a privileged Catholic Church. "Neither philosophically nor politically can one separate Christianity from the Church, and the Church has become, in the eyes of the people, one of the greatest forces of oppression in the world."[25]

The attack on the Church, therefore, belonged, as far as Jaurès was concerned, to the realm of politics, and was not a matter of conscience. He considered it totally desirable. So long as the State guaranteed free-dom of worship, man's religious quest could proceed unimpeded. What frustrated it, after all, was its association with a Church so long a center of reactionary politics.[26] Thus, as Jaurès observed the signs of *ralliement* and the consequent pause in secularizing the State, he was both sus-picious and critical.

What did it really mean for Catholics to recognize the Republic? It was all quite formal and completely opportunistic, Jaurès wrote, unless the Church recognized also the principles of reason and free thought on which the Republic presumed to rest. Could the Church, or would it, accept "a religious conception in harmony with science and history?"[27] He had only to roam the rural Midi, he wrote, observing at firsthand the near-fanaticism of many priests, to learn the answer.[28]

It was not long before the action of the Catholic hierarchy in France justified his fears. In January, 1892, right before the papal encyclical, five French Cardinals published a long letter to Catholics, approved by Lavigerie but far from conciliatory in tone. The Cardinals paid lip serv-ice to the Republic, Jaurès noted, but then proceeded to attack freedom of conscience, secular education, civil marriage, in fact the entire frame-work of institutions on which a free society rested. Summing up his observations, Jaurès expressed his essential distrust of the *ralliement*. "The Church is emotionally attached to the monarchy, and the monarchy is dead."[29] The Church would not change by accepting the Republic, but the Republic would change in accepting the Church.

The social program of Catholicism, so spectacularly displayed in *De Rerum Novarum*, seemed to him an even more dangerous deception than the *ralliement*. The growth of socialism was the point of departure for both Jaurès and the Pope, but they moved in opposite directions. The growing determination of workers to alter the social order thrilled

Jaurès while it frightened Catholics and capitalists. But instead of running from the problem, the astute Pope Leo sought to answer collectivism with a kind of Christian socialism.

Jaurès was not impressed. Traditionally the Church had offered nothing besides charity to men crippled by insecurity and misery.[30] Pope Leo's new encyclical at least recognized the magnitude of the social problem created by industrialism. But while Jaurès praised the message for its recognition of labor's plight, he denounced both its caricature of socialism and its feeble proposals.[31] What measures, short of socialism, could possibly achieve that fair return for the workers which the Pope had set as his goal? While realistically exposing the terrible social conditions created by capitalism, Leo had rejected the only valid way of ending them.[32] Answering the clerical charges of materialism and human debasement, Jaurès once again summed up his version of socialism: "It seeks to develop all the faculties of man, his power to think, to love, and to will."[33]

III

"We were being led quite openly into an authoritarian Republic—the Republic of important names, of captains of industry and great financiers. This was not the result the parties of the Left expected when they had organized to defeat Boulanger."[34]

So wrote Andler years later in recalling the trend of politics in the 1890's. Almost everyone was calling himself republican now, but political leopards don't often change their spots. The Opportunists, soon to be called Progressists, found their marriage of convenience with the ralliés an effective coalition against socialism, but it was hardly consonant with their oft-repeated program of purifying the Republic. Jaurès now harbored few hopes about the politics of moderate republicanism; if any of them lingered on, they died with the workers of Fourmies in the Department of the Nord.

The fusillade de Fourmies of 1891 was the bloodiest episode in the early history of the May Day movement in France.[35] The idea of May Day originated in the United States where, on May 1, 1886, more than three hundred thousand embattled American workers walked off their jobs to demand the eight-hour day. In that early period of the international labor movement, when workers were easily intimidated, the courage of these Americans inspired their most militant European comrades. At Bordeaux, in November, 1888, Jean Dormoy, the leader of the Parti ouvrier français in the Allier, persuaded the Fédération nationale des syndicats, a national labor organization founded largely by Marxists, to sponsor a one-day strike for a legal minimum wage and an eight-hour working day; thus, on February 10, 1889, groups of workers in some sixty cities demonstrated simultaneously. Later that year, the representatives of world socialism, a weak minority but convinced of their ultimate success, met in Paris to organize the Second International, essentially Marxist in inspiration and revolutionary in outlook. At that first Congress, Raymond Lavigne, the pioneer of Marxism in the Gironde and Secretary of the Fédération nationale des syndicats, proposed for the first of May an international workers' strike on behalf of the eight-hour day. The motion was adopted, and the May Day movement was born.

In spearheading the drive for social reforms, the Guesdists, who professed themselves revolutionaries, were following the lead of Marx himself. The *Communist Manifesto*, after all, contained proposals for a number of concrete reforms; in the same vein, the platform of the P.O.F., which Guesde had composed in 1880 under Marx's watchful eye, ended with a list of immediate political and economic goals. For genuine reforms, the Marxists argued, like the raising of wages or the shortening of the work day, would strengthen the proletariat in its struggle against capitalism. Furthermore, the campaign for those reforms would rouse the workers from their apathy, school them in collective action, and, because of the bitter resistance they were certain to encounter, sharpen their class consciousness. For the Marxists, neither social reforms nor democracy were the paths to socialism; and at the turn of the century, in their bitter battle against reformist socialism, they would seem openly contemptuous of both these techniques. But for the present, in their struggle to reach the workers and to organize them, the campaign for reforms seemed an important source of propaganda.

On May 1, 1890, following the directive of the Second International, workers in some 150 French cities demonstrated peacefully for the eight-hour day. It enhanced the influence of the P.O.F. and the Fédération nationale des syndicats which had organized most of the strikes. In 1891, when the Blanquists, the Allemanists, and the Possibilists also supported the movement, the May Day demonstrations were more widespread but also much more tumultuous. In several cities — Bordeaux, Roanne, Lyon, Saint-Quentin, Charleville — the strikes were forcibly broken up and some of their leaders arrested. But in Fourmies, May Day, 1891, was a day of violence and death.

Though not a large city (in 1891 it had a population of 15,895), Fourmies was heavily industrialized. The great majority of its workers, women and children included, earned their living in the several textile mills which made the city a leading producer of woolen goods. For a year at least, Fourmies had been a center of economic misery and social tension. Faced with a temporary decline in the textile market, the manufacturers, though they still reaped substantial profits, cut the wages of their workers. To protect themselves, the employers collaborated with the local priests to establish a *syndicat mixte*, a sort of pseudo-union inspired by the ideas of Pope Leo XIII; furthermore, they organized a *Société industrielle*, a common front of employers against their workers.

By 1891, however, the textile workers had struck several times, and a minority among them were determined to form a union. Their leader was the Marxist Culine who had organized the local P.O.F. and now strove to unite the textile workers against the manufacturers. Other Guesdist leaders came to his assistance. On April 12, 1891, Paul Lafargue addressed a meeting of more than 500 workers at Fourmies, and so did Victor Renard, who had organized a textile union at Saint-Quentin. Thus, as May Day approached, the workers of Fourmies, not all of them but probably a majority, prepared to demonstrate for an eight-hour day, higher wages, and a union.

The employers, inspired by fear and anger, urged the mayor, Bernier, to prepare the police for action and to ask the Prefect of the Nord for military help. Bernier complied, and so did the Prefect, who sent two infantry companies to Fourmies on the eve of May Day. During the morning of May 1, a clash between the police and some 1500 *manifestants* took place before one of the textile mills; momentarily dispersed, the workers regrouped and demonstrated before the city hall. In the afternoon, after the luncheon respite, an even larger crowd gathered in the central square of Fourmies. Ordered to leave, they defiantly refused. Mounted police then rode down on them, indiscriminately striking at men, women, and children. Hurling stones at the police, the workers held their ground until troops arrived and occupied the square. At about five o'clock, the soldiers opened fire. The *fusillade de Fourmies* lasted less than four minutes. When it was over, nine had been killed, four of whom were under twenty, and thirty-three wounded, including a two-year old child.

The events at Fourmies had immediate and widespread repercussions. In one public meeting after another, several sponsored by the Guesdists, some by the Blanquists, even one by the Boulangists, speakers denounced the government for its part in the tragedy. In the Chamber of Deputies, on May 4, several socialists launched a bitter attack against the government and especially the Minister of the Interior, Jean Constans. Ernest Roche, once a Blanquist but more recently a Boulangist, told the story of Fourmies in every shocking detail. He concluded with these angry words: "If there were justice in France, if we deputies were the kind of men we are not, M. Constans would pay with his own life for the death of those innocent people." But Constans easily survived the attack. Building his defense around the report of the Prefect of the Nord, Constans blamed the tragedy on the dangerous agitators who had whipped the workers into a frenzy. For the troops and the local administration, he had only praise. When Alexandre Millerand, a Radical moving toward socialism, demanded an official inquiry, the republican majority rejected the proposal. Instead, they adopted a motion which extended sympathy equally to the workers and to the soldiers who had fired on them. As its sponsor, Adolphe Maujan, said: "The republican party must lead the socialist movement and convert it into something orderly and peaceful."[36]

Jaurès followed all these events closely, and they influenced his development as a socialist. After the first May Day strikes in 1890, he wrote enthusiastically about the working-class solidarity which was developing. But he was concerned primarily about the reform itself, the eight-hour day. It was a humane measure which would lessen the weight of the long, grueling work day; but more than that, he argued, it was an economic measure, which might, partially at least, resolve the problem of unemployment. Yet at this stage of his development, when he still had no firsthand contact with the labor movement, Jaurès questioned the technique of street demonstrations. If the workers had gotten out of hand, their lawlessness would have been a perfect excuse for suppressing the strikes; for "at the first show of violence, the bourgeoisie calls upon the government to repress the workers."[37] It was far better, he insisted, to influence the deputies, to educate the public, and to win the eight-hour day by parliamentary action.

In 1891, however, Jaurès approached the May Day movement with greater militancy. He no longer questioned the street demonstrations. Instead he was outraged by the tragedy at Fourmies. He found in it grim evidence that socialism, not clericalism or monarchism, had become the enemy of the republican moderates. Yet when he first wrote on Fourmies, Jaurès still appealed to the good will and the common sense of the Freycinet ministry. The working-class movement he wrote, was a legitimate, a necessary political force. In its May Day strikes, it was using democracy — freedom of speech, of press, of assembly — not to overthrow society but to demand a decent life. He urged the ministry to face up to the social problem, to recognize and accept the working-class movement.[38]

The aftermath of Fourmies, however, dashed Jaurès's hopes for reason and generosity. On May 11, the government arrested both Culine and Lafargue on the charge of instigating the violence. The evidence against them consisted of quotations of speeches attributed to them. On July 4 and 5, they were both tried before the Cour d'assises of Douai by a jury of "capitalists, industrialists, and landed proprietors."[39] After five minutes of deliberation, the jury returned verdicts of guilty, and the Court meted out sentences of six years imprisonment for Culine and one year for Lafargue.[40]

Jaurès was now moved by anger and compassion. Culine, a worker and the father of four, a courageous leader who had organized a peaceful meeting, had been sent to jail, while the murdering troops and the officials who ordered them out won the plaudits of the Chamber. "His real crime," Jaurès wrote of Culine, "is to have been a socialist and an organizer of a workers' demonstration." So long as socialism was a movement of much theory and talk, it was harmless enough; but now that it had reached the stage of action and organization, "a sector of French society has succumbed to fear and hatred."[41]

It was like a final dismissal of the party with which he had once sat. But if the bulk of republicans would not, as he hoped, lead France step by step to a new social order, how could socialism evolve? Suppose, he thought, suppose the Radicals, the most energetic among them anyway, paved the way. "There are Radicals like Clemenceau," he pointed out in stressing this possibility, "who proclaim that their movement cannot remain purely political, that new social questions have been raised. . . . And there are socialists like Benoît Malon outside the government and Millerand and Basly in the Chamber who are reformist. They believe that a true social revolution can be accomplished by law and without any violence in the streets."[42] But what of the fundamental issue of property, which was destined to separate Radicals from socialists and to shatter their hope of collaboration? What of the social struggle which was destined to convert Clemenceau and his friends into archdefenders of law and property? On these questions, Jaurès was silent; he wrote instead as though the latter-day Jacobins, carrying forward the work of 1793, would league themselves with the socialists to create, peacefully and democratically, a new social order.

IV

In these important years of his development, Jaurès did not enroll in any of the organized socialist parties. Had there been a single large party, representing a coherent, class-conscious proletariat and committed to an effective program of action, he might well have joined it. But such was hardly the case; instead, the socialist movement bore all those marks of weakness and immaturity — factionalism, cultism, doctrinal scholasticism — which could only have discouraged him. Divided into at least seven distinct groups, none of which could claim more than a few thousand vocal adherents, French socialism suffered not only from the arid quarrels of its leaders but especially from the peculiar development of French capitalism.[43] In the last three decades of the century, France, to be sure, experienced considerable industrialization, but not so much as to replace small-scale, workshop production or to destroy the peasantry; so slow was her rate of growth, in fact, that as an industrial power she trailed badly behind both England and Germany. "All the power used in French industry in 1890," J. H. Clapham has written, "would only have driven a few squadrons of the capital ships in 1920."[44] Thus, by 1896, 85 per cent of all industrial establishments in France employed fewer than five workers, while industrial concentration was limited mainly to certain metallurgical and textile enterprises.

Such were the conditions which imposed upon the French socialist movement its numerical weakness and doctrinal confusion. Outnumbered and dispersed, the industrial workers did not constitute a highly coherent, class-conscious proletariat; often of peasant or artisan origins, they — the minority who actually protested against their dismal lot — espoused doctrines which echoed the associationism of Blanc, the insurrectionism of Blanqui, and the mutualism of Proudhon. Only where industrialization had created a compact and disciplined working force, in the Nord, for example, or the Pas-de-Calais, did the Marxism of the Parti ouvrier français make real headway. In the decade and half before World War I, when the pace of French industrialization and urbanization quickened, the socialist movement would grow larger; but even then, and it was the basic cause of its weakness, the party would never enroll anything like a majority of all the workers. Neither a genuine mass party on the one hand nor a highly centralized core of militants on the other, it lacked the numbers to control elections or the discipline to attempt revolution.

By 1890, the Possibilists had scored some notable successes in local elections, while the Guesdists had increased their influence among the most militant workers. Yet these factions remained small, and they dissipated their energies by bitterly accusing each other of betrayal to the socialist cause. Even within their ranks, the quarrels went on, so that the Left wing of the Possibilists, angered by what seemed to them the opportunism of the majority, broke off in 1890 to found its own party, headed by Jean Allemane, which was essentially antipolitical and anti-intellectual; among the Guesdists, doctrinaire astringency so disturbed some that Clovis Hugues, erstwhile collaborator of Guesde, finally labeled him a "Torquemada in glasses." Jaurès spent his socialist life working for unity and tolerance within the movement, and was of no mind to opt, permanently and passionately, for one approach to socialism as against all others.

But despite his independence, Jaurès had direct and friendly contacts with the Marxist party. The leaders of the local P.O.F. in Toulouse, hopeful of recruiting him into their ranks, asked him to their meetings, invited him to speak, and finally arranged his historic first meeting with Guesde himself. Fourteen years older than Jaurès, Jules Guesde had been in the radical movement since the late days of the Second Empire. Ending in 1876 his five years of post-Commune exile, he had returned to France and, in the following decade, devoted himself to the establishment of the Marxist party. A tireless organizer and a skillful speaker, Guesde was already a mighty figure in European socialism. He was, as the syndicalist Mermeix once put it, "Marxism speaking French."[45] In March, 1892, he arrived at Toulouse for a speech, and Albert Bedouce, then a Guesdist militant in Toulouse, accompanied the young philosopher to his meeting with the Marxist chief.

Jaurès went to the rue Peyrolières in Toulouse, where Guesde had a large, ill-furnished room in the Hotel d'Espagne. The whole night through the two men discussed socialism.[46] The words are unrecorded, but one can imagine Jaurès' defense of reformism, his appeal to an educated proletariat and a free electoral system. And one can imagine equally the responses of the Marxist, whose view of democracy in a bourgeois society was compounded of scorn and disbelief. The meeting was immensely stimulating to both men. Jaurès found Guesde challenging and courageous; yes, he would think more deeply about the Marxist philosophy of history. Guesde, attracted by the high intelligence of Jaurès, turned to Bedouce as the dawn crept into the room and said: "It's been a good day."

Far more the sectarian than the theorist, Guesde was not the kind of *philosophe* who could cope convincingly with serious questions and criticisms. Jaurès never enrolled in the P.O.F., but he certainly did not sever his contacts with the Marxist movement. He followed its literature, expressed open admiration for its organization, and in *La Dépêche* on April 20, 1892, openly praised its program. Not much more than six months later, he accepted that very Marxist program as the basis for his own electoral campaign. Nonetheless, as he prepared again for public action, his socialism remained a complex convergence of ideas, the two main strands of which were idealism and materialism.

4

Idealism and
Materialism, 1892

I

"The whole art of higher education," Jaurès once wrote, "is
to link analysis and synthesis together in the life of the mind. . . . That
is the secret of great poetry, great science, great action."[1] It was also the
key to his philosophy.

In the crowded months between 1890 and 1892, wedging the research
in between politics and teaching, he brought to completion the two theses
which he presented and successfully sustained at the Sorbonne. Within
the pages of the long French thesis, *De la Réalité du monde sensible*,
and the supplementary Latin work, *De primis Germanici socialismi
lineamentis apud Lutherum, Kant, Fichte, et Hegel* (*On the Origins
of German Socialism*), he worked out his theories of metaphysics and
history, and built at the same time the basis for his system of socialism.

On the central issue of his philosophical work, the nature of the real
universe, Jaurès took a position between positivism on the one hand and
absolute idealism on the other, which one historian of philosophy has
called "metaphysical positivism." It was linked to a philosophical tradition, originating in nineteenth-century France with Maine de Biran,
which sought to go beyond positivism and "to perfect knowledge of

the spiritual life."² As Jaurès once pointed out,³ he was indebted to the rigorous logic of Aristotle, the skepticism of Montaigne, the humanism of Rabelais, the cry for justice in the Bible and in Rousseau; he owed even more to those philosophers, especially Spinoza, Leibnitz, Kant, and Hegel, who had confronted contradictions and sought an ultimate reconciliation; and in the most immediate professional sense, he owed most to those two important teachers of the École Normale, Jules Lachelier and Émile Boutroux, authors respectively of the consequential works, *Du Fondemont de l'induction* (1871) and *De la Contingence des lois de la nature* (1874).⁴

What is the universe, what is God, what is man? — in answering these questions he would define reality. As he had already done in his philosophy course at Albi, Jaurès rejected the idealistic conception that the real exists only in the subjective consciousness. He posited the world of objective matter but contended that this did not completely explain reality. The table exists, as the senses testify; one can see it, touch it. Yet what the senses reveal are not the particles of matter which lie at the root of things, but a "substantial unity" that the mind has contributed. The stone, which seems whole and at rest, is composed of "a certain number of chemical components, but these molecules . . . oscillate perpetually under the action of certain agents — gravity, electricity, magnetism, heat."⁵ "Without mind, therefore, without the profound idea of unity, of individuality . . . there would be for us no substance."⁶ So Jaurès came to his first and fundamental proposition, that reality is a synthesis of matter and mind, the objective and the subjective; "the real is what is intelligible."⁷

Reality is that constant fusion between rational man and material universe. "The consciousness lodged in the brain is not isolated from the world, but is, on the contrary, tied to it."⁸ Space, the vast environment, is crucial. In the dialogue between space and the sensory organs, all the colors, sounds, and smells come to be differentiated. Space communicates and the mind transforms. Nothing is isolated; everything is fused. "How many times, in roaming through the fields and along the pathways, I have felt myself part of the earth I was treading — that I was in it and it was in me."⁹ With a lyrical cry of joy he pictured the universe as a constantly evolving harmony. "The Infinite is not a static house, but as Buffon put it, moving architecture."¹⁰

Unlike the rigid positivists of Martin du Gard's *Jean Barois*, Jaurès believed in God. Certainly it was not an anthropomorphic God or God the Creator; it was not God as a Being, but as a Becoming toward which the universe evolved; it was God in a pantheistic sense, "the order and harmony of things."¹¹ With Dante he sang a hymn of praise to this unity. "When Vergil and Dante, after having descended through the circles of the underworld, wished to find the living again, they took another route; they came out on the other side of the earth and the poet shouted: 'And we came to the stars again.'" When individual was linked to nature, when individual was tied to individual, in this universal harmony there was universal joy, and that was the reign of God. Sadness was rooted in isolation and discontinuity, "each center of sensitivity . . . impenetrable to the others." Reflecting the tragic sense of life, Jaurès believed that the effort to achieve complete harmony was bound to fail. "It is what renders the life of the world so dramatic. The battle is never fully won." But, far from pessimistic, he could add that the battle likewise "is never fully lost."[12]

Jaurès' philosophy was rich with consequences for his social theory, its ends and its means. If the reign of God was harmony and unity in the universe, then socialism, ending the conflict of classes, replacing competition with coöperation and isolation with community, abolishing private property for collectivism, was its earthly analogue. Jaurès conceived of socialism, lyrically and religiously, as the emergent unity of mankind. Finally achieved would be the long-awaited City, at once the City of Man and the City of God. No more, at last, would one see those "mute and sad phantoms circulating in the city fog, devoid of all contact one with the other."[13]

He returned constantly to the theme of harmony and its beneficent results. Consider one example of what socialism would mean, he urged, consider art. Steeped in European culture and *au courant* even with the most contemporary creative movements, Jaurès knew well enough how many significant works of art had appeared in the nineteenth century. Yet he bemoaned certain trends of the times, the isolation of artist from public, the replacement of large human themes by the "cult of the uncommunicable self,"[14] the absence of beauty in the life of the multitudes.

A great work of art, he felt, is like communism; in it, the artist, the creator, transcending the narrow and confining limits of his ego, has given his work an eternal and objective value; it is communism since it endows all of humanity with the greatest riches of the human spirit, and since each passing generation draws new meaning, strength, and joy from the eternal, unalterable, yet constantly renewed masterpiece."[15]

But what had happened in the bourgeois age? At its earliest trumpeting the artist felt exhilarated, liberated, until its individualism proved to be isolation and not freedom. The artist was alienated, his vision no longer whole, his outlook pessimistic. "How shall I grasp you, o infinite universe! It is the suffering of Werther, of Obermann, of Stendhal, of

Flaubert; it is the yearning of Loti; it is fervent yet frustrated aspiration."[16] So it was even with the giants. "The century starts with Goethe and declines with Victor Hugo. They were prodigious"; but they too, victims of the age, "were incapable of delineating a clear direction in the universe and in society."[17] Reviewing the drama, of which he was especially fond, Jaurès once praised Ibsen and Hauptmann, but criticized them for never fully understanding the course of human history.[18] The theme of great art was "humanity itself," the most sensitive evocation of "the joys and sufferings, the hopes and dreams of the people."[19] But now, "there is no one humanity, no human unity; men are too divided by the antagonism of classes; the privilege of property has created among them too many rivalries, has opened too many chasms. . . ."[20]

So it was socialism, passing beyond mere existence to the full life, that would lead the artist to confront the largest, most universal themes. But what of ordinary men and women, were they not too crude to respond to beauty and too stupid to learn from art? Jaurès, revealing his commitment to equality, denied it. "There are not some who are common and others who are intellectual. Within every man is both the commoner and the philosopher."[21] It was true that the working day was now too enervating and education too inadequate. "How can you expect that after twelve, fourteen, or fifteen hours of work in a factory . . . man's thoughts will rise, dreamlike, above all the raucous noise of the machine?"[22] And in contemporary society the masses were ill-prepared to understand art. "Ah, the aristocrats know all the refinements of the French language so well, but our society has done nothing to enable peasants and workers to understand those works of art created by the geniuses of other generations."[23]

When socialism arrived, there would be security, but beyond that leisure and education, the time and capacity to contemplate and reflect. What would art then do, what would it mean? It would be, in painting, writing, architecture, and music, a spiritual experience fused with daily routine, the beautiful penetrating the mundane. Not a note in all of this forecast latter-day concerns over "too much leisure" and dehumanizing *kitsch*. This was faith, as William Morris had it, that "science and art will flourish only in the new society, where the enjoyment of them will be part of life itself."[24]

From his philosophy, Jaurès clarified not only the goal of socialism, but also the means of attaining it. Reality he had said was an interplay of objective matter and subjective conception. In his behavior man was thus both determined and free, swept up by outside forces yet capable of influencing them. In regard to the nature of man, Jaurès accepted only in part the physiological determinism which reduced states of consciousness to molecular action in the brain, and utilitarian ethics, which attributed all human action to brute selfishness. Both positions, starting from certain demonstrable truths, erred on the side of simplicity, ignoring the fusion of the original determinism with a powerful voluntarism.

Strongly influenced by Darwinism, Jaurès thought in evolutionary terms, and found in the course of animal development the origin of moral instincts. Like Kropotkin, he tried to show that in the evolution of animal life "the purely selfish drives give way, little by little, to aesthetic and altruistic drives. . . . By inundating the vision with sights which exceed the immediate needs of the animal, by suffusing the hearing with sounds that exceed its needs, the universe offers the animal more than just the means of survival. . . . It develops the need, the joy, the delight of melody and harmony." When man emerged he already possessed "a primordial and permanent instinct, a sympathy for other human beings. . . . From the beginning of his long development, man had what can be called a sense of unity." Modifying selfishness, therefore, was an altruism "which, guided by reason, can subordinate the ego to ideals and even, if necessary, sacrifice life to duty."[25] Thus it was man the moralist who created history, just as history created man. Social change, Jaurès once wrote, was the result of "self-conscious egotism, the impersonal dialectic of history, and the deep conscience of humanity."[26]

In his supplementary Latin thesis of 1892, *On the Origins of German Socialism*, he sought to illustrate that theory, to demonstrate that German socialism was not only a response to material conditions but also a culmination of philosophic idealism. "Socialism was born in the German spirit," Jaurès wrote in setting out his theme, "long before the abnormal growth of its big industry and those other conditions necessary for economic socialism."[27]

Touching only briefly on the social theories of Luther, Kant, Fichte, Hegel, Marx, and Lassalle, Jaurès could in no way claim to have written a serious and exhaustive history. Nor was that his purpose. His work was rather an essay of interpretation, a vehicle for posing and answering some fundamental questions about the growth and development of socialism; and though, in the course of his demonstration, he twisted the significance of certain texts (finding elements of socialism in Luther's denunciation of usury, for example, or in Fichte's *geschlossene Handelsstaat*), he set forth cogently a socialist theory which sought to reconcile Marx and the moralists.[28]

What are the sources of class consciousness? Where, in other terms, are the roots of an expanding socialist movement? In posing the problem, Jaurès called into question orthodox Marxism, which considered socialism a function not of morality but of history, a product not of human ideals but of the inevitable struggle of classes. What Marx had presumably taught, his disciples repeated; and more than thirty years were to pass before the Marxists, Georg Lukács in particular, would seriously confront the complex problem of class consciousness.

Against Marxist teaching, Jaurès made his case for the power of ideals in moving men and creating history. In Germany itself, he insisted, where orthodox Marxism was the official creed of Social Democracy, the socialist consciousness took root in the moral idealism of Luther, Fichte, Kant, and Hegel. Before Marx and Lassalle taught that socialism would inevitably emerge from historical and economic evolution, these men had preached the ideal of justice and impregnated German society with a collectivistic ethos. In proclaiming the rights of the community over the individual, the restraint of the one in the interest of the many, they had formulated a profound theory of freedom and simultaneously planted the seeds of socialism:

Only that man is free, Louis Blanc once said, who has not only the right but the means and the power to act. In our philosophy as well as in our economic theory, we French have often considered each individual will as autonomous, separate, isolated, sufficient unto itself; in this way, the claim that all men are equally free; thus our economic dictum: "Every man for himself." The Germans, on the contrary, have linked each individual will to the universal order, both human and divine. The human will is perfected only by obedience to God; and in civil society, political freedom is perfected only by obedience to the standard of justice which regulates relations among men.[29]

What was the core of Luther's revolutionary critique, asked Jaurès, if not his sensitivity to human corruption and his relentless insistence upon moral duty? For once having delivered man from the yoke of Rome, Luther subjugated him to God. He denounced human sin and commanded man to live in the light of God, not later but now, not in the hereafter but in society: "Justice will not flower in the cold regions of death, but in life itself. . . . What is Christ if not God present in the affairs of the visible universe?"[30]

So it was that the impassioned Luther preached the reign of justice on earth. In his pamphlet against usury especially, where "one almost hears the voice of the suffering masses," Luther was denouncing "injustice, avarice, and the human proclivity for sin and crime. . . . Let us admire the rich socialist harvest in this pamphlet. . . . With rare perspicacity, he recognized the reproductive power of wealth when it was left unregulated; he saw how it could impoverish the rich and intensify the misery of the poor. . . . In his book on *Capital*, Karl Marx cities Luther often, enlarging upon his argument and refurbishing it."[31]

The Lutheran Reformation thus left a rich legacy for socialism: "The Germans . . . insisted that individual freedom can be assured only through the power and regulation of the community."[32] And in the later history of German thought and philosophy, Jaurès insisted, that principle was in many forms repeated. In Kant, who linked human freedom to "the fulfillment of duty and obedience to the moral law"; in Fichte, "whose passionate love of pure justice brought him close to the French of 1789 and 1848"; in Hegel, who regarded the State as "that perfect union of individualism and universalism," Jaurès traced an idealistic tradition which, he argued, had prepared the way for the German socialist movement.[33]

But Marx, he realized, had taught otherwise: "To Hegelian idealism Marx opposed economic materialism; events do not emanate from ideas, but ideas from events; history and political economy do not depend on philosophy, but philosophy depends on history and political economy."[34] Yet Jaurès, who had so carefully and sympathetically read the Marxist texts, especially *Capital*, did not deny either the achievement of Marx or his central insights; only those who have examined Jaurès superficially or selfishly can ignore the strong Marxist component in his socialism. He praised Marx not only for his labor theory of value, "the cornerstone of socialism" as he called it,[35] but especially for his systematic description of economic development and historical change. How superior he found Marx to those bourgeois economists, who "treat capital and labor as eternal economic categories. Marx, on the contrary, traces the dialectical process in political economy; the inevitability of progress necessarily changes the relationship of things and ideas; nothing is eternal except the law of the dialectic itself."[36]

Thus Jaurès, who proclaimed the power of the ideal, agreed equally with the materialism of Marx. Nor did he consider this contradictory. Yes, capitalism, suffering its internal contradictions unto death, would finally yield to socialism. But without the component of idealism, how could the Marxists answer the two "pressing" questions, which he now posed? One centered around the role of the individual in history. If events inevitably led to socialism, was it at all useful to form a socialist movement? Seeking confirmation of his own position, Jaurès found a useful passage in Marx who, in writing about social change in the preface to *Capital*, had referred to the possibility of "shortening the period of gestation and mitigating the aches and pains of new birth." The idealist in Jaurès pounced upon this phrase, as though to prove that the system of Marx himself, if not of Guesde, was large enough to embrace the action of both history and man: "Is it nothing to shorten the period of gestation and to mitigate the pains of birth? In so doing, man can snatch

several centuries away from agony, tears, and injustice. If man under-
stands the true course of affairs, he guides them, hurries them along, and
he is truly revolutionary."[37]

The second question centered on the problem of finality, whether or
not mankind, guided by its ideal of justice, can shape the new society,
whether that new society will be the final human triumph or yet another
transition in the process of history. If history were an impartial and relentless evolution, then would not socialism be another passing moment,
devoid of any particular moral value? "If only the brute fact existed,
this socialism, which seems like a wonderful religion of justice to the
people, would become only the worship of fact."[38] But no, the march
of events was a moral journey, and socialism, "the victory of humanity
itself," was its goal. Whether the Marxists admitted it or not, socialism
was a powerful movement because it was the hope of the people: "Lassalle
would never have fired the hearts of men with hope if, in the dialectic
of history, in its results, he had not shown the triumph of eternal
justice."[39]

Thus, Jaurès sought not to separate but to fuse, to reconcile the French
school and the German, to integrate into a single powerful theory the
aspirations of mankind and the impersonal dialectic of history: "Dialectical socialism harmonizes with moral socialism, German socialism with
French socialism; and the hour is approaching when they will converge,
when all the forces of conscience, when the aspiration for dignity and
genuine freedom will unite with the immanent dialectic of history and
the universe."[40] The Marxists, as Lafargue proved two years later in his
historic debate with Jaurès, would dissent. Guardians of the dialectic, they
rejected the appeal to morality as delusive, an echo of all that bourgeois
piety about justice in an unjust society. They feared that idealism would
yield only political compromises and inconsequential reform; they insisted that the revolution would be determined by history and then
shaped by it. Over the years, as his experience widened and his social
analysis deepened, Jaurès would draw even closer to Marxism; but he
never abandoned his idealism. Socialism would emerge in the course of
history. The inner contradictions of capitalism would bring the system
down; but its immorality would move men to act and to prepare the
reign of Justice. For "at the very core of capitalism is the negation of
man."[41]

II

Speculating once about the path to collectivism, Jaurès drew up a list of
the steps that could be taken at once. "First there must be an education
for the people which is more than just an empty word."[42] Before every-

thing else, he named education. Let men learn; let the suns of knowledge drench them; let them compare the potentiality of life with their present condition — and what great will-to-socialism might not follow! At every stage of his career, before 1892 and after, Jaurès was the propagator of education, among the socialists its most active promoter.[43]

There were some in the camp of French socialism, especially among the Guesdists, who raised skeptical questions about the significance of education. Could men fight for ideals that were not simply rationalizations of their class position? And even if so, could education under capitalism be anything but ruling class propaganda, rather than a scientific grasp of the universe? Jaurès pondered these questions, but did not succumb to fatalism or yield his affirmative stance. In that twilight of the age of reason, he kept his faith in a rational people. The street mobs of the Dreyfus period were a decade away, and, in twentieth century terms, even they were small.

In part, his confidence in the power of learning was the indestructible legacy of his own career. For despite inauspicious origins, Jaurès had come to understand his world through education, and that understanding had led him to socialism. At heart he always remained the *normalien*, dedicated to letters and convinced of the power of human reason. In his study of the École Normale, Hubert Bourgin sketched two pictures of Jaurès which show him as perhaps the greatest of the *normaliens*. Bourgin described Jaurès at a learned gathering, then in the school library: "At the dinner to celebrate the tenth anniversary of *l'Année sociologique*, held at the home of Emile Durkheim, he [Jaurès] occupied the place of honor, but without affectation, vanity, or pretension; and if the extensive part he took in the conversation, if his obvious indifference to culinary delights prevented him from really enjoying the duck in orange sauce, he eclipsed without the slightest effort, and without annoyance to anyone, all the learned professors then present."[44]

Then, in the fine library of the École Normale, where Jaurès frequently browsed among books on all subjects, Bourgin would see him, "the humanist, the professor, the philosopher, the dialectician, standing in a corner of the room and discussing with two or three friends the great questions of literature, history, metaphysics, or ethics."[45]

But his belief in education was more than an expression of gratitude for his own opportunities. It was a position implicit in his philosophy, and explicitly stated many times over.

For the true happiness of man, he held, was not to be confused with his trivial pleasures; it was rather the product of discovery, the full, even painful discovery of self and society. That discovery, and the actions it induced, depended on knowledge. Ignorance produced not bliss but immobility, a hollow kind of mute existence. "Happiness," the twenty-three-year-old teacher had told his students at Albi in 1883, "is a glowing and intelligent light, which clarifies all the details of life and all sides of human nature."[46] Bertrand Russell once set down as the chief aims of education the blossoming in man's character of vitality, courage, sensitivity, and intelligence.[47] For Jaurès too, education was the key to self-realization; it enabled men to develop their latent talents and to pursue ends larger than the immediate. "Forced into a routine by their occupation and their profession, men can all too easily become dull and insensitive; eventually, if they are to live full lives, they must recover the enthusiasm of their youth and understand the wonders of the world."[48]

Beyond individual awareness, however, there was collective action. Once alive to the vastness of life, once struck by the truth about an immoral society, men would be stirred, their wills propelled. Why, he asked, do the rich and powerful fear education for the poor? "The intellectual equality of all will make social inequality untenable. . . . For that reason, we hear all of those objections to the spread of 'elite' education which, as the critics say, can only lead to unrest."[49] Enlighten the people, enable them to understand the world, its past and present, its limits and potentialities, and they will muster the courage to live meaningfully.

And what is courage? It is to learn a trade and do it well. It is to understand society and "to prepare . . . a social order more expansive and more fraternal, where the machine will be the servant of the worker. . . . Courage is to love life and to view death with calm; it is to seek the ideal and to understand the real; it is to act and give support to great causes, regardless of gain; it is to seek the truth and to speak it."[50]

So Jaurès led the socialists in their fight for a decent educational system. The most orthodox Marxists, who insisted that education under capitalism could be little more than class propaganda, considered the effort futile. Jaurès found support for it in the writings of the great socialist theorists. In Blanqui,[51] for example, "who has too often been written off as a mad insurrectionist. From the very start of his career, he understood that the work of revolution must be, before everything else, a work of education. . . . He said one day to a friend: 'The Revolution does not begin in the workshop; it begins in the school.' "[52]

Jaurès went further and sought support in Marx himself, whose complexity, he implied, had suffered at the hands of economic determinists. "According to Marx," admitted Jaurès, "the economic evolution of society governs the intellectual and moral evolution of humanity." Yet within the framework of history, Marx had explained, "each individual develops his own nature, here selfish and appetitive, there affectionate and loving."[53] Properly understood, Marx would not deny but rather affirm the capacity of men to nurture ideals and to seek their realization. Nor would he deny, especially from the evidence of his own life, that even under capitalism, rational men, though with considerable effort, could grasp the truth about society.[54]

In its essential spirit, however, Jaurès' educational philosophy reflected less the teachings of Marx than the faith of the Enlightenment and the French Revolution.

Jaurès' study of eighteenth-century thought was lifelong, and his indebtedness, political as well as philosophical, profound. From his earliest days at the École Normale, when he first discovered what Bersot, the school's Assistant Director, called "ce courageux XVIII° siècle," he returned time and again to the wisdom of the *philosophes*. His writings abound with glowing references to their theories, their courage, their essential radicalism before traditional institutions. But he avoided the obvious and the sentimental, and while he praised their great accomplishments, he also criticized what he considered their weaknesses.

So, Jaurès respected and admired Voltaire, whose masterful attack on the Church had crumbled its intellectual pretensions, and Rousseau, who felt, more profoundly perhaps than any other, the joys of nature and the cruelties of society. But as a socialist, he accepted neither Voltaire's defense of inequality nor Rousseau's ultimate pessimism, his distrust of revolutionary action and his futile reveries of a golden past. Jaurès was more deeply indebted, more closely linked to Diderot, whose "rêve panthéistique ardent," as he was to describe it in *L'Armée nouvelle*, was the spark for his own religious flame, and especially to the Encyclopedists, whose optimism and faith in enlightenment had conditioned society for the great Revolution.

The *philosophes*, especially those who theorized about education — Condillac, Helvétius, Holbach, de Tracy, Condorcet — had made of education the great lever of social change. Radical in their belief in human reason, convinced "that man could improve his lot by modifying the social organism," they expected that once educated, he would "clear away outworn superstitions, prejudices, delusions, and inequalities."[55] For Jaurès, who had rooted his theory of history partly in Marxist soil, education was no Aladdin's lamp which, vigorously rubbed, would convert the world to justice. But it was at least an important element in the progress of humanity, a way of rousing the conscience of men, and on that he was one with the *philosophes*.

They had urged, as Jaurès did in his own time, the broadest knowledge for the people. What was their fundamental message, if not to "love life, to have universal curiosity about all of life?" And because they practiced what they preached, they had, with their boundless energy, popularized the learning of the day. Jaurès pointed to them as the best of educators, who "seemed to reveal to men, to all men, the ways of society, whose science offered them knowledge of time and space, whose history unveiled to them the civilizations the past."[56]

Jaurès defended them against those, like the historian Taine, who accused the *philosophes* of turning men into abstract and impractical dreamers. Their efforts, on the contrary, were direct and practical; and their disciples, the revolutionaries of 1789, "had a profound knowledge of reality, a clear understanding of the difficulties they faced."[57]

In the essential democracy of their educational philosophy, Jaurès felt, they had made their greatest contribution. The *philosophes* believed not only in the regenerative power of education, but also in the possibility of educating the humblest of men. "In other words," as one historian has summed it up, "not alone a few geniuses but mankind in the mass was capable of unbounded intellectual achievement."[58]

To that faith Jaurès paid a tribute, flowing over twenty large pages of his history of the French Revolution, when he analyzed the educational plan of Condorcet. Philosopher, historian, and mathematician, Condorcet had carried the spirit of the Enlightenment into the Legislative Assembly of 1792. There, on April 21, 1792, he had submitted an outline for an educational system, designed, as he said, to enable all men "to provide for their needs, assure their well-being, know and exercise their rights, understand and perform their duties." How did Jaurès view it? "It was a beautiful and grand plan of universal education, . . ." he wrote. "It was the product of science and reason, it was the enlightenment of the eighteenth century, which he sought to pass on to all persons."[59] In concluding his commentary on the proposal, Jaurès left little doubt of his identification with its idealism: "it is the philosophy which offers all to all and which seeks to make every man one of the elect. What grandeur of hope and faith, what sublime appeal to the humble to shake off their religious resignation and social degradation, to raise themselves so high that there will no longer be anything above them but the truth!"[60]

The *philosophes* were not socialists, and Jaurès was well aware of it. Their social outlook, formulated in the circumstances of the eighteenth century, was not collectivist, though almost to a man they "understood that real democracy was incompatible with a marked inequality of fortunes."[61] But their fight for unfettered learning, their enthusiasm for translating knowledge into reform, the essential egalitarianism of their approach — all of this was tonic to Jaurès. And finally, it was their courage that inspired him, their unflinching stand against those in authority, who, as a biographer of Helvétius has written, "aimed to enslave the people by stupifying them."[62] "Before evidence of evil," he had told his students at Albi, "a man must neither fall silent nor compromise; he would be denying his reason and wasting his chance to act."[63] And he added: "As for myself, I feel enriched when I find a man of integrity, and I do not know but that this quality may not be the finest among human virtues."[64]

III

"No matter what anyone may say," Jaurès once cried from the floor of the Chamber of Deputies, "if today on the soil of the Republic there are thousands of schools where millions of children are raised in the light of naturalistic morality, science, and reason — we owe it to the spirit of the Revolution."[65] To that tradition Jaurès belonged when he pressed hard for a free and effective educational system. If he believed that only socialism could offer a completely honest and scientific knowledge, it did not deter him from his campaign to improve, by democratic means, the educational system of the Republic. That fight was most fully developed at this earlier stage of his socialism, rather than later, when the blunter issues of class strife consumed his time.

For most republicans, as for Jaurès, a free educational system meant a shearing away of clerical influence. In the Third Republic it became an article of republican faith, whether expressed by the moderate Opportunists or the more flamboyant Radicals, that the Church had to be ousted from the schools. The deputy Paul Bert, a disciple of Jules Ferry, had expressed that attitude very well when he wrote that "the realm of reason belongs to the teacher, that of faith to the priest."[66]

Thus, the reigning republicans had managed to push through a series of laws between 1879 and 1886, which established a considerable number of new normal schools; suppressed the letters of obedience qualifying nuns to teach; provided free and compulsory primary education; modernized the curriculum; eliminated religious instruction from the schools; and culminated at last in the hotly debated law of October 30, 1886, reserving teaching positions in primary schools for nonreligious personnel.[67]

The passage of these laws, however, did not ensure either their acceptance or their execution. Catholic leaders assailed the State monopoly of education as an unjustifiable infringement of the freedom to teach. The Catholics argued effectively, for they accused the republicans of suppressing liberty in the name of protecting it. That clerical spokesmen raised the issue of freedom to teach only after the Church monopoly of education had been broken was assuredly true; but the republicans could hardly dispose of these charges merely by attacking the motives of the Catholics. It was Bert, perhaps better than anyone else, who formulated the republican answer to these charges: "Freedom (to teach) is *not* the due of those who would use it to undermine all other freedoms."[68]

The republican counterattack was systematically developed by the historian Émile Bourgeois. In principle, Bourgeois agreed with Condorcet that "a power which prohibits the teaching of opinions contrary to its own undermines the freedom to think and thus to perfect its laws."[69] But the freedom to teach, according to this doctrine, was meant to guarantee the expression of all ideas. It was not meant to permit Church schools which inculcated only hatred of the Republic.[70]

If Jaurès had been a Guesdist, he might conceivably have stood aside from the debate, considering it part of the struggle between capitalists and clericals for the control of men's minds. But feeling as he did that human reason could be released in the democratic Republic, he took an active stand against clerical education. He was concerned, of course, about the antirepublicanism preached in Church schools; but he objected most vigorously to the absolutism of Catholic education, to its fatalism about inequality and its acceptance of irrational myths. "In our country," he wrote bitterly, "the peasants and workers are fed the propaganda that all republicans are Freemasons and that all Freemasons hold meetings presided over by the devil himself."[71]

Against the dogmatic education, Jaurès called for " a constant pursuit of truth,"[72] a system of free, secular education which would make men masters of their environment.[73] In scores of articles and speeches, he praised the educational program of the Third Republic, but urged its expansion and improvement. As a republican deputy, he had proposed several educational reforms, but in so doing, he found that his bourgeois colleagues were influenced less by their commitment to education than by their fear of taxation and their distrust of the masses. Jaurès made his pleas, but he won few converts.

Primary education, "the only real wealth of the masses," as he once called it, received his greatest attention. One day in the Chamber, he listed the obstacles to an adequate system of elementary education: poor attendance, shortage of schools, overworked and badly trained teachers.[74] He reminded his colleagues that there could be no teaching without teachers and that there would be few teachers without suitable compensation. Without better salaries, smaller classes, and unimpeded freedom, he warned, teachers would continue to move into other fields.[75] As a good republican and still not a socialist, Jaurès was depressed by the failure of his colleagues to respond to his appeal; but in 1894, he could answer the argument that more and better schools would mean higher taxes by proposing to take the money out of the expenditures for the army and the Church.[76]

As a former professor in the lycée, Jaurès could and often did offer experienced advice on the system of secondary education. When an important Extra-Parliamentary Committee, under the chairmanship of Alexandre Ribot, inquired into this question in 1899, Jaurès was one of a select number of intellectuals called to testify. What, he was asked, would be the best curriculum for the lycées? Refusing to list specific courses, Jaurès chose rather to discuss the aim of a secondary education. The curriculum, he replied, ought to be broad and flexible enough to develop the reasoning faculties of the student and to rouse his enthusiasm. "What is really important," he told the committee, "is not to throw a mass of facts at the young student or to judge him on details which may or may not have stuck in his memory; the teacher must be sensitive to the student and determine through his examinations whether the student has really thought and studied."[77] But though Jaurès believed in a flexible curriculum, he always insisted that Catholic schools, if they were to continue to exist, had to meet certain minimum standards set by the State.[78]

At the heart of lycée education, Jaurès proposed the study of classical literature and philosophy, the plinth on which any real education rested; upon this foundation he would develop a full program of modern and scientific studies. Thus, when it was proposed in 1890 to divide the secondary schools in two, one group to produce intellectuals and the other technicians, Jaurès attacked the scheme. For to deny the unity of all learning was to distort education.[79]

As for higher education, Jaurès was a fervent supporter of the proposal to turn the local, isolated faculties at Lyon, Montpellier, Toulouse, and elsewhere into significant regional universities. He envisioned them as great centers of local culture, the focal points for a kind of regional renaissance. Furthermore, such universities would end the artificial separation between faculties and reveal the essential unity of knowledge.[80] One day, he wrote, "each discipline will be only one particular aspect of a unified system of thought, and students will master through their higher education the entire science of existence."[81]

IV

How, then, should one summarize Jaurès' socialism? In its inspiration, it was strongly idealistic. With Kant, Jaurès believed in the power of moral ideals, man's quest for justice especially, to move history and to help shape it. He was neither of the positivists, like Comte or Spencer, who worshiped evolution and called it progress, nor of the determinists, who embraced socialism only because they considered it inevitable. The goal — the reign of justice, the unity of mankind, a world without the castes, the classes, the wars that separated men from each other, in short, the collectivist society — was all-important. To reach it, men had created the history of the past and they would found the socialism of the future. Others, like Eduard Bernstein and the socialist Revisionists, content with reforms under capitalism, would later proclaim that the movement was everything and the end nothing. Jaurès would never join them. If his method was peaceful and evolutionary, his goal was revolutionary. The collectivist society, he felt, would be the culmination of a great human endeavor; it was a cause he couldn't betray. He would never be, he promised in 1889, one of those "Pharisees of democracy, who accept the principles of a just society, but not the sacrifices it demands."[82]

In a very special sense, therefore, his socialism was religious. Certainly, Jaurès had rejected formal theology and broken forever with Catholicism. Christianity, he charged, had become a pseudoreligion, its institutions oppressive, its charity hypocritical, its doctrine a mass of lies and myths. But in socialism, in the harmony and unity of mankind, Jaurès foresaw a genuine religion, the triumph of man's moral aspirations and the deepest expression of his love. Impossible under capitalism, which destroyed fraternity; ignored by positivism, which enshrined brute fact, religion would emerge only in the just, the truly human society.

But Jaurès' socialism was equally materialistic. Unlike the absolute idealists, he accepted the material universe and its shaping influence. The economic transformation of society, the internal development of capitalism, as Marx had described it, determined the direction of history and presaged the triumph of socialism. Was it then a contradiction to believe at once in freedom and necessity, in the human will and the law of history? Jaurès denied it. Like Hegel (*Alles was existiert, ist vernünftig*), Jaurès believed in the identity of opposites, in the unity of contradictions, in short, in the dialectical process. "His mind strove for unity," Romain Rolland once wrote of Jaurès, "just as his spirit craved freedom."[83]

His socialist philosophy, which embraced both the moral and economic determinants of history, was complex, yet powerful and effective. It resembled the "integral socialism" of Malon; even more strikingly, it resembled the "scientific idealism" of Peter Lavrov (1823–1900), that remarkable Russian *philosophe* and revolutionary.[84] Yet Jaurès was more Marxist than Malon and more reformist than Lavrov. His eclecticism was his own and original. Beyond sectarianism, he could examine the proposals of rival socialist schools and appreciate them all. Reformism and revolution, federalism and centralism, syndicalism and politics — Jaurès would ultimately fit them all into a unified plan of action.

But by 1892, though Jaurès had established the intellectual foundations of his socialism, he had observed the social struggle only from a distance.

He had neither led the working classes nor walked at their side. Of the class struggle, he still had no firsthand knowledge. His belief in democracy — the conviction, like Lassalle's, that the State could be the instrument of socialism — was intact. But the time of testing was at hand. In Carmaux, Jaurès would join the struggle of the miners against their employers; in the Chamber of Deputies, he would before long lead the socialist attack against the conservative majority; and from those experiences, he would emerge a more militant, a more impassioned socialist. Jaurès would never abandon his idealism or lose his faith in democracy. But as he came to understand the power and program of the ruling class more clearly, he would evolve with that understanding. Marxists like Guesde, who preached simple, categorical truths, tended to distrust Jaurès. But when, in later years, he recognized the revolutionary implications of the Dreyfus Affair; when he campaigned so powerfully against colonialism, militarism, and war; when he insisted on a constant evolution of socialist thought and method, his spirit was more like Marx's than theirs.

The point is an important one. For if Jaurès was never a Marxist, neither, as he asserted in a famous epigram, was Marx. His disciples in the Second International, lacking his intellectual depth, converted his full-bodied philosophy into a mechanistic economic determinism, which did justice neither to his humanism nor to his historical insight. Jaurès, who was no man's disciple, nonetheless became Marx's spiritual *confrère*. For both men were enflamed by the same burning indignation against man's degradation; both were inspired by the same vision of a free and harmonious society, resolving at last, as Marx wrote in his *Economic and Philosophical Manuscripts*, "the conflict between existence and essence, between objectification and self-affirmation, between freedom and necessity, between individual and species"; and both, finally, were driven, out of conscience and courage, to act. "For it is the boldness of action," Jaurès cried, "even more than the boldness of theory, which has given man wings."

PART II

Years
of Militancy
1892-1898

Vous avez interrompu la vieille chanson qui berçait
la misère humaine et la misère humaine s'est réveillée
avec des cris, elle s'est dressée devant vous et elle
réclame aujourd'hui sa place, sa large place au soleil du
monde naturel, le seul que vous n'ayez point pâli.

1893

Toujours notre société violente, chaotique, même
quand elle veut la paix, même quand elle est à l'état
d'apparent repos, porte en elle la
guerre, comme la nuée dormante porte l'orage.

1895

5

Carmaux
1892

I

Though the Tarn was largely agricultural, its extensive deposits of coal were the basis for both mining and manufacturing enterprises. In the heart of the coal basin, on the left bank of the Cérau, ten miles to the north of Albi, lay Carmaux, in 1892 a city of almost ten thousand people, mainly miners, glass workers, and their dependent families. The sight of the nineteenth-century mining community was no less cheerless in the Tarn than in Wales or West Virginia. The ugly pits, the periodic mine disasters, the layers of grime were all there.

In the last decade of the century the industrial centers of France witnessed considerable social tension, and Carmaux was no exception. It was a time of action by workers and very real concern among employers. Both the action and the fear sprang from the rash of strikes and the growth of unions which followed hard upon their legalization in 1884.[1] At the very outset, the labor unrest had an essentially economic cause and the strike movement an economic objective. Both were obviously grounded in the uneven distribution of the national product. In the mining industry, for example, where labor agitation was almost chronic for three decades, profits soared while wages rose very slowly. If the wages and profits in 1850 are taken as the base number 100, then the wages for miners stood at 161 in 1890, while the profits of the owners had risen to 236.[2] Thus, while the daily pay of the mine workers rose, the increase hardly reflected the industry's increasing productive capacity.[3] Nor were wage scales in line with the harshness of working conditions in the mines, where men fell victim to explosion, suffocation, anemia, and tuberculosis; and like workers in most other trades, the miners suffered that ultimate insecurity of periodic unemployment.[4] Thus, through unions and strikes, the workers sought to improve their condition and to win for their families at least a modicum of security. As their determination and discontent grew, so did the number of strikes; in 1893 alone there were 634, involving 170,123 employees.[5] By no means were all these strikes successful, or even partially so, but in some instances the workers won concessions which, in the context of the times, seemed fairly impressive.[6]

Against this upsurge, employers fought back bitterly. Not only did they resist the specific demands of their workers but they even denied, despite the act of 1884, the very right of unionization. Writing of labor conditions in France at the turn of the century, even so moderate a critic as Daniel Halévy was struck by the determination of management to prevent the establishment of unions.[7] The resistance of French capitalists, as shortsighted as it was unyielding, helped to change the direction of the labor movement. Workers found themselves forced to strike as often for the existence of their unions as for economic gains; and since the issue was power — whether management could continue, unchallenged, to set the rules of industrial life — strikes now became bitter, at times bloody, clashes between the classes.

If their experience after 1884 disappointed the workers, it did not domesticate them. Led on by men, often from their own ranks, who came to despair of simple economic action, they thought increasingly of political action. If they could unite for strikes, they could just as well organize their numbers to wrest from their employers' hands the reins of political power. For a minority of class-conscious workers, that prospect became the great hope, but for management it was the great fear. The same universal suffrage which had been the bold contribution of the bourgeoisie in the eighteenth century could well turn into its undoing in the twentieth. What was at stake, of course, was domination of the government. Whoever controls the office, controls the spoils; such was the penetrating insight of Stendhal, and it was well borne out by the growth of the great capitalistic dynasties, like the Decazes, the Schneider, and the Reille.[8] But the privileges that friendly governments had yielded, hostile governments, as the French Revolution had amply demonstrated, could ultimately take away.

The fears of French capitalists were not without foundation. Socialists were already denouncing a political order in which, as Eugène Fournière later put it, "the power of money paralyzes or corrupts parliaments, intimidates and dupes the masses."[9] That view was spreading among the most militant workers, along with their determination to organize for political action. To the owners, their notions of industrial organization rooted in patriarchalism, all of this reflected a dangerous insubordination which had to be effectively restrained. They would thus harass politically conscious workers, curtail their activities, even dismiss them. In response, the workers would protest their right to organize politically and to challenge the conservative parties at the polls. Some of the bitterest strikes of the period, therefore, were essentially political, strikes to determine whether workers could freely participate in politics. Twice in the decade of the 1890's conflict flared up in Carmaux over that issue, and out of that swirl of events, Jaurès would emerge as the impassioned spokesman of the *carmausins*.

II

Jaurès, already thirty-two at the start of 1892, was still a stranger to the strike movement. But in his writings, he had clearly revealed his knowledge of the labor problem and his concern over the unequal relationship between capital and labor: "Employers have enormous power. They have capital; they own the factories that house production, the machines, the motors that move the machines, and the raw materials."[10] The workers, lacking capital and deprived of learning, had only their manpower. Unions, he felt, could help to redress the balance, and the unimpeded right of organization became the essential starting point of his labor philosophy.[11] He attacked without quarter the opposition of employers to the development of unions and especially their frequent resort to the lockout. Here was a practice doubly shocking to him; not only did it hamper organization, but it also reduced the workers to impotence and destroyed their self-respect. For though "the machine without the man who moves it is nothing, its value nonexistent, the man without the machine dies of hunger."[12]

In these early reflections, Jaurès proposed a second approach, as important to him as flourishing unions — the use of universal suffrage through which the numerical strength of the workers could manifest itself. Let labor organize and establish sympathetic parties. Then the workers would find political leaders, ready to clarify issues for the rank and file, to expose false panaceas like Boulangism or company paternalism, and to sponsor progressive legislation.[13] His deep faith in democratic politics became somewhat less lyrical over the years as a certain early optimism wore down, but now he could make a stirring analogy between the march of the Ten Thousand described by Xenophon and the march of the workers to their liberation: "When the Ten Thousand, after their long and cruel march, first through enemy lines and then through the desert, saw at last the blue sea which would take them back to their homeland, they could not at once believe it, so often had they been victims of mirages; but at last they shouted in unison: the sea! the sea!"[14]

At the end of the democratic march, what else would the workers see but socialism? After 1889, when he had in mind his own election defeat, he stressed the recourse to politics as the best solution for the labor problem. He had to go no further than his own experience to understand that the economic élite depended on political influence to safeguard its power. He returned many times to the lessons of the elections, noting how the Marquis de Solages had scored his own victory by implying to desperately insecure workers that their employment hinged on his success.[15] And he drew an important conclusion, that the control of the State was so important to the capitalists of France and the surge of democracy so dangerous to them that they would resort to underhanded tactics. Thus, when Solages became a member of the board of directors of Carmaux's important glass factory, Jaurès insisted that "he [Solages] has moved into that position, not for industrial but for political reasons."[16] He implied thereby that the workers in the glass factory would also be subject to the political pressure of the Reille-Solages group.

As his position on labor matured, it came to rest on two principles which transcended mere union bargaining — that only socialism could really free men from economic insecurity, and that workers, to be genuinely fulfilled, could not live by bread alone. Union action would yield temporary relief, but its deeper significance lay in bringing together the workers who could then unite politically to move toward socialism.[17] And at the end of that effort they would enjoy not only abundance but dignity. For Jaurès weighed the life of workers on those moral scales which measure man's wholeness. It is in this vein that he wrote in his famous essay "Au clair de lune," which appeared in La Dépêche de Toulouse on October 15, 1890: "So it is that up and down the scale the social order produces only slaves, for those men are not free who have neither the time nor the energy to live with nobility and dignity."

III

The most significant political duel in the Tarn over the last decade of the nineteenth century was fought between Jaurès, who represented socialism, and the House of Solages, which stood for the sanctity of property. Traced in the documents as far back as 1028, the Solages family came by marriage into large landholdings in Carmaux in 1724. But it was Gabriel de Solages in the very next generation who really founded the fortune in mines and industry.[18] The great mining fortunes were largely the result of an important royal decree of January 14, 1744, by which the government agreed to grant concessions to private individuals for exploitation of the subsoil. Seizing upon this arrangement, Gabriel de Solages obtained extensive mining rights by a Royal Decree of September 12, 1752. Not to be outdone, his son François-Gabriel benefited from Napoleon's generosity, acquiring some 8800 hectares of land by a grant of February 16, 1801.

In addition to its mines, the Solages family eventually came to own a glass factory, forests, and an iron mill. This economic empire was secure enough until the 1880's. By that time, one began to hear demands in the successive legislatures of the Third Republic for revision of that basic mining law of April 21, 1810, which granted private concessions in perpetuity. As recently as November 19, 1889, several Left-wing deputies (Joseph Ferroul, Eugène Baudin, Antide Boyer, Valentin Couturier) had proposed the nationalization of the mines; and as strikes spread throughout the mining areas, the demand for either regulation or nationalization increased.[19]

But more serious by far for the present Marquis de Solages and the Baron Reille was the labor unrest which had begun in the 1880's to upset the smooth running of their economic machine. Their regime had been patriarchal, semifeudal, and profitable for half the nineteenth century. They had depended upon and received complete loyalty from their peasants-turned-miners, who had traditionally attributed their employment to the beneficence of their employers. Never had these mute toilers considered political action against their masters, any more than they had voiced their economic grievances. But the march of events was too much for even a marquis and a baron to master, and by the 1860's and 1870's an inchoate mass was being transformed into a more self-conscious proletariat. The intrusion into the Tarn of the Albi-to-Toulouse Railroad in 1864, with a trunk line to Carmaux, meant not only wider contact with the outside world but also the appearance of a more modern capitalistic firm, the Société Mancel, charged with building the line. This almost inevitable economic evolution did not augur well for the tranquillity of the Solages empire, and a strike in 1869 was like handwriting on the wall. Still, the absence of either labor unions or a real political consciousness hampered a serious workers' movement until a strike in February and March, 1883, though itself a failure, ushered in a new era of militancy. By now, the miners were openly reassessing their relationship to their bosses; they were beginning to feel that the Solages clan had built its fortune from their labor.[20] Despite the failure of their 1883 strike, the workers managed to turn their temporary and informal organization into a union soon after the law of 1884 went into effect.

But what posed the greatest potential problem for the Solages establishment was the growth of a socialist consciousness among the workers, which brought them into contact with Jaurès. His relations with the *carmausins* had developed slowly. As a very young professor, selected for the republican list in the elections of 1885, he had gone to Carmaux to meet the workers. He addressed them one night in one of his first experiences with an audience of men embittered by their lot and crude in their behavior. Parrying the taunts of some skeptical hecklers at the start, he had won over most of them by the end of his speech. Still, Jaurès in these years had not forged a real bond with the miners. The control by the company over their weekly paycheck was a more powerful weapon than his oratory, as the 1889 elections effectively proved. But then, if Jaurès rallied to their cause, backing their union and their strikes, might not the support of the workers become steadfast? And might they not, by closing ranks behind him, become a powerful political group?

The miners had almost gone out on strike early in 1892, when they had presented twenty-eight demands on February 19, three-fourths of which had to do with wage increases. The company made its own offer in response, which proved to be unsatisfactory to the workers. A strike had been decided upon when Laurent, Prefect of the Tarn, successfully urged arbitration. The arbitration decision was rendered on March 18; the workers resumed their jobs on March 21; and a pattern for settling future disputes seemed to be assured.

But the labor trouble finally exploded into a strike later in 1892 over an issue that was specifically political rather than economic. The crisis centered around the bespectacled but rugged person of Jean-Baptiste Calvignac, a militant socialist and secretary-general of the miner's union, whom the workers had audaciously elected mayor of Carmaux. When management, indignant at what seemed an act of insubordination, refused to grant him enough free time to perform his political duties, Calvignac simply took the time, for which dereliction he was fired on August 2. The two conflicting positions were clearly enunciated. The workers charged that the company was striking a blow against their right of suffrage, while the partisans of managment insisted that a worker could not be retained who did not fully perform his duties.[21]

For the next two weeks, the company persistently refused to arbitrate the matter, on the grounds that it involved no real question of working conditions. By August 15 the miners, angry and ready for more direct action, held an explosive meeting. Resentment over the company's attitude reached such a fever pitch that at six o'clock that evening a group of the most irate unionists invaded the home of Humblot, the director of the company who had issued the order for Calvignac's dismissal. Receiving from the miners an ultimatum to rehire Calvignac, Humblot chose rather to resign, while the Marquis de Solages, apprised of the "atrocity," made a hasty escape to Albi with his household entourage of twenty-eight. The next day, August 16, 1892, the strike of the miners of Carmaux began its grueling ten-week course. The streets were empty, the pits were gaping holes, and the miners' wives mustered courage to face the ordeal.

In the moderate and conservative press, Baron Reille reiterated that no worker who persistently absented himself could possibly be retained.[22] *Le Temps* supported the company's rationale, calling attention to the many petty merchants and professionals who willingly accepted economic loss in order to discharge public functions, and implying thereby that miners and lawyers, for example, enjoyed the same economic staying power.[23] This important organ of moderate republicanism summed up the issues of the strike at the end of August by asserting that Calvignac had the *right* to become mayor, but the company had the equal *right* to discharge him.[24]

To expose what he considered the distortions in most of the press commentaries, Jaurès immediately wrote about the strike in *La Dépêche*. Retracing the sequence of events, he sought to present facts which had been suppressed in the public discussion.[25] It was only when Calvignac, an avowed socialist, became mayor of Carmaux, defeating the company candidate, that he was fired. The request for two free days a week to discharge political duties was considered impossible by the company. "Impossible? [snapped Jaurès] The entire issue is concentrated there. For if the company was unable to grant just two free days a week to a worker elected mayor by universal suffrage, it was because it consciously sought to destroy the effectiveness of the popular vote; it thus struck a blow at universal suffrage; and by making a mockery of the ballot, it wantonly provoked the workers to strong action."[26]

Would not the two days off each week have been granted, he asked, if they had been for some obsequious worker doing the company's bidding?

Actually the issue became for Jaurès one of human dignity, of the struggle by the workers to free themselves from the control of their employers. "At Carmaux there are over 2000 miners, and Baron Reille who governs them doesn't even know them by sight. He lives in Paris during the winter and in Saint-Amans in the summer. . . . The workers of

Carmaux are merely so many coins for him, accumulating in his cash-drawer."[27]

By mid-September Jaurès was charging the company with violation of a law of February 2, 1852, which made it a crime to intimidate a voter by threat of dismissal from employment. It was almost impossible, he granted, to enforce such a law on behalf of domestic servants, but it was crucial to apply it for industrial workers. "For if there is no absolute freedom, there is slavery."[28]

As the strike dragged on, the workers showed that devotion to cause which was necessary in the face of near-starvation and of 1500 troops, one for every two strikers, called out by Premier Loubet. Jaurès exhorted them to have courage, assuring them that the significance of their struggle extended even beyond the proletariat to all those artisans, peasants, and shopkeepers at the mercy of capitalism.[29] Manifesting a new militancy under the impact of events, he sounded the demand, already voiced by certain socialists, that the law of 1838 be invoked, empowering the state to nulify any mining concession whenever the public safety was endangered by a work stoppage.[30] Such demands went unheeded in 1892; and the French government was far more responsive to an extensive series of articles in Le Temps, which described the working conditions of the miners as actually rather enviable.[31] Neither in the hazards of mining nor in the refusal of management to arbitrate did Le Temps locate the origin of the dispute, but rather in the alleged revolutionary aspirations of the workers.[32]

Thus did opinion divide and tempers flare. October came, and the cause of the workers was strengthened by the active assistance of certain socialists who gave freely of their oratorical and moral support, both out of sympathy for the strikers and hope for recruitment. Duc-Quercy of the P.O.F.; Baudin, socialist deputy from the Cher; Millerand, Viviani, and Gérault-Richard, those new vedettes of socialism, made hortatory speeches at Carmaux. The danger of such intervention was not lost upon management, and there is good reason to believe that they were sponsoring agents provocateurs, like the anarchist Tournadre, to precipitate violence which would completely discredit the workers' cause.[33]

The break in the strike came finally through the intervention of the socialists in the Chamber of Deputies. In the session of October 18 Eugène Baudin and especially Alexandre Millerand, recently recruited from Radicalism, leveled an attack against Baron Reille, accusing his company of dragging out the strike to punish the audacious workers. When Millerand finally moved that the government seize the mines on the basis of provisions in the laws of 1810 and 1838, Reille capitulated and agreed to arbitration of the dispute.[34]

Jaurès seized upon Reille's decision and spelled out what he considered its significance. Here was an employer powerful enough to impose unemployment for many weeks on almost 3000 men simply by his refusal to submit a dispute to arbitration. By agreeing now to an outside judgment, Reille was actually admitting that he could have adopted that course sooner.[35] It was clearer than ever to Jaurès that such power by private employers constituted the highest barrier to the full freedom of workers. For many others, the same events yielded a very different lesson, of course; and so well-known a conservative as the economist Paul Leroy-Beaulieu wrote in the *Economiste français* on November 12, 1892, that the government had remained shockingly powerless in the face of a revolutionary threat.

The arbitration decision was to be handed down by Loubet, then president du conseil, with Millerand and the two Radical leaders Clemenceau and Pelletan pleading the case of the workers. By October 30 the arbitration sentence was rendered, and from every point of view it was a compromise, calling for the reinstatement of Calvignac, who was to have leave of absence while fulfilling his political duties, the retention of Humblot by the company, and the rehiring of all the strikers, except those nine convicted by an Albi court on October 3 for invading Humblot's house.

The decision satisfied neither the partisans of capital nor the extremist socialists in the union. For the former it seemed like a dangerous capitulation; for the latter it appeared a concession to management. And, according to well-founded reports, "the workers returned to the mines singing the *Carmagnole* . . . but adding new couplets about the marquis backed into the barrel of a gun and the baron at the end of a cannon."[36] But Jaurès, who was prone to read great victories even into indecisive battles, saw in the result a great blow struck for the freedom of the workers. The immediate consequences, he wrote, were the capitulation of Reille and the safeguarding of universal suffrage; but the far-reaching results were the achievement of solidarity by the workers during the long, hard strike and the potential use of that unity for further political action.[37]

In a very real sense, the political force of the workers was now considerably strengthened. For the strike had an epilogue many weeks later in January of 1893. The Marquis de Solages had come under heavy attack, and so widespread was the hostility to him in the Tarn that he resigned from the Chamber on October 14, thus opening the way for a special election. The socialists of his district, enthusiastic about the prospects of victory, were fully determined to wrest control of the district from the hands of the Reille-Solages group; to run against Jean-

Baptiste Héral, the former Opportunist deputy who now enjoyed solid backing from the local capitalists, they wanted a candidate who would campaign, openly and forcefully, as a socialist. But who?

Many of the workers favored a local man, someone who could win votes even in the villages beyond Carmaux; increasingly, therefore, they mentioned Jaurès, who had so eloquently espoused their cause during the tensest days of the strike. But the most vocal of the local socialists, militant workers like Berton of the miners' union and Aucouturier of the glass workers' union, were ardent Guesdists, scornful of bourgeois intellectuals so lately come to socialism; they insisted upon an unquestioned revolutionary who, whether successful or not, would espouse from every platform the principles of Marxism. First they approached Duc-Quercy, who had carried the banner for the embattled workers of Anzin, Decazeville, and Carmaux, but they couldn't persuade this inveterate revolutionary to abandon the strike fields for the halls of Parliament. They thought then of Louis Camélinat, the old Communard who had already carried socialism into the Chamber in 1885. But the supporters of Jaurès, convinced of their man, of his idealism and courage, stood their ground. The showdown then awaited the meeting, historic though none could then have known it, where the socialists would argue the question and choose their candidate.

Writing years later in *Le Populaire du centre* (July 30, 1916), Vincent Auriol, whose information came from none other than his father-in-law, the glass worker Aucouturier, described that meeting and its outcome:

Jaurès, who lived in the neighboring district, attended. The battle that took place was heated. . . . But when Jaurès spoke, he completely captivated the audience. On behalf of the minority, Aucouturier then spoke up, promising Jaurès the coöperation of the Guesdists and thus, in 1893, long before the party unity of 1905, effecting socialist unity in the Tarn: "We have fought you, Citizen Jaurès, but the majority is with you. We will work hard for your election. If your course is the right one, you will have no more faithful and devoted friends than we." And that was true.

Jaurès thus became the candidate of the working classes of Carmaux, and when he accepted as his platform the 1892 program of the Parti ouvrier français, openly and unreservedly, he not only quieted the doubts of the local Marxists but also reached another milestone in his own socialist evolution.

Campaigning hard against M. Héral, drawing especially on the events of the recent strike to attack the Reille-Solages group, Jaurès won the by-election of January 8, 1893, by a vote of 5317 to 4843. If there was any doubt that he was the workers' choice, it was dispelled when the vote was analyzed. The second district of Albi comprised five cantons, four of which — Monestiès, Pampelonne, Valderies, and Valence — were rural; the other, Carmaux, was not. Though Jaurès ran behind Héral in all the nonindustrial areas, he piled up a majority of 1172 in Carmaux, more than enough to ensure his victory.

This dramatic turn in Jaurès' fortunes affected the members of his family rather differently. Adélaïde, resigned to losing her son to public life, was confirmed in her belief in his eventual greatness. For Louise, preoccupied always with her immediate surroundings, it meant a Parisian ménage and perhaps even luxury. But others were apprehensive and even upset that one of theirs had taken up the hated doctrine of socialism. M. Bois might have profited from being the father-in-law of a deputy, but not one of the extreme Left. And among the provincial and conservative Barbazas some sparks flew, especially from that crusty aunt of Jaurès, who summed up the event with no little cynicism: "He has turned socialist to make some money. He is a good husband, and the beautiful Louise needs money." [38]

The novelist Barrès, no intimate of Jaurès, nonetheless wrote of his return to Parliament: "He [Jaurès] will bring into the discussion and diffusion of socialist ideas the wisdom of a philosopher and historian." [39] The consequences for French socialism, in fact, were far greater than Barrès predicted.

IV

The years from 1889 to 1892 had been a vital interlude for Jaurès, a period of organizing and maturing his thoughts. Back in the Chamber in 1893, he was considerably more forceful and dynamic than before. No longer did he regard the republican majority with equanimity, but he charged that it had "consistently capitulated before the power of money, and it has never made its force felt." [40] What had characterized the rule of the Opportunists? "They have not produced a single progressive law in four years," he wrote sweepingly, ignoring certain pieces of labor legislation in 1892. Now, certain new men had joined the ranks of the moderates. There was the rather austere bourgeois from Lorraine, Raymond Poincaré, and then the flexible, ambitious *gascon*, Louis Barthou. But they had used their new influence "not to initiate new and vital policies, but to lead an old wagon, which is stuck in the mud, to the end of the road." [41]

Less than a month after Jaurès launched this attack on the government party, it was May Day. This year, 1893, the socialists of Paris had a special reason to demonstrate, for only a short time before Premier Charles Dupuy had closed down the local bourse du travail. That labor exchange, transformed in recent years from a kind of employment clearing house into a center of revolutionary agitation, had both frightened and disturbed the opportunist leadership. Now, on this May Day, socialist and labor groups were determined to make a defiant gesture by attempting to hold their meeting in the hall of the bourse du travail.

Failing entry, however, they took to the streets, and a rousing, antigovernmental meeting was in full swing. What happened while militant spokesmen were making their speeches has been reported in two very different versions, one by the socialists and the other by the police. Eugène Baudin, one of two deputies arrested that day, gave his version to a reporter for *Le Gaulois*: "Vaillant had just finished his speech when police descended on the crowd. I rushed forward at once and urged them not to use force, but at that moment I received a blow that knocked my hat off. I was surrounded by police who grabbed my arms and others who paralyzed my legs by kicking me. Dumay [another deputy] was next to me. Seeing this monstrous aggression, he shouted: "But you're hitting a deputy!" The police, as though hearing nothing, seized Dumay, grabbed me, and led us to the police station.[42]

The most controversial aspect of the arrest, the abuse of parliamentary inviolability, was treated lightly by *Le Temps*, which declared on May 3 that "it is suspended in cases of flagrant crimes." The crime in question, according to the official police version, was Baudin's violence, both verbal and physical, against officers of the law.[43]

Jaurès was indignant. He believed too strongly in republican government to watch with dispassion what seemed to him its corrosion. In the press he stressed the attack on freedom of assembly, the denial to socialists first of a meeting hall and then of the street itself.[44] In the Chamber he pressed the ministry to explain its violation of parliamentary immunity in the arrest of deputies. He disposed of the official police version of the May Day events as a fraudulent invention,[45] and pleaded with the government, whatever its antisocialist bias, to respect the right of opposition.[46] The ministry was sure of its majority, however, and when the question of Baudin was put to a vote, the government was authorized to proceed with the prosecution. It would be the beginning, Jaurès predicted sadly, "of systematic persecution of socialism."[47]

But sadness was always bested by an irrepressible optimism; Jaurès was back in Paris now, the Paris of students and artists, which engulfed and refreshed his spirit. He punctuated his crowded schedule with walks through the Latin Quarter, and as he wandered around the Left Bank, he recalled: "What I feel most there (and permit me, for once, a personal confidence) is the sense of continuity in my life. To the goals of universal happiness and human perfection, which excited me as a student, I have, I feel, remained faithful in what are called politics, and I am grateful to socialism for showing me the way to reach them." The very streets of the student quarter were like links between his youth and his maturity. "Despite the small alterations in the Sorbonne and Louis-le-Grand, the rue Saint-Jacques, narrow and secluded in the light of the moon, still has that special quality by which persons and things seem to elude both time and history." But now, in his walks, he saw something the young *normaliens* had ignored — the gatherings of socialist workers and students. "Not sentimental dilettantes and virtuosos of social mysticism, but militants who have grasped the doctrine in all its harshness and accepted it, young bourgeois wishing to end once and for all the oppressive and corrupt regime of the bourgeoisie."[48]

V

The general elections in the fall resulted not only in Jaurès' return but also in the final collapse of the old monarchist and Boulangist threats. The moderate republicans won 279 seats, but the Progressists gave the declining Right a lease on life by making overtures toward it. It was a time of social unrest, and the moderates tended to line up with all enemies of the extreme Left. What disturbed them, of course, was the mounting threat of socialism. Instead of twelve, the socialists now numbered thirty-seven; their votes, more than four times the number of 1889, had passed half a million.[49] It was hardly enough to threaten the social order, but it showed a drift toward socialism, so much so that *La nouvelle Revue*, with considerable exaggeration, declared: "One has to have courage nowadays to be a reactionary."[50]

Where did the socialist support come from? What were the bases of the socialist movement? Socialism was still a mixture of small parties and local unions, of clubs and federations, of depressed workers and bourgeois intellectuals.[51] It was the pottery workers of the Haute-Vienne, organizing the Cercle de l'avant-garde socialiste; it was the leather worker, Jacques Dufour, spreading Marxism in the Indre; it was J.-B. Lebas, opting for socialism after reading Deville's summary of *Capital*; it was the wealthy Léon Blum, conditioned for socialism by a radical grandmother; and the poverty-stricken Albert Bedouce, converted to Marxism by Dr. Bach, an ex-Communard in Toulouse. It was the product of labor organization and socialist propaganda, of despair and of hope. It was revolutionary, and yet, by 1893, it was essentially political and increasingly parliamentary.

For Jaurès, the election of 1893 meant the end of political isolation; he was now part of a coherent, vocal, and, in this legislative session, very fraternal group. "For those who, like me, had come to socialism by solitary paths, who had never been part of the organized parties, who

had never suffered the ordeals of the earliest period of propaganda, this
new and cordial familiarity with the old, experienced hands was exciting and invigorating."[52]

"How young we all were then," he recalled nostalgically in 1913,
"even the old socialists! . . . Within a few weeks, indeed within a few
days, a wonderful socialist fraternity developed."[53] That fraternity,
though it was subject to far greater internal tensions than Jaurès later
admitted, was formalized on November 8, 1893, by the creation of the
Union socialiste, which coördinated the parliamentary efforts of the
socialists. That working unity was effective enough, observed *Illustration*, so that socialists "vote, interrupt, and argue with the unanimity
of a Greek chorus."[54]

So Jaurès belonged with the socialists, and back in the Tarn, among
his old bourgeois republican sponsors, that realization created consternation. He had fallen, or so it seemed, among the enemies of individualism. The most distinguished of the republican notables, Senator Bernard
Lavergne, was determined to go to the root of the matter and to find out
precisely how far Jaurès had slipped.

Lavergne was no conservative; at seventy-eight he had a record of
radical republicanism which dated back to the Second Republic of 1848
and included sincere efforts on behalf of secular schools and social reforms. But he was a strong defender of individual property; and in September of 1893 he launched an extended public debate in the pages of
La Dépêche where he asked Jaurès some blunt questions about his ties
with collectivism and Marxism. More than twice the age of the socialist
deputy, Lavergne was still hopeful that he might recover the younger
man for his own brand of republicanism. Jaurès was polite and respectful
in his replies, but rather than backtracking, he firmly maintained his
position and, what is more, used this debate to amplify it by a detailed
description of collectivism.

"M. Lavergne begs me to repudiate collectivism. I will not do it; for
I believe that collectivism, properly understood, is the hope of the future."
So he began on September 25, 1893, and he remained equally unequivocal
throughout the three-month debate. Lavergne had asked whether he
was a Marxist. "Again, I must answer yes, insofar as Marx is a collectivist." Citing the major economic doctrines of Marx — the theories of
value and surplus value, the concentration and centralization of capital,
the inevitable downfall of capitalism — Jaurès added simply, "These
truths I make my own."

But socialism was more than Marxism, he went on; it was also the
revolutionary and idealistic tradition of France carried to its ultimate
and logical conclusion. Finally triumphant, French socialism would be

republican, humanitarian, passionately democratic. And above all, he said, addressing himself to the petty-bourgeois disquietude of the Tarn, it would not destroy individualism but would encourage "individual energies" and preserve "individual property wherever legitimate and necessary."[55]

As the weeks passed, Jaurès sketched his own picture of a collectivist society.[56] His earlier sentiments on labor now gave way to the view that only the socialist organization of industry could guarantee security and well-being. What a later age would call the challenge of automation was already an issue for Jaurès in 1893. "The truth is that mechanization poses a problem to the present social order which it will not be able to resolve, and its impact will ultimately be fatal. For the machine is increasingly replacing man. . . . What will you do with wage-earners? . . . It means that the nation will be obliged to proclaim and organize the right to work. . . . To do that, the nation will have to control the means of production."[57] Returning over and again to the theme of individualism in a collectivist order, Jaurès denied the inevitability of an oppressive state bureaucracy, but envisioned rather, in the tradition of Louis Blanc, an era of worker control over production.[58]

There could be little doubt now about Jaurès' commitment. But for any who still wondered how militant his socialism would be when it was expounded not on the printed page but in the Chamber itself, the answer was quickly at hand. It was late in November, 1893, when Jaurès, interpellating for the socialists, launched an extended attack on the ministry of Charles Dupuy — and revealed the dimensions of his socialism.

Dupuy, who had advanced from an insignificant teaching career to the forefront of Progressist politics, opened the new legislature with a conservative ministerial declaration that dampened the spirit of the exuberant socialist group. A week later, on November 21, Jaurès was recognized by the president of the Chamber, Casimir-Périer. When he began to speak, there was still considerable disturbance in the House. But the voice and manner were compelling, and soon silence fell over the Chamber.[59]

"The ministerial declaration is perfectly clear," he charged, "it is a declaration of war on the socialist party." But socialism was a tide that could not be easily stemmed. It was not the work of agitators, as the government was charging. "No, gentlemen, the truth is that this movement is a product of history; it comes from endless and timeless sufferings. . . . The truth is that in France the socialist movement has emerged both from the Republic which you have founded and the economic order which has been developing for half a century." The crucial rights of union organization and free, secular education, which the Opportunists themselves had extended in the 1880's, were the keys to the transition from capitalism to socialism. It would not be easy, that he knew. "Though you cannot openly destroy your work of secularism, you can place the Republic under the tutelage of the Papacy. . . . You do not dare to destroy the unions, but you find ways, without changing the laws, of actually suppressing their freedom." It was all to no avail, shouted Jaurès. The struggle against the people was doomed to fail. Almost exhausted from his philippic, the orator concluded with a motion of censure against the "reactionary policy of the ministry."

The result was electrifying. Though the motion of censure failed, it signaled the emergence of Jaurès. Camille Pelletan, the cultured, cigar-smoking veteran of Radicalism, rose to his feet to lead the heavy applause from the Left. Édouard Vaillant and Marcel Sembat, militant Blanquists, were deeply moved. Alexandre Ribot, that redoubtable foe of all radicalism, voiced the question others had in mind when he asked Jaurès what was responsible for his dynamism since returning to the Chamber. "I was too hesitant before; I was like a volcano spewing forth ice," explained the now secure *tarnais*.[60] But the Carmaux strike, the constant stream of articles on social problems, the building of a comprehensive philosophical position — all of this thought and experience had released the volcano. Four days later, on November 25, Dupuy, under sustained attack, resigned. The entire episode had launched Jaurès among his colleagues of the extreme Left.

Even the Marxists of the Parti ouvrier français were willing to welcome "this devil of a man," as Lafargue called him. "The miners of Carmaux," continued Guesde's collaborator, "have richly paid their debt to the socialist party, which led their strike to victory, by taking Jaurès away from teaching and pushing him into politics again."[61] But the winds of fellowship did not blow Jaurès into the Guesdist camp, and he continued to propagate a socialism that was strongly moral in its appeal. By the start of 1894, his stature had grown and with it his socialist influence. For the Marxists it seemed time to spell out in debate the difference between their own materialism and Jaurès' idealism, to point out, wherever possible, the error of his way. And where better to hold such a debate than before the socialist students of the Latin Quarter, who might be lost to Marxism if they were seduced by Jaurès' idealism?

This was an almost unbelievable age of public discussion, and socialists eagerly lectured to audiences on the most complex and academic subjects. So it was that on January 12, 1894, Jaurès and Lafargue faced each other in a debate on *Idéalisme et matérialisme dans la conception de l'histoire*, and what followed has come down as one of the lasting moments in the history of French socialism. There were the students, an overflowing crowd of them, alive as their predecessors in 1848 to the hope for great changes, poor, intellectual, craving for the right words. Jaurès was never better than with students; he was their most eloquent professor. And Lafargue, such a complex bag of contradictions, wealthy but a Marxist, certain of human destiny yet a suicide in 1911 — this Lafargue compelled attention with his razor-edged tongue and brilliant presentation.

They met, with no intellectual holds barred, and both seemed exhilarated by the challenge. Jaurès spoke first and presented his already familiar theory. What he sought to do, in his perpetual quest for unity, was to show that idealism and materialism, far from excluding each other, were both parts of a valid historical theory. "There is not, in fact, a single idealist who does not avow that a higher ideal of mankind can be realized only with a previous transformation of the economic system; and on the other hand, there are few advocates of economic materialism who do not ultimately appeal to the ideal of justice."[62]

Without denying the central assumptions of materialism, Jaurès considered them inadequate to explain the progress of history. Sketching briefly theories he had already elaborated in other writings, he spoke to the students that night of "certain predispositions and tendencies" that were already embedded "in the first brains of nascent mankind."[63] Over long ages that human sensibility had developed — the aesthetic sense, the urge toward abstraction, the instinct of sympathy, the longing for community — which now characterized man. They were human ideals, innate and independent, growing stronger over the ages, furnishing men's goals and spurring their action, which had helped to direct and shape history.

Lafargue, lucid and learned, attacked this idealism with his astringent brand of Marxism. The course of history, the line of progress from earliest origins to the eve of socialism, had been determined by material evolution alone — by economic transformations and their consequent social struggles. Had the moral thinking of mankind so advanced over the centuries as to account for human progress? So Jaurès had said, but Lafargue denied it:

It has been said that in the old military societies labor was despised; that is not entirely exact. The heroes of the *Iliad* tended their flocks and worked their land . . . the patricians of Rome and Greece took off sword and armor to get behind the plow; the feudal noblemen of the Middle Ages began their apprenticeship to knighthood by serving as pages and squires for noble families; what was despised in those ages was the sale of labor.[64]

Yet that very practice, so morally debasing, had become the backbone of modern capitalism.

The concept of justice was neither the culmination of mankind's moral advance, as Jaurès insisted, nor the force behind the great socialist movement: "The ideal of Justice, which, according to Jaurès, lies dormant in the mind of primitive man, doesn't actually enter the human mind until the appearance of private property. Primitive men have no notion of Justice; they don't even have a word to describe it."[65] Such an ideal was neither necessary nor even conceivable in a communist society; for it was private property which alone inflicted injustice upon mankind and called forth the demand for justice. Yet justice, as nurtured in bourgeois society, was a pious idea at best and a deceptive one at worst; its aim was to alleviate the worst conditions of capitalism, to distribute its goods more equitably and to meet distress with charity: "The ideal of Justice does not conflict with the established order, but rather accommodates to it."[66] The reflection of bourgeois individualism, it aimed for a quantitative change, not a qualitative transformation.

In their heightened class-consciousness, Lafargue argued, and in their drive toward communism, the masses responded not to the misty ideal of justice but to hard economic realities; their direction was not toward *justice formelle et distributive* but toward *communauté et fraternité universelles*; and their success was assured not by their moral claims but by the relentless dialectic of history. "The masses have understood the laws of history, for one of their proverbs runs: 'Man is tossed about and God leads him.' "[67] God, for this Marxist, was the economic system. Thus he painted for the students the picture of universe and society both propelled by great material forces beyond the voluntary control of men. "If we are communists," he summed up, "it is because we are convinced that the economic contradictions of capitalist production are leading us inevitably to communism."[68]

As a confrontation of two theoretical approaches to socialism, the debate was a classic, unsurpassed in the literature of the movement. But beyond its intrinsic value, it was an important reflection of certain divisions within French socialism, differences of mood and approach, which, though they might be temporarily ignored in the interests of unity, would never disappear. Working from a clearly defined theory of power, the Marxists distinguished sentimentalism from socialism, quantitative gains from genuine revolution. But in the process, they could ignore the most generous impulses, oppose the most humane measures, and blind themselves to the world of real men and their needs. Jaurès sought to supplement the Marxist view of history rather than to reject it; he sought to articulate the communist goal rather than merely to assume it.[69] For he insisted upon what he saw and sensed and knew — that men were not moved by bread alone, that their indignation and idealism, their hopes and dreams were also the creative stuff of history. He sought to harmonize, to synthesize the two approaches; the Marxists, distrustful of the Independents and convinced of their own doctrine, hewed closely to their line.

But these were hard years for the socialists, embattled years. The conservative bourgeoisie sought to isolate them and curtail their freedom. Before the common danger, the theoretical argument took on less importance, and the socialists, materialists and idealists alike, linked arms for survival.

6

The Conservative
Offensive, 1893-1895

I

French politics between 1893 and 1895 whirled like a car-
rousel and astride the highest horses were the leaders of the moderate
republicanism, now called Progressists. First it was Charles Dupuy who
clutched the brass ring and became Premier; then it was Jean Casimir-
Périer; and when it was neither of them, it was the wily Ribot who
crooked an experienced finger and snared the prize.[1] It led Jaurès to
comment that "all of French politics has been reduced to a little game in
which Périer and Dupuy nonchalantly exchange offices."[2]

The successive ministeries were, from the socialist viewpoint, cut of
the same conservative cloth. The "new spirit," as it was termed by the
old Gambettist Eugène Spuller, Minister of Education in the Casimir-
Périer Cabinet, described the growing *détente* between republicans and
clericals to effect a working coalition against the extreme Left. Monseigneur Ferrata, a churchman of no mean standing, was a ready disciple
of the "new spirit," urging "the appointment of conservative elements
to counter the socialist parties which are threatening society."[3] Jaurès
summed up the direction of the ministries as neither new nor spirited,
but rather as a final form of monarchism in which "big capital is king,

the most powerful and the last of kings."[4] He looked over the rising *vedettes* of moderate republicanism — Paul Deschanel, Raymond Poincaré, Charles Jonnart, Georges Leygues, Louis Barthou — able young men, none of them much older than Jaurès, who were destined to fill the ministries and take the lead in the Chamber. He concluded that their basic aim was not much more than "to keep their influence."[5]

So Jaurès buckled down to the hard work of socialism — debates and interventions in the Chamber, speeches and meetings for the cause, wide reading and research, a steady stream of newspaper articles. He rose early each day and spent mornings in his cluttered little study mastering the material for the afternoon sessions of the Chamber. He lunched around eleven, heartily, to assuage a substantial appetite, and then walked at a brisk pace to the Palais Bourbon, observing everything — bookstalls, shops, the river itself — with unabashed enthusiasm. "Jaurès is a child, an overgrown child," Ribot had once said.[6] And, in truth, he never quite lost the child's capacity for discovery and dreaming.

Dupuy, the Auvergnat who had carried his unimaginative republicanism to the highest reaches of French politics, fell from office on November 25, soon after the new Parliament convened. It was then that the key figure of the Anzin Mining Syndicate, Jean Casimir-Périer, received the call from President Carnot to form a ministry. This he did by December 3, including in his moderate republican cabinet three old *gambettistes*, Spuller, Raynal, and Antonin-Dubost, and one professional soldier, General Auguste Mercier, as Minister of War. Dupuy, meanwhile, was elected president of the Chamber of Deputies.

Casimir-Périer's government began its five months of existence with a fairly strong majority behind it. But the ministry was timid about social reform, and that provoked criticism from the socialists. Yet their bitter opposition to Progressist leadership developed in the face of a more fundamental and immediate challenge. For in the first weeks of Casimir-Périer's leadership, the government proposed certain laws which seemed to Jaurès and his friends serious threats to their freedom of expression.

France had come to that agonizing period when, because of social ferment and the organization of workers, men of property, both large and small, were gripped by an irrational fear of revolution. Despite obvious signs of their loyalty to the democratic process, the parliamentary socialists continued to season their speeches with revolutionary rhetoric. At this moment, therefore, when their movement was strong enough to make an impact yet weak enough to stimulate hopes of suppression, moderates and conservatives were tempted to challenge its very right of expression. Especially now, in 1893, nonsocialists were spurred to action. For this was a time of terror, bombs, and anarchism, and the bourgeoisie were making few distinctions between men who sought to legislate private property out of existence and those who proposed to blow it up. Yet socialists were not anarchists, far from it, and the great challenge before them, as Jaurès realized, was to mark that distinction clearly while safeguarding, despite violence on the extreme Left, the fullest measure of self-expression.

II

The French anarchists traced their lineage back to that learned son of a poor cooper, Pierre-Joseph Proudhon. He had formulated a social theory which aimed to end authority "whether in the form of Church, State, land, or money."[7] So attractive was this anti-authoritarian doctrine to most later anarchists that, whatever their individual differences, almost all of them expressed their debt to him. By the 1880's, when the post-Commune years gave way to a decade of agitation and organization, anarchism won converts, not numerous but devout, among anti-statist artisans, libertarian intellectuals, and near-desperate proletarian outcasts. The movement lived mainly through its literature, the newspapers, pamphlets, and books of such dedicated propagandists as Émile Gautier, Jean Grave, Charles Malato, and Émile Pouget.

What did the anarchists preach? What was their good society, and how did they propose to reach it? No single answer suffices; for if all anarchists agreed that the goal was perfect freedom, a society without coercion and restraint, they reached no such common accord on the actual terms of such a society. Thus, while the *anarchistes individualistes*, the purest among them and the least realistic, admitted of no social organization at all, the *coöpératistes* envisioned a society based on voluntary association and the *syndicalistes* on worker-controlled shops. On matters of tactics, the anarchists were no less divided. While the *propagandistes par la parole* sought to convert men by preaching the evils of coercive society and the virtues of anarchism, the *propagandistes par le fait* hoped, by individual acts of violence, to destroy the oppressors and win over the masses. Revolutionaries by conviction, convinced that man was born free but that private property especially had enslaved him, the anarchists were nonetheless the bane of the socialists' existence.

It was an ancient struggle, older even than the First International, pitting pure libertarians, the least realistic of theorists in an age of increasing complexity, against social planners, who recognized that freedom is never absolute. In the 1880's and 1890's, the quarrel between Marxists, advocating a collectivist society directed by a central authority, and anarchists, attacking centralism as coercive, had lost none of its bitterness. Theoretically, anarcho-communists, who envisaged a collectivism based on small, voluntary groups, and those non-Marxist socialists, who preached association and coöperation, might have managed some measure of collaboration. In practice, this proved impossible.

The socialists, whether revolutionaries or reformists, centralists or decentralists, all organized for political action. For the Possibilists and Independents, success at the polls and social reforms would gradually lead from capitalism to socialism; for the Marxists, they would organize the proletariat and prepare the revolution; for the Allemanists, they would complement and support direct economic action. But the anarchists, irascible critics of the socialists, denounced their parties and their motives. Though their criticisms were sometimes valid (socialist opportunism *was* a danger and parties *could* become bureaucratic), their asceticism destroyed their sense of reality and forced the socialists into protracted debates. It was the tactical problem, then, which divided socialists and anarchists; and when the anarchists finally resorted not to political action or organized revolution but to random acts of violence, the gap between them became unbridgeable.

By the 1880's, some French anarchists, emulating their Russian comrades, began to protest with bombs and to wreak vengeance by assassination. Through acts of violence, often directed against men in high places, they proposed to strike directly at organized society; then, they felt, the State would be seriously weakened, while their "propaganda by the deed" would convert the masses to anarchism. The work of *révoltés*, a handful of half-desperate, half-idealistic men, terror nonetheless shaped the whole movement. Most anarchists, though they didn't plant dynamite themselves, defended the violence as a valid protest and blamed a coercive society for provoking it. Terror finally dominated the anarchists; it preoccupied their theorists and colored their public image. But when the government retaliated, and here was the danger, it threatened the existence not only of anarchists but also of socialists.

In the 1880's acts of violence were still relatively rare; by the early 1890's they had become frequent, and the so-called era of *attentats* (outrages) reached its height.

On December 9, anarchism struck in the Chamber itself. From the public gallery, one Auguste Vaillant threw a bomb which exploded among the deputies; though only one of them, Abbé Jules Lemire, was seriously wounded, most of the others went sprawling beneath their desks for safety. According to a popularly accepted version of the events, Dupuy, presiding over the Chamber, rapped for order and in a notable display of *sang-froid* stated resolutely: "The session will continue."[8] The Vaillant episode sent a shock through French society, and demands for control over extremist activities now filled the air. "Any society, and especially a democratic one," *Le Temps* declared editorially on December 12, "has the right and duty, in the name of universal suffrage, to quarantine and silence those who are in constant revolt against its laws."

The republican majority took action with unprecedented speed, and on December 12, both houses had enacted legislation which drastically altered the liberal press law of July 29, 1881. In essence, the government was now empowered to seize or suppress newspapers, not only for demonstrable and direct provocation to crime, but also for what was vaguely called "indirect provocation."[9] The Casimir-Périer ministry could conceivably use such a law against a wide range of opposition papers, and yet, aside from the criticism by socialists and a few Radicals, notably Goblet and Pelletan, this change won overwhelming support in the Chamber.

The defenders of social order were not yet finished. The extremist press was bad enough, they felt, but freedom of assembly for dangerous persons constituted an even greater threat to society. Establish tight controls over meetings, urged the moderate and conservative press.[10] And especially, strengthen the control of the Prefects over the police, lest the mayors, some of whom were socialists, should frustrate efforts to protect law and order.[11] Again Parliament responded with alacrity, and on December 15 a second proposal was sweepingly approved, this time by a vote of 464 to 39, which empowered the government to suppress organizations or forbid meetings suspected of hatching criminal plots.

The era of *attentats* was a nightmare for the socialists. As they viewed developments, the working-class movement had been dangerously invaded by unthinking bomb-throwers, who, no matter how sincere, could only encourage wild delusions among the workers. Guesde, though he had made impassioned appeals for revolution a decade before, condemned anarchist violence, declaring that "socialism will succeed only by the peacefully expressed will of the people."[12] Behind this attitude was his participation in the struggle between Marx and Bakunin, between scientific socialism and anarchist irrationalism.

Jaurès was no such direct heir of past disputes. Nor could he regard without deep sympathy the selflessness of young terrorists who neither sought nor were able to escape the death penalty, and the sense of despair which had driven them to violent acts. He studied their biographies, read their words, and could hardly deny them his sympathy. There was a strange and haunting purity about Ravachol who, however unbalanced, went to his death for throwing a bomb in the boulevard St. Germain on March 11, 1892, leaving these final words: "I hope that the jurors, who have thrown my devoted friends into despair by sentencing me to death, carry the memory of this sentence in their consciences; as for myself, I will bow my head to the blade of the guillotine courageously."[13]

Jaurès thought about that tragic young man, Auguste Vaillant. Was he evil, inherently wicked? No, cried Jaurès, his words formed in his burning conscience, he was the victim of society — abandoned by his parents as a boy, driven to petty crime for survival, moved by it all to a hatred of life, and longing, as he had said at his trial, to die for something meaningful.[14] Out of his compassion Jaurès signed, along with other leading socialists, an appeal for clemency, which failed, however, to move President Sadi Carnot.

But personal sympathy altered not at all the doctrinal opposition of Jaurès. For him the anarchists were twice wrong: wrong in their violent methods and wrong in their individualistic aims. For though the great theorists of anarchism had set down a community of free men as their goal, Jaurès, out of either superficiality or special party pleading, accused the anarchists of espousing an unhampered individualism.[15]

The most immediate threat of anarchism to the socialist cause, however, was neither doctrinal nor theoretical. It was rather, as all the socialist leaders agreed, the discrediting of the working-class movement, the easy association in the public mind of bomb-throwers and militant reformers. "The door is opened to all sorts of crimes," wrote *Le Temps* on December 14, 1893, "when respect for law vanishes and violence is condoned." Such words were vague and the categories even vaguer. Were the socialists to be excluded too from the community of the respectable? So long as they both trod anticapitalist ground, anarchists and socialists were constantly being lumped together.[16] As Jaurès and his friends viewed it, anarchism was not the real danger to French capitalism, but rather socialism, its parties, unions, election victories, propaganda. The Republic, because it had granted democratic freedoms, was a thorn in the side of the conservatives, and their procedure was now clear. For under cover of the anarchist threat, they had pushed through what the socialists labeled the *lois scélérates*, the "infamous laws" threatening the civil liberties of every left-wing group.[17]

Anarchism stayed alive, like a hissing serpent that on occasion struck, and on February 12, 1894, Émile Henry threw a bomb in the Gare St. Lazare, which wounded twenty persons and killed one. Eight days later a bomb in the rue Saint-Jacques found another victim. The authorities now stepped up their surveillance of the Left, and the socialists felt increasingly threatened. On April 30, 1894, Jaurès expressed the socialist opposition when he interpellated the ministry on its repressive tactics.

Jaurès moved directly to his subject that day. What had been happening in France since the laws of December were enacted? Men of socialist sympathies, though living peacefully enough, had been harassed and manhandled. "Why," he cried out to the ministerial benches, "why, in these past few months, have you become so suspicious of the militant workers? Why have you multiplied searches and arrests among the poor on the basis of the vaguest standards, the silliest pretexts, and completely anonymous charges?"[18] The random terror of anarchists, he concluded accusingly, had become the excuse for controlling the political activities of the working class.

But, continued Jaurès, it was even more than that. The government was using *agents provocateurs*, and when anarchist outrages didn't occur, the authorities invented them. At the Vaillant enquiry, the charge had already been made that the police had encouraged that unfortunate anarchist.[19] Jaurès had not spoken loosely when he had noted, a month before, that "capitalism and anarchism can be seen fraternizing on the boulevard des Italiens."[20] Were the deputies incredulous? Then Jaurès now offered them proof drawn from his experience in the Carmaux strike of 1892. It had been the anarchist Tournadre who had gone among the Carmaux workers saying: "What good is your strike with its weeks of useless suffering while the company lives on profits and the socialist deputies lead a good life at your expense?" He had proposed the easy solution — money for dynamite and then flight to London if that should be necessary. When asked the source of his funds by the suspicious socialist miners, the anarchist had replied: "There are capitalists in Paris, the heads of great industries and stores, who are friendly to me and my associates." This same Tournadre, added Jaurès, had left behind him in Carmaux a trunk containing two friendly letters, one from the Baron de Rothschild and the other from the Duchesse d'Uzès.[21]

The meaning seemed clear to Jaurès. It reflected the "new spirit" at work. If the ministry had intended simply to prevent anarchist disorders, it would not have drawn laws that could be used against socialists, the very men preaching to workers the futility of anarchism. But its aim was larger, nothing less than to silence socialism. "A long time ago," Jaurès wrote sweepingly, "the men of Panama vowed to destroy freedom of press and speech."[22]

The ministry won its vote of confidence overwhelmingly, despite Jaurès' peroration. And public opinion did not unite behind his views, far from it. Nonsocialists of all shades supported restrictions on press and assembly to fetter dangerous ideas and organizations.[23] The editorialist of *Le Matin* spoke for a large body of moderate and conservative opinion when, in summing up the significance of the recent laws, he wrote, on July 24, 1894: "The freedom of speech is far from being universal and absolute. And it is the same with writing, especially in the press."

To the Left the ministry thus symbolized reactionary rule. But even to the friends of order, it appeared as something less than a distinguished government. Its days were thus numbered, and in May, 1894, almost without warning, its majority disappeared on the issue of union rights for state employees. The Minister of Public Works, Charles Jonnart, was a competent young politician whose actions were influenced by his ties through marriage with the powerful Aynard banking family. Since it had not been precisely indicated in the 1884 trade union law whether the right of association extended to government employees, Jonnart refused to grant free time to workers on state railways to attend union conferences. The socialists joined in a debate which roused not only the Radicals but even some moderates who felt committed to the right of association. Casimir-Périer risked a vote of confidence on May 22, and fell from office on the unfavorable result. Lafargue, certainly exaggerating the role of the socialists, nonetheless underscored their vigilance when he wrote that they were "the only ones who have fought and brought down ministries."[24]

But the spirit of the Chamber and the leadership of the Progressists remained intact. By the end of May, a ministry had been formed again by Dupuy, who filled his Cabinet with the future leaders of France. It consisted of Louis Barthou at the Ministry of Public Works, Félix Faure at the Ministry of the Navy, Théophile Delcassé at the Colonial Office, Raymond Poincaré at the Ministry of Finance, and Georges Leygues at the Ministry of Education. General Mercier remained, fatefully, at the War Office. For the socialists, little had changed but the names.

III

On June 21, 1894, Jaurès interpellated the Dupuy ministry. The issue was the same, only the details were different. The subject now was academic freedom and his interpellation was directed to the thirty-six-year-old Leygues, who would probably have preferred a less scorching baptism of fire.

It was Spuller, his predecessor at the Office of Education, who had undertaken earlier in the year to bring the political activities of teachers under surveillance. From his desk in the Ministry of Education he had theatened with disciplinary action, even dismissal, those teachers and professors who actively participated in politics. Now Leygues would have to defend that policy against the criticism of the socialists.

Jaurès discussed in turn three kinds of political participation from which, he charged, teachers had been excluded. There was the matter of petitions to Parliament, which Spuller's directive of February 10 had specifically prohibited. To Jaurès this was nothing less than an infringement of every citizen's right to criticize authority. "There is no infallible power; there are no infallible laws; there is, therefore, no unerring administration."[25]

When teachers went beyond the simple petition to deeper political involvement, he went on, they ran the risk of dismissal, especially if they were of the Left and had won public office. Jaurès cited a case from his own constituency in Albi. A young teacher named Marty, of excellent professional reputation, had been elected to the municipal council. But after tangling with the moderates of the area, especially Senator Barbey (a decade before a supporter of the young Jaurès), he had been dismissed from his teaching post. From this one illustration Jaurès drew a broad conclusion — that when teachers were both politically active and radical, their livelihood was jeopardized.[26]

Finally he came to the socialist teachers, the men who neither petitioned nor ran for office, but who openly professed their socialism. Were they any the less good teachers? Had they violated the scientific spirit? Jaurès categorically denied it, and none better than he, a great teacher and a socialist both, could challenge the positivists and their doctrine of objectivity. The issue was a crucial one, nor has it become less so since Jaurès debated it. The bourgeois republicans hadn't wrested control of the schools from the clerics, after all, only to pass it on to a corps of socialists. When they insisted on the objectivity of teachers, they implied, in more cases than not, an acceptance of the present social order; and the more the teachers, usually underpaid and sensitive to social problems, turned toward socialism, the more the republican officials tried to silence them.

But no, Jaurès insisted, there was no contradiction between the inquiring spirit and moral conviction, between classroom competence and political commitment. The frightened bourgeoisie would restrict the activities of their teachers and remove them from the mainstream of life; yet the spokesmen of the French Revolution, full of hope for a new and better social order, had urged teachers "to grasp all the vital ideas of the century, to participate in all the great movements for freedom and justice."[27] For when teachers understood the human condition, when they worked for its improvement, then, cried Jaurès, they brought to their classrooms a vitality, a profundity, a high seriousness, which both inspired and awakened the young.

The speech, though it was a fervent defense of freedom, attracted few supporters in the Chamber; instead it was followed by a spirited attack against insidious propaganda in the classroom. By the time the debate finally came to a close, Jaurès had failed to exact from the ministry any concrete guarantees for socialist teachers. But he had so effectively summed up the case against academic neutralism that his words could only have had a bracing effect on those teachers whose resolve was weakening before the threat to their careers. At least, his influence seemed pernicious enough to antisocialist spokesmen so that they devoted considerable time and space to countering his arguments. Thus, Francisque Sarcey, the noted critic of *Le Temps*, was diverted from his endless campaign against all that was new in the theatre to direct an attack against Jaurès. In an article for *La Revue bleue*, he sallied forth as the champion of the nonpolitical teacher, whose energies were concentrated totally on his classroom and his students and not dissipated in outside politics. The school, wrote Sarcey, was not made for the teacher; "no, it is the teacher who is made for the school. . . . M. Jaurès, who speaks glibly of the rights of teachers, seems oblivious to the rights of the lycée."[28]

At once and in the same review, Jaurès responded to Sarcey's article: "He is quite mistaken. The teacher who participates in the political struggle, who is therefore exposed to the watchful eye of all parties, must be more careful than others to discharge his duties faithfully and fully."[29] But Sarcey's argument, he suggested, was really trivial and quite beside the point. At the heart of teaching were curiosity and breadth of vision. Curtail the experience of the teacher, warned Jaurès, confine him to dead texts and time-worn tradition, and he will know little of human reality and convey less.

Jaurès won no parliamentary victories for academic freedom in 1894. But it was important that teachers, especially the young socialists among them, should have heard so eloquent a voice raised in their defense. Hemmed in by the guardians of social order on the one side and strong tradition on the other, they could stand up, full of renewed courage, confident that on their behalf they had a spokesman, one from their own ranks, who so easily commanded attention. Throughout his life, Jaurès would number countless teachers and professors among his friends and correspondents; he enjoyed nothing so much as to discuss with them the problems of teaching and the fruits of their scholarship. He could not help but instill in them something of his own socialist faith, and it is not too much to say that for the impressive spread of socialism among teachers, especially in those years-to-come of the Dreyfus Affair, no one was more responsible than Jaurès.[30]

IV

In June, 1894, Sadi Carnot, President of the Republic, made a ceremonial trip to Lyon. Elected in 1887 on the resignation of Grévy, he had filled his seven years with honest and trivial service. As his term drew to a close, Carnot continued to perform his decorative functions. On June 24, he opened an exposition in Lyon and presided over a banquet, climaxing it with an unexceptional patriotic toast. Then he was off to the theatre for a command performance; but as Carnot's carriage passed through the rue de la République, a man rushed wildly from the crowd, lunged into the open vehicle and stabbed the President in the chest. Three hours later Carnot was dead.

The assassin was an Italian anarchist, Santo Caserio, who had fled Italy to avoid imprisonment. This act, which he considered just revenge for the French prosecution of anarchists, sent a shock through the country. On June 27 the two houses of Parliament met, and indicated their mood by raising Casimir-Périer to the Presidency. With 451 votes to the 195 cast for Henri Brisson, candidate of the Left, he entered the Elysée as a symbol of all that the socialists opposed.

The crime at Lyon almost inevitably brought before the Chamber proposals, even more comprehensive than six months before, for the control of extremist activities. And it was, in fact, on July 9 that a sweeping measure was introduced to suppress "anarchist ideas," whether in the press, meetings, private gatherings, or even personal letters.

The socialists tried to block or at least delay passage of such a law. The next day, July 10, Jaurès made a major address in favor of fiscal reform, an intervention which presented the socialist approach to the tax structure and simultaneously revealed the social conservatism of the ministry. Lift the heavy burden of taxes from the backs of the poor, he urged, and raise revenue instead by progressive levies on income and inheritance. When the moderate Jules Roche denounced this as nothing less than confiscation, a new tyranny over the rights of the individual, Jaurès shot back. "We have so often heard these surcharged words about the potential tyranny of the people. But while this potential tyranny is decried, the actual tyranny of capitalism continues."[31] On July 11, Le Temps led the spirited attack on Jaurès, calling his proposal an assault against "the work, the honor, even the life of the citizens." And two days later, Minister of Finance Poincaré brought to a decisive close this debate on what he called "the seizure of large fortunes."[32] Jaurès' effort was resoundingly defeated, 364 to 142, though not before he had made it clear that the proper function of republican rule ought to be reform, not repression.

For the next two weeks bitter controversy raged in the Chamber over what became the third and vaguest of the lois scélérates. Opponents of the proposal demanded of Lasserre, reporter for the committee which had drawn it, that he give a precise definition of "anarchism" as he understood it. As he defined it, anarchism was like a capacious umbrella, covering many shades of social protest, indication enough of what wide latitude the government would have in applying the law. Furthermore, the measure foresaw a breach in the historic protection by jury trial, for the cases of the accused were to be heard before special and secret "correctional tribunals." It seemed to the socialists, and to a fair sprinkling of Radicals, that civil liberties were being peeled away like leaves from an artichoke.[33]

The socialists made a sustained attack. The Allemanist Victor Dejeante even charged on July 24 that a *coup d'état* was in the making. "Look at the Eighteenth Brumaire and the Second of December! The makers of these *coups d'état* declared that they wished to combat the Anarchist idea, when their real objective was the destruction of the Republic. We say that the real objective which you pursue by your measure is identical."[34]

As the debate neared its end, Jaurès went to the tribune. A mask had been ripped away, he charged, and all the class selfishness of the bourgeois government was now exposed. What was this proposal, he asked, but a way for the Prefects "to rid themselves in any village of persons who bother them — sincere democrats, Radicals, socialists?"[35] Thoughts had undoubtedly crossed his mind of the Tarn, where Reille and Solages had strong influence over departmental officials.

Now, towards the end of the two-week debate, he startled the majority by introducing an amendment, certain to fail in votes, but unmistakable in its meaning: "All men in public life who have sold their votes — or been involved in financial scandals — will be judged as the real cause of anarchist propaganda." Defending his amendment, he called on all his oratorical powers. "When the same bark carries the corrupt politician and the murdering anarchist into hell, they will find much to talk about, for they will be complementary products of the same social order." In conclusion, he called for censure of the ministry, and the House, obviously shaken, supported Dupuy by what was first announced as the slight majority of 42 votes. Successive recounts reduced the margin to four and then one. The Left was sure that the Government was tampering with the vote, and an unidentified deputy cried out: "It's a Panama scandal in the voting urn."[36]

The next day, July 26, the majority had recovered both composure and purpose, and the third of the *lois scélérates* passed with a substantial majority. Jaurès had few illusions, he wrote a few days later, about a state that "can punish words whispered into the ear of a friend, suppress both jury trial and publication of court proceedings, [and] permit judges to label as anarchist anyone they please."[37] Jaurès' fears were not idle; the first victim of the law against the "anarchist threat" was Jules-Louis Breton, a Blanquist socialist.

For the anarchists themselves the days of terror were numbered. Since the start of the decade that most remarkable of anarchists, the Russian prince and outstanding scientist, Peter Kropotkin, had protested that tactics of terror could only isolate them from the people. Such protests, added to governmental repression, persuaded the French anarchists to change tactics by 1895 and to turn increasingly to the union movement as their center of influence. Thus the socialists, still fighting the *lois scélérates*, would soon face the anarchists on yet another front.

V

In the waning summer Louise packed the trunks, Jean loaded books into suitcases, and the Jaurès family went south to Bessoulet — to breathe the fresh air of the Midi. When the Chamber of Deputies was not in session, Jaurès took on a full schedule of speaking engagements, and wherever he went, he found time to visit the museums, the libraries, and the monuments. Once he traveled to Lille, taking with him for reading matter on the train a book in English, on Dante Gabriel Rossetti. While in that city, he sought respite from politics in the municipal art museum where he found masterpieces of Goya, Rembrandt, and Ruysdael. But by the autumn of 1894, Jaurès was again fighting for socialist freedom, this time in a head-on clash with President Casimir-Périer.

On September 29 a sensational article appeared in a flamboyant little weekly newspaper called *Le Chambard*. Entitled "A bas Casimir!" it was written by the young socialist editor, Gérault-Richard, whose use of invective was proportionate to his desire for the limelight. His subject was a provocative one, the unpopularity of President Casimir-Périer. The President was, in fact, a haughty man who had expected to receive from the people the approval he craved. His handsome appearance, his position as one of the genuinely wealthy capitalists of France, his well-developed sense of importance at forty-seven — all encouraged this vanity. But as he traveled around France the reception he received was at best unenthusiastic. Gérault-Richard, sparing no insults, now undertook to "explain" his unpopularity to the Chief Executive.[38]

"Casimir-Périer is right to hate the people," he began. "Rarely has a feeling been so thoroughly reciprocated; his hatred is returned to him a hundredfold." And why? asked Gérault-Richard. The people could not forget the deeds of his family, its rapacity and exploitation. "The crimes of the grandfather," he went on, thinking now of the Chief Minister of Louis Philippe, "have profited the grandson, since they assure him leadership in the kingdom of exploiters." But part of that legacy was the hostility of the people. "Today, the citizens are silent when he passes. Tomorrow the cry will echo: 'Down with Casimir!' which means 'Long live the Republic of the Workers!' "

The attack could hardly pass unnoticed. Gérault-Richard, who had already been prosecuted thirteen times for offenses under the press law, was now haled before the Cour d'assises on November 5 to face almost certain punishment under the stiffer press code. He approached Jaurès for help, thinking no doubt of the powerful effect his oratory could have even in a court of law. The generosity of Jaurès was well-known; his critics considered it love of flattery, a desire to feel important. But when he agreed to go before the Cour d'assises, he was thinking not only of defending an undisciplined editor but even more of pleading for freedom of expression and exposing the world of Casimir-Périer. It was a strange turn of events. For in his advocacy of Gérault-Richard, Jaurès was defending a man who not only envied him but made him the butt of his sarcastic humor; and in carrying his defense into the courtroom he found himself in surroundings which were unfamiliar and confining.[39]

But permitted by the president of the court to plead for Gérault-Richard, he began at first with good legal comportment and then gradually, as though he couldn't restrain himself, he released a flood of explosive words.[40] Jaurès addressed himself to the issue of free expression. Why, he asked, should the right to criticize stop with the person of the President? And why should socialist propaganda be considered the cause of the President's poor showing in France? His unpopularity was far less the product of bad publicity than of the conservatism he espoused and the family tradition he represented.

Leaving aside the actual charge against Gérault-Richard, Jaurès now sketched with telling detail, proof of his research, the history of a family which had enjoyed privilege and power.[41] Stretching back to the maneuvers of Claude Périer, the President's great-grandfather, who had gained the Anzin concessions through his influence under the French Revolutionary Directory, the record as he unfolded it was consistently antilabor and repressive. It was the grandfather, the first Casimir-Périer, who had indelibly stamped on the family tradition its "authoritarian Orleanism, greedy, selfish, and bloody." Even before he became the minister of Louis Philippe he had tripled his fortune; "he kept his eye peeled in our tortured society for commercial and industrial disasters and enriched himself on the defeat of the vanquished." Then, holding power under the Orleanist Monarchy in 1831, he had crushed in blood the rising of the desperate Lyon silk workers.

That was the tradition, cried Jaurès, which the present Casimir-Périer carried into the Élysee. What did it mean for the Third Republic to raise such a man to the Presidency? "Every regime must have its symbol, a visible sign, by which it betrays and reveals its soul. We wanted to create the Republic of great money-changers and usurers: very well, the estate where the President of the Republic resides, where he convokes his ministers and signs decrees, where he promulgates laws and receives, in the name of France, the representatives of nations, is the home of usury, and when the French Republic touches that soil, it is the spirit of usury which contaminates it."

At the climax of his denunciation, Jaurès cried out to a shocked audience: "I swear that I prefer for our country the houses of prostitution where the monarchy of the Old Regime died to the treacherous banking house where the honor of the bourgeois Republic is dying."

It was too much for the judges. The president of the court called him to order. "You are comparing the house of the President to a house of prostitution!" A determined Jaurès replied: "I am not comparing it; I am putting it below." And he went on, unveiling the story of Anzin, its oppression of the miners, its fantastic profits. It was as though he could not stop, for he spoke "in the name of a century of silence."

Against that tradition, Jaurès concluded, Gérault-Richard had struck a blow for freedom. When he had finished, bursts of applause crackled through the air; the class struggle had been carried into the courtroom. But the jury supported the government's case, and when it rendered its verdict, the judges meted out to Gérault-Richard the maximum penalty of a year in prison and a three-thousand-franc fine.

The reaction of the antisocialist press was extremely hostile to Jaurès' performance. It was a travesty of legal procedure, they charged, because he had strayed far beyond the point of law and stressed totally superfluous issues. But more than that and worse, it was blatant demagoguery and a danger to the organized rule of law.[42] The socialists, however, were stirred by the event — this denunciation in the prophetic tradition of the money-changers in the temple. La petite République printed the trial record and Jaurès' plea in a brochure which had a considerable sale.

As 1894 drew to a close, Jaurès had no illusions left about the Progressist ministries. Hardly a move they made seemed to him above reproach.

VI

On November 1, 1894, la Dépêche de Toulouse, reporting a case of espionage committed by an officer of the French army, offered the readers the name of the offender. "The guilty officer is named A. Dreyfus; he is of the Jewish race and religion; he is an artillery captain, born October 9,

1859." In fact, there had been as yet no confession by Dreyfus, nor had a trial been held to determine guilt or innocence. But several papers, following the lead of Édouard Drumont's anti-Semitic *La libre Parole*, assumed the guilt of the officer under arrest.[43]

In the period from the arrest on October 15 until the trial on December 19, 1894, a penetrating study, even of material printed in the newspapers, might well have set one to questioning the validity of the case against Captain Dreyfus. But Jaurès, absorbed as he was in his struggle with the Progressist ministries, was hardly moved to speculate about a possible injustice to an army officer. Nor had he felt it necessary to reply to the stream of fantastic charges against the loyalty of Jewish soldiers, which had been appearing in *La libre Parole* since its inception in 1892.

Yet late in November even so resolute a reactionary as Paul de Cassagnac expressed concern in *L'Autorité* about the possible conviction of an officer on the basis of a single document (the famous *bordereau*)[44] attributed to Dreyfus on the testimony of so-called handwriting experts. Then, when General Mercier, the War Minister, interviewed by *Le Figaro* on November 28, asserted that the proofs against Dreyfus were essentially conclusive, a handful of deputies and editors questioned the propriety of such an expression of opinion before the trial had begun. Finally, the decision to conduct the trial *in camera*, in large measure because the evidence against the accused was too flimsy to stand wide public scrutiny, roused a newspaper controversy in which due process of law stood at the center of the debate. At none of these points did Jaurès intervene. He spoke for the first time on some aspects of the case after the trial had ended on December 22 in a verdict of guilty and a sentence of imprisonment and exile for life.

The penalty, it was claimed, had been the most extreme possible, since Article 5 of the 1848 Constitution had abolished the death sentence for political crimes. Thus stymied, Mercier sought to plug the hole in the law by presenting to the Chamber on December 24 a bill to restore the death penalty in cases of espionage and treason. At this point Jaurès intervened, not for Dreyfus, whose guilt he hardly questioned, but for the better treatment of the simple soldiers in the French army. Speaking for the socialists, he cried out: "We urge the Chamber to grant precedence to consideration of a law to revise Articles 221, 222, and 223 of the code of military justice, which impose the death penalty on a soldier even for a momentary act of insubordination to one of his superiors."[45]

In the course of his speech Jaurès implied that an irregularity had attended the court martial of Dreyfus, resulting in special leniency toward an officer by judges of the same military caste. The judges could have sentenced the traitor to death under Article 76 of the military code, he argued. Premier Dupuy reported testily that Jaurès had made his plea on behalf of his party of internationalists who were seeking to undermine the army. Tempers rose to the breaking point and Dreyfus was forgotten. Barthou, answering the charge that the government shielded traitors, accused Jaurès of lying. The *tarnais* roared back at once: "You are the liars, those of you who are trying to win back your popularity by exploiting patriotism."[46]

For this intemperate reply, Jaurès drew not only temporary expulsion and official censure for violating Article 124 of the rules, forbidding insults or threats to a member of the government; he also received a challenge to a duel from Barthou. Jaurès' actions won him strong support from strange bedfellows. The Guesdist weekly, *Le Socialiste*, pointing to his exposure of false patriotism, declared on December 30 that "his words, like the lash of a whip, slashed an ineradicable mark across the mask of Dupuy and Company." At the same time, his criticism of leniency brought Jaurès the support of *La libre Parole*.[47] The duel with Barthou, fought ludicrously enough on Christmas morning of 1894, produced two shots and no hits. Once relieved of this burden, Jaurès took to the forum and to the press to explain these extraordinary events. In the course of these explanations, he attributed the failure to utilize Article 76 of the military code to "the enormous Jewish pressure which has been far from ineffective."[48]

The mob fury which accompanied the degradation of Dreyfus on January 5, 1895; the constant exploitation by the anti-Semitic press of the "Jewish syndicate" theme;[49] the efforts of a handful of men to begin the slow, difficult process of tearing away layer after layer of falsehood in the search for truth in the case — these actions and reactions went on without drawing comment from Jaurès, otherwise working so passionately for a socialist France. Coming in the wake of the Gérault-Richard trial, the events surrounding Dreyfus fitted all too easily into his picture of class justice.

VII

On the first day of the New Year, 1895, *La Revue des deux mondes* summed up the political life of the past twelve months: "If we had to indicate in a few words the chief characteristic of the session which has just ended, we would say that it belonged to the socialist party."[50] For the conservative editors of the journal that was a plaintive cry, not a shout of joy. It was indication enough that the parliamentary socialists, a handful of men, had won converts in the country, displayed vigor and vigilance in the Chamber, and even thrown the defenders of capitalism on the defensive.

But it was far from the end. Soon after the turn of the year, on January 6, 1895, Gérault-Richard, who had been canonized as a hero of freedom in the unforgettable speech of Jaurès, won a clear-cut victory in a special election for the Chamber of Deputies from the thirteenth *arrondissement* of Paris. The socialists in the Chamber moved suspension of his sentence, but by a vote of 309 to 218 that proposal was beaten.

The polemic of Jaurès and the election of Gérault-Richard were tough meat for the refined digestion of Casimir-Périer. Furthermore, Premier Dupuy, though linked with the President politically, scarcely hid his dislike of Casimir-Périer. "They had little in common," one historian has commented, "perhaps because of the unbridgeable gulf, noted by Barrès, between heirs and scholarship boys."[51] Thus, the Premier seldom consulted the President and barely informed him of passing events. Then, on January 15, 1895, when the Dupuy ministry fell apart on the issue of railroad concessions,[52] Casimir-Périer, faced with the prospect of calling on the Radicals to form a government, decided to resign. The next day he sent to Parliament his last message, the final word of a man deprived, as he wrote, of any effective influence.

If the socialists welcomed the departure of Casimir-Périer, they were little cheered by the immediate consequences. The more things change, runs the French adage, the more they remain the same. On January 17, 1895, the two Houses met at Versailles to choose a new President. In a test of strength with the Left, which solidly supported Brisson, the moderate republicans enjoyed the help of the monarchist Right in favor of Félix Faure. The accommodating Faure set Catholic fears at rest by denying, contrary to the evidence, that he had once fallen among Masons.

On the second poll Faure won handily, 430 to 361, and into the Élysee marched probably the most pretentious of French presidents. Sporting the finest clothes, assuming the airs of a snob, boasting at fifty-four of an all-round physical prowess, he was conservative, friendly to both Church and army. Clemenceau, stressing Faure's extremely conservative connections, quipped that he was an ideological egg "laid by Aynard and hatched by Léon Say."[53] And Jaurès wrote with scarcely veiled scorn of the "foppish *parvenu* who has pushed his way into politics by giving great dinner parties and attending fashionable affairs."[54]

But even worse from the socialist standpoint was the ministry that followed, which was headed by Ribot and retained most of the Progressists of the previous Cabinet. But Jaurès, convinced that men would fight for their highest ideals, was not discouraged. One day in February, addressing Poincaré, Minister of Education in Ribot's Cabinet, he spoke up for those young Frenchmen seeking guidance toward those ideals. "I understand their interest in Spinoza and Hegel." It was not enough to anchor education in "the narrow positivism of Littré, which is only a poor imitation of . . . Comte." Men searched for something more than the truths of science; "humanity in this world is like a great commission of inquiry which no governmental interference, no metaphysical or secular absolutes ought ever restrain or dupe."[55]

VIII

Time and again in these recent months Jaurès had stood forth as the defender of civil liberties. Yet his defense of freedom seemed hollow to antisocialists, who regarded socialism as the great threat to individual rights. Jaurès pondered this criticism and then defended socialism as the source of genuine freedom. "Will socialism suppress human liberty?" he had already asked in his Latin thesis. "Is it wrong and unjust that the law should intervene in the contractual relations between men? But the one who is poorest is not free; his chief tyrant is hunger."[56] Jaurès questioned the so-called freedom of an unequal society, which compelled men to accept almost any terms of employment. "To conceive of freedom only in its negative aspect, to think of it only as the absence of law, would make the inhabitant of Constantinople, not subject like the Parisian to regulations over hygiene and roads, not forced to send his children to school, a free citizen while we are the victims of tyranny."[57]

But after three tumultuous years of involvement, Jaurès resumed the argument with unprecedented fervor and conviction. The spokesmen for liberalism pointed to democracy and economic individualism; one, they asserted, guaranteed political equality, the other *les carrières ouvertes aux talents*, and together the essential freedom of man. But Jaurès riddled the liberal rhetoric and its assumption that power now belonged to the many and not the few:

To be sure, a worker occasionally rises to the rank of capitalist and a capitalist falls to that of worker. But let us face the essential truth that in French society a group of men, privileged through education and wealth, wields the decisive political and economic power. . . . The peasants and the workers comprise two-thirds of the nation; yet there is hardly a handful of workers in the Parliament and not a single peasant. . . . I know from firsthand experience how the powerful manipulate and control elections; I know of certain regions where the rich are the only voters, or at least control far more votes than the poor.[58]

The essence of freedom, Jaurès agreed, was the capacity to act, to create, to function in the fullness of one's powers; but it was a travesty to speak of freedom when the class system enriched the few and impoverished the many, when the State guaranteed the dominion of the powerful over the weak: "Contemporary society is weighed down not only by militarism, but by an arrogant bureaucracy. . . . Whenever they have felt it necessary to guarantee the conservative Republic or to assure their success at elections, the ruling republicans have sent into battle their legion of bureaucrats, high-ranking and low — prefects, tax-collectors, judges, professors, and teachers."[59]

And yet it was socialism, according to liberal rhetoric, which would destroy human freedom: "Once the nation controls all wealth, we are warned, we will suffer first expropriation, then despotism, bureaucracy, and complete enslavement!"[60] Rejecting what could only have seemed to him a caricature of socialism as a vast prison house, Jaurès undertook — and that despite the skepticism of the Marxists — to suggest the workings of a socialist society, its institutions and their human impact.[61]

A socialist government, once in power, would move immediately to the collectivization of private property, the root cause of injustice, greed, even starvation and war. On this, Jaurès allowed neither compromise nor half-measure.[62] Yet the regime would fail in its purpose, it would distort the revolution, unless, in the process of collectivization, it could assure both economic growth and human freedom: "All workers must receive the full value of their labor; initiative and invention must be stimulated; the freedom to consume and to choose one's job must be respected; an investment fund must be created."[63]

The problem, Jaurès realized, would be to reconcile freedom and authority, to harmonize the duties of the citizen and his rights, to control the resources of the nation while releasing the energy of the individual; it would be to realize institutionally the productive values of St. Simon and the human values of Fourier:

A central planning commission could not possibly wield all the power or resolve all the problems in this vast and complex world. . . . The government would have to decentralize, granting both autonomy and initiative to local groups. . . . Unions in the same trade would federate locally to form a sort of corporation, which would elect leaders, a local economic council, and delegates to the national planning commission. . . . Yet, if each of the corporations were absolutely independent, the result would be an economic State within an economic State. . . . Thus, a central planning commission, elected, composed of representatives of both the separate industries and the nation as a whole, would have the final authority — to allocate resources, to ensure proper investment, and to determine prices and wages. . . . Thus would socialist society be both disciplined and free, centralized and varied, planned and spontaneous.[64]

Written in the heat of the political battle, these articles of Jaurès' were nonetheless thoughtful and richly detailed.[65] Yet it would be tendentious to deny that they raised more questions than they answered; they hardly suggest the painful difficulties, the very contradictions that inhere in the relationship between freedom and planning, industrial democracy and collectivization, socialism and bureaucracy. What gives them enduring value is their insistence that these problems *must* be resolved, that freedom, though it is not the antithesis of collectivism, cannot be the handmaiden of despotism. His passion for the free life enriched the socialist tradition, endowed it with deep human value. In the final analysis, his response to the enemies of socialism was also a warning to its friends:

We socialists, we also have a free spirit; we also feel restive under external restraint. . . . If we couldn't walk and sing and meditate under the sky, if we couldn't drink in the air and pick flowers when we chose, we would even accept the present society, despite its misery and incoherence; for though its freedom is a deception, it is a deception which men still agree to call a truth and which sometimes grips their hearts. . . . Rather solitude with all its perils than coercion, rather anarchy than despotism, whatever its disguise.[66]

For Jaurès socialism meant freedom — freedom from poverty, yes, but even more from a life lonely, fragmented, loveless. In the new society, as he would so movingly describe it in *L'Armée nouvelle*, man would finally fulfil himself:

La force des instincts, la chaleur du sang, l'appétit de vivre ne seront atténués, mais les puissances instinctives seront disciplinées et harmonisées par une haute et générale culture. La nature ne sera plus supprimée ou affaiblie, mais transformée et glorifiée. Vraiment, par l'avènement de l'ordre réel, de la justice réelle, dans les rapports de la communauté humaine, il y aura un *fait nouveau* dans l'univers, et la conscience de ce fait nouveau, des hautes possibilités du monde, permettra les vastes renouvellements de l'esprit religieux.

7

Carmaux
1895

I

On May 25, 1895, there appeared a letter in the pages of *La Dépêche de Toulouse*, signed by Rességuier, head of the large glass factory in Carmaux. Responding to a threatened strike by the glass workers' union, he hurled a threat of his own. Should the workers walk out, he warned, they would come back only on his terms. Thus began a long, complex series of events which precipitated Jaurès once again into the struggles of Carmaux. This time there was no doubt anywhere about his strong identification with labor against capital. In the two years that had elapsed since his return to Parliament, he had consistently written and spoken in defense of striking workers.[1]

In Rességuier both the workers and Jaurès found an extremely rugged opponent, a self-made man with a passion for defending what he had built. He had early established himself at Toulouse as a merchant in the bottle trade, but when competition from Carmaux vendors disturbed him, he moved into that city and soon monopolized the products of its glass factory. By 1856 he had bought into the factory and in 1862 he built another plant. By 1884 his factory was producing some 32,000 bottles a day, but continuous expansion brought that figure to 100,000 per day in

1891. The position of his company in the economy of the area was improved by the preferential freight rates Rességuier won from the Midi Railroad Company. It was also enhanced by its owner's unscrupulousness; in 1890, for example, a court had found him guilty of stealing from a rival house, Alain Chartier and Company, a patented process for making a more economical mold. Rességuier's business was a tribute to its builder, and he guarded it jealously. Now almost eighty, though in good enough health to make frequent pleasure trips to Paris, he was not likely to be flexible and yielding.

The glass workers who challenged their employer were a kind of labor élite in Carmaux, enjoying twice the pay of the miners and harboring generally more radical views on politics and religion. It was almost inevitable that they should organize to strengthen their bargaining position. They had little experience with organization, however, until 1887 when Rességuier, looking for skilled labor, rather thoughtlessly brought to Carmaux some highly trained but extremely class-conscious workers from Montluçon, who were then out on strike. It was one of the new militants, Aucouturier, who spearheaded the union's drive and even got Resseguier's early paternalistic support. A strike then broke out in 1891 over the issue of substandard bottles. The company had followed the practice of selling the inferior bottles cheaply but, by the piece-rate system, paying the workers nothing for them. The union demanded and won acceptance of the practice of breaking the rejects, thus lessening the company's haste in labeling bottles as inferior.[2]

By 1895, though the advantages of working for M. Rességuier were widely proclaimed throughout the Tarn, the actual conditions of employment did not fully support the propaganda. There was bitter hostility, for example, between the workers and M. Moffre, son-in-law of Rességuier and a key administrator of the company, who imposed what the union considered a brutal regime in the factory. And there was the issue of the company's change of policy on the matter of rejects, which amounted to granting the workers half-pay for defective bottles that the company then sold. The prospect of a strike in 1895 was made all the more serious by the increasingly uncoöperative attitude of management, since a work stoppage at that time could operate to its advantage. Not only was there then an enormous inventory of bottles (almost six million) which could be disposed of during a strike, but also the strike might serve as the pretext for lowering wages and breaking the union. With a conservative ministry in Paris and a capitalist solidarity in Carmaux (the Marquis de Solages had recently joined the Board of Directors of the glass company), management was ready for action.

What seemed to underlie the more obvious calculations of the Carmaux management group was a determination to break, once and for all, the political control over the city administration which socialists had exercised since the election of Calvignac as mayor and the return of Jaurès to the Chamber. Their specific goals were to forge an effective alliance of assorted monarchists, Bonapartists, and conservative republicans, to wrest the city hall from unfriendly socialist hands, and eventually to recover the Chamber seat occupied by Jaurès. The first of these objectives was entrusted to one Dr. Sudre, physician for the mining company, who, acting as a kind of political mastermind, began to reorganize the Right by combining into one force all the enemies of socialism.

But the success of Reille, Solages, Rességuier, and their friends in achieving the second objective, the elimination of Calvignac, was even more spectacular. The opponents of the socialist mayor found a convenient pretext in 1894 for registering a complaint against him with the Prefect. Since Calvignac had neglected to revise the electoral lists, as prescribed by law, he was charged with negligence, suspended by the Prefect, and dismissed by a Presidential decree of March 12, 1894. The socialist municipal council then resigned in a body, thus necessitating new elections. Again the *carmausins* voted in the socialists who, immediately defiant of the higher authorities, proclaimed Calvignac mayor once more. But his election was again voided, and the socialist councilors decided to turn over the mayor's functions, during the year of his suspension, to their comrade, the deputy mayor Mazens, who solemnly agreed to withdraw at the end of that time. But when the year was up, in April, 1895, Mazens, susceptible to the pressure of the Prefect, refused to leave. In a stormy council session, Calvignac and Baudet, secretary of the glass workers' union, were reported to have denounced their ex-comrade as "traitorous and venal." Such insults against an elected official were excuse enough to dismiss Baudet from the council and to bring Calvignac to the bar of justice, where he was sentenced to forty days in prison and made ineligible to hold office for five years.

It was a striking victory for the companies, this elimination from the politics of the two most militant socialists among the workers. But management, which had expected the compliance of the labor force, celebrated prematurely. The defiant *carmausins*, nominating both Calvignac and Baudet for places in the coming cantonal elections, used the polls on July 28, 1895, as a place of protest against what they considered infringement of their political rights. They were both elected, Calvignac to the *conseil général* and Baudet to the *conseil d'arrondissement*. The exasperation of the management group was now virtually boundless, and a potential glass workers' strike shaped up as a showdown between capital and labor in that area.

As it actually happened, the immediate issue of the strike in '95 was again political. After Baudet had been elected to the *conseil d'arrondissement*, he was accused by the glass company of absenting himself too frequently from his job. Unauthorized absences were frequent in a trade inducing so much exhaustion and had certainly never been cause for dismissal; but on July 30, 1895, Baudet and Pelletier, secretary of the union at the Bousquet d'Orb plant in the Hérault, both of whom had left jobs from July 21 to 27 to serve as delegates at a congress of glass workers, were summarily fired.

When the company refused any negotiation on the matter the union decided to strike. Jaurès, conscious of the company's power of endurance, of the great sacrifices demanded of workers on strike, sought to head it off. The Chamber was not in session during the summer months, and he was passing some time at Bessoulet, when, on August 1, he received a telegram telling him of the trouble. Jaurès was momentarily relaxing, enjoying both a good meal and conversation with Georges Renard, who had become editor of *La Revue socialiste* after the death of Malon in 1893. Leaving everything, he rushed at once to Carmaux and urged caution upon the workers. So far was he successful that he was able to represent them that day in an interview with the director Moffre and to transmit their sincere desire for a peaceful settlement. The workers were ready to accept new regulations on absences and even to accept stiff penalties, short of dismissal, for Baudet and Pelletier. Such was the nature of the first intervention by Jaurès, which was attacked by *Le Temps* on August 3 as a deliberate socialist attempt to stir up trouble.

As it happened, it was an employer lockout which forced the workers to strike. The formal request for arbitration, made by the union on August 2, was rejected flatly by Rességuier three days later. Nevertheless, Jaurès urged an immediate return to work, whatever the fate of Baudet and Pelletier. This was the course the glass workers decided upon when they discovered on August 8 that the factory was closed against them. Jaurès now became spokesman for workers, releasing to the newspapers the explanation of what had happened: "He [Rességuier] wants the strike at any price in order to break the union; it is not enough for him to have fired Baudet and Pelletier; it is not enough to have refused the arbitration asked by the workers; he is now opposed to any resumption of work."[3] Rességuier pleaded a very different case before the public through his own newspaper, *Le Télégramme*, where he outlined the good working conditions enjoyed by his men and viewed the Baudet-Pelletier case as a kind of last straw of misbehavior. "In fact, the question which is actually posed today is whether the company will retain control of its business or whether the union will dictate policy."[4] Thus were the battle lines sharply drawn between union and management, socialist and conservative, Jaurès and Rességuier.

The lockout became an important source of socialist propaganda and several leading militants carried the case of the Carmaux glass workers to the entire nation. "How," asked Jaurès, "how can anyone in France, in the industrial centers, in the great republican cities, remain deaf to our appeal when we are denouncing a pact of famine entered into against men of courage, who ask nothing more than their basic freedom?"[5] He traveled to Paris on the first day of September to address an audience of some ten thousand who packed the Tivoli-Vauxhall to hear his explanation of the strike. He analyzed the dismissals of both Calvignac and Baudet as part of the counterattack by the Reille-Solages clan against the growing political power of the workers. And he reached heights of moving oratory when he concluded with an exhortation to courage. "Courage," he cried to the embattled strikers, "the proletariat of France, the proletariat of Paris is with you!"[6]

The socialists went to work on Rességuier with their heaviest artillery, and Gérault-Richard, one of the most aggressive of their publicists, dug up and capitalized on the story of that entrepreneur's theft of patents from the Chartier Company.[7] The press, which was unfavorable to the strikers, was at least as active, hammering away constantly at such themes as the minority control of the strike, the violent attitude of some of its leaders, the right of employers to discharge employees, and the sabotage of production by labor.[8]

The case against Rességuier was strongly enhanced on September 3, however, by the resignation of Sirven, vice president of the glass factory, in protest against the intransigence of the president. It seemed like the best evidence thus far that Rességuier was deliberately prolonging the strike. Sirven went even further: in accusing the president of imposing the lockout without previous consultation with the stockholders, he was documenting the very personal nature of Rességuier's war on the workers.[9] Evidence of this sort gave vigor to the socialist case, and it was in an atmosphere of real enthusiasm that Millerand, Rouanet, and Jaurès rode to Carmaux to address the workers on September 14. Millerand, who had rather played down in his own mind the stories Jaurès told of police interference, now came face to face with it; for no sooner had he arrived at the doorway of his hotel, where he started to converse with two friends, than the police broke up the "meeting." The deputies spoke that night in the packed Salle du Capitole, and it was Jaurès who had the spotlight. He swept up history in the grand manner, placing the labor movement in the great stream of contemporary events. At the heart of his speech was a description of the forces against the strike:

"While our enemies attack us for interfering in the strike, they are themselves intervening through their judges, police, prefects, and troops; they are intervening on behalf of capitalists, who can so easily hold out; and against workers, who are deprived of bread; on behalf of the strong against the weak." And he uttered a warning in his conclusion, which carried the strike to the very doorstep of revolution. "When two principles are in conflict in a society and when one of them involves the complete negation of the other, there is no longer any solution possible except revolution."[10] Jaurès was hardly a man of violence; on human grounds, he opposed it. But he was learning from this great labor conflict how difficult it was to build peacefully a world of justice and brotherhood.

The forces arrayed against the strikers and their friends seemed like a formidable and solid phalanx. The police had not remained neutral, and both Jaurès and Gérault-Richard took to the press early in October to denounce the brutality directed against the strikers by the government. This campaign, Jaurés revealed, was being masterminded on the spot by the chief official in the department, the Prefect of the Tarn, Pierre Doux.[11] After several years in the administrative service, Doux had been assigned to the Tarn in February, 1894. When appointed, he had indicated to Jaurès his willingness to coöperate with all sincere republicans and his special desire to learn more about socialism. Once in the Tarn, however, Doux learned instead that effective power lay with Baron Reille and his friends, and the ambitious Prefect, his critics charged, then undertook on their behalf to "fill Carmaux with *agents provocateurs* and police."[12] His hostility to the unions and socialists of Carmaux is demonstrable from certain unpublished documents. In a letter to the Minister of Justice on June 20, 1895, he had urged the dissolution of the glass workers' union on the ground that it was fomenting revolution.[13] And somewhat before that, Doux had written bitterly of the socialists to the same minister. "The intention of Jaurès and his friends is clearly evident. Today they are protesting in a closed hall, . . . but tomorrow they will carry their protest into the street."[14]

It was the Blanquist Marcel Sembat who bluntly accused the Prefect of having become "the pliant instrument of the hatred and bitterness of an industrial tycoon, whom a man as temperate as Senator Ranc has unhesitatingly called both mad and power-hungry."[15] That judgment was reiterated even by the monarchist Cassagnac, anxious to expose the egoism of the Republic by reciting the record of the Prefect's partisan behavior.[16]

The intervention in the strike of unsympathetic government officials touched off an explosion in the first week of October. A number of strikers, including the leader Aucouturier, were arrested and brought to trial in Albi on October 5, charged with uttering highly inflammatory remarks. Jaurès and some fifty glass workers attended the trial, which turned out to be at least as inflammatory as the alleged remarks. According to many observers, the prosecutor Bertrand, making his charges against the strikers, suddenly broke off his analysis, pointed a finger at Jaurès (a deputy and merely a spectator at the trial), and cried to the judges: "It is this man, gentlemen, who has perverted the minds of the workers by his unreasonable ideas, and who, by his very presence here, . . . has attempted to put unfair pressure on the court."[17]

The socialists could ill afford, morally or politically, to let such accusations go unanswered. On October 18 a delegation of indignant socialist deputies, Boyer, Chauvin, Lavy, and Millerand, carried complaints against Doux and Bertrand directly to Premier Ribot. Ribot made a cursory investigation, questioned the officials involved, and presented their formal denials of partisanship. Though both Jaurès and Gérault-Richard openly offered to prove the charges, no moves were made to examine the proofs.[18]

Meanwhile Rességuier, who was being turned into a hero of capitalism because of his last-ditch opposition to unionism,[19] was far too rugged an independent to put his fate exclusively in the hands of friendly political officials. If his men were recalcitrant, he could find others, and he began to bring in replacements, particularly glass workers from Rive-de-Gier. His agents used all sorts of incentives, like providing travel expenses, while concealing the unpleasant truth that these workers would be acting as "scabs."[20] Some of those who came under false pretenses left at once, but others stayed. Most of the beleagured strikers, loyal to their cause and shored up by friends like Jaurès, held their ground. But the introduction of scabs was discouraging, and a trickle of hungry *carmausins*, believing the company would never have to bargain, began to resume their jobs.[21]

Rességuier, more than just holding firm, began to strike out in all directions. Thus he instituted on October 8, 1895, a suit for 100,000 francs against Jaurès and the management of both *La petite République* and *La Dépêche de Toulouse* for organizing an illegal, conspiratorial attack against him. Sembat could ridicule the action and refer to the glass tycoon as a madman,[22] but there were others who felt that a successful suit would "discourage the politicians from fomenting strikes."[23]

The tension was boiling to the point of explosion. To the socialist deputies it seemed as though the leaders of capitalism and the bourgeois Republic had combined in a reign of terror against the workers and their friends. Now it was the strike fund that irritated the management forces, a fund put together by sympathetic contributions from many corners of France, a symbol of solidarity though hardly a solution to the problem of maintaining the idle *carmausins*. To put an end to this show of idealism, the authorities on October 15 arrested the two treasurers of the fund, both widely known for their honesty, and charged them with theft. An irate Jaurès now forced a public showdown. He interpellated the Ribot ministry for two days, October 24 and 25, on its role in the Carmaux strike, and his oratory was pitched in its most impassioned key.

Jaurès reviewed all the major themes of the affair. In Carmaux, he charged, there had developed a united front among the major economic interests, symbolized by the presence of the Marquis de Solages on the Board of Directors of the glass factory. This coalition expected political support, for the preceding Dupuy ministry had already sent sufficient police to Carmaux to keep the workers in line. When Dupuy heatedly denied the accusation, Jaurès replied sharply: "Monsieur Dupuy, your entire policy belies your protest."[24]

In assessing the blame for the strike he made much of the constant provocations by the company which reached their high point in the dismissal of Baudet and Pelletier. He went step by step over labor's caution, his own intervention with Moffre, the union's plea for arbitration, and the eventual lockout by management. He then centered his attack on the serious political implications of the widespread police interference with public meetings and speeches and even the ordinary comings and goings of the strikers. Such tactics, he charged, could only destroy freedom of speech and assembly.

With considerable detail he illustrated the kind of pressure applied by the Prefect to persuade workers to go back into the plant. There was the story of Agnès Dumas, who was told by Doux that she could have a post as schoolteacher if she got her brother and father to return to work. And there was the glass worker, home from the army on a two-week leave, informed that he could stay for three months if he would only resume his job. Jaurès wheeled upon Premier Ribot and promised documentary proof of these stories, but the government was offering no denials. Summing up his interpellation, he declared that the concrete issues of wages and hours were less important in the lives of the men than "their freedom and their right to organize."[25]

Leygues, the Minister of the Interior, was no match for Jaurès in the debate either intellectually or oratorically. But he did his best to construct the government's case. He repeated the most favorable parts of Rességuier's record, such as his high wage scales, his early recognition of the union, and his willingness to compromise on the issue of rejects.[26] But even Leygues had to admit that the company had been intransigent in refusing to bring the dispute to arbitration. He went on, however, to defend the behavior of Doux, especially his arrest of strikers who sought to obstruct the right to work for those willing to return to the plant. Finally he produced a telegram from Bertrand denying the action in the courtroom attributed to him by Jaurès. All in all, it was not a strong defense, but the majority nonetheless supported the government by a vote of 273 to 176.[27]

For the Left in France the interpellation was a great event, bringing the labor problem graphically before the public and unveiling a Jaurès of great forcefulness. Pelletan, veteran of many political battles, felt that "the speech today reveals a new Jaurès. Now he is the complete orator . . . well equipped with facts and the master of raillery as well as indignation."[28]

For the Right, for the promanagement forces, it was a partisan attack on capitalism,[29] a scandalous performance,[30] and a figment of Jaurès' morbid imagination.[31] But the attack which the deputy from the Tarn had leveled against the Ribot ministry quickly took its toll. From that onslaught the socialists went on to another on October 28 over irregularities in the financial administration of the Chemins de Fer du Sud. By a vote of 275 to 196 Ribot fell on that issue and was replaced by the first Radical ministry of the Third Republic.

This political victory for the Left didn't persuade Rességuier to capitulate. As November wore on, it became apparent that the workers, starved and helpless, were beginning to go back to work on the company's terms.[32] Though the strike may have advertized the struggle of the workers for political and economic security, though the socialist leadership leveled the charge of governmental collusion with private capital, though Jaurès' attacks were probably responsible for the transfer of Prefect Doux from the Tarn at the end of November, the strike did not succeed in breaking the company's will. That failure was underscored by a group of socialists themselves. The *allemanistes*, strong advocates of such direct economic action as the general strike, sharply attacked the dragging of the labor problem into politics.[33]

But the affair was far from over, and the Carmaux glass strike took a sudden, dramatic turn from its apparent dead end onto a new road. Though Rességuier's company would not capitulate in a strike, the dignity and the independence of the workers could perhaps be saved by the establishment of another glass factory, coöperative and worker-owned, a *verrerie ouvrière*. The history of the Carmaux glass workers' strike would thus become an important chapter in the development of the French coöperative movement.

II

The question of who first suggested the coöperative glass factory has no conclusive answer.[34] But it is certainly well established that the plan could never have materialized without the initial gift of 100,000 francs by one Madame Dembourg. A wealthy eccentric who engaged in philanthropic activities while skimping on her own household expenses, she turned the money over without strings to Henri Rochefort, the radical and cantankerous editor of *L'Intransigeant*. The 100,000 francs represented, however, only a quarter of the sum needed for a new factory; the rest eventually came from coöperatives, unions, and private contributions.[35]

In so complex an undertaking with such an assortment of stockholders, serious complications were bound to crop up, all to the delight of the antilabor interests.[36] One of these complications centered on the location of the *verrerie ouvrière*. It was soon obvious that Albi represented a more satisfactory setting than Carmaux because of its better housing for the workers and its cheaper coal supply for the plant; at Carmaux the Marquis de Solages could be expected to charge exorbitant prices for coal from his mines. The proposed move met with strong opposition, however, from the merchants and artisans of Carmaux, who contemplated with considerable rancor the loss of some 2000 customers. An arbitration committee, composed of Millerand and René Viviani, finally weighed the facts and on January 6, 1896, decided for Albi. In the months that followed, both government spokesmen and the antisocialist press insisted with some validity that Jaurès, who was so intimately connected with the new project, had lost prestige in Carmaux because of this decision.

The plans for the new glass factory made good progress despite the obstacles. Rességuier, between fury and fear, relentlessly pressed his court suit against Jaurès, *La Dépêche de Toulouse*, and *La petite République*. The distinguished corporation lawyer René Waldeck-Rousseau, whose prorepublican ministry three years later received such strong support from Jaurès during the Dreyfus crisis, drew up the brief which rested on Articles 414 and 1382 of the civil code. The trial court in Toulouse finally threw the case out, denying that these Articles, which covered damage to reputation, applied to legitimate intervention in a strike situation.[37] But the decision of the appeals court, rendered on June 30, 1897, reversed the original result. Infuriated by the verdict, Jaurès attacked the administration of justice in France as essentially one-sided: "Even before my own intervention and that of the republican newspapers, Rességuier's paper insulted the strikers, assaulted Baudet, attacked the union. . . . And I don't even recall the number of insults published against me."[38] Yet there had been no prosecution of those activities. The awarding of 15,000 francs to Rességuier was felt by many critics to be a serious threat to future freedom of the press for the Left.

The will of the men, so long put to the test in Carmaux, pushed the new factory toward completion. Skilled glass workers turned into carpenters and masons to build the factory that would be theirs. Jaurès, however, agreed with many other socialists that it should belong to all the workers, represented by the unions, the coöperatives, and the socialist groups that were backing it. Against the Marxists, who insisted upon a *verrerie aux verriers*, a factory owned by the local glass workers, he opted for a *verrerie ouvrière*.

The quarrel, which broke with sudden fury, illustrated the deep division over tactics between the Guesdists and their socialist rivals. Despite their solidarity in the Chamber, where conservative pressure forced them into close collaboration, the several socialist factions still clung to their separate views. For Guesde and his followers, coöperatives, like trade unions, were essentially schools of propaganda, instruments for uniting the workers and developing their class consciousness. Coöperators, syndicalists, reformists, the assorted disciples of Fourier, Proudhon, Blanc, or Malon, were like the utopians whom Marx had consistently opposed. When the Guesdists battled against Possibilism in the 1880's, or when they consistently denounced reformism in the years before World War I, their argument was always the same: the new society could never be created within the framework of the old. Thus, in supporting a simple coöperative glass factory, the Marxists hoped to create not a genuine socialist institution but an annex of the Parti ouvrier français.

To other socialists, however, followers of Brousse or Malon, for example, consumer and producer coöperatives seemed like steps toward socialism. A *verrerie ouvrière* at Albi, they argued, would not only belong to the entire working class, but it would plant another socialist seed in capitalist soil. Jaurès, however, was not so convinced a partisan of coöperatives. After the strikes at Carmaux and the struggle against the Progressists in the Chamber, he had a realistic understanding of power in capitalistic society; it had pushed him close to the Marxists. Yet he was aware of the coöperative movement, and he had undoubtedly read the writings of its leading theorists, like Charles Gide; his articles on socialist organization in *La Revue socialiste* in 1895 demonstrated Jaurès' complete familiarity with the history of the coöperative movement. Though he hardly believed that coöperatives were *the* answer to capitalism, he did consider them useful in associating the workers and training them for collectivism.

A *verrerie ouvrière*, Jaurès thought, responded to the hopes and aspirations of many workers. Thus, on this issue, as on the question of the general strike, he was willing to oppose his Marxist friends. Furthermore, (and this was not the least of his considerations), a *verrerie ouvrière* would unite socialists of many factions into a single working-class enterprise. So he came out for the *verrerie ouvrière* and sought to bring the quarrel to an end. From the Chamber of Deputies, on January 11, 1896, Jaurès wrote a letter to the glass workers, which read in part:

This unfortunate misunderstanding need not divide us permanently. . . . I hope that after this quarrel the bitterness will disappear and that socialist solidarity will triumph over all. I deeply regret that I am temporarily incapacitated because of exhaustion and illness. One has to learn how to reconcile himself to his limited powers, which are hardly adequate for the constant struggle. But I assure you that I have not forgotten your cause. . . . Very shortly, I will take up your cause again in the press. Courage and Unity![39]

Finally, the majority of the glass workers and their leaders opted for the *verrerie ouvrière*. On the *comité d'action*, whose forty members would guide the fortunes of the enterprise, sat representatives of the socialist groups, the coöperatives, and the unions, which had invested in it. Representing many branches of socialism, they were all convinced, even a syndicalist like Fernand Pelloutier or a Blanquist like Victor Jaclard, of its socialist value. For Jaurès, it represented the victory of unity over division, of solidarity over individualism: "In struggling for itself, the proletariat struggles for all humanity. In raising itself from the lowest depths, it raises all the rest. Humanity is thus glorified by itself and for itself."[40]

Nine grueling months passed, and on October 25, 1896, the *verrerie ouvrière* was ready to open. At the celebration banquet in Albi, Rochefort referred to Jaurès as its guiding spirit.[41] Jaurès gave the main address, reserving the most moving passages for tribute to the heroic wives of the glass workers, "who constantly exhorted their husbands to resistance."[42] Then, at the end of the banquet, the ex-professor of philosophy, who had traveled so long a road from the lycée to the glass factory of Albi, mounted a table and led the assemblage in singing a rousing version of the revolutionary *Carmagnole*.[43] Rochefort ignited the flame in the first furnace, and the festivities ended with cries of "Vive Jaurès! Vive la République Sociale!"

But fury broke loose the next night in Carmaux when Jaurès sought to address another celebration meeting. From the time he arrived at the railroad station until he reached the assembly hall, he was jostled by the police and greeted by catcalls from part of the crowd. At the meeting itself Jaurès was addressing 4000 listeners when the police broke in to halt the proceedings.[44] Returning to Paris on October 28, he minced no words in blaming these events on the conservative Minister of the Interior in the Méline Cabinet, Louis Barthou.[45] He was not alone in this accusation, for the Radical Paul Doumer charged that "against Jaurès and the socialists everything was permitted."[46]

Again Jaurès went to the floor of the Chamber, and on November 5, 1896, he interpellated the government over the most recent events in Carmaux. He charged the public officials with complicity in the events of October 26. Why were so many special police in Carmaux, he asked, unless the government had knowledge of a previously arranged hostile demonstration? They were on hand, he suggested, turning directly to Barthou, ". . . to permit hostile groups to organize against us right from the station; then, if we should bypass them, they were there to break up friendly gatherings along the way, to empty the streets of Carmaux and to give the illusion that we were important only to our enemies. Then, at the public meeting they were to break up and dissolve the session, on the slightest pretext, or no pretext at all, if necessary."[47] It was a fact, shouted Jaurès, that when he finally began his speech on that night, he had the devoted attention of his audience until sixty armed police invaded the hall and broke up the meeting. His meaning was clear — that the entire affair was a plot, well directed by the Minister of the Interior and the Prefect, to prevent him from speaking.

Barthou replied testily in a very bitter session that the hostility in Carmaux was both real and spontaneous, the product of resentment over locating the glass factory at Albi. It was with considerable relish that the minister spoke of a wedge between the workers and Jaurès. When the final vote on the interpellation was taken, the government prevailed by a margin of 308 to 222.

In the conflict of interpretation with Barthou, Jaurès had the weight of facts on his side. For though it was undoubtedly true that bitterness lingered in Carmaux, it was closer to the mark to explain the events of October as another chapter in the social struggle which was being openly waged again in Carmaux in 1896. Already thinking ahead to the general elections two years hence, Dr. Sudre had written to the Marquis de Solages on February 2, 1896, stressing the need for a solid organization against the terrible threat of socialism. "Whatever the cost," he had asserted there, "we are going to win out."[48] As a result of Sudre's effort, the conservatives and moderates of Carmaux formed the Cercle républicain progressiste. And it was this group, aided by the police, which disrupted the socialist meeting and silenced Jaurès.[49]

Despite opposition by public and private forces, the *verrerie ouvrière* set out on its colorful history in 1896. It did not progress without considerable internal difficulties over finances and administration. So diversified in its sponsorship, it was subjected to many stresses and strains. The anarchists, for example, objected from the start to the imposition of regular industrial discipline in the plant and championed four workers dismissed for open disobedience.[50] Yet the *verrerie ouvrière* weathered these storms and stood for years as a tribute to the courage of the glass workers.

For Jaurès, the founding of the *verrerie ouvrière* was an important experience. This first contact with a coöperative prepared him for his later appreciation of the coöperative movement. Especially in the years between 1899 and 1905, when he believed most fervently in evolutionary socialism, he spoke enthusiastically of coöperatives as one means of reaching the new society. Under the influence of such a convinced coöperator as Professor Marcel Mauss, a *normalien* like himself and a nephew of his friend Durkheim, Jaurès openly supported those coöperatives whose aim was expressly socialist. In 1899, he attended the opening of the Boulangerie Socialiste in Paris; in 1900, in his celebrated lecture on Bernstein and Revisionism, he spoke of both coöperatives and trade unions as important instruments of socialism; in *La petite République* on February 24, 1903, he wrote appreciatively of Charles Gide. And even in those years after 1905, when he fought one bitter battle after another against the bourgeois ministries, he remained an "integral socialist," convinced that coöperatives, like trade union action and social reforms, helped to link the old society to the new.

But the struggle to found the *verrerie ouvrière* had a more immediate impact on Jaurès. For it had taught him how difficult it was to limit the power of private enterprise, even through both economic and political action. But that very difficulty strengthened the bond between the socialists and the workers, between Jaurès and the *carmausins*.

III

The glass strike had a profound effect upon Jaurès' thought. It taught him more than he had heretofore known of the power of management, gave him evidence of the links between private enterprise and public authority, and convinced him that the political power and social maturity of the masses were their greatest weapons against the old order. At the level of direct experience, where social theory either comes alive or dies, it brought into his outlook a new, almost romantic fervor about working men and women. Having submerged himself in their milieu, he came up for air, more than ever on their side. For all of those intellectuals whose knowledge of mundane affairs was, in the main, derived from libraries and statistics, he urged involvement, "making contact with working people who have infinitely less book learning, who are interested in receiving insights and clarification from teachers, but who have penetrated to the core of real life, social life, its complications, difficulties, and vicissitudes, with greater depth and truth than the schoolmasters."[51]

But it was more than all that. The history of the Carmaux strike, linked to the conservatism of the Progressist ministries, upset Jaurès, and led him for a time to a new and extreme position on the State. In 1895, taking to the pages of *La Revue socialiste*, he wrote a series of strongly worded articles in which the nature of the State was categorically defined in Marxist terms. "Theoretically, today's State," he reflected, "especially the republican State, is the expression and the organ of the common will and the public interest. In fact, however, it is the servant of certain classes which have, either through a lucky turn of events or through the underlying laws of society, effective preponderance."[52] History had recorded the drama of the conflict of classes, and in that struggle the State had always been — what it continued to be — an instrument of the ruling class. "Today the real struggle is between the Proletariat, that is, between those, whoever they may be, who have no other resources except their daily labor, and Capital, which exacts from them its remuneration. . . . And because there are classes, the State must constantly use force. . . . The permanent intervention of the army at Aubin, at Ricamarie, at Decazeville, at Fourmies, at Carmaux, attests very well that there is, at the heart of our society, a class struggle."[53]

As for reforms, Jaurès was momentarily skeptical. Improvements which were desirable in principle, he charged, become deceptions under capitalism. If the eight-hour day were voted, it would probably mean the imposition of the "speed-up" system on workers. If employers were forced to contribute to pension funds, they would no doubt reduce wages in retaliation. No, it was impossible, he now thought, to work through the capitalistic State. "A reactionary and repressive policy will end in a revolutionary explosion; and a reformist, radical policy will end either in the deception of the workers or the opposition of the industrial bosses."[54]

Jaurès was on new ground, further from his earlier republican base than he had ever traveled. For the moment the Marxist image of class struggle suffused his vision of society. But Jaurès could no more expunge his deep faith in a marching humanity than he could deny the evolution of capitalism. Offer hope for progressive reform, and his thought would again whirl on an idealistic pivot. To many, his fluctuations revealed contradiction and inconsistency. Gustave Téry, once his collaborator at *La petite République,* asked him how he could justify his shifting perspective, and the philosopher laughingly replied: "I have often compared socialism to the heart; it has, like the heart, pulsations, rhythm, alternate movements of expansion and contraction. . . . Is it surprising to observe in the organic development of my thought the same phenomena of systole and diastole?"[55]

In a striking metaphor, Jaurès captured the spirit of his philosophy. For the key to his thought and action was unity — in his intellectual makeup, the fusion of ancient wisdom and modern, of Greek, German, and French philosophy; in his socialist method, the alternate rhythms of participation and opposition, reform and revolution; in his ultimate goal, the harmony of all mankind, "une civilisation d'hommes libres . . . l'universelle humanité."

"As for myself," Jaurès wrote in *La Revue socialiste* (June, 1895), "this perpetual struggle between the classes and among human beings . . . depresses and disgusts me. The socialists, *avec passion,* seek the means for ending it." It was a cry of pain and a cry of love. Before the prospect of transforming a fragmented, an unjust society, Jaurès had to act, restrained neither by dogma nor by respectability. He would fight for the reforms, which could strengthen the working classes; and those working classes — each day, as capitalism progressed, more numerous and better organized — would then, "par l'ironie dialectique des choses," create the socialist community.

8

Radicals and
Syndicalists, 1895-1896

I

Ribot was an experienced hand, already fifty-three, when he formed his ministry in January, 1895. A masterful debater and parliamentarian, he used his considerable skills to hold his moderate majority together and to fend off attacks from the Left. Under his subtle lawyer's touch, France didn't march forward or back; she took half-turns from the waist and maintained an uneasy status-quo.[1]

But the growing demands of the working class and its leaders were difficult to contain. Jaurès' polemic during the Carmaux strike had shaken the ministry badly, and though it survived on October 26, it fell just two days later. Rumors of parliamentary corruption, reminiscent of Panama, circulated ominously through the corridors of the Chamber, raising the name of the Chemins de Fer du Sud, a railroad in Provence whose financial difficulties were shrouded in a suspicious secrecy. When Minister of Justice Ludovic Trarieux refused to release to the Chamber the results of an inquiry into the administration of the railroad, a resolution of no confidence was voted, 275 to 196, and Ribot resigned.

The Radicals had supplied the bulk of the opposition votes, and President Faure reluctantly turned to their leader, Léon Bourgeois, who managed to put together by November 1, 1895, the first all-Radical ministry in the history of the Third Republic. After years of Progressist rule it seemed a startling change. The firebrands of Radicalism, Clemenceau and Pelletan, were conspicuously missing from the ministerial list; but some of the choices, even among men of the second rank, offered prospect for reform. A civilian went to the War Office at last, Godefroy Cavaignac, whose militaristic sympathies were as yet unknown; at the Ministry of Education sat Émile Combes, once a seminarian but now strongly anticlerical; at the Ministry of Finance was Paul Doumer, later a pillar of colonialism but now an ardent advocate of the progressive income tax.

And at the apex was perched Premier Bourgeois, who also took the Interior portfolio. "He had a pompous and austere look about him," wrote Georges Suarez, the biographer of Briand. "He cultivated his fine, ebony-colored beard, expressed his commonplace thoughts in a mellow voice, and wrote like a rural constable."[2] Not a very flattering portrait, it nonetheless caught something of the unexceptional quality of Bourgeois. At forty-four, he had moved steadily up the political ladder in the prefectoral service, endearing himself to his friends by a ready dispensation of favors. "He is the leader not so much of a party," someone had quipped, "as of a clientele."[3] But Bourgeois had pushed himself into the foreground also by passing as a social philosopher, espousing a doctrine of "solidarity" which at least recognized the failure of liberalism and conceived of welfare legislation as the basis for a new community;[4] for private property, widely diffused, he had the characteristic Radical devotion.

On November 4 Bourgeois read out his ministerial declaration, which was striking both for its omissions and professions. Not a word was uttered about revision of the Constitution or separation of Church and State, proposals which had long been the standard fare of Radicalism.[5] But he put his ministry unequivocally on record for progressive taxation of income and inheritance, a decent system of workers' pensions, and a satisfactory plan for arbitrating strikes — all of which might presage a turn in French public life if, and it was the crucial unknown, the Radical group, a minority of 140 in the Chamber, stood unflinchingly behind the program.

The parliamentary socialists, whatever their origins and party affiliations, could hardly help but welcome this prospect of social reform and relief from high tension. They had all come to accept, even the Marxists among them,[6] a program of immediate improvements in preparation for socialism, but they had been frustrated in their efforts by the conservatism of Progressist ministries. Now their parliamentary caucus, the Union socialiste, speaking through the voice of Gustave Rouanet, pledged support for the ministry, essential if it was to survive, so long as Bourgeois honorably fulfilled his promises.[7]

Yet it was a decision hedged in by the uncertainty over tactics that dogged the socialist movement for long years. If society was divided into hostile classes and the State was a coercive instrument of the bourgeoisie, as the militants had taught, it was pointless to think of coöperation with any sector of the ruling class. If, furthermore, the socialists participated in common action with the Radicals, they might well find themselves propping up a capitalist order with half-hearted reforms.[8] And yet, what was the alternative for a group, however enthusiastic and energetic, which was less than half a hundred strong, too large to accept impotence and too small to effect changes alone? If the socialists stood aside from all collaboration, hewing tightly to the line of collectivisim, they could become, more easily than monks, pure but remote ascetics. Were they then to offer the poor and the abused nothing but golden promises?

Jaurès, who wrestled with the problem over the entire span of his public career, more often than not supported working arrangements with the Radicals for limited but desirable objectives. Philosopher though he was, he was essentially a man of action, viewing politics as a goad to social evolution. He was driven by the imperative of taking socialism from the drawing board and setting it into motion, of effecting those basic reforms which would pave the way to collectivism. He thought, long and deeply, of the multitudes whom he served. He wanted to move with them and for them, to be done, as he once put it, "with that monotonous exercise of daily polemics against Power. . . . If we want the battered and bruised proletariat to recover some confidence in methodical and regular action, we must press hard for a policy of freedom and reforms."[9]

But where and how to muster the strength for that work? In a country like France, Jaurès mused, where the urban proletariat was as yet no majority, the socialists had to look beyond their own working-class followers to that large democratic mass which, though not collectivist, might struggle against reaction. He reminded his party of the legacy of the French Revolution, which had provided the nineteenth century with the tradition and the classes of the Jacobin Left, not socialist but certainly democratic and Leftist.[10] The petty bourgeoisie, descended from the historic Montagnards, formed the hard core of the Radical movement; without their support, Jaurès felt, the fight against Progressist rule might become only hollow heroics. So it was that he studied Radicalism carefully, reflected on its potentiality, and encouraged its militancy. Even as he was making his own commitment to socialism, he applauded the "socializing tendency" among the most articulate of the Radical leaders, those who had already become known as Radical Socialists.

Thus, in the early 1890's he extended a friendly hand to Clemenceau, sharpest wit among the Radicals, who leveled at moderates and reactionaries alike a barrage of barbed criticisms. So different in temperament, the two men were often to be thrown together in the course of affairs. "Clemenceau — composed, like a solid block, of nerves, muscles, and flesh, an immediate sense of reality, a brusque grasp of the means, an elliptical speech where words were concentrated, compressed into telling phrases, an incisive voice, bitter, where bantering becomes ferocity without transition. . . . He was pale, almost ashen, and spoke as if he were firing bullets."[11] Between this realist and the socialist visionary, there was a tremendous contrast. But since Jaurès' first entrance into the Chamber in 1885, they had been cordial to one another, as their public writings indicated; and especially after 1889 Jaurès followed with sympathetic interest the increasing bluntness of Clemenceau's criticism. For by then the Radical chief was openly speculating about a mixed social system, a kind of coëxistence of individualism and collectivism.[12] And never did Jaurès applaud him so warmly as when the Tiger cried out in the Chamber of Deputies after the May Day repressions of 1891: "One must have the courage to say it; the Fourth Estate is rising and will soon have power."[13]

The other stalwart of militant Radicalism, Camille Pelletan, voluble critic of conservatism both as deputy and editor, impressed Jaurès even more. With Pelletan, so bohemian in habit and appearance, the inevitable cigar half-hidden in a bushy beard, the paralyzed right arm hanging limply at his side, he felt almost a comradeship. Especially from the time of the Carmaux strike in 1892, when the Radical had joined the socialists in their campaign for the miners, Jaurès had come to look upon him as friend and ally.[14] Even years later, after many a bitter doctrinal battle had been fought, Le Temps with considerable exaggeration could refer to Jaurès and Pelletan on March 17, 1911, as "the Siamese twins of the Extreme Left."

But a marriage of convenience meant neither submission nor permanence, and Jaurès, from the earliest years of his socialism, drew that conclusion clearly. Unlike certain Independent socialists, he refused to blur differences, but instead persistently criticized what he considered the ineptitude of the Radicals in a modern industrial society.[15] To a socialist philosopher like Jaurès, they lacked not only a grasp of contemporary capitalism but also a clearly conceived goal for humanity. Clemenceau, influenced by English experience, was pragmatic and, in the fashion of his mentors Mill and Spencer, concerned mainly with the autonomy and property of the individual. Jaurès, on the other hand, belonged to European philosophy, to the tradition of Kant, Hegel, and Marx; his thought was idealistic and his goal collectivist.[16] Radical political practice, impoverished in theory, was like smoke without fire; its effect, he felt, could ultimately be only trivial.

Yet Jaurès returned over and again to the benefits that could come from temporary coöperation between Jacobin and socialist forces. Though their objectives were different,[17] they could, by uniting in elections to support the stronger of their two candidates on the second ballot, by joining then in defense of social reforms, halt the tide of reaction. The most intransigent socialists, responsive to the pure line of class struggle, questioned the value of alliances, even temporary ones, with bourgeois politicians. Socialists, they argued, ought rather to expose the failings of Radicalism than join it at elections; and some even proposed in the 1893 elections to throw their support behind Clemenceau's conservative opponent. Jaurès reacted at once and with sharp opposition to the suggestion that a man who had fought clericalism and supported the Carmaux miners was a greater danger to socialism than a conservative of the Right; and in public print he offered to speak for Clemenceau in his constituency.[18]

On the morrow of the 1893 elections, brimming with excitement over the trend to the Left, he hoped for common action, especially with the extremists among the Radicals. "I have stated that there are several degrees of socialism," he wrote with less precision than usual, "and I include as socialists those like M. Pelletan, who advocate the active intervention of society into the economic relations of men in order to sustain the weak and disinherited against the strong and rich."[19] But the two years that had passed between the fall of the first Dupuy ministry and the investiture of Bourgeois had transformed his attitude toward the entire middle-class party. By now, even the left wing of the bourgeoisie seemed irritatingly inept, and in March, 1895, he was writing in *La Revue socialiste* that "for Radicalism, capitalism is a legitimate monarch not to be dethroned but only disciplined with a whip. A strange and ephemeral conception which is the equivalent in economics of constitutional monarchy in politics."[20] But in November, before the prospect of a more favorable political climate, Jaurès, once again optimistic about coöperation on the Left, urged his party to stand firmly behind Bourgeois. With varying degrees of enthusiasm the socialists fell into line; if reformists like Millerand and Viviani embraced the policy, revolutionaries like Guesde and Vaillant at least accepted it. And at the center of the socialist phalanx, like a bridge between the factions, stood an indefatigable Jaurès.

II

The Radical interlude was no Roman holiday for the socialists. Though the siege guns of reaction were momentarily silenced, Léon Bourgeois was neither willing nor able to make the world safe for socialism. It was quickly evident, within the first two weeks of the new ministry, that if the socialists, anxious to effect reforms, meant to support the government wholeheartedly, they were destined to find themselves in positions of compromise. So it was on November 14, 1895, that Julien Dumas, a deputy of the Right hoping to embarrass the Radicals, proposed modification of the *lois scélérates*. Bourgeois, who had expressed strong reservations about these measures when they were passed, now foresaw an overturn of his government if he accepted the proposition. Vacillating in his reply, the Premier condemned the principle of the laws while insisting that the time was not yet right for either repeal or alteration.[21] The socialists, Jaurès and the others, hardly broke an embarrassing silence, and when the issue of confidence was raised that day, most of them went down the line for the ministry. Both Guesde and Viviani justified the behavior a day later by calling into question the sincerity of the Dumas maneuver. It was, they charged, a trap for the ministry, and they, the socialists, would not be party to any plan for bringing back the Progressists.[22] Both the Marxist and the Independent implied what Jaurès had so often insisted — that the bourgeois party was not undifferentiated and that the Radicals might genuinely aid the cause of reform.

Not all socialists were so sanguine about piecemeal change, however, and as the militants in the Chamber trod their path of collaboration, they heard around them the warning voices of criticism. The Allemanists especially, organized as a party in 1891 through a schism among the Possibilists, were full of suspicion about socialist political activity. Their leader, Jean Allemane, a compositor by training and a worker by identification, believed, as he once wrote, that "the people have been victimized every time they have entrusted the defense of their interests to those who belong to the bourgeoisie."[23] Scrutinizing the activities not only of their own five deputies in the Chamber but of the entire socialist deputation, they cast accusing, often bitter aspersions on the new policy of *détente*.

Over the months the socialist deputies thundered a little as of old, as though demonstrating that they were still collectivists and not just the Left wing of Radicalism. Vaillant went to the rostrum in January, a poor orator but with a fervid Blanquist sincerity, to urge relief for the unemployed. But his program, which centered around social security for idle workers, neither roused interest nor rallied support among the republicans.[24]

Again in March, with France embroiled in another colonial venture, the socialists separated from the ministry, this time on the issue of Madagascar. Over a decade before, on December 17, 1885, the French government had established a vague protectorate over that vast East African island which especially tempted the sugar interests. The native tribes were restive and rebellious, however, and by September, 1894, responsive to the demands of the procolonial group, led in the Chamber by Eugène Étienne, Parliament had voted sixty-five million francs for a decisive military expedition. But the venture misfired badly; lacking proper transport and medical supplies, the campaign foundered in a morass of disease and death. Now the government and the colonial deputies returned to Parliament, seeking further credits for a military expedition. The socialists, though strongly ambivalent on questions of imperialism, could hardly accept without protest a campaign which promised to enrich a few investors at the expense of the nation. "You always invoke the honor of the flag, or markets opened to trade, or the benefits of our expanding civilization," shouted Gérault-Richard. "The government begins by involving itself in expeditions and comes finally to Parliament only to ask for men and money."[25] The socialists abstained from voting funds for colonial purposes, and yet this opposition, not supported by other groups, scarcely affected the life of the ministry.

So, in spite of discomfort and occasional deviation, the socialists, in general, closed ranks behind Bourgeois. "You have seen us struggle for years with revolutionary strength and energy against your governments of reaction," cried Jaurès, thrusting a warning finger at the Right and Center in the Chamber, "and that same vigor will return if it becomes necessary." But the socialists were more than negative and intransigent; they were "capable of following and practicing a method and a discipline," he went on, and they were determined to back the Radicals until noble promises became effective laws.[26]

Moderates and conservatives, confronted for the first time with the Radical threat, thundered their opposition and pursued a course of obstruction. The biggest storm that broke in the less than six months of the Bourgeois ministry, arose, not surprisingly, over a threat to the sanctity of property. The issue which rallied the socialists solidly behind the Radicals while driving the Right and Center into frenetic opposition was the proposal to introduce into the fiscal system a graduated tax on income. As conceived by the government, the measure was eminently moderate, calling for a levy on all incomes over 2500 francs, running in increasing scale from one percent on incomes of 2500 francs to five percent on those of 50,000 francs or more.[27] But more fundamental than the terms, as both supporters and opponents recognized, was the new approach to the fiscal system, so long a mélange of duties on land, doors, windows, furniture, and licenses. A new direction was now indicated, however dimly, and the rich were to bear a larger part of the burden of taxation which now rested so heavily upon the poor.

Unrestrained attacks issued from moderate and conservative quarters,[28] but on the tax proposal the ministry remained faithful to its promises. By March, 1896, despite the opposition of the budget committee presided over by Georges Cochery and dominated by the Progressists, the Minister of Finance presented the measure to the Chamber for debate. It was then that Jaurès took charge for the socialists, occupying the tribune for several hours on March 22 to speak on behalf of this basic reform.[29]

M. Cochery's committee, without indicating any alternative, was urging further study of the fiscal system, but Jaurès decried the suggestion as deceptive. "In answer to the government's fiscal program, the budget committee offers no project or principle of its own. . . . The committee has left that to other ardent polemicists, outside its own ranks. . . . It has left it to M. Leroy-Beaulieu to declare that every personal tax . . . is unequal, arbitrary, violent, and inquisitorial. It has left it to M. Georges Michel or M. Jules Roche to declare that personal and progressive taxes are engines of civil war and social disorder." But that opposition could be only temporary and finally futile. "You must realize," cried Jaurès, "that the most complex organisms are the most adaptable, and that Lamarck's famous formula, 'Need creates the organ,' is true, especially in human societies. If, then, there is a great need for fiscal justice in this country, as you yourselves admit, you will not halt the relentless march of democracy by quibbling over details." And he cited to the prosaic budget committee the words of Homer: "The snow fell on the banks of the sea, but the surging waves came and the snow was melted."

Jaurès developed his argument with rigor, seeking to answer each objection in turn. Cochery, and Paul Delombre, reporter for the budget committee, had spoken of the income tax as contrary to the spirit of France, which they equated with individualism and privacy. But how inadequate, exclaimed Jaurès, to identify the spirit of a nation by so ephemeral an institution as its fiscal policy. "It is only in great periods of history, at the highest reaches of art, philosophy, and life, that you can grasp the essentials of the French spirit, just as in the tangled forests . . . you can sense the direction of the wind only by the large movements of the treetops." Leroy-Beaulieu, the foremost economist of laissez faire, had raised another kind of objection. In a burst of morality, he had charged that the measure, by proposing to tax joint family incomes, would encourage illicit relationships to the detriment of legal marriage. But Jaurès, robustly enjoying this concern over the sanctity of the hearth, doubted that the income tax would corrode the private morality of the French. "We have been told that two lovers would be persuaded not to legalize their relationship so as not to combine their incomes. Gentlemen, they were about to submit to legal marriage; they were climbing the stairs of the City Hall; but on the last step they met M. Doumer and they fled in terror."

The government's proposal, Jaurès freely admitted, was hardly definitive; but its inherent method was valid, and "by the logic and force of events you will eventually have to give it a more extended application." Nor was this fiscal reform, despite the charges of its opponents, a socialist measure. "In fact, you can institute a progressive income tax, and you will not have advanced by one minute the transformation of capitalist into socialist property. . . . Tomorrow as today, after the tax as before, you will still see in the industrial order the same concentration of production and capital, the same development of corporations and mechanization, the same separation, each day more brutal, between the capitalist minority and the wage-earning multitudes."

No, the essence of socialism was still collectivism, and Jaurès insisted upon that principle. Why, then, should the socialists fight so militantly for the proposal? "If we support the income tax," he explained, identifying the movement with his own idealism, "it is simply because it introduces into the body of our fiscal laws a deep concern for man." Turning to the deputies of the Right and Center, he charged them with contempt for a genuine individualism; "you do not want to see the anonymous mass, on which social and economic laws weigh so heavily, transformed into a vibrant diversity of individuals; you do not want to discern in that obscure crowd, crushed by your impersonal taxes, individual faces, happy, suffering, or ravaged." For his party, Jaurès cried, "it is not a socialist tax any more than it is a tyrannical or an inquisitorial tax; it is simply and totally . . . a human tax."

The socialists, basking in the humanistic warmth spread by Jaurès, were exultant over his effort, and *La petite République* printed his speech in pamphlet form. Moderates and conservatives, however, now greeted him with obloquy and attack. Joseph Reinach, the old Gambettist, accused him of seeking "to choke off the radiant future which lies before democracy."[30] And *Le Journal des débats*, well practiced in traducing Jaurès, charged, on March 23, that he had become the avowed enemy of private rights in France. The debate was far from over, as the opposition paraded speaker after speaker to the rostrum of the Chamber. Finally, on March 26, Doumer made his final long defense of the proposal before it was put to a definitive vote. Interrupted and challenged by the old stalwart of the Centre gauche, Léon Say, and the very conservative

Progressist, Jules Méline, Doumer held his ground while rejecting all substitute proposals. Thus, on March 27, the Chamber was ready to vote on the Radical proposal which would have introduced a graduated income tax to replace several other levies. When the results were recorded, a sufficient number of moderates, convinced apparently that fiscal reform could no longer be held back, had crossed over into the enemy camp, and the measure was approved by the slight margin of 286 to 270.

"Another socialist victory," crowed Gérault-Richard, thinking especially of the decisive intervention of Jaurès.[31] But this first triumph of the Bourgeois ministry proved also to be its last. With the support of the socialists it had carried its reforming will into the Chamber; before the Senate, however, it would fulminate, founder, and fall.

The Upper Chamber, a citadel of conservation, came suddenly alive to act as the champion of social order. Hoping to bring down the ministry, it followed a course of endless criticism. The senators first seized on a minor issue, maintaining that the Minister of Justice had been guilty of a serious breach of office when he transferred the inquiry into the Chemins de Fer du Sud from one judge, whom he accused of dilatory tactics, to another. The ministry stood solidly behind the transfer, however, and the Senate on February 11 voted censure of the government by the strong majority of 156 to 53. But what now? Should the ministry resign in the face of an unfavorable vote in the Senate, or should it hold to the unwritten principle that only the Lower House, expressing popular, universal suffrage, could overturn governments? Refusing to step down, Bourgeois carried his case before the Chamber and won a vote of confidence. The ministry thus survived in February, but that was only the beginning of the senatorial campaign. Over the income tax, and it was here and nowhere else that the heart of the opposition was located, the Upper House again voted censure while the Chamber reiterated its confidence. Throughout the country vocal minorities now divided in heated partisanship, and when President Faure made a trip through Southern France in late February, he was greeted with alternating cries of "Vive le Sénat! A bas le ministère!" and "Vive Bourgeois! A bas le Sénat!"

On April 2 the senators voted censure of the ministry a third time, and the Easter holidays relieved what had become a feverish tension. In a portentous gesture the Senate adjourned, without passing on the government's request for credits to carry through the military expedition in Madagascar. The socialists suspected a plot-in-the-making, and one of them, Henri Turot, spelled it out with considerable insight: "On April 21 [the day Parliament was to reconvene] the Senate would refuse credits; the ministry would then be forced to withdraw under this threat of seeing the entire legal life of the country suspended. A ministry of the Right would then be constituted and the dissolution of the Chamber at once proclaimed. In sum, a new *Seize-mai!*"[32] For the moment, however, the Bourgeois ministry refused to give way, either on the income tax or on its alliance with the Extreme Left. Its will-to-resist, in fact, reached something of a high point on April 14, when Bourgeois, to the delight of the socialists, ordered the reopening of the Paris bourse du travail, closed since the early months of Dupuy's first ministry.

Meanwhile the Senate was excited in mid-April by an adverse verdict on the tax rendered in the conseils généraux of the departments, to which the ministry had gone for a test of national sentiment. The socialists, fearful that the Radicals might give up their fight in the face of an adverse decision, minimized its importance. What difference would it make, asked Louis Dubreuilh, if all eighty-six departmental councils rejected the tax? "Chosen generally from among the great landed proprietors and captains of industry, these cantonal office-holders are inspired only by their own class interests."[33] But for the Senators, about to reconvene, the result of this test was like a call to resistance.

In the heat of battle Jaurès, as was his wont, stepped back for a moment to put rampaging events into a large perspective. On April 19, he wrote in *La petite République* a long review of Gabriel Deville's new book, *Principes socialistes*; and if there were those among the socialists who looked at the fight for an income tax as the signal to transform socialism into a kind of advanced Radicalism, this essay gave them no comfort. For Jaurès implied once again that reforms and coalitions to achieve them could yield but limited benefits. "The State," he wrote in the very midst of the Bourgeois era, "which is, according to conservative economists, the eternal and necessary form of human association, is actually only a historical form. . . . It exists along with the antagonism of classes as the means of coercion for the dominant class." Yet democracy was the new battleground of the struggle. "By the play of universal suffrage, the oppressed and exploited class can today capture a few of the institutions thrown up against it and inaugurate, by its infiltration of the State, a reformist period in preparation of the Revolution." His mélange of materialism and idealism, revolution and reform, was thus intact, however different his theory might have seemed on the socialist Left among the Guesdists or on the socialist Right among the Independents.

Two days later, on April 21, when Parliament reconvened, Jaurès was back in the front line, aiming his fire directly at the activities of the Senate. As though anticipating a faint-hearted stand by the Radicals, he sought to strengthen their militancy. "Let the ministry affirm its will to life and victory," he exhorted, "and it will be crowned with success."[34]

And Bourgeois would need all the courage he could muster in these days of April. For the Senators, holding in their hands the fate of Madagascar, declared that they would vote no credits so long as the incompetent Radical ministry remained in office. So bold a decision was it that even President Faure considered it "almost revolutionary."[35] Jaurès, linking the action back to the attempted coup of *Seize-mai*, denounced it as the worst crime against democracy in twenty years.[36]

For two critical days, while tempers on both sides flared, the fate of the ministry depended on the will of Léon Bourgeois. The Premier could have followed an extreme course, by-passing the Senate action and issuing credits by executive decree. But he was of a timid temperament, and on April 23, 1896, anxious by now to quit power, Bourgeois submitted his resignation. The first 170 days of Radicalism had come sputtering to a close. *Le Temps* welcomed the collapse as both desirable and proper, since "neither in the Chamber nor in the Senate, nor even in the country, has there ever been a majority in favor of a Radical policy." But Vaillant, expressing the widely felt socialist resentment, wrote off Radicalism as "without courage or audacity."[37]

The demise was bitter medicine for Jaurès, who hoped for Radical courage even when he doubted it. The real enemies of social progress, he insisted, still resided in the Right and Center, and without spending time in useless recriminations against the ministry, he centered his attack on those who had brought it down. Rally the Left in the Chamber, organize defiance of the Senate, turn defeat into victory — that was his working program. On the morrow of the Bourgeois resignation he exhorted his colleagues in the Chamber, like Mirabeau inspiriting the National Assembly against the king, to stand firm against "the very negation of the Constitution and universal suffrage."[38] By the time the day had ended, the deputies, by a vote of 291 to 250, affirmed their resolve "to pursue a policy of democratic reforms."

The next evening, April 25, Jaurès, sharing a platform with Pelletan and Gérault-Richard at the Tivoli Vauxhall, instructed an overflowing crowd of ten thousand on the meaning of the present crisis. The appearance of Pelletan indicated well enough that the Left wing of Radicalism still stood solidly beside the socialists, and the veteran Radical seemed to justify Jaurès' confidence when he shouted out a fiery challenge: "People of Paris, you took the Bastille in 1789; you made the Republic in 1848 and in 1870; you fought in 1830; there are other Bastilles to demolish! They say, Parisians, that you are asleep! Prove that it is not so."[39]

When Jaurès spoke, he hammered away at the resolve by men of wealth and their representatives to halt the march of progress. Their power, he warned, was formidable, but the strength of people was even greater. "And the people will pulverize the reactionary bloc." But even as Jaurès foresaw inevitable victory, the winds of French politics had changed course and blew again in the direction of the Progressists, indeed, of the most conservative men among them.

President Faure, casting around for a successor to Bourgeois, went logically to the moderates who had engineered his downfall. The socialists imputed to the conservative president the basest of motives; Félix, they said, was driven by the desire "to recapture his popularity in the world of high society."[40] By May 1, 1896, a sad day for the French Left, a Progressist ministry was formed by Jules Méline, which included Barthou at Interior and Cochery, the spokesman for the anti-income-tax forces, at Finance. "Only Dupuy and Constans are missing," Vaillant wrote bitterly.[41] But the next day, May 2, the new government was approved in the Chamber by the narrow margin of twenty-eight votes. The courageous resolve of a week before had disappeared as a crucial number of moderate deputies made their way again to the conservative camp. "Thanks to M. de Mackau, the Duc de La Rochefoucauld, Baron Reille, and the Abbé d'Hulst, M. Méline has forced on the nation the insolent decisions of the Senate."[42] So read the manifesto of the socialist deputies, who already sensed that the new ministry, so warmly supported by *Le Figaro, Le Gaulois, Les Débats,* and *Le Temps,* would create close ties between the ruling Center and the clerical-aristocratic Right. Two years later, in the dying days of the Méline government, they had collected a mass of evidence to document their suspicions.

Jaurès dissected the experience with Radicalism, examined the parts, sought, as he did with all concrete events, to derive from it some working principles. He considered the Radical performance distressingly faint-hearted. In part, he sensed, it was the result of division within the group itself. For if there were extremists like Pelletan, willing to work with the socialists, there were others who either doubted or denied the wisdom of such a course.[43] But their special weakness, Jaurès felt, was doctrinal, and he wrote wearily and without illusions of Radicals, "protesting against the fruit, while protecting the roots of the plant."[44]

Yet, however inadequate, they were preferable to Progressists. Soon, in 1898, there would be general elections, a crucial test for the future of socialism. Could the militants do anything, asked Jaurès, but join forces with willing Radicals to oppose the Progressist candidates?[45] Here, however, he drew the line. Among some ambitious men in the movement, those with dreams of high office, the word was being dropped that if socialists could coöperate with Radicals at elections and in the Chamber, they might even accept a ministerial portfolio or two in a Radical government. Jaurès rejected the suggestion flatly, as firm on the question as the

Guesdists. One day socialists would form a ministry, he predicted, but it would be uniform and collectivist. When socialism "is only one element," he explained, "it will turn out to be nothing . . . its ideals will not be realized but compromised."[46]

The tactics proposed by Jaurès were flexible, but in his own view, so long as the goal of socialism remained clear, not opportunistic. Yet the movement was growing, attracting adherents neither Marxist nor revolutionary. For them Jaurès' words were like the basis of a new reformism.

III

On May 30, only a month after the April political crisis, some six hundred socialists, Jaurès prominently among them, went to the Porte Dorée, 275 avenue Daumesnil, in the Saint-Mandé district of Paris. They congregated to break bread together at a mammoth banquet, to listen to speeches by Jaurès, Vaillant, Guesde, and especially Millerand, and to celebrate their recent victories. For between the fall of Bourgeois and the Saint-Mandé meeting, socialists had campaigned hard in the municipal elections of early May and come away with their biggest prize to date.[47] Socialism was in the air, despite bourgeois hostility and governmental repression, and the optimism of Jaurès and his friends, their faith in inevitable victory, was irrepressible.

But even in their jubilation, the most thoughtful socialist leaders were strangely troubled. With the movement divided into several distinct parties, all of them anxious to reach the New Society while insisting to their confused electors upon different routes; with socialism diluted by the superficial and vague yearning of ex-Radicals and assorted reformers, it was no easy task to identify a socialist and to single out the party. The ultimate success of the movement, Jaurès had long insisted, depended upon unity and a common though flexible program. But then, he had no such vested interest as Guesde, Vaillant, or Allemane in maintaining the existing factions. To him there was but one socialism, broad and capacious; to them their own parties, so saturated with their energy and spirit, represented the only true belief. Standing apart from the factions, Jaurès saw their essential similarities, not their historic differences; inside the factions, the militants nurtured their separate identities.

The road to unity, mined with doctrinal differences and self-interest, would inevitably make rough travel, but now, in the late spring of 1896, socialists took a leap toward that goal. At the Saint-Mandé banquet, socialists of all factions but the Allemanist agreed for the first time on the basic and irreducible principles to which they all had to adhere. The chairman of the evening, Alexandre Millerand, spelled out with cool lawyer's logic the terms of what become known as the Saint-Mandé program.[48] A former Radical, and foreign to the revolutionary tradition, Millerand thought of the socialist movement as broad, peaceful, reformist, casting wide its net and blurring its principles somewhat at the edges. He was especially well-suited for stating a minimum program.

What did it mean, asked Millerand, to call oneself a French socialist? It was, before all else, to believe in collectivism while approaching it through peaceful reforms; to seek mastery of the state, though by democratic means; and to feel a bond with workers everywhere while nurturing a patriotic devotion to the revolutionary tradition of France. So much that had been alien to the Guesdists and Blanquists but espoused by Jaurès—reformism, democracy, patriotism—was now set beside collectivism and internationalism. Yet Vaillant, long an advocate of a unified party, lent the program his support.[49] Impressed by this show of fellowship, Jaurès foresaw success for socialism and spoke enthusiastically of the new society. And it was none other than Guesde who now offered up the toast in praise of the Saint-Mandé program. Accepting the democratic premise, Marxists and Blanquists thus walked across the field of socialism to meet Jaurès, whose spirit had dominated the proceedings.[50]

In fixing their attention on the impending unity of their movement, the socialists ignored the confusion inherent in the Saint-Mandé program. Neither Guesdists and Blanquists on one side nor Jaurès on the other would lose sight of their socialist objectives or lack the courage to fight for them. But nothing was said at Saint-Mandé about class struggle, and many a recent convert to socialism looked upon the program adopted there as a safe and sane blueprint for social reform. The Saint-Mandé program was broad enough to encourage unity among diverse groups; but it was moderate enough to fit a parliamentary party of reformist tendency. For that reason, it fed the suspicions of those revolutionaries in the trade union movement who had long accused the political socialists of opportunism.

IV

In the last week of July, 1896, Jaurès crossed the English Channel and took a train to London. Every foreign culture fascinated him, and because of his wide reading he was rarely a stranger in new lands. The great English writers—Shakespeare especially—he knew in the original; the historian Daniel Halévy seems hardly off the mark in writing of Jaurès that "he read everything." But his spoken English was never quite coherent, and it was surely no small amusement to the staid English when the ebullient, bright-eyed, portly Frenchman stopped them on streets or in pubs to converse in hopelessly broken English.

The purpose of his trip, however, was other than cultural. Jaurès was attending for the first time a congress of the Second International, an event of considerable importance in his career as a socialist of European fame.[51] Furthermore, that meeting in London was a crucial one, especially to the delegates from France; for here in 1896 they would make decisions and strike attitudes bearing heavily on the relations, increasingly strained for almost a decade, between socialism and syndicalism.

In the years following the Commune, the workers, out of fear and repression, fell silent. Emboldened by the hard conditions of their lives, however, they had moved gradually toward organization. By the end of the 1870's, even before the law of 1884, they had founded unions in various trades, essentially peaceful, reformist, and economic in orientation. A decisive change, the development of class consciousness and a revolutionary spirit, accompanied the revival of socialism; for the Marxists, especially, taught the workers that collectivism must be their goal and political action their means. Capture the State, they exhorted, expropriate the capitalist class, and take control of the productive machinery. Anything short of that, charged Guesde and his followers, like bargaining over wages and hours, was trivial or, worse than that, delusive. For the masters of capitalism would always, by the very nature of the system, extract their profits from the toil of the workers. Thus, when the Marxists lent their support to unions, they were encouraging not agencies of collective bargaining but centers of socialism.

The socialist message had considerable appeal to workers anxious to barter their dismal present for a happier future. By the 1880's, even though many unions remained professional corporations, economic in nature and reformist in outlook, an increasing number, as in Carmaux or in the Marxist stronghold of the Nord, were revolutionary and pledged to socialist politics.[52] And when, in 1886, national and regional unions in various trades organized a central body, the Fédération nationale des syndicats et groupes corporatifs de France, it was controlled by the Guesdists, who viewed it as a recruiting camp for the Parti ouvrier français.

But the Marxist success in shaping the union movement, even at its pinnacle, was challenged within the very ranks of revolutionary labor. Increasingly were heard the voices of militant workers, who, though they professed socialism as their end, sharply questioned the strategy of political action. Depressed and embattled in their relations with their employers, they sought more direct and immediate tactics for overturning capitalism than the tedious process of building parties and winning elections. The long-range conquest of the State little impressed those who daily confronted authority in shop or factory. Skepticism about socialist politics burst into outright hostility among the most vocal workers, who imputed to the politicians, bourgeois after all and remote from their milieu, motives of self-aggrandizement through public office. What sort of revolution was there, they asked, what hope for socialism, when politicians, certainly among the Possibilists but even among the Guesdists, first won elections and then lost their fervor?[53]

So the tables were turned on the political socialists, and militant workers, laying claim to the revolutionary mantle which had adorned the Marxists, proposed that the way to socialism lay not through politics but only through the direct action of the unions. The union, the *syndicat*, became the irreducible nucleus of the revolutionary movement to those who were now called "syndicalists." For when the workers of a plant massed together in a struggle against the capitalists, the very directness of the class conflict generated an *élan* unknown in election campaigns. And through their solidarity the workers forged a weapon far more effective and powerful than elections — the strike, the crippling of production, the vital proof of their collective force.

Yet the partial strike, the conflict between workers and employer in a single plant, never threatened to bring down the whole capitalistic system. But if the partial strike were suddenly generalized, if at a crucial signal all the unions could be galvanized into common action, then, with the entire economic life of the nation paralyzed, the revolution might quickly reach full flood. A seductive simplicity attended the theory of the *grève générale*; in contrast to the rationalism and complexity of Marxism, it offered up a revolution swiftly, decisively self-made, without elections, deputies, or parliaments. First mentioned in French labor circles around 1885 and openly proposed a year later by Joseph Tortelier, an itinerant carpenter of anarchist persuasion, the general strike soon became the most widely discussed of syndicalist ideas.

The Guesdists, fighting hard against what they considered the irrational deviation of syndicalism, managed to hold on to their influence in the Fédération des syndicats while officially condemning the tactics of the general strike in their party congress of 1888. But syndicalism, its attraction increasingly strong, came to dominate the bourses du travail, those peculiar labor institutions whose stormy history commenced in 1887. On February 3 of that year, the Left-wing municipal council of Paris, providing a building as a central meeting hall for the Parisian unions, launched the first bourse du travail. Housing an employment agency, an educational center, and a legal aid service, it was the model for other bourses du travail throughout France. Especially in the Paris bourse but also in the thirteen others that were established by 1892, pure syndicalist doctrine flourished, revolutionary and antipolitical. Confronted with bickering and division among the socialist parties and made cynical by frequent revelations of corruption in French politics, the most vigorous workers responded to the revolutionary call of the bourses du travail.[54] And those bourses became a major force in French syndicalism when, on February 7, 1892, ten of them sent representatives to a congress at Saint-Étienne and created a central organization, the Fédération des bourses du travail de France. The labor movement now spun not on one but rather two national pivots.

The success of the Fédération des bourses was assured by 1895 when the key office of Secretary-General was filled by a remarkable young man, Fernand Pelloutier, destined to become in his very short life the head and heart of the early syndicalist movement.[55] Almost a legendary figure of purity and dedication when he died prematurely at the age of thirty-four in 1901, Pelloutier, tubercular, a huge head teetering on a wizened body, gave his every breathing moment to the labor movement. Of humble bourgeois origins, he passed through a Marxist period in Saint-Nazaire, where by 1892 he helped to found the local Guesdist party. But he was equally instrumental in setting up a bourse du travail, and, in collaboration with a rootless but ambitious extremist, Aristide Briand, Pelloutier began to press hard for the tactics of the general strike. His Marxist connections were thus quickly severed, and after passing through the anarchist sieve, he made his career with the Fédération des bourses where his antipolitical credo became a flying red banner.[56]

Pelloutier's quarrel with the socialists was more than a tactical one. His vision of the future society, which furnished the ideals of the syndicalist revolution, was markedly different from theirs. Like the anarcho-communists, he identified the good society with freedom and equality, with the voluntary association of free citizens. Where and how would these citizens come together? Not simply in general communities (communes), as the anarcho-communists taught, but in *syndicats*, the essential social and productive cells of the new society. In every locality, workers in each industry would form a *syndicat*, which would manage production on behalf of the commune, the ultimate owner of all property; each *syndicat* would send delegates, freely chosen, to a community council, the organ of local administration; each commune would then send its delegates to a federal council, charged with whatever larger administrative tasks might be necessary. It was a theory which rested on a fervent belief in what Proudhon called "the capacity of the working class for self-government." Pelloutier realized that the workers were still plagued by ignorance, that they weren't ready yet to run the industries of France; like certain later syndicalists, Alphonse Merrheim, for example, during the revolutionary ferment of 1919 and 1920, he feared a premature revolution, before the workers were ready to control their own destinies. For that reason, he made of the *bourses du travail* centers of education. What did it matter if the preparation were long and arduous? Unlike many revolutionary syndicalists, Pelloutier was patient. The new society, if it were to be a good one, would belong to the working classes themselves and not, as the Marxists seemed to anticipate, to a dictatorship on their behalf.

The Guesdists, their goals questioned and their tactics scorned, now saw their influence erode even in the Fédération des syndicats. In September, 1892, the Fédération convened at Marseille, and Briand, acting as Pelloutier's alter ego, hurled the challenge of the general strike in the face of the Marxist leadership. The assembled workers would not be denied this potent new weapon, and the Congress adopted a report favorable to this syndicalist device. But Jules Guesde was not one to watch silently the repudiation of Marxism among the workers. Soon after the Congress of 1892, he took to the pages of his own weekly newspaper to denounce the general strike as "a deceptive mirage."[57] Certain it was that the Guesdists would fight the syndicalists to the bitter end for the control of the Fédération des syndicats, and the showdown came in Nantes in 1894. First it was the P.O.F. which met, between September 14 and 16, and under its tight Marxist leadership the general strike was unceremoniously rejected.[58] But in the debate on the question, one social-ist, an observer at the Congress and not officially a party member, argued that the general strike could be accepted as one of several working-class weapons. It was Jaurès, already trying to find some sort of bridge between two groups fighting the same enemy. No, the general strike was hardly a panacea, he agreed; yet why could it not be used to apply pressure in the support of major legislative reforms, the eight-hour day, for example, or pensions for workers?[59] But the Guesdists demurred, erecting instead a solid wall against syndicalist infiltration.

A scant twenty-four hours intervened between the end of the P.O.F. meeting and the start of the union convention. But the results were decisively different. Briand, speaking glowingly of the general strike, touched off a heated debate. When the Congress, by an almost two-to-one vote, approved the principle of the general strike, the Marxist sector withdrew from the organization, and the Fédération des syndicats virtu-ally crumbled into dust. The syndicalist leaders regrouped their forces, however, and in 1895 at Limoges a new organization was founded, the Confédération générale du travail (C.G.T.), part revolutionary, part reformist, but devoted to working-class liberation through economic ac-tion. So it was that by 1896 the political socialists, while maintaining a grip on many local and regional unions, had suffered the triumph of syn-dicalist leadership in both the national federations of organized labor.

An anarchist plot, cried the Guesdists in explanation of the syndicalist tide. And when one scrutinized the roster of leaders in the Fédération des bourses du travail, where the names of avowed anarchists like Paul Delesalle and Georges Yvetot cropped up beside that of Pelloutier, their accusation rang true. For once checked by the *lois scélérates* in their tactics of terror, the anarchists had sought, and successfully, to establish a beachhead within the union movement. But to brand the entire syndicalist movement as anarchist was to propagate a consequential half-truth. Many syndicalists, probably most, were socialists, collectivist in their aim. Though some believed that only the revolutionary strike could achieve the new order, others were advocates of action on both the economic and political fronts.[60] And within the very ranks of organized socialism were the Allemanists, espousing at all their congresses the doctrines of revolutionary unionism. When Guesdists and other parliamentary socialists wrote off syndicalism as the bastard child of anarchism, they were expressing deep resentment over failure to control the great federations of organized labor. But more than that, they were fighting to retain control of the socialist movement itself, for in a surge of confidence the leaders and theorists of the unions, claiming a closer kinship with the workers, were seeking to lay hands upon socialism and to reshape it in a syndicalist mould.

Two methods and a single professed aim — it might have strengthened socialism immeasurably, but extremists in both camps eschewed coexistence. Those syndicalists most committed to anarchism would have no truck with greedy politicians. Guesdists, emboldened by the anti-anarchist actions of the Second International, would make no peace with the wild men of the general strike.[61] Yet the consequences of division, then schism, could be catastrophic for a movement whose total energies seemed hardly enough for the struggle against capitalism.

The fourth Congress of the Second International, meeting under the muggy skies of London in the summer of 1896, thus promised to be crucial. For world socialism in general the Congress of London would address itself to the question of proper and legitimate tactics. But for the French delegates in particular, drawn from unions, bourses du travail, and the several political factions, the meeting could decide who spoke for socialism in France and with how many voices.

On the eve of the Congress of London, however, most signs pointed to a bitter struggle for control. Rouanet, expressing the parliamentary viewpoint, warned the syndicalists that no delegate would be accepted as a socialist who did not advocate political action.[62] Augustin Hamon, a prolific sociologist turned anarchist, replied testily in *Paris* on July 24 that anarchocommunists were certainly socialists and fully entitled to attend the Congress.[63] But tension mounted when several unions delegated men whose anarchist connections were unmistakable. So Jean Grave, the chief libertarian theorist, who was called, "the Pope of the rue Mouffetard," represented the steel workers of Amiens; Émile Pouget, who had learned his social philosophy from the revered old woman of anarchism, Louise Michel, was sent by the slate workers of Trézale; and Joseph Tortelier, who had first popularized the idea of the general strike, was the choice of a union from the Seine.[64] It would be all too easy in London for the political socialists to lump anarchists and syndicalists together and to deny them both a place in their movement.

But Jaurès understood, rather better than most of his comrades, the complexity of great social changes. Was not the French Revolution the product of both Jacobin political action and insurrectionary street action? Reformist though he was, he was more eager than the Guesdists to include within the ranks of French socialism the advocates of both peaceful political action and direct economic action.[65] But anarchists, he was convinced, were beyond the pale, and if he were to work effectively to keep the revolutionary trade unionists within the socialist movement, he would have to distinguish carefully between anarchism and syndicalism. That, as it turned out in London, he failed to do.

V

On July 27, at 11 A.M., with delegates from twenty nations gathered together at Queen's Hall, Langham Place, the presiding officer, Covey of the British Miners' Federation, opened the Congress of London and called for a show of good sportsmanship. "I am rather afraid," he declared in a classic understatement, "that we sometimes speak hastily. I am rather afraid that ambition to a large extent influences our motives. I believe that we ought to lose sight, as far as it is possible in human nature, of our parties."[66] This spirit of British reserve was little shared by most of the continental militants, as was quickly evident when Paul Singer, the 280-pound giant of German Marxism, roared from the rostrum his party's demand for unmodified allegiance to political action. So hectic was the fray following this challenge that when one French anarchist, the young mechanic Paul Delesalle, tried to rush to the podium, he was hurled down the half-dozen stairs of the platform by a French student, Franklin-Bouillon, then serving as an interpreter.[67]

Though the agenda for the Congress was long and varied, the issue that enflamed the learned doctors and toiling workers was acceptance or rejection of the Zurich resolution which had restricted the label of socialism to those who accepted political action. When the first day's session reached its uproarious end, the French section met separately to adopt a position on the resolution; what followed was described by the anarchists as "the most significant episode in the conflict between Marxists and revolutionary socialists, politicians, and workers' delegates."[68] Pelloutier effectively led the opposition, while the Guesdist Deville undertook the reply. When the final poll was taken, the principle of political action was voted down by the slightest possible margin, 57 to 56.

For the political socialists, Jaurès included, the result was intolerable. It was one thing to accept syndicalist action as part of the working-class drive but quite another to be inundated by an anarchist wave. That same night, therefore, the minority favoring the Zurich resolution held their own meeting at the Horse Shoe Hotel to chart a course of action. In the discussion, Jaurès charged that a considerable number of anarchists had infiltrated the Congress in bad faith, obtaining designation from unions with which they had only the most marginal connections.[69] The assembled delegates, convinced that they, veterans of long and hard struggles against bourgeois parties, had a right to represent French socialism, agreed to seek recognition as a separate group.

When the full sessions of the Congress resumed on July 28, the debate over the Zurich resolution dragged on for hours until, exhausted and overheated, the antagonists were ready for the division. The vote was by delegation, and in the final tally the controversial resolution was approved 17 to 2 with one abstention.[70] No sooner had the Congress thus declared itself than Millerand strode to the podium, urging official recognition of the French minority group as a separate delegation. Émile Vandervelde, that brilliant lawyer from Brussels who would soon stand out as the undisputed leader of Belgian socialism, criticized, though himself a partisan of political action, this precedent of splitting delegations. And when he questioned Millerand's facile and unqualified designation of trade unionists as anarchists, he was warmly supported by Vaillant.[71] But the Congress, following the lead of the disciplined Social Democrats from Germany, voted 15 to 5 for Millerand's proposal, and the schism in the French working-class movement was a formal reality.

Jaurès, who considered the move a response to anarchist tactics, did not at all intend to drive genuine syndicalists from the movement of socialism. And when he rose the next day, this orator whom the militants of the International were discovering almost for the first time, he spoke of several paths to socialism. Fresh from the direct clash with capitalism in Carmaux and the daily battle with its representatives in Parliament, he urged the Congress to recognize that the working class needed all of its weapons. But turning directly to the syndicalists, Jaurès first lauded the strike and the power that inhered in it, but then added that its success depended increasingly on the political influence of socialism: "You may have traitors in any party, but the worst traitor and most dangerous foe is he who, as you go out to fight, says 'Leave your weapons at home.' . . . Formerly in cases of strikes all the political machinery was used against the men. Now there are socialist members of Parliament who can stand by the side of the workers and use some of the political machinery on their behalf."[72]

In this attempt to embrace both approaches to socialist action, to instruct extremists of both groups in the benefits of collaboration, Jaurès sought to heal wounds, but at a very late hour. Many delegates, no doubt disturbed by the dangers of rigid formulas, were deeply moved; "burst after burst of applause followed Jaurès all through both speech and translations, and finally nearly the whole Congress rose to their feet waving hats and handkerchiefs in one tremendous roar of cheering. It was the speech of the week."[73]

The French syndicalists, however, and their Allemanist allies ignored Jaurès' plea for harmony, and on the last day of the meeting, August 1, resumed their attack on political socialism. Under consideration was the report on economic action, and the head of the Railroad Workers, Eugène Guérard, pressed for approval of the general strike. It was not to be, however, as the Congress, while voting the importance of union activity, adhered to the formula that collectivism would emerge from "a system of legislative measures."[74] By the time the French delegates crossed the Channel again, the war between socialists and anarchists had virtually killed collaboration between the unions and the parties of the workers.

VI

The bitterness and recriminations of the London meeting played havoc with Jaurès' hopes. Yet, when he summed up the meaning of London some eight days later, he stressed for the readers of *La petite République* what he considered the positive achievements of the Congress. The international socialist movement, so formless and disparate in its early years, had finally, he felt, strengthened itself with definition and discipline. Furthermore, though he continued to advocate tactical flexibility for world socialism, Jaurès warmly defended the imposition of some internal discipline. So he could write in explanation of the anti-anarchist moves: "A Congress meets to make certain common decisions on the basis of common principles; it is not an Academy where hostile philosophies are debated. . . . That is why we asked to be constituted as a separate delegation where the intervention of anarchism would not determine our position."[75]

Overanxious to write of events in a positive light, Jaurès made few public references to the deepening antagonism between the trade union movement and the parties. It was all too obvious to the working class, however, when hostile accounts of the Congress were spread prominently across the pages of newspapers and pamphlets. Guérard expressed a widely held syndicalist viewpoint when he charged the political socialists, a minority after all, with "creating a very deep schism" by constituting a second delegation at London.[76] The anarchists, even more bitter, poured their sarcasm on the ambitions of political socialists; one day, wrote the publicist Sébastian Faure, the inquisitorial Guesde would be Minister of the Interior, the learned Jaurès Minister of Education, and the patriotic Rouanet Minister of Foreign Affairs.[77]

The Guesdists, confirmed in their tactics by the International, were exultant, ready once again to fight for party control over the unions. But Jaurès, though he neither could nor would deny the central political drive of the working class, demonstrated through his actions in the months and years that followed a different attitude. He "was not a party man in the last legislature," wrote the socialist poet Charles Péguy of the years between 1893 and 1898.[78] That was proved many times over, especially when Jaurès kept a firm and friendly hand extended to the leaders of syndicalism.

His ties to the openly socialist unions such as the organized miners and glass workers of Carmaux, whose leaders were important members of the socialist parties, remained close. His relations with the reformists within syndicalism, those spokesmen in the C.G.T. who pleaded, as he did, for economic and political action, were marked by strong and reciprocal respect. But beyond that, Jaurès could never deny, however much he disputed their tactics, either the sincerity or the value of the revolutionary syndicalists. Even as he was attacked in their press and accused of a debilitating reformism, he read their literature and debated with their leaders as though they belonged, except the complete anarchists among them, within the large constellation of socialism. So it was, for example, that his friend Dr. Clauzel wrote to Pelloutier on September 14, 1900, to tell the indomitable syndicalist that Jaurès "is reading your book [*La Vie ouvrière en France*] with great interest; and when he finishes, he will gladly give it his warm-hearted consideration in *La petite République*."[79]

"One of the reasons for the weakness of the C.G.T. in its early years," the outstanding historian of French labor has written, "was the atmosphere in which it operated."[80] There was too much talk, hopelessly romantic, about barricades and guns and sudden, massive strikes. Jaurès fought the irrationalism in the syndicalist dream while respecting the working-class *élan* that inspired it. He would wrestle long and hard, for all the years that followed, with the problems of a fruitful partnership between the party and the unions.

But Jaurès was a deputy, a socialist deputy, and it was the autumn of 1896. The Progressists, more conservative than ever, were back at the helm of French government; and for the present, neither Radicals nor syndicalists were quite so immediately important as the policies of the Premier of France, Jules Méline.

9

The Méline Era
1896-1898

I

One day early in 1898 Jaurès walked briskly from his apartment in the rue Madame toward the Chamber of Deputies. At his side was a young and enthusiastic socialist, the *normalien* Charles Péguy, excited to be conversing with the learned deputy who was his hero. Approaching the Palais Bourbon, they noticed on the boulevard a small man with "an alert eye; a tenacious look; the prominent nose of a judge or lawyer; greying or white sideburns; lips straight, tightly drawn, pinched, evil-looking, willful, churlish, and thin; looking simultaneously like trickster and prophet. . . . Jaurès said: 'It's Méline; he still has life in him, that old one.'"[1]

Almost two years before, on April 29, 1896, when Jules Méline first formed his ministry, he had manifested even more life. Already close to sixty, he sat first in the National Assembly in 1872, and later in the Chamber of Deputies; during those twenty-five years as a deputy from the Vosges, he had consistently demonstrated his republicanism and his conservatism. As spokesman for the spinning-mill owners and the substantial landlords of the east, Méline had become the staunchest parliamentary advocate of high protective tariffs; in fact, the sharp increase in the schedules of 1892 had been, up to the time of his ministry, his greatest legislative monument.

Surrounding himself with younger men of unimpeachable conservatism ("the young Machiavellis of the tired bourgeoisie," Jaurès called them[2]), Méline directed his ministry toward what he termed a policy of "appeasement." All that was not quite so peaceful as it sounded, however, for if it meant sidetracking secularism and reform, it also involved resuming the offensive against the extreme Left.[3] It was evident from the very first vote of confidence won by the Premier that his ministry would enjoy strong majority support; for the ralliés and even a fraction of the more determined monarchist Right, finding Méline's social program totally acceptable, fell into line behind the Progressists. Somewhat uneasy in their support of the old Gambettist who was now Premier, the Rightists claimed that in their chosen course they were defending the Catholic faith. Jaurès, however, brusquely rejected that apology; "religion is only a rein on democracy for them, and their real objective is to protect their fortunes against the threat of socialism; they mean, like Méline, to defeat the income tax, shackle the unions, and strengthen the Senate."[4]

As the months of Méline's rule slipped into years, his ministry, faithful to its announced policy, withdrew plans for an income tax, permitted congregations once dissolved by Ferry to reorganize, and took scant note of the pressing problems created by industrialism. On one issue, however, Méline was incited to bold lawmaking — the issue of tariffs. His campaign for high protection, a crusade already fifteen years old, endeared the Premier to large landed proprietors and even to those less affluent peasants who were concerned over foreign competition in French markets. "His heart beats only for cereals," someone had once quipped of Méline.[5] But for urban workers, threatened with high food prices, his heart was not the key to the Premier's anatomy; in their circles he was known as Méline-pain-cher.

The socialists, confronted now with a ministry even less conciliatory than its Progressist predecessors, set out on the double offensive of attacking its policies within the Chamber while building their own support outside. The point of convergence, the link between these two campaigns, became the rural problem; for if the socialists could expose Méline's favorite nostrum for agricultural distress and simultaneously set forth a more convincing program, they might succeed, as indeed they had to in a France still predominantly rural, in undermining the ministry while winning to their side the population of the villages.

The opportunity for the socialists was linked to the sickness of the countryside, for which the politicians of the Center had persistently proved poor doctors. Over the last decade the signs of rural distress had multiplied, and none had been more telling than the perceptible drift of population from village to city.[6] In leaving the land to seek their fortunes in an uncertain urban milieu, families were responding to a deep frustration induced by the sharp drop in agricultural prices, or by the inequality of land ownership, or, if they were not owners but workers, by the heavy burden of long hours at low wages.[7]

Yet the task of planting the red banner in green fields was no easy one for socialists, as their conspicuous lack of success among peasants had amply illustrated. From its revival around 1880, the movement had remained primarily urban — hardly surprising when one considers the effect of collectivist doctrine on villagers, whether owners or not, whose dreams of happiness invariably took the form of privately owned fields. To socialists in general, and especially to Marxists, the peasant vision of individual property was a hopeless mirage. Not only was it impossible to achieve (had not Marx taught, in both the *Communist Manifesto* and *Capital*, that individual landed property, subject like industry to the law of capitalist concentration, was destined to disappear?),[8] but it was, by its very stimulus to the ownership instinct, dangerous to suggest. Thus, when the socialists first organized a political party at the Congress of Le Havre in 1880, their program, worked out by Guesde and Lafargue with the active collaboration of Marx and Engels, called for "the collective ownership of land, ores, and farm machinery as quickly as possible." The concrete needs of the villagers thus went unattended as socialists persuaded themselves that the abstract promise of security under collectivism would assuage the land-hunger of the peasants.

Most villagers, little inclined to become forerunners of today's *kolkhozniki*, not only failed to disappear as a social element but resisted easily enough the appeal of Marxism. By the start of the 1890's it was perfectly obvious that socialism, if it were to succeed as a political movement, had to accept the peasantry, landholding or not, while offering an immediate program consonant with a realistic view of the countryside. The moment of reorientation coincided with the emergence of Jaurès in the movement; and none was better equipped, by origin and doctrine, to make the socialist appeal both immediate and meaningful to the peasantry.

In January, 1893, when Jaurès announced his candidacy for the Chamber, spokesmen for socialism could write, as Millerand did, that his victory would represent the conversion of "rural as well as urban workers."[9] And when he had won, Jaurès himself took up the same theme, implying that peasants were embracing a socialism they had traditionally eschewed. For, as he explained, the villagers did not enjoy that prosperity and stability attributed to them in popular political parlance;[10] rather they were beset by complex and serious difficulties. Here were small proprietors and tenants, faced at once with excessive land taxes, rents, and interest rates; there were farm laborers, their lives squeezed away between endless hours of work and miserable wages. The disgruntled peasants were no longer safe for capitalism, predicted an optimistic Jaurès, and his victory was proof enough that socialism "has become a friend to those who, until now, ignored or feared it."[11]

In fact, he exaggerated in attributing his success in January to support by the villages; for it had been the socialist workers of Carmaux who had supplied the margin of victory over the opposition of the four predominantly rural cantons. Yet his analysis was really only premature, and in the general elections of August, Jaurès' victory rested not only on Carmaux but also on the support of two rural cantons. Then it was that one could point, with horror or with joy, to the startling truth that Jaurès was carrying socialism into the traditional centers of conservatism.

Superficially at least, it was incongruous that a *philosophe* should have been able, in the intimacy of political contact, to draw peasants into the socialist orbit. His good friend, the Belgian Émile Vandervelde, suggested an explanation when he referred to Jaurès as "a peasant of genius calibre."[12] The judgment, if taken too literally, is badly misleading; for there was nothing in the finely philosophical nature of Jaurès to suggest a Breughel rustic. But what was obvious to observers both in and out of the villages was his spontaneous attraction to the countryside, its fields and their cultivators. It was so deep a sympathy for village life that it could not be mistaken by peasants for a public pose. As a young student of twenty, Jaurès had already written to his friend Salomon of the idyllic joy he felt during summer holidays in the Tarn, listening to "the songs of our peasants, . . . those chants of love and mirth."[13] And eighteen years later, in the heat of political battle, he would write thus of his visits among the villagers in his constituency: "That friendly, personal contact with the robust, democratic peasantry envigorates me and increases my enthusiasm for new and expanded efforts on their behalf."[14] "He knew the humble folk," one critic has written, "he felt their pains."[15] His approach to the rural problem was empirical and free of dogmatism.

Over the four years of his first parliamentary experience, when he still hoped that bourgeois republicans would rally to social justice, he returned often, in press and forum, to the plight of the villages.[16] Inexperienced though he was, Jaurès managed to see through the inaccuracies of most contemporary descriptions of the peasantry. Half of those listed as landed proprietors, he pointed out, were holders of such tiny plots that they were endlessly threatened by poverty. As for countless others — the *métayers* who sharecropped the land, the *fermiers* who rented it as cash tenants, and the laborers who worked it for others at day wages — they lacked even the minimum security of proprietorship.[17]

When he faced up to the question of effective legislative action, Jaurès questioned the prompt and easy solution of high tariffs; and he broke with most of his Opportunist colleagues when he charged, as he did in the Chamber debate of March 8, 1887, that while protectionism screened out competition for big landed proprietors, it offered no relief for the rural masses.[18] In the many months that followed, as he moved toward and assumed his socialist position, he wrote increasingly on the rural poor, proposing now reduced taxes for small owners, then social security for agricultural laborers. With socialism the fixed point on his horizon, however, he had a purpose larger than immediate relief. Jaurès hoped to enlighten the villagers, to reveal to them the social roots of their distress, and in so doing to guide them toward a common meeting ground with the urban proletariat. And in exposing the nature of the class system in the countryside, he was never more graphic than when he wrote, early in 1891, about meeting a gentleman from the West who spoke freely about his affairs: "'The spirit of insubordination and aggressiveness is spreading into the countryside. Didn't one of my tenants ask for a lowering of his rent? And simply because he spends more than his father.' The same gentleman added a little later, in a very offhand manner, that he had just lost 40,000 francs at Monaco, the equivalent of perhaps three or four years of the tenant's rent."[19]

Yet it was no easy matter to pierce the traditionalism of the villages, to encourage that *entente* of workers and peasants which alone might provide the votes for a peaceful transition to socialism. "When I explain to the peasants those fiscal and social reforms which will give them access to landed property," he wrote of the obstacles, "even when I enable all those who drudge away their lives for others to catch a glimpse of the day when they will harvest for themselves, I find that what they lack most is confidence in the possibility of these great changes."[20] Thoughtful observer of the relentless round of rural life, Jaurès knew what resignation, what feeling of inevitability suffused the spirit of the peasants. "Their greatest weakness," he reflected almost a decade later, "is excessive humility before Nature, the tendency to accept what is, in the social as well as in the natural order, as immutable and inexorable. Even today, even after the prodigious inventions of science, even after the application of chemistry and mechanics to the labor of the fields, progress, when they do accept it, seems accidental, almost surprising.

They still have no idea of the slow but infinite evolution of the human race. Life for the peasant is like a tiny raft on a motionless ocean."[21] The very force of events—the growth of concentration in land ownership, the rise of the standard of living—would work great changes, Jaurès felt sure. But he hoped for a conscious effort by the peasants themselves to guide and hurry the events. And therein lay the challenge for socialists: "we must work feverishly to rouse among them the ideal of social justice; we must group them and organize them."[22]

The most significant of the socialist groups, the Parti ouvrier français, undoubtedly moved by electoral considerations rather than the idealism of Jaurès, finally came to grips with the job of capturing peasant interest. In 1892 at their Congress of Marseille, the Marxists, preparing for the general elections of 1893, dropped their doctrinaire stand on collectivization of land and adopted a fourteen-point program of agricultural reforms.[23] Thus, by the time Jaurès agreed to stand for the Chamber on the program of the P.O.F., the party had reconciled itself to the immediate needs of the peasants, just as the *tarnais* had accepted the Marxist laws of economic development. The relationship between Jaurès and the party was symbiotic, and as he blew into the movement a strong draught of idealism, he was himself invigorated by association with determined militants. This he showed clearly enough when he went out of his way, in April, 1893, to express deep sorrow over the death of De Fitte, his old Marxist antagonist in the municipal council of Toulouse. "He had a wonderful spontaneity," he wrote in a letter to *La Dépêche*, "an *élan* and vivacity of spirit, a colorfulness of speech and thought which served so well to propagate our ideas in the Midi."[24] "Our ideas," as Jaurès understood them, were not "enclosed in a narrow doctrine and an exclusive sect."[25] Rather did they develop out of a philosophy based on great human ideals and the laws of history.

But the matter of a socialist appeal to the peasantry was hardly settled by the formulation of the Marseille program. The Marxists had so long espoused collectivization of the land that antisocialists derided their turnabout as a deceitful bit of electioneering.[26] From many a pen came the dire warning that peasants who began by embracing socialism would end by losing their land. And that was only half the problem. Within the socialist movement itself the agricultural program became another of those doctrinal difficulties that could scarcely be resolved by a single formula. For if it was evident that socialism could win few rural converts without supporting immediate reforms, it seemed equally obvious that the bolstering of private property in the villages was an incongruous plank in a collectivist program. Thus, while Guesde propounded his Marxist catechism to the workers of the Nord and Vaillant preached

Blanquist *élan* to the militants of Paris, it was Jaurès, more than anyone else, who sought to raise the socialist approach to the peasants from
opportunism to the level of theory.

II

One night in October, 1893, Jaurès sat up late, reading Quinet's *Les
Révolutions d'Italie*. In the account of the struggle by the Florentine
working class against the nobility and the bourgeois patriciate in the
late Middle Ages, he was especially struck by the ruling-class propaganda
spread among the neighboring peasants, stories of the rapacious intentions of the workers, which successfully divided the rural and urban
masses. How strikingly like the present, thought Jaurès! For by "trickery
and calumny" antisocialists were now generating the same fears in the
French villages, hoping to drive a wedge between workers of field and
factory.[27] *Le Temps*, for example, charged repeatedly that under collectivism the state would become a behemoth-owner, devouring all
property titles as its own.[28] More directly aware than most socialists of
peasant susceptibility to such allegations, Jaurès worked carefully at
refuting them. Contemporary collectivism, he pointed out, far from
being sort of latter-day tribal communism, was complex and adaptable,
expressing itself through a variety of institutions and even various forms
of property. Thus, while others, both enemies and proponents of collectivism, exchanged insults on the level of generalization, Jaurès now
attempted, in his instructive public debate with Senator Lavergne, to
reveal its complexity, especially as it affected the villages.

Projecting himself into the socialist future, he sketched a picture of
property organization consonant with both the ideals of a collectivist
society and the aspirations of a land-hungry peasantry.[29] Leaving aside
the question of vastly increased production, which has dominated most
contemporary socialist theorizing, Jaurès concentrated on variety in
the land system. Whenever there was no exploitation of one man by
another and whenever each cultivator was guaranteed the right to
work and to live decently, then village organization conformed to the
irreducible standards of socialism. So it was that Jaurès envisaged two
kinds of farmsteads for a socialist France: "there will be what we can
call small family operations and then what we can call collective farms."

To the poor small landowners the socialist government would come
not as an expropriator but as a friend, reducing the crushing burden of
taxation, suppressing debts, and extending cheap credit for land improvement.[30] Then, exercising its right as the ultimate owner of all
property, the government would oust from the land the absentee owners who drew rents from tenants, and the capitalistic proprietors who

exacted their wealth from the work of farm laborers. *Métayers* and *fermiers*, holding their land from the community, would find their obligations reduced to just proportions. And farm workers, so long the victims of the worst conditions, would be organized into coöperative groups, tilling the land together, and recompensed, each one, according to his contribution in labor. "By working, a man will possess," he wrote in summing up his views on collectivism; "and to possess he will have to work."

Socialist solidarity, effectively created as a reaction to Progressism, brought Jaurès and the Marxists into close community. By 1894, Guesde was endorsing Jaurès' description of rural collectivism while applauding his many interventions in the Chamber for social reforms.[31] On April 8, 1894, the two men traveled to Fleurance, deep in the Midi, to address a socialist meeting. Jaurès denounced the charge that socialism threatened small holders with expropriation, and the Marxist chief wholeheartedly supported him. And when Guesde rose to speak at a banquet held later that evening, he turned to Jaurès, moved for the moment by the remarkable creativity of his young comrade, and said with considerable emotion: "I can die now, since there is a man like Jaurès who will continue my work and bring it to fruition."[32] As for Jaurès, even when he spoke of justice and reforms, he reflected the influence of Marxism. So, some two weeks after the meeting at Fleurance, he emphasized the slow but sure trend toward concentration, in land as well as in industry, for "in the Cher, the Nièvre, the Allier, large holdings are constantly developing; whole parishes now belong to two or three men."[33] But for the present, both Jaurès and his friends among the Marxists, though convinced that economic evolution would ultimately lead to rural collectivism, agreed to fight for better conditions for the peasants. In the fall of that year, 1894, Jaurès attended the twelfth annual Congress of the P.O.F., held at Nantes between September 14 and 16. Here the Guesdists again adopted the reform program approved two years earlier at Marseille. It was a significant concession to reformism, which finally influenced Marxist tactics throughout the decade; during the Dreyfus affair and its aftermath, the Guesdists would do penance for their sin; but now, confronted by the inescapable problem of spreading socialism in rural France, they escaped the confines of their doctrine.

But though that program promised to win votes for socialist candidates, it created consternation among some of the most influential theorists of international socialism. When the P.O.F. opted again for reformism at Nantes, Engels, already deeply concerned over the attempt of Georg von Vollmar, leader of the Bavarian wing of German Social Democracy, to water down Marxism, leveled a solid attack against the position. Writing in the German socialist organ, *Neue Zeit*,[34] Engels insisted that the problem of agriculture could be treated only by reference to the laws of capitalist development. It was both deceptive and futile to stand before the peasants as defenders of their individual holdings. "The capitalist form of production has struck a fatal blow at small agrarian property," he wrote. "It is in decline and will inevitably disappear." Even though the French Marxists knew that and said it, they sought to proffer aid to small owners. And if all this was only an electoral strategem, Engels went on, it was the grossest kind of tactical error. "We will never make socialists out of peasants protecting their property, any more than out of artisans hoping to remain entrepreneurs." Of course, he conceded, there was a socialist obligation to the peasants, but it was fulfilled by instructive propaganda, explaining to the peasants the forces of capitalism which daily victimized them. Hardly an effective electoral appeal, the procedure outlined by Engels nonetheless opened a long debate, one that has recently reverberated in Russian and Chinese accents, on the role of the peasant in a socialist society.[35]

At least one organized group of French socialists, the Allemanists, constantly alerted to signs of compromise by socialist politicians, scored the reformism of Guesde and Jaurès as rank opportunism.[36] As the conflict over agricultural policy simmered within European socialism, it promised to boil over when the Second International held its Congress at London in 1896. Indeed, a scant month before that meeting, the Marxist Charles Bonnier wrote to his party chief Guesde that he was engaged in a protracted debate with the German theorist Kautsky over the merits of the P.O.F. program.[37] Engels' criticism failed to sway either Jaurès, who could never remain mute witness to distress, or Guesde, who heard enough from various departmental sections of the P.O.F. to know that the villagers would be lost to socialism unless its program catered to their needs.[38] Their determination to reach the villages with proposals for immediate reforms was finally rewarded at the Congress of London. When the delegates of international socialism devoted their fifth session, on July 30, 1896, to the problem of agriculture, they decided against imposing a hard and fast program applicable to all countries.[39] Coinciding with the opening months of the Progressist resurgence under Méline, this action at London was a green light to French socialists to challenge the protectionist formula of the Premier with a reform program of their own.

"In the socialist group as then constituted in the Chamber, the leading orators all became specialists," Péguy wrote of the years 1893 to 1898. "Vaillant generally spoke on labor problems; Guesde on questions of labor or socialist theory; Millerand, so reasonable and even a little opportunistic, on governmental and foreign policy matters."[40] But it was Jaurès who spanned all fields; and whatever the subject, he collected a mass of data, worked out a strong position, and ended by giving the major socialist speech. So it was with agriculture, and by the summer of 1897, he was ready to present the socialist program on the peasant problem.

III

"Let us be fair," wrote the Catholic apologist De Cheyssac in Le Ralliement. "Félix Faure has done everything possible to encourage the overtures of the Pope and the Catholics. M. Méline has shared his views."[41] Here, then, was open reconciliation of the republican Center and the clerical Right, and Jaurès denounced this reconciliation. "You cannot openly and officially destroy the republican secularism," he wrote, apostrophizing the Premier, "but you can put your Republic under the patronage of the Papacy. Yes, it is the policy of Leo XIII which guides you. From the Vatican you now take your political line, and since you can't eliminate the laws of secularization, you can at least introduce the clerical viewpoint as much as possible."[42]

Respectful parliamentarian though he was, amiable, even decorous in the corridors, Jaurès was no player of political games. A flame of resentment, ignited whenever he sensed contempt for democracy, burned within him. The Méline ministry would hear from him at length in defense of his party and faith. This was evident when he gave notice, as early as December 14, 1896, that he intended to interpellate the Premier on the very subject of his agricultural program. Méline chose to ignore the announcement for a considerable time, and, in an extraordinary delay, the socialist interpellation was placed on the agenda, not in the cold months of winter but rather in the sultry days of June, 1897, when the Chamber sweltered under the summer heat. Nor was Jaurès then accorded the right of delivering his address on consecutive days, but instead he was forced to put his discourse together on three successive Saturdays, beginning on June 19 and concluding as late as July 3. Jaurès, however, made good use of the intervening months; his preparation for the interpellation was elaborate, his grasp of detail firm. In addition to printed sources, he had read the responses to a questionnaire which socialists had sent out to the villages and which constituted, in a minor way, a new body of cahiers de doléances.

What followed, when he finally began his long intervention on socialism and the peasantry, has come down as one of his most celebrated orations. At his full powers, a dozen crowded years having intervened since he began political life, Jaurès had become, in the rich brocade of his discourse, an artist of the spoken word. "Neither in Cicero nor De-mosthenes," one critic has sweepingly written, "can you find such an efflorescence of images; no one except Bossuet can reasonably compare with Jaurès in that art."[43]

Yet, as many a witness has testified, Jaurès' oratory was neither polished nor practiced. The socialist Viviani, by contrast, was a finished speaker, a former student of the Comédie Française where he had perfected his manner and composed his gestures.[44] But Jaurès broke all the rules in the book, thrusting a clenched fist aimlessly through the air, pacing too much at random, taking off weakly like an uncertain pilot. Whence, then, derived his power of discourse? In part, as any extensive reading of his speeches demonstrates, it flowed from a deep reservoir of culture, where the temporal issue merged with the eternal principle, where all segments of knowledge were rationally concatenated. But beyond this power to impress, his words had more — a capacity to link him to an audience beyond the listening one. Trotsky, no mean master of the word, listening often in his years of exile to speeches at meetings and Congresses, made this penetrating observation: "For Jaurès, oratory had no intrinsic value. That is, though the most powerful speaker of his time and perhaps of all times, he was *beyond* oratory; he was always superior to his speeches, as the artisan is to his tools."[45] The word, as Trotsky indicated, was a means for Jaurès and not an end, a way of proposing and momentarily effecting the harmony of mankind. "He knew instinctively how to express the needs of the masses," recalled the aged Guesdist Bracke but a few years ago. "And when he had found the metaphor that summed up the spirit he sought to convey, he was off: a bird, a forest, a leaf, the fruit, the sea — one spoken word, whether uttered by himself or someone in his audience, set him off on a flow of interconnected words."[46]

As Jaurès now embarked on his long analysis of the peasant problem, he traded a few words with Méline which revealed, for a moment, the Premier's contempt for the small but vociferous socialist group. Jaurès had just asserted that if the Premier had been as assiduous in supporting democratic reforms as in pressing for tariffs, "then the rural masses would already be enjoying the attention they so richly deserve."[47] Méline at once retorted: "If you had interpellated less, that would have been done." But Jaurès brushed this defense aside: "I can hardly imagine into what a bottomless pit of reforms we would have fallen if the socialists hadn't interpellated!"

In truth, he went on, reforms had not been on the agenda of this minis-try, nor on that of most of its predecessors. The life of the villagers was the record of timeless suffering, imposed by successive social systems and unrelieved by successive political regimes:

Continuously for eighteen centuries — under the whip of huge Gallo-Roman estates, under the hierarchical rule of feudalism, under the exploitation of bourgeois and financial ownership — constantly, they have watched their wheat and wine, the richness, strength, and joy which burst from the earth under their tools and effort, flow into the hands of others, some parasitical minority. For themselves — the pain of toil and the trouble of sowing; for themselves — the grueling work of tearing out each wild root; for themselves — the fierceness of clearing the unyielding woods; for themselves — snatches of sleep in the stable and tending to the cattle before starting the day.

Too patiently and too long had the peasants endured these conditions, and in the name of a thinking humanity, Jaurès expressed hope that they would finally express their self-interest: "Yes, let their appetites awaken, the appetite for pleasure and joy, for good food and plentiful drink, for enlightment and life; spurred on by those aroused instincts, their consciousness, now inert and dormant, will erupt, and they will show their determination to throw off the parasitical classes who squeeze them dry."

The worst threat of democracy — and Jaurès repeated this in many forms throughout his lifetime — was inertia, the failure to will and the inability to act. But when the villagers came to self-consciousness, seeking satisfaction of their needs, they would uproot a system of exploitation, and by the transmutation of all great social struggles, their own self-interest would turn into the interest of humanity. Was it then crude and vulgar, this appeal to appetite? No, cried Jaurès, there was nothing hallowed about the resigned asceticism of the poor. Only when they had abandoned their fatalism could they advance to a higher and fuller appreciation of life. Crude materialists there were, but they were the ones "who would continue to dull the peasant senses through privations, instead of stimulating them by hope and desire." Republican governments, one after another, had refused that stimulation, fearful lest the villagers should militate for change, and instead had romanticized a bare and crude round of existence. The spokesmen for the bourgeois party had screened off village reality with a curtain of platitudes about widespread ownership and rugged independence. Jaurès, in the name of socialism, now began to paint a very different picture of the countryside. The ministry, talking of low farm prices and proposing tariffs, had treated the rural problem superficially; for Jaurès, it was deeper and older than Méline was willing to admit.

Sweeping past the obscurity and complication that seemed always to attend the foggy debates on price schedules, Jaurès went directly to what he considered the core of the agricultural problem — the inequality and insecurity which characterized the life of the peasant masses. When he asked why it was so, he answered with a class analysis of the villages, claiming that, behind the façade of a landholding peasantry, the exploitation of labor and the concentration of property went on apace. Armed with statistics, especially the 1882 decennial census on landholding (and why, asked Jaurès, had the Ministry of Agriculture, in 1897, still not published the 1892 report?), he was able to bring out two central facts — that a very large percentage of villagers were not proprietors at all, and that among those who were, a striking inequality prevailed.

The figures revealed that, despite the several categories of landowners, almost half the peasants owned little or no land. The 800,000 tenants (*fermiers*) and the 500,000 sharecroppers (*métayers*) held their farms from absentee owners, often under terms so harsh that most of their labor was turned over, in cash or kind, to their landlords. But the three-and-a-half million agricultural workers, whether the *domestiques de ferme*, who were billeted at the farm, or the *journaliers*, hired by the day, constituted the rural proletariat, devoid of land and worked to excess by their landed employers. "I don't know of any other condition," said Jaurès, the reports from his village inquiry lodged in his memory, "and I don't believe that one exists, which is more servile, more terrible than that of the farm domestic. . . . And you, gentlemen, you who always talk about the defense of individualism, I ask you if there is any debased form of communism so tyrannical as the existence imposed on these domestics, who haven't a scrap of property or even any assured rights, who never enjoy a single hour of privacy, either at table or in their dwelling." As for the day workers, averaging 350 francs a year, they were already victims, as their chronic underemployment proved, of advancing mechanization. There was, Jaurès knew it, a ready response by the bourgeoisie to these propertyless masses. Guizot had said "*enrichissez-vous*," and then turned his back on the Orleanist poor. His spiritual descendants in similar accents still proposed to the landless that they quit their dependency by becoming proprietors. "I ask the Honorable M. Méline, I ask the Honorable M. Deschanel . . . if it is on an annual wage of 500 to 600 francs, further reduced by unemployment, that you imagine these workers will buy a piece of land."

From the plight of the rural proletariat, Jaurès turned to the condition of the proprietors. He adduced figures to reveal that 28,000 owners at one end of the spectrum held as much land as six million at the other. It seemed evident that if a distinct minority enjoyed abundant property, most peasant-owners suffered an insecurity compounded of fragmented holdings, high taxes, and consequent indebtedness. But the figures revealed also the trend toward concentration of ownership. Though that tendency had progressed more hesitantly in France than in England, for example, leaving intact a substantial percentage of small holders whom the socialists proposed to relieve, it nonetheless meant that the landless were destined so to remain, while some of today's owners were ticketed for extinction. Even the spokesmen for capitalism, when their guard was momentarily down, admitted that Marxist truth, claimed Jaurès. He quoted from memory part of an article in the *Economiste français*; written by the dean of orthodox economists, Leroy-Beaulieu, it had apparently accepted as both inevitable and desirable the disappearance of small, inefficient tenures.

By the time Jaurès rested on the first day of his speech, he had traced what he considered the inescapable dimensions of the actual rural problem. But for most of his republican colleagues, far better-humored about the high-or-low-tariff debate than this disturbing discussion of social structure, the speech had seemed disturbingly unreal. Yet Jaurès proposed, as he mounted the tribune for the second successive Saturday, to puncture the realism of Méline and his ministers, who, in hoping to save the profits of big market farmers, were posing as friends of the peasants.

It was June 26, and all semblance of reasonable weather had disappeared. The Chamber was a virtual inferno, but Jaurès, heavily attired as usual, made only passing reference to the temperature and moved at once to the attack.[48] The Premier had proposed — it was obvious to all — but a single cure for the ills of agriculture, and that was protection. To the socialists, of course, this was neither profound nor effective, treating a single symptom of the problem without ever going to its cause. For the moment, however, Jaurès was willing to meet Méline on his own ground and to discuss the usefulness of tariffs in guaranteeing a healthy home market for French producers.

Socialists were hardly doctrinaire free traders, Jaurès insisted, in defining his party's attitude toward protection.[49] Unlike nineteenth-century liberals, who made a panacea of free trade, they viewed tariffs, in a world of uneven economic development, as occasionally necessary. "Certainly a socialist nation will maintain many points of contact with the outside, but it will not welcome the products or labor of foreign countries until it has brought its own domestic production to the maximum, and it will import foreign products only when they enhance its own development."[50] By this striking piece of economic realism, suggesting economic nationalism, Jaurès did not mean to embrace protectionism. Though useful on occasion, tariffs, as a systematic policy and unaccompanied by strong measures to redistribute purchasing power, brought few benefits to society. Not only had new acts of protection encouraged similar foreign barriers against French products, but, as he pointed out, they had ultimately failed to ensure a larger home market. And why? Because the masses, so badly underpaid, lacked the power to consume; because "you do not have the courage, you do not have the political and social capacity to ask of the rich, the possessing classes, that they make the concessions necessary to raise popular consumption in proportion to national production."

Jaurès was now at the heart of his case — that no fundamental solution was possible for agriculture short of socialism. And the very poverty of the ministerial program, he optimistically predicted, would encourage its growth. For as the plight of the peasant grew, so would his militancy; from the economic realities would emerge a new idealism: "And while the Christian bell tolls vainly on the horizon the rhythms of ancient thought and Oriental dreams, the tocsin of distress and ruin, resounding on the great plains, is awakening the peasant for the first time to the noblest of thoughts and the highest of aspirations."[51]

When he returned on July 3, it was to sum up the socialist case. His party had a reform program, one similar to the Marseille doctrine of the P.O.F. Jaurès moved swiftly now through the major proposals — a minimum wage law for farm workers, the extension of cheap credit to indebted proprietors, the community ownership of the processing plants (dairies, distilleries, refineries). He promised that his party would fight without quarter to push through these measures. But France was in the second year of *mélinisme*, and Jaurès had few illusions left about the leaders of Progressism, "all those new men, all those young men, the Turrels, the Poincarés, the Barthous, the Burdeaus, and, beside them, at the periphery of power, the Deschanels and the Dupuys."[52]

Perhaps, even in this class-dominated State, the pressure for reforms might be successful; it was the hope that made Jaurès a democrat and a republican. But only when socialists had captured power, effecting their revolution through the ballot, was a real transformation of the villages possible. Addressing himself to the peasants, he urged them to put their trust in socialism, to combine with industrial workers to ensure its victory. "It is the law of history that never, from the beginning of time, has the peasantry, whatever its strength and economic preponderance, been able to accomplish by itself any great social and historic change." The bourgeoisie, still frightened by the knowledge of what the urban and rural poor, together, had been able to achieve in 1789, were working assiduously to split and divide the masses.

What a piece of dupery, cried Jaurès, was their charge that all peasants would be deprived of their property! Under no circumstances would collectivism crush the individual. "Its very first concern *is* the individual, the right of the individual to fulfill himself in freedom." Exhausted and overheated but swept to a climax by the very force of his idealism, Jaurès reached the end of his historic speech with these words: "It is for the people to conquer power!"

He returned to his seat in the Chamber, and his socialist colleagues, transported by the power of his invocation and its political significance, showered him with congratulations. And to wring from the speech its fullest propaganda value the socialists announced in *La petite République* on July 6 that it would be reprinted in a brochure within the week, available to all comers for only thirty centimes. Conservatives and moderates, however, upset by this appeal to the villages, hastened to the attack, both inside and out of the Chamber. Speaking at Vesaul on July 4, Méline accused the socialists of organizing a collectivist tyranny where neither private property nor individual rights would survive.[53] The antisocialist press, too, swept aside as "hypocrisy and duplicity" the beautiful image of a collectivist order.[54]

They were wise to fulminate, wrote Gérault-Richard; for it was nothing less than their conservative predominance which was threatened once peasants linked arms with workers. "And Jaurès' speech, we are certain, will have the most fruitful results; with an unfailing power of demonstration he has analyzed the agricultural crisis, shown its causes, intensification, and results, linked it to that universal evolution which concentrates all means of production in the hands of an exploitative minority, constantly smaller in number and greater in power. He has forced the exponents of social conservatism to face the fatal weakness of their doctrines and desires."[55]

Two of those exponents struck back. Paul Deschanel, addressing the Chamber on July 11, offered, in a very polished discourse, an effective reply. Rather than denying *en bloc* Jaurès' allegations, he admitted a number of defects in rural organization and called for both parliamentary reforms and voluntary mutual aid societies in the villages. "M. Paul Deschanel," commented Jules Lemaître, obviously pleased with the intelligence of this anticollectivism, "very fortunately opposes *free* association to the *coercion* of socialism." But the critic could not suppress some uneasiness about Deschanel's encouragement of both state-sponsored reforms and laissez faire. For he added, "I am afraid that the form and measure of state intervention may be rather difficult to fix in such conditions."[56]

It was the economist Leroy-Beaulieu, however, cited by Jaurès as both predicting and advocating the end of small holdings, who replied most indignantly. Accusing the deputy of falsifying his views, he composed an entire brochure to demonstrate that socialists "have no scruples about mutilating . . . the theories of their opponents."[57] In trying to correct the impression left by Jaurès, Leroy-Beaulieu referred readers to the discussion of agriculture in his *Traité d'économie politique*, where he had concluded that "large and small holdings can coexist and be of service to each other."[58] Jaurès went at once to check the texts, his speech, and the writings on which he had drawn. It was true, he admitted in print, that he had cited as a direct quotation what was actually a summary of Leroy-Beaulieu's thought. For this he promised rectification in the Chamber; "I dont want anyone to say that a socialist would alter even the nuance of an opponent's thought." But in what was crucial—the economist's actual meaning—Jaurès admitted neither error nor falsification. For he had been completely accurate, he concluded, "when I said (and I said nothing else) that M. Leroy-Beaulieu has proposed as a remedy for the agricultural crisis the transformation of the old rural economy into capitalistic farming."[59]

The long debate on agriculture, touched off by the intervention of Jaurès, occupied many more Chamber sessions until it was concluded late in the autumn of 1897. In the months that followed his speech, the 1892 statistical report on agriculture was published, revealing, as though in substantiation of Jaurès, that the number of proprietors had declined by 138,000 in the decade after 1882. But the majority in the Chamber concluded the debate by a profession of antisocialism. Jaurès moved a resolution on November 21 in the light of his analysis, which foresaw "a public inquiry into the state of rural property and into the condition of farm workers." Rejected by a vote of 348 to 152, that motion gave way to one by Deschanel, approved by all but the socialists, stressing the superiority of a private property system to collectivism.

But the motion and the vote were anticlimactic. They reduced to nothing the immediate legislative effect of Jaurès' speech. That was certainly true. But it was harder to destroy its political and social effect. More than a skirmish in the war on *mélinisme*, the discourse was an attempt, stronger than ever before, to tie peasants to workers. And as its warm phrases eddied slowly through the countryside, who knew but that they might not rouse the villagers from their historic traditionalism?

IV

When he was young, Jaurès made and reported a discovery: "I have acquired the very difficult art of loafing," he wrote to his friend Salomon, "the art of vegetating calmly for an entire day without studying, or reading, almost without thinking. It's an admirable art, and I want to cultivate it; it should be a great resource for keeping good humor and inner serenity when one grows old and worn-out."[60]

Both humor and composure Jaurès retained, in remarkable degree, even at the height of his career. The joys of idling, however, were but a fond memory during the endless days of combat. For just as he surpassed all socialists in oratory and philosophy, so he led them in dedication to parliamentary duties. The day of the deputy, as Jaurès lived it, stretched well beyond the Chamber session. When the president of the Chamber signaled adjournment and the hall buzzed with the din of departure, he remained in his seat, studying the agenda for the following session to chart a plan of action and, more often than not, to detect a maneuver-in-the-making. During the occasional periods of recess, while deputies circulated freely in the corridors, his vigilant eye and ear prepared him for many a covertly conceived political deal. Especially in these years of social conservatism, Jaurès scrutinized every passing issue, lest an unchecked ministry work against the people.

As the summer of 1896 gave way to autumn, the Méline government was certainly up to something, for it seemed bent on uniting the nation with pomp rather than dividing it with social issues. A great pageant was in prospect, the visit to France of the young Russian Tsar Nicholas II and his beautiful Tsarina Alexandra. Excepting only the Shah of Persia, no crowned head had passed before French eyes since 1870, and the preparations for the October reception created, in high society and low, excited anticipation. M. Crozier of the Protocol Service, charged with the geometry of etiquette, stepped suddenly from the shadows into the spotlight, while President Faure prepared to indulge his seasoned appetite for pomp. The security of France, the greatness of the nation, the alliance against Germany — all of these phrases circulated through the half-serious discussions of purpose. But it was, after all, a matter of foreign policy, a realm of national activity properly reserved to experts and removed from partisanship.

Yet that view, to the unconcealed distress of both moderates and reactionaries, was not shared by Jaurès and his friends. Persuaded that the State was a fulcrum of class interest, they detected in all of its policies, whether foreign or domestic, a common and conservative denominator. Though the direction of diplomacy was presumably set by concern for the safety and resources of the nation, considerations said to transcend separate group interest, the socialists openly expressed their suspicions that these lofty objectives often hid less exalted purposes. So it was that Jaurès, suspicious of the meeting between the republican Méline and the autocratic Nicholas, became an increasingly searching critic of French foreign policy.

In the early decades of the Third Republic, the feelings of most Frenchmen were directed by the realities of both geography and history. Immediately to the east of France, united since 1870, populous, productive, and self-confident, lay Germany. The fear that such a power might serve its greatness at the expense of France was based on more than a glance at the map. Burned into the national memory were the events of 1870–71, when a well-disciplined Prussian army had marched to victory, while Bismarck had annexed, as the staggering prize of war, the provinces of Alsace and Lorraine. Gone from the French nation were the rich soil, the coal and iron reserves, the textile and metallurgical mills which gave these territories their immense economic value; but gone also were Frenchmen, kin to those who still called Paris their home, or Nantes, or Bordeaux, or Toulouse. This "terrible right of conquest," as the *Frankfurter Zeitung* called it on August 17, 1870, was certain to distort all future relations between France and Germany, to suffuse the French atmosphere with a vapor, one part fear, one part resentment, one part revenge.

Bismarck sensed the French mood and realized its dangers. He had constructed the Triple Alliance by 1882, a secret defensive agreement among Germany, Austria-Hungary, and Italy, to discourage aggression from the west; he had encouraged France to forget the provinces and nourish her greatness in the vast expanses of the African desert; and, all the time, he had kept a watchful eye on vast, mysterious Russia, binding Tsardom to Germany, first in the League of the Three Emperors (1872), and then, when Austrian-Russian rivalry in the Balkans made that impossible, in the secret Reinsurance Treaty of 1887. Yet in France the spirit of *revanche* persisted; and when Boulangism carried it to a feverish pitch in 1887, Bismarck sought and obtained large increases in German armed strength and created a mood of crisis.

Where did Jaurès then stand? As always, he was for peace among nations, the only objective consonant with his humanism. But when he came to assign blame for the crisis of 1887, he spoke as a proud republican and patriot. Why, he asked, had this tension arisen? "On the other side of the Rhine, there are hidden but powerful forces, wavering between war and peace, capable of starting a conflict, even against the German will. In France, there is only one will, expressing . . . a deep love of peace but an unyielding courage in the hour of danger."[61] For Jaurès there was as yet but one struggle in history — the traditional one between the Old Régime and bourgeois democracy. In monarchist Germany, he felt, forces of war, military and bureaucratic circles, operated dangerously and beyond the popular reach. In France, a democratic republic, the will of the people was omnipotent and peaceful.[62]

But what of the army, the caste of monarchist officers and the mass of conscripted men? Did not the French army cherish aggressive hopes, or at least feed the hopes of chauvinists? Not according to Jaurès, who gazed upon the barracks of France through thickly idealistic lenses. He saw what he dreamed of — an army like the one Carnot had organized in 1793, a *levée en masse*, the defender and promoter of democracy. And when he saw conscripts from his own Midi returning home on leave, he was moved to write proudly:

All these young men, or almost all, seem animated by a very fine spirit; the most intelligent among them enthusiastically note how, in a military discipline that was formerly a mixture of insult and punishment, the respect of man for man has been making progress. . . . The regiment is not only a great school of patriotism, but also the greatest school of democracy. When the popular masses, workers and peasants, are conservative, it is especially because of the social forces that dominate them. From time to time they work for great proprietors, and without much reflection, they follow them in their voting. In the regiment the narrow circle which enclosed them is broken; they enter the great French family where there are no other masters but honor and dignity.[63]

But at no time, not even in his political youth, did Jaurès join the *revanchards*; in none of his writings, even his most patriotic, did he preach hatred of Germany or berate her civilization. Too young in 1870 to retain bitter and vivid memories of the Franco-Prussian War, the kind that never die, he belonged to a generation capable of accepting the facts of history, however unpleasant, and of seeking a *modus vivendi* with Germany. He came to his maturity, furthermore, at a time when German intellectuals and artists exerted a powerful influence on the cultural life of France. The historians Monod and Lavisse, who made veritable pilgrimages across the Rhine, considered Germany the second homeland of every thinking man; the philosophers Lachelier and Boutroux, who so directly influenced Jaurès, made Kant their god and their students his disciples. The most challenging of German thinkers — whether Hegel, Schopenhauer, or Nietzsche — had their French followers who, when they were not Germanophile, were at least convinced that German civilization added up to considerably more than Bismarck and Prussian militarism. The time would come again, and it was not far off, when anti-German feeling would sweep through the world of letters. But Jaurès, who had drunk so deeply from the well of German thought, could never surrender to the irrational demands of chauvinism.

Not that he ignored the question of Alsace and Lorraine, or considered it closed. For Jaurès, as for most Frenchmen, the loss of the provinces was a national tragedy, a violation of right and a standing threat to peace. But the Boulangist solution, the holy war of revenge, clashed with his ideal of a peaceful, democratic nation, and he rejected it out of hand. Standing unequivocally against aggression, Jaurès appealed rather to time and patience as the only solutions to the problem: "Our duty is simple. It consists of remaining well armed; talking little but thinking a great deal about Alsace-Lorraine; of honoring the dignity of France by rising above cowardly and childish attacks on the Germans in France; and of choosing our leaders and policies in domestic affairs without reference to foreign powers."[64]

Jaurès' spirit was both proud and peaceful. It recalled nothing so much as the vigilant republicanism of Gambetta.[65] But as an understanding of French purposes in international relations, his views were markedly superficial. Jaurès spoke of the nation as though there were no divisions, except between monarchists and republicans, which bore on its policies; he spoke of the people as though their will alone shaped and directed history. And in all this, he was poles apart from Guesde and his small band of Marxist followers.

The militants of the P.O.F., armed with a set of simply phrased axioms, traversed the land exposing as false the idea of la patrie.[66] Forty years before, when democracy and social reforms had not yet begun to affect industrial society, Marx had said that the workers had no fatherland. Now leaders like Guesde, too absorbed in building a movement to recognize the changing environment, reiterated the charge.[67] Only the state was real, taught the Guesdists, not the nation; and like army and diplomacy, it was a weapon of the ruling class. The peaceful ideals of the people? They were empty, futile; short of socialism, nothing would stay the aggressive course of capitalism.

It was a strident teaching, far different from the thoughts of Jaurès. And yet, was there not within it a method of analysis which could alter his understanding? Once convinced that there were special interests, would he speak of the "national interest"? Once aware of organized power, could he remain sanguine about the people's power? Whatever the potential changes, however, one thing was certain — that, as in many other matters, on questions of war and peace, Jaurès would carry into socialism an idealism and an original experience.[68]

By 1890 Jaurès was in full transition. As recently as a few years ago, Bracke wrote about that evolution: "Don't say that Jaurès was converted to socialism; it's an absurd expression. Think of it, rather in this way: Jaurès understood. From that point on, everything was changed, within him, for him, through him."[69] The warning of the old Guesdist is valuable, underscoring as it does a continuity in the experience of Jaurès. The republican deputy was as deeply devoted to peace and the harmony of mankind as the later socialist militant. What changed were the means, not the ends; what emerged was the conviction that only socialism, ending private gain, was the way to peace.

Jaurès now looked across the Rhine to the militants of German socialism. Here, he felt was the real hope for the future of Franco-German relations; for once the Social Democrats had won power, he predicted, old disputes would be resolved and the damage of 1870 repaired.[70] It was the start of a long and almost unbroken devotion to German socialism, a courageous movement, as he saw it, whose leaders, Wilhelm Liebknecht and August Bebel, had dared to denounce the annexation of Alsace-Lorraine; a successful movement, which had survived harsh anti-socialist laws to capture almost one-fifth of all votes in the elections of 1890. But this optimism trapped him into exaggeration. Thus, when Bismarck resigned his office on March 20, 1890, Jaurès, ignoring the decisive clash that had developed between the Chancellor and Kaiser William II, read into the event "the growing strength of the socialist party." The prospects were already bright, he concluded, for "the redemption of France and the avenging of the nation."[71]

But while Jaurès thought of Franco-German accord, many others did not. If Boulangism had collapsed, the rankling desire to do something about Germany remained, and it led, at the turn of the new decade, to the making of a Russian alliance.[72] It had long been evident that Tsardom, locked in Balkan rivalry with Germany's Austrian ally, was the least reliable partner in Bismarck's diplomatic system. But when the proposal of a Franco-Russian *rapprochement* was first raised in France, by *revanchards* out of chauvinism and monarchists out of political sentiment, it found little support among old republicans — Ferry and Floquet, for example — who still distrusted this darkest of European monarchies.[73]

Yet the drive for a Russian counterpoise to German strength picked up considerable steam by 1890. Operating in the shadows of international affairs, certain French financiers, who, in extending a large loan to Russia in December, 1888, had begun to form a decisive link with the Russian debtor economy, pressed hard for close political ties.[74] At the center of French affairs were republicans of a new school, closer than their predecessors to the monarchist-clerical party of the Right and free of moral sensitivity about Tsardom. Anxious to get tough with Germany, they sensed their opportunity in the evident availability of Russia as an ally. For, in fact, the fall of Bismarck, placing the reins of German diplomacy in more numerous and less adept hands, had resulted in the alienation of Russia from the German alliance system.[75] The colossus of the east, now isolated, stood open to overtures, even from republican France.

It was the very competent Ribot who dominated the Foreign Office for three years (from March, 1890 to March, 1893) and during three ministries. Turning what Barrès called "his fine pianist's head" in Russia's direction, he maneuvered for a specific agreement. The negotiations, marked by Tsardom's tantalizing hesitancy, dragged slowly on until a public display of Franco-Russian friendship gave them an emotional charge. In the summer of 1891, a French naval squadron set sail for Russia, putting in at Kronstadt on July 23. The reception for the French, by both public officials and ordinary citizens, was fervent to the point of ecstasy; and the happy sailors could hardly have known how much they forwarded diplomacy as they went to the bosom of Mother Russia. On July 25 the officers of the French squadron were feted by the Tsar and Tsarina, who stood at attention as a Russian band played the revolutionary *Marseillaise*. When the reports of these extraordinary events were received in France, popular elation was at once evident. The climate was now right for an agreement, and it resulted on August 27 in the form of an *entente cordiale*, drawing the two powers together "for the maintenance of peace."

Jaurès followed the events closely, though what he understood was limited by scanty public information. The display of warmth between two peoples was evident; the motives of the key figures were not. After Kronstadt, he applauded the friendly atmosphere, first as a proud republican. "They have always criticized the Republic . . . for having isolated and weakened France," he wrote of the monarchist-clerical party. "Let them now compare the condition in which the last of our monarchies, the Empire, left France, and the international position which twenty years of republican freedom and patriotic wisdom have given to our country." And he continued as a patriot, pointing out the defensive advantages of the new friendship: "The Triple Alliance will be very hesitant to attack both the French and Russian armies."[76]

In this judgment, a reflection of his earlier republican views, Jaurès questioned neither the intentions of French policy-makers nor the extent of actual commitments. Other socialists, however, shouted their opposition, though their arguments were neither uniform nor sharply analytic. The Marxist Lucien Roland, contemptuous of relations with reactionary Russia, attacked "the second-rate politicians" who, "frightened by Corporal William have fled into the arms of Cossack Alexander."[77] Guesde simply tossed out the suspicion that Russia would flirt with France "only to get *carte blanche* in the Balkans from the Hohenzollerns."[78]

While the majority applauded and a handful of socialists objected, French politicians and military men worked feverishly to convert the *entente* into a definitive military agreement. In the summer of 1892 the government sent handsome and courtly General de Boisdeffre off to Russia, the second-in-command of the French general staff. The general worked out a military agreement with the Russian Chief of Staff, and could even report back to Paris that "although the Tzar may genuinely desire peace, he is not particularly alarmed by the idea of war."[79]

The die was being cast in the affairs of Europe; "the great military powers," wrote Engels in 1893, "are like two great enemy camps — France and Russia on one side, Germany and Austria on the other."[80] French socialists, Jaurès among them, grew apprehensive. They began to plumb the depths of foreign policy, listening all the while to opponents who charged them with the worst of sins — disloyalty. An indignant Jaurès answered, even for the Guesdists among them:[81] "If we, the French socialists, were indifferent to the honor, security, and land of France, we would be committing a crime against both country and humanity. For a great and free France is essential to mankind. In France democracy has triumphed in its most logical form, the Republic; and if France were to fall, the whole world would suffer."[82] But secret diplomacy, warlike provocations, alliances with reaction — what had these to do, demanded Jaurès, with defense of democracy? Between patriotism, as he defined it, and internationalism, as the socialists preached it, he saw perfect accord. For at the heart of each he found love of mankind and devotion to peace.

In October, 1893, a squadron of the Russian fleet arrived. Putting in at Toulon, officers and men were treated to a half-delirious show of affection. But this time, at the dawn of Progressism, Jaurès did not share the enthusiasm. What was it really about, he wanted to know, this *rapprochement* with Russia, bounded on one side by secrecy, on the other by ecstasy? "The responsible ministers," he cried, "must tell the country in what manner, in what spirit they have negotiated, if, in fact, *they have negotiated.*"[83]

But secrecy persisted, and suspicion about the Franco-Russian agreement grew deeper on the Left. In Russia, Tolstoy called it "an association of warmongers."[84] Jaurès, sensing in it a community of conservative interest, kin to the Holy Alliance, denounced the "monarchist-clerical-bourgeois front" now raised against socialism.[85] Threatened in their supremacy, the dominant classes would even unchain violence; peace, thought a sober and unillusioned Jaurès, had become a fast-fading dream under capitalism. A severe indictment, but he carried it directly to the floor of the Chamber in 1895, speaking there at length on the nature of war.

It was March 7, and Ribot, architect of Franco-Russian unity, was at the head of his third ministry. Under discussion was the military budget for the coming years, a budget larger than hitherto requested. Why this increase in military preparations, why this trip to the brink of war? It was class struggle, charged Jaurès, which was responsible for the recourse to war. For it was class struggle which made armies essential and Bonapartism possible. "So long as a handful of men in each nation possess the significant means of production and exchange; so long as they govern other men; so long as that ruling class . . . depends, for its protection against possible mass uprisings, on military dynasties or on the professional armies of oligarchic Republics; so long as Caesarism can profit from this deep class division . . . then armed conflict will break out among the peoples of the world."[86]

War, then, was diversion from internal crisis, augmentation of State power against potential rebellion. But even worse, cried Jaurès, it was something inherent in the contradictions of the social system. Producing too much and distributing too little, capitalism touched off "those great colonial rivalries. . . . Our chaotic society, even when it professes peace or appears relaxed, carries war within it, as the sleeping cloud carries the storm." There was but one road to peace, he concluded, and it was socialism.

Yet, despite this note of determinism, Jaurès intensified his criticisms of foreign policy as though he felt, out of idealism or hope, that the human will could deter the forces of aggression. It was an unclear position, reflecting in Jaurès the dualism between the social theorist, taking the long view of affairs, and the democratic deputy, aware from daily battle that policies might be altered.

But hope could entrap Jaurès. Peace was so commanding a goal that he tended to magnify every sign that seemed to point to it. The Social Democrats of Germany, increasing their influence and professing their brotherhood, would, he felt sure, check aggression east of the Rhine. But that old Marxist Duc-Quercy, observing the German comrades at close range in Berlin, was less sanguine about their influence: "Given the political constitution of Germany, action in the Reichstag, compared to our parliamentary action, is of absolutely no importance," he wrote to Guesde. "When we judge German affairs, we are duped by an optical illusion. Pen in hand, behind closed doors, the Social Democrats are wonderfully audacious. But it goes no further than that."[87]

It was hope again that led Jaurès to an omission. For years he had made no critical analysis of colonialism, while the spectacular tide of imperialism after 1880 carried the French flag into the far-flung reaches of Africa and Asia. It was a movement well supplied with propagandists and pressure groups. In 1890 a Comité de l'Afrique française had been formed, counting among its leading members, like the *ralliement* in microcosm, ex-Boulangists, Catholic Rightists, and influential republican moderates — Eugène Étienne, Félix Faure, Gabriel Hanotaux. By 1895 this organization to preëmpt an empire in Africa had been joined by others — the Comité de l'Asie française, the Union coloniale, the Comité de Madagascar — each anxiously eying some profitable "backward" land.

In the Chamber it was Étienne, the influential deputy from Oran, who spoke most consistently for the French colonial destiny; outside, Paul Leroy-Beaulieu, chief among the apologists, proclaimed that empire was the natural consequence of greatness. And from May 30, 1894, when Hanotaux, an inveterate digger into diplomatic archives, began a four-year tenure as Foreign Minister (broken only by the few months of Radical government), colonialism became a cardinal principle of French policy.[88]

The drive was too fruitful of results to have escaped Jaurès' attention. Here, empirically, was the cause of many small wars, and, potentially, of a major one. But in the little he wrote and spoke about imperialism until the end of the 1890's, he centered his criticisms rather on faulty administration than on the idea of colonialism. It seems a strange position for one who fought so hard against all forms of human subordination. How, then, does one explain it?

Perhaps, at that deep level of consciousness where early impressions hang on, his old admiration for Ferry, the tough republican who had defied the Right with a secular school system and overseas conquests, encouraged his tolerance for the recent empire. But two factors are indisputable. First, in his fervent desire for a Franco-German *rapprochement*, the very cornerstone of European peace, as he saw it, Jaurès considered empire-building, with Germany's consent, a solution for the tension over Alsace-Lorraine. And then, he had a noble dream about colonies — that life there could be improved and the natives respected, that France had a genuine mission to spread her civilization. Though, like most socialists, he deplored the "startling corruption" of imperialism, Jaurès felt it worthy for socialism, while opposing further conquest, to fight for improved conditions within the vast lands already occupied.[89] And in the case of Madagascar, unlike Gustave Rouanet and Vigné d'Octon, he didn't even oppose fresh conquest. In England, old William Morris harbored no such illusions about imperialism: "And what is all this for?" Morris asked in the May Day issue of *Justice* in 1896. "For the spread of abstract ideas of civilization, for pure benevolence, for the honor and glory of conquest? Not at all. It is for the opening of fresh markets to take in all the fresh profit-producing wealth which is growing greater and greater every day; in other words, to make fresh opportunities for *waste*; the waste of our labor and our lives."[90]

But by 1896 the immediate issue was Progressist predominance, and the uses to which Méline, Faure, and Foreign Minister Hanotaux would put the diplomacy of the nation. Security of France, concern for Alsace and Lorraine, *ententes* for defensive purposes — all of this was part of Jaurès' realistic policy. But the determined goal of peace, the conviction that France, as the revolutionaries of 1793 had proclaimed, must stand as friend to oppressed mankind — this was his socialist program. Capitalism, as he viewed it, was unstable and a danger to peace. The ascendancy of the Progressists showed it; and behind their pious patriotism Jaurès sensed chauvinism and a threat to democracy. His deepest suspicions had been aroused, especially when Tsar Nicholas and his beautiful Tsarina agreed to visit France in 1896.[91]

V

Only in June, 1895, did Hanotaux, for the first time, speak of an "alliance" between France and Russia. The word came as no suprise, but the terms of such an alliance and their implications remained vague and secret. The Foreign Minister insisted, to the distress of open *revanchards*, that the agreement was peaceful in intention and defensive in nature. And, in fact, the articles of the secret agreement bore him out. For Tsarist Russia, with no interest in Alsace-Lorraine, had been unwilling to enter into concrete engagements until, by the terms of the Alliance, that French aim had been placed in check. What Hanotaux did not reveal, nor could he at that juncture, were the potential involvements for France in far-distant Russian enterprises. For in courting Russia as the answer to the Triple Alliance, France had won a partner whose maneuvers were played over vast stretches of land, from the Balkans to the China Sea.

Checked to the south by Austrian rivalry and German resistance, Russia had fixed upon China, immense, populous, defenseless, as the most profitable field for expansion. But the Celestial Empire appealed not only to the bankers and militarists of debtor Russia but also to market-seeking capitalists of the highly industrialized countries. China should have been a vast enough feeding-trough for the west, but, appetites being what they are, intense rivalry was certain to develop.

Russia had staked out Manchuria, almost an extension of Siberia, as her logical field of enterprise. Port Arthur on the Liaotung Peninsula could provide a port which, unlike Vladivostok, would be open all year to the Russian fleet. Beyond that, there were railroads to be built and timber to be cut; and if these enterprises required French capital, Russian speculators would profit nonetheless. A good plan, until Japan spoiled it. Emerging in the mid-nineteenth century from prolonged dormancy, Japan, by the 1890's, had superimposed a modern industrial and military society on an essentially feudal structure. With a home population shorn of purchasing power, her industrialists required markets; with an army and navy modernized and large, her militarists clamored for action. In 1894, Japan attacked a hopelessly outclassed China; by March 13, 1895, the treaty of Shimonoseki had added to the Empire of the Mikado Formosa, the Pescadores, and, to the horror of St. Petersburg, the Liaotung Peninsula.

Russia wavered between a possible partition of Manchuria and a determination to oust Japan from the Asiatic mainland. In April, 1895, St. Petersburg received German approval for a policy of expulsion, but not British approval. It was now up to France, and Hanotaux lent support to Russia's policy. By a strange detour the new alliance had led France into a joint action with Germany to safeguard Russian interests in Manchuria. On April 23, 1895, notes to Tokyo from Russia, France, and Germany demanded evacuation of the Liaotung Peninsula, and the outnumbered Japanese withdrew. In the months that followed, Russia triumphed and French bankers profited. St. Petersburg arranged a loan to China for payment of its war indemnity to Japan, but Paris provided the money, and at four per cent; St. Petersburg organized a Russo-Chinese bank to obtain railroad concessions and provide loans, but Paris supplied the capital.

In the Turkish Empire too, Russian moves came increasingly to involve the French. The diverse nationalities within the orbit of Turkey, groaning under the rule, both repressive and ineffective, of Sultan Abdul Hamid II, broke into sporadic rebellions, the signs of a dying order. The Armenians, long subject to cruel repression, had been presumably safeguarded by the European powers in the Treaty of Berlin of 1878,[92] but the Sultan nonetheless inflicted upon them, starting in October, 1894, a wave of terrible massacres. A year later the terror was repeated, this time in Constantinople itself; by the summer of 1896 the prospect for the Armenians seemed extermination. England, in decline at the Sultan's court since its conquest of Egypt, espoused the Armenian cause in order to bring pressure on Turkey. But Russia, her own influence at stake, backed the Sultan against the British while abandoning the Armenians to their tragic fate. Again, as in Manchuria, St. Petersburg called for support from France and Germany, and again it was forthcoming. In Paris, once more, financiers were active, urging Hanotaux to support a sultanate which then absorbed nine per cent of all their foreign investment. The diplomacy of imperialism was now at its height, and if its rich details were curtained off from public view, Jaurès' assiduity had enabled him, from the outset of the Méline ministry, to sense its main lines.

"Because France has become the servant of Russia's Far Eastern ambitions, so menacing to Chinese territorial integrity, she has become suspect in China and will be ousted from the Chinese market to the profit of England." So began Jaurès in opposing the Tsar's impending visit. The comment was, if anything, realistic, measuring the effects of Franco-Russian unity on French commerce. But the loss, as he saw it, was more than markets; it was moral leadership. "Because the Tsar wants to maintain intact the abusive and violent regime of Turkey until that day when he will be able to intervene alone and seize everything, France has stood by, without protest or whisper, while the most atrocious massacres in history have been committed. And even now, has France agreed to a blockade of Crete, choking off, for the benefit of the Turks, a justifiable native insurrection, simply to please Russia, the self-styled guardian of Turkey?"[93] And why? The France of Méline and the Russia of Nicholas, charged Jaurès, were of a single kind, reflecting in each case the dominion over state and society of an uneasy capitalism:

The time has passed when one could say that the Tsarist social system was so far removed from our own that no possible similarity existed between Russian and French reaction. Industrial and capitalist civilization has penetrated Russia; there are large factories in St. Petersburg and Moscow, just as in Paris and Roubaix; and only recently, on the morrow of the Tsar's coronation, forty thousand factory workers in the capital went out on strike. . . . Despite an absolutistic regime, which prohibits all meetings, working-class propaganda has continued . . . under the very eyes of a stupified police. . . . The Parisian workers have been asked to shout lusty approval of that regime; . . . Tsar Nicholas is now one of the guardians of capitalism; let Leygues and Trarieux and Rességuier join the parade and acclaim him.[94]

Yet there was no gainsaying the enthusiasm that everywhere broke loose as the Tsar's arrival drew near. It was a pageant, and the proletariat, weary of the humdrum, awaited it too. Jaurès now pleaded openly, exhorting the working classes to cut through the deception, to work harder for a new order. "O, people of France, send up your dream, and then further still; for as high as it flies, the socialist ideal will never be beneath it."[95]

When the Tsar reached Paris, however, on the sixth day of October, almost a million Frenchmen pushed and shoved their way along the Champs-Elysées to catch a glimpse of his Imperial Majesty. Sumptuous feasts, command performances at the Opéra and the Comédie-Française, military parades and unctuous speeches, crowds and more crowds — for two festive days Paris celebrated while high-ranking officials harvested the field that diplomacy had ploughed. So orthodox a republican as Radical Henri Brisson, president of the Chamber, said elatedly: "French democracy has testified that its institutions do not preclude a sense of coherence, a steadfastness, a unanimity of aim."[96] But Jaurès, obviously distressed by this popular outburst for an autocrat, worked to break the emotional spell, to recall the public to a sober truth — that in diplomacy the price of obscurity could well be aggression.[97]

Speaking for socialism, he now intervened often in the Chamber and with a command of detail on the half-hidden course of French diplomacy. Foreign Ministers are wont to prefer privacy, but democracy, thought Jaurès, feeds only on discussion. What good was foreign policy, or any policy, if it resulted not in the enhancement of life but in its destruction? Hanotaux, the ministry's voice on diplomatic questions, listened, a pointed goatee thrust forward, hands revolving in nervous rhythm, as Jaurès, in essence, put that question to him. The issue was the slaughter of the Armenians, 100,000 of them, and he sought to dissect the position of the European powers. About England's solicitude on behalf of the victims he had few illusions: "the insatiable need of capitalist expansion is constantly at work, and noble human emotions, as sincere as they may be, turn easily into protectorates."[98] Tsardom's game was even more reprehensible; for St. Petersburg planned nothing less, he charged, than to seize Armenia once the Sultan had exterminated the ones who might "inject the virus of independence into the Russian Empire." But France, cried Jaurès, what was the policy of revolutionary France, emancipator of all the oppressed? Hanotaux had spoken of the Armenians as trouble-makers, agitators. Jaurès, turning to the ministerial benches, called it a lie; "Before all the bloodshed, before horror and barbarism, before viola-tion of French honor and every human right, not a cry has come from your mouths, not a word has formed in your consciences; you have watched it all in silence, you accomplices of total extermination!" The moral polemic may have stung, but it did not sway the deputies. When Hanotaux described French aims as peace in Europe and maintenance of the Russian tie, the Chamber first and the press afterwards lent him wide support.

The policy-makers, in fact, were wary of the Turkish issue, so much so that Hanotaux warned Russian Foreign Minister Mouraviev in 1897 of French neutrality if war broke out in the Near East. But Faure, filling in an important detail, put it this way to the same Russian: "We would not even suggest that we could engage in a Near Eastern military action so long as Germany remains armed and ready. We will do it only if the question of Alsace-Lorraine is included."[99] Jaurès knew nothing of whispered caution in the diplomatic wings. When he rose again in March, 1897, to question the ministry's foreign policy, his accusations cut like blades. Where, he asked, were the decisive influences behind French diplomacy? "I am justified in saying that heavy financial interests have

208 | YEARS OF MILITANCY

weighed, and still weigh upon our conduct in Near Eastern questions."[100] Hanotaux exploded, protesting "with all my strength against such words." Méline called the accusation "odious." Jaurès continued, accustomed by now to bitter encounters with the ministry. The other great influence was Russia, determinedly pulling France into its eastern schemes. And why, why had the government accepted this subordination? Because Tsarist Russia was one with it, because it was Méline's ally against French democracy. As he uttered these charges, shouts of "censure" went up, while over the din the Premier asserted: "No one has ever spoken in such a manner!" But Jaurès was relentless. And from his store of historical knowledge he drew concluding words, the words of Benjamin Constant when he defended his right to attack the Villèle ministry: "Do you want us to add the silence of the Opposition to the silence of all the heads that adorn the walls of the Seraglio?"[101]

Do not despair, Jaurès exhorted impatient socialists and rebellious syndicalists. The age of Méline was but a moment in history. By its inherent contradictions, capitalism was destined to collapse; by their unified action, the working classes would shape the new society. Patience and courage — to these virtues he made his appeal, the patience to live through a period of transition, no matter how agonizingly long it seemed:[102] "The true role of socialists, of revolutionaries, is not to become isolated in social asceticism . . . and, like Flaubert's Saint Anthony looking at the sun rising on the desert horizon as 'the resplendent face of the Lord,' to gaze far off for the dazzling face of new man. Their role is to commit themselves to today's society and, through their action, to strengthen the elements which can transform it."[103]

More quickly than even Jaurès had expected, events in Mélinist France led to agony and disruption; shouts mingled with groans, and through the tumult one word assailed the ears — "Jew" — become, in the climate of the 1890's, opprobrious.

VI

In late April, 1895, Jaurès sailed to Algeria. Though he welcomed the trip as something of a holiday, he was actually off on a socialist mission.

Algeria was not a happy land. The Arab masses, deprived of their tribal status but denied French citizenship, had lost first their land and then their hope of freedom. The depression of the 1890's, caused in the first instance by the sharp drop in Algerian wine exports to France, crushed both the masses and the petty *colons*, forced then to turn to local money-lenders, often Jewish, for survival. Their misery choked their reason, and soon they blamed it all — the depression, the exploitation, the loss of land and freedom — on the Jews.

In such conditions Algerian socialism was born. Daniel Saurin, its first real leader, was like a mirror of the movement: a dedicated socialist; courageous enough, before any other Frenchman, to demand independence for Algeria; yet a confirmed anti-Semite. Twice the Algerian socialists had organized congresses, in Constantine and in Bône, to spread their propaganda. Neither had been a success, but they planned yet a third one, this time in Algiers, for April, 1895. They invited Jaurès (his prestige and advice could only help their cause), and he accepted.

Algeria was a revelation for him; in fact, it was a series of revelations. He found a privileged French community, *colons*, soldiers, administrators, living on the land and labor of the Arabs; an Algerian people deprived of their historic past and their national future; such misery that all the rhetoric about the French civilizing mission became a colossal lie. But he also found anti-Semitism, a turbulent anti-Jewish spirit which had infected both the Arabs and the French, a violent anti-Jewish campaign which threatened reason, justice, and life itself.

Jaurès was startled, shocked, but he was also educated. He had never been greatly concerned about anti-Semitism; like many socialists, he had even expressed views, especially during the Panama scandal, which were the stock-in-trade of the professional anti-Semites. But now, for the first time, he learned about the dangerous uses of anti-Semitism — how it divided the masses, how it protected the ruling classes, how it shielded colonialism from attack. It was an important lesson; for anti-Semitism, like a terrible virus, was seriously infecting France as well as Algeria.

In metropolitan France, the Jews were not numerous, and if discrimination requires large numbers of victims, there should have been little anti-Semitism. By 1880 there were perhaps eighty thousand Jews in the country, about half inhabiting Paris, the rest scattered among the Sephardic communities of Bordeaux, Nantes, and Toulouse. Over the last two decades of the century, France did experience an influx of larger proportions, derived from those Jews who had fled the pogroms of Russia. Raising the total to almost two hundred thousand, and representing a more distinctly foreign, Yiddish-speaking group, these newcomers provoked a greater sensitivity to the existence of a Jewish community. But, as later western experience has amply shown, the objective conditions of a minority's existence — numbers, wealth, morals — are less important in the growth of anti-Semitism than the subjective needs of the majority.

By 1886, when lingering economic depression and political instability were destroying the routine of French life, a polemicist, powerful of pen, set out to discover the cause of national decline. It was Édouard Drumont, sprung of old peasant stock in the Ardennes, who peered out through thick-lensed glasses and saw in the Jews the true enemies of

French welfare and virtue. His observations and deductions he published in two long volumes, *La France juive*, a sustained diatribe against Jewish financiers, especially the Rothschilds, and the "Jewish way of life," so corrosive to the homely virtues — family, faith, hard work — which he attributed to traditional France. Unswervingly devoted to the cause of anti-Jewish propaganda, Drumont found an increasingly large and diversified following for his one-track trip through history. When he founded his Anti-Semitic League in 1889, support came to him not only from the ambitious but frustrated Marquis de Morès, but also from the outcast proletariat of Paris, the slaughterhouse workers of La Villette.

By April, 1892, success had sufficiently crowned his efforts so that Drumont launched *La libre Parole*, a daily newspaper devoted to the single cause of anti-Semitism. It took a demonic ingenuity to uncover enough Jewish malevolence day after day to fill a newspaper. And, in fact, *La libre Parole* threatened to sag with dull hearsay when it was saved by a scandal. Panama made Drumont, just as he, in a certain sense, made Panama. In the corrupt activities of two Jews, the Baron de Reinach and Cornélius Herz, *La libre Parole* found the issue for denouncing Jewish influence while augmenting its own.

Jaurès was a son of the provinces, of the small-town life where Jews were not favorably talked about and not frequently seen. Nothing in his early milieu led him to special concern for their plight, and none appears in his early writings. But, by 1892, when organized anti-Semitism had imprisoned the reason of a growing number, Jaurès spoke out against it. Several influences had by then left their mark upon him. At the École Normale, where comradeship was close, Jaurès had counted a considerable number of Jews among his friends, young men, like himself, with excellent minds and wide intellectual interests. If Bergson was never his intimate, others, like Lévy-Bruhl, certainly were.[104] In addition to friendship, Jaurès experienced intellectual discovery which awakened in him a respect for all that was seminal in the history of western thought. Thus, the prophets of the Old Testament, the Jewish masters of philosophy and science shone as brightly as any others in his intellectual cosmos. For his socialist philosophy rested on the premise of human equality and harmony. By no mere accident did he quote, over and again, the lines from Michelet: "If all, even the humblest, do not enter Heaven, I will remain outside."

When he definitely entered the socialist movement, Jaurès fortified his understanding with the analyses and warnings of the Marxists. No one in all of France centered deadlier attacks on Drumont than Guesde. The chief of the P.O.F. took him on, along with Morès and Jules Guérin (soon to be head of the Anti-Semitic League), in a public debate at the

Salle des Mille-Colonnes on July 8, 1892. Divesting his movement at once of racist doctrines, Guesde went on to denounce Drumont's blaming of the Jews for the ills of society. "It is neither finance nor Jewry which is destroying the proletariat," he declared. "It is the bosses, . . . each one more Catholic than the next, who are responsible for the misery of the workers."[105]

But besides speaking out against anti-Semitism, the Marxists also offered a theory to explain its appeal and growth. It was the product of economic and social insecurity, they argued, the desperate groping of the petty bourgeoisie, threatened with extinction by big capitalism, to find the cause of their misery. Thus, they hit upon the Jew as a convenient, emotionally satisfying surrogate for the bitter truth — that capitalist concentration was sending them to their irrevocable doom. Though the economic determinism of the Marxists led them to simplify rather crudely the complex problem of anti-Semitism, they were nonetheless able to cast light on its appeal.

Such were the influences on Jaurès when he made his first extended public comments on the Jews: "I have no prejudice against the Jews; in fact, I favor them, since they have long been among my best friends. I don't like racial arguments, and I adhere to the idea of the French Revolution, however outmoded it may seem today, that there is only one race and it is mankind." Decisively he served notice on Drumont and his friends that he was not of their number. He went further, instructing his readers in Jewish accomplishment — the biblical tradition of social protest, the philosophical masterpieces of Maimonides or Spinoza, "in whom moral beauty and intellectual force become one."[106]

But what of Drumont's charges and the evidence against Jewish financiers that were the stock-in-trade of *La libre Parole*? Jaurès denied very little, repeating, in fact, some of the best-known examples of Jewish involvement in sordid financial enterprises.[107] The professional anti-Semites of the 1890's had said little he had not heard in the small towns of the Tarn or read in the charges of older French socialists, Fourier and Proudhon especially, and even contemporaries like Malon and Chirac.[108] But once having recognized Jewish participation in unsavory activity, he drew no anti-Semitic conclusions. The cause of corruption was gain, and the appetite for gain belonged not to the ethics of Jews, but to the morality of capitalism. "You only want to oust *Jewish* financiers from places of privilege," wrote Jaurès in answer to Drumont and Morès. "But once the Jews are eliminated, there will be Christians to take their place."[109]

Socialism, by abandoning the ethics of capitalism and guaranteeing the security of all, would, as Jaurès foresaw it, write the finish to anti-Semitism. It was a simple formula, but no more so than the one that had satisfied the Second International since its Congress of 1891. There were a few delegates to the Brussels meeting of that year who had urged a forceful campaign against the spread of racialism. But when Abraham Cahan, later the editor of the *Jewish Daily Forward* of New York, proposed a special resolution against anti-Semitism, the Belgian Jean Volders, expressing the majority viewpoint, opposed separate treatment for an issue that was only "an offshoot of the social question."[110]

After 1892 Jaurès fell silent on the question of anti-Semitism. Yet the climate of opinion was becoming perceptibly infected. What explains Jaurès' silence? The burden of work in Parliament and the press? The conviction, shared by most of his friends, that socialism would solve it all? These factors were undoubtedly present, but also, it may be assumed, there was a serious underestimation of the emotional impact of Drumont and others on an all-too-susceptible public.[111] When Jaurès traveled to Algeria, however, in the spring of 1895, he saw and heard enough to bring him back to the issue.

In Algeria the Jewish community had long been under attack, almost from the time the French government bestowed voting rights on it by the Crémieux decree of 1870.[112] The Arab masses, enjoying neither political prerogatives nor the slightest economic security, turned against the Jews, whom they most often encountered as merchants and money lenders.[113] French settlers encouraged the strong anti-Jewish feelings — especially the entrepreneurs, who disliked their Jewish competitors, and the Radicals, who resented Jewish support of Opportunist candidates.[114] Drumont had been quick to recognize Algeria as a fertile field for his doctrine, and the entire fourth section of *La France juive* was ominously entitled "Crémieux and the World Jewish Alliance."

By 1895 the depression, which should have revealed the weaknesses of Algeria's colonial economy, intensified the anti-Jewish movement instead. Jaurès listened to the local socialists, who blamed the great Arab chiefs, French officers and bureaucrats, and especially the Jews for the suffering of the masses. He did not contradict his hosts; exploitation by Jewish money-lenders, he agreed, was deplorable. But the "Jewish explanation" was too superficial and anti-Semitism, especially when it spread to the socialist movement, a dangerous deception. Colonialism, Jaurès insisted, was the cause of Algeria's misery, and the answer to it was equality for the Arabs, not extermination of the Jews. A few years later, in several brilliant articles for *La petite République* (July 1, December 29 and 31, 1898; May 25 and 30, 1899), he would raise a lone but revolutionary voice on behalf of full citizenship for the Arab masses. But even now, in 1895, he spoke out against French colonialism in Algeria and exposed the tactics of anti-Semitism. "They have lost their fine native schools," he wrote of the Arabs living under the enforced predominance of French culture. "They have lost the tradition of family-owned property which supported them in bad times and cared for them in old age. Their crafts, producing artistic and luxury goods, have been ruined by industrial imports. The Arab proletariat has been crushed — by expropriation, by unemployment, by miserable wages." But the French *colons*, working on the time-tested principle of divide-and-rule, had encouraged the Arabs to vent their hatred against Jews. "When they [the Arabs] see the French form anti-Jewish leagues, when they hear . . . shouts of 'Down with the Jews,' they believe that great changes are about to take place and they join the movement."[115] It was a cruel deception, charged Jaurès. To strip the Jews of voting rights, to legislate against their freedom would solve nothing. "When a socialist France frees the petty *colons* and the natives from debt, when it sponsors improvements on the land and in the ports, then will a new life emerge in Algeria."[116]

For Jaurès, the events in North Africa were a disturbing revelation. But he was now aware that behind a smokescreen of hate a whole system could flourish and prevail. In Algeria it was imperialism. And in France, where anti-Semitism was daily evident, might it not be antirepublicanism? "They were enthusiastically received in the clerical world," Caillaux wrote of the works of Drumont. "It was a milieu hostile to the laic laws, always ready to invent plots, easily persuaded that Jews, republicans for the most part, were fanning the anticlerical movement, trying to circumscribe the Catholics. The crowd of the envious and jealous who tightened their fists at the sight of prosperous Jewish enterprises marched in step with the editors."[117]

By the time Méline's reign began, the day of testing had arrived. For voices were being raised, sporadically at first, then in greater numbers, denying the guilt of Captain Dreyfus, the Jew who languished on Devil's Island for high treason. Converging as it did with the anti-Semitic movement, the case became a crisis.

VII

Marius Bernard, called Bernard Lazare, was a literary critic, author of a history of anti-Semitism, and one of the few Jews other than the unhappy victim to distinguish himself in the Dreyfus Affair. A philosophical anarchist, whose goodness of heart was to captivate Péguy, Lazare already suspected in the early months of 1895 that Alfred Dreyfus had been wrongly sentenced. In February of that year he so informed Mathieu, Dreyfus' brother, who from the start had believed in Alfred's innocence.

Mathieu proposed that Lazare write a brochure exposing the weakness of the case against his brother; he consented with the alacrity of a man who has found his mission.

By spring he had written, in simple, lucid style to avoid misunderstanding, *Une Erreur judiciaire, la vérité sur l'affaire Dreyfus*, calling into question the flimsy proofs against the accused and the failure to attribute to Dreyfus a valid motive for treason. Waiting for a propitious moment to publish the sensational document, Lazare and Mathieu agreed on the fall of 1896; by November 6, three thousand copies of the brochure had been printed in Brussels. After sending them out to members of the press and Parliament, Lazare insistently visited key personalities in the dim hope of enlisting open support for judicial review, or revision, as it was generally called.

He harvested little. The Catholic *rallié* De Mun refused to discuss the matter at all; the Radical Goblet wrote to Lazare that he had "neither qualification nor reason for intervening in this affair."[118] But his hopes must have been higher when he visited Jaurès, who never spoke more eloquently than when justice was at stake. They sat down together, Lazare with "bifocals set firmly across a large nose, barring and screening a pair of big, kind, shortsighted eyes, . . . his gaze lit by a flame fifty centuries old,"[119] and Jaurès, ruddy and buoyant. The socialist listened intently, disturbed perhaps by his memory of Lazare's hostile articles in *L'Écho de Paris* after the Congress of London. What Lazare said that day is unrecorded, though he probably reviewed the evidence and arguments of his pamphlet. It planted a seed in Jaurès' mind; he would study the documents further. But for the moment, he would not be diverted from his struggle with *mélinisme*, and he sent Lazare away. Jaurès still saw no connection between the case of Dreyfus and the forces of anti-Semitism, clericalism, and militarism. And like most of his fellow socialists, he had little innate sympathy for one who was both bourgeois and an officer.[120]

While Lazare and Mathieu made their weary rounds, the course of the Affair was changing in the War Office itself. In general, the upper military caste of France was antirepublican and clerical, aloof and professional, uncontaminated by the democratic ideas of the Third Republic. If Auguste Mercier, War Minister at the time of Dreyfus' conviction, was essentially apolitical, Charles de Boisdeffre, the Chief of Staff, was a devout Catholic, influenced by his Jesuit confessor, Père du Lac. In the important Statistical Section, the branch of the War Office devoted to counterespionage, the chief was Colonel Jean-Conrad Sandherr, an Alsatian convert to Catholicism from Protestantism and a rabid anti-Semite. On his staff was Major Joseph Henry, a peasant by origin, brave but essentially ignorant, who had risen through the ranks to arrive finally in the Statistical Section for which he had neither training nor competence. Among such men, dedicated to a powerful war machine against Germany, jealously guarding the prestige of the army, Dreyfus' conviction was an irrevocable *fait accompli*. The same should also have been true of Lieutenant-Colonel Marie-Georges Picquart, an Alsatian Catholic and anti-Semite who replaced Sandherr at the Statistical Section on July 2, 1895. But the human personality defies prediction, and Picquart, under orders from Boisdeffre to establish Dreyfus' guilt once and for all, arrived, through an unswerving integrity, at the opposite conclusion.

For Picquart discovered, first, that French documents were still being delivered to the enemy, and then, that another officer, Major Ferdinand Walsin-Esterhazy, had been dealing with the German Embassy.[121] A professional military officer with an unreasonable passion for women and gambling, Esterhazy was in constant quest of money and pleasure. He was one of those whom society can never restrain. "He might have been an elegant and treacherous gypsy," wrote the critic Julien Benda, who had seen him at Courbevoie in 1892 during his military service, "or better, a great wild beast, alert and master of itself."[122]

Picquart's investigations led him on until he had determined, by September, 1896, that Esterhazy had actually written the *bordereau*. When the startling realization had sunk in, that there was no substantial evidence against Dreyfus, he went to his superiors, first to the ineffectual Gonse, assistant Chief of Staff, and then to Boisdeffre. No one seemed interested, and the bewildered Picquart finally laid the evidence before old General Billot. But Méline's Minister of War likewise followed the path of least action. Gonse then turned on Picquart and vowed that the case would never be reopened. But the colonel, propelled by a conscience that could not acquiesce, cried out: "It's abominable, General. I will not carry this secret to my grave."[123]

The General Staff was plagued and worried. Henry, so simple-minded, so devoted a servant of the army, thought to tighten the noose around the Jew by fabricating new and incriminating documents. Billot, Boisdeffre, and Gonse, meanwhile, temporarily disposed of Picquart by transferring him first to Châlons-sur-Marne and then to southern Tunisia.

The case of Dreyfus, by 1897, still trickled in the narrowest tributaries of French life. Lazare's pamphlet was incomplete, Picquart's proofs unknown. Who could suspect (who would dare?) that the army, defender of the nation, was the corrupter of its honor? Even the majority of Jews "looked upon the beginning of the revisionist campaign with circumspection and suspicion."[124] "The Hebrew adopts the hostilities and the alliances of the land where he was born," wrote Froude in his life of

Disraeli; and it was true of French Jews that they avoided those situations which could cast suspicion on their patriotism.

A few men, it is true, supported Lazare and Mathieu, and they were the earliest Dreyfusards. Arthur Ranc, the old Communard who was now a Radical Senator, sensed foul play, and Joseph Reinach too, the Jewish follower of Gambetta. But by mid-1897 the tiny movement won the crucial support of Auguste Scheurer-Kestner, vice-president of the Senate. Scheurer had been a founding father of the Republic, and like most founding fathers, he lived on a pedestal of patriotic respect. Of his prestige and influence there was little question. One fateful July day in 1897 he met with Louis Leblois, a lawyer close to Picquart, and the colonel's discoveries, already revealed to Leblois, were passed on to him. With the information of both Lazare and Picquart, Scheurer-Kestner was convinced of Dreyfus' innocence; he reported his conclusions to Mathieu and also, discreetly but firmly, to his fellow Senators. As he had expected, his words made their way to Méline. It was the hope of men like Scheurer and Reinach, who shared with the Premier discipleship to Gambetta, that the government would itself undertake revision. They were moderates, these political men, not revolutionaries. But they were destined for disappointment. The old Méline first checked on the case with General Billot, and then, assured by his Minister of War that the proofs were conclusive, lapsed into immobility. In the War Office, meanwhile, General Gonse, his monacled assistant Major Du Paty de Clam, and the ubiquitous Major Henry worked overtime to forestall an Esterhazy ending to an otherwise satisfactory melodrama.

By November, 1897, the atmosphere had grown tense in Paris. News of Scheurer, Reinach, and their campaign spread about, galvanizing journalists of the Right into vigorous action. Those who now read the incendiary words of Drumont, Millevoye (*La Patrie*), Judet (*Le petit Journal*), or Arthur Meyer (*Le Gaulois*) were witness to a crusade. For the conviction of Dreyfus was the first article of faith in a program that insisted upon the supremacy of Church and army.

Louder voices and sharper pens now appeared in the camp of the Dreyfusards. Clemenceau, forcibly retired to private life in the wake of the Panama scandal, still craved the political limelight; for not even the close friendship of writers like the Goncourts or artists like Monet and Rodin could fully sustain so inveterate a politician. But as the defender of Dreyfus, Clemenceau once again commanded public attention. In October, 1897, he began to write regularly for a new and uncompromising Dreyfusard daily, *L'Aurore*.[125] His support of the cause was certainly unexpected. "They bore us with their Jew," he had said at the start of the revisionist campaign.[126] Why, then, should Clemenceau have changed so decisively? He had an eye for the main chance, and he seized it; so said his critics. He would break out of the political grave, to which even the Radicals had assigned him; he would climb back into public life, this time on the sagging shoulders of Dreyfus. That undoubtedly was a factor, as the human being on Devil's Island was not. But ambition alone cannot account for a campaign which exposed Clemenceau to danger and revealed him at his courageous best. Principle, certainly, was a motive, the principle of a free, individualistic, secular society. "What was the essence of the Dreyfus Affair?" he asked at Zola's trial in 1898. "The struggle of the French Revolutionary tradition against the blind authoritarianism of caste."[127] Personality too was a factor, the intractable personality of Clemenceau, who throve when he set himself squarely against the foibles of mankind. His faith in men may have been eroded in the muddy waters of Panama, but not his love of turbulence. Clemenceau, who loved innovation in art, relished iconoclasm in politics. He could take on the army and even the Church, and he chose to do so, an untamed Zarathustra delivering the barbarians. And once having chosen, he never wavered. He sat at a desk in the rue Franklin, turning out daily articles with biting sarcasm.

All the while the case began to dominate Jaurès' thoughts. Eight years before, when he had been making his way into socialism, Lucien Herr had placed erudition and renowned powers of persuasion at his disposal; again, in 1897, the librarian of the École Normale intervened crucially to persuade Jaurès of the innocence of Dreyfus. By the summer of that year Herr had already studied the case with Lazare and learned, through Lévy-Bruhl, a relative of the Dreyfus family, of Picquart's discoveries. That September he was spending considerable time in the countryside near Paris with Léon Blum, now a talented young critic, once, in 1890, a student at the École Normale. "Lucien Herr, astride his bicycle, came to see me almost every day," Blum later recorded. "One day he said, point-blank: 'Do you know that Dreyfus is innocent?' "[128] Herr was a convinced man, and he never veered from his conviction.

In the autumn he contacted his friend Jaurès. Two *philosophes*, who swept up history in their capacious minds, they spoke a common language, served a common goal. Herr was, if anything, persuasive. He didn't harangue but he guided. He spoke now of the key documents, he dissected the case against Dreyfus; he suggested the revolutionary implications of a campaign for justice. When they parted, Jaurès reviewed matters in his own mind. He was influenced by Herr, as he had been by Scheurer and Lévy-Bruhl. But he was more than an individual; he was the outstanding leader of a growing socialist movement, and he couldn't afford mistakes. "The parliamentary socialists listen to no one but Jaurès," the socialist Delacour had blurted out with an edge of sarcasm. "All the others bow down before him. Jaurès is the Pope."[129] He would study and watch; but he would wait before he moved.

By November 15, 1897, Mathieu, convinced that his evidence warranted strong public action, sent a letter to the Minister of War, openly naming Esterhazy as the author of the *bordereau*. However reluctantly, the War Office was now forced to conduct an inquiry into the charges, a responsibility handed over to Brigadier-General Gabriel de Pellieux. For the Dreyfusards the investigation at first backfired. In two enquiries, Pellieux interrogated all the principals — Mathieu, Scheurer, Leblois, Picquart, Henry, and Esterhazy. He concluded that while there was no case against his bohemian fellow officer, Picquart had been guilty of a serious breach of discipline in revealing information to the outsider Leblois. In its complex strategy, however, the War Office decided on an Esterhazy court-martial. Hoping once and for all to quash the revisionist campaign, the military chiefs, looking ahead to an acquittal, thought to lay at rest the suspicions against Esterhazy. In their fear of exposure — of error, crime, deception, or prejudice — the implicated officers had abandoned caution. On December 4, General Gaston Saussier, Military Governor of Paris, ordered the court-marital of a confident Esterhazy.

The case shook Méline's aplomb; his solid conservative coalition had, for almost twenty months, fenced in all serious political disruptions; but the noise over Dreyfus had grown disconcertingly loud. And while he continued to treat the affair as a purely judicial concern, it had already spilled over into politics. The anti-Semitic and Rightist press, in denouncing the Dreyfusards, were condemning the Republic. The republican groups, Progressist, Radical, socialist, still feeling out their ground, sensed that the case would overflow the courtroom.

Jaurès, deliberate and determined, groped toward a public position. In the closing days of November, he raised questions about the conduct of the case rather than its verdict. Documents which bore heavily on the original conviction had been unavailable to the accused and his lawyer;[130] Picquart, who had discovered irregularities, had been sent off to Tunisia; the Minister of War, confronted with substantial suspicions, had remained silent. Why, demanded Jaurès, why had there been no answers from the proper authorities? Now he took a step, a decisive one, down the long road which led finally to the full battle against anti-Semitism and militarism. The central issue, he wrote, was whether, through exaggerated patriotism or hostility to a Jew, "military judges can strike a man down without legal guarantees."[131]

On December 4, the Chamber session was devoted in large part to the fast-growing Affair. The deputies of the Right, agitated by news of

Esterhazy's court-martial, demanded assurances from Méline that the Army would not be sacrificed to benefit a traitorous Jew. The Premier, his politician's ingenuity never sharper, placated the critics. The Esterhazy case, he argued, had nothing to do with the guilt of Dreyfus; the two events were separate; neither was political; both were judicial. "There is," he cried with finality, "no Dreyfus case."[132]

A firm declaration it was, yet insufficient for the Comte Albert de Mun. Once a cavalry officer, then a partisan of Catholic social action, de Mun emerged as the authentic voice of Catholicism in the Chamber, unqualified in his hostility to the principles of '89, forthright in his advocacy of Church and army. Denouncing a covert plot to subvert the officers' corps, he demanded that Billot confirm, unequivocally, Dreyfus' guilt; the Minister of War, satisfying all but a troubled minority, readily complied. Then it was the turn of Millerand, the one socialist to speak that day. But how and for what? Draping the patriotic mantle around his ample shoulders, Millerand denounced the leaders of revisionism and rapped the ministry for its delinquency in answering their troublesome accusations. The session ended, not surprisingly, in the adoption of Nationalist Marcel Habert's motion, which upheld both army and ministry while heaping scorn on the "odious campaign" of the Dreyfusards. When the vote was taken, Guesde, Vaillant, and Jaurès abstained.

Jaurès, his mind moving back and forth over the issues, his keen, nervous eyes roving among his colleagues, sat silent that day. But four days later, he put Méline's words to the test of logic. It was absurd, wrote Jaurès, to deny the connection between the two cases; for if Esterhazy wrote the *bordereau*, then Dreyfus did not.[133] A second step: convinced of legal impropriety, he now suggested ministerial complicity.

As a group, however, the parliamentary socialists remained neutral, equally hostile to the two opposing parties, both of them presumably organized — Jewish capital on the one hand and clerical, military reaction on the other. Publicly, Jaurès refused to break from the group; but he revealed his true feelings when he exhorted his party to do battle for justice. "For when the arbitrary power of the judge increases, the welfare of mankind declines."[134]

The Affair now consumed Jaurès. Several times he saw Leblois, who guided him through the intricacies of the testimony.[135] He spoke with Scheurer-Kestner, and was moved by his sense of dedication. "Whatever strength and life I have left," the old Gambettist avowed, "I put to the service of oppressed innocence."[136] But as the weeks passed, Jaurès still waited.

It is Péguy who has best unraveled his mood. As *normalien*, Péguy learned socialism at the desk of Lucien Herr. But as a child of workers and a son of Orléans, he had felt it, long before, in the marrow of his bones. "Perhaps he never learned anything," Andler once wrote of Péguy. "He knew by instinct."[137] To his friends, he was almost a saint, this "small, square-shouldered man, closely buttoned into his skimpy jacket, with huge hobnailed boots on his feet—two keen, bright eyes in his open peasant's face."[138] His essentially religious goal he called socialism, a dedication to man's internal development, full, free, integral. It led him to Jaurès.

At Sainte-Barbe the portraits of Ignatius of Loyola and Calvin looked down upon Péguy, but the spirit of Jaurès guided him. From the École Normale, in the 1890's, he marveled at the deputy from the Tarn. "Péguy assigned him the mission of representing in daily politics all those ideals which were discussed at the desk of Lucien Herr. . . . Jaurès would be virtue in socialism, courage, strength, generosity."[139] Péguy had but one standard for judging him—moral perfection. And if Jaurès proved to be a man and not a god; if he belonged to the masses and not to Péguy; if he was a political reality and not a schoolboy's ideal, what broken illusions might not lie around Péguy's impossible image?

The Affair gripped the *orléanais*. The flame of Jeanne d'Arc, kindled by the defence of justice, would revitalize French life. Péguy went with his friend Jérôme Tharaud, one day early in 1898, to see Jaurès, hopeful that the *tarnais* would lead the Dreyfusards. They found him in his crowded study, poring over documents of the case—a facsimile of the *bordereau*, the handwriting of Dreyfus, the handwriting of Esterhazy. "He was worn out, hoarse, troubled, sad." About to go to the Chamber, Jaurès invited the two *universitaires* to accompany him. As they walked, they talked, mainly of the Affair. The young enthusiasts urged Jaurès, regardless of the views of others, to enter wholeheartedly into the case. And Jaurès blurted out: "You can hardly imagine how tormented I am! What I do in the Chamber and what you know about from the papers is nothing compared with the kind of work I am forced to do in private socialist meetings. Our enemies are nothing. But our friends! You can't know how battered I am. They devour me because they are all afraid of not being elected. They pull at the back of my coat to keep me from going to the tribune; I am already drained, a hollow shell, exhausted by these internal ravages, worn out in advance."[140]

In the spring of 1898 there would be elections, and for those who made success at any price the objective, entanglement in the Affair was a threat. Jaurès would have expected faintheartedness from the Radicals, and in that he was not disappointed. Goblet, Mesureur, Bérard, Lockroy, men of the republican Left, shied away from participation. Bourgeois found safety in magisterial silence. Pelletan wrote that "the crime of Dreyfus appears less and less doubtful."[141] But among the socialists also there were moderates, led by Millerand and Viviani, who would set principles aside, at least until the votes had been counted. There were others who could hardly believe that the Jew might be innocent. "In the elections of 1893," Jaurès later explained, "anti-Semitic and Rochefortist elements infiltrated socialism."[142] Now he faced the cruel alternative of holding to a party unity he so much desired or sustaining without full support the ideal of justice.

But Guesde and Vaillant were socialists of a different stripe. Their course of action, wherever it led them, had as its objective the success of socialism. When the socialist deputies gathered to discuss their strategy in the Affair, the moderates urged abstention: "It's a dangerous question and we shouldn't intervene," declared Millerand, Viviani, Jourde, and Lavy. But Guesde and Vaillant, sensing the growing danger of militarism and nationalism, retorted: "No, we must give battle."[143] What they said was tonic to Jaurès.

The court-martial of Esterhazy took place behind tightly closed doors on January 10, 1898. The verdict of acquittal, a foregone conclusion and announced the next day, was greeted among the military spectators with triumphant cries of "Long live the army! Down with the Syndicate!" But the War Office was not yet satisfied. Picquart, whose unbreakable convictions had led him to disclose military information, was highly vulnerable. On January 13, he was charged with breach of discipline, and by order of Billot placed under arrest in the fortress prison of Mont-Valérien.

It was a moment of deep frustration for the Dreyfusards. "We were motionless and crushed," Léon Blum later recalled.[144] But the case now took clear shape in Jaurès' mind. He had not declared publicly that he believed Dreyfus innocent; nor can one prove from the available documents that he had said so privately. But he was convinced, it is certain, that the trial had been a travesty and that the antirepublican Right, which had apparently died in the *ralliement*, had again come to life. The old legions of monarchism and Boulangism drew close together, rallying to the single standard of ultranationalism. Their foyers of influence were Church and army, their Pretorian guard the patriotic and anti-Semitic leagues; their program was militarist, clerical, and antiparliamentary, their appeal violent and irrational.[145] Jaurès had already noted in Algeria the emotional power of anti-Semitism and the kind of goods it concealed. In France, he felt, it was even more dangerous; for under the guise of upholding nation and faith against Jews and antipatriots, the Republic itself and its democratic process were endangered. But that was not the worst of it; the government of Méline, as Jaurès had long felt, inclined toward the Right, moved by its conservatism to defend army and Church.[146]

For socialists, thought Jaurès, it was a time of decision. They had to defend the Republic, which was their field of action; they had to fight for justice, which was their central ideal. Socialism, he felt certain, would emerge in the economy through the very progress of capitalism; but it would burn in the hearts of mankind only when men fought, out of love and brotherhood, for the victims of injustice.

The future of the movement could well hinge on the growing conviction of Jaurès. If the bourgeois parties failed in republican defense, might not the socialists, courageous and united, take the lead? If Jaurès' moral fervor cauterized the corruption of public life, might not adherents, especially from the world of the university, flock to socialism? "The everlasting honor of Jaurès," wrote Andler years later, "will be . . . to have understood that justice, to be revolutionary, must be integral. . . . It was necessary to ensure the socialist future, the future of Marxism itself, by a doctrine eloquently human."[147]

VIII

Émile Zola exploded a bombshell on January 13. Enraged by the acquittal of Esterhazy, France's most renowned novelist made history with a long open letter to President Faure. On January 12 he took the document to the officers of *L'Aurore*, where it was labeled *J'accuse!* and printed the next morning. If Zola longed to be the Hugo of a later age, he succeeded overnight. His letter was an attack on the chief members of the War Office, well documented, dramatic, and unsparing. In essence, the generals were accused of violating Dreyfus' rights and hiding Esterhazy's guilt. It was an act of conscience that ended in defiance: "Let them dare to take me to the Court of Assizes and let the examination take place in the light of day. I am waiting!" Within a day almost 300,000 copies of *L'Aurore* had been sold, and Zola, to some a hero and to others a traitor, shook the national conscience.

The parliamentary Right, led by De Mun, served notice of its intention to interpellate the ministry on its reaction to the letter. The socialist deputies caucused on January 13 in preparation for the session of the fourteenth. If, as was expected, the Right demanded legal action against Zola, how should the socialists react? Their meeting was a stormy one. Zola was a bourgeois, argued the moderates, and socialists had no business at his side. Guesde was revolted by what seemed to him rank opportunism. "Rising, as if suffocated by the language of the moderates, he walked to the window of the meeting room, threw it open, and cried: 'Zola's letter is the greatest revolutionary act of the century.'"[148] Unanimity was hardly the order of the day, but Jaurès, encouraged by Guesde and Vaillant, decided to act.

The following day, De Mun demanded assurances from both Méline and Billot that the army would be avenged. Republican chiefs — Barthou, Poincaré, Dupuy, Hanotaux — not one of them spoke. The Radical opposition was likewise silent, until Cavaignac rose as defender of the army. Both Méline and Billot, when they responded to the Right, gave satisfaction, and the Premier promised that charges would be brought against Zola. Jaurès could no longer contain himself. In an atmosphere uncongenial to serious criticism he rose to denounce the pretensions of the Right and the complicity of the ministry. Why, he asked, had Méline spoken of the case only when the Right demanded it? Why had he threatened the free speech of Zola and not the power of the generals? Under the guise of patriotism, cried Jaurès, the Republic was being delivered to its ancient enemies. But his words were coldly received, and even on the Extreme Left, he drew only scattered applause. Méline won his vote of confidence that day, but in a confused, rather frightened Assembly more than a hundred deputies abstained.

On the morrow of Zola's letter, Jaurès' fears seemed amply justified. A wave of anti-Semitism swept through the major cities of France, and for defense of the fatherland, assorted anti-Semites, nationalists, and monarchists unleashed their attacks on Jews and other Dreyfusards. The rioting hit hardest in Algeria, where traditional anti-Semitism converged with Antidreyfusard agitation. For four days, from January 18 on, a pogrom engulfed Algiers, spreading out finally into Oran and Constantine.

But while *J'accuse!* provoked violence, it also generated republican defense. Men long sheltered in the world of letters and learning took heart from Zola's example and plunged into the rough waters of politics. When a petition was circulated in favor of revision, it included among its three thousand signers some of the most renowned French intellectuals and artists — Anatole France, Reclus, Monet, Proust, the Halévy brothers. A new political consciousness was forming in the corps of the learned, among writers and teachers especially, and Jaurès' idealism, once fully released, was destined to draw many of them beyond the Affair and into socialism. Marxists and syndicalists scorned these intellectuals. But Jaurès, who was one of them, would defend, encourage, and, what is most important, lead them. All of which would strongly affect the composition of the socialist movement and the ideology of the teaching corps.[149]

On January 19 the parliamentary socialists published a manifesto on the mounting crisis, which failed, even at this late hour, to grasp either its present gravity or future potentiality. Bearing the signatures of all the socialist deputies, including Jaurès, it described the Affair as a power struggle between rival factions of the ruling class. By exploiting the guilt of Dreyfus, clericals hoped to discredit all Jews, Protestants, and free-thinkers in public office; and by proclaiming his innocence, Jewish capitalists, supported by their Opportunist allies, sought to rehabilitate themselves after their disgraceful involvement in financial scandals. In words tinged almost as much with anti-Semitism as with anticlerical-ism, the manifesto called down a plague on both factions and warned the workers against involvement with either.

Was there then no socialist stake in the crisis? "The proletariat," ad-mitted the deputies, "cannot remain insensitive to injustice, even when it affects a member of the enemy class."[150] The workers had to carry on a continuous and simultaneous struggle against clericals, army chiefs, professional anti-Semites, and capitalists (both Jewish and Christian), whose power and pretensions daily subverted the reign of justice. But that participation could never mean class collaboration; for if socialist workers lined up with bourgeois Dreyfusards they would lose sight of both the class struggle and the goal of socialism. "Between Reinach and De Mun," warned the manifesto, "keep your complete freedom."

The socialist deputies thus continued to proclaim a neutrality which, in the face of the grave crisis, must have discouraged Jaurès. Why, then, did he support and sign such a manifesto? No doubt he realized that any more positive stand would have destroyed the unity of the socialist deputies who, for a variety of reasons, were reluctant to be drawn into the Affair. But he also recognized that in exhorting the workers to struggle for justice, the manifesto could stand as a call to action. By twisting the real meaning of the socialist proclamation, Jaurès found his mandate for participation.

On Saturday, January 22, the Affair again consumed the Chamber. Cavaignac, a Radical steeped in militarism, announced an interpellation of Méline, and anticipation ran high in Paris. The spectator seats were filled to capacity for the session; among the onlookers was Gabriele d'Annunzio who thrilled to scenes of strife. Cavaignac opened the de-bate, demanding of the Premier the definite proofs against Dreyfus that would destroy the revisionist campaign. Méline's response was a classic of evasion. Proofs existed, he assured them, but he produced no documents. Rather he turned, a thin-lipped old man, and attacked the Dreyfusards: Zola, who "has used his pen to besmirch the army chiefs," and the socialists, Jaurès especially, who "are preparing us for a new edition of *La Débacle*."[151] The Premier was wildly applauded; the Rightists demonstrated as though their day had dawned; and Cavaignac came forth to praise Méline's words and withdraw his interpellation.

Jaurès was no longer to be restrained by the hatred of his enemies, the caution of his friends, or the decorum of the Parliament. It was an Isaiah who mounted the tribune, flushed with anger, propelled by moral indignation. Méline had spoken of *La Débacle*, and Jaurès thundered: "The downfall came once from the court generals, shielded by the Empire; it is coming again from the Jesuit generals, shielded by the Republic." Bedlam followed, and the orator was sharply reprimanded by Brisson, the presiding officer. But Jaurès roared on, accusing Méline of courting antirepublicans and nationalistic fanatics: "The cry of 'Death to the Jews' has howled through the streets, and those responsible are your supporters!" The Republic, the democratic way of life, was dying. "Since this Affair began, we have been dying of lies, equivocations and cowardice." Tumult filled the hall as Jaurès, turning first to the ministerial benches and then to the Right, cried out: "The charges against Zola are based on nothing but lies and cowardice!" Brisson again called him to order. Then, as Jaurès resumed, a voice crackled through the din, the voice of the deputy from Nîmes, the Comte de Bernis, monarchist and distant relative of the Marquis de Solages. "You are part of the Syndicate," accused Bernis, referring to the alleged plot of Jewish bankers and Dreyfusards. Jaurès stopped short: "What did you say, M. de Bernis?" "I said that you must be part of the Syndicate, that you are probably the mouthpiece of the Syndicate." "M. de Bernis," cried Jaurès, almost beside himself, "you are a miserable coward."

The Assembly broke up in near-riot. Bernis rushed toward the podium seeking vengeance. Eluding the grasp of Gérault-Richard, he found Jaurès and twice struck him on the back. Reason and honor had both vanished. Deputies shouted and flailed their arms on the floor of the Chamber; in the gallery, d'Annunzio looked on, exhilarated. Brisson, who had been desperately ringing the presidential bell, finally dismissed the Assembly. But the melée continued out into the halls, where an irate socialist threw an inkwell at Bernis' head.

Like the debris-ridden calm after a storm, the Chamber was glumly quiet the next day when Jaurès resumed. He put a direct question to Méline, asking him to answer "yes or no." Had the defense been denied access to decisive evidence in the Dreyfus court-martial? Méline, however, doggedly refused to comment. "He mimics a deaf-mute," Clemenceau wrote in *L'Aurore* on January 26. But by the end of the debate, when the vote of confidence was recorded, Méline won handily, 360 to 126. Reinach watched his colleagues, even those who were aware that a terrible injustice had befallen Dreyfus, fall silent. Dupuy was one, Barthou another. "Several who should have spoken, or better yet, acted, Loubet, Fallières, Béranger, Waldeck-Rousseau, Magnin, took refuge in the famous excuse of Sieyès: 'What good my glass of wine in this flood of gin?'" And why this general abdication? Even an old Opportunist like Reinach sensed the reason: "They voted with Méline to vote against Jaurès."[152]

The *tarnais* was very much alone those days. He hoped he stood for his party and the people. In that, he was undoubtedly too optimistic. The socialists were then divided, and would long remain so. As for the people, only a minority ever plunged wholeheartedly into the Affair, whether on one side or the other. The bourgeoisie were too easily diverted; for France was arriving in the twentieth century, on bicycles (409,000 in 1897) and even in automobiles (1200 in that same year). As for the masses, deprived of expensive pleasures, they were, too many among them, debased by alcohol or attracted to demagogues. "What will we socialists do," asked a perplexed Jules Guesde, "with a humanity so degraded? We will come too late; the human materials will be rotten when the time arrives to build our house." But Jaurès had faith that when people knew the truth they could act upon it. He continued, then, to talk and to battle. This commended him to Guesde. "Jaurès," said the old Marxist, "I love you, because with you the act always follows the word."[153]

Zola's trial opened on the seventh of February. The Minister of Justice had drawn the charge against the novelist very cleverly, limiting it to but one of his accusations — that the judges at Esterhazy's court-martial had, under orders from above, acquitted a man they knew to be guilty. Thus, the defense lawyers were prevented from dealing with Dreyfus' conviction, for which they could produce evidence, while forced to defend a charge that was ultimately a surmise. As the trial moved along, Delegorgue, the corpulent judge, consistently disallowed both evidence and witnesses that he presumed irrelevant to Esterhazy's court-martial. But the leading generals testified, whitewashing their activities and heaping criticism mainly on Picquart. On the fifth day, February 12, the defense called friends of Zola to testify as to his stature and integrity. Jaurès was the most important among them, and he used his appearance to warn, once again, of the military threat to the Republic.

He awaited the hour of his testimony in the Salle des Pas-Perdus of the Ministry of Justice, reciting for his companion, Anatole France, some of the loveliest verses of minor seventeenth-century poets. In his testimony Jaurès went directly to the procedure of the Esterhazy trial, questioning the closed-door hearings, the bad treatment of Picquart, and the absence of a serious inquiry. "It thus appears . . . that the trial was conducted, not to reach the truth and justice, but to exonerate the great military chiefs."[154] The violation of justice, Jaurès claimed, was no secret among the deputies; yet they had been paralyzed into inaction by their opportunism or their prejudice. "Endless numbers of deputies, of all groups and parties, have said to me: 'You're right, but what a shame that this Affair should have broken just a few months before the elections.'" It was not Parliament but a mighty pen that revealed the truth. In prosecuting Zola, the ministry, the army, and the Church were wreaking vengeance on a man who had too long defended the downtrodden and exposed their oppressors. "They prosecute in him the man who defended the rational and scientific interpretation of miracles; they prosecute in him the man who, in *Germinal*, announced the drive of an impoverished proletariat, rising from the depths of suffering and ascending toward the sun." "They can prosecute him," he concluded, "they can hunt him down, but I think I speak for all free citizens in saying that we bow down before him in deference." In the courtroom, despite the presence of ultranationalists, his eloquence had a moving effect. In the country, socialists, even in the P.O.F. federations, found leadership and guidance.[155]

But none of it helped Zola. Despite the evidence that had slipped through, especially in the testimony of Picquart, demonstrating Dreyfus' innocence, the verdict of guilty was returned. The Court imposed the maximum sentence under Article 31 of the 1881 Press Law, fining Zola three thousand francs and ordering him to prison for a year.[156] The toughs of the anti-Semitic and patriotic organizations received the verdict with shouts of "Long live the army! Death to the traitors!" In Paris, Jewish stores and synagogues were pillaged. In Algeria, under the leadership of Drumont and Max Régis, soon to be elected mayor of Algiers, anti-Semitic rioting increased.

The Chamber of Deputies debated the situation in Algeria on February 19, and again Jaurès came forward. The Radical deputy from Algiers, Paul Samary, defending the outburst of anti-Semitism, read to the Chamber a list of provocative Jewish malpractices. To solve the problem, he concluded, France had first to abrogate the rights of citizenship for Algerian Jews. Jaurès would have none of it; he knew too much now of the uses and abuses of anti-Semitism. It was imperialism that he arraigned that day and not the Jews. At the climax, he turned to his fellow socialists and called them to their human mission: "Our duty as socialists, is not to preach reactionary and deadly hatred against the

Jews; no, it is to call attention to the suffering and exploited among the Jews, who, standing at the side of oppressed Arabs, should form, with the European proletariat, a party of all those who toil and suffer."[157]

IX

As spring approached in 1898, the Méline ministry let its opportunity slip by. Though well enough supplied with evidence to carry through revision, the government made no such move. Hopeful that the Affair would blow over, fearful that revision would rouse too many passions, concerned that the conservative Republic should survive, Méline pursued a meaningless policy until April 7, when the deputies went home to prepare for the May elections.

Arrived back in the Tarn to campaign, Jaurès found formidable barriers already raised against him. The employers of Carmaux, planning since 1896 to ensure his defeat, disposed of limitless resources. "The campaign which they're waging against Jaurès," wrote Lafargue to Guesde, a year before the elections, "is merciless; they will keep him from making a single speech in the district."[158] Primarily, the capitalists had money, and during the campaign of 1898 the Marquis expended 19,858 francs, a staggering amount compared to the resources of Jaurès.[159] Solages was able to flood the constituency with propaganda, and to make those donations to organizations and individuals which guaranteed votes. But the power of money was most evident in the mines and factories themselves, where the employers could (and did) put pressure on their insecure workers. "When a candidate for office is the chief capitalist of a district," wrote Jaurès, "when he alone is responsible for the work and the very life of thousands of families, when he can control the employed by threat of dismissal and inveigle the unemployed by the promise of jobs, then this economic power, in the hands of only one candidate, is particularly dreadful."[160]

In its electoral propaganda, the Solages group appealed, especially in the rural villages, to the fears of anticlericalism. Jaurès, it was charged, was an enemy of religion, an agent of Freemasons and Jews. When the *tarnais* walked through the hills and across the valleys to talk with his people, he found that some among them had been swayed. He stopped at Saint-Christophe to pass the time with an old peasant who asked him: "You're the one who wants to throw down the churches, aren't you?" And Jaurès replied in *patois*: "And what, my friend, would I do with so many stones?"

The tactics of the Solages forces fell beneath any standards of decency. The Antisocialist League, founded in 1896, had been renamed the "Cercle républicain progressiste"; but it remained what it always had been, an organization to break up the meetings of socialists and to intimidate their supporters. The case of Dreyfus was used against Jaurès, but even if the Affair had been no issue at all, he would have faced, as a socialist and a militant, the organized power of the employers.

His own resources, all equally important, were mind, heart, voice, and feet. He climbed through the countryside, appeared in mountain villages, like Larivière, where they had never seen a deputy, spoke in the local dialect, ate heartily of the local food. "He talked to the people wherever he could, in barns, in stables, standing atop the husks or on a barrel; even cow manure didn't bother him. One day a rooster began to crow just as he started to speak. An old woman cackled: 'You hear? Even the chicken tells you to be quiet.' 'It is doing the work of a chicken! Now let me do mine.'"[161]

The only chance for Jaurès rested with the *carmausins*. If he could win a thumping majority in Carmaux, he might overcome expected losses in the villages. The well-directed employers' group thus spread the charge that Jaurès was responsible for the city's economic depression. The Verrerie ouvrière, on which so many *carmausins* had pinned high hopes, was going badly in the face of sustained competition from Rességuier's factory. Jaurès stood accused in the opposition propaganda of forcing a futile economic enterprise on the glass workers, and the *carmausins* read posters — "Jaurès, Misère!" "Jaurès — L'Affameur."

On a national scale the campaign of 1898 brought forth a realignment of groups. Since the *ralliement* and the "new spirit," the Progressists and the Right had coalesced in common opposition to candidates of the Left. Now a revivified Right, drawn from several traditions, came into the open as an antirepublican party. Anti-Semites around Drumont, Boulangist patriots like Dèroulède, old monarchists behind the Duc d'Orléans, and ultra-Catholics represented by the Assumptionist organ *La Croix* united to support men of their own.[162] Méline and his Progressists, led by the shrewd Barthou, sought to build a conservative republican party around the Premier's formula: "Neither reaction nor revolution." Radicals and socialists, divided by an Affair they had wanted to ignore, were unable to present a common front against the Progressists. "Pelletan blames me," Jaurès later wrote, "for having played into Méline's hands by stirring up a matter which divided the republican party. . . . But what merit would there have been in beating Méline if we became, in the process, the slaves of clerical mendacity and military arrogance?"[163]

The first ballot was cast on May 8, and Jaurès awaited the results with his *carmausin* comrades at the Café Filaquières. A messenger on bicycle carried in the figures from distant villages, and by 1 A.M. the stunning result had become clear. Jaurès was beaten by Solages; his 5515 votes could not match the 6702 for the Marquis. At 9:50 the next morning Jaurès wired his friends in Paris: "I have been beaten by a large majority. Under pressure of the employers, the region has yielded. Long live the Social Republic!"[164]

Guesde, facing similar pressure from the capitalists of the Nord, went down to defeat in Roubaix.[165] Goblet of the Radicals was likewise defeated, while Drumont and three supporters, running as anti-Semites, won four of the six seats from Algeria. But the worst of all for the socialists was the loss of Jaurès. Between the first ballot and the second, on May 22, the Left mapped its strategy, and the socialists proposed a plan to salvage victory for the *tarnais*. He would become *parisien*. Charles Gras would withdraw in the second district of the fifth Paris arrondissement, and Jaurès would run for that fairly safe seat. Though appreciative of the offer, Jaurès demurred: "To recover my health, weakened by five years of endless activity, and to look after that of my family, I must have time to relax." Moreover, this was his chance to study again, "to live once more in the quiet world of ideas, to touch the farthest horizons of thought and enlightenment." And, finally, he could never desert the Tarn. "I will never quit Carmaux unless Carmaux discards me."[166]

By the time the final election results were tabulated, the political picture was vague and unclear. The socialists had recovered sufficiently to return forty-two deputies; the Radicals (and Radical-Socialists) elected 170; the Progressists were still dominant with 250 deputies, including a young newcomer, Joseph Caillaux; and the Right held on to its former position. The republicans were still very much in control of Parliament, and the future hinged on the tendency, whether toward the Right or the Radicals, of the Progressists.

The new Chamber assembled on June 1 amid shouts by the Drumont faction of "Down with the Jews!" Two weeks of instability followed, as Radicals and socialists, avoiding the issue of Dreyfus, attacked Méline's sympathy for the Right. On June 14, after two hectic years of power, the Premier suffered an unfavorable vote and submitted his resignation to an unhappy Félix Faure. Two more weeks of political crisis came finally to an end when the Radical Brisson ascended to the Premier's office, and, more fatefully, the Antidreyfusard Cavaignac took over the War Office.

Jaurès was no longer in the Chamber. But he was back in Paris and deeply involved in the unresolved Affair. It disquieted some of the socialists. "One evening," Léon Blum recounted, "Jaurès stopped by my place after leaving the Chamber, where he occasionally sat in the Gallery of Former Deputies. He told me that some socialist deputies had accompanied him as he walked toward the Champs-Élysées. One of them, almost furious, said: "Well, Jaurès, are you going to keep up your campaign? Don't you see that you're threatening all of us, that our voters will associate us with your position? . . . Jaurès had answered: 'Your voters will soon know the truth; what they will blame you for then are your laxity and cowardice; then you'll beg me to go to them with excuses on your behalf.' And Jaurès added, smiling broadly: 'I know myself too well; I will go.'"[167]

Behind him lay the action and thought of a militant, before him a memorable campaign for justice. All that, and Jaurès was not yet thirty-nine.

PART III

Years
of Anguish
1898-1906

Par la faute de la société qui s'obstine contre lui à la violence, au mensonge, et au crime, Dreyfus devient un élément de révolution.

1898

Mais d'abord,, mais avant tout, il faut rompre le cercle de fer, le cercle de haine où les revendications même justes provoquent des représailles qui se flattent de l'être, où la guerre tourne après la guerre en un mouvement sans issue et sans fin, où le droit et la violence, sous la même livrée sanglante, ne se discernent presque plus l'un de l'autre, et où l'humanité déchirée pleure de la victoire de la justice presque autant que sa défaite.

1903

10

Defense of
the Republic, 1898-1902

I

At sixty-eight, Henri de Rochefort was master of the vitriolic word. When he described the bovine Charles Dupuy as "a cow gazing at a passing train," he was demonstrating his power of congealed malice. A handsome man, a shock of white hair crowning a thin, tense face, Rochefort looked half-aesthetic, half-fanatic. For almost twenty years, as a tireless polemicist in *L'Intransigeant*, he had heaped scorn on what he considered a corrupt and mediocre Republic. At the beginning of the Affair, he had not been notably Antidreyfusard; young Léon Blum believed, in fact, that this old battler against the Second Empire, himself victimized by a military court in 1871, would find a place of importance in the campaign against the army and the Church.

But it was not to be, and Rochefort turned instead into an increasingly bitter pamphleteer against the Dreyfusards. This development puzzled Blum, who finally attributed it to resentment over the founding of a rival daily, the pro-Dreyfus *Aurore*, by his old collaborator Vaughan. Zévaès, however, dug more deeply to find in Rochefort's thought a continuity of ardent and uncompromising patriotism which finally pushed him into the camp of his former enemies.[1]

By the spring of 1898 Rochefort was spraying charges against the Dreyfusards like an uncontrolled volley of buckshot. In June, he centered his attention on Jaurès, and hardly a day passed that *L'Intransigeant* did not carry some accusation against him. Jaurès' bourgeois origins, his early contacts with Opportunism, his position as "mouthpiece of the traitors" were all exposed.[2] But Rochefort made what he deemed his most telling disclosure when he revealed that Jaurès' family still maintained traditional ties with the very Catholic Church he was publicly attacking. "I can see him now," wrote the pamphleteer, conjuring up a picture of Jaurès as a second Saint John, "a cross in his hand and nothing but a sheepskin across his shoulders to cover his nakedness."[3]

Rochefort's barrage was but the opening salvo in a campaign of calumny that tracked Jaurès to his grave. Many later attacks he would ignore, but now, to defend his socialist integrity, he answered the major accusations of *L'Intransigeant*. "M. Rochefort charges me with being very rich, and if it were true I would hardly apologize for it," he admitted. "In fact, I wish that the militants of our party were free of money worries. . . . As for myself, I live by my work and my work alone. If I couldn't lift my pen tomorrow, I would be reduced to poverty." But what of the revelation about the Catholicism of the Jaurès family? "My wife and mother are practicing Christians. I have neither the right nor the slightest inclination to interfere with their freedom of conscience." There *was* a socialist duty toward one's family, he granted, but it was other than control over personal beliefs. "The essential concern for us . . . is to safeguard our children against a confining clerical education."[4] And that, he stressed, he had always done.

If the assaults on Jaurès were designed to discourage his socialist activity, they failed. In the weeks that followed the elections of May, he made a decision which kept him in Paris and at the front of daily combat. Rejecting the chance to return to the university, he accepted an offer from Millerand, editor of *La petite République*, to compose that paper's daily political editorial. It was not only a position of real influence, but it came also as a welcome economic windfall. Cut off from the daily stipend for deputies, Jaurès found his financial circumstances precarious. Louise would soon give birth to a second child, their son Louis; Madeleine, already nine, required clothes and schoolbooks; the apartment in the rue Madame was becoming conspicuously overcrowded. The thousand francs a month from the newspaper work, while no princely sum, was at least sufficient to cope with these expanding family wants.

And those were the only material worries Jaurès had, for he himself remained, as he had been from early youth, indifferent to personal possessions and appearance. His tightly packed day was an all-absorbing round of books, articles, speeches, and meetings. In the morning, before he composed his column, he generally read at the library of the École Normale, and the young *normaliens* who caught sight of him then long remembered what they saw. "The misfortune of his defeat only made him greater in our eyes," recalled the Tharaud brothers; "on his powerful shoulders, it seemed to us, he bore, like a caryatid, the full weight of bourgeois hatred. While awaiting the next elections and a change of luck, he spent his leisure hours in rereading the Greek orators; I can see him yet, carrying under his arm Lysias' speech against grain speculation."[5]

Behind his desk at *La petite République*, where he might fill twenty or more sheets in a large, bold hand to produce a single article, he was serious and fully disciplined. "You didn't see much of Jaurès," Francis Jourdain later recalled. "He was in his little office, always working. Jaurès was certainly not arrogant, but he had no time for idling. Of course, he regretted it, because everything interested and enriched him. Yet even though he did so many things, he never seemed overworked. He would come to the end of some enormous job, unruffled as a peasant, never feverish or nervous."[6]

Jaurès took up his editorial duties in days of high tension. History, he felt, had thrown out to socialism both the challenge and the opportunity to safeguard the Republic and to guarantee its progress. But the movement, still badly splintered, would fail in its mission unless it moved effectively toward unification; and the great obstacle to unity, he believed, lay less in differences of theory than in the vested interest of the long-established organizations. Thus, to soothe those feelings bound to be sensitive, Jaurès proposed unification by stages. "It isn't a question of dissolving the existing groups immediately; they represent an important historic tradition." But why not call an annual congress to assure the movement a common and coherent direction? "I believe that in a general party congress the best socialist thought will emerge to inspire us. The words of old-time militants," he pointed out, treating pioneers like Guesde and Vaillant with special deference, "will perfect the education of our newcomers."[7]

On June 7 Jaurès found a golden opportunity to press his point home. Socialists of all factions sponsored a "Great Punch" at the Tivoli Vauxhall, and an enthusiastic crowd of workers and students turned out to hear their leaders. Jaurès, the presiding officer that night, spoke of the present crisis and its implications. But he spoke most fervently of socialist unity. "Since Reaction has formed a bloc," he cried out, "Revolution must form a bloc. . . . To achieve unity is to forge the weapon of social revolution!" But though his words swayed the crowd, they were less enthusiastically received by the leaders of the existing parties. "Some persons, too much in a hurry, would like to see the death of the very groups from which French socialism derives its strength."[8] So responded Vaillant, indicating well enough that while they approved unification in principle, the Blanquists were reluctant to dissolve their party.

The Marxists, if not hostile, were at least cautious. "I have noted with interest the attempts to unify the socialist forces," Lafargue wrote to Guesde. "It has to come, of course; it's necessary for the development of socialism. . . . There is no sense in fighting against the inevitable, but we should try to direct a unified party toward our own goal."[9] The relations between Jaurès and the party chiefs became strained over the unification issue. Personal resentment cropped out, and once again, as though past years had proved little, old militants viewed Jaurès as a "newcomer," dictating (or so it seemed to them) the dissolution of their historic groups. In the months to come, as friction developed over participation in the Affair, this initial strain became a breach.

II

Godefroy Cavaignac, the strong man of the Brisson ministry, entertained no doubts whatever about the guilt of Dreyfus. In examining the dossier on the case, the Minister of War found certain documents, recklessly forged by Major Henry, which he accepted as conclusive evidence against Dreyfus. Especially was he impressed by a letter, purportedly written by the Italian military attaché Panizzardi to his German counterpart Schwartzkoppen, openly referring to relations with Dreyfus. Fabricated by Henry in October, 1896, this document, known later in the case as the *faux Henry*, became Cavaignac's sharp-edged sword against revisionism. Thus, for the Dreyfusards, this ministry seemed certain to be a crushing disappointment.

Jaurès watched the indecisive feints of the Brisson government with scarcely veiled impatience. While intensifying his daily attacks on anti-Semites and ultranationalists, he berated the republican government for its hesitancy in undertaking revision. But even as he campaigned, Jaurès was increasingly isolated within his own movement. The socialist moderates, who stood behind Millerand, had consistently steered clear of the Affair on grounds of expediency. Not so Guesde and Vaillant; but these old battlers were in the throes of second thoughts about participation. Never did they doubt that an injustice had been committed; but they questioned the value for socialists of an extended campaign for a single victim, and a bourgeois at that. Jaurès, however, accepted no such narrow reading of socialist duty. "There is no action more socialist," he insisted, "than to denounce the crimes of the great chiefs, who tomorrow may march beside the capitalists and the priests."[10] But once again there was strain on the Extreme Left, and at the very moment, thought Jaurès, when its honor was at stake.

In the political arena, the sorry spectacle continued. On July 7 Cavaignac appeared before the Chamber to put at rest all doubts about the guilt of Dreyfus. The *bordereau*, he began, was of no value, since its author was actually Esterhazy. Unruffled by this startling admission (had not the *bordereau* been the basis of conviction?), he waved before the House new documents, especially the *faux Henry*, which, he assured his listeners, sealed the case against the traitor. Cavaignac's performance drew wild cheers from Drumont's anti-Semites and Déroulède's resurgent nationalists. But the Radicals, proud that one of their own had brought forth the proofs, appeared no less exultant. For the rest, assorted republicans and socialists, the Minister of War had, in the words of Millerand, "eased the public conscience."[11] By a unanimous vote (with only a handful of abstentions), the Chamber ordered the posting of Cavaignac's speech outside every City Hall in France.

That night Mathieu Dreyfus was like a man without limbs. Knowing that his brother was innocent, he was yet unable to move. With Lucien Herr, he went to Blum's house, and the three of them sat silent and sad before the rubble of their cause. Then, as Blum later recalled, the bell rang insistently. Jaurès stood framed in the doorway, "triumphant, beaming." He too had attended the session, and he alone had understood its meaning and its ultimate consequences. Revision, he told his friends, was now a certainty, and he went on to explain his bold conclusion. "Méline was invulnerable because he kept quiet. Cavaignac is talking, debating, and so he will be beaten. The documents which he has just adduced — well! — I tell you they're forgeries; they smell of forgery. They are idiotic forgeries, manufactured to cover others. And I will prove it. The forgers have come out of their hole, and we have them by the throat. Don't despair any more. Join me and rejoice!"[12]

On July 10 Jaurès subjected the *faux Henry* to detailed criticism, which brought a storm of abuse down on his head. Papillaud, Drumont's sharpest pen at *La libre Parole*, charged nothing less than that his defeat had deranged him mentally.[13] But from the Extreme Left Jaurès suffered another and more serious kind of repudiation. In a strongly worded manifesto on July 24, the P.O.F. charged that Dreyfusards and Antidreyfusards were equally "enemies of the working class and of socialism."[14] Guesde and Vaillant, memories of the Commune and a hundred bitter strikes burned in their memories, could not bring themselves, either doctrinally or emotionally, to march beside Reinach or a knot of bourgeois professors. It would distort the clear-cut struggle between classes; it would reduce socialism to pious moralism. Despite their collaboration with the Bourgeois ministry less than three years before, possible only on the assumption that middle-class parties could be differentiated one from the other, Guesdists and Blanquists returned to their earlier intransigence, where an undifferentiated bourgeoisie was the enemy and the State its weapon. But Jaurès, who drew distinctions and welcomed fruitful alliances, resisted, out of his faith in the power of democracy, the politics of isolation. However dramatic the later issue of Millerandism, their fundamental division, as both Jaurès and Guesde agreed in their Lille debate two years later, developed here, in the Dreyfus Affair, over the tactics of collaboration.

The days of anguish were upon Jaurès. Where and how would he move? The answer was not long in doubt. There was work to be done; justice had to be served. On August 9 Jaurès sat in his office at *La petite République*; he leaned forward at his desk, and wrote in large letters across the top of a blank sheet the simple words *Les Preuves*. The next day, a long article appeared. And from then on, day after day, with never a pause, he dissected the case against Dreyfus until he had torn it to shreds. Despite his rigorous examination of evidence and his insights into the army's machinations, it was no mere *roman policier* which Jaurès composed. At the very start of the series, he spelled out his view of the socialist stake in revision. Comrades of his had argued that the fate of Dreyfus, a bourgeois and an officer, was of little concern to the proletariat. To this argument he answered: " — if Dreyfus has been illegally convicted and if, as I will prove, he is actually innocent, then he is no longer an officer or a bourgeois; in his misery, he has been stripped of all class character; he is nothing less than mankind itself in the deepest pit of despair. . . . We cannot, in the name of socialism, turn our backs on despoiled mankind."[15]

For a solid week, from August 13 to 20, Jaurès examined, questioned, and denied any link between Dreyfus and the *bordereau*. From August 25 and for four successive days, he analyzed the evidence presented by Cavaignac, centering his attention on the *faux Henry*, "a forgery, manufactured by the crudest kind of operator." Introduced only because the *bordereau* could no longer be used against Dreyfus, the Panizzardi letter withstood no real test of logic. Yet Cavaignac had accepted and defended it. "Truly, I ask myself if we are not all dreaming!"[16]

The Minister of War, though still convinced that he was right, was nonetheless shaken by Jaurès' articles, and he ordered a careful examination of the entire Dreyfus dossier by one Captain Cuignet. The results were crushing for both the War Office and the Minister. Cuignet discovered that the Panizzardi letter was indeed a forgery, manufactured by Henry out of parts of two separate documents. Hopeful that Henry could offer a convincing explanation, Cavaignac pushed the inquiry to its limits. On August 30, in a session attended by Boisdeffre and Gonse, the War Minister interrogated the trapped major. Confronted with the evidence, Henry broke down and admitted his forgery, blurting out in self-defense: "I acted for the good of the country." That hardly satisfied the War Minister, who saw his case, if not ruined, at least badly damaged. The interrogation over, Boisdeffre, who had trusted Henry, wrote out his resignation, while Cavaignac ordered fortress-arrest at Mont-Valérien for the major. The next day, August 31, in the blazing heat of mid-afternoon, Henry, alone in his cell, slashed his throat with a razor, drowning his case against Dreyfus in a pool of blood.

What followed bordered on chaos. Esterhazy, now a proven traitor, fled to Belgium and then to England. Cavaignac, still determined to resist revision, submitted his resignation. As for Brisson, this was not his finest hour. The Premier bent a little in all directions and finally yielded to the military. Though the job before him was reparation of a now obvious injustice, he appointed as the new Minister of War General Zurlinden, Military Governor of Paris, who promptly ordered prosecution, not of Du Paty and the other implicated generals, but of Picquart. Brisson stood firm for a moment and dismissed Zurlinden on September 17, but replaced him with yet another antirevisionist officer, General Chanoine. The initiative for retrial, which obviously would not come from inside the ministry, was thus left to the Dreyfusards on the outside. Lucie Dreyfus, wife of Alfred, submitted to the government a formal petition requesting revision, and on September 26, six of the eleven Cabinet members, Brisson included, voted to forward her application to the Court of Criminal Appeals. "A decisive step has been taken," wrote Jaurès, "but the battle is far from over. The party of falsifiers will try to control public opinion with lies."[17]

Even as he wrote, his words were validated by the actions of others. The young Charles Maurras was using the pages of the monarchist *Gazette de France* to turn Henry into a martyr for the Fatherland. "Your unlucky forgery will be acclaimed as one of your finest deeds of war."[18] In September, Déroulède was reorganizing his League of Patriots, and at noisy public meetings shouting threats against Jaurès and others of the Dreyfusards. The Anti-Semitic League meanwhile was sending its shock troops into the streets, there to pick victims for what *La petite République* called their "despicable brutality."[19]

Jaurès intensified his fight against these elements. By September 25 he had cast his recent articles in book form, and, for one franc fifty, readers could follow his trenchant analyses of *Les Preuves*. In October, he was writing of larger socialist objectives than mere revision. He urged, as the first prize of victory, the integration of the army within the cadre of the nation, a theme that was almost to obsess him until his death. Special military courts and schools, he insisted, had to be swept away. The old army had to yield to a new one, based not on professionals but on citizens' militias. But in proposing such extensive aims, was Jaurès simply yielding to an incorrigible optimism? Given the diversified origins of the Dreyfusards, could they ever agree on a reorganization of French institutions? Beside Jaurès marched not only Clemenceau, with a record as a reformer, but also moderates — Yves Guyot and Senator Trarieux — with no such record at all.[20] Furthermore, the movement had been growing larger, as certain Progressists and Radicals, at first conspicuously silent, found it expedient to join the Dreyfusards. All that was obvious enough to Jaurès; but in insisting upon the socialist stake in the Affair, he proceeded on several working assumptions: that the movement had yet to develop a clear direction; that the progressive bourgeoisie would collaborate with the socialists in curbing the power of Church and army; that the leadership in the Affair might fall to the socialists if they entered it unified and purposeful. For a few exciting months around the turn of 1899, that last condition seemed almost realized as labor unrest touched off ominous military movements and sent the socialists scurrying together for safety.

Late in September of 1898, the construction workers of Paris struck, and the Federation of Railwaymen, considering the time ripe for pressing home their own extensive demands, prepared a national strike. The Central Committee of the Confédération générale du travail, guided then by a rather ineffective Secretary, Lagailse, thought the time had come for the much-discussed general strike. As the leaders of the C.G.T. reckoned it, a railway strike, involving both State and private employees, was certain to be considered illegal (the 1884 law on unions and strikes, it had been ruled, did not extend to public employees) and to provoke repressive action. The impact of governmental reprisals would then rouse such widespread resentment among the mass of workers that they would join the strike out of sympathy, thus generalizing it into the long-awaited revolution. In a secret letter to all major unions, the C.G.T. urged vigilance and action. But while the militants of syndicalism prepared for revolution, so, in its own way, did the government.

Apprised of the contents of the C.G.T. letter, the authorities acted swiftly. The railway workers were warned that, should they strike, they would lose both their jobs and their unions. As a result, the great majority of workers refused to walk out, and the hope of a railway strike evaporated almost overnight.[21] But the Brisson ministry nonetheless poured troops into Paris, some sixty thousand of them, on the pretext of main-

House in Castres where Jaurès was born

Jaurès at the École Normale Supérieur. Jaurès is second from the left
in the first row. Bergson is third from the right.

Jaurès and the glass workers of Carmaux
during the strike of 1895

Jaurès at the Mur des Féderés, 1913,
with Vaillant at his right

L. Blanc

GRÈVE DE GRAULHET (Tarn). - M. J. JAURÈS à Graulhet

Jaurès with strikers at Graulhet, 1910

Sketches of Jaurès
as orator, 1910

Jaurès
in his library

Jaurès pleading for peace
at Pré-Saint-Gervais, 1913

Jaurès and Viviani at the trial
of Captain Dreyfus, Rennes, 1899

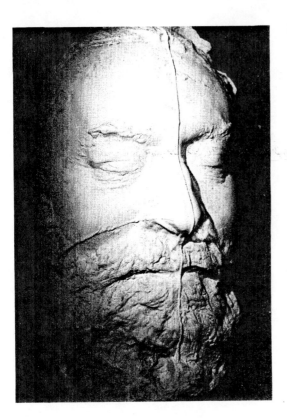

Death mask of Jaurès

Carmaux miners
at the burial of Jaurès
in the Panthéon, 1924

taining order. As the army occupied the depots and patrolled the main boulevards, rumors spread through the city that a military coup was imminent. The army chiefs had used the strike threat to occupy the city, and now they intended to overthrow and replace civil authority. Suddenly, it was Guesde and his followers who were genuinely worried. The Republic, which they had but recently written off as a weapon of the ruling class, now seemed as vital to them as it had always been to Jaurès. Thus, from the P.O.F. came a bold initiative to unite the socialist factions into a coherent fighting legion within the army of the Dreyfusards.

What set Guesde at variance with his own recent views, it should be noted, was something more than the threat to Paris. In the steady stream of information which he received from the P.O.F. Federations, he learned that neutrality in the Affair was damaging to his party's strength. "Because we seem to oppose all forms of bourgeois republicanism," he read in a letter from the Federation of the Deux-Sèvres, "many people take us for the allies of monarchist reactionaries."[22] With a party chief like Guesde, the welfare of the P.O.F. came before anything else; quite obviously, conditions justified a retreat from his recently held position.

The Marxist leaders sent out a call for a meeting of socialist groups, and on October 16 with all factions responding, an historic conclave took place in Paris. Jaurès presided. "Oh! undoubtedly quarrels would start up again tomorrow and the bitterest of polemics would divide us," recalled Zévaès, a young Guesdist at the time of the meeting. "Some, the shooting stars of socialism, would desert the way of revolution for the path to the ministry; but at this moment, everyone was moved by the gravity of events."[23] In consequence of the session, a temporary Comité de vigilance was established, comprising all the outstanding leaders of socialism (Jaurès, Guesde, Vaillant, Brousse, Millerand, and Allemane among them), which was made responsible for formulating a common socialist policy. Organized to meet a crisis, the Comité became only the first step toward the much larger purpose of final organic unity. By December it was dissolved and replaced by a permanent Comité d'entente socialiste, representative of all five affiliated organizations, including the newly-established Federation of Independent Socialists. In the half-year that followed, militants of all factions shared platforms in every major city of France, and it seemed only a matter of time before a national congress produced the unified party that would shape the destiny of France.

III

"I should like you to take a picture of my infant son, now six months old. When shall I bring him to your studio?" So wrote a proud father to a photographer in the last days of 1898. In the Jaurès family now settled in larger quarters at 7, avenue de Chalet, in Passy, little Louis was the center of attention. A few weeks later, the father wrote to the photographer again: "We are very much pleased with the two proofs you have just sent. We should like to have a dozen of each."[24]

But the Affair took Jaurès away from his moments of diverting privacy. Parliament reconvened on October 25, 1898, and it took but a single session to ring down the curtain on the Brisson ministry. His own War Minister, General Chanoine, rising to answer nationalist interpellations, shocked Brisson, though not Déroulède, by reasserting Dreyfus' guilt and denouncing the Cabinet's decision to accept Lucie Dreyfus' petition. With this bombshell, Chanoine also threw in his resignation and stalked from the Chamber. The stunned Premier denounced the betrayal of his minister and shouted his support of revision; but it was to no avail. Nationalist denunciations inside the Chamber were counterpoint to Guérin's vulgarities outside. Failing on a vote of confidence, the unhappy Brisson was forced to resign. By November 1, a new ministry was formed, but it augured nothing of originality or boldness. For President Faure had entrusted the national destiny to Charles Dupuy, hardly a refreshing new face in French politics, who, in his indecisive ministerial declaration, managed to heap praise equally on both civil and military authorities.

In the midst of this domestic storm, lightning struck on the foreign front. The Fashoda crisis was upon France, when the nation went to the brink of war with England over control of the Upper Nile Valley. As early as March, 1896, the expansion-minded Hanotaux had ordered one Captain Marchand to march from French Equatorial Africa into the unclaimed Sudan, with Fashoda on the Nile as his objective. Marchand's forces, no more than two hundred Senagalese troops and a dozen officers, moved doggedly east through incredibly difficult jungle country until, on July 10, 1898, they raised the French flag over Fashoda. But by mid-September, the British proconsul, Lord Kitchener, arrived there from Egypt, commanding twenty thousand troops and determined to oust the French from what England considered her sphere of influence. To capitulate or to push expansion — these were the alternatives which confronted Dupuy's Foreign Minister Théophile Delcassé.

Forty-six in 1898 and for almost a decade the deputy from the Ariège, Delcassé had been a disciple of Gambetta, a *revanchard* in the League of Patriots, and an imperialistic Under-Secretary in the Ministry of Colonies. At the outset, he favored aggression rather than capitulation. But the Russians, technically correct in contending that their alliance did not extend to conflict with England, advised Delcassé to yield. The Germans might conceivably have helped, but it was too much for a smoldering *revanchard* to strike a bargain with Prussians. And standing alone,

France could hardly cope with the superiority of the British fleet. Thus, on November 3, France yielded, and Marchand was ordered to withdraw from Fashoda. But even as French troops were returning to their native soil, through Ethiopia and across the Red Sea, Delcassé was calculating the chances of turning this British enemy into a future ally against Germany.

Jaurès, reacting sharply to the new crisis, yet another sign of disarray in capitalist society, wrote three times in two weeks of Fashoda. But even in that short span of time his views lacked uniformity as he floundered once again on the question of imperialism. Writing before the crisis had been resolved, he accepted the principle of expansion, protesting only the methods involved. "Certainly, France was right in trying to link up the basins of the Congo and the Nile by a series of forts. But in doing so, she should have avoided anything that might have irritated or vexed England. . . . Let's recognize right off that England has important rights through her long occupation and organization of Egypt."[25] What he proposed was a kind of fair bargaining among the interested powers in the division of Africa. Once the crisis had subsided, however, Jaurès conceded nothing to the patriots, but accused successive ministries of playing fast and loose with peace. "Two years ago, the Méline ministry begged the parliamentary opposition not to question its request for credits to provide funds for an African expedition. We nonetheless asked if there was any danger of military involvement. We were told that there was none, and so the vote followed without debate."[26]

But in his final reflections on Fashoda, Jaurès was bitterly critical. Arraigned now was not the Progressist party but the capitalistic system itself. Peace, he charged, "has been left to the whim of chance. But if war breaks out, it will be vast and terrible. For the first time, it will be universal, sucking in all the continents. Capitalism has widened the field of battle, and the entire planet will turn red with the blood of countless men. No more terrible accusation can be made against this social system."[27] The peace was preserved in 1898, but a deep fear of war had seized Jaurès. And even as he worked to safeguard the Republic, he felt it essential to wrest it from the hands of the bellicose and the greedy.

On the first day of 1899 the League of the French Fatherland (Ligue de la Patrie française) came into existence for the express purpose of fighting against a retrial for Dreyfus. Its guiding spirit was Maurras, already in full sail on an antirepublican voyage that spanned half a turbulent century. Around him he gathered a handful of nationalist and anti-Semitic intellectuals, bitter opponents of the Dreyfusard *clercs*. Barrès, Mistral, Coppée, Bourget, Brunetière, Vandal, and Rambaud — novelists, critics, historians — were among the giants of the League; but it was Jules Lemaître, perhaps the most quoted critic of his day, who spoke authoritatively for it.

Jaurès spared no feelings in denouncing the literary Leaguers. He spoke out of opposition to their politics, but even more, he attacked them for subordinating their minds to unreason. An intellectual fully prepared to meet other such on their own level, Jaurès was doubly effective. Few among the leading Dreyfusards could have struck such body blows at Brunetière, Barrès, and Bourget, for few could have known their work so well. "After having applied a futile method to the study of literature, M. Brunetière has finally taken refuge beneath the heavy arches of the Church," Jaurès wrote of the editor of La Revue des deux mondes, who had tried to reduce literary history to an evolutionary science. "He is trying to recover from his professional failure by claiming the failure of science in general." And M. Barrès? "He cannot forgive himself for failing to assert his 'I' in the Dreyfus Affair; so he is now with the Academy, that is, with the 'barbarians.'"[28] As for Bourget, he was driven on by the excesses of his vanity. "The courageous actions of Zola have aggravated Bourget's detestable jealousy. What course then was open to him? To stand behind Esterhazy! Thus, after having flattered the salons for their adultery, he now praises them for their reactionary politics."[29] Among the "generation of 1885," as Albert Thibaudet has written of the writers after Renan, "emotion, intuition, and skepticism argued with reason, religion, and philosophy; those inner experiences argued with science, a system of external experience."[30] Sensitive to every seismic change in the foundations of intellectual life, Jaurès saw danger in this challenge to reason, and in combatting the literary Leaguers he felt that not only was the Affair at stake but nothing less than the cultural direction of France.

For a moment, however, the newly founded League scored a triumph. Responding to their propaganda, Dupuy proposed that the Dreyfus case be transferred from the Criminal Appeals Court to a wider panel of judges, the United Appeals Courts, considered less favorable to the Dreyfusard cause. A bill embodying the proposal was brought before the Chamber and approved; in the course of debate, Minister of Justice Lebret appealed to a sentiment rather less exalted than justice. "Gentlemen," he warned his colleagues, "think of your constituencies!"[31] Once again revision seemed hopelessly blocked. But in February, with chance at the wheel of history, the Affair took a sudden new turn.

President Faure had been no friend of the Dreyfusards. Snobisme, near-monarchist pretensions, strong Catholic ties — all these had linked him rather to the camp of the nationalists. But on February 16, his sporting nature did him in. Early that evening, while entertaining one Mme

Steinheil in the Presidential suite, he succumbed to a cerebral hemorrhage, bitter fruit for one who loved not wisely and too late. In the death of Faure, the Dreyfusards saw their golden opportunity to win control of the Presidency. "I vote for Loubet," Clemenceau wrote at once, and the suggestion swept through republican ranks. The sixty-one-year-old Loubet seemed ideal — conservative enough to pass muster with some of the Progressists, yet revisionist enough to satisfy most of the Dreyfusards. The Rightists and their allies among the Progressists opposed him, of course, and chose as their candidate the unyielding Méline. But when the two Houses assembled for the vote on February 18, 1899, Loubet was elected, and by an almost two-to-one majority.

The noisiest of the nationalists and the anti-Semites, upset by the turn of events, planned their revenge. "In a week we will have driven Loubet from the Elysée," promised Jules Lemaître.[32] They chose to strike on February 23, the day set aside for the state funeral of the late President, when the royalist followers of the Duc d'Orléans and the League of Patriots gestured at a coup against the established Republic. After the service at Notre Dame, an overwrought Déroulède, flanked by Barrès, Guérin, and two hundred others, raced in among the processional troops then returning to the barracks. Déroulède, beard flying in the day's sharp wind, shouted at Roget, the strongly Antidreyfusard commander: "To the Elysée, General!" But Roget, whether because of deafness or discipline, failed to respond; his sword pointing toward the barracks, he marched his troops back to their quarters. The attempt failed miserably, but for Jaurès it seemed a strong warning. He reiterated what he had so often said — that the antirepublican movement was desperate and organized. There were those in France who detested the people and wanted to destroy their democracy. He exhorted his own party, organized in the interest of those very masses, to unite for action: "Socialists, militants of the Revolution, tell the people the truth. Arm yourselves and your comrades. If you remain divided, you will fall beneath the sword."[33]

The hour for firm ministerial action was most certainly at hand. But when Dupuy moved at all, it was not toward but away from a review of the judicial crime. At the start of May, he appointed Camille Krantz, an avowed Antidreyfusard, as his Minister of War. Jaurès was enraged, revolted. When would republicans come forward to defend human rights in the Republic? In that spring of 1899, he traveled from one corner of France to another, attacking the nationalists, urging the ministry on to actions he knew it wouldn't take. Finally, on May 13, he arrived in the socialist city of Marseille, and his campaign to rouse the conscience of a nation reached a momentary climax. Accompanied by Gérault-Richard, Pressensé, Zévaès, and Jean Psichari, son-in-law of Renan, he was hailed by more than thirty thousand *marseillais* who lined the streets from the railway station to the Hôtel de Noailles to catch sight of him. From the balcony of the hotel, he spoke to them, and they listened with rapt attention as he improvised a kind of historical poem to this ancient Phocaean city. The next evening, at the Alhambra, speaking before eight thousand, Jaurès described in detail the "ignominious drama which has been unfolding for two long years."[34]

The pendulum now oscillated nervously in an indecisive France. On May 31, Déroulède, brought before the Court of Assizes of the Seine for his actions of February 23, was permitted to shout defiant obscenities against Loubet, and was then acquitted. But on June 3, the nationalists suffered a check when the United Appeals Courts, confronted with too many irregularities in the original court-martial, ordered a retrial for the unhappy prisoner wasting away on Devil's Island. The next day, June 4, the nationalists took their revenge. It was a festive Sunday, the day of the annual steeplechase at Auteuil, and the sport of kings attracted to the racecourse not only aristocratic dandies but also bourgeois republicans, including the one-time peasant from Montélimar, Émile Loubet. Despite the tense political atmosphere, Dupuy, whether deliberately or stupidly, provided no special police protection at Auteuil, and on his arrival the President was met with hostile catcalls from young monarchist extremists. One of them, the Baron de Christiani, played for Orleanist immortality by bursting into the Presidential box and bringing his walking stick crashing down on Loubet's top hat. A hero to his friends, Christiani exhorted them to action, and the general melée which followed ended only when police reinforcements arrived and hundreds of arrests were made.[35]

To many—socialists and bourgeois Dreyfusards—the danger had never seemed greater. As Jaurès understood it, the threat was twofold: it was the pretension of the Right to the domination of caste and religion, but it was also the duplicity of bourgeois republicans, in their own way hostile to democracy. Dupuy was one of them. "He has hesitated and betrayed the Republic," Jaurès wrote bitterly.[36] The inaction of the Premier finally depressed even a considerable bloc of moderates, and when they deserted the ministry on June 12, Dupuy suffered a vote of "no confidence" and fell from office.

Once more France was in a political crisis. The solution Millerand proposed was "a cabinet of republican concentration, faithfully reflecting the full array of democratic forces."[37] It seemed strange, on the surface, that Millerand, at first so hostile to the Dreyfusards, should now enthusiastically support a popular front among them. But those who looked more closely seemed to understand that his robust careerism gave unity to his successive positions; and a movement which once was a threat to his parliamentary seat might yet be the springboard for ministerial heights.

Jaurès responded to the crisis just as quickly. He felt that the Republic was in serious danger and had to be saved *now*, lest it collapse under the blows of its enemies. Five years later when Guesde fought him at the Congress of Amsterdam, the old Marxist would assert that the Republic had been in less danger in 1899 than in the time of Boulanger. And in retrospect, when it is recalled that the Prefects, the courts, and local and national administration remained essentially loyal to the Republic, Jaurès' fears seem exaggerated. But he responded to the stimuli of the day. And what he saw were powerful thrusts, noisy threats, violent street actions against republican society. Could the Republic last while the Church, the army, and the Leagues rampaged unchecked? Jaurès doubted it.[38]

IV

President Loubet sought to resolve the ministerial crisis with Raymond Poincaré, hardly a front-runner among the Dreyfusards. Four days of negotiation demonstrated that if Poincaré had become a revisionist, he remained at heart a Progressist. "He's another Dupuy," wrote Clemenceau, as he observed the attempt to form a government with members of the ministry just repudiated. By June 17, having failed to work out a viable combination, Poincaré gave up. But in the course of these otherwise meaningless negotiations, one event was to take on significance. A day before he abandoned his effort, on June 16, Poincaré received a surprising visit from a man of the Left.[39] It was Millerand, who had come, unsolicited and in secret, to offer advice on the formation of a government. Include a socialist, he suggested, arguing that such a move would give representation to all defenders of the Republic. The startled Poincaré asked his visitor if he had a particular socialist in mind. Millerand offered the name of Viviani, the talented orator of the Independents, who, as he pointed out, was moderate enough to collaborate with a nonsocialist ministry. Both men knew perfectly well, as they traded words in Poincaré's study, that Viviani was too young and inexperienced for such a role, while Millerand, now that Jaurès and Guesde were out of the Chamber, was the virtual leader of his party in Parliament. Could Millerand, his critics later asked, have been thinking of anyone but himself, even while he named another? It seems unlikely that so ambitious a man would have proposed this radical departure from traditional socialist policy on ministerial participation unless the personal stakes warranted the risk. As it turned out, Poincaré rejected the idea, and for the moment Millerand's proposal had no practical effect.

By June 18, 1899, Loubet sought to end the crisis by calling on René Waldeck-Rousseau, a republican moderate who had held himself aloof from the recent political turmoil. The choice was a serious one, for in appearance and background Waldeck-Rousseau passed for a distinguished republican. "His impassivity, his British-like figure, accentuated even more by the cadaverous quality of his face, was startling in political circles, where cordiality and personal effusion were more customary. . . . Always dressed in impeccable English style, artistic and cultivated, he rather liked being called the 'Pericles of the Republic.'"[40]

In 1899, Waldeck-Rousseau was fifty-three and a Senator. A wealthy bourgeois and an outstanding lawyer, he had served both Gambetta and Ferry as Minister of the Interior and had been primarily responsible, in fact, for bringing to fruition the 1884 law which facilitated the right of association. His public role in the revisionist campaign had been negligible; but, like his father in 1848, he believed deeply enough in republican institutions to take strong measures on their behalf. When he agreed to try for a ministry, Waldeck-Rousseau jotted down in a private diary, on June 18, his central purpose: "To put an end to factious agitation and to impose on everyone respect for constitutional law."[41]

For two crowded days Waldeck-Rousseau searched for the magic combination, a ministry of strength and prestige. With the insubordination of the army chiefs preying on his mind, he gave his deepest thought to the War Office. He decided that he would himself take the portfolio of War Minister, while appointing as his chief assistant General the Marquis de Gallifet, "a magnificent soldier in Italy, the Crimea, Mexico, Algeria, and at Sedan."[42] Near seventy, the handsome old Gallifet had outlived a stormy youth to become an officer renowned for his arrogance, competence, and discipline. But even more important in the swirl of 1899, this reserved aristocrat was actually a convinced republican, converted to that position out of admiration for Gambetta's patriotism. Yet the appointment of Gallifet was bound to cause consternation on the Left. Despite his republicanism, he was the very officer who had directed the slaughter of Communards during Bloody Week of 1871. The present crisis might demand many expedients, but for old militants of the Commune, whose memories were the epic poems of the socialist movement, the appointment of Gallifet was not one of them.

Realizing that he would need socialist support, Waldeck-Rousseau heeded the advice of experienced politicians like Reinach and Ranc. At their suggestion, he thought to balance the appointment of Gallifet with the inclusion of a socialist, one whose prestige and moderation were equally high, Alexandre Millerand. When he dangled the ministerial plum before the socialist lawyer, Millerand, as might have been foreseen, reached for it like a man long hungry. He understood, even better than Waldeck, that the move would rouse bitter controversy among his comrades. The socialists were almost certain, in the first place, to view with suspicion any move by Waldeck-Rousseau, whom they knew as the attorney for big business, a leading public spokesman against collectivism, and in 1898 an active campaigner again Jaurès in the Tarn and Guesde in the Nord.[43] But even if they could lend their temporary support to a government of republican defense, socialists were bound, in the second place, to demur before the prospect of participation in a ministry dominated by the representatives of capitalism. On that issue of tactics, their teaching had been unequivocal, and no one had emphasized the prohibition any more than Jaurès in his *Cosmopolis* article of 1898.[44]

To overcome the opposition of his party, Millerand knew that he would need powerful moral support, and almost at once he visited Jaurès, probably confident that the *tarnais* could be swayed by their personal friendship. Jaurès listened as Millerand, comrade of a hundred campaigns, told him of Waldeck's offer. Reasonable and persuasive, Millerand dwelt on the advantages of acceptance — salvation of the Republic, the increase of socialist influence, the extra pressure for reform. The arguments were cogent, but Jaurès envisioned at once the divisive quarrel that would rage over participation in a Waldeck-Gallifet ministry. What then would become of the long-laid plans for unity? Jaurès thus pleaded with Millerand to reject the offer, though it became quickly evident that his friend had come not for advice but only for support. The lawyer pressed his case, but Jaurès promised only one thing, that if Waldeck-Rousseau managed to form a government of republican defense, he would support it. In return, he extracted from Millerand the promise to discuss his offer with the other socialist deputies. "I told him that he had no right to keep secrets, and he agreed at once."[45]

By nightfall of June 19, however, Waldeck-Rousseau gave up his attempt to form a ministry, beaten momentarily by the hesitation of the revision-minded Progressists. When he had solicited their support, Waldeck received oblique replies from Leygues and Poincaré, who, concerned as they were over Radical and socialist influence in the proposed ministry, demanded Progressist predominance as the minimum price of their support.[46] Thus, by the morning of June 20, some eight days after the fall of Dupuy, Loubet began to search once again for a new Premier. In turn, and without success, he approached Delcassé and Brisson. He even recalled Léon Bourgeois from the Hague, where the Radical leader was serving as the French representative at the Disarmament Conference. But Bourgeois, comfortable in his role as an international peacemaker, made little more than a gesture at forming a government, and then gave up. "The angel of arbitration has flown off to the Hague," wrote Jaurès, implying that Bourgeois had again lacked courage. "When the danger is over, he will return to head an impressive ministry. He will preside proudly, along with his fellow Radicals, at the celebrations for the Exposition of 1900."[47]

By the afternoon of June 20, Loubet appealed to Poincaré again, who once more failed in the mission. Two full days had been added to the widening crisis when the President retraced his steps and returned to Waldeck-Rousseau. On the evening of June 20, Waldeck traveled to Clairfontaine where he was a guest at the beautiful chateau of General Gallifet. Millerand and Jean Dupuy, owner of the influential *Petit Parisien*, joined them there, and together these men composed a ministerial list. It was to be Waldeck-Rousseau himself at Interior, Millerand at Commerce, Jean Dupuy at Agriculture, Delcassé at Foreign Affairs, and Gallifet at the War Office.

For Millerand the hours of secrecy were numbered; now he could hardly avoid open discussion of ministerial participation with his socialist colleagues. What he could do, however, and with consummate skill, was to reveal only half the facts. On June 21, the parliamentary socialists met in caucus at the Palais Bourbon to evaluate their role in the political crisis, and Millerand finally spoke about an offer to join the ministry. But what he revealed were the outlines of his previous negotiations with Waldeck-Rousseau, which, since they had come to nothing, had only abstract theoretical interest. But since the issue had been raised, Millerand pointed out to his colleagues, he thought they might profitably state a position on socialist participation in a bourgeois ministry, just in case he or some other socialist should again be approached with such an offer. His omissions were, of course, as significant as his comments. He gave no indication that he, Millerand, had initiated the discussion of socialist participation with Poincaré; nor did he feel it necessary or wise to mention that Gallifet was to be part of the same ministry.

Dealing with what seemed to them an academic question of tactics, the socialist deputies took up the question of participation only superficially. As Millerand was later to point out,[48] no one spoke of the class struggle or its relationship to ministerial collaboration. In fact, since socialist opposition to participation had been stated many times over, a detailed discussion may well have seemed superfluous. Instead, the question on which the conversation turned was whether a socialist could enter a ministry, not as a representative of the party, but rather as an individual. Since neither Jaurès nor Guesde was among the deputies, Vaillant spoke with the most authentic voice of authority. "I told him, [Millerand]," Vaillant later recalled, "that if a socialist entered as an individual, the party would in no way be committed to the government; and I swear that Millerand, if he didn't actually say anything, at least nodded his head affirmatively. I took note of that and left the room."[49] But when Millerand left the meeting, he was satisfied that no theoretical barrier had been raised against the action, which he had, in fact, already taken.

On Thursday, June 22, the French press carried startling political news. Waldeck-Rosseau had formed a ministry, drawn mainly from the ranks of Progressism and Radicalism.[50] But the reins of the new government rested in the hands of three men, the Premier, Gallifet, and Millerand. When the socialists received the news, most of them were incredulous, especially the Blanquists and Guesdists. Of course, so careful an observer as Vaillant had long expected that Millerand would one day "seize a ministerial opportunity."[51] But he could scarcely have believed that any socialist, under any circumstances, would choose to sit in a ministry beside the "Butcher" Gallifet. Thus, Vaillant, half believing that the newspapers had published false information, sent a special delivery letter to Millerand, urging him to repudiate the printed report. His message said nothing about the principle of participation; it centered exclusively on the issue of Gallifet. Vaillant received no direct reply, but the next day, June 23, he, along with the rest of the deputies, found in the *Journal officiel* Waldeck-Rousseau's complete ministerial list. On it was Gallifet, and also Millerand.

If surprise was universal among the socialists, disapproval was not, and therein, as Jaurès had feared, lay the seed of discord. Among the Independents in the Chamber and at the offices of *La petite République*, the reaction to the new ministry was favorable. But among the militants of the major organized factions, their patience already worn thin by their uneasy alliance with the Independents, resentment and anger mounted quickly. On June 25 the Blanquist deputies announced their withdrawal from the Union socialiste; and at the same time the deputies of the P.O.F. published their first official statement in a manifesto which condemned participation, not merely on the issue of Gallifet, but on principle. For as the Marxists insisted, the collaboration of a socialist with the enemies of the working class could only result in blurring the clear lines of class struggle.

For eight months party unity had seemed to be the immediate and greatest objective of French socialism; but Millerand's action had suddenly raised an almost insurmountable barrier to that goal. Yet, there is good reason to believe that among certain socialists, Guesdists especially, who were extremely uneasy about the potential influence of the Independents in a unified party, the new controversy was a welcome one. "Fortunately I think that Millerand's maneuver will give us an excellent pretext for restoring sane ideas among socialists," Bonnier wrote to Guesde. And he added significantly: "We can now force Jaurès' hand."[52]

And Jaurès — how would he react to this new dilemma? For a moment he was confused; a clear line eluded him, probably because none existed. To support Millerand might mean destruction of socialist unity; to reject the ministry might mean destruction of the Republic. On June 23 he made his way to the rue d'Ulm, to Lucien Herr and the familiar confines of the École Normale.[53] Herr had urged the visit in order to persuade Jaurès to stand behind the ministry. Others in the *équipe* of *La petite République* had argued the same position, but unlike them, the librarian could not be suspected of political opportunism. Jaurès listened intently as Herr explained how this ministry could turn the Dreyfus Affair into a great republican victory — carrying through revision, throttling the ultranationalists, checking the influence of the Church and the army. Herr talked on, as though he could anticipate every objection Jaurès might raise. Millerand's action, he admitted, was unfortunate, but it was a *fait accompli*, and it had to be accepted. Only one thing mattered now, the safety and progress of the Republic. And almost as an afterthought, he added an argument which Jaurès would later use many times over. "What a triumph for socialism that the Republic cannot be saved without calling on the party of the proletariat!"

When Jaurès walked away from the Ecole Normale, he was a man dominated by certain thoughts and pressures: Herr's words, his own friendship with Millerand, his hope that he could rally a united socialist movement behind the ministry, and above all, his belief that socialism could never desert the Republic. His decision was thus evident. He would support the ministry and Millerand's participation. The consequences, he knew, might be personal pain and anguish; the Marxists might rail against him and the workers misunderstand him. But he would function by a credo he repeated often: "A man should know how to be popular; but he should know how to go on without popularity."

The next day, June 24, Jaurès wrote out his conclusions for the public. The threatened Republic, read his article, needed a strong ministry, and Waldeck-Rousseau promised to head one; Waldeck needed an energetic Minister of War, and Gallifet fitted that description; the Republic needed the socialists, and Millerand was answering the call. "For myself and on my own responsibility, I approve Millerand's action in entering this fighting ministry."[54] His words undoubtedly influenced many rank-and-file socialists and strengthened the Independents in their support of Ministerialism. But simultaneously, the veneer of unity peeled off the whole movement like paint flaking off an old house. On June 25 the high command of the P.O.F., following the Blanquist lead, ordered its deputies to withdraw from the Union socialiste. And if there was any question as to how deep a division now cut across the socialist movement, it was answered on June 26, when Waldeck-Rousseau appeared before the Chamber of Deputies to seek approval for his government and his program.

The hall rocked with tumult that day. From the start of the session, the followers of Guesde and Vaillant, manifesting their contempt for Gallifet, shouted: "Assassin! Murderer! Long live the Commune!" They were joined, in an alliance of the extremes, by the nationalists of the Right, who were determined to block approval of this revisionist ministry. From the ministerial benches, the unbending Waldeck-Rousseau stared impassively at his howling critics. Millerand, "his moustache trembling on his lip, looked bedraggled, like a huge cat just caught in a downpour."[55] Gallifet, his expressive face fixed between a scowl and a smirk, wheeled round to the shouting deputies and barked: "Assassin! Present!"

The prospects for a vote of confidence seemed poor. Lined up against Waldeck-Rousseau were the deputies of the Right; the Mélinist Progressists; a few Radicals, like Pelletan, of Communard sensibilities; and half the socialist deputies. When Waldeck-Rousseau tried to speak, the sheets of his speech trembled in his hands, and his words were drowned out by the roar of insults. "I spoke for no more than ten minutes," he later recalled, "but I remained at the podium for an hour."[56] Yet even without words, his meaning was clear enough. He meant to carry through revision and safeguard the Republic. When the all-important vote was finally cast, the ministry managed to survive by the slim margin of 263 to 237.

The session was fraught with political significance. In his winning vote, Waldeck-Rousseau had help from several groups, which constituted his republican majority. From the Center, he won the support of part of the Progressists, persuaded by the influential banker Aynard that it was better to cast their lot with a moderate like Waldeck-Rousseau than to risk an unknown future. Some two years later, in May, 1901, these Progressists were to formalize their organization in the Alliance républicaine démocratique whose leading members dwelt at the heights of French capitalism.[57] Thus, from the start of his tenure, Waldeck-Rousseau was linked to an important group of economic conservatives who found a comfortable home within the new government.

On the Left, the Premier won almost solid support from the Radicals, many of them doctrinaire anticlericals who were determined to curb the power of the Church, and from twenty-five socialists (nineteen

Independents, two Allemanists, and four Guesdists), whose votes provided the margin of victory. But the new Premier even received the covert help of his noisiest critics on the Extreme Left. For when the vote was cast, the Blanquists and most of the Guesdists, seventeen in all, abstained. "They shouted angrily," commented Jaurès, "they demonstrated their hostility; but in the final analysis, they did not vote against the ministry."[58]

Yet, though the revolutionaries were unwilling to sacrifice the Republic either to the Right or to sheer chaos, the undeniable fact remained that the socialists were entering the new era of republican defense badly divided. Cut off from the revolutionaries (as the socialist opponents of Ministerialism were called), the ministerial socialists had little chance to influence public policy. Against the Progressists, they could hope for little better than a standoff. And the only common denominator of reform thus remained anticlericalism. When Jaurès predicted real gains for socialism under the new regime, he misrepresented the nature of the majority. On the other side, the Blanquists and Guesdists, in choosing the ranks of the opposition, abdicated their role in the Dreyfusard reformation.

For the moment, one consideration crowded the others from Jaurès' mind. France finally had a revisionist government; and since the ordinary session of Parliament ended on July 4, the ministry would at least survive the retrial of Dreyfus in August. As it turned out, the government lasted considerably longer than that. It ended only three weeks less than three years after it had been formed.

V

"You live very well up in the clouds among pure ideas, but you live badly on the solid ground of real life. . . . You are a socialist monk, not a normal socialist man."[59] That sharp criticism, directed at Guesde, came from Raymond Lavigne, chief of the P.O.F. in the Gironde. The charge of unreality was motivated by Guesde's determination to commit the entire P.O.F. to Antiministerialism. If that were done, warned Lavigne, the Marxists would lose countless followers who hoped for major social reforms. But Guesde was not to be deterred. While Vaillant had been upset originally by the presence of Gallifet in the ministry, the austere Marxist had immediately opposed any socialist collaboration in a bourgeois government. The struggle over Millerandism, after all, was only a dramatic symptom of a conflict, evident early in the Dreyfus Affair, over certain fundamental questions: whether or not all bourgeois parties were the same; whether or not fundamental reforms were possible.[60] Under the stimulus of the Millerand case, Guesde and his closest associates reverted to an earlier position, as they began to repudiate their decade-long compromise with parliamentary democracy.

On July 10, six men, including Guesde and Lafargue for the Marxists and Vaillant for the Blanquists, met at the home of Alexandre Zévaès to draw up a joint manifesto for their two parties. Zévaès held the pen, Vaillant added a few phrases, but Guesde was unquestionably the author. The manifesto, which was published on July 14, contained a stinging message: "The socialist party cannot share political power with the bourgeoisie. In their hands the State can be nothing but an instrument of oppression and conservatism." The Ministerialists were practicing "a false political method, compounded of compromise and deviation. . . . Party of opposition we are; party of opposition we must remain, entering Parliament and other elective assemblies as though we were in an enemy State, only in order to fight the enemy class and the political groups that represent it."

The words broke like thunder over the socialist movement. To those who now stood behind the government — Independents, Allemanists, Possibilists — the manifesto seemed like an attack on their understanding, and even more, on their integrity.[61] But to Jaurès especially, who had given so fully to the cause of socialism, its meaning appeared both mistaken and ungenerous. Exasperated yet still composed, he answered his "teachers, educators, and friends, Vaillant and Guesde."[62] In essence, as Jaurès realized, the manifesto challenged the value of progressive reforms; by implication it repudiated social change by democratic means. But if socialists abandoned reformism, he warned, the movement would sink to the level of "sterile and intransigent anarchism."

Such a reaction from Jaurès and his friends was predictable. But what undoubtedly startled the revolutionary leaders was the criticism aired by their own rank and file. From the Gironde, Lavigne sent a scorching letter to Guesde, denouncing his "aggressive attitude toward Jaurès and Millerand. . . . You have had good intentions for our party; I have no doubt of that. But don't come to us later and say that you were led by your subordinates, that they pushed you into this extremism of yours. . . . Insults and insinuations instead of considered and precise arguments will only drive the masses away from our program."[63] During the rest of July reports flowed in, which indicated to Guesde that several P.O.F. federations were opposed to the spirit of the manifesto. "I am convinced," wrote Lafargue, taking cognizance of the universal respect for Jaurès among ordinary socialists, "that if Jaurès had not been so obviously indicated [in the manifesto], the reaction would have been different."[64]

The confusion and conflict in the ranks of the movement led the Possibilists to propose on July 17 that the question of Ministerialism be debated and resolved before a general socialist congress. Marxist and Blanquist leaders, looking for a method of orderly retreat, quickly endorsed the plan. The Ministerial groups likewise accepted the proposal, though Jaurès objected to an agenda limited only to discussion of the Millerand case. At his suggestion, the socialist groups agreed to address themselves to unification at the proposed congress. By August of 1899, a Comité d'entente socialiste had been established and was making the arrangements for what promised to be the most important congress of the French socialist movement.

Behind this temporary *détente*, however, the tensions had scarcely disappeared. Despite years of close association, Guesde and Vaillant grew increasingly estranged from Jaurès and, until 1905, they were to write and say many acrimonious words about each other. With Vaillant, who later became so intimate a friend and collaborator of Jaurès, the quarrel seems to have been exclusively doctrinal. A learned man, who, according to Bracke, "grew each day by his endless reading, observation, and reflection," [65] Vaillant was not of an inflexible temperament. An admirer of English freedom as well as German philosophy, a disciple of Blanqui as well as of Marx, he was insensitive neither to democracy nor to the varieties of social action. But he was convinced that Jaurès had gone too far in the acts of collaboration and reformism, and he fought him on those grounds.

With Guesde, it was rather different. His influence on Jaurès had been considerable, which the latter had never denied. Together these two men had represented that systole and diastole of socialism to which Jaurès so frequently referred. Why, then, the sudden bitterness in their relationship, the tone of personal vindictiveness against Jaurès in the private correspondence of Guesde and the other leaders of the P.O.F.? What was on the surface a conflict over socialist theory, was at bottom a clash of personalities. The doctrinal dispute was evident enough. Though Jaurès respected Marxist principles, Guesde and his followers never accepted Jaurès' idealism; they were, at best, indulgent toward what seemed to them a hangover from his early bourgeois republicanism. Now, on a question of tactics, a conflict which had been latent burst into the open.

But beneath the formal issues, there were undoubtedly factors of a psychological sort which intensified the clash. Guesde, aging, fatigued, and unwell, saw in the P.O.F., its organization, tactics, and principles, the greatest justification of his life. He had become, as the papers of the Guesde Archives amply indicate, a party chief, with neither the time nor the resources to alter his intellectual framework. The Marxism he had learned he repeated; but while the times changed, his phrases did not. Jaurès, flexible, complex, confusing, seemed a threat to Guesde's party, doctrine, and leadership.

Thus, when Guesde agreed to a general socialist congress, he was thinking less of a real debate on tactics than of a confirmation of his own viewpoint. Between August and December, he turned to German Social Democracy, the font of authority in world socialism, for aid and comfort. And in a steady interchange with the septuagenarian Wilhelm Liebknecht, he received them.[66] "As to Millerand," Liebknecht wrote in his most didactic mood, "you must stand firm. It is nothing short of treason that he remains in a ministry on which Gallifet has stamped his mark."[67] So, while the public pronouncements of leading socialists glowed with the prospects of unity, the private documents were laden with signs of schism.

VI

In July and August, the government of Waldeck-Rousseau created a revisionist climate. Gallifet moved quickly to remove the officer corps from interference in politics. Those officers who had been conspicuously associated with Antidreyfusard activity were reprimanded or transferred; a few were even dismissed. Then, on August 7, the second court-martial of Dreyfus began at Rennes, and Jaurès traveled there to report for his newspaper readers this latest climax of the Affair.

"I cannot describe how deep my feeling of pity was when I first saw him a week ago," he wrote from Rennes. "His whole presence reveals depths of unspeakable suffering."[68] Jaurès was reacting to the appearance, after more than four years of confinement on Devil's Island, of the broken, white-haired Alfred Dreyfus. It seemed to Jaurès that justice would no longer be deferred. But the case was tried before seven officers, little different in their prejudices from their implicated colleagues of the General Staff, and there was no guarantee that the rule of law would triumph over esprit de corps.

For a solid month the trial dragged on, a recital once more of familiar charges, denials, and assumptions. Again Mercier insisted on Dreyfus' guilt, and again Picquart disproved it. The seven military judges permitted everything, and a saddened Jaurès sensed that they were dominated by their attachment to caste. "If they condemn Dreyfus again," he wrote, "they will do it to save Mercier, Gonse, Boisdeffre, and Du Paty de Clam."[69] On September 9, the judges, voting five to two, returned a verdict of guilty against Dreyfus, though, because of what they called "extenuating circumstances" they changed the prisoner's sentence from a life term on Devil's Island to ten years of imprisonment.

"A new Austerlitz!" cried Drumont after the verdict became known. "It's a great and marvelous victory for France against the crowd of Jews and internationalists."[70] But for Jaurès the decision was "monstrous. To convict an innocent man a second time is a crime without precedent."

Yet now, more than ever, with the innocence of Dreyfus "known the world over," he viewed the future optimistically. "As for us, who have waged this rough but noble battle for almost two years, we have never been more fully confident of eventual victory."[71]

The Dreyfusards had one important trump card. They knew they could count on the good will of Waldeck-Rousseau and his ministry. What baffled them most was the matter of procedure, whether to demand another trial or to work for a Presidential pardon. A day after the verdict at Rennes, Reinach met with Jaurès and Clemenceau at the offices of *Le Radical* to map out strategy. Reinach, whose chief concern was justice for Dreyfus the man, opted strongly for a pardon so that the misery of the victimized captain would end at once. Clemenceau voiced strong opposition, for unless the corruption of justice were exposed by a clear-cut verdict of innocence, "the fight would end without victory."[72] Jaurès at first backed Clemenceau, not for lack of mercy but out of dedication to the larger cause of justice. The next day, however, Mathieu pleaded with Reinach to intervene with the Premier in favor of a pardon; his brother, he wept, would never survive further imprisonment. Reinach agreed, and when he sounded out Waldeck-Rousseau, he found him favorable to the idea of a pardon. Clemenceau, unmoved by arguments about one man's suffering, remained opposed, but Jaurès, convinced that the struggle against the corrupters would continue even after that single act, endorsed the plan to seek Presidential clemency.

The wheels turned quickly once the pardon was agreed upon by the leading Dreyfusards. The Minister of War formally requested that the President reverse both the sentence and the act of degradation. On September 19, Loubet complied, and by nightfall Alfred Dreyfus, a man who had been to hell and back, returned to his family. "The incident is closed," Gallifet declared in a manifesto issued to the press. Jaurès knew otherwise. Dreyfus had been saved, and so had the Republic. But work of recovery and reformation still lay in the future.[73]

In the autumn months Waldeck-Rousseau gave the Republic the strong leadership it had lacked. He went after the noisiest rabble-rousers on the nationalist and anti-Semitic fringes in order to snuff out the lingering hope of a *coup d'état* against the Republic. Déroulède and some twenty others, rounded up in August and charged with plotting against the State, were brought to trial in November. Though the majority were acquitted, the most vocal of them, Déroulède and Guérin, were given prison sentences of ten years.

Then, on November 16, Waldeck-Rousseau appeared before the Chamber to unveil his legislative program for republican defense. Moderate, even cautious in such proposals as the curtailment of courts-martial and the liberalization of the 1884 trade union law, the Premier was most imaginative in calling for a new law on associations, the essential though unstated aim of which was to eliminate or hamstring the clerical congregations. Nothing in this program was socialist, and, like the Dreyfusard cause in general, it roused no enthusiasm in the organized labor movement.[74] Yet Jaurès lent his support and prestige to the Government of Republican Defense, identifying the interest of socialism with a program not even remotely collectivist. In defending his position, he stressed again and again the importance of democracy in the evolution toward socialism. Once the Republic was secure, he reasoned, the socialists, if they were united and purposeful, could utilize its institutions in guiding France toward a collectivist society. But again, unity was all-important, and for that reason the forthcoming congress of socialist organizations was uppermost in his mind.

As the last month of 1899 began, the socialists readied themselves for their historic congress, which opened at the Salle Japy in Paris on December 3.[75] The huge hall was cold during the six days of meetings, but everything else — issues, voices, tempers — generated ample heat. Some seven hundred delegates represented 1452 diverse socialist groups. The tightly organized Marxists and Blanquists together controlled a bloc of 830 votes, while the Independents, Allemanists, and Possibilists could count for certain on no more than 550. Jaurès realized that he faced a difficult battle, uphill all the way, to win broad support for the tactics of collaboration and a program of reforms. His intellect and his voice were powerful weapons, but he sought also a strong and friendly ally. His man, he felt, was Briand, who, in the controversy between Jaurès and Guesde, chose Jaurès.

"His association with Jaurès," Suarez wrote candidly, "held greater advantages for him [Briand] than an alliance with Guesde."[76] The Marxist chief practiced self-abnegation and expected it of others. But Jaurès, thought the ambitious Briand, was no ascetic, and he could be counted on to interpret socialist office-holding as a gain for humanity. If Jaurès had doubts about a man who was a Boulangist in 1889, who was run out of Saint Nazaire for paying court to the wife of a local banker, who had been in and out of the syndicalist movement, he suppressed them. When he looked at the warm, handsome face of Briand, he apparently saw only a loyal comrade.

The major controversy at the Congress, the conflict that absorbed the delegates over four successive days, centered on the question of tactics. On the second day Jaurès spoke at length, trying to reconcile the concept of the class struggle with tactics of ministerial participation. The class struggle, he affirmed at once, was undeniable in contemporary society. There existed a "fundamental antagonism" between the bourgeoisie and the proletariat, and for that reason the working class needed a separate political party to carry on its struggle. But how that battle was waged belonged to the realm of method, not principle, and any successful political method required flexibility, variety.

The socialist party, he reminded the delegates, was engaged in daily politics, and though it was easier just to recite old revolutionary slogans, its responsibility to the workers demanded that it influence the bourgeois State as much as possible with its own men and ideas. In the imperfect world of politics, socialists had constantly to choose the better of two courses, even though it might fall short of ideal socialist action; for by cumulative gains, they would evolve toward their final goals. Nothing in all this was new or heretical, Jaurès pointed out. They had all, Guesdists and Blanquists included, followed that method in their support of the Bourgeois ministry. They were following it whenever they elected socialist mayors, who were required, after all, to maintain law and order within the cadre of the capitalist State. Millerand's entry into the Waldeck-Rousseau ministry simply carried socialist influence one step further.

Yet suddenly, after adhering to so fruitful a line of political action, the so-called revolutionaries concluded that the State was impenetrable, every reform delusive and every victory hollow. "Citizens," cried Jaurès, "once we had to cut through the false teaching of the iron law of wages, which would have discouraged the workers from struggling to improve their conditions; now we have to cut through the equally false notion of the iron law of the State; . . . we must fight not from a futile distance, but from the very heart of the citadel."[77]

The understanding of the French Marxists, he charged, was distorted by their rigid determinism. Guesde had been so convinced of the iminence of a capitalist collapse, recalled Jaurès, that he had predicted a socialist society by 1900. Such certainty was, in fact, the most delusive sort of utopianism: "If we can't predict exactly when and how capitalism will collapse, we must always be ready for it, but we must also work for those reforms which . . . will prepare the way."

The revolutionaries had charged, Jaurès continued, that Ministerialism was an open invitation to opportunism and personal corruption. That danger was admittedly latent in all public action. But the prohibition of political participation could only weaken socialism while presumably safeguarding its purity. The better answer to the danger of opportunism was, as Jaurès and his supporters were proposing, to establish party controls over the actions of socialist officials.[78] "We are all good revolutionaries," cried Jaurès in conclusion. "Let us make that clear, and let us unite!"

Deafening applause came from the ministerialists, but not from the revolutionaries who, stung by his personal references to Guesde and Lafargue, had interrupted and heckled throughout the oration. No doubt it was uncomfortable to be reminded of changing social and political realities: of increased productivity in Western capitalist countries, or of slow improvements in the condition of the working class. For all of that modified the socialist conception of revolution.[79]

But support for Jaurès came at once from Briand, who, as Pelloutier observed, "put the Guesdists on trial by recalling to them that, though they had once been opposed even to participating in elections, and then to formulating a minimum program, they had continuously modified their original intransigence, like all other socialists."[80] Through this barrage, Guesde kept a strict silence, and only on the third day did he rise to answer. "Tall, thin, dessicated, his eyes ablaze like black fire, he spoke quickly, releasing his words without any apparent style."[81] Guesde brought before the delegates the teachings of other Marxists; the German socialists, he asserted, had posed the question of ministerialism, and Liebknecht had concluded ——

At that moment, as the name of the renowned Social Democrat was mentioned, the Allemanist Joindy shouted: "Down with Liebknecht!" "Imagine a man," wrote Pelloutier, "shouting in Notre Dame, at the moment when all heads are bowed before the Holy Sacrament: Down with God! and you will have a rough idea of the shock and then the anger which passed over the faces of the Guesdists."[82] Bedlam broke loose in the hall as Joindy tried to explain that he was protesting against anti-Semitic remarks made by Liebknecht and conveniently cited by Drumont and Rochefort. Order was restored only when Joindy was expelled from the hall. What Guesde then said had been heard many times; his speech was important only because he, the leader of the P.O.F., delivered it.

On December 6, four days after they had begun their debate, the weary delegates were ready for a vote. But before it was taken, Briand was back on the rostrum, defending the revolutionary general strike in order to needle the Guesdists, and, if possible, to drive a wedge between them and the Blanquists. At the climax of his speech, he let fly the words that would, almost eight years later, come back to haunt him: "Go into battle with the ballot, if you judge it sound, and I will find no fault. I have been a voter; I have been a candidate, and I will undoubtedly be both again. Go then with picks, swords, pistols, and rifles, and, far from disapproving, I will do my duty by taking my place in your ranks. But do not discourage the workers when they try to unite for an action which is their own and whose efficacy they trust."[83]

264 | YEARS OF ANGUISH

Through all the talking and shouting, Jaurès hoped that the Congress might work out a temporary combination of viewpoints. In the Resolutions Committee he worked hard for an acceptable compromise, and that seemed to have been accomplished when the Committee agreed on a single resolution (only the seven Blanquists opposed it), which was to be placed before the entire Congress. In part, it read: "While admitting that exceptional circumstances may arise in which the party would have to examine the question of socialist participation in a bourgeois government, the Congress declares that . . . the entire strength of the party must be turned toward winning elective offices only — in the Communes, the Department, and the State." Thus, though the party's tactics were to be flexible in times of emergency, the practice of Ministerialism was in principle prohibited.

During the Committee debates, the P.O.F. had supported the resolution, but Guesde soon discovered that it was unacceptable to some of his most uncompromising followers. Therefore, he struck a bargain with Jaurès: to rally his own men, he would present an amendment, so phrased that the Congress could take a clear stand, yes or no, on Ministerialism; but while speaking for this amendment, he would put his party behind the Committee's main resolution. Thus when the time for voting arrived, Fournière, the chairman, read Guesde's amendment, which was put in the form of a question: "Yes or no, does the class struggle permit a socialist to enter a bourgeois government?" But when Fournière called on Guesde to speak for his amendment, the Marxist replied: "No! The reading suffices." In refusing to speak for the Committee's resolution, Guesde had broken a promise and endangered the possibility of an acceptable compromise. Jaurès lost his sang-froid completely. Brick-red, he rushed to the rostrum and shouted: "Guesde, it's an act of disloyalty! Guesde! Jules! Jules! It's treason! Guesde, you must speak in the name of your party!" Pelloutier found himself "overcome with emotion; Jaurès appeared so sincere and Guesde so culpable."[84] The din was deafening, but Jaurès went on: "You are dishonored! You have fallen! You have broken your word! . . . If there has been only a misunderstanding, you must clear it up; if there has been a betrayal, you must bear the responsibility." Guesde finally came forward to defend his honor, but in the course of his brief statement he offered no explanation of his broken promise.

The vote was cast first on Guesde's amendment, and by a count of 818 to 634, Ministerialism and the class struggle were declared incompatible.[85] The delegates then turned round, as though no contradiction were involved, and overwhelmingly (1140 to 240) accepted the Resolution, which approved Ministerialism in exceptional circumstances.

Neither logic nor integrity was served by these successive votes, but temporary unity was. These actions enabled the delegates to sit together for two more days while they hastily approved plans for a new party, the Parti socialiste français, to be governed by annual congresses and guided by a General Committee.[86] By nightfall of December 8, the International had been sung, the red banners unfurled, and the goal of unity, on paper at least, attained.

The Congress over, Jaurès played down its obvious dissensions while accentuating in his public statements its positive accomplishments. In his willingness to smooth over differences in the interest of unity, he even found good words for the Guesde amendment: "Personally, I'm not at all upset over that vote. It's not bad for the party to erect barriers against unrestrained and dangerous ambitions."[87] But there were other commentators, neither so generous as Jaurès, nor so sanguine about lasting harmony. "I congratulate you warmly on your superb victory," Lavigne wrote to Guesde. The Congress, he went on, was a solid defeat for "Jaurès, le pauvre."[88] And Pelloutier wrote tellingly to the anarchist Delesalle: "Each socialist faction means by unity a monopoly of its own policy; for despite appearances, Jaurès is as sectarian as Guesde, though in the interests of a narrow and sterile reformism."[89]

For a brief time, and in the afterglow of the Congress, the socialist deputies restored their single parliamentary caucus, and it seemed as though the optimism of Jaurès might be justified. But when days passed into weeks, the skeptics proved to be the better prophets. Beneath the formality of unity, the division over socialist tactics continued. The resolutions of the Congress had solved very little. The General Committee of the new party was dominated by Antiministerialists, and the parliamentary group by Ministerialists. Between the two, the clash was virtually inevitable, and when it came, it killed unity for four full years.[90]

VII

The quarrel over tactics was not confined to the French movement. Wherever parliamentary and capitalistic institutions flourished, conflict developed within socialism. But while the controversy remained essentially tactical in France, in other places, notably Germany, the division was also, in a very fundamental sense, doctrinal. For the very essence of what was called German Revisionism was a repudiation of the principal tenets of Marxism.[91] Jaurès sympathized with the spirit of free inquiry and the great intellectual capacity of Eduard Bernstein, the leader of the German Revisionists. But at a strategic moment, he spoke out against Bernstein's teaching. Coming as it did soon after the Salle

Japy Congress, his criticism of Bernstein was no doubt influenced by a desire to cultivate the best possible relations with the revolutionaries. In its essential argument, however, his discourse on Bernstein was a restatement of the position he had held for almost a decade.

Bernstein was a Berlin Jew who had spent twelve years of exile in England (1888–1900) absorbing Fabian influence, until he felt impelled, in 1896, to challenge the central axioms of Marxism in a series of articles for *Neue Zeit*. The replies were hostile enough to bring Bernstein back into the debate in 1899 with a book, *Die Voraussetzungen des Sozialismus und die Aufgaben der Sozial demokratie*, setting forth his arguments in detail. He questioned in turn the materialist conception of history, the Marxist theory of value, the increasing misery of the working class, the trend toward capitalist concentration (Bernstein pointed out the diffusion of ownership through shareholding), the growing intensity of capitalist crises, and the polarization of society into two sharply antagonistic classes. The chief defender of Marxism was the indefatigable editor of *Neue Zeit*, Karl Kautsky, who admitted no basic modification in socialist doctrine. Aware of the potential impact of Bernstein's book, Kautsky sought to demolish it in a volume of his own, *Bernstein und das Sozialdemokratische Programm*. He did his work well enough so that the Revisionists were outvoted at the Congress of Hanover in 1899; but Bernstein's influence certainly did not disappear, and in 1900 he himself was elected to the Reichstag.

Into this doctrinal quarrel stepped Jaurès. One February evening in 1900, he went to the Hôtel des Sociétés Savantes, where a meeting had been organized by a group of socialist students. Allemane was the chairman, Jaurès the orator, and "Bernstein and the Evolution of Socialist Method" the topic. "In the controversy between Bernstein and Kautsky, I am with Kautsky."[92] So Jaurès began, ranging himself immediately with the Marxists. Bernstein, he felt, had made a significant contribution; "he has forced us all to verify our fundamental conceptions and to adapt them to changing realities." For "as great as Marx was," he wrote some time later, "he did not fix socialist thought for all time. It must change and develop, like reality itself."[93] But it was one thing to test theory against experience, and quite another "to break with the general traditions of international socialist democracy. I feel, and I will try to show, that Marxism contains within itself the means of completion and renewal."

Jaurès went on to defend the central Marxist theses — the theory of value, the materialist conception of history, the dialectical process. "After hard study, and after analyzing the attacks against the theory of surplus value, I find that it manages to stand up very well. For the fact always remains that the capitalist cannot draw profit, except from part of his workers' toil." Bernstein's rejection of Marx's theory of history brought the longest retort from Jaurès. Certainly, history was not shaped by a narrow set of economic determinants; nor was such a contention valid Marxism. "Marx never intended to say that economic forces acted alone and at once, . . . although I know Marxists in France who are shocked by Engels' apparent revision of their narrow construction." Other forces — science, democracy, religion — gave shape to daily life, Jaurès asserted, but the form of production and ownership ultimately determined the general character of the society: "It is like a strong breeze above everything, which stirs the many different trees. Each one responds with its own rhythm and vibration, and the whole forest, while shaken and driven in a general direction, deflects this strong breeze and helps to determine its direction."

To Bernstein's neo-Kantian voluntarism he added the dialectical process. "A revolution occurs when a social order develops an inner contradiction which can be resolved only by passing to a new social order." Bernstein had denied, through his observations of new class phenomena, that a revolution was imminent between two sharply antagonistic classes, the capitalists and the workers. While Jaurès agreed on the complexity of the class structure, he did not conclude that class antagonisms were thereby muted, but rather that they were different and constantly evolving. Thus, socialists were obliged to study, as Marx himself had done, "the slow and subtle transformations in the nature of the class structure."

When he passed to the question of tactics, Jaurès was neither with Bernstein nor with Kautsky. "I maintain against Bernstein that the proletariat and the bourgeoisie are and remain . . . radically distinct; and I maintain against Kautsky that we must not be afraid of contacts between the proletariat and other classes. It is impossible for a class to act without increasing the area of contact between himself and the rest of human society." Why not collaborate with the bourgeois progressives, where there were common battles to be fought and victories to be won? "We want revolution, but we don't want perpetual hatred. . . . Ah, what a joy it is for men who are hated and despised to find themselves collaborating for a moment, coöperating for a day! . . . And what joy there will be, sublime, universal, and eternal joy, when all men finally and definitively live together!"

As both analysis and strategy, the speech on Bernstein was an important document. On the level of theory, Jaurès again developed his synthesis of materialism and idealism, which served, throughout his socialist experience, as his guiding philosophy of history. If anything, he stated more explicitly than ever before the *primacy* of the class struggle in historical change; it was a subtle shift in emphasis which would become apparent after 1905 especially. But once he had accepted several important revisionist propositions, his final judgment on Marxism appears somewhat evasive. If a new white-collar class had, in fact, appeared to swell the ranks of the bourgeoisie; if property-holding peasants and shopkeepers suffered no such rapid extinction as Marx had predicted; if the living standards of workers in advanced industrial societies improved, however slowly; if the State, even under bourgeois control, had become an instrument of social reform, then the Marxist dogmas of class struggle and capitalist collapse were subject to extensive revision.

Unlike those socialist alchemists who sought to repudiate Bernstein by juggling statistics or ignoring facts, Jaurès praised his honesty and insight, while maintaining the ultimate validity of Marx's analysis. That conclusion he considered neither contradictory nor illogical. For on the basis of both his own economic investigations and his direct political experience, Jaurès rejected the full implications of Bernstein's revisionism. The struggle of antagonistic classes, he felt, would remain a moving force in history; neither the rise of a new middle class nor the lingering on of the old altered the essential fact that the goods of society were unjustly divided between those few who controlled the means of production and the many who did not. Nor could he agree that capitalism, whether through increased mass purchasing power or through colonial expansion, had permanently by-passed economic crises; even before the great depression of 1929 destroyed such optimism, Jaurès believed that capitalism might mask but could never eliminate the dilemma of too much production and too little consumption. And finally, though he deeply believed in amelioration through reforms, he was equally convinced that no social system short of collectivist socialism could permanently provide full employment and fair distribution. To accept Bernstein completely, he felt, was to transform socialism into a reformism shorn of identity and significance; that course Jaurès refused to follow. Still, like most leaders of the Second International, he passed too lightly over issues raised by Bernstein which were destined to affect the fate of socialism and limit its success.

The lecture on Bernstein, of course, was as much a tactical weapon as a statement of theory. Even as the schism within French socialism deepened, Jaurès strove for party unity, the sole basis for a strong and influential movement. No party, he realized, could unite Marxists and reformists unless it recognized collectivism as its goal and democracy as its means. Thus, through the medium of his oration, Jaurès implicitly warned against two excesses in French socialism — the tendency of those

Independents who had scrapped Marxism for a vague pragmatism, and the tendency of those revolutionaries who had turned Marx into an oracular god. Only by preventing the victory of the extremes, he reckoned, was unity possible. Thus, in the midst of Millerandism, Jaurès appealed to Marxists as well as reformists, and proposed a movement based on the insights of both. Only those who underestimated his dedication to unity or his devotion to collectivism could have been wholly perplexed by his behavior after the Congress of Amsterdam in 1904.

Six weeks later, Jaurès was in Bordeaux for the National Congress of Independent Socialists. One *bordelais* criticized him for having just spoken before the local P.O.F., bitter rival of the Independent group. Jaurès answered sharply that he was not simply a spokesman for the Independents, but an orator for the entire socialist party. "And in Bordeaux," he added, "there is only one great socialist force, and it is the P.O.F. Federation of the Gironde."[94] Such were his efforts to reach out to diverse factions, urging them to coöperate. But, as Jaurès was soon to learn, it was more difficult to unite the proponents of reform and revolution than to fuse his own idealism and materialism.

VIII

In the evening, when they have finished their long and arduous day, workers go to the "people's university" of their quarter. There, upwards of one hundred and fifty, perhaps even two or three hundred of them, listen to discussions of science, history, or economics. . . . Generally, it is not a question of a single lecture on one isolated topic, but rather there are several successive lessons devoted to the same subject. This eliminates empty generalizations and accustoms the workers to serious and detailed examination of questions. A discussion period follows the lecture when students ask for further explanations, without any embarrassment at all.[95]

So wrote Jaurès of the *universités populaires* immediately after he, along with Anatole France and Allemane, had spoken at the inauguration of the workers' school for the first and second arrondissements of Paris. The idea of offering regular lectures and courses for the proletariat reached back at least to 1886, but it was not until April 23, 1898, that the first people's university was founded by the workers of the typographical union. In the next few years, the movement flourished, spreading to most of the working-class districts of Paris. From the cultural and academic worlds the schools recruited their faculties, and from Jaurès came warm and enthusiastic support. The people's universities, he felt, would contribute significantly to the creation of a thoughtful proletariat, shaken from the torpor of resignation, awake to the potentialities of man while prepared to accept his limitations. "The workers don't want to wait for the total transformation of society before they start thinking," wrote Jaurès.[96] His exuberance, as it turned out, was premature, for within a few years, when the initial enthusiasm of workers and intellectuals waned, the people's universities disappeared.

But it was symptomatic of the cleavage among the socialists that the same experiment which stirred Jaurès' hope drew unqualified opposition from Guesde and Lafargue. "This movement," complained Lafargue, "is an attempt by intellectuals to capture the minds of the workers. . . . The only science the workers need is socialism."[97] All of the latent Guesdist hostility to the *universitaires* of socialism came to the surface, and it required but a superficial knowledge of recent events to realize that their criticisms were directed at Jaurès. Yet while this sharp difference of opinion over the people's universities revealed disunity, it was a minor symptom compared to the deep division of opinion over the Waldeck-Rousseau ministry and especially Millerand's position at the Ministry of Commerce.

Since taking office, Millerand had been an active minister, proposing a series of reforms which, he averred, would create peace and harmony in France's industrial society. At the heart of his program was the conception of a balance between responsible unions and privately owned industries, both of them coöperating, under the guidance of the State, in improving working conditions and increasing productivity. Turning his back on class war, Millerand was aiming for industrial peace. Toward this end, he proposed labor councils to negotiate collective contracts, compulsory arbitration of labor disputes, laws to reduce the hours of work and to expand the coverage of social security.[98] Did any of this add up to socialism? Hardly anyone, in or out of the working-class movement, believed it. "The ideas of the Honorable M. Millerand," noted *Le Temps* "do not differ essentially from those of the most moderate of his colleagues or predecessors."[99] Syndicalist leaders in both the Fédération des bourses du travail and the C.G.T. denounced the reform proposals as an attempt to mute labor's revolutionary cry. "They wanted to tame us," charged Victor Griffuelhes, the ex-Blanquist who emerged as spokesman for the revolutionaries of the C.G.T.[100]

In public print, however, Jaurès supported Millerand's program, calling it a source of strength for the workers in their march toward socialism. He even came out for measures like the Millerand-Colliard Law, which were most heatedly disputed within the organized labor movement.[101] At first glance, a startling position, for did it not drive a solid wedge between Jaurès and the revolutionaries of the socialist and syndicalist movements? That he was willing to compromise to help safeguard the ministry appears certain. But this alone does not seem to explain his position. More than most of his socialist colleagues, he grasped the central paradox of unionism, that however revolutionary its rhetoric and goals, its very raison d'être was amelioration of existing social conditions. Among certain trade union leaders, this objective was bluntly proclaimed, and Keufer, Baume, and Moreau publicly applauded Millerand's efforts. But in practice, even the revolutionaries demanded better conditions for the working classes; and when the government remained neutral toward their activities, they achieved some measure of success. It is probably true, though there is no way to measure it, that no such breach existed between Jaurès and the rank and file of the trade union movement as might be assumed from the pronouncements of certain syndicalist leaders in the labor press. As for the Guesdists and the Blanquists, adepts in the revolutionary texts, they offered little that was concrete on the transition from capitalism to socialism, while Jaurès, alerted to changing conditions and techniques, was at least seeking to construct a program of socialist action.

Two vital and probing questions, however, might have been raised about Millerand's reform efforts, and on the Extreme Left they were, in fact, formulated. In the first place, in trying to integrate workers within the cadre of existing industrial society, weren't the proposals of Millerand and Waldeck-Rousseau similar to the currents of corporatism which were already flowing through French social thought? The Blanquist de La Porte stressed the point when he clashed with Jaurès in May, 1901, at a meeting of the Comité Géneral of the Parti Socialiste Français. Arguing against compulsory arbitration, de La Porte compared it to the corporatist schemes of "the Christian socialists, especially De Mun."[102]

In retrospect, his apprehension probably had more justification than even de La Porte realized. For from several sectors of the French political community the drive toward an enforced class collaboration had picked up steam. Not only were Christian socialists preaching a medieval corporatism to harness the struggle of classes, but even the increasingly pessimistic liberals, devoted in theory to the system of the self-regulating market, were advocating forms of regulation and control. Thus, when so prominent a spokesman of liberalism as Waldeck-Rousseau sponsored the law of 1884, which encouraged trade unions, the militants of the labor movement instinctively felt that the measure aimed to enclose the working class within the walls of a regulated capitalism.[103] And even within the socialist tradition itself, when the roots reached down to Proudhon, the goal set for social action was the harmony of classes, not their conflict. "For Proudhon," Dolléans once wrote, "the revolution meant not the antagonism of classes but their collaboration; *reconciliation* was the sign that the revolution had been achieved."[104] Such, in fact, was the outlook of Millerand, conditioned early by Radicalism, and destined, after he left socialism, to move toward the Right. But it was qualitatively different to propose collaboration between masters and workmen in an age of small shops, as Proudhon did, than to apply the same method in a period of industrial capitalism.

Jaurès, who had been criticizing social Catholicism for over a decade, was hardly seduced by the tenets of corporatism. Thus, while defending compulsory arbitration, he insisted that its socialist value was in no way diminished because it was advocated by Christian corporatists for their own purposes: "Whenever revolutionary socialism makes progress, it will be surrounded by the penumbra of false socialism. . . . The fact that the nonsocialist parties usurp part of our program is hardly a reason to drop certain of our demands. . . . Since the Church can no longer count simply on the faith of its followers, it is trying to trap the workers with a handful of reform proposals."[105]

Nor was Jaurès so blindly loyal to Millerand or so sanguine about his motives that he abandoned his doubts about the program devised in the Ministry of Commerce. "Too often, Millerand has failed to take account of the class struggle in today's society," he charged. "Thus, when he has spoken of the necessary alliance between the republican bourgeoisie and the republican workers, he has given it a significance which it cannot have."[106] What else could Jaurès have intended by so direct a criticism than to warn of the impossibility of permanent class peace?

But even if the tactics of collaboration were considered temporary and Millerand's labor program advantageous to the workers, a second question loomed large. Was it possible, given the structure of the French urban economy, that any regulative machinery could intervene effectively between capital and labor? As late as 1906, one-third of all industrial and commercial wage-earners still worked in those many tiny enterprises which employed fewer than ten workers and generally escaped State regulation. The rest worked for those large establishments which were already transforming France, though more slowly than in either England or Germany, into a large-scale industrial society.[107] Against the owners of these powerful enterprises, it was at least questionable whether any bourgeois government could muster either the will or the strength to enforce its social laws.[108]

From both his scrutiny of economic records and his first-hand knowledge of capitalism in the Tarn, Jaurès may have felt that workers in small and large establishments alike would derive limited benefits from economic reforms. Why, then, did he lend such strong support to Millerand's program? Probably he was guided by his understanding of history, his conviction that the seeds of new societies have always been planted in the soil of the old: "Researches into the most remote past, in the succession from the iron to the bronze age, for example, show that there were periods in which old and new civilizations coexisted. The bourgeois revolution, one of the swiftest known in history . . . was not produced all at once. . . . And as we knew, the new revolution will be even more complex, vaster and deeper than the bourgeois revolution." [109] Thus, a mechanism like compulsory arbitration, by forcing otherwise recalcitrant owners to bargain with their workers and by wrenching from them a fraction of their gains, might strengthen the proletariat for its decisive thrusts against the system.

Faced with the eternal paradox of working for social improvements while preparing the new society, Jaurès fell back on analogy crossed with intuition. No incontrovertible evidence justified the assumption that reforms would strengthen the proletariat rather than prolong the capitalist system. But both logic and observation fortified his conviction, spelled out in the lecture on Bernstein, that since social misery, economic crisis, and political coercion were inherent within capitalism, the workers could never be permanently reconciled to the prevailing system. And intensive study of the French Revolution persuaded him (as it did Tocqueville) that a class steadily strengthened by concessions within the cadre of the old society was actually emboldened in its revolutionary will.

Yet another consideration influenced his position. In justifying Millerand's program, he was lending vital support to the ministry; and the ministry, whatever its other shortcomings, promised to drive hard against the Church and the army, eliminating from bourgeois society the last vestiges of aristocratic influence and curtailing the power of coercive institutions. [110] So long as the ministry was willing to cleanse the Republic, he would not abandon it. And that will seemed manifest when Waldeck-Rousseau introduced his Law on Associations and ordered dissolution of the Assumptionists, while General André, the anticlerical *polytechnician* who replaced Gallifet at the War Office, proposed to ventilate army headquarters with a strong gust of republicanism. [111] To these efforts Jaurès gave wholehearted support, recognizing in clericalism and militarism a threat to the minds, souls, and bodies of free men. At the dawn of the twentieth century, he already sensed the dilemma of the age — that as men were forging the tools to build a good society, their freedom to reason and think clearly was in danger. Watching the military parade in Paris on Bastille Day, 1900, he was moved to write of the automatism which could undermine democracy: "Automatism among great crowds of men has something very disturbing about it.

Each moving unit was like a fortress, impenetrable by reason or thought. Like a bloc of steel, heavy and overwhelming. . . . The army passed, mute, probably insensitive to the criminal provocations of the nationalists, but so distant from the people, so isolated from life by its very inner mechanism that it may one day yield to the most execrable commands."[112]

But if Jaurès persuaded his friends by these arguments, he had little evident success with his opponents. As the socialists prepared for two congresses in September, first the meeting of the Second International and then the conclave of the Parti socialiste Français, it was evident that the antagonism between Ministerialists and Antiministerialists had not only continued but deepened. Yet the impact of Jaurès' daily articles and frequent speeches worried the Guesdists. "Last night, I talked with Anseele, Adler, and other socialists of different schools," Lafargue wrote Guesde from Berlin. "They are all more or less for Jaurès. They don't know the situation in France, taking their information only from *La petite République*. To them Jaurès is still the great man of the Dreyfus Affair."[113]

Lacking a forum in which to answer Jaurès regularly and systematically, the Guesdists wanted a daily newspaper. Confined to their little weekly, *Le Socialiste*, they could hardly cope with such Ministerialist dailies as *La petite République* and *La Lanterne*. The will to publish a daily had long existed among the Marxists; they lacked only the money. The money was suddenly offered, however, by an eccentric multimillionaire, Alfred Edwards, former royalist, son of a physician to Abdul Hamid of Turkey, and once owner of the eminently respectable *Matin*. Thickset, burly, and arrogant, Edwards was the brother-in-law of Waldeck-Rousseau, whom he hated, and by allying himself with the Antiministerialists, he sought to embarrass the ministry. Though a liability to the revolutionary socialists because of his background, Edwards nonetheless gave them a newspaper, *Le petit Sou*, which served, from its first issue on September 2, 1900, as a forum for unrestrained criticisms of the Ministerialists and especially of Jaurès. A permanent breach between the French factions was in the making unless the International could resolve their differences.

On September 23, 1900, some eight hundred delegates from three continents gathered in the Salle Wagram for the Fifth Congress of the Second International. The revolutionaries thought that the leadership of the German Marxists would ensure a strong resolution against Ministerialism. But within the International, the currents of reformism (not only in France, but also in Italy, Belgium, and Germany itself) were strong enough to induce a spirit of compromise. Jaurès sensed a conciliatory mood among the Germans when he accompanied Singer to the Mur des Fedérés, where the German left a wreath at the scene of the Communard slaughter. As they were leaving, Singer turned to Jaurès and said: "We can't accept the entry of a socialist into a bourgeois ministry; but I can't help marveling at the fact that, while workers were shot down here thirty years ago, the socialist party has now grown so strong that the bourgeoisie had to call on one of them when freedom was in danger."[114]

Kautsky undertook to write a resolution which would uphold Marxist principles while simultaneously offering some satisfaction to the Ministerialists. On September 26, his handiwork was presented to the Congress by Vandervelde, and it revealed Kautsky as a master of compromise. Condemning ministerialism in principle though accepting it in certain emergencies, the resolution read in part:

The entry of a single socialist into a bourgeois ministry cannot be considered as the normal beginning for winning political power. It can never be anything but a temporary and exceptional makeshift in an emergency situation. Whether, in any given instance, such an emergency situation exists, is a question of tactics and not of principle. The Congress does not have to decide on that. But in any case, this dangerous experiment can only be of advantage if it is approved by a united party organization and if the socialist minister is, and remains, the delegate of his party.[115]

Jaurès was elated with the resolution; it gave him, he felt, real ammunition for the national congress. "More and more," he wrote the following day, "the socialist party is learning to distrust doctrinaire formulas, which are soon contradicted by the experience of life."[116] There was vigorous opposition to the resolution, however, led by Guesde and the learned Italian criminologist Enrico Ferri, who together proposed an amendment prohibiting participation under any circumstances. "When the socialist child grows and becomes a young man," cried the eloquent Ferri, "the capitalists change their tactics. No more persecution; instead, hypnotism."[117] But when the vote was cast, the Guesde-Ferri amendment was defeated, and by a tally of twenty-nine to nine the Kautsky resolution was adopted.

On September 27, the foreigners left the Salle Wagram, and the next day the French socialists returned for the second annual Congress of their tenuously united party. The past week's proceedings, it was at once evident, had only intensified their factionalism. A clash came at once over the very first question, the verification of credentials. Ministerialists, their opponents charged, had created artificial socialist groups to pack the meeting, and the accusation was partially true. Confronted with the well-organized Marxist and Blanquist organizations, the Ministerialists had sought, under Briand's direction, to manufacture a majority. "His methods perhaps were not very clean, but they were effective."[118] Throughout France, Bracke commented sarcastically, there occurred a "miraculous proliferation of groups; they grew . . . like mushrooms. Leaving aside the bus drivers' union, divided into as many sections as there were depots in Paris, it was a little startling to see groups springing up in areas traditionally unreceptive to socialism."[119] In the Credentials Committee, Briand tangled with Bracke, one of the few genuinely erudite Guesdists, distinguished translator of Euripides and commentator on Aristophanes. In the course of one stormy session, Bracke even lunged at Briand as though to choke him. The questionable credentials (136 of them, and all belonging to the Ministerialists) were finally placed before the entire Congress, where, by the narrowest of margins, they were accepted, thus ensuring a majority for Jaurès and his friends. From that point on, the Guesdists were truculent, and finally schismatic.

Three of the four Committee reports, drawn up by Antiministerialist majorities, were frontal attacks against the parliamentary group, and it fell to Briand to return the fire.[120] Heckled and interrupted, especially by Lafargue, Briand turned to "the millionaire Lafargue, who spends his life in a chateau and leaves it only to play the demagogue at socialist congresses." But Briand could go no further. At that moment, one Andrieux burst into the hall, blood spurting from his hand. The Guesdists, pushing forward to see what had happened to their comrade, learned that Andrieux had been stabbed in the corridor. Lucien Roland of the P.O.F. demanded immediate expulsion of the aggressor. The Ministerialists rejected the demand, and from the angry Guesdists came shouts of "assassins!" Rising then in a body, they flooded, like a tidal wave, into the corridors and toward the door. The Guesdists left the hall, the Congress, and the unified socialist movement. The Blanquists, however, stayed on, largely because of Vaillant's reluctance to sever the frayed threads of unity completely. During the rest of the Congress, the old Blanquist took up the attack against the Ministerialists, but the resolutions of his faction were now easily beaten.

Jaurès, who had participated little in the antics of the first two days, viewed them, no doubt, with mixed emotions — satisfaction that his own position would prevail, apprehension that the new schism would deprive the party of much-needed militancy, and hope that the Guesdists could be induced to return. On the last day, September 30, he read the report for the Committee on Party Unification, which reflected his own basic sentiments: "The Congress proclaims that the full and definitive unity of the socialist party must be realized with the least possible delay. In spite of temporary divisions, the Congress affirms the continuity of the socialist party, and decides that a new General Committee — will consult at once with all the political and economic groups in the party on the method of organization and unification."[121] Cries of "Vive l'Unité!" filled the hall, and, as the Congress of the Salle Wagram drew to its close, the resolution was passed by acclamation.

Jaurès had spoken of "temporary divisions," but he was too optimistic. The Guesdists, crystallizing the split in party ranks, called for a new socialist party, and on September 30, they set up a committee to lay its foundation. By October 9, on the other hand, the new General Committee of the socialist party was elected, and the powerful role of secretary was filled by the most irritating of the anti-Guesdists, Aristide Briand. By the end of October, the split between the factions was dramatically revealed when Jaurès and Guesde had an opportunity to confront each other in public debate before a working-class audience. The P.O.F. Federation of the Nord invited them to Lille for a discussion of socialist tactics. Both men accepted the invitation, and a classic moment in French socialist history was assured. With Delory, the Marxist mayor of Lille, presiding, the two men took the platform on the appointed night to debate "the two methods."[122] But the words had all been heard before and the results, except for the chronicle of socialist debates, were negligible. By the end of 1900, it was perfectly obvious that unity was at best a hope, not a reality.

IX

The new year opened in pain. "I must apologize to the socialists of the eleventh arrondissement," Jaurès wrote in January, "for being unable to attend tonight's meeting as scheduled. To my deep sorrow I have been incapacitated by an almost complete collapse of my voice."[123] A month later, he was forced to cancel all speaking engagements indefinitely because of a "serious throat infection which has afflicted me."[124] The cumulative strain of countless speeches in rooms where he sweltered with heat or shivered with cold had taken its toll.

But nothing slowed down his pen or his persuasive personal conversations. In May the Parti socialiste français would hold another annual congress, and the whole question of collaboration, especially Millerand's role, was bound to be challenged by Vaillant and his followers. As Jaurès contemplated that showdown, he realized that his most effective weapon must be the record of the Waldeck-Rousseau ministry. If he could demonstrate that this government was different from its reactionary predecessors, energetic in republican defense and sincere in social reform, then he might not only defend Ministerialism but also prevent another schism in the party. As the months passed between

January and May, he tried, on a number of issues, to make such a demonstration. In each instance, however, he found his support of governmental actions sharply attacked by the Antiministerialists.

On January 15, 1901, the Chamber began to debate the Law on Associations, and Waldeck-Rousseau was faced with strong and varied opposition. The Catholic De Mun charged him with legislating the "de-Christianization of France."[125] The conservative Ribot defended the right of Catholics to teach. The Radical Pelletan, arguing on the other side, appealed for the suppression of all congregations.[126] Waldeck-Rousseau remained resolute in the face of the opposition. To Catholics and conservatives, he declared in the Chamber on January 21: "We must either be with the Revolution and its spirit, or with the Counter-Revolution against public order." To the Left, he drew the distinction between the Church, which he viewed as a vital institution in French life, and those of its organs which remained unreconciled to the Republic. In this position, a compound of resolution and moderation, he had the backing of Radicals like Bourgeois and Brisson, and ministerial socialists led by Viviani. Outside the Chamber, he won the vital support of Jaurès.

While any distinction between the Church and its congregations struck him as "false and artificial,"[127] Jaurès welcomed the measure because it was moderate enough to win a majority, yet forceful enough to limit clerical power, especially in teaching.[128] Skilled in the art of politics, he realized that most achievements are built on compromise; and devoted to the "evolutionary revolution," he was willing to traverse the road to socialism slowly, a step at a time. But the Antiministerialists were of a different mind.[129] Their position was best summed up in Zévaès' unsuccessful amendment, supported by both Guesdists and Blanquists, which proposed immediate suppression of all congregations.

The conflict between Jaurès and the Antiministerialists was sharpened, however, when the ministry had to take a stand on the conflict between capital and labor. From the early winter to the late spring of 1901, labor disorder spread through the mining and metallurgical communities of the Saône-et-Loire, reaching a climax in the pits around Montceau-les-Mines. The demands of the miners, a daily wage increase of twenty-five centimes, was flatly rejected by the companies, even though coal prices had been increasing for some time. Rather than grant any concession, the company dismissed 450 of the striking workers.

The ministry was immediately involved when the Premier ordered troops to the strike fields to maintain order and to protect property. But it was even more deeply implicated when the Comité fédéral of the National Miners' Federation assumed leadership of the dispute and threatened to call a general strike unless the ministry promised pensions for workers, an eight-hour day, and minimum wages for miners. Waldeck-Rousseau, replying in the Chamber on March 8, agreed to support laws on pensions and hours, but refused either to withdraw troops or to interfere with wages, which he considered a totally private matter between workers and employers.

Not questioning for a moment the justice of the miners' cause, Jaurès denounced the action of the companies in unqualified terms: "The capitalistic system is thus revealed in the full flush of its iniquity. Its very essence is to crush the innocent."[130] But the ministry, subject to the influence of socialists and even of certain Radicals, had proved itself something other than the direct representative of capitalism. Waldeck-Rousseau was bourgeois, to be sure, but his response to the workers was "in marked contrast to the antilabor hostility of the Méline ministry."[131] It was possible, Jaurès was in effect asserting, to filter progressive influences through the State.

But the miners rejected the Premier's offer. Meeting at Lens in April, a national congress of miners decided to put the general strike to a referendum, and when it was held on April 28, the vote favored it by a three-to-two majority. Jaurès intervened at once to try to prevent it, contacting the government, on the one hand, to ensure its integrity on reform proposals and, on the other, M. Cotte, the secretary of the Miners' Federation. The general strike, he argued, was effective only under certain conditions, when it was well organized both as to ends and means. Otherwise, it was "revolutionary romanticism," an idle gesture which misused the workers and compounded their misery.[132] The promised reforms, on the other hand, would improve their conditions, lending a modicum of security to their lives. In the back of his mind, however, another thought may well have held sway — that a general strike would split the republican majority in the Chamber and bring down the ministry before its work was completed. But was it really a sound decision, to moderate the workers' demands for the sake of anticlerical and antimilitary reforms? In the Lille debate, Jaurès had answered that question in reminding Guesde of some well-known words of Marx: "We, the revolutionary socialists, are with the proletariat against the bourgeoisie, and with the bourgeoisie against aristocrats and priests." For a number of complex reasons,[133] Jaurès' role among them, the threat of the general strike and the actual partial strike sputtered to a halt by the first week of May.

Throughout the labor crisis, the attitude of the revolutionaries, both in socialism and in syndicalism, conflicted sharply with that of Jaurès.

In the Chamber debate of March 8, the Antiministerialists, led by Déjeante, Vaillant, and Zévaès, brushed aside Waldeck-Rousseau's concessions to demand immediate withdrawal of troops from the strike fields and then nationalization of the mines. As for the syndicalists, embittered by the collapse of their plan for a general strike, their hero was not Jaurès, but the emaciated Pelloutier, who, by dying of hemoptysis on March 13, 1901, gave syndicalist hagiography its first saint.

Did Jaurès then lose support among the great mass of workers? Though it is impossible to know accurately, it is improbable. They continued to pour into meeting halls and to throng onto fields to listen to him and to be caught up by his incomparable oratory. Was it possible, after a dozen embattled years of contact, to suspect him of inconstancy? Even Charles Rappoport, who became so bitter a critic of ministerialism, would write to Kautsky, attacking Jaurès not for duplicity but for poor judgment: "Jaurès is personally honorable, but not his entourage."[134] If his honor seemed unassailable, his position did not. Thus, when it was finally time for the annual party congress of 1901, he had signally failed to impress the revolutionaries with the validity of ministerialism.

In the last week of May, Jaurès went to Lyons for the Third Congress of the Parti socialiste français. Hardly had the meeting opened, when the Blanquist Amédée de La Porte moved a resolution of expulsion which sought to place Millerand "outside the party" because of his entry into a bourgeois ministry. The Ministerialists countered with another resolution, artfully composed by Briand, which would have placed Millerand "outside the *control* of the party." Only once during the Congress, in the debate on the de La Porte motion, did Jaurès speak, reiterating his faith in the ministry, and then dwelling at length on the crucial point of expulsion. He resented and resisted the method of purging members from party ranks. Once Millerand had been expelled for treason, he cried, all of his supporters would be future victims. Heated denials flew back, especially from Jean Longuet, but Jaurès had made his point. The de La Porte motion was decisively beaten, 910 to 286.

When the vote was announced, echoes of earlier congresses resounded through the hall. Émile Landrin leaped to his feet, declaring that the Blanquists had no alternative but to bolt the party. At that signal, Vaillant and his followers, less disciplined in their departure than the Guesdists, flocked toward the door, singing the *International* in defiant voices. From that moment until April of 1905, the French socialist movement was split in two.[135] Jaurès walked the streets of Lyons once the Congress had ended. His anguish was great. "We are in a narrow alley; from two opposing rooftops we are drenched by hard heavy rain. Oh, let the beautiful sun of socialist unity come to dry us off!"[136]

X

In the summer of 1901, Jaurès, spent and depleted, returned to his family. He visited the aged Adélaïde, now near her eightieth year, but still possessed of the Barbaza brightness. He spent time with Louise. In particular, he sought out his children — Madeleine, a girl of twelve, and Louis, a sturdy little three-year-old. But the winds of politics blew wildly, and in the end they carried sadness into his home.

Madeleine, though she appeared to be physically well, ailed psychologically. A mother lost in her own small interests and a father absorbed in public life had apparently failed her. While the family lived in the vicinity of the Luxembourg Gardens, she studied at the Collège Sévigné; when they moved to Passy, she transferred to the Lycée Molière. Before the end of the 1900–1901 school year, she dropped out because of illness and went south with her mother and brother to rest at Bessoulet. Responding to her traditional Catholic instincts, Louise sent the girl to a convent in Villefranche-d'Albigeois to prepare for her first communion. Jaurès stood aside, respectful of his wife's beliefs and patient with her indiscretions. On July 7, 1901, Madeleine, in a long white dress, received first communion; her relatives then gathered at Bessoulet to celebrate.

The story of Madeleine's communion spilled into public print through the efforts of a former schoolteacher in Toulouse, one Lamouère, who carried a ten-year-old grudge against Jaurès because he had failed to receive a municipal subsidy for certain inventions while the *tarnais* was a member of the municipal council. Writing in *L'École laïque*, Lamouère implied that Madeleine had always been enrolled in Catholic schools. On July 11, a few days after the story appeared, Jaurès wrote in *La petite République*: "She [Madeleine] has not had, and will never have, any but secular teachers." As for the first communion, he held it to be strictly a private family matter.

The Guesdists, in fact, treated it as such. "As for that affair," Bonnier wrote to Guesde, "it hardly interests us whether the girl has her communion or not."[137] But for others, of both the Right and the Left, the *cas Madeleine* became very much a public issue. And for no one more than for Urbain Gohier. A brilliant though scurrilous journalist, Gohier had once been an astringent critic of republican socialism and secularism for the monarchist paper *Le Soleil*. When he rallied to the Dreyfusard cause, however, he began to bestow his practiced invective on militarism and clericalism. A self-styled socialist, Gohier aspired to status on the Left, and by so sensational a gesture as denunciation of Jaurès, he would at least achieve notoriety. His own explanation of his tirade pictured him as a man bitterly disillusioned by Jaurès: "He had filled me with hope and enthusiasm . . . now he has made, as well as thousands of others, pay for those fervent hours with inexpressible disgust."[138]

The tempest over Madeleine's communion finally spread to the rue Portefoin, home of the General Committee of the Parti socialiste français. Its agitated Allemanist members, having grown restive in the Ministerial camp, demanded a hearing on the near crime of Catholicism in a socialist home. For six weeks, members of the General Committee raised voices, brought fists down on the table, and agreed finally to hold a hearing. On an appointed September day, the inquisition took place. "Jaurès sucked lozenges to soothe an inflamed throat. Never had he been so unhappy, crushed by the callousness of others."[139] Willm, whose own purity was later (and with much better reason) suspected, spoke for the Allemanists: "You can't make daily denunciations of officers who go to Mass, while handing your own daughter over to the priests."[140]

Jaurès replied at length, and he published the substance of his argument some five weeks later: "In most families of the republican bourgeoisie and the socialist proletariat, the women are neither clerical nor free-thinking, neither fanatical nor devout. . . . If their heads, the fathers, are not believers, they offer no protest. . . . But, except in a very few cases, they remain attached to their traditional Catholic faith. . . . Without intolerance, they still link the great events of life — birth, marriage, death — to a religious tradition." So it was with his own wife. As for his beliefs, Jaurès asserted, they were clearly on the record. "I have been free of formal religion since my adolescence." But he would never impose his beliefs on others. Nor did he feel that his position in the movement required some especially circumspect behavior: "I am one militant, like other militants; one man, like other men."[141]

The hearing sank to the ludicrous. Someone suggested that Jaurès ought manage his wife more authoritatively. Briand promised that, if elected to the Chamber, he would introduce a measure forbidding baptism without the consent of both parents. Finally the hearing ended when the General Committee agreed to seek guidance on the issue from the forthcoming Congress of Tours.

Gohier, however, only stepped up his attacks, denouncing the disparity between Jaurès' public appeal and his private behavior.[142] Jaurès finally exploded with rare fury against "this poor, malicious, incoherent, deluded character" who "knows nothing of socialism, who has neither curiosity nor common sense."[143] Running out of new charges, Gohier resorted to an old one, that Jaurès was rich from journalism. "During the entire Dreyfus Affair," retorted Jaurès, "from the Zola trial to the Rennes trial, the amount of work I put in had rarely been equaled, I believe, in the history of journalism." For that, he had received a sum not half as much as the salaries earned by writers in the capitalist press.

Gohier then trained his fire on *La petite République*, identifying Jaurès, of course, with the activities of the paper. On the ground floor of its building, Gohier revealed, *La petite République* ran a shop where exorbitant profits were made on goods manufactured cheaply by prison and convent labor. Jaurès replied at once: "Just as Urbain Gohier is powerless to control the administration of *L'Aurore*, so I am powerless to control the administration of *La petite République*."[144]

Thus did the autumn of 1901 turn into a time of torment. His own child, quite innocently, had been a cause of his misery. Nor was poor Madeleine ever able to bring her father happiness. By the time of his death, he had seen her twice the wife of worthless husbands and once the mother of a subnormal child. He did not live to see Louis killed at the front in 1917 before he was twenty.

XI

"Work . . . is an interior light," wrote Jaurès, "a defense against stupidity, vilification, cowardice, and betrayal; it brings serenity and frees one of bitterness."[145] Work was his prescription for these difficult days. In addition to his regular round of activity, he threw himself into the task of writing history, and history on a grand scale.

In 1898 the publisher Jules Rouff had approached Jaurès with a proposition. Rouff would publish a multivolume series, under the title *L'Histoire socialiste de la Révolution française*, which would carry the history of France from 1789 to the end of the nineteenth century, if Jaurès would plan, edit, and contribute to the work. Delighted with the challenge, Jaurès immediately accepted. In working out the plan, he left for himself the sections on the Constituent Assembly, the Legislative, and the Franco-Prussian War. He then persuaded certain socialist colleagues — Guesde, Deville, Andler, Herr, Dubreuilh, Labusquière, and Gérault-Richard — to contribute the rest. But several of them had neither his energy nor rich preparation. Before the work was completed, the list of contributors had changed considerably. Thus, Guesde, whether from illness, as he himself claimed, or from his inability to produce a genuinely scholarly work, failed to write the history of the Convention. His replacement was Jaurès, who, by 1903, produced the two enormous volumes covering the years 1792 to 1794.

In all probability, Rouff was originally thinking of a popular work — vivid, dramatic, but not essentially original. Jaurès, however, relished the challenge of another sort of history — long, detailed, new in material and interpretation. The socialists, he hoped, would do what men of the academy had not: they would write a full-bodied and original history of France, marking them as the true heirs of the Enlightenment. So it happened that Jaurès, a professional philosopher turned politician and journalist, sought achievement in yet another field. His resources for the task were peculiarly rich. Steeped in the record of history through his omnivorous reading, he had long made the French Revolution a subject of special study.[146] Furthermore, he brought to his history two qualities rarely found among professional academicians: an active political involvement which nourished his powers of interpretation, and a style of writing which was vivid in description and lucid in analysis. To both of these strengths Léon Blum alluded in his review of the work: "One senses on every page of his book the swift flash of intuition which finds the truth underlying apparent disorder. I can't conceive of any comparison for the prose of M. Jaurès, except that of Victor Hugo. It is much more poetical than oratorical, for M. Jaurès does not write as he speaks; he speaks as he writes."[147]

But did he have professional method, the capacity to search out and select from the sources? Without doubt Jaurès understood and met the rigorous demands of the historical craft. In the years between 1899 and 1903, he was often seen at the Archives Nationales, the Bibliothèque Nationale, the Carnavalet — where he pored over many hundreds of printed and manuscript sources. The results of his efforts were judged by Aulard, then the most renowned academic authority on the French Revolution, in these words:

Up till now, M. Jaurès has been famous as a philosopher, an orator, a polemicist. One might have feared that in undertaking historical studies, he would reveal himself as a philosopher, orator, and polemicist. But he has proved himself an historian, in the full meaning of the term, and he has produced, as far as it is possible in history, a work of truth, scientifically inspired and executed. . . . It [his documentation] is marvelous, and no historian of the Revolution has even come close to his achievements. . . . He judges; he is eloquent; he is moving; but all his judgments, emotions, eloquence, and irony come out of the facts he has adduced and the texts he has cited.

After listing the varied sources consulted — newspapers, memoirs, letters, parliamentary debates — Aulard offered professional criticisms which later historians have amplified. Jaurès often failed to give complete citations; he ignored some subjects; he tended to be verbose and digressive. But Aulard then concluded: "These weaknesses are merely the result of the conditions under which M. Jaurès has worked. In two or three years he completed what any other person, less well endowed, would have taken at least twenty years to produce."[148]

Philosopher by training, Jaurès was absorbed in nothing so much as the theory of history. In a revealing letter to Bernstein, he gave a clue to his own approach: "I have done my work by going back . . . to the original sources and documents; the method of historical materialism, when . . . it is not debased by absolute childishness, as Lafargue has done here and Mehring in your country, is an excellent guide."[149] In general terms, Jaurès, like Marx, was concerned with an eternal problem — the relationship between man and events, the shaper and the shaped. He solved it this way: "In history, we must take full account of both economic evolution and human grandeur. Thus, our interpretation of history will be at once materialist with Marx and idealistic with Michelet."[150] The problem of interaction between these two forces challenged Jaurès at all stages of his work, and as he progressed in his writing, he wove an increasingly complex tapestry. In the earlier volumes on the Constituent and the Legislative, he tended to separate intellectual and economic factors, placing them side by side in an unsatisfying dualism. But in the magisterial volumes on the Convention, he finally approached that dynamic fusion of human will and material phenomena which resembled life itself.

The central pivot of his interpretation was the movement and clash of classes. The Revolution, Jaurès wrote, turned on the drive-to-power of the French bourgeoisie. Burke was wrong, and Taine after him, in contending that the Revolution had no roots in the French past. "The Revolution was no accident," wrote Jaurès. "It was no sudden and wild creation of a generation of *idéologues*. It was the magnificent culmination of social and intellectual forces, long developed by the aggressive bourgeoisie and by courageous theorists."[151]

In their scramble for gain, middle-class merchants and industrialists (whose pioneering exploits in manufacturing and mining Jaurès described from a plethora of new documents) had become both progressive and revolutionary — progressive because they expanded production, revolutionary because they had to destroy the cadre of the feudal State. Thus, he judged capitalism, for all of its attendant human misery, as a liberating force. The eighteenth-century social critics, who would have restricted it on behalf of pastoral "socialism," drew a sharp reply from him: "The workers in manufacturing were instinctively much more with the revolutionary bourgeoisie, who created and expanded industry, than with reformers who, in the interest of morality and simplicity, wanted to drive the passive herd of men back to the common pasture, drenched in the morning dew."[152]

But in writing of the emergent and then triumphant bourgeoisie, Jaurès avoided crude generalizations about class composition and motivation. "Too often in reading histories," he remarked somewhat later, "you have the impression that the combatants of the Revolution are only abstractions, ideas in action."[153] Because he considered a class to be composed of living men, moved here by ideals and there by self-interest, he was able to suggest the essential complexity of the Revolution. Consider his treatment of the bourgeois deputies who filled the Convention.

The word "bourgeois" designates a class not only complex and contradictory, but ever-moving and changing. . . . theorists of the Revolution, they came to establish the grandeur, not the egotism of the bourgeoisie. They didn't want to meddle with the principle of individual property . . . But they were perfectly capable, in the interest of the Revolution and for the safety of the new society, of demanding great sacrifices of property-holders. . . . A class is egoistic only when it opposes, out of narrow self-interest, the advent of a new stage of social development, which the movement of events and ideals has prepared.[154]

His perception, that the nature of a class is kaleidoscopic, replete with inner tensions and divisions, was grist for his own political mill. Had he not applied it only recently, when he separated Mélinists, unwilling to safeguard the Republic, from Dreyfusards, ready to accept advanced reforms for its defense? So it was among the members of the Convention: "If you applied literally the method Marx used in his *History of the Eighteenth Brumaire,* you would have to find in the clash between the Girondists and the Montagnards the expression of a class conflict. But history is marked not only by class struggle; there are also struggles of parties. As I understand it, outside of economic affinities or antagonisms, there are constellations, formed out of personal passions, pride, and ambitions, clashing with each other at the surface of history and producing great disturbances." It was not that the Girondists were more bourgeois than the Montagnards; nor was their view of a laissez-faire society a sordid one: "I am not forgetting the magnificent picture of future society, happy, and prosperous, which Vergniaud painted in his great speech on the Constitution. But in 1793, the only real way of saving civilization was to save the Revolution, and the Girondists were abandoning it."[155]

Yet, even the Montagnards went so far and no farther. For whatever the internal divisions within a class, wrote Jaurès, no one of its major factions ever forgets its essential interest. Behind the Montagnards were the Paris masses, loosely organized by the Enragés. "Fearing overthrow by the movement of Jacques Roux and the other street leaders, the Montagnards found it useful to canalize popular passion into a purely political movement. To denounce the Girondists and to strike out at them was to gain time."[156] Their success doomed both the Girondists and the social movement. But that was possible only because the popular movement was still immature and incoherent: "When Varlet and Jacques Roux gave assurances that they wished to retain property, while in the same breath they demanded prosecution of speculators and monopolists, they were hopelessly incoherent. . . . Their doctrine prepared the way for communism, but only because it was contradictory and impotent."[157]

While concentrating on class, Jaurès remained sensitive to personality. Full-bodied men strode through these thousands of pages, creatures and creators of history. Danton? "He was nothing less than the spearhead of the national defense. It was he who ignited hearts and souls with his dauntless confidence. It was his energy which created the energy of others."[158] Robespierre? "His grandeur lay in a sort of tender regard for the souls of the people, for the humble wisdom of the poor." But in completing his picture, he added (and perhaps Guesde flashed before his eyes as he wrote): "But there was something of the priest and sectarian in him, an intolerable pretension to infallibility, . . . the tyrannical habit of judging all by the standards of his conscience."[159] Marat? "His death was a great misfortune for the Revolution. . . . He would perhaps have prevented the violent campaign of the Hébertists against Danton, and thus conciliated Danton and Robespierre."[160]

Nor did Jaurès ignore, any more than Michelet did, the incomparable force of collective heroism:

On contact with all this new and enthusiastic energy, the army of invasion, weary, sick, devoid of sustaining ideals, felt its own misery more deeply. . . . It was the supreme defeat, imposed by inner discouragement, by a sense of futility. Since defeat was far more in the hearts of the invaders than in their ranks, Kellerman and Dumouriez could not at first grasp the meaning of that great day. But Goethe, clairvoyant poet, who had accompanied the Prussian army, noted immediately the fullness of the event: "In this place and on this day begins a new era in the history of the world." It was September 20.[161]

Croce once wrote that "every true history is contemporary history." While there is no evidence that Jaurès read his younger Italian contemporary, he shared, in large measure, that point of view. For even as he sought to clarify the present, was he not warning the Guesdists against ignoring human idealism? Durkheim, his old comrade of the École Normale, while lecturing at the University of Bordeaux, had said that "socialism is not a science, a sociology in miniature; it is a cry of pain."[162] For Jaurès, such a judgment was like a kernel of truth wrapped in husks of exaggeration. But to ignore the kernel was to misunderstand the force of the social movement. Yet was he not likewise warning the overeager Ministerialists against permanent class collaboration? Consider his judgment of Mirabeau's attempt to reconcile the king and the Revolution:

"No, no, it was not possible for any man, no matter how great, to struggle against destiny, to wrest the old monarchy from its reactionary instincts and to endow it with a revolutionary soul."[163]

And, finally, was he not reëmphasizing his devotion to the revolutionary process, peaceful if possible, violent if necessary? That he accepted violence yet felt compassion for its victims is clear; violence disfigured revolution, but it did not destroy it: "What good is it to philosophize about these sad things?" he asked in writing of the September Massacres. "The justification of the Revolution has not been destroyed; for the enormous social change which resulted can't be judged by a temporary outburst of fury. On the other hand, I don't like cowardly apologies. It's certain that the massacre of unarmed prisoners . . . represented a blackout of reason and humanity."[164]

But the age of revolution through terror, he hoped, lay in the past. The very violence of the French Revolution had ushered in an era of democracy, and therein was one key at least to social change: "I pass into the hands of our friends the torch whose flame has been blown about by so many savage winds. . . . A tormented but immortal flame which despotism and counterrevolution will persist in extinguishing, and which, always relit, will light the way to socialism."[165]

Jaurès' search into the revolutionary past enormously enriched his knowledge of social structure and historical change. He learned, and consequently taught, more that was essential about the eighteenth century than any of his political contemporaries; in the process, he deepened his understanding of his own society and its evolution. As a young republican, when he still imagined that the bourgeoisie would extend to the working classes the liberty and equality it had proclaimed in the revolutionary decade, he considered socialism the natural culmination of the French Revolution. By 1893, events at Fourmies and Carmaux had destroyed that earlier faith, and he could write: "The bourgeoisie has done its work, and we must do ours." The victory of socialism, in other words, depended upon the organized working class and its effective political action. But when he had reflected on the lessons of his research, he would write in La petite République (June 9, 1900): "None of the great assemblies from 1789 to 1793 foresaw the triumph of nineteenth-century capitalism. That was an economic phenomenon, which democracy alone could hardly have produced. In the same way, democratic action by itself will not abolish capitalism."

Jaurès' premise was the essentially Marxist one — that technological and economic developments were destined to transform capitalism and to produce its fatal contradications. But human effort, the idealistic component of historical change, remained vitally important. The revolutionary assemblies, bourgeois in program and composition, had created those liberal institutions, which served the ends of capitalism; in the same way, the working classes, clear as to their ultimate goals, could lay the foundations of socialism even within the cadre of capitalist society.

Jaurès thus arrived at a solid intellectual justification for his support of the Waldeck-Rosseau ministry and the Combes government that would follow it. Against the sectarian Guesdists, who constantly invoked Marx in their opposition to collaboration, he defended his position in an essay (*La petite République*, November 17, 1900), significantly entitled "Le vrai Marxisme." "True Marxist tactics" he derived from a celebrated letter, which Engels had written to Bernstein on September 22, 1882. Exasperated by Guesde's simplicity and inflexibility (the same kind of *simplisme*, which had once caused Marx to exclaim: But I am not a Marxist!), he had sharply criticized the P.O.F. line: "Guesde just doesn't understand that in France we probably can't travel from *la République à la Gambetta* to socialism without passing through *la République à la Clemenceau.*"

With his customary generosity, Jaurès defended Guesde's early propaganda. Since the days of Babeuf, he noted, socialists had mingled indiscriminately with radical republicans, and it was to Guesde's great credit that he had so vehemently insisted upon their fundamental differences. Yet Engels' letter was a very significant commentary on the complexity of Marxist tactics: "Marx often declared that it would be blind and absurd to look upon all groups outside the proletariat as one homogeneous reactionary mass. . . . It is this position, a position *très compliquée et très nuancée, très révolutionnaire à la fois et très enveloppante*, it is this truly Marxist position, which . . . prevails today in French socialism."

Democracy, Jaurès taught, was a magnificent instrument of progress, the best means ever devised for peaceful social change. But it was not, as he would warn Millerand at the Congress of Bordeaux in 1903, "a sort of extraordinary, supernatural God." It was a human, an imperfect institution, limited in its effectiveness by the power of money and propaganda. Nor did he rule out revolution, even in the democratic age, at the crucial moment of social change. His contemporaries, whether reformist or revolutionary, generally missed the point, but he did not condemn violence in itself, only its misuse and excesses: "The revolutionaries of 1789, 1830, and 1848," he would write in 1908 in his long essay on the Franco-Prussian War, "condemned the *coup d'état* of 1851; but they did so not because of its violence but because it was violence in the service of reaction, *une parodie de la force*. Violence is valid and justified when it serves historical progress and forwards the movement of people toward greater freedom and more universal justice." But for the present, the socialists had the opportunity, unmatched in their political experience, to serve the working classes and to strengthen them by intelligent, vigorous democratic action.

XII

"In France after the turn of the century, as in Germany a decade earlier, the young people began to declare themselves Nietzscheans." Thus observes a penetrating historian of modern European thought. A page later he adds: "At the École Normale Supérieure the influence of Lucien Herr, the librarian, and of Jean Jaurès, the great socialist alumnus, began to wane."[166] Only two years before, Dreyfusard intellectuals — Andler, Blum, Bourgin, Roques, Simiand, and Péguy — had enthusiastically collected articles by Jaurès into a volume, *Action socialiste*, to give some guidance, especially to French youth. But by 1902 many young intellectuals were seeking wisdom from other prophets. Some had discovered Nietzsche, whose aphoristic brilliance withered bourgeois conformism, Christian morality, democracy, and socialism. They thrilled to his call for heroes transcending mediocrity to find truth and beauty.

Jaurès had read Nietzsche, and on one occasion at least he had defended him against the ill-conceived attacks of Lafargue. But if he granted Nietzsche's stature as a provocative thinker, he rejected the final implications of his teachings. In February of 1902, Jaurès went to Geneva, and in three lectures at the Cirque Rancy commented on the central doctrines of Nietzschean thought.[167] The bourgeois age, Jaurès asserted, had, as Nietzsche taught, resulted in the stifling of human potentiality and the propagation of false materialism. Yet Jaurès' prescription was not the development of a few isolated Zarathustras, but the achievement of a socialist community. "It is not true that to be free we must cut ourselves off from humanity . . . we want all of mankind to be supermen."

When Jaurès returned to France, he faced the general elections of 1902 and a vigorous campaign in the Tarn to regain his Chamber seat. To do battle with his erstwhile opponent, the Marquis de Solages, he went back to the villages and towns of his electoral district. The issues in the forthcoming elections were outlined in *La Revue de Paris* in April by Léon Blum.[168] No longer was defense of the Republic the central challenge, he pointed out; that had already been accomplished. The real question was the direction of the established regime, whether it would press on with the institutional and social reforms begun under Waldeck-Rousseau. Blum indicated that a clear-cut division had developed between a party of order and a party of progress: "On one side is the liberal spirit, in the historic meaning of the word; on the other side is the democratic or Jacobin tendency. . . . It is natural that on one side the moderate republi-

cans, *ralliés*, royalists, Bonapartists, Caesarian nationalists, and nationalists of *La Patrie française*, and on the other side, Gambettist republicans,
Radicals, and Socialists should unite at the ballot box."[169] But if Blum
thought there was a coherent progressive coalition, at least one contemporary historian has denied it: "Was there anything in common between
a great anticlerical bourgeois and a miner of the Pas-de-Calais or a glass
worker of Carmaux? The various tendencies, 'Left Republican,' 'Radical,' 'Radical-Socialist,' 'Independent Socialist' did not add up to an
organized party."[170]

Jaurès knew that. He nourished few illusions about leaders of the
Alliance démoçratique like Poincaré. But if the Left wing of the governmental coalition should carry the day, he reckoned, if Radicals and socialists should form the majority, then no one could hold back the era of
reforms.[171] In his own particular campaign, Jaurès again confronted the
power of organized wealth and the influence of the Church. Yet even
though the Marquis spent 24,743 francs (5,000 more than in 1898), the
glass workers and miners received Jaurès enthusiastically wherever he
spoke. The opposition, of course, didn't melt away, and, in fact, it included the Antiministerial socialists, who put Lavigne into the race
against Jaurès. In the end, however, the *carmausins* voted for Jaurès and,
despite Guesdist propaganda, for the prospect of reforms.

The first ballot was cast on April 25, and outside the offices of *La petite
République* thousands gathered for word of the socialist candidates, especially Jaurès. The hours passed; the vote was collected slowly in the second district of Albi. Finally, words were scrawled across a screen set up
in front of the building: Jaurès Elected! Carmaux had been decisive, and
the *tarnais* had scored over Solages, 6543 to 6154. Téry, witness to the immediate reaction of the Parisian workers, recorded it: "There was an
ovation from which the city shook, and a human flood inundated the
street. Police, troops, horses, all were swept aside by the hurricane of
joy."[172]

When the second ballot had been counted on May 11, the size of the
Leftist victory became clear: some 350 seats were now held by the Ministerial coalition against 230 for the opposition. Within the victorious coalition, the 220 Radicals and Radical-Socialists and the thirty-six Ministerial
socialists constituted the decisive group. The efforts of these freshly organized Radicals had paid off. The socialists, wrote a hopeful Jaurès, "are
determined to support the earnest effort for reforms, which will have
to be made by a Radical ministry."[173]

On May 28, the Parti socialiste français held a victory banquet at the
Porte Dorée. Viviani, just beaten, was consoled with the honor of presiding. Jaurès, the party's greatest deputy, was the principal speaker.

Everyone's mood seemed festive, but Jaurès introduced a sober note into the proceedings, a warning to both the Radicals and to his most ambitious comrades: "The Radicals are going to exercise power. The socialist party will influence their actions and guide their direction. But it is important to avoid confusion of socialism with the program of the Radicals. . . . Socialism should be the spur of the Radical Party until the latter, completely exhausted, gives up power."[174]

The immediate prospects, thought Jaurès, were bright. Before the new Chamber met on June 1, Waldeck-Rousseau, pleading illness though actually disconcerted by the new Radical preponderance, resigned. The Chamber then met for its organizational session, and its Leftist majority easily elected Léon Bourgeois president over Paul Deschanel. It was thus clear to Loubet that only a Radical Premier could organize a ministry, and on the suggestion of Waldeck-Rousseau, he called on Émile Combes, a little old man then Senator from the Charente-Inférieure. By June 10, Combes was able to offer the Chamber a ministry composed of seven Radicals and three Moderates.

Five days later, Jaurès was in good enough spirits to fill his newspaper column with a devoted commentary on "the superb cuisine of Toulouse."

11

Left Bloc to
Socialist Unity, 1902-1906

I

For the first half of his sixty-seven years, Émile Combes had been either a student of theology or a teacher of Catholic philosophy; in the last half he had become a practicing physician and a Radical politician. The transition from religious dedication to secular practice had been swift, but not without complexity. Influenced in turn by his study of Abelard's controversy with Saint Bernard (the subject of his doctoral thesis), the liberal Catholicism of Lacordaire, the positivism of Quinet, and the moral *mystique* of Michelet, Combes nursed disquieting doubts about Catholic dogma, and finally rejected it. The Superior of the Grand Séminaire of Albi, aware that the seminarian was no longer a true believer, refused him higher orders, though encouraging him to continue in Catholic education. Such, in fact, was the course Combes followed. But while teaching at Pons (Charente-Inférieure), this son of a simple tailor married into a family of local bourgeois notables who sponsored his study and practice of medicine. Out of friendly contacts with Masonic and republican milieux, Combes won backing for a political career which took him from the mayor's office in Pons to the Senate, and finally to the exalted position of Premier.

293

But three decades in the clerical mold were not easily brushed aside, and Combes retained, even when his dedication was to the law of progress rather than to the law of the Church, the inflexibility of a sectarian. His religious spirit remained central, though his God no longer spoke to him through Catholic dogma, but rather through the laws of science and morality. When he fought the Church, he was less renegade than a heretic, angered by the institutional barrier to truth.[1]

A small man, slightly bent, with a pointed white goatee, he usually wore a long, black frockcoat, and looked for all the world like a victorian Mephistopheles. For the large questions of finance, defense, or foreign policy, Combes had neither education nor concern. But for carrying the attack against clerical influence, he had almost explosive energy. From the moment he formed his ministry, his single-minded purpose was evident. Out of his interest in anticlericalism, he reappointed André to the War Office, charged Pelletan with the Ministry of the Navy, and took for himself the Ministry of the Interior. At the Foreign Office, meanwhile, he left the secretive Delcassé virtually unchecked in his game of diplomatic chess, and at the Ministry of Finance, where tax schemes were hatched and promoted, he placed Maurice Rouvier, long-time favorite of the *haute banque*.[2] "Two Ministers in the Cabinet," *Les Débats* perceptively commented, "will prevent us from falling into a revolutionary abyss; they are MM. Rouvier and Delcassé."[3] The Radicals had an approach to the Church question; for the rest, they were timid, divided, and essentially unsure. "They have never really understood very well," Halévy once observed, "where big interests begin and little ones end."[4]

Neither the *mystique* of Combes nor the doctrine of the Radicals attracted Jaurès to their cause. Nor did he, as Péguy once claimed, consider "le petit père" Combes a great man. Yet, from the first day, he was on the side of the ministry, convinced that the Church threatened the mind of France, and hopeful that strong socialist pressure might force the Radicals to enact a program of social reforms. On June 10, 1902, the deputies heard Combes read out a ministerial declaration full of progressive promise. Three days later, Jaurès, making his first major speech in more than four years in the House that had so often resounded with his words, delivered the socialist response: "We want to collaborate with the Left in a program of republican defense and social reforms; but at the same time, we intend to move toward those higher goals for which the proletariat has organized."[5]

Jaurès hardly departed from that formulation throughout the thirty-one consecutive months of the Combes ministry. If the government carried through a reform program, he conceded, the working class would be fortified, and democracy improved. Yet this ministry, or any progressive bourgeois government, could be only a transition and no more. Once its immediate goals were reached, the socialists would work for the collectivization of property. Make no mistake about it, Jaurès warned his bourgeois allies, there was nothing immutable about individual property: "It is not a sacred institution; like all institutions, it is mutable. Was it an unchanging institution when the Revolution suppressed feudal rents? . . . Is it immutable when you claim the right to expropriate, on grounds of public utility, the land the peasant doesn't want to yield to a railroad company? . . . We will give substance to our conceptions by proposing practical and specific laws. We will aim for the transformation of the major capitalist services into public services, run by the organized workers and the State."

Though Jaurès offered the government his qualified support, others were openly hostile. From Ribot, who feared Combes's anticlericalism, came the sharpest rebuke: "You don't want peace; you want violence." But when heads were counted, the coalition of the Left was easily victorious, and the ministry won a resounding vote of confidence for "an energetic policy of secularism, social reforms, and solidarity." The Left had emerged as a bloc, its four constituent groups linked in support of certain reforms.[6] What loomed ahead was the prospect of a disciplined majority, and it led Combes to a bold move. By July 2, he called together representatives of the parties of the Left bloc; they formed a central committee of the majority, the Délégation des gauches, which was to meet regularly with the Premier and to collaborate with him in the introduction and passage of his program.[7]

From conservative critics of the government, fearful of the majority and hoping to discredit it, the word spread about that through the Délégation des gauches Jaurès had become "the real master of the country."[8] He was the new "grey eminence," they charged, a latter-day Father Joseph, appeasing his appetite for power by steering the ministry into dangerous and uncharted waters. But if anyone hoped that because of such talk Combes would sever his ties with Jaurès and the governmental socialists, he was deluded. The Premier categorically declared at Tréguier (September 13, 1903) that he would do nothing to disrupt his majority.

My opponents think they can disturb me by picturing me as a prisoner of one of these groups; or perhaps they hope to worry public opinion about my political tendencies . . . in lieu of facts, they cite the name of a deputy, who is viewed as the director of the ministry. If they expect to hear me disavow my friendly relations with this deputy or his group, I want to set them straight. Like the entire Chamber, regardless of party affiliation, I admire the amazing talent of the deputy; his group is one of the important elements of the majority. I have the same cordial relations with them as with members of other groups in the majority.[9]

By the fall of 1902, the importance of Jaurès' role received recognition when the Délégation des gauches, meeting on October 17, chose him as a candidate for one of the four vice presidencies of the Chamber during the 1903 session. On January 13, 1903, the unprecedented happened, and Jaurès, benefiting from tight discipline among the Radicals, won election as vice president, despite angry protest from both the Right and Center.[10]

Was it, as his critics charged, a long-smoldering ambition which drove Jaurès to participate in the bloc? Ambition, no doubt, played its part. By his own admission, frequently made, Jaurès was no ascetic, and he enjoyed recognition of his efforts. In a life that provided so little shelter for his personal sensibilities, in which calumny was an everyday occurrence, the admiration of his own people in Castres or Carmaux, obviously impressed by his national importance, bolstered his morale. At home, Louise basked in her new importance, and his foyer glowed.

But if personal ambition had been his only guide, would he have moved to the Extreme Left? A life with the Center would have been far more profitable. Jaurès participated in the Délégation des gauches, one may safely assume, because he believed in it. Dedicated to the parliamentary process, he looked at its method as one of order and discipline, enabling the majority to develop a program and to convert it into laws: "It is excellent that the government's proposals should come as no surprise to the majority, and that the ideas of the majority should be no surprise to the government."[11] But even more than its method, he supported its objectives — those republican reforms upon which the entire Left could agree.

It was a position, however, that cost him dearly. The closer Jaurès and his friends moved toward governmental collaboration, the farther they traveled from the most militant centers of the working class. For the Marxists and Blanquists, now organized in the Parti socialiste de France, socialist participation in the Délégation des gauches was another gigantic step toward the degeneracy of socialist principle and honor. Who joined the bloc, asked Guesde's friend Bonnier, except "those easily tempted by favors or public office?"[12] Jaurès had said repeatedly that the fruits of the Affair would come in the form of reforms. But the concern of the ministry, replied Guesde, was fixed only on anticlericalism, that time-tested "capitalist maneuver for diverting the workers from their struggle against economic slavery."[13] The revolutionaries were increasingly convinced that whatever the collaborationists were — reformers, Jacobins, agents of goodwill — they were no longer socialists. Thus, Louis Dubreuilh, militant Blanquist, could write: "There is nothing in common — no relationship, no affinity — between the incoherent gang whose chiefs dine with presidents and ministers, who vote support in the Assembly for the murderers of the proletariat, who play leading roles in the theatre of bourgeois philanthropy, and the party of the working class, organizing for the Revolution against all the forces of the social order."[14]

In the national labor organizations, the politics of the bloc strengthened the hand of those leaders who had long charged that socialist politicians were respectable bourgeois in thin disguise. Meeting at Montpellier in September, 1902, the Fédération des bourses and the C.G.T. finally amalgamated into a single Confédération générale du travail which was avowedly nonpolitical. Though the new C.G.T. was institutionally complex (among the constituent groups were national federations in specific trades, bourses du travail, and departmental unions) and doctrinally mixed, its influential leaders were markedly anarchosyndicalist. Led by Griffuelhes, Pouget, Yvetot, and Delesalle, the new C.G.T. embarked on what Dolléans described as its "heroic age," scornful of any tactics but those of revolutionary intent.[15] At the C.G.T. Congress of Amiens in 1906, Griffuelhes made a revealing statement about the labor movement in these years: "There was a coalition then of anarchists, Guesdists, Blanquists, Allemanists, and other scattered elements — all working to isolate the unions from the State. That coalition has been maintained. It has been the life of the C.G.T."[16]

But the cost of bloc politics must be reckoned in moral as well as revolutionary units. Inspired Dreyfusards, like Lazare and Péguy, who had once hailed the leadership of Jaurès as the basis for the regeneration of France, now denounced it as a prop for vindicative anticlericalism. From the start of his ministry, Combes had set out to give the Law on Associations a new and vigorous application. "The objective of the 1901 law, as Waldeck-Rousseau had conceived it, was to prevent the congregations from forming a "state within a state." But Combes turned it into an instrument for abolishing first congregational teaching, and then the congregations themselves."[17] To maintain the bloc, Jaurès defended an anticlericalism that was undeniably harsh and, in the view of his critics, totally ungenerous.

Combes moved by calculated stages. At the outset, he struck at the unapproved schools of the authorized congregation. The previous government had decreed (January 31, 1902) that authorized congregations (mainly those of women) required no special approval for schools established before July, 1901. It had been a significant decision, since most Catholic primary education was carried on by the teaching sisters of these congregations. Combes, overriding the previous ruling, proceeded at once to close some three thousand schools.

Solidly supported by his parliamentary majority, the Premier moved next against the congregations seeking authorization under the law.

Gathering up fifty-four applications from male orders, Combes sent them to the Chamber where their requests for authorization were lumped together and considered simultaneously. On March 28, 1903, by a vote of 304 to 246, they were rejected en bloc. In June, the same procedure was applied to the applications of eighty-one congregations of women, and with the same result. Police now went to work, closing religious houses, dispersing their members, and shutting down their schools. By October, 1903, some ten thousand congregational schools had been closed, though more than half of them were reopened, ostensibly as secular schools.

Against this show of force even some of the most renowned republicans — Goblet, Monod, and Waldeck-Rousseau — raised their voices in protest; in the Senate, Clemenceau, back in Parliament after a nine-year absence, now flayed encroaching State power as vigorously as he had once fought clerical power: "We have guillotined the King; long live the State-King! We have dethroned the Pope; long live the State-Pope! We have banished God: long live the State-God!"[18]

Combes took scant notice of the protest. By December, 1903, he made his final move against congregational schools, introducing a measure to strip all religious orders, authorized or not, of the right to teach. Though the debate was intensely bitter and the Premier's majority dwindled, the bill passed in the Chamber by the end of March, 316 to 269. Throughout the ministry's drive against the congregations, Jaurès lent it his support. His position was not based, as was that of the historian Aulard, for example, on positivism. Nor was it based on the belief, apparently held by Combes, that Catholicism could be suddenly uprooted and discarded. Had he not written of the futility of Robespierre's attempt to establish, overnight, a new civic religion? "He [Robespierre] was very shortsighted to imagine that Christianity could be easily replaced by a national religion. The divinity of Christ had dominated man's conscience for eighteen centuries."[19] Jaurès' position rested on the conviction that a democracy required free and inquiring minds, and that Catholic education did little more than impose dogma. In the course of the final debate on congregational teaching, he summed up his thought, turning it on the distinction between the unrestricted freedom to believe but the qualified freedom to teach: "Freedom to all of you, believers, to propagate your beliefs and faith, from soul to soul, from mind to mind, whatever the long-range consequences. . . . But at the source of the nation's intellectual life, in its system of education where the minds of the young are formed, there must be State control; education must be free of dogma; its aim must be not to inculcate absolute ideas but to develop in our youth the power of reason and the love of truth."[20]

All the while that he allied himself with the provincial politicians of

Radicalism, Jaurès was sustained by his hope for the large reforms to which the government seemed committed. The Combes ministry had hardly been installed when General André introduced a bill to reduce military service from three years to two;[21] some months later, a reluctant Rouvier, under the direction from the Chamber, produced the semblance of an income tax proposal;[22] but beyond those horizons, if the Left bloc survived, lay the whole field of social legislation — pensions for workers, protection of the aged and ill, reduction of the work day — which the ministry might cultivate.

A worthwhile socialist risk? Not to Péguy, who began, in the current of 1902, to question Jaurès' moral stature. His disillusion came gradually. In January, 1900, he had stalked out of the socialist publishing house which he directed (refusing the party discipline imposed by Herr, Blum, and three other trustees), and founded his own journal, *Les Cahiers de la quinzaine*. There, in the early issues, Péguy heaped his unqualified praise on Jaurès. In the third *Cahier*, he ran on for fifty pages, trying to capture in words the spiritual depth of Jaurès: "Like all true socialists," wrote Péguy, "he is deeply philosophical and deeply poetic; these two great qualities are perfectly fused in him."[23] In 1901, he defended the recourse to politics: "It seems to me indispensible that certain revolutionary socialists should engage in political action; if they didn't, all political action would be directed toward crushing the revolution. . . . They say that the métier of politics is a dirty one. . . . We should then extend the most sincere gratitude to citizens who are willing to submit themselves to it."[24]

But the politics of the Combes ministry were something else again. They revolted and tortured Péguy; he saw what Barrès called "the great pity of the churches of France." For a year he followed the moves of the Left bloc, and by June, 1903, he openly criticized Jaurès for gilding them with his oratorical brush: "Jaurès has become what he almost never was in the previous legislature, a parliamentary chief. . . . The great *philosophe*, the fine artist, the man of wisdom no longer reigns: a minor orator has taken over." And for what had Jaurès destroyed his inner self? For opportunism and deception — for "politics": "To run Catholicism with Anticatholic and Catholic demogogues, to achieve liberalism while monopoly reigns, to reach socialism through the bourgeois State, to achieve antimilitarism with generals, to practice anticolonialism with ex-naval officers, and to prepare the social revolution with reactionary Radicals — all this is very complicated; it is very evil. Such are politics."[25]

Jaurès, who once spoke of the world as "cruelly ambiguous," had ample evidence of it. He had taken a position which seemed to him justified by his grasp of history and his idealism. Yet it isolated him from the revolutionaries on the Left and the moralists among the Dreyfusards. Whether Jaurès or any man of daily political action could long have satisfied Péguy's standards is doubtful. Whose program, in practical terms, could have coincided with Péguy's goal — "to inaugurate, to restore, a new, old order; new, antique, in no way modern; an order of labor, a workingman's order?"[26]

But the separation of his party from the Parti socialiste de France and from the C.G.T. was more consequential because it divided the working-class movement and hurried both sides to the extreme limits of their positions, until Jaurès exaggerated the accomplishments of the Left bloc while the revolutionaries denied them completely. In unity, the organizations of the Left might have avoided excesses induced either by isolation or collaboration; without it, they lacked the balance for creative action. At the side of the Alliance démocratique ("so full of hatred and disdain for socialism," Jaurès later wrote[27]) and the new Radical équipe, the tarnais was led into compromises and forced into apologies. But in the years of the Combes ministry, one consideration overrode all others for him — that France now had a "democratic government, which capitulates before neither sword nor Church."[28]

That was the crux of the matter. "The two great threats to the French Republic," Jaurès would assert at Amsterdam in 1904, "are clericalism and Caesarism." The Guesdists, intellectually paralyzed by an economic determinism which parodied Marxism, brushed the warning aside; neither anticlericalism nor antimilitarism, they repeated, only anticapitalism. But Jaurès, fresh from his study of the great Revolution, insisted that the present prepares the future; that intellectual freedom and political democracy, the greatest gifts of the bourgeois revolution, were the keys to that preparation; that priests and officers, if left unchecked, would stifle free inquiry and destroy the Republic.

"Some day," Jaurès would remark at the Congress of Toulouse in 1908, "when the whole story can be told, we will prove that our influence, especially in regard to the separation of Church and State, was often decisive." Within the Délégation des gauches, J.-L. Breton would testify at Toulouse, it was Jaurès who, "in nine cases out of ten worked out the compromise motion which all its groups could accept." Jaurès would support the Bloc too uncritically; without the comradeship of the revolutionaries, he would be trapped by illusions, underestimating the ministry's commitment to the bourgeoisie; persuaded of its sincere desire for social reform; even convinced that European governments, already swept up in the race for arms and colonies, would arbitrate disputes, disarm, and federate. Eventually, for the sake of socialist unity, he would renounce collaboration and move to a much more critical position. But

not until the Bloc, under his guidance more than anyone else's, had reduced the influence of the Church and the army. These he hailed as
major reforms, vital to the proletariat; the recent history of France is
ample proof of his wisdom.

II

Early in September, 1902, the Italian socialists, their revolutionary wing
flapping against a reformist body, congregated at Imola to air their dis-
agreements. In dispute were the party's tactics since 1900, the policy of
supporting Zanardelli's bourgeois ministry, which had been considerably
less unfriendly than its predecessors to the Socialist Party and the trade
unions. The revolutionaries of the Left wing, ably directed by Enrico
Ferri, denounced the policy of collaboration, bearing down heavily in
their propaganda on the ministry's sporadic action against strikers. How,
they demanded, could deputies who called themselves socialists vote the
budgets of such a government or support its foreign policy? What better
proof was there of the ministry's warlike intentions than its recent renewal of the Triple Alliance? At Imola, the moderates, headed by Ivanoe
Bonomi, were in the majority. But before their tactics were endorsed (as
they were), they received important help from the outside.

A hush fell over the tempestuous sessions at one dramatic moment,
when Andreas Costa, a revered founder of the party, read a letter from
Jaurès. Costa had written to him, asking him how he felt, as a Frenchman
and a socialist, about the support given to the Triple alliance. In his reply,
Jaurès endorsed the position of the moderate socialists; through their
influence, he maintained, the Triple Alliance was becoming a force for
peace. "In your foreign policy," he wrote in the letter Costa now read to
the delegates, "your contribution has been important. For the Triple
Alliance, which is an essential counterpoise to our chauvinism and to
wild Franco-Russian ambitions, is gradually losing its aggressive character. We can even foresee the day when all European powers will be
part of a federation which will be able to end the destructive race in
armaments."[29] Jaurès' specific objective was to aid the cause of his fellow
reformists in Italy, and toward that end his intervention was effective. But
the party squabble in Italy was more the pretext for than the cause of his
strong words on foreign policy. For Jaurès, increasingly apprehensive
about war, was anxious to discuss every possible force for peace.

Since 1898 he had watched imperialism spread swiftly across continents, upsetting the traditional cultures of Asia and Africa while threatening the tranquillity of the West. The Spanish-American War, the Boer
War, and the Boxer Rebellion were the preface to an era of expanding
armaments and ambitions. In the swirl of overlapping rivalries and ten-

sions, the competition between England and Germany for markets and naval supremacy and the antagonism between Japan and Russia over China (intensified when the Tsarist army occupied Manchuria in October, 1900) seemed the greatest immediate threats to peace. On January 30, 1902, the Chinese question took top priority. Japan, now dominated by military extremists, negotiated an alliance with England, each signatory agreeing to neutrality if the other went to war with a third power over China or Korea, each agreeing to armed intervention if the other went to war with two or more powers. An eager Japan had thus made her diplomatic preparations for a showdown with Russia.

But even when the top layers of tension were stripped away, Europe's international relations suffered from long-standing antagonisms: German fears of a Russian attack; Russo-Austrian rivalry in the Balkans; persistent French dreams of *revanche*. At the Quai d'Orsay, under Combes as under Waldeck-Rousseau, Delcassé moved with energy and without check toward large diplomatic goals: to combine a reinforced Russian Alliance and new agreements with Italy and England into a tough anti-German coalition; and to use that diplomatic strength for expansion into Morocco and, if feasible, for a showdown war with Germany. Only a small knot of personal diplomatic representatives — the brothers Cambon (Paul in London and Jules in Washington), Camille Barère in Rome, and Nisard, his chief assistant in the Foreign Office — shared Delcassé's secrets and understood his ambitions. The public at large knew nothing of them and the Parliament little more than that. "He deceived by his silence," Caillaux was to write of Delcassé, "and he deceived also by a flow of words, behind which he concealed his carefully meditated plans."[30]

In August, 1899, the Foreign Minister traveled to St. Petersburg, and there he negotiated a significant revision of the Franco-Russian Alliance. Whereas the agreement had previously stated as its objective "the maintenance of peace," the revised version set as its aim "the maintenance of the European balance of power." So flexible was this formulation that it could satisfy equally *revanchards* in France and Balkan imperialists in Russia. Delcassé, who brought the precious new agreement back to France taped across his chest, joyfully described it to President Loubet as "the means of realizing our dreams."[31] While the Alliance expressed mutual ambitions, money created mutual dependence. French investors began to pour their francs into the bottomless well of Russian loans, eight billion francs between 1898 and 1900, 485 million in 1901, and 145 million more in 1903 (to complete the Trans-Siberian Railroad). The editors of great Paris dailies (*Le Temps, Le Journal des débats,* and *Le petit Parisien* among them), already dipping into the ample largess of

M. Raffalovitch, Paris attaché for the Russian Ministry of Finance, busily manufactured public confidence in Russia.[32] On the unimpeachable authority of both the Quai d'Orsay and the press, French investors, many of them petty bourgeois, bought Russian bonds and waited eagerly to reap the rewards of their patriotism.

Curtained off from public view, however, were the economic risk of investment in so unstable a country and the political risk of involvement in Russia's Far Eastern ambitions. For by 1902 the Tsar had fallen under the influence of expansionists like A. M. Bezobrazov, who flatly rejected any compromise with Japan over Manchuria and Korea. Though apprised of the facts, Delcassé concealed them and backed the Russians as war threatened in the Orient. On the morrow of the Anglo-Japanese Alliance, France and Russia released a joint declaration (March 20, 1902), stating that, in the event of hostile acts by other powers in China, they would "take measures necessary for defense of their interests." Among ambiguous statements of policy, that one was sure to become a classic.

Jaurès scrutinized the passing events and intensified his criticism of the Russian Alliance. Standing hard against public sentiment, he charged that France had nothing to gain but danger from her involvement with Russia. "Russia has no desire to back any offensive of ours," he wrote in answer to the *revanchards*. "But she has interests of a high order in Asia. In Afghanistan, Persia, and the area of the Persian Gulf, she has an intense rivalry with England. Above all, she has great designs on China." Delcassé had assured everyone that the Franco-Russian Alliance had no other aims than the Open Door and the territorial integrity of China. "But it's not the declaration of principles that counts; it's their application," retorted Jaurès. "Does the present action of Russia in Manchuria conform to a policy of respect for China's independence?" Peace for France, and indeed for all of Europe, was being endangered by Russian policy; yet France still clung to the Alliance, giving aid and comfort to the Tsarist imperialists because French policy-makers nourished hopes of *revanche*. "There is only one way to loosen a Franco-Russian tie which has become too tight. It is to assure peaceful and courteous relations between France and Germany."[33]

Such were his thoughts when Jaurès wrote his letter to Costa, promptings of peace and reconciliation that separated him from his friends in the ministry. For in the very same September days when he was writing about the peaceful intentions of the Triple Alliance, André and Pelletan were lending the prestige of their high offices to saber-rattling speeches against Germany and Italy.[34] In the more conservative sectors of the bourgeois press, in *Le Temps* and *Le Journal des débats*, Jaurès' words met with shock and contempt. He had dared to speak kindly of Germany, and he had questioned French intentions. The press picked on one phrase in his letter to Costa (that the Triple Alliance was "an essential counterpoise to our chauvinism") to bring into question Jaurès' patriotism, and even his clear reason. "Unlike the German socialists," wrote *Les Débats*, "our French socialists have no compunction about supporting foreigners against their own fellow citizens."[35]

On September 18, and then almost daily for two weeks, Jaurès defended his position.[36] French society, he charged, was shot through with chauvinism, "in its press and literature, in its schools and universities, in the speeches of its generals and Ministers of War." Against this irresponsible bellicosity, he welcomed any counterpoise, even an opposing alliance system. The Triple Alliance was not "a thing in itself." It was good or bad, depending on the spirit which animated it. But for twenty-five years, he asserted, it had served the cause of peace. "It has held our dangerous aspirations in check by setting up a formidable defensive coalition against our chauvinism."

But Jaurès moved beyond the immediate debate over the Triple Alliance to lay down some general principles about the European State system. He accepted the nation-state as the basic unit in world politics, and neither as socialist nor as internationalist did he anticipate that it would soon wither away. What distressed him was not the existence but the anarchy of the state system, the unrestrained will to compete and to fight. Standing alone, each state felt either insecure enough or free enough to succumb to the temptations of war; but in combination, whether through alliances or federations, they felt sufficiently secure or restrained to keep the peace. Thus, the immediate problem, to move from chaos to some semblance of order, was soluble enough. If the rival alliance systems were linked by increasing contacts, by agreements on arbitration and disarmament, they might form the outlines of a European federation. And none of this, insisted Jaurès, was a pipe dream, for the will of mankind was peaceful and the influence of socialism salubrious.[37]

"M. Jaurès evinces a startling ignorance of contemporary history," retorted *Les Débats*. From its inception, the Triple Alliance had been an instrument of war, blunted only by France's ties to Russia and by her increasing military preparations. To disarm was thus to invite disaster. *Si vis pacem, para bellum*; this was realism, maintained the critics of Jaurès, time-tested and free of misty utopianism. But the "preparations for peace," Jaurès had warned, all too easily encouraged the will to war. In reply, *Les Débats* fell back to the simplest order of realism — that war was, after all, natural and inevitable: "Universal peace is a dream. . . . Even if socialism should one day triumph, we are not convinced that human nature would have changed so much as to eliminate war from society."[38]

The words flowed from a wellspring of anger and hope when Jaurès replied to the argument of inevitability:

If it is true that nations will forever be forced to kill in order to defend themselves; if it is true that the spirit of fraternity will never win over man's aggressive nature, then humanity has embarked on a futile journey. . . . I can understand the favor *Le Temps* occasionally shows toward the most intransigent socialists. For they too proclaim that there is no chance for peace and harmony so long as there remains a single root of capitalism. . . . They differ from *Le Temps* only in that they foresee the total and forthcoming collapse of the system, while *Le Temps* thinks of it as eternal; but they agree that while the system lasts, it is chimerical to preach and to work for peace. . . . As for myself, in foreign policy as in domestic, I reject such foregone conclusions.[39]

A dozen years before war engulfed the world, Jaurès had begun a campaign, unbroken until his death, to create a climate of peace. From the Radical ministry, however, he received scant help or encouragement, for if it differed from its predecessors in domestic policy, Combes' government resembled them in foreign and colonial affairs. The Premier, whose interest never really strayed far from the religious battle fronts, lent active support to expansionism. Thus, under pressure from the colonial bloc, he chose Jonnart, a favorite of the Alliance démocratique, as Governor-General of Algeria, and assured Étienne that he had authorized "whatever repressive measures are necessary for the security of our position."[40]

Pelletan's provocative, anti-German remarks did move the Premier to a partial retraction; but in a speech at Saint-Jean d'Angely (September 22, 1902), he excused his minister's words as "just a figure of speech." Jaurès replied at once. Something more fundamental than literary form was at stake, he felt, when a man with Pelletan's broad culture could refer to the civilization of Luther, Lessing, Goethe, and Wagner as "German barbarism." "The Radical Party," he observed, "has inherited the same unfortunate contradiction which vitiated the French Revolution: on the one hand, repudiation of conquest; on the other, the will to conquer."[41] Having thrown his support to the Left bloc, Jaurès chose not to desert it over foreign policy. But he reserved the right to criticize on matters of diplomacy and defense, hoping that socialist pressure might influence the course of affairs.[42]

In January, 1903, discussion moved from the press to the Chamber of Deputies. On the sixteenth, Dejeante of the revolutionary socialists interpellated General André on his order forbidding soldiers to enter bourses du travail, where they might find antimilitarist propaganda. On the nineteenth began the general discussion of the budget as Deschanel and Ribot, both strongly critical of peace efforts, spoke at length in favor of a strong defense establishment for France. The two separate debates converged on the twenty-third, when Joseph Lasies, stalwart of the Nationalist Right, demanded that "the Holy Father of the Socialist Church," as he called Jaurès, explain his words on the Triple Alliance.

When Jaurès rose, he faced critics who questioned the very sanity of his peace appeal. His goal, therefore, was to persuade the Chamber that peace was not only desirable but possible. "The fact which dominates our times," he cried, "and which serves as the basis for our party's actions, is that peace is now possible in Europe; I mean lasting, total, definitive peace."[43] Thirty-two years had elapsed without a major war among the great European powers. "Never, through all the clash of hatreds," he intoned, "never, through all the dark chaos of peoples and races, through the thick web of passions and the savage jungle, where beasts of prey have roamed for centuries, has the light of peace shone for so long a time." The Alliance system had placed aggressive designs in check; and from a defensive stalemate, the nation-states of Europe were already "evolving in a peaceful way, developing friendly contacts, moving toward a federation of Europe."

Men like Ribot had accused Jaurès of lulling the French into a false security, weakening the fibre of their courage, making them unfit to resist attack. He answered by redefining courage, locating its sources not in "verbal heroics" but in the inner spirit: "Moral strength is inseparable from physical; they are fused, one into the other. . . . Endow the nation with life-giving and healthy vigor: strength from work, thought, justice, and freedom. And if these sources of its life are some day threatened by the force of a foreign power, they will serve as a magnificent reservoir of courage. . . . There are only three things which undermine the courage of a people — deception, apathy, and cynicism."

From the Left an ovation, generous and spontaneous, greeted Jaurès as he returned to his seat. His speech had touched the sensitive center of man's idealism. On the streets, among the people of Paris, the vendors hawked reprints of the January 23 issue of the *Journal officiel*, and some ten thousand bought copies to read Jaurès' bracing words on peace and disarmament. But when André declared that he had asked the Minister of Justice to prosecute certain syndicalists for distributing antimilitarist propaganda to soldiers, he won an overwhelming vote of support, 441 to 55 (with Jaurès among the minority). And in the antisocialist press, "the best guarantee of peace" remained "the military force of France."[44]

In mid-summer, with peace uppermost in his thoughts, Jaurès visited

the old lycée at Albi to deliver the major speech at the annual distribution of prizes. He looked forward to this *Discours à la jeunesse*.[45] The
future, he knew, depended on the youth, on their willingness to stand
for justice and peace. There were already disquieting signs that the educated among them were abandoning reason for instinct, the goal of
brotherhood for the mysticism of religion. But in the current of 1903,
admiration for Jaurès, especially among these students of the Tarn, remained high. In a very intimate way, he belonged to them. Almost forty-
four years old and wearied by the tumult of politics, he began on a minor
note of melancholy: "It is a great pleasure for me to return to this
lycée of Albi and to speak here once again. Great pleasure and yet rather
sad. For when we return after a long interval, we can measure how much
of our lives has flown by and disappeared into the past. Little by little,
time steals life away from us and all at once we see a great part of it
behind us. . . . But what does it matter that time saps our strength, if
we have used our days for some significant accomplishment, which keeps
part of us eternally alive?"

The accomplishment toward which he turned the excited minds of
his young listeners was peace, beautiful and definitive peace. For twenty
centuries man's hope had been thwarted by the wars of Rome, or of
the Church, or of the Revolution:

What then? Will peace always flee from us? And will the cry of mankind
continue to mount toward the golden stars, always frantic but always doomed?
. . . No! . . . There is no complete certainty in history. I know how much
sickness there still is in the joints of nations, where a minor irritation can suddenly turn into a general inflammation. . . . Peace is difficult but not impossible. The appeasement of prejudices and hatreds; more comprehensive
alliances and federations; international arbitration and simultaneous disarmament; the coöperation of mankind in work and in learning: that will
be, young friends, the greatest goal and the supreme glory of the coming generation.

The task required courage, concluded the *tarnais*, a courage far more
fundamental than that needed for the wielding of arms: "Humanity is
damned if, in order to prove its courage, it must eternally kill. Courage
today is not to cover the world with a black cloud of war. . . . Courage is not to let force resolve conflicts which reason can solve. Courage is
the exaltation of man; force is the abdication of man!"

III

The socialists who gathered in April of 1903 as delegates to the Fifth
National Congress of the Parti socialiste français were as certain as the

308 | YEARS OF ANGUISH

characters in Mauriac's novels to find Bordeaux a somber city. But whereas the novelist's *bordelais* wrestled with sin, the socialists were still struggling with tactics. Though the party had been twice split, first by the exodus of the Marxists and then by that of the Blanquists, the inevitable Left, Right, and Center remained. For the Parti socialiste français was more complex, less uniformly reformist than its revolutionary critics either understood or admitted.

Since the Congress of Tours in March, 1902, when the party had charted a purely reformist course, the opposition from the Left had grown until, on the eve of the Bordeaux meeting, it was a full-scale revolt against the leadership of the Parti socialiste français. In ten departmental federations at least, socialist workers and their local leaders, Marxist in outlook and insurgent in spirit, were determined to wrest control of the party from the opportunists of the Palais Bourbon. Conceivably, they might have switched their allegiance to the Parti socialiste de France, but they had little sympathy for Guesdists and Blanquists who, in rejecting all practical action, had turned their party into a sect of purists. These Left-wing mutineers didn't distrust Jaurès personally; nor were their socialist principles essentially different from his. But they considered him too indulgent toward others, especially toward Ministerialists like Millerand, who were draining the party of its socialism and destroying its integrity. To the Left wing the Congress of Bordeaux was like a last reprieve. Unless it acted decisively and at once, unless it expelled Millerand and censured his followers, the Parti socialiste français could only degenerate and die; but if, like German Social Democracy, it combined realism and Marxism, if it were at once reformist and revolutionary, it would ultimately expand and thrive.

All of these calculations and aspirations are abundantly clear in a series of letters from Jean Longuet to Karl Kautsky. As the grandson of Marx and the son of a courageous Communard, Longuet always felt a rather special responsibility to safeguard sound socialist principles, and it is not surprising that he should have emerged as a leading strategist for the Left-wing minority or that he should have been, despite his membership in the Parti socialiste français, on friendly terms with Kautsky, Marx's most dedicated disciple.[46] No sooner had the Congress of Tours ended in 1902 than Longuet wrote not only of discontent within his party but also of the reluctance among the insurgents to join the Parti socialiste de France: "Quite obviously, the Ministerialists have become more and more impossible. . . . Unfortunately, the Guesdists and Blanquists have followed so foolish a course that most of the French workers are even less impressed by them. . . . At present, these revolutionaries expend all their time and energy attacking not the reactionaries

— the forces of feudalism and clericalism — but only the Radicals and the Ministerial socialists! So that's what passes for Marxism!"[47]

A year later, when Longuet wrote to Kautsky on the eve of the Bordeaux meeting, he reflected the determination of the left-wingers and revealed something of their strategy:

Some of my friends and I are spearheading a drive to expel Millerand from the Parti socialiste français, which contains not only terrible Ministerialist elements but also some very dedicated socialists. . . . To be sure, you might say that Millerand's expulsion won't solve all the party's problems and that certain members of the same stripe will stay in. But I think that if we manage to get rid of His Excellency, we will thereby serve warning on the Devilles, the Rouanets, and even on Jaurès, who will no doubt oppose the expulsion.[48]

How widespread, then, was the Left-wing revolt? In an article for *Le Mouvement socialiste,* Hubert Lagardelle's strongly Antiministerialist review, Pierre Renaudel, another of the Left-wing strategists, spelled out the answer: "The Federations of the Aube, the Charente-Inférieure, the Oise, the Savoie, the Seine-Inférieure, and the Yonne have joined with the Nièvre to demand first a thorough exposure of Millerand's record and then his expulsion. The Federation of the Rhône has made the same point, as has the Federation of the Vaucluse."[49] And in the important Federation of the Seine, Renaudel pointed out, the majority, though rejecting a motion for expulsion, had voted a resolution of censure against Millerand. No one could doubt, least of all the well-informed Jaurès, that the Congress of Bordeaux would become a battleground and the debates a bitter contest.

But Longuet and Renaudel, though they could write resolutions and talk to federation leaders, were neither colorful nor impassioned enough to lead the Left-wing minority into battle. That command fell at Bordeaux to a hopelessly nearsighted, almost meek-looking schoolteacher, who nervously stroked his goatee as he whispered his words. It was Gustave Hervé who, though he hardly looked the part, would soon become the *enfant terrible* of French socialism. A professor in the lycée of Sens and an active member of the socialist Federation of the Yonne, Hervé had already displayed his intractable temper and unrestrained vocabulary in a series of antimilitarist articles in the *Pioupiou de l'Yonne.* To conscripts in the army he had preached insubordination and even desertion; of patriots he had spoken with unsparing contempt: "So long as there are barracks, . . . I would like all of their filth and dung piled high in the largest courtyard of the quarter, and with all the troops watching and military music blaring, the regimental flag planted there by the Colonel."[50] Suspended from his teaching position by the Minister of Education and brought to trial on the complaint of the Minister of Justice, Hervé had been successfully defended by Briand before the Cour d'assises of Auxerre. For if they thought his language offensive, the Dreyfusard socialists of Paris found something heroic in the violent antimilitarism of the young provincial. At the end of November, 1901, they had made him guest of honor at a banquet where Jaurès praised him for showing that "the true France is the France of philosophy, peace, and the Enlightenment."[51]

At Bordeaux, Hervé emerged as spokesman for the Left.[52] Millerand's crime, he asserted, lay not in advocating collaboration and reformism but in treating these tactics as permanent and irrevocable. By so doing, Hervé charged, Millerand was destroying the revolutionary *élan* of socialism. From the Right wing of the party, Joseph Sarraute leaped to Millerand's defense. Representing that faction which considered socialism as only a more serious version of Radicalism, he ridiculed as outdated and totally unrealistic those who still preached the rhetoric of revolution. As soon as the French socialist movement organized politically, argued Sarraute, it set forth a program of reforms and fought to achieve them through parliamentary action. And why? Because through democracy the State had ceased to be a monopoly of the ruling class but had become an instrument of the majority. Millerand was thus wholly justified, Sarraute concluded, in defending the institutions of the democratic State and working within its confines.

For Jaurès, this moment could only have been painful. In expelling Millerand and censuring his supporters, the party would, by implication at least, discredit the bloc; but by repudiating the Left wing, the party stood to lose its most dedicated socialists. When he mounted the platform and began to speak, it became quickly evident that he would opt neither for the Left nor the Right but for unity. The socialist house, he argued, was large enough for all its tenants. So he deplored the folly, indeed the sheer laziness of hewing to a single, narrow line of socialist thought and dismissing all others. Political democracy, he insisted, was a great boon to the proletariat, and in joining the Left bloc, the party, justifiably, had sought to protect it. But some reformists, he warned, were too sanguine about the present state of affairs. The class struggle was still society's sternest reality, and democracy could affect it little until, under socialism, power was widely diffused; for only then would workers effectively show their strength. So Jaurès called for a synthesis of viewpoints, each partially valid, a policy of immediate collaboration and ultimate separation, of preserving democracy while organizing for socialism. As for Millerand, Jaurès rebuked him sharply for blurring the lines between socialism and Radicalism; but he criticized equally the attempt to expel him from the party. Instead of dividing the movement further, cried Jaurès, the Congress had to bend its every effort toward a reunion with those who had already left.

But for the Left wing Millerand's expulsion had become an irreducible minimum program; on that, they were adamant and united. Thus, in the special committee appointed to consider Millerand's fate, their motion, drafted by Renaudel and demanding expulsion, was narrowly adopted. As the Congress debated the resolution, its success seemed almost assured. But once again, Jaurès was at the podium, this time to deliver an emotionally charged appeal to reject the resolution. Why? Undoubtedly, to preserve unity. To hold the party within the bloc until it had fulfilled its promise. For that, he felt, he had to save Millerand. Against Renaudel's motion, he posed one of his own. Millerand was not mentioned by name, but every deputy would be required henceforth to act in accordance with general views of the party. "Free thought and scientific inquiry" were at the same time set down as indispensable in socialist deliberations. A compromise, and a relatively weak one, but it worked. When the two motions were placed side by side for a vote, Jaurès' resolution was adopted, though by a small margin, 109 to 89.

For the moment, the party held together, but it had not yet reached the limits of its inner dissension. Beaten only at the last moment, the Left-wingers were more determined than ever to control the party or leave. "The splendid fight we had in Bordeaux," an exultant Longuet wrote to Kautsky, "us poor little *genossen* against all the great ministerialist leaders and the victory nearly won in such conditions is a new proof of the great mistake made by our friends, guesdists and blanquists when they left the party." Then, in a reflection, which virtually forecast the conditions of socialist unity two years later, he added: "If they had been there, since a long time the party would have expelled all those acting against our principles and the others would be obliged to walk right."[53]

So, for all his feverish activity, Jaurès had won no real victory at Bordeaux. Nor could he so long as *millerandisme* continued to plague the party. If he expected either the Left or the Right to be guided by his resolution, he was only deluding himself. And if he still hoped that the revolutionaries would rejoin such a party, he was far too unrealistic. That illusion, if he really harbored it, was soon broken on the rock of German authority. The Marxists of Social Democracy arrived at their Dresden Congress in September, 1903, determined, once and for all, to condemn revisionism; and in so doing, they were bound to strengthen the resolve of the revolutionaries in France. When their long debates ended, the Social Democrats adopted a resolution which seemed categorical and inflexible:

The Congress most decisively condemns the Revisionist endeavor to alter our twice-tested and victorious tactics based on the class struggle. . . . If the Revisionist policies were adopted, it would become a party content with merely reforming bourgeois society. Further, our party Congress condemns any attempt to gloss over the existing, ever-increasing class conflicts for the purpose of turning it into a satellite of bourgeois parties.[54]

To the revolutionary socialists of the Parti socialiste de France, the Dresden Resolution was considered authoritative, and at their Congress of Reims in September they unanimously endorsed it in only slightly modified form. A scant year later, at their Lille Congress, these Guesdists and Blanquists, approving once more what was now called the Reims-Dresden resolution, agreed to offer it at the forthcoming Congress of the Second International as a fundamental code of socialist action.

Jaurès understood well enough that the weight of international socialist opinion had been thrown behind his opponents. And he was irate that foreign theorists, the German Social Democrats especially, who, he felt, misunderstood both French conditions and the potentiality of democracy, should presume to set rules for France. Privately, he expressed anger and exasperation; to his supporters he revealed his doubts about Social Democracy; a movement which had not even won universal suffrage in all the German States or effective power for the Reichstag, he insisted, was neither so strong as it appeared nor so infallible. Studying the German arguments carefully, reading the Social Democratic press intensively, he prepared for the coming showdown; he would not be overwhelmed, that was certain enough, by the prestige of Social Democracy. If Jaurès, out of his deep concern for socialist unity, was publicly more restrained, his determination to fight at the coming international congress was nonetheless clear. "The most serious mistake that the socialists of one country can make," he wrote, "is to judge the political action of other socialists without taking into account differences of political and social background. Many Germans theorists make this mistake when they judge the tactics of the Parti socialiste français."[55]

IV

In its fundamentals, the social system had not much changed in three years of progressive bourgeois rule. The working poor still suffered the pangs of hunger, still endured conditions that warped their lives and deprived them of security. What was it like for the mass of Frenchmen and their families? Consider one historian's description:

At the base of the social pyramid there were, around 1906, seven million wage-earners in industry and commerce, 2,700,000 day-workers in agriculture, and some four or five million small artisans, poor peasants, and hard-up tenants and sharecroppers.

How, then, did these masses live, who constituted the overwhelming majority of the working population? From day to day, without the slightest security for the morrow, always threatened by sickness, accident, unemployment. No savings, no holidays, no day off. The aged — those whom the pressure of work hadn't killed off — were thrown to the rubbish heap, reduced to asking for handouts. In Paris, a million inhabitants had hardly enough air to breathe; a third of the dwellings were terribly unsanitary, without running water or light. . . . The conditions of labor were frightful. . . . The annual rent represented a month's wage, sometimes more. The worker, driven to despair by his fatigue, low wages, fines, and dismissal, his dismal hovel, his pressing debts, the illnesses of his family, sought escape in drink. . . . It was, we are told, *la belle époque.* But not for everyone.[56]

Jaurès knew these facts all too well. It was the suffering of the many that had brought him to their side and kept him there. Never, over the long years, did his sympathy for them waver. What seemed to change in the period of the bloc was his view of the components of the labor problem. At the root of working-class poverty he found, as before, the system of capitalism, the exaction of industrial profits from the long hours and low wages imposed on labor. Nor did he feel that the system was perceptibly moving toward a more equal distribution of wealth. When the Minister of Finance, in the summer of 1903, released a long statistical report on declared inheritances, Jaurès scrutinized it as an indication of the national distribution of wealth. What he found struck him as a conclusive answer to economists like Leroy-Beaulieu, who wrote frequently of the trend toward equality. "In 1902," he pointed out, "the total amount left by the twenty-seven wealthiest of the deceased was higher than that left by the 243,000 poorest, who represent the vast majority of the people. . . . The decisive and glaring fact is that after a hundred years of capitalist democracy, . . . the great class of workers possesses only a miserable scrap of the public wealth."[57]

But now Jaurès posed the State as a third force between the two conflicting classes. Compared to the repressive State of the 1890's, the government of Combes, supported by a Left-wing majority, seemed to him closer to neutrality, willing to support impartial arbitration and to send troops to the strike fields for the sake of order rather than repression.[58] As proof, he cited the many complaints lodged by management against alleged governmental sympathy for the strikers. Thus, though the class struggle had been naked and unrelieved in the days of Carmaux, and would seem so again in the current of 1906 and 1907, the years of the Left bloc struck him as an interlude when the State, through arbitration and legislation, was attempting to bring order into the chaos of industrial relations.[59] At no time during these years did Jaurès reveal his thoughts more clearly — his attachment to the workers' cause, his criticism of capitalism, his confidence in arbitration — than during his direct participation in the prolonged textile strikes of the Nord.

In the fall of 1903, tension between capital and labor centered in the densely populated country around Lille and Armentières. In March, a strike had broken out among the textile workers in the valley of the Lys. Though their strike was spontaneous in origin, the workers had clearly formulated demands from the first: application of the wage scales agreed upon in the industry in 1889 but never observed by the mill owners; institution of the ten-hour day, as foreseen by the Millerand-Colliard Law, without any cut in wages; and uniformity of hours and wages for all mills in the region.

By October the strike had become widespread and occasionally violent, and the government ordered M. Vincent, Prefect of the Nord, to intervene. Convening representatives of capital and labor, the Prefect tried to work out an agreement; such was his success that he managed to settle all differences except one. The strikers demanded that half the increase in wage rates, scheduled for April 1, 1904, to guarantee their salaries after the reduction of hours, should be paid to them at once. The employers, claiming the hardship of competition and low profits, refused to make this concession. When the Prefect then proposed arbitration of the one point in dispute, labor approved but management did not. To break this stalemate, Jaurès intervened.

Traveling to the scene of strife, he mixed with the strikers, visited their dwellings, learned of their plight, and three times spoke before their overflowing crowds.[60] At Armentières he called "the attention of all of working-class and republican France to the misery, the grievances, the violated rights of the great mass of textile workers." At Caudry he expressed his shock and indignation at the living conditions of the workers: "What I saw yesterday at Armentières has burned unforgettable memories into my heart and my spirit. . . . In that city, the queen city of cloth, I saw beds without a scrap of cloth to cover the naked bodies of children. . . . Tiny, poverty-stricken dwellings where families with seven or eight children are huddled together without air, without light, without furniture, without anything that makes life human. . . . I am shocked by the selfish indifference of our civilization."

The defenders of management claimed that international competition, especially from German textiles, was responsible for the depression of wages. "An industry which cannot survive without constantly lowering the wages of its workers," retorted Jaurès, "is finished. There is a level below which human beings cannot sink." At Cateau, he praised the workers for an effort that could lead to the reform of an anarchic and outmoded industry: "This struggle is a blow for progress, for the rationalization of production as well as the organization of the working class."

On November 7 Jaurès addressed the Chamber on the textile strike. "Gentlemen, the refusal of management to agree to arbitration, as proposed by the Prefect and accepted by the workers, is the cause of the present crisis."[61] From that blunt beginning, he went on to review the origins of the strike, the demands of the workers, the conditions of their lives, and the course of the negotiations. He denounced as beyond justification the order of existence imposed on the textile workers, "where the shortest period of sickness or unemployment throws them into a sink of misery, an abyss of ignominy from which nothing can save them." Spokesmen for the industry pleaded competition and low profits. "And I say that the textile industry has fallen to its present level of anarchy because the bosses, instead of finding prosperity through improvement of their products and rational management of their plants, engage each other in disastrous competition which always ends in the cutting of wages. . . . The capitalists have lost their balance in our time, and they waver between extremes of industrial centralization and absolute anarchy."

Management struck back in the person of Jules Dansette, a deputy whose family had long prospered in the textile trade. To the charge of recalcitrance which Jaurès had hurled against the owners, he replied: "They cannot accept arbitration because they have already gone as far as they can; they would have to shut down their plants if they were forced to concede more." In turn, Dansette attacked the workers for violence, the ministry for failure to protect company property, and the socialists, especially Jaurès, for provoking and prolonging the strike. Dansette drew this last and most sensational charge from *Le Travailleur*, the Guesdist newspaper of Lille, which accused the governmental socialists of supporting the strike merely to improve their labor record before their appearance at the Congress of Amsterdam.

This rebuttal scarcely coped with the detailed particulars set forth by Jaurès. When the Minister of Commerce, Georges Trouillot, agreed in substance with the case against the textile manufacturers, wide support was assured for the course of action Jaurès was proposing. Over some objections to "direct governmental interference in the conflicts between capital and labor,"[62] the Chamber voted, 512 to 2, for immediate resumption of arbitration and a full-scale inquiry into the conditions of the textile trade.

In the aftermath of the Chamber session, the strike ended, and though arbitration was again rejected by management, the Prefect of the Nord helped to create labor-management councils to effect settlements of further disputes. For Jaurès it demonstrated how important friendly governments could be for the cause of labor. "Who will deny the services rendered to their comrades by the socialist mayors of Armentières and Houplines? . . . And the most unanimous vote of the Chamber, though it didn't force the employers to accept arbitration, at least helped to resolve the conflict."[63]

His critics in the labor movement accused him of unrealistic optimism; neither was the State so neutral, they insisted, nor arbitration so effective as he believed. But when these critics questioned his devotion to the cause of labor, they were men carried away by their own dogma. For among the rank and file of the working class, Jaurès was rarely doubted, he was revered. "I shall never forget," recalled François Mauriac, "what my friend Jean Guéhenno told me — how as an insignificant worker from a Breton town and in the course of a strike, he stood for hours against the columns in the market place where Jaurès was supposed to speak, and what he then derived from the man: faith in the mission of the working class, an indestructible confidence in life, dismal though it might be, a light which guides him still, after so many long years."[64]

V

The seven months that stretched from the opening of the 1904 legislative session to the Congress of the Second International at Amsterdam were laden with disappointment for Jaurès. The thread that linked many diverse events together was the gradual disintegration of the Left bloc through desertion from the inside and attacks from without. As early as January 13, it was already signaled when some twenty Radicals and old Progressists broke discipline to vote against and thus defeat Jaurès' candidacy for one of the vice-presidencies of the Chamber. He lashed out at those "Radicals or pseudo-Radicals, hungry for ministerial power," who were hoping to upset the ministry by provoking socialist desertion. But they were wrong to think that Jaurès cared so much about an official post or that his party could be so easily turned from its course: "How badly they understand socialism. We are all the freer now to support the essential work of the Republic."[65] Jaurès was thinking of the next important moves of the government: separation of Church and State, passage of the two-year army law.[66] His friends had to withstand attacks upon them, work closely with the majority, and support Combes until those goals had been reached.

But within his own party, the Left-wingers showed a mounting contempt for the tactics of collaboration. Too often, they charged, the party deputies had voted against the spirit of socialism just to support the ministry. And especially was this the case during the Chamber session of October 30, 1903. The day before, Lépine's Paris police had raided the bourse du travail where some three thousand workers were assembled to protest against the levying of monetary charges by government employment offices. Using the revolutionary rhetoric of the C.G.T. as their excuse, the police fired upon the workers and wounded well over a hundred of them.

In the tense parliamentary session that followed, Jaurès deplored "the blind and sterile" recourse to violence, which had become the stock-in-trade of certain syndicalist leaders, and once again stated the case for rational political action. But in sharper language, he attacked Lépine and the brutality of his police. Combes, called upon to answer for the government, expressed deep regret over the incident and directed words of censure against Lépine. It was a weak defense, which won over neither the revolutionary socialists nor the majority of the reformists. Yet Jaurès and thirteen members of his party, loyal to the bloc, threw their support to Combes.

In the Interfederal Committee, the central administrative body of the Parti socialiste français, the representatives of the departmental federations, though they lacked authority to discipline the deputies, voiced bitter criticisms of the *élus* and especially of Millerand.[67] Tension mounted in the party until, on January 4, 1904, it broke. On that day, in a sudden climax of a long struggle, the Federation of the Seine, now under Left-wing control, expelled Millerand from its ranks and, as a consequence, from the Parti socialiste français. "Our party is suffering from religious atavism," Gérault-Richard wrote sarcastically "Periodically, we have to repeat our dogma and excommunicate our heretics."[68] But Longuet was exultant; the party, he felt, had turned an important corner. "I am very glad with the present situation of socialism in France," he wrote to Kautsky. "It is not as we should like to see it, but everybody begins to see what we *move*. . . . More and more there are possibilities of *bringing together* all French socialists in one party — and a party with a revolutionary majority."[69]

Jaurès, however, said nothing publicly. He was undoubtedly concerned lest any comment should deepen the party split. But more than that, he seemed strangely confused, torn between conflicting loyalties and positions. He had led the party into the Left bloc because he believed that institutional and social reforms would pave the way to socialism. But the cost of collaboration — the evident heresy of Millerand, the antisocialist votes of his party, the easy confusion between reformist socialists and Radical-Socialists, and, above all, the roaring discontent of the party's rank and file — was staggeringly high. What could Jaurès say, after all, to express his belief both in the reformist politics of the party and the revolutionary spirit of its insurgents?

By the time the Parti socialiste français convened for the Congress of Saint-Étienne in February, 1904, it had sunk to its nadir. Glum delegates were informed that paid memberships had dropped from eleven to eight thousand since the Congress of Bordeaux, while two Federations, those of the Yonne and the Somme, had broken away completely. The Left-wingers, emboldened by the expulsion of Millerand, were ready to act. The party could be saved, they felt, and its socialist spirit resuscitated only if control passed to the departmental federations where the Left now predominated. What they proposed, therefore, was a change in the party rules, empowering the Interfederal Committee to discipline the deputies and thus to control their activities in the bloc.

Jaurès listened as a parade of delegates deplored the record of the ministry and the antisocialist deviations of party deputies. He questioned neither their sincerity nor the validity of some of their charges. But still, he felt, he had to play for time. Until the Dreyfusard program had been enacted into law, until the Church and the army had been effectively disarmed, he was determined to support the bloc, and without restrictions. When he finally spoke, he conceded a great deal to the opposition case: "We realize that the government hasn't always acted with complete good will; and we also know that when its will has been good, its policies have at times been sabotaged by its administrative officials." But on the whole, the ministry had a progressive record; it had been a worthy ally for socialists: ". . . and the time has come for us to be concerned not only with espousing pure principles but also with acting upon them through practical reforms."[70]

His oratory was effective, and so was the compromise he suggested. Agreeing with the insurgents that some sort of discipline was desirable, he proposed a change of rules, which was unanimously adopted by the Congress. For on paper, it seemed to answer the criticisms of the Left; but in practice, it soon proved to be hardly any change at all.[71] Party wounds had not healed. As often happened in the socialist movement, noble words and a meaningless resolution had merely preserved the outer form of unity. At best, Jaurès had gained only time. A little later in the year, when Millerand joined a Centrist and Rightist attack on Combes, he had good reason to worry about his record of defending his former friend.[72]

His course of action in the last year of the Combes ministry was full of twists and turns. On February 6, 1904, Japan severed diplomatic relations with Russia; two days later, the Russian fleet at Port Arthur was shelled, and a Russo-Japanese war, long feared and anticipated by Jaurès, now threatened the peace of Europe. With involvement in a Far Eastern war a distinct possibility, he turned on the ministry in anger and demanded information about French commitments.

"It is really extraordinary," he wrote, "that neither the text nor even the exact meaning of the treaties with Russia have been revealed to the nation. If we should be led by secret commitments to the brink of war, the country would never forgive those who, for a decade, have smothered in a cloud of patriotism all those questions which the socialists have tried to raise." [73] Neither the explicit statement he sought nor the French engagement he feared actually resulted. Had England felt compelled to aid Japan, France might well have been forced to war; but the conflict remained localized, and the majority of the French settled back to enjoy a quick Russian victory.

Jaurès, however, foresaw other results. Run by "corrupt financiers, parasitical courtiers, dishonest bureaucrats, grasping admirals, empty-headed Grand Dukes, a pack of sharp-toothed wolves," Russia seemed to him no match for a modernized Japan. Long before the fall of Port Arthur (January 2, 1905) shocked the French into sober reappraisal of their invincible ally, he ridiculed those newspapers which interpreted every Russian retreat as a masterpiece of strategy: "Flaubert, who collected examples of human stupidity with an embittered delight, would have found some fine specimens this busy season; his laugh would have resounded from the Seine to the Neva." [74]

In these early months of 1904 Jaurès was sustained by the happy anticipation that at least one of his problems would soon be resolved. His relations with *La petite République*, where he had once found friends and a forum, had become painful and strained. Gérault-Richard, concerned more with its solvency than its integrity, had involved the newspaper in certain highly questionable enterprises. On the ground floor of their building, the management of *La petite République* had opened a number of shops where clothing and household goods, manufactured in prisons or monastery workshops, were offered to the public at conspicuously low prices. The revelations of Gohier, the C.G.T., and others were shocking but true.

In 1903, therefore, Herr and Blum proposed a new daily for Jaurès, one which he would edit. He was enthusiastic, and he speculated about the style of such a newspaper. It would be popular yet serious, political yet literary. The monetary barrier was hurdled through the efforts of Blum and Lévy-Bruhl. Using their influence in well-to-do Jewish circles, they found most of the 880,000 francs which constituted the original fund of capital. Jaurès welcomed the investors, unaware as yet how frequently his enemies would accuse him of serving Jewish finance.

Herr gave the new daily its name — *L'Humanité*. Jaurès' prestige brought to it a large and remarkable staff of contributors: for political analysis Allemane, Briand, Pressensé, Viviani, Herr, Andler, and Longuet; for the arts Anatole France, Léon Blum, Jules Renard, Gustave Geffroy, Abel Hermant, and Henry de Jouvenel; for questions of education, Gustave Lanson; and, as news editor, Daniel Halévy. Looking over the list, Jaurès proudly announced to Briand that it contained seventeen *agrégés*. "We shall have the most talented men in Paris." To which the practical Briand replied: "Yes, but where are the journalists?"[75]

On April 18, 1904, the first issue of *L'Humanité* appeared. Those who snatched up 130,000 copies that day, out of eagerness or curiosity, discovered a newspaper which included among its features an old story by Georges Sand and a new one, *La Vieille*, by Jules Renard. They found also the first of more than two thousand articles that Jaurès would write for *L'Humanité*, this one a statement of purpose from the editor: "To welcome all communications bearing on the life of the working class; . . . to support all organizational efforts of the proletariat; . . . to give all free minds, through precise and extensive information, the means of understanding and judging the events of the world by themselves." There followed days and weeks of enthusiasm and revitalized comradeship. Jaurès spoke optimistically of the newspaper's financial prospects: "We will reach 140,000. There will be a tremendous overhead, but we can show a profit. At 70,000 daily, the paper will cover its expenses."[76] Year after year the financial crises at *L'Humanité* amply disproved this optimism.

On May 17 both the sales of the paper and the cause of anticlericalism were stimulated when *L'Humanité* published a sensational papal document, confided to Jaurès by the Prince of Monaco. Pope Pius X, successor to the worldly Leo XIII on the latter's death in 1903, was a cross between "a village curé and an archangel with a flaming sword."[77] Neither he nor Merry del Val, the thirty-eight-year-old, inexperienced Spanish Cardinal who became his Secretary of State, was endowed with flexibility or wisdom enough to fend off an impending showdown with France. Instead, their intransigence actually hastened it. Thus, when President Loubet paid an official visit to King Victor Emmanuel of Italy, the Pope, recalling that Italy had despoiled the Vatican of her lands, considered it a major insult. His Secretary of State delivered a note of protest to Nisard, the French Ambassador, and then sent copies to all powers maintaining diplomatic relations with the Vatican. This note, which the strongly anticlerical Prince of Monaco gave to Jaurès, first appeared exclusively in *L'Humanité*. Revealing as it did a rash and ill-advised interference with the diplomatic activities of France, the document produced a general embarrassment ranging from disquietude to bitter resentment.[78]

Combes reacted at once by recalling Nisard from his post in the Vatican and leaving only a chargé d'affaires behind. Jaurès, speaking before a capacity audience at the Cirque d'Hiver on May 28, applauded this spirit of decision, and rang out an appeal for separation of Church and State.[79] The climate of opinion was hot with excitement. In the Chamber the Catholic Right tried to minimize the importance of the papal note, but even from the antigovernmental Center Ribot raised his influential voice to protest against clerical interference with "political society." By the end of the debate on the Premier's course of action, Combes won an overwhelming vote of confidence (427 to 95). One substantial pretext would now suffice for the definitive break with the Vatican, and two French bishops supplied it.

When the Bishops of Laval and Dijon, known for their republican sentiments, were ordered to Rome to explain alleged transgressions of their holy office, they appealed to the Premier, who refused to permit their appearance while denouncing Rome's action as a violation of the Concordat. Pius X would give no ground; the bishops, unwilling to precipitate a schism, resigned. But the Premier, backed by most of his ministers, broke off diplomatic relations with the Vatican. As the last hours of the Established Church ticked rapidly away, Jaurès foresaw a significant victory for French democracy. "The Concordat, which confers part of the public power on a privileged religion, is a conspicuous residue of the Old Regime in a society presumably founded on human freedom," he told an audience at Rouen. "After secularizing marriage, the family, and the school, we will finally secularize the State by the great reform we call Separation."[80]

L'Humanité and its early campaigns were like an anodyne for Jaurès' pain, but they were not enough. He suffered deeply from the quarrels in his party, the schism within the movement, the fitful convolutions of the bloc, the terrible truth of hope deferred and promise unfulfilled. "The world of empirical morality," observed the Goethe whom he read through a whole lifetime, "consists for the most part of ill will and envy." How often and how nostalgically he must have thought back to those days of friendship with Guesde or Péguy!

One day, as though seeking the road back, Jaurès went to the small shop at Suresnes where they printed *Les Cahiers de la quinzaine*. He asked for Péguy, who was not there, and he promptly left. When Péguy appeared at the shop, the excited printers told him that Jaurès had been looking for him. It puzzled the poet, who hadn't seen the *tarnais* for many months. What happened next was revealed by Péguy in the *Cahiers* (November, 1905) and retold by Daniel Halévy:

It appeared to Péguy that this visit from an older man, and one of the busiest in France, should be returned. He called on Jaurès, wondering why he had asked for him, but without discovering. He found a saddened, disillusioned man, entirely absorbed, perhaps to the point of exhaustion, in the labor of running *L'Humanité*, which he was busy taking over. "I have to go out," he said to Péguy. "Come along with me." He liked talking and walking together. Péguy could call to mind other walks made memorable by Jaurès' conversations and recitations. Jaurès could let his memory flow, and out would come enchanted streams of poetry from Lamartine, Hugo, Racine, Ronsard, Villon. Péguy had the same gift. It made a lovely game, and they used to cap one another's cantos and exhortations from tragedy. But the day came when Jaurès had no voice left for poetry. Near the Champs-Elysées, he called a cab: he was in a hurry. Péguy made a last-minute attempt to solve the riddle. Jaurès might have wanted to talk to him about his paper. He took the bull by the horn and said: "I can't collaborate; I belong to the *Cahiers*. But I have got some very gifted friends, faithful ones. If you try them, you will not regret it." "It's not collaborators I need," said Jaurès, "I have got more than enough. What worries me is the question of support." The cab was there waiting. Jaurès started to climb in. Péguy ends the story thus: "A last handshake. He got in heavily and sat all crumpled up in his cab which went off jerkily. I never saw him again. So I never knew why suddenly, the day before, after a long interval and with no warning, he came to see me at the printer's. Perhaps at the critical moment, some dim regret, a sort of dull remorse, beset him."[81]

Péguy had seen clearly the shadows of fatigue across Jaurès' face. But the circle of Père Sorel, where Péguy imbibed the wisdom of France's most erudite engineer, had so far separated him from Jaurès that he failed, one feels, to grasp the vital powers of recovery in the *tarnais*. Socialism was and remained a way of life for Jaurès, the source of prodigious energies and boundless hopes. Defeat or despair were only temporary. "Even if socialists were to extinguish for a moment all the stars in the heavens," he once wrote, "I would still walk the darkened road which leads to justice, to that divine flash which alone can rekindle all the suns in all the vast stretches of space."[82]

VI

"In 1904, before the Congress of Amsterdam, Jaurès came to Toulouse. He spoke at the Capitole, and I can recall so very well all the details of that meeting. Guesde was supposed to answer Jaurès, but because of ill-ness he was replaced by Cachin. Outside on the streets, vendors were selling Cachin's pamphlet, *Le Banquet du roi*. The insults hurled at Jaurès shocked me greatly. . . . But I can still hear Jaurès raise his cry of hope — that unity would soon be realized."[83]

Vincent Auriol's reminiscence is doubly revealing. He recaptured, in the first place, something of the bitterness and recrimination which char-acterized the quarrel among the socialists as the meeting at Amsterdam approached. The Second International would render final judgment on the debate in France, as all the militants realized, and that realization threw the great and minor orators on both sides into a frenetic, unre-strained campaign to win over the socialist public at home and abroad. Everything was thrown into the boiling pot of contention — theory, tactics, personal motives, and, in at least one instance, even primacy in erudition, according to an anecdote which Bracke, a trained classicist as well as a Marxist, recounted fifty years later:

Before Unity, Jaurès had quoted a beautiful verse of Homer in one of his speeches. But that verse existed neither in the *Iliad* nor the *Odyssey*. After some searching, I realized that he had actually hemstitched together parts of two separate Homeric verses. I eagerly reported the discovery to my friends: "Jaurès had a dream, in which he entered the Elysian fields and met Homer, who made him a present of an unpublished verse." That story bothered Jaurès terribly. It was, remember, before Unity, and surrounded as he was by Hellen-ists, including my own student Psichari, he was no little annoyed to be tripped up by a Guesdist.[84]

But of equal importance was Auriol's recollection that in the heat of battle Jaurès managed to speak hopefully of unity. On the surface, at least, the quarrel over tactics reflected an irreconcilable conflict. If, then, the Second International should pronounce an interdiction against the tactics of collaboration, as everyone expected, wouldn't the consequence be the permanent division of French socialism rather than its unity? To those who accepted at face value the bitter attacks by each socialist group upon the other, that conclusion must have seemed inescapable; but not to Jaurès, who realized that neither party was so monolithic as less astute critics believed. The Parti socialiste français, despite resist-ance from the Right, had twice admitted the wisdom of the Marxist International: first, when its Congress of Tours had voted to prohibit any further uncontrolled ministerial participation; and then, when it had finally ousted Millerand, an action which by now was scarcely ques-tionable. But more than that, the Left-wingers, who spoke with increas-ing authority in party councils, had disguised neither their contempt for the *élus* nor their desire for a reconciliation with the revolutionaries.[85]

As the politics of the bloc ran their course, Jaurès seemed to welcome their influence on party policy.[86]

On the other side, within the Parti socialiste de France, he felt that some leaders, rather less intractable than Guesde, would ultimately approach their socialist rivals in a conciliatory spirit. Hadn't Vaillant, after all, always shared his faith in party unity? Generous and realistic, he might moderate the stridency of Marxists; or so Jaurès hoped. Thus, some months before Amsterdam, when Jaurès wrote at length about Blanqui's theory of revolution and rescued him from the ranks of the "putschists," he was actually addressing Vaillant. "According to Blanqui," Jaurès wrote early in 1904, "the essence of revolution was to create a political and social milieu in which all citizens could educate themselves and work out freely and coöperatively the terms of a communist society."[87]

But what about the leaders of the Second International, especially the vociferous Germans, armed with both the Dresden Resolution and the 1903 election results?[88] Once again, Jaurès felt that actualities were different from appearances. Thus, though leaders like Bebel and Kautsky were determined to extirpate Revisionism from world socialism, they probably intended to press their case no further than to the limits of compatibility with socialist unity.[89] If spokesmen for the conspiratorial parties from those countries (Russia, Bulgaria, Hungary, Serbia, Japan) where the struggle was still naked and brutal were certain to be unyielding, others, like the Austrian Victor Adler and the Belgian Vandervelde, were more conciliatory and certainly more influential. Jaurès would go to Amsterdam as determined to make his case as the Marxists were to repudiate it. But he had a sure sense of timing, and he understood the fact that the presumably deadly opposition between reformism and revolution had already become, in practical political terms, rhetorical.

Jaurès traveled to Amsterdam with Briand, arriving in the charming Dutch city on August 13. In a new setting Jaurès was exuberant again. The canals delighted him, as did the busy, winding streets, and the clean, neat houses. At the opening session of the Congress the next day, his delight turned into exhilaration, when delegates of twenty-two nations met in the beautiful Concertegebouw, mingling beneath a huge banner which read: "Workers of the World, Unite!" The international fraternity, which came alive that first day, was symbolized by a firm handshake between Katayama of Japan and Plekhanov of Russia, whose countries were then locked in war.

Almost at once, the Congress broke up into committees, the most important one charged with drafting a resolution on socialist tactics and method. All the *vedettes* of world socialism were members of that committee — Jaurès, Guesde, Kautsky, Bebel, Rosa Luxemburg, Vander-velde, Ferri, Victor Adler, Pablo Iglesias, Ramsay MacDonald, Daniel DeLeon, Plekhanov — and for three days they debated in the *petite salle* of the Concertegebouw. None was more active in the debate than Jaurès, who was direct, intimate, and "free of all the pompous formality of great public meetings."[90] He was bothered, as they all were in a day before simultaneous translations, by the barrier of language. At one point, when he was ready to answer a strong attack by the Germans, he asked: "But who is going to translate for me?" Little Rosa Luxem-burg, the brilliant and polylingual Polish Jew who was to contribute her powerful mind and revolutionary courage to German Social Democ-racy, replied: "I will, if you will accept, Citizen Jaurès." Smiling broadly, Jaurès accepted the help of his bitter opponent, noting that "our struggle does not exclude collaboration."[91]

At the outset of the debate, Guesde moved that the committee accept the Reims-Dresden resolution as its basic formula for socialist action. This proposal was countered by Vandervelde and Adler, who introduced a motion more moderate and conciliatory in tone. Instead of an explicit condemnation of Revisionism in its manifold forms, the Adler-Vander-velde motion simply declared the class struggle to be the basis for so-cialist tactics; and rather than a final prohibition on ministerial participation, it repeated the warnings laid down in Kautsky's resolution of 1900. The guiding lines in this alternative motion were thus less dic-tatorial, though its basic principles differed little from those of the Reims-Dresden resolution. The debate that resulted, therefore, centered rather on the spirit than the actual wording of the two proposals. In the sharper resolution, with its disciplinary tone, its proponents found their defense against the corrosion of socialist doctrine.

At the height of the committee debate, Guesde and Jaurès faced each other once again, the ailing but dedicated Marxist in his sixtieth embattled year, the thoughtful and tireless philosopher in his forty-fourth. At Amsterdam their differences reached a climax, and then, when they had said all they could, they relaxed their antagonisms for a decade. Jaurès now defended the record of his party and its deputies. Through their common front with bourgeois progressives, he claimed, they had helped to safeguard the Republic, so threatened from the Right during the Af-fair. Under Waldeck-Rousseau and Combes they had helped to liberate the minds of men from the shackles of clericalism; they had promoted international peace, the indispensible condition for a life of full measure, by pressing for negotiation; and they had fought for social legislation in collaboration with a progressive majority.

Guesde answered with unsparing criticism, which revealed his deep suspicion of reformism. Denying his own position of 1898, the old Marxist minimized the danger to the Republic during the Dreyfus Affair, and concluded that it would have disappeared, as at the time of Boulangism, without socialist participation. Anticlericalism, he went on, was more a deception than a gain when it was pushed by bourgeois leaders, a deflection of the working-class assault on their capitalistic imperium. Guesde riddled the argument that socialists had promoted peace, parading before the receptive committee members evidence that the Ministerialists had supported the government's budgets for the army and navy, and reminding Jaurès that he and his friends had even voted funds for colonial enterprises. As for social welfare laws, he answered scornfully that nothing had been won which could not have been secured without tight socialist collaboration. At the climax, Guesde turned on Jaurès and accused him of promoting a false conception of socialism, reducing it to an advanced stage of the eighteenth-century democratic revolution. But no, cried Guesde, socialism was the inevitable consequence of capitalist development; the tradition of the French Revolution had little bearing on the character of the ruling class or on the nature of capitalism; the tactical position of socialism could not be shaped by differences in local history and institutions.

The committee sided with Guesde, though its members scarcely doubted Jaurès' integrity. They were persuaded that a great French party needed sound principles; but they were equally persuaded that it required both of its outstanding leaders. Thus, by the time Vandervelde reported to the full Congress, the committee had acted three times: first, it rejected the Adler-Vandervelde motion by a vote of twenty-four to sixteen; then it endorsed the Reims-Dresden resolution, twenty-seven to three, but with ten abstentions; and finally, it accepted the motion, sponsored jointly by Kautsky, Bebel, Ferri, Adler, Troelstra, and Vandervelde, that there should be in each country only one unified socialist party, just "as there is only one proletariat."

On August 9, Vandervelde summed up the committee's report before the full assembly, and the debate began. Jaurès knew that the weight of opinion fell on the so-called revolutionary side; but he felt certain that time was on his side, and that he might safeguard the socialist future by waging a successful fight for the more flexible Adler-Vandervelde motion. "The more the socialist party becomes accustomed to freedom and responsibility," he wrote, "the more it will reject absolute dicta on tactics, which can only constrict the action of the working class."[92] With that thought in mind, Jaurès rose before the final tribunal of world socialism and delivered one of the memorable orations in modern socialist debate.[93]

On one basic principle, he began, he agreed with the Dresden resolution — that "the party of the proletariat must be autonomous in its goals, organization, and method." But was it sound to scorn reforms, these "important steps toward final liberation," as props of the capitalistic order? Even the Dresden resolution proposed an all-out fight for political liberties and social legislation. In France, socialists had sought to wage that fight in collaboration with the progressive bourgeoisie, those Radicals who represented a broad stratum of democratic peasants, artisans, and shopkeepers, and who were pledged to vote for an income tax, social security, and even the nationalization of public utilities.

It was a serious error to consider the bourgeoisie en bloc, warned Jaurès: "In the days when Guesde and I worked side by side to spread the word of socialism, I often heard him say that of the thirty-eight million Frenchmen, there weren't more than two hundred thousand who had class interests directly opposed to collectivist socialism. . . . It would be foolhardy, even criminal to abandon the amorphous, heterogeneous, inconsistent democratic mass to its own devices. The socialist proletariat, organized into a separate class party and hostile to big capital, must influence and guide it."

The worst of blunders would be to prohibit the parties in democratic countries from nudging a progressive majority toward socialism. Yet that was the essence of the program now being dictated to the International by the German Social Democrats. In complete command of the hall, Jaurès had suddenly electrified the audience. Not since the expulsion of the anarchists had the tactics, accomplishments, and even the revolutionary will of German Social Democracy been so directly challenged; nor ever again, until the World War sundered socialist unity, would it be so authoritatively assailed. But now Jaurès, who had already invested his hopes for European peace in Social Democracy, and who would stand accused most of his life as a Germanophile, blurted out, for the first and last time, all of his inner doubts about the German movement: "I say, without any hesitation, that by internationalizing their Dresden resolution, they are foisting on world socialism the uncertainty and hesitation which grip them. At this moment, what weighs most heavily on Europe and on the world, on the guarantee of peace and freedom — is not the bold attempt of French socialists to safeguard progress and peace, but the tragic impotence of German Social Democracy."

Only time, not discretion, could stop Jaurès now. He excoriated the Social Democrats with the intensity of a democrat and a revolutionary who resented judgment by socialists experienced in neither democracy nor revolution:

On the morrow of the elections last June, when you won some three million votes, one fact became evident to all — that though you showed a great force in propaganda and recruitment, neither the traditions of your working class nor the terms of your constitution enabled you to convert that mirage of power into genuine political action. Why? Because you cannot act either as revolutionaries or as parliamentarians! . . . Historically, there is no revolutionary tradition among your workers. They never conquered universal suffrage on the barricades. They received it from above. . . . Because you lack a revolutionary tradition, you have a kind of disdain for those who have a genuine revolutionary will. . . . And even if you were the majority in the Reichstag, socialism would not be master. For your Parliament is only a pseudo-Parliament. . . . You have shouted in your newspapers: *Unser das Reich! Unser die Welt!* No! The Empire is not yours, since you are still unable to extend hospitality to international socialism in your own capital.

As his time ran out, Jaurès urged the delegates to understand the growing force of democracy, for which many were unfortunately ill-equipped, and not to frustrate "the full development of international socialism."

The applause was deafening. It had been a speech of daring and passion. But at two that afternoon, the delegates heard the less eloquent words of Bebel.[94] "The Pope of socialism," as Jean Bourdeau, the cynical but well-informed correspondent for *Les Débats*, called him,[95] was obviously pushed to the defensive by Jaurès: "Certainly, Germany is a reactionary, feudal, police state, the worst governed country in Europe," he began. "But we scarcely need anyone from the outside to come in and teach us how dismal our conditions are." A republic? Perhaps it was preferable, he admitted, "but we wouldn't get our heads broken for it; it's not worth the trouble."

A thunder of "bravos" greeted that remark, and it was obvious enough that only a minority among the delegates shared the republican faith of Jaurès. "Bourgeois monarchy, bourgeois republic, both are class states. . . . The monarchy is not so bad, nor the republic so good as you suggest." Rejecting the contention that local differences were anything more than superficial, Bebel moved on to his main argument — that the Dresden Resolution would prove a good guide for socialists of all countries.

Thus were the battle lines drawn. Before the division, the delegates unanimously approved the resolution calling for a single unified party in each country. Adler then proposed his motion as an amendment, which only barely failed to pass when the delegations divided evenly in the vote, twenty-one to twenty-one. At that long-delayed point, the Reims-Dresden resolution was finally adopted twenty-five to five, but with twelve abstentions. Reformism, presumably, had been defeated. How, then, would Jaurès react?

"M. Jaurès finds himself caught between two blocs, the International and the Radical. After the decisions at Amsterdam, he must choose."[96] So wrote Bourdeau, and many others echoed his words in the conservative press. The conservatives were right; the burden *was* on Jaurès; in his judgment, then in his decision, he would seal the fate of his movement. Was he angry when he returned from Amsterdam, ready to quit the International? If so, he would carry thousands with him into some political limbo. But no! Jaurès would not leave or decry his defeat. If the conservatives harbored hopes (as they surely did) that socialism would now die from division, they were doomed to frustration. Better than any other witness, Gustave Téry has described Jaurès' mood after Amsterdam: "He was anything but crushed; it was no use for us to recall the many speeches urging censure of his policy. . . . If he claimed he was the victor all the same, it was not because he overestimated himself. No, he really believed it, frankly and deeply. And what is more, he was right, despite the votes for Bebel."[97]

Jaurès' reaction undoubtedly startled some and certainly annoyed others. When he talked of victory, he was thinking especially of unification in the French socialist movement. But, then, would the new party be forced to abandon daily political efforts on behalf of the working class? Jaurès sensed that no such course was really possible. "At each crucial moment," he noted, "all socialists have supported the policies of secularism and social reform proposed by the present ministry."[98] The facts supported him, as did Marcel Sembat, the Blanquist, who bluntly admitted that "since the Russo-Japanese War, we have consistently supported the government."[99]

In the weeks that followed the Congress of Amsterdam, Jaurès clarified his position. On September 25, before some three thousand *carmausins*, he promised his enthusiastic support of unity; but he insisted also that socialism had to avail itself of the opportunities of democracy. Among some of the revolutionaries, his attitude and potential influence caused apprehension. "Jaurès is the most brilliant, far-sighted, and clever battler," Rappoport wrote to Kautsky, "and he may yet put socialism on a reformist basis."[100] But others were elated that their greatest tribune would be among them. According to Sembat, it was Vaillant especially who had faith in Jaurès, and who "overcame the qualms of the revolutionaries."[101] For, as they ultimately sensed, Jaurès was a revolutionary and a republican, a Marxist and an idealist. "Of a capacious spirit," Trotsky was later to write ,"he had a physical repulsion for all sectarianism. . . . He was an eclectic, but an eclectic of genius."[102]

Jaurès' reaction was not without its disappointments for some — conservatives hoping for a schism in the collectivist Left; enterprising

Ministerialists, their hands outstretched towards the reins of power; and the eager Louise, daydreaming about life as a minister's wife. But for Jaurès Amsterdam opened another phase of his political life. He would abandon neither his belief in democracy nor his fight for reforms; on the benefits of the bloc he would never recant; but neither would he deny the class nature of the socialist struggle or its revolutionary dimension. Now he would become more critical of socialist relations with the bourgeois Left; he would leave behind the compromises that had troubled him and weakened his position; he would devote himself, even more than before, to building a large, unified party. In terms direct and categorical, Vandervelde described the new Jaurès: "There is no doubt that in the story of his life we can distinguish two periods: before Amsterdam and after. Before, he was a socialist, no one doubts it, from his head to his toes. But he became involved in marginal activities, in reforms and causes which had little direct bearing on socialism. After Amsterdam, he became, above all, the man of unity. Detached from a number of his old friends — Briand, Viviani, and others who joined up with the bourgeois parties — he drew closer to Guesde and especially to Vaillant, the spur to his socialist conscience."[103]

VII

"The telegram which informed me of the decision taken at Amsterdam rang in my ears like a death knell. . . . From that day on, I anticipated that my ministry was doomed."[104] This reaction of Combes was somewhat premature. True enough, the two socialist parties, as early as August 30, had begun to draw up the terms of unification, one of which was certain to be withdrawal from the Délégation des gauches. But it was not until January 13, 1905, that a committee, drawn from both groups, finally settled upon a "Pact of Union" as the basis for debate. In the intervening months, Jaurès, at the head of the socialist delegation, fought as vigorously as ever to keep the Combes ministry afloat.

His efforts were vital. By the full autumn of 1904, the ministry was being assailed not only from the Right and Center, where clerical and antilabor feelings ran high, but also from the Left bloc itself, where personal ambitions, vulgar rivalries and genuine moral considerations were producing a growing number of dissidents.[105] By late October all the discontented elements made common cause against the government over the strange events known as the *affaire des fiches*.

When General André took over the War Ministry, he found, as was evident enough during Dreyfus Affair, that the officer corps was dominated by conservative, clerical, antirepublican men who frequently won advancement because of their views, just as republicans lost out because of theirs.[106] Determined to right what seemed an obvious injustice, André overhauled the system of promotions, substituting the authority of the War Minister for that of the General Staff. But how could one man, trying to safeguard the Republic from its enemies, ascertain the views of more than twenty thousand officers? Reports by superiors, he knew, were prejudiced. André thus felt that in making promotions he needed help from outside republican sources — deputies, Prefects, the League of the Rights of Man, and especially the Freemasons. Through an intermediary, Anatole France's son-in-law Captain Mollin, the War Office received a steady stream of reports from Masonic head-quarters in the rue Cadet, where M. Vadecard, Secretary General of the Grand Orient, mobilized the lodges of France into a great informa-tion service.

In less than four years, the War Office had received several thousand *fiches* (forms on which reports were made), many containing worthless bits of hearsay, but others revealing the hostility of many officers toward the secular Republic. Though the *fiches* were filed away secretly, word of their existence spread about; and the whole system finally blew up when one Jean Bidegain, assistant to Vadecard at the Grand Orient and a self-confessed anti-Semite, sold a batch of *fiches* for a comforting forty thousand francs to Gabriel Syveton, Secretary of the Ligue de la Patrie française. Syveton shared his harvest with Guyot de Villeneuve, a deputy of the nationalist Right wing, who then used the *fiches* as live ammunition against the ministry in the Chamber debate of October 28.

Selecting the most glaring examples of Masonic interference, Guyot de Villeneuve first read off to a startled House comments about "dirty Jesuits" and then attacked this entire system of espionage. André made matters even worse for himself when he neither denied nor defended the *fiches*, but merely promised an investigation. The Combes ministry would have died that day but for the intervention of Jaurès, who in-sinuated that the reactionaries were concealing their hatred of a reform ministry behind a smokescreen of honor and public morality. "What you can never forgive the Minister of War," he cried out to the Right, "is his willingness to undertake the difficult task of restoring republican-ism in the army."[107] He urged the Left to maintain its *sang-froid* until the affair of the *fiches* had been further investigated and to recall those tragic days when the military chiefs had dishonored the nation. André's actions were part of the struggle, like the Law on Associations and the eventual separation of Church and State, to excise the pernicious influ-ence of clericals and militarists. He urged republicans to weigh the consequences of "ousting a government which has kept peace, in order to turn the country over to the merchants of war and imperialism." Thus, the speech became an apology, politically inspired and uncritical, but it ensured victory for the ministry, though by a scant four votes.

On November 4, the attacks against André were resumed. This time he answered in a prepared speech in which he justified use of the *fiches* in order to safeguard the Republic. "The effect was dismal," Combes later admitted, "a dull and monotonous speech without verve or dignity."[108] Leaders of the Alliance démocratique, dissident Radicals, and Millerand, still a man without a party, all denounced the recourse to espionage. And again Jaurès came forward to defend the ministry.[109]

"The real question is whether we are going to allow reactionaries to reverse the truth by denouncing those very republican officers who have so long been victimized by a system of spying and prejudice." From the Right came indignant cries: "Prove it!" demanded Syveton. "I want the floor," roared Millevoye. Jaurès persisted, citing cases of officers who still forced their subordinates to attend religious services. Pugliesi-Conti broke in with a familiar charge: "Your daughter received her first communion; yet you associate yourself with those who denounce officers' wives for going to Mass." "Of course!" shouted Jaurès in reply. "I see by your 'subtle' interruption how low you can sink." Pugliesi-Conti, almost beside himself, raced into the well of the House screaming inarticulately. Above the din, Jaurès cried: "This isn't the first time I have had to face the howling nationalist pack!" As the noise subsided, he concluded with his central argument—that the officer corps had become top-heavy with aristocrats and that "the duty of the Republic is to eliminate these influences of caste and privilege."

Jaurès' words rallied the socialists and many Radicals to the side of the government. But the lineup against Combes and André was now formidable, and the ministry might well have fallen but for the uncontrolled violence of Syveton. A highly unsavory character, accused at one time of stealing funds from the Ligue de la Patrie française and at another of having sexual relations with his daughter-in-law, Syveton leaped at André and struck the Minister of War hard across the face. The deputies, unwilling to condone such violence, voted, 286 to 276, for the motion of support for the ministry put forth by Jaurès, Berteaux, and Bienvenu-Martin.

His stand on the *affaires des fiches* damaged Jaurès as both socialist and moralist. Like certain other votes in support of the ministry, when the government had used force against the workers or when it allocated funds for the secret police, this defense of espionage lacked essential integrity. By denouncing secrecy and spying when they damaged his friends while defending them against his enemies, Jaurès had fallen to the level of opportunism. In thus protecting the government, he lent credence to the charges of moralists like Péguy that the republican majority was an unholy coalition of ambitious men. Until the separation of Church and State and the reduction in the term of army service became law, Jaurès assumed the responsibility, despite the decision at Amsterdam, of preserving the bloc; and the attacks upon it, he realized, were inspired by the political self-interest of the Right. Yet the *affaire des fiches* should have persuaded him that the Radical ministry had lost its moral credit and that the socialists could win no real victories by covering for political chicanery.

Though the ministry survived on November 4, its days were obviously numbered. On November 15 André resigned, replaced at the Ministry of War by Maurice Berteaux, the stockbroker-Radical. Syveton, meanwhile, who boasted about his attack on André, was scheduled for a trial on assault charges, but on December 8, a day before the proceedings were to begin, he was found asphyxiated in his study. Suicide or murder? Countless theories swirled through press and conversation, but the final truth has always remained obscure. What seemed clear to Jaurès, however, was how conveniently the rot of degeneracy masqueraded as ultrapatriotism. "This great nationalist party, the party of honor and of virtue, incarnated first in Esterhazy, has now taken the shape of Syveton!"[110]

Jaurès was right to worry about the new nationalism, rampaging again after a few years of containment and making its greatest appeal to French youth. In November, young nationalists of the Ligue de la Patrie française ostentatiously demonstrated before the statue of Jeanne d'Arc; *L'Humanité* ridiculed the exhibition in an unsigned article, which ended on a note of sarcasm: "We await the inevitable telegram from M. Déroulède." From his Spanish exile, that veteran chauvinist addressed a bitter message to Jaurès on November 30: "I look upon Jeanne d'Arc as the most sublime heroine of our heroic history. François Coppée and his young demonstrators are far more necessary for the nation than you and your disciples. I consider you, M. Jaurès, to be the most detestable corrupter of the public conscience who has ever played the foreigner's game in France."[111]

For three days his secretary Bilange concealed the wire from Jaurès. When he finally read it, Jaurès reacted in a manner totally out of keeping with his socialist and humanistic principles. He challenged Déroulède to a duel in a message which read in part: "The socialist party, to which I am completely dedicated, condemns, and rightly so, such barbaric methods of settling disputes. My excuse is that I did not provoke this controversy, and I am reacting to a wholly unjustified provocation."[112]

On December 4, Jaurès boarded a train with his seconds, Gérault-

Richard and Deville, and headed for Saint-Sébastien on the banks of the Bidassoa. The duel was unexpectedly delayed when Spanish authorities refused to allow it. Both sides then requested and received permission from the French government for Déroulède to enter France temporarily, and on December 6 the duel was fought at Hendaye. Two shots were exchanged, no hits were scored, and that evening an exhausted Jaurès returned to Paris.

"Let us now have a good loud laugh," chortled *Les Débats*, "and avow that we have never witnessed so fantastic an escapade. M. Jaurès, socialistic, fraternal, portly, racing in hot pursuit of the long, narrow silhouette of M. Déroulède, exiled Boulangist."[113] Even among his friends, however, his behavior must have appeared inexplicable. Socialist honor, after all, was never won on the dueling field. More than any other, this event reveals the momentary confusion and frustration that had overtaken Jaurès. Despite his plea at Amsterdam, the Dreyfusard movement had not really regenerated France; despite its moderate accomplishments, the Left bloc was disintegrating; despite the dictum of the International, the socialist movement was still divided. It was as though the violence of Déroulède was the last straw, more than Jaurès could endure. In a difficult time of transition, when one political phase was closing and the next had not yet begun, he lost his cool reason. But by the turn of the year, he returned to the political lists, prepared to salvage the program of the Left bloc and to fight for the unity of all socialists.

On January 10, 1905, the Right, the Center, and some fifty dissident Radicals joined forces to elect Paul Doumer, rather than Brisson, president of the Chamber for the 1905 session. Doumer had traveled far from his earlier position as a leading advocate of the income tax. Once having accepted Méline's secret offer to go to Indo-China as Governor-General, Doumer was an increasingly "realistic" Radical. When he returned from the Far East in 1901, well accustomed to command, he expected to play a major part in republican politics. But when his old friendship with Combes yielded him little, he became a bitter critic of the ministry. His election made it clear that the government could not long survive.[114]

On January 14, the government faced an angry interpellation on its general policy. Combes was reproached for every sort of disreputable behavior: the collection of the now famous *fiches*, espionage into the private lives of deputies to enforce discipline in the Left bloc, vindictiveness in his anticlericalism. In a lengthy reply Combes equated support of his ministry with the safety and progress of the Republic. But Ribot, keeper of the morals that day, declared that "a nation of honor and dignity" could hardly accept "the Premier's dilatory and deceptive answers." Jaurès was at the rostrum to score the intentions of moderates and conservatives, who were "utterly indifferent to moral issues when they involved Esterhazy and his ilk." Dissecting the coalition against the ministry, he revealed a self-interested union of monarchists and nationalists on one flank, and their erstwhile enemies, "men of finance, speculation, and shady adventures on the other."[115]

The Premier squeaked through with another narrow vote of confidence, 287 to 281, and all the socialists were part of his majority. But the *élan* of the Left bloc was gone. Leaders of the Alliance démocratique and the dissident Radicals were presiding over its death; within his own ministry Delcassé refused even to speak to Combes; and at the Elysée Loubet, harassed by his Catholic wife, openly withheld his sympathy. On January 18, 1905, two years, seven months, and ten days after taking office, Émile Combes resigned and the era of republican defense was over. "The time had come," M. Chastenet has remarked with evident satisfaction, "for a return to realistic politics."[116]

That realism was embodied in the septuagenarian Maurice Rouvier, who formed a government which brought the Progressist Poincaré to the Ministry of Education and the colonialists Étienne and Thomson to the Ministries of the Interior and the Navy respectively; the banker-Premier remained at the Ministry of Finance and the presumably indispensable Delcassé at the Foreign Office. Five second-rank Radicals completed a government which left Jaurès and his friends "greatly disturbed."[117] "M. Ribot has entered; M. Jaurès has departed," *Le Journal des débats* happily reported (January 29, 1905). "All the Progressists have followed their chief into the inner councils; all the socialists have exited with theirs."

In his ministerial declaration Rouvier kept a banker's silence on the issues of income tax and social security. The whole tone of his pronouncement was deflationary and conservative, so much a reflection of his Cabinet's big business connections that Clemenceau quipped: "It's not a ministry; it's a board of directors." In such circumstances, most of the socialists would come to regard the dictum of Amsterdam as their guide to policy. Jaurès realized this, even before Rouvier had completed his ministerial list. For when Briand found him at the offices of *L'Humanité* to report that Rouvier had offered him the Ministry of Education, Jaurès gave his friend this unequivocal answer: "We are about to realize unity; this is no time to jeopardize it with another case of Millerandism. You ought not think of such a move." An embittered Briand submitted but then told his friend Buré: "This evening I obeyed him for the last time."[118] And that was literally true.

Yet, for a few brief months, socialists threw their support behind

Rouvier, who promised to complete two reforms initiated under Combes — separation of Church and State and the two-year military service. By April 21, 1905, the two-year measure passed definitively into law, while the Committee on Separation, carefully guided by its reporter Briand, brought a detailed proposal before the Chamber for debate.

The Church issue, in its final phase, revealed deep divisions in the French spirit. Those who hoped for the extirpation of religion from national life, uncompromising freethinkers like the Blanquist Maurice Allard, thought to expropriate the property of the Church and to strip Catholicism of the material means of its survival. Others, who wanted to eliminate hierarchical authority from religion, like the Radical Brisson, sought to turn separation into a successful Reformation. But opposed to them were more conciliatory leaders, Jaurès and Briand especially, whose dedication to the separation of Church and State was accompanied by solicitude for the nation's religious sensibilities. They hoped to rein in the passions of extreme anticlericals while winning support from reasonable Catholics; if, as they reckoned it, the State could be secularized without destroying either freedom of conscience or the private practice of religion, then the schisms of the First Republic might be avoided. For Jaurès, time, patience, and enlightened education were far more powerful weapons than force.

The mark of harshness or generosity showed up most prominently in the debate over the disposal of Church property. Since separation would cut off State stipends, only its property could enable the Church to survive. The extreme anticlericals wanted to nationalize clerical wealth, imposing a crippling poverty on the Church. "Let the clerical proprietors disappear," cried Pelletan before the Chamber.[119] But Jaurès and Briand, both of whom had gauged the attitude of responsible Catholics, countered with a plan, incorporated into the proposed law as the fourth article, for the creation of congregations called *associations culturelles*; composed mainly of lay Catholics, these congregations would inherit churches, presbyteries, and other property, thus providing both the form and the means of Catholic survival.[120] In the fight for Article Four Jaurès and Briand took their strongest stand against extremists both for and against separation.

Briand bore the main burden of a debate that stretched over three months; but it was Jaurès who gave the liberal proposal its philosophy. To the impatient opponents of Article Four, he expressed his belief that a free Church in a free State would either adapt itself "to the progress of secular thought and scientific criticism" or perish.[121] Already, he pointed out, a vanguard of priests were trying "to reconcile the Gospel and the rights of man, . . . priests democratic at heart and free in spirit." He was thinking mainly of the Abbé Loisy, whose *L'Évangile et l'Église* (1902) and subsequent writings had created a sensation by their rational criticism of biblical miracles. Jaurès welcomed these efforts to eliminate dogma from the spiritual core of religion. They seemed to him a preview of further accommodations to science and democracy, which a separated Church would have to make:

To believe that God is an author who composed or dictated the Bible as Milton composed or dictated *Paradise Lost*, and that each word of the Bible is the direct expression of divine thought as each word of the Aeneid is the direct expression of Vergil's thought is infantile. . . . The human spirit can find God above or beneath all events; but it does not find him at the surface of these events. . . . Eighteen centuries ago, Christianity broke out of the confines of the Hebraic tradition to enter into fruitful contact with the vast Hellenic world. It knew how to adapt and expand without destroying itself. Why can't it renew itself that way today?[122]

The sharpest critics of Article Four came from the Left side of the Chamber, where Allard and Charles Dumont wanted to cut all ties between the "associations culturelles" and the Church of Rome. But in the final showdown vote on April 22, Article Four was adopted, 509 to 44, and an overjoyed Jaurès exclaimed: "The separation has now been made!" His cry was premature, however, and the debate dragged on almost ten weeks longer until finally, on July 3, the Chamber voted, 341 to 233, for the entire proposal. And only when it was ratified in the Senate on December 9 did the separation of Church and State become a legal realty. "Our law is one of liberty and peace," wrote Jaurès, hoping to reach out and assure all believers. Some there would be "who will attack us as sectarians and Jacobins. . . . But here is the answer to them: separation respects all beliefs, does not restrict any church, and guarantees full freedom of conscience."[123]

With the separation of Church and State, another barrier to the democratization of France had been scaled. Thus, when Jaurès looked back upon the two successive ministeries he had supported, he had few regrets. "They were calumniated and attacked, as all governments are which act strongly," he declared in the midst of a criticism of Rouvier's government. "But at least . . . they had a policy and a will; they devoted their efforts to fulfilling their program."[124] For the future, Jaurès thought, socialists would wage ceaseless battle for other reforms, social and economic, and they would welcome help from progressives of the bourgeois camp.[125] Yet neither among socialists nor Radicals were there many who thought, in the summer of 1905, that collaboration could be based on more than a temporary identification of interests. In spirit and in form, the Délégation des gauches had vanished. But in its place the socialists acquired a force of their own, the elusive, long-awaited unified party.

VIII

On the eve of unity, the Parti socialiste français suffered its final case of tremors. The "Pact of Union" laid the foundations for a revolutionary party which should carry a relentless attack against the bourgeoisie; socialist deputies, according to the new discipline, would form a separate group, uncompromised by alliances with middle-class parties.[126] Yet the party was not thereby consigned to a fruitless sectarianism; in spelling out the terms of its program, the Pact of Union combined, as Jaurès did, a revolutionary *ethos* and reformist tactics. Thus, though collectivism was its final goal, the party was to champion those reforms which would prepare the new order; and though collaboration with the bourgeoisie was in principle forbidden, the party might, if the interests of the masses warranted it, lift that ban temporarily.

The National Council of the Parti socialiste français, where the delegates of the federations and a minority of the deputies now formed a Left-wing majority, approved the Pact of Union on January 10. But most of the party deputies, *millerandistes* without Millerand, had little sympathy for the new revolutionary line; on January 30, when the parliamentary group met to set its course of action under the new Rouvier ministry, their simmering resentment abruptly exploded. Jaurès stood loyally behind the Pact of Union, but Briand, who had already tasted parliamentary popularity in the debate on separation, spoke for the opposition. And when he proposed that the party continue, unchanged, its support of the bloc, he carried a majority of the deputies with him. The controversy was then thrown back to the National Council where, on February 7, Jaurès and Pressensé clashed head-on with Briand and Augagneur. Genuinely angered by the eleventh-hour tactics of his erstwhile comrades, Jaurès moved unqualified acceptance of the Pact; put to a vote, his resolution carried easily with a three-to-one majority.

But neither party discipline nor the prospect of unity nor even the sentiment of rank-and-file socialists subdued the fractious deputies. On February 9, they met again and voted, nineteen to four, to uphold the Left bloc. But to break this intraparty deadlock, they proposed that a national congress be summoned. The National Council agreed, and in late March delegates packed off to Rouen for a special congress of the Parti socialiste français.

At Rouen the deputies supported their cause vehemently, even defiantly. Gérault-Richard and Breton predicted the direst consequences if the party withdrew from the bloc: the effort to separate Church and

State might fail; Rouvier might become prisoner of the Progressists. But it was Briand, stung by the imputation that the *élus* had been corrupted by power, who heaped scorn and sarcasm on their critics. Addressing himself to the Left-wingers, he accused them of malice and envy: "He [the *élu*] has the confidence of the masses, and because of that, you treat him like some kind of pariah. You never miss the chance to humble and humiliate him, instead of giving him . . . the confidence and support he needs. . . . You are never so happy as when you can point out that there are deputies in the party who are unworthy of confidence."[127] Alliances and bargains? They were the backbone of politics, and there were none, even among the self-styled revolutionaries, who could escape them. "Why, then, do you condemn us?" demanded Briand. "I for one have had enough of this hypocrisy!"

When Jaurès rose to speak on March 29, the last day of the Congress,[128] he must have felt torn by conflicting emotions. On the one hand, he could scarcely accept at face value the accusations hurled against the party's *élus*. But on the other hand, he placed certain objectives above others, and unity seemed a more important task than a sermon on the subtleties of political action. Thus, the focal point of his speech was a defense, though modulated, of the decision at Amsterdam: "Though it could be foolish and dangerous to restrict the daily actions of the great national socialist parties with abstract and general principles, we would commit the worst of mistakes if we ignored the warnings which international socialism has given us." Gérault-Richard had argued that refusal to vote the budget, as commanded by the Pact of Union, could endanger the life of the Republic. But that action, countered Jaurès, was to be a symbol of protest rather than a threat to a "reformist government or a reform supported by the working class." In urging acceptance of the Pact, Jaurès seemed to soften its tone. If we but unify, he appeared to be saying, the differences we have will melt away.

His oratory and prestige helped the cause of unity. Voting by federations, the Congress unanimously approved the Pact and ordered the deputies to dissociate themselves from the Left bloc at once. The decision upset Briand terribly, and he had only contempt for the role of Jaurès. To his friend, Édouard Julia, he blurted out: "Convince him [Jaurès] of something, of certain tactics, of a certain program. After a thousand discussions and arguments, he shares your opinion. But let someone else come along to say the opposite, and he deserts you."[129]

After Rouen, unity was assured. On the twenty-third day of April, 1905, delegates of the Parti socialiste de France, the Parti socialiste français, and several autonomous federations met together in Paris for the first time in almost six years. They were holding the Unity Congress in the Salle du Globe. The debate over tactics had dragged on for years and the preparations by the Committee of Organizations for months. Suddenly it was all over in three days. With the fatigue that often accompanies final accomplishment, the delegates went through the motions of approving the Pact of Union and pledging their eternal loyalty. By the time night fell on April 25, a new Socialist Party was born, the Parti socialiste, section française de l'internationale ouvrière (S.F.I.O.).

Both in its statement of principles and in its internal organization, the S.F.I.O. reflected, on first glance at least, the predominance of the revolutionaries.[130] The new party seemed destined not only to sever its ties with the Left bloc but even to repudiate the reformist program which socialists had so long supported. For several Ministerial deputies whose ambition and ideology were tightly linked to the bloc, the S.F.I.O. represented a dangerous and unrealistic retreat into political asceticism; Augagneur, Colliard, Deville, Boyer, and Zévaès, all of whom had bitterly opposed the Pact of Union at the Congress of Rouen, refused to join the new party, while Briand, in a strong speech at Saint-Étienne on October 1, virtually read himself out of it.[131]

But Jaurès recognized, far better than those who bolted the party, that the S.F.I.O. would neither abandon its program of reforms nor permanently rule out alliances with the Radicals. Withdrawal from the bloc and renewed emphasis on revolutionary propaganda—these, he felt, were essential, not only to safeguard the integrity of socialism but also, and especially, to ensure its unity. In accepting these conditions, however, and in leading the Parti socialiste français into the S.F.I.O., Jaurès acted on the premises, later validated by history, that unity was the key to strength and that the S.F.I.O. had to call upon essentially revolutionary tactics—great demonstrations, strikes, street rallies, mass petitions—and electoral, parliamentary action to achieve socialism.[132] Thus, when Bourdeau, writing in *Le Journal des débats*, accused the S.F.I.O. of contradiction and confusion, of participating in democratic politics while preaching revolutionary abstention, Jaurès replied, and in so doing, he revealed his understanding of the new party:

On the one hand, Bourdeau explains, socialism . . . roots itself in democratic collaboration and uses it to achieve immediate reforms; on the other hand, by the growth and organization of the proletariat, it must act as a hostile class party. . . . What he sees only as a contradiction is actually the law of every higher organism, which becomes more complex as it develops and perfects itself. . . . So, in the life of the socialist organism, there must be a double movement of concentration and expansion, a rhythm of struggle and *détente*, analogous to the systole and diastole of the heart.[133]

As an uneasy coalition of moderates and revolutionaries, the S.F.I.O. was fully acceptable to neither. Even after the dispirited Independents left, the moderates who remained were more often than not social reformers who had little stomach for the revolutionary rhetoric of the Marxists or the bombastic threats of the syndicalists. As for the revolutionaries, especially the Guesdists among them, they were far from comfortable in a party inundated with moderates. On the one hand, they could scarcely bury overnight their long-cultivated hostility towards Jaurès and his friends; and on the other hand, they were of that breed of militants who thrive more on controversy than on harmony. Thus, Bonnier wrote revealingly to Guesde some months after unification: "Have you noticed that unity always create a kind of stupor? . . . We never have the vigor to win battles except when we're alone—against everyone! From that point of view, the years between 1898 and 1904 were perfect."[134]

"What, then, was this party?" asked a perplexed Daniel Halévy. "I will define it in a word: it was Jaurès. It was his reflection. He created it. He kept it together."[135] A penetrating observation, for in Jaurès alone socialism was both evolutionary and revolutionary, democratic and insurrectionary. He embodied the faith of the reformists, though he warned them against diluting socialism into another brand of Radicalism; he praised both Marxists and syndicalists for their militancy, though he attacked them for their intransigence. Even more than Vaillant, Jaurès belonged to the entire party. "An eclectic of genius," as Trotsky called him, an incomparable orator and a brilliant *philosophe*, he towered above his comrades; and though some were jealous of him or suspicious, he became, without official title or special position, without a political machine to rally the majority behind him, the undisputed leader of the S.F.I.O.

But Halévy added a final word to his observations on the S.F.I.O.: "Then Jaurès died, and the party went to pieces." So long as Jaurès held in balance the aspirations of reformists and revolutionaries, he could cover over the essential contradiction that plagued every socialist party which was unwilling either to organize a revolution or to abandon hope of one. So long as he led the party, he could chart a middle course which none of the factions would consider a betrayal. And it was a remarkable achievement—to make republicans of revolutionaries and insurgents of reformers, to assault the State while working within it, to combine the preachments of Marx and the slogans of '93. But it was a dangerous game. Though Jaurès could keep the party together because he spoke, and with great sincerity, its several languages, the tactical and programmatic divisions remained. When he died, the party would lose his unique talents but not its persistent factionalism.

Once unity had been achieved, Jaurès bent all his efforts toward protecting and preserving it. On the morrow of the Unity Congress and in the months that followed, his words and actions increasingly reflected the spirit of Amsterdam and the Pact of Union. His criticisms of the Radicals became sharper, until he virtually wrote them off as sincere reformers; his overtures to the syndicalists became more frequent, as he urged a fruitful collaboration between the S.F.I.O. and the C.G.T. The year that linked the Moroccan Crisis of 1905 and the Pas-de-Calais strikes of 1906 was a crucial time of transition, when Jaurès sought not only to allay the suspicions of the revolutionaries but also to reorient himself and the parliamentary socialists to the politics of opposition.

IX

On March 31, 1905, Kaiser William II, helmeted, sword hanging from his side, revolver in his belt, marched off his imperial yacht and set foot in Tangier.[136] Within a few hours he was back on his yacht, but the next day a communiqué from the German legation broadcast to the world his words to Sultan Abd-el-Aziz: "I expect that a free Morocco, under the sovereignty of the Sultan, will remain open to the peaceful competition of all nations on a completely equal basis. . . . My visit to Tangier was designed to inform all that I have decided to do everything in my power to safeguard German interests in Morocco." The target of his declaration was France, already far advanced in her plans for creating a Moroccan protectorate. The effect was a considerable threat of war. The events that followed from this *coup de Tanger* propelled Jaurès into the forefront of the campaign against French aims in North Africa.

In pushing their plans to annex Morocco, French expansionists were not without convincing arguments: the contiguity of Algeria and Morocco; the inability of Sultan Abdul Aziz to maintain order in the borderlands between the two countries; the Sultan's increasing indebtedness to a consortium of French bankers. The imperialists were especially helped, however, by the diplomacy of Foreign Minister Delcassé. The Madrid Convention of 1880, signed by the twelve powers carrying on trade in Morocco, had guaranteed both the open door and the most-favored-nation treatment for each signatory. Delcassé thus set about to win separate support from each of the most interested powers for a privileged French position.

By the accord with Italy, he brought one power into line. He looked next to England, whose interest in Morocco had been staked out by a colorful Scottish adventurer, Harry MacLean. Despite numerous points of controversy between Paris and London, both Delcassé and his ambassador to the Court of St. James, Paul Cambon, were persuaded that England, dangerously isolated at the time of the South African War, might be receptive to French diplomatic overtures. By April, 1903, Lord Lansdowne, the British Foreign Secretary, informed Cambon that England was ready for serious discussions.

In Morocco, meanwhile, military action supplemented diplomacy. By September, 1903, Colonel Lyautey, fresh from an apprenticeship with Gallieni in Madagascar, was sent to the Sud-Oranais in Algeria to put down border disturbances. But in his capacious view, he was there to promote the manifest destiny of France.[137] Colonial circles exulted over the drift of events. "The greatness of a country is relative," commented *Le Temps*. "It diminishes if it remains stationary while that of other powers grows. Against the strength of Germany, Russia, England, and the United States, we can hold our own only by expanding into Africa."[138] Eugène Étienne, addressing a banquet of the Union Coloniale in 1903, spoke more bluntly of the benefits of imperialism: "My friends! What a wonderful field for your activity! It is in Morocco that you will find phosphate deposits and iron mines, wheat fields and olive plants! It is there you will find markets for the cotton goods of Rouen and the Vosges! Wool to supply our weavers in Roubaix and Tourcoing! Railroads to build, harbors to develop! . . . And I will tell you a secret. My old friend Delcassé is negotiating right now with England. In exchange for some concessions in Egypt, we will have a free hand from the Moulouya to the ocean, from Tangier to the Sahara!"[139]

The tumult of colonial excitement disturbed Jaurès, though it was not until the fall of 1903 that he spoke out on Morocco. And when he did, he fell into serious inconsistencies. At the center of his analysis he singled out and assailed the "military and colonial party, which dreams of seizing Morocco through armed action."[140] He gave some clues to the identity of these plotters: the big *colons* of Algeria; ambitious officers; profit-seeking capitalists;[141] and conservative politicians hoping to divert the ministry from its work of reform. "Such is the plan of M. Ribot, spokesman for the opposition, and of M. Doumer."[142]

But his opposition was tempered by certain considerations. In the first place, as a moving spirit in the Délégation des gauches, he consistently drew distinctions between "military and colonial coteries" and the Combes ministry. Whatever suspicions he may have harbored of Delcassé were fairly much under cover so long as he supported the government.[143] Furthermore, he accepted as valid both a French interest and a French mission in North Africa. It was important "to police the Sud-Oranais vigorously and vigilantly," and then to carry to Morocco the benefits of Western civilization: "If France doesn't try to annex the country and to develop an exclusive influence there; if she can give just recognition to English and Spanish interests, it will be easy to bring about a lasting accord. . . . The most fanatical Arabs won't reject great public works, the building of railroads, the digging of mines, all of which can modernize Morocco."[144]

Whether penetration could be peaceful, or, even if it could, whether its benefits would be equally shared, were questions Jaurès did not ask. Thus, Camille Sabatier, former Radical deputy from Algeria and an expert on North Africa, labeled this position meaningless. "The Foreign Minister, the colonialists, and M. Jaurès have all sung the praises of 'peaceful penetration.' . . . The trouble is that this phrase owes its success, I fear, only to the diversity of interpretations which the parties have given it, only to the equivocation embedded in the phrase."[145]

Meanwhile, Delcassé's design neared completion, and an Anglo-French *entente* was concluded on April 8, 1904. It was iceberg diplomacy; part of the agreement was in open view, the rest concealed from the public until 1911. By the first article of the public declaration, France agreed to British preponderance in Egypt, while England recognized French interests in Morocco. By Article Two, France pledged to respect the sovereignty of the Sultan, while England recognized the French claim to bring order and reforms to Morocco. But the terms of the secret agreement, contrary to the spirit of the public pronouncement, foresaw the partition of Morocco between France and Spain. The way to the protectorate now seemed open.

Delcassé, however, had more in mind than a North African empire. "The tactics of Delcassé, which I [Combes] approved and encouraged from the start, consisted mainly . . . of encircling Germany."[146] His diplomatic moves were designed to win allies, not only for the conquest of Morocco but mainly for the certain showdown with Berlin. In his Moroccan policy, he seemed to be testing the anti-German strength of his recent agreements. For while laying the groundwork of a French protectorate with Rome, London, and Madrid, the Foreign Minister ignored Berlin, a policy almost certain to create misunderstanding. Though not a power with vital interests there, Germany could properly claim that she was second only to England in the carrying trade to Morocco. And as long as national prestige was at stake, she was sure to inflate the importance of these relations. But Delcassé chose to behave deceptively. Less than three weeks before completing the accord with England, he finally informed Prince Radolin, the German Ambassador to Paris, of the negotiations, but denied that they threatened the status quo in Morocco.

The facts soon contradicted these assurances: the mission of the

Comte de Saint-Aulaire, who arranged, on behalf of the Banque de Paris et des Pays-Bas a loan of sixty-two million francs guaranteed against Moroccan tariffs; the publication of a Franco-Spanish declaration on Morocco; and the military maneuvers of Lyautey, which took French troops well into Eastern Morocco. Colonial and industrial circles in Germany seethed with resentment over this *tunisification* of Morocco without a franc of compensation for Germany.

By the time the Chamber came round to a full-scale debate on the Anglo-French *entente* in November, 1904, Jaurès had intensified his criticism of Moroccan diplomacy. The Congress of Amsterdam had intervened, where the socialists of the world, Jaurès among them, had denounced the perils and burdens of imperialism.[147] Furthermore, by piecing together words, actions, and surmises, the *tarnais* uncovered more of Delcassé's aims than the Foreign Minister explicitly revealed, and his conclusions upset him. Thus, though the debate on the treaty fell during those critical weeks when he was trying to save the Combes ministry, Jaurès led an intensive socialist probe into the meaning of French diplomacy.

He warned against the danger of the Anglo-French *entente* if it should tempt policymakers into a protectorate over Morocco or into a war with Germany. "So it seems absolutely essential for the government to say clearly . . . that the treaty carries within it no hidden seed of hostility towards any nation of the world."[148] As for Morocco, Jaurès attacked military operations beyond the defensive and economic development placed in the hands of greedy private investors. "Once the financiers have become masters of Morocco," he cried, "France will be pushed into a war of occupation." But Delcassé returned to the rostrum to assure the Chamber that French aims were both peaceful and generous. And so satisfactory did his reply seem to the majority that he won a strong vote of confidence, though without the support of the socialists.

Thus armed, Delcassé moved decisively toward the long-anticipated protectorate. In January, 1905, he instructed Saint-René Taillandier, his minister to Tangier, to seek the Sultan's approval for a plan of French control over the defenses and economy of Morrocco. The Taillandier mission with all its overtones of Tunis, triggered off a hostile reaction in Berlin, which finally resulted in the Kaiser's trip to Tangier. By that action the Germans were saying, in effect, that if the French were to alter the status quo, Germany, like Italy, England, and Spain had to be compensated, or at least consulted at an international conference. If not, the alternative might be nothing less than war.

Delcassé nonetheless encouraged Saint-René Taillandier to press on with the French demands. But others, Rouvier included, were not nearly so convinced as the Foreign Minister that Germany was bluffing or that France's allies could protect her through any crisis. In the Chamber Delcassé's refusal to negotiate with Germany roused considerable opposition. On April 19, as the crisis of war mounted, a score of deputies launched an attack. It was Jaurès, no longer influenced by ties either to the ministry or to the Radical bloc, who led the attack for the socialists. For his reticence on matters of foreign policy these five years past he had paid dearly. Not only had he given ammunition to adversaries, like Tardieu of *Le Temps*, who effectively reminded the public that he had led no consistent campaigns against Moroccan diplomacy until the fall of Combes, but he had let valuable time slip by while imperialism was in the making.

Nor had he spoken out publicly against those socialists, the most moderate among the reformists, who openly welcomed colonialism as a source of national prosperity. Like the Fabians in England or Bernstein in Germany, Millerand and his disciples, Joseph Sarraute especially, identified empire and "national interest." They were "social imperialists" for whom colonial markets were a source of prosperity and a rising standard of living at home. Jaurès flatly rejected their position. For him, reformism was a method of achieving socialism, not for adjusting the masses to capitalism. But under the Combes ministry, when his influence depended in part on the support of the *millerandistes*, he did not draw the distinction clearly enough. In 1903, in fact, Lucien Herr had to remind the young Albert Thomas that on colonial and international questions, Jaurès and Millerand were poles apart. Now, however, Jaurès leveled a bitter attack against Delcassé and his diplomacy. In so doing, he clarified his own position and identified the socialist movement with the struggle against imperialism.

"By his trip to Tangier," Jaurès began, "the German emperor has signified that he will accept neither the aims of France's Moroccan policy nor its consequences. He has signified that he did not consider himself bound by the meaning you have chosen to give the Anglo-French accord, an agreement of which he was never officially notified."[149] The failure to consult with Germany, the secrecy and selfishness of French diplomacy, had created the present crisis. The guiding hand behind that dangerous policy was that of Delcassé, whom Jaurès now excoriated: "Step by step, all the alliances and *ententes* which had been created by this country have been compromised, falsified, and misdirected. . . . You expanded the Franco-Russian Alliance; you contracted the accord with England, which could have been the high point of your life, and suddenly, by a fatal miscalculation, . . . you decided to treat Germany as a negligible quantity.

The fate of millions, Jaurès felt, dangled over the abyss of war, and so long as he could speak out he would denounce that high price of imperialism. He pointed in another direction, toward peace with Germany, before the nation's blood was spilled for revenge or a protectorate. "In seeking a settlement, we will neither lessen nor weaken French prestige. Only one thing — to continue blindly along the course you have set — would besmirch our national honor."

Vaillant and Pressensé joined in the socialist attack, and its total effect was greater than usual. For Delcassé was criticized also from the benches of the Center, and even when Premier Rouvier spoke, it was evident that he favored negotiations with Germany. Rouvier, it should be noted, was an internationalist, extensively connected in European financial circles; he mingled with those bankers and industrialists who were already participating in colonial projects with their German counterparts. There was little reason, he felt, to resist an agreement with Germany.

Despite the Chamber session, the Foreign Minister refused to bargain with Berlin, maintaining throughout that German moves were only a bluff. And even if a war were to break out, the Foreign Minister seemed ready to accept the challenge. "I have Europe on my side," he boasted to his friend Maurice Paléologue. "England supports me and will even go to war. . . . I will not open negotiations. My position is excellent."[150] His intractability increased in direct proportion to British commitments. Unwilling to stand by while Germany built up her navy and expanded her markets, London appeared ready to support French resistance to Berlin.[151]

But was Russia, then locked in the jaws of Far Eastern defeat and domestic revolution, prepared to back her ally in a showdown with Germany?[152] The influential Paris dailies tried to minimize Russian defeats. But Jaurès called lie to their apologetics: "The plain truth is that Tsardom and not the Revolution have led Russia to bankruptcy. It is Tsardom, the regime of autocracy, waste, corruption, and stupidity, which has exhausted the resources of a great people, which has unleashed ruinous wars, which has driven the country into debt and the masses into desperate revolution."[153] "Only in the future," he later added, "when Russian democracy has overthrown the Tsar, the Grand Dukes, and the ravenous financiers . . . will both Russia and France be assured of peace, security, and dignity."[154]

Despite Delcassé's dependence upon Russia, Rouvier chose to bypass his Foreign Minister and to negotiate with Berlin. It was already late, the Premier realized; in May, Tattenbach, Berlin's envoy to Fez, persuaded the Sultan to reject the proposals made by Saint-René Taillandier. On June 1, Bülow telegraphed these ominous words to Radolin: "We would have to make the only logical assumptions possible if France, after the Sultan's declaration, irrefutable from the standpoint of international law, were to persist in Delcassé's policy of intimidation."[155] When Rouvier learned from the Italian government that Germany intended to cross the French frontier if France pressed into Morocco, the Premier was prepared, even at the cost of dismissing Delcassé, to come to terms with Berlin.

On June 5 and 6, 1905, history was made at the Elysée. The Cabinet met in a long, stormy session, the prize the head of either Rouvier or Delcassé. The debate centered on the Foreign Minister's determination to conclude a concrete military alliance with England. Retorting that this would lead to a war for which France was unprepared, Rouvier threatened to resign unless Delcassé's policy were reversed. When the entire Council of Ministers lined up with the Premier, the Foreign Minister, checked after almost seven years at the Quai d'Orsay, announced his resignation and left the meeting.

After the fall of Delcassé, events moved swiftly toward a diplomatic resolution of the crisis. Rouvier, now himself at the Foreign Office, yielded to the German demand for an international conference, and by July 8, certain general principles — the independence of Morocco and the internationalization of reforms on the one hand, the recognition of special French interests on the other — were set down as its aims. The first Moroccan crisis thus abated, and the preparations for the Algeciras Conference, which opened on January 6, 1906, were under way.

In the critical weeks of June, it was an impassioned Jaurès who emerged as spokesman for the Socialists. He spared neither fact nor fury in his campaign against "that hallucinated Lilliputian called Delcassé,"[156] and in favor of negotiations. Then, in the months during which the Conference of Algeciras was organized, he lent the same intensity to his appeal for an international agreement to frustrate "the impatient greed of our financiers."[157] And in that tense year from the debarkation at Tangier to the settlement at Algeciras, he hammered out a position on foreign policy, both as to analysis and action, which for a decade guided the Socialist Party and its working-class followers until World War I rendered it void.

What, then, was the underlying cause of crises like the one that broke across Tangier? Jaurès' categorical answer was imperialism: "The economic competition of one nation against another, the lust for gain, the need to open new markets at any price, even that of a shooting war, simply to extricate capitalist production from its own inner disorder, all of that keeps contemporary humanity in a state of permanent war tension."[158] The roots of war were sunk in the present social system.

Nor were capitalists the sole agents of that system, but at their side were certain allies — generals, journalists, politicians — all of them linked by the universal desire for personal gain.

Thus, in the first Moroccan crisis, as in the successive crises that were to follow, Jaurès assigned to each implicated power a share of the responsibility. The guilt of France? "The *colons* of Algeria, generals who wanted to rise further, colonels who wanted to become generals, captains who wanted to become colonels, all of them hoped for a nice little war, an invasion over the frontier, which would lead them right to Fez. . . . And then there was M. Delcassé, who didn't want a military expedition into Morocco by the generals, but who wanted to conquer it all by himself!"[159]

The German responsibility, he felt, was quite evident in the "brutality" of the *coup de Tanger*. But England too bore a heavy share of guilt: "The ones who are most affected by German competition are the shippers, the great maritime capitalists who have been forced to lower the transportation costs of millions of tons of merchandise. . . . Since they have dominated English industry by their outlay of capital, since they control the great London press, they were able to plunge England into the Boer War, and they then hoped to involve England and France in a war against Germany."

Was there, then, no way out of this thick tangle of rivalries? Fatalism rubbed hard against the grain of Jaurès' idealism. "There is no inevitability, no certainty. . . . In this very indecision, human action can accomplish a great deal."[160] Democracy gave men a chance to manifest their will, to cast a beam of public light on the activities of their policy-makers. "Too long has the Minister of Foreign Affairs governed alone," insisted Jaurès.[161] There was a way to peace, and he tried to indicate it: "Between England and Germany war is not ineluctable. In serving as a friendly intermediary between these nations, we would make our diplomacy far-sighted and honorable."[162]

But there could be no peace without the will, and that will, Jaurès felt, had ultimately to form among those who suffered most in war, the laboring masses. Their guide, by default of all other parties, the increasingly chauvinistic Radical group included, had to be the organized working-class movement. Yet Jaurès was not so sanguine as his critics charged about the impulses of men or the influences upon them. If peace was possible, it was also difficult: "Part of the working class is still either indifferent to political action, or insufficiently moved by socialist idealism, or even captive of crude and emotional nationalism. Millions of peasants have not yet extended their vision to the international horizon." But at the end of his thinking, he still had an optimism born of the possible:

"For we know that slowly, even painfully, the influence of an alerted working class is growing."[163]

The immediate goal toward which Jaurès directed his campaign, an international settlement of the Moroccan crisis, was reached, temporarily at least, at Algeciras. During the Conference, Italy and Spain, who were tied to France by secret treaty, England, even though governed now by a Liberal government, and Russia, dependent on French loans to bypass her new Duma — all supported French aims, leaving Germany flanked only by Austria and Morocco. On April 7, 1906, the powers signed the Act of Algeciras, which rested on the two principles of internationalization and special French rights. While the independence of the Sultan was decreed, along with the Open Door in economic relations, France was given a central place in the new Moroccan State Bank, and, especially, in the administration of the country. "It is a reasonable settlement," wrote Jaurès, "which seems not to wound anyone's pride. To reach that decision, did we have to keep the world in suspense and turmoil for almost a year?"

The Conference was far from perfect, as Jaurès well realized. By virtually isolating Germany, it created a German-Austrian intimacy which would have serious consequences in the Balkans. By granting special privileges to France, it fed, despite overtures to internationalism, the French appetite for a protectorate. Jaurès cast an apprehensive glance into the future: "France would be culpable if she were to forget that from now on the Moroccan question is international, regulated internationally."[164] Yet whatever dangers inhered in the Act of Algeciras, and for the next six years he would have dozens of occasions to record them, he could do little else than rejoice that an agreement had been reached and by peaceful means.

In the days of Tangier and the months that followed, nationalism blew hard across France, like a biting wind. Intellectual polemicists — Barrès in *Bastions de l'est* and Maurras in *Kiel et Tanger* — equated patriotism with revenge east of the Rhine. Péguy in his *Notre Patrie* summed up the new current, assigning all the blame for the threat of war to Germany: "Everyone has always known," he wrote, "that the threat of a German invasion is present; indeed it is imminent. . . . It is an inner, collective realization, a deep and sobering knowledge."[165] The struggle for the loyalties of Frenchmen was now a deep one, and Jaurès was assailed by the nationalists as utopian, pro-German, antipatriotic, even traitorous.

To these charges he had persistently replied that peace was the most realistic policy of all; that the realities of German militarism had never escaped him; that his love of country was as deep as his roots in the Midi; that his appeal was to man's reason, not to his blind faith. But his critics attacked him with another weapon when they linked him, as chief among the Socialists, with the currents of unrestrained antipatriotism swirling through the C.G.T. and the Hervéist wing of the S.F.I.O.

The leaders of revolutionary syndicalism, their hostility toward the capitalist State both sincere and boundless, looked upon anti-militarism and antipatriotism as great, thick walls to separate the working class from contamination by that State. Their arguments against the army were effectively simple: it was the fighting arm of the bourgeoisie, the strike field its chief battleground, and the proletariat had no stake in serving it. Thus, the *Manuel du soldat*, first published by the syndicalists in 1902, proposed to working-class conscripts the alternatives of deserting or spreading revolutionary propaganda in the barracks.

But what of *la patrie*? Had the workers no obligation to defend their native land? "The Fatherland of the worker," retorted Griffuelhes, "is his stomach."[166] Such was the attitude of the syndicalists who, at the C.G.T. Congress of Marseilles in 1908, agreed to meet any declaration of war with a revolutionary general strike. And such also was the teaching of Gustave Hervé within the confines of the Socialist Party itself. The nationalists thus charged that French syndicalists and Socialists were preaching an internationalism not matched by the chauvinistic trade unions and Social Democrats of Germany.[167]

Both the Scylla of ultranationalism and the Charybdis of antipatriotism, felt Jaurès, were dangerous. Socialism, in his view, had to hold in balance loyalty to both the nation and to the brotherhood of man. The extremism of Hervé finally impelled him to speak out and to clarify his stand on patriotism. In the midst of the Moroccan crisis the philosopher and the schoolteacher met head on in a public debate at the Elysée-Montmartre, where Jaurès spelled out his views.[168]

The fault of Hervé, he began, was not in his attack on "an idol which is called *la patrie*; for free spirits, and no one is a Socialist who is not a free spirit, there are no idols." But it was his gross misconception of the value and force of the nation-state, from which individual men derived their identity and their special experience. Nor would the triumph of communism alter that truth. "All nations, each endowed with its own individual spirit, language, literature, sense of life, memories, hopes, passions, soul, and genius must comprise the great communist society of the future."

So there was no sense arguing, as Hervé did, that workers would lose nothing if their nation were conquered. Frenchmen feel themselves Frenchmen, cried Jaurès; they would fight to defend their native soil and, if subdued, to liberate it. Nor was it true that under the Republic workers had nothing to defend. Marx and Engels asserted in the *Communist Manifesto* that "the workers have no Fatherland." But their words reflected an age before democracy had endowed men with the instruments of their liberation.

Hervé had charged that the republican State was a weapon of the ruling class, its so-called national purposes in sharp conflict with the brotherhood of workers. Every war, even those passed off as defensive, had to be met with insurrection and military strikes. In reply, Jaurès denied nothing of "the wars of hatred and murder" under capitalism. But neither as Socialist nor as democrat could he view life through the narrow lenses of Hervé, or accept the total isolation of the working class from the cadre of the nation. "The truth is," he concluded, "that the complex relationship between duty to the nation and duty toward internationalism cannot be resolved in advance, either by mechanical slogans or by ready-made formulas."

In the struggle for peace, Jaurès sought to keep his party politically effective, integrated within the nation, skilled in the ways of diplomacy, alerted to the needs of national security. Yet in the same struggle he had recourse to the international appeal, to the brotherhood of workers as a collective force against war. If it were possible to fuse loyalty to the national soil with loyalty to mankind, then Jaurès would do it.

X

Loubet's historic term at the Elysée drew to a close in January, 1906, and on the seventeenth the remnants of the Left bloc held together long enough to defeat the candidacy of Doumer; the majority raised to the Presidency a corpulent, sixty-four-year-old republican from Gascony, Armand Fallières. From that point on, however, the ties between the Socialists and the bourgeois parties, weakened since Amsterdam, broke under the strain of mounting social strife.

In the first week of March Rouvier fell from office, victim of the riots accompanying the inventories of Church property; by the thirteenth a new government was formed by the Radical politician, Ferdinand Sarrien, whose character, quipped Combes, "was to have none at all."[169] To form his ministry, Sarrien called on some of the stalwarts of Radicalism: Bourgeois took over the Quai d'Orsay and Clemenceau, in the first Cabinet post of his already advanced career, the Ministry of the Interior. Drawing even from the fringes of Socialism, Sarrien invited Briand to become Minister of Education. This time, the erstwhile revolutionary would not be denied. He took his offer to Jaurès, who persuaded him to lay it before the National Council of the party. He agreed, but when his proposed action proved unacceptable to the Council, Briand walked out of the Socialist Party and up the ladder to power.[170]

Such appointments gave the Sarrien ministry a leftist hue. But several other ministers coated it with the familiar colors of Progressism. Two staunch Algerian colonialists, Eugène Étienne and Gaston Thomson, occupied respectively the Ministries of War and Navy. But more significantly, those triumvirs of moderate republicanism — Poincaré, Barthou, and Leygues — were back in office, older than in the 1890's and not one whit less conservative. In the wave of bitter strikes that now broke across the industrial front of France, it was almost certain that relations between the Socialists and such a ministry would crumble on the rock of class hostility.

Once again the miners demonstrated the insurgency of the workers, some forty thousand of them striking in the Nord and the Pas-de-Calais by the beginning of April. "The strike has been provoked by the sharp rise in the price of coal," claimed Rouanet, "by the extraordinary prosperity of the mining companies over the last four or five years."[171] But *Le Temps*, speaking in the interest of the companies, located the cause in "the hidden dictatorship of the C.G.T. over the mass of workers."[172]

The government intervened in the labor unrest, but without the *sang-froid* of the Combes ministry. Clemenceau, as Minister of the Interior, increased the number of troops in the strike fields to twenty thousand, one for every two workers. His purpose, he asserted, was not only to prevent disorder but to protect nonstrikers from violence. On April 11, the miners were joined by several thousand postal employees, who went out on strike in Paris; Barthou, the Minister of Public Works, expressing the government's position that public employees could neither organize nor strike, fired them. "M. Barthou . . . has at least proved," applauded *Le Figaro* on April 14, "that the principle of authority has not been entirely abandoned." Then, on April 30, 1906, in a climax to government toughness, Griffuelhes and several other officials of the C.G.T. were arrested on charges of fomenting insurrection against the State.

In this highly charged atmosphere, France prepared for the general elections of 1906, and party lines were now tightly drawn. On the Right, conservatives, nationalists, Catholics — opponents of separation, the income tax, and labor insurgency — formed a common front. On the Extreme Left, the Socialists, following the tactics adopted the previous October at the Party Congress of Chalon-sur-Saône, prepared to run their own candidates on the first ballot, while allowing the Federations to act on the second ballot "in the best interests of the proletariat and the social Republic."[173]

But between these extremes, there was a mass of republican candidates and their supporters, calling themselves Left Republicans, or Radicals, or Radical-Socialists, or (in the manner of Briand and Millerand)

354 | YEARS OF ANGUISH

Independent Socialists. Linked together mainly by their common support of the Law of Separation, they constituted the Left and in a political atmosphere suffused with the spirit of anticlericalism and reformism, they were bound to benefit.

In the second electoral district of Albi, Jaurès again faced the combined power of clericalism and capitalism. The Marquis de Solages, who spent 15,461 francs for this campaign, toured the villages denouncing Socialist desecration of the churches. Jaurès, however, preached his collectivist doctrine and defended the Law of Separation. In Carmaux, on April 7, a surging crowd of four thousand heard him warn the workers that a vote for Solages was a vote against their fellow miners then locked in battle in the Nord and the Pas-de-Calais. In the final stages of the campaign, the Marquis resorted to force. On May 6, which was election day, "a gang of five or six hundred partisans of Solages, the most violent of his followers, including all the officers of his company, gathered in the main squares. . . . Before the polls opened, the Socialist mayor tried to enter the city hall but was surrounded, pushed about, even hit." The Marquis and his men demanded control of the polling places, and "the mayor finally had to telegraph the Prefect for armed force to disperse the crowd surrounding the city hall."[174] But when the votes were counted, Carmaux came through for Jaurès, who defeated the Marquis de Solages on the first ballot, 6427 votes to 6147.

By the time the final election results were in on May 27, it seemed clear that victory belonged to the Left. The coalition of the Right lost almost sixty seats, to emerge with 177. On the extreme Left, the Socialists, gathering almost 900,000 votes, elected fifty-four, an increase of thirteen deputies. But the major victory belonged to the coalition of Left Republicans (90 seats), Radicals (115), Radical-Socialists (132), and Independent Socialists (20), who together controlled a solid majority of almost 360 seats. But in this constellation of the Left were many, especially among those labeled Radicals, who, as Pelletan complained, were opportunists riding to victory on the crest of public sentiment. As for the Left Republicans, they were the most successful of chameleons, old Opportunists, Progressists, members of the Alliance démocratique, whose social sympathies were far more with Ribot than with Pelletan. Was it conceivable, given such a majority, that the Left bloc could be revived? Jaurès laid doubts to rest in mid-June, when he clashed with Clemenceau, kingpin of the ministry, in a brilliant if bitter Chamber debate.

On June 12, 1906, in a moment of social strife, Sarrien read out a ministerial declaration unexceptional in tone, even in its routine promises of reform. Replying for the Socialists in an oration that spanned two sessions, Jaurès countered with the case for collectivism.[175] The real measure of the government, he cried, was to be taken not in its glib professions of good will but in the vigor of its attack on the striking miners. Jaurès' targets were clear — Clemenceau and the Radicals. Memories of Dreyfusard battles fought in common evaporated in the heat of a social struggle that separated the *tarnais* and the Tiger forever.

Arguing that troops were necessary against the violence of the striking workers, Clemenceau had drawn a sharply etched picture of anarchistic, C.G.T.-led strikes. "But if the Minister of the Interior had applied the same selectivity in revealing all the company's injustices from which the miners have suffered for so many generations," replied Jaurès, "he could have produced a totally different picture." The symptoms of the social problem were inequality and its attendant poverty; its source, the regime of private property. "Don't you believe that a society where the mines, factories, and land will be owned by a collectivity of producers, rather than monopolized by a small minority, will be more just and humane?" The transformation he foresaw was not violent but legal. Through laws of expropriation, based on the principle that the public interest was superior to the private, the nation could proceed to collectivism, even while indemnifying the owners. Was this not the method, asked Jaurès, consecrated by the French Revolution itself?

"On his bench," noted *Le Matin* on June 15, "Clemenceau didn't flinch. He didn't look at the orator. Legs crossed, torso thrust back, he stared into space. . . . Jaurès, exhausted, wiped perspiration away with his handkerchief and his hands." As he reached the climax, he threw down the gauntlet to the republican majority: "There are moments in history when men must choose sides. One hundred years ago, when that great Revolution broke out, Mirabeau, Vergniaud, Robespierre, and Condorcet were also uncertain and confused. . . . But finally, they decided; they dared; they knew that the old world was crumbling, and they had to sweep away the debris to launch a new society. . . . We are now at such a moment and you are offering empty phrases, partial solutions, hesitation. You have fallen behind the will of the people." The applause was tumultuous on the Extreme Left where Jaurès was again leader of all the Socialists. But elsewhere the oration met with varying degrees of criticism. It was a useless speech, charged Ranc, offering nothing but pious hopes.[176] Jaurès prefers a collectivist bureaucracy to the "fertile freedom of capitalism," wrote *Le Temps* on June 16. But the main reply came from Clemenceau, rising, after thirteen years' absence, before the very House which had witnessed so many of his triumphs and defeats. His voice was older and weaker than before, but his words no less barbed. On June 18, he spoke for the ministry.[177]

"M. Jaurès orates from great heights, where he creates his magnificent mirage, while I work down on the plain, on the hard earth which yields so little harvest." So began Clemenceau, wrapping up in an image the contrast between the dreamer and the realist. Jaurès has spoken of governmental brutality against the workers, snapped the Tiger, "but at the time of the strikes at Châlons, he uttered not a single word of censure against his friends in the Waldeck-Rousseau ministry whose police shot down the workers."

It was a telling blow. Barrès, who watched it all as a deputy, saw Jaurès "grow pale."[178] Only later did Jaurès reply: "Yes, it is true that we were often given that terrible and tragic alternative of either accepting deplorable acts against the proletariat or conspiring with the reactionaries to overthrow ministers whom they hated. But at least, under those ministers, the working class had a certain freedom of movement."[179]

Clemenceau continued, denying that he had wronged the working class, insisting that his aims were law and order. "I ask you," he cried, addressing himself directly to Jaurès, "if you were the Minister of the Interior—a misfortune that could conceivably occur—would you let strikers pillage and ransack the houses of workers, whose only crime was their refusal to strike? . . . I ask you, if you were in my place, what would you do when one of your Prefects telegraphed you: 'They are pillaging the house of a miner?' Have the courage to answer; say whether or not you would protect the lives of nonstrikers." Jaurès said nothing, and Clemenceau nailed down his victory: "By not answering, you have spoken eloquently!"

Once the debate had ended, Jaurès returned to that point, seeking to expose Clemenceau's solicitude for "yellow unions" and "scabs" as part of his drive against legitimate labor organization. "I have always said that violence might well damage the cause of the proletariat, provoke reaction and panic, and above all, identify Socialism with brutality and barbarism. . . . But having said that, let me add that I am not duped by the hypocrisy of the ruling class. For under the pretext of preventing violence against so-called 'free workers,' they hope to cripple the legitimate action of the proletariat."[180]

Toward the end of his long discourse, Clemenceau turned to the Radical reform program: the eight-hour day, the income tax, the nationalization of natural monopolies. "That is my program," the Tiger growled, "and if you Socialists now claim it, it is because you have expropriated it." "Very well," retorted Jaurès, so often the witness to verbal good intentions, "we will see if you will enact it into law." When Clemenceau moved to his conclusion, he countered collectivism with his oft-repeated philosophy of individualism. "You have invoked the example of the great revolutionaries. You have said to us: 'Do as they did, choose sides!'

I have long since chosen — *against* you and *for* the just and free development of the individual. That is the program I oppose to your collectivism."

But Jaurès was not yet finished; he mounted the tribune for one last word.[181] "Gentlemen, I come before you pricked all over by arrows that only a skilled and still youthful hand could have let fly." Once having paid that tribute to Clemenceau's debating genius, he returned to his case. "A wonderful description by Jaurès of two actions," exclaimed Barrès, "that of the employer and that of the worker forced to resort to violence. Such a speaker! How he releases wellsprings of enthusiasm!"[182] In the final analysis, Jaurès could accept nothing of Clemenceau's basic philosophy: "Your doctrine of absolute individualism is a denial of all the vast movements of progress which have shaped history; it is a denial of the French Revolution itself!"

So the debate ended, impassioned and historic. The great Paris dailies enthroned Clemenceau as victor. "He has exposed the childishness of socialism," asserted *Le Figaro*.[183] But Barrès thought otherwise. "Whatever one thinks of him, Jaurès was the master."[184] On June 21, the ministry won its vote of confidence, but the Socialists were in the opposition. Yet that simple act scarcely sums up the significance of the prolonged debate. For political battle lines were drawn in those June days of 1906 that remained intact until war came to make them obsolete.

When, on July 12, the Court of Cassation finally reversed the verdict of the Rennes court-martial and declared Dreyfus innocent, it symbolized for Jaurès the end of a political era. In Castres, on July 9, Adélaïde Jaurès died in her eighty-fifth year, and that marked the end of a personal era. The Dreyfusard days were over; the warmth of Adélaïde's affection was gone. But the final, impassioned days of Socialist leadership lay ahead. An enormous undertaking it would be — to fling himself against big capital, unfriendly ministries, increasing militarization, and resurgent nationalism. But he had prodigious powers, and it was Trotsky, in a wonderful passage, who best captured them in words:

Beside a Voltaire, a Boileau, an Anatole France in literature, the Girondists, a Viviani, a Deschanel in politics, France has produced a Rabelais, a Balzac, a Zola, a Mirabeau, a Danton, and a Jaurès. It is a race of men potent in their physical and moral muscularity, unequaled in their courage, profound in their passion, powerful in their will. One had only to listen to the ringing voice of Jaurès, to see his enlightened look, his imperious nose, his thick and unyoked neck to say to himself: There is a Man! [185]

PART IV

Years
of Passion
1906-1914

Messieurs, oui, nous avons, nous aussi, le culte du passé. Ce
n'est pas en vain que tous les foyers des générations humaines
ont flambé, ont rayonné; mais, c'est nous, parce que nous
marchons, parce que nous luttons pour un idéal nouveau, c'est
nous qui sommes les vraies héritiers du foyer des aïeux. Nous
en avons pris la flamme, vous n'en avez gardé que la cendre.

1910

Citoyens, si la tempête éclatait, tous, nous socialistes, nous
aurons le souci de nous sauver le plus tôt possible du crime
que les dirigeants auront commis et en attendant, s'il nous reste
quelque chose, s'il nous reste quelques heures, nous
redoublerons d'efforts pour prévenir la catastrophe.

1914

12

The New Insurgency
1906-1911

I

At first glance, there were signs enough in France between 1906 and 1913 to suggest significant economic growth and even prosperity. Industrial production, probably the best mark of a nation's vitality, expanded steadily over those years, fifty-five percent in the metals, twenty-nine percent for all of French manufacturing; in fact, per capita industrial production rose fifty-seven percent in France between 1901 and 1913, a rate higher than for Europe as a whole (thirty-seven percent) and even for Germany. Thus, the national productive wealth, estimated at 274 billion francs in 1906, stood at 302 billions in 1913. In the cities and towns, Frenchmen ate and dressed somewhat better; the per capita consumption of sugar, coffee, wool, and cotton, an important measure of living standards, rose noticeably over the seven prewar years. And in the villages, the rural population, still half the nation, appeared to benefit from tariff protection, improved technology, and rising world prices for farm produce.

Yet these data, especially since they are selective, can be deceptive, and only if their implications are examined more closely can one understand why, in the midst of such seeming prosperity, the working-class move-

361

ment could grow both in numbers and in militancy. For all that France increased her production over these prewar years, she continued to lag considerably behind England and especially Germany as an industrial power. Cast-iron production, to take one example, rose in France from 2,540,000 tons in the 1896–1900 period to 5,207,000 tons in 1913; in Germany, however, production over the same period rose from 7,425,000 tons to 16,764,000 tons. France was stirring economically, but she still had not reached (nor would she ever reach it under the Third Republic) that level of productivity which, when accompanied by just distribution, can produce a sharp rise in the standard of living. In part, her population stagnation was to blame; in part it was the continuing preponderance of her rural population; in part, it was her high proportion of self-employed artisans and shopkeepers (in 1906, wage-earners comprised 58.4% of the industrial working force in France and 81.3% in Germany). For the S.F.I.O. and the C.G.T., both of which aimed for power in a country where the industrial proletariat was a minority and the property-oriented petty bourgeoisie a major force, such economic and social conditions created serious difficulties; but on the other hand, because they forestalled any dramatic improvement of living conditions under capitalism, both the socialist and trade union movements found widespread support for their attacks on the social system.

And especially was this the case since the benefits of an expanding capitalism accrued far less to the urban and rural masses than to the masters of the factories, the mines, and the transportation system. The villages were home not only to the small minority of prosperous proprietors but also, and far more conspicuously, to landless agricultural workers whose depressed wages and long hours created, in the Midi especially, serious social unrest. Urban workers, badly housed, laboring twelve hours a day, deprived of the most basic elements of social security, benefited little from the increasing national productivity.

Beneath the glittering surface of *la belle époque*, as André Siegfried wrote, "one breathed, politically and socially, a new air; from the fall of Delcassé, the climate of the twentieth century was one of war and social struggle."[1] Both the C.G.T. and the Socialist Party, the one through strike action and the other through political propaganda, hammered away at an order which, they charged, was dominated by privileged capitalism. In response to these attacks successive republican governments and their parliamentary majorities, espoused "moderation, order, and patriotism."[2] France was entering the era of Radical leadership and conservative policies.

On October 18, 1906, Sarrien, suffering from a combination of ennui and enteritis, resigned as Premier. With indisputable logic President

Fallières entrusted the formation of a ministry to the strongest man of the Sarrien government, Georges Clemenceau.[3] Now in his sixty-fifth year, Clemenceau showed conspicuous signs of age. "A bowed, stocky figure, bald except for a shocking fringe of white hair, his sharp eyes shrewd and cynical, the Mongolian caste to his dark, high-boned face more marked than ever. A strange-looking old man, always wearing immaculate grey gloves to conceal his chronic skin ailment."[4] But his senses were still acute, and he remained, as he had been for twenty-five years, one of the most mordant debaters in the parliaments of the Third Republic.

Like the advent of Gambetta, the arrival of Clemenceau had been long delayed and much anticipated. And like the Great Ministry of 1881, his three-year reign created little but disillusion on the Left. Both the nature of the man and the temper of the times were the fertile seeds of his failure. No qualities of political greatness were conspicuously lacking to Clemenceau except humanism. Few who achieved high office in these years were so vigorous in action and so incisive in understanding. What was missing, especially in these late years when accumulated experience imprisoned his spirit within walls of cynicism, was a philosophical solvent for his misanthropy. Once the disciple of John Stuart Mill, he had parted company with that most humane of the Utilitarians to join forces with Hobbes and Darwin. "Hunger and physical love," he once remarked, "yield all the actions of man."[5] Clemenceau saw men, pushed by their instincts, roaming a jungle they called society. "Organic phenomena," he wrote, "are inevitably driven by the laws of the universe."[6] No comforting belief in freedom of the will tempered his harsh determinism.

Yet Clemenceau chose not to withdraw from so uncongenial a world. "I can change nothing and neither can you," he wrote to his grandson. "We never ask to come into this world; nonetheless here we are. When one falls into the water, one has to swim, and above all to ignore discouragements."[7] Upon the shoulders of an intelligent élite fell the heavy obligation of leading the rest and of bringing order out of the chaos which threatened. Against the aggressors beyond the Rhine they would organize the strength of France; "ever since Cain and Abel, the lower passions — the common lot of all — have armed brother against brother. When my brother comes to me with blade unsheathed, I intend to protect against the hand of Cain the land where my people have lived and will live after me."[8] And against the fury of the workers they would hurl the weight of the State. "The real France," he cried, "is founded on property, property, property."[9] Certain it was that in a period of international and social tension, Clemenceau would work to safeguard property against the workers, and the army against the antimilitarists.

Ultimately, his efforts shook the party structure of France. The moderates, who had always distrusted him, lent Clemenceau their support; the Radicals, whose symbol he had once been, divided over his leadership; and the Extreme Left offered him consistent opposition. Beneath the flag of the Left, the eternal Center flourished as the republican bloc gave way to the national front.

The government which Clemenceau formed was, on the basis of its personnel, avowedly Leftist. The key positions went to men whose labels read Radical or Radical-Socialist, and, in the cases of Briand and Viviani, socialist. But in a period when Barthou, that outstanding alumnus of Progressism, called himself a Radical, those designations were unclear and almost meaningless. On November 5, 1906, the Premier read a ministerial declaration which emphasized the themes of national defense and social reforms. Appealing thus to both Left and Center, he scored an easy victory, winning his vote of confidence, 376–94. The Socialists abstained, and the next day Jaurès clarified their reasoning: "We wished to signify that we would judge the ministry by its actions, not its pious declarations."[10]

Jaurès and his friends recognized no ally in Clemenceau, and even his early feints in the direction of reform failed to disarm them. The Premier did, for example, create a Ministry of Labor, which he entrusted to the erstwhile socialist, René Viviani. Then on February 7, 1907, over the strenuous protests of the conservative press, his Minister of Finance, Joseph Caillaux, a haughty bourgeois fallen among self-styled Jacobins, introduced the government's income tax proposal. But all this, the Socialists felt, was a ministerial ploy; for when Clemenceau and his colleagues came to grips with the growing labor crisis, their attitude was tough and repressive.

In 1907 France experienced a succession of bitter strikes, which the ministry, acting in the name of order, proceeded to break. In March, when the dockers of Nantes struck, the government sent in troops who fired on the workers and killed at least one. Also in March, when the electricians of Paris walked off their jobs and threw the capital into semi-darkness, Clemenceau forced them back to work with threats of permanent dismissal.[11] But the government faced its most serious labor problem when the schoolteachers organized a union, the Syndicat des instituteurs, and brought to a head the long-standing, never-resolved question of their rights as state employees. Unlike either Waldeck-Rousseau or Combes, Clemenceau announced, unequivocally and at once, his opposition to the organization of civil servants. After submitting to Parliament a measure to prohibit unions among government employees, he sent, on April 6, a strongly worded letter to the Syndicat des instituteurs, criticizing especially their affiliation with the C.G.T. The teachers' union, supported by other groups of organized State employees, responded the very next day with a manifesto, posted on the walls of Paris, which denounced the stand taken by Clemenceau. The government promptly retaliated, dismissing from their jobs not only Marius Nègre, Secretary of the Syndicat des instituteurs, but also several postal workers whose names appeared on the manifesto. The C.G.T. then entered the dispute with public denunciation of "Clemenceau, Briand, and Viviani, who have passed to the other side of the barricade."[12]

The conflict between Clemenceau and the teachers had flared up during the Easter recess of Parliament. When the deputies returned, the ministry was faced with no less than eighteen interpellations, most of them hostile. On May 7, Alexandre Blanc, Socialist deputy from the Vaucluse, launched his party's assault against the Premier and the Minister of Education, Aristide Briand. The workers, Blanc charged, were suffering at the hands of renegades, leaders who had courted them while aspiring to high office but who deserted them when in power. From this angry beginning the debate raged on for several days. Deschanel struck out at pernicious anarchist influences in the labor movement, while Vaillant inveighed against a "government run by police and troops."

But it was Jaurès' speech which carried the debate to its climax. When he rose to speak, he was a man with a mission, the Socialist mission which, despite the pressures and compromises of politics, shaped his life. "Whatever the world thinks," Bishop Berkeley once observed, "he who hath not much meditated upon God, the human mind, and the *summum bonum*, may possibly make a thriving earthworm, but will indubitably make a sorry patriot and a sorry statesman." The "thriving earthworms" were evident enough in French politics, but Jaurès was not among them. "There are times like the present," he averred one day in the Chamber, "that are particularly uncongenial to courage and idealism."[13] But against the tide of cynicism, irrationalism, and self-interest, he swam hard, buoyed up by his trust in reason, his faith in Socialism, his love of humanity. He came now before the Chamber aflame with idealism and indignation, to demand both security and freedom for French teachers.[14]

In his speech of May 10, Jaurès defended the right of teachers to organize unions and even to affiliate with the C.G.T. "Men liberate themselves only by liberating their brothers-in-chains," he had once written.[15] Now he lauded the courage of teachers who, he felt, were also fighting for all other public employees and, in fact, "for workers in general."[16] But what of the government's charges that C.G.T. was a hotbed of anarchists and antipatriots? Was it not illogical, as Clemenceau and Briand claimed, that employees of the State should affiliate with an organization dedicated to the destruction of that very State? Jaurès' reply was perforce a defense of the C.G.T. He did not deny that extremists had infiltrated the labor movement, but he differentiated between the handful of insurrectionary leaders and the mass of rank-and-file members. Anarchists there surely were in the C.G.T., but "they enjoy no such preponderant influence as the government has attributed to them."

As he spoke, the Chamber rumbled with half-audible protests. Clemenceau and Briand exchanged a few words, then laughed. This disturbed Jaurès' train of thought. Wheeling round to the Premier, he concealed none of his anger: "When you were in opposition, you excoriated the great bourgeoisie. But now that you are in office, you prefer to strangle the workers." Jaurès had descended to the plain of political in-fighting where he sought to expose those who had seduced the workers only to deceive them. His attack was centered, however, not on Clemenceau but, in the manner of higher tragedy, on his old brothers-in-arms, Briand and Viviani. On May 11, he carried his case directly against these now-independent socialists.

Nothing could have been harder for Jaurès than to denounce men who had been his close friends. "However serious are the issues which divide men and break their bonds," he confessed, "you cannot wound old comrades without wounding yourself."[17] But he wrenched himself free of all personal qualms to deliver a powerful indictment of the socialist as renegade. Briand, once the persuasive spokesman for the general strike, was obviously vulnerable. "I should like to ask the Minister of Education," cried Jaurès,

what difference there is between the idea of the general strike which he once preached, and the idea of the general strike which now makes the C.G.T. so suspect that it is almost a crime to associate with that organization. . . . Here, in essence, is what M. Briand said to the workers: "Emancipate yourself by legal action. Emancipate yourself by violent action. But there are two kinds of violence, and the romantic kind, the violence on the barricades, is outmoded. . . . I counsel you, as a friend, to follow the most expedient, useful and modern form of revolution, the general strike." . . . And then he said — nor should one forget it at a time when the government is prosecuting men for antimilitarism — he said: "Soldiers will certainly be sent to confront workers, who are their brothers. . . . Should their officers insist on ordering them to fire, their guns will indeed be fired, but not in the direction the authorities expect."

When Jaurès thundered out his conclusion, he severed all lingering ties with Briand and cast him, once and for all, from the ranks of Socialism: "When he assumed office, the Minister of Education declared: 'I have come here with all my ideas intact. I disavow none of them.' Yet it is he who dares to strike us down! I have but one word for the minister: We want no more of your policies! We want no more of you!"

The Socialist attack on the ministry had taken the form of personal recrimination, and two days later, on May 13, Briand replied in kind. A great deal was at stake for Briand: acceptance by the Radicals and the moderates as a trustworthy leader; consolidation of his evolving views on social order; a future of considerable personal influence. In tone and gesture, Briand affected hurt, amazement, innocence; it was the performance of a virtuoso politician. His defense of the general strike, he insisted in defiance of his own words, was not akin to the doctrine preached by leaders of the C.G.T. His speech at the Salle Japy in 1899, which Socialists never tired of quoting, was part of his plan to split Guesdists from Blanquists. "It was to enable you to recruit a majority," Briand asserted, addressing Jaurès; "it was to enable you to build a reformist party."[18]

The time-tested defense for the cornered politician is an angry attack. Briand now turned on Jaurès, accusing him of supporting reformist governments under Waldeck-Rousseau and Combes while assaulting a similar ministry under Clemenceau: "What ingenuity you used during the Waldeck-Rousseau ministry to persuade the working class to collaborate with all republican groups! How deeply you dug to find excuses when circumstances forced the government into obviously antilabor actions. . . . Well, M. Jaurès, I have continued along the way you marked out."

Only as he neared the end of his self-defense did Briand speak of the strong measures he had ordered against the teachers. They were dictated, he insisted, by no antilabor spirit but by a determination to prevent the classrooms of the nation from becoming *foyers* of revolution. What Briand preached was his own version of *raison d'état*, and Barrès, who sat in the Chamber as a deputy, wrote perceptively: "his speech was made before him by Rouher. It even smacks of Bismarck."[19]

The moderate and conservative dailies hailed a new hero in Briand. "He has made the transition from revolutionary nonsense to political truth," declared the monarchist *Gaulois* on May 14. "We would be ungenerous if we did not express our admiration for M. Briand's speech," the conservative *République française* admitted the same day. "He has championed order, discipline, and authority." Authority, in fact, was the key to the new conservatism, authority exercised by men who still protested their allegiance to the Left.

Jaurès returned to the rostrum for a final rebuttal. Briand had won strong support in the Chamber when he asserted that in assuming a governmental role he was merely following a course charted by Jaurès himself. "But M. Briand is mistaken. . . . I have always contended that the Socialist Party cannot stand aside from any valid struggle. . . . But I have said equally that we would never lead the workers into any political alliance which did not serve the final goal of socialism. . . . If I have been guilty, it is for not having spoken out before; it is for contributing to prolong certain illusions about socialist participation in a bourgeois government. But now, gentlemen, all the veils have been torn away."[20]

From the issue of the teachers and their right to organize, the discussion had widened until it revealed, as in the days of Méline, a chasm between the middle-class parties on one side and the Socialists and syndicalists on the other. On May 14 Clemenceau closed the debate with a sharp indictment of the C.G.T. The Premier even asserted that he would have dissolved the C.G.T. except for the illegality of such an action under the association laws of 1884 and 1901. His credentials as a defender of social order were thus good enough to bring him the solid support of the moderates. Despite the defection of twenty Radicals and the opposition of both the Socialists and the Extreme Right, the government won its vote of confidence, 323 to 205.

In the twenty months that followed this debate, Clemenceau and his associates combined wile, threat, and repression to protect the established order. To cope with an incipient rebellion by workers and peasants in the vine country of the Midi, victims in 1907 of a depression in the wine trade, the Premier sent troops by the thousands into the critical area.[21] When, in the spring and summer of 1908, strikes broke out among the construction workers of the Seine-et-Oise, at Draveil-Vigneux and Villeneuve-Saint-Georges, the police charged the strikers, killing two of them on June 1; and on July 30 troops opened fire at a workers' protest rally, wounding fifty and killing four. In self-defense Clemenceau spoke of sabotage, antipatriotism, and the rights of nonstrikers. The fruits of his labor policy, according to Dolléans, were 104 years in prison sentences, 667 wounded workers, twenty dead workers, and 392 dismissals.[22]

Yet the consequences of repression, as history has demonstrated, do not always conform to expectations. Clemenceau may have thought to cripple the C.G.T., but he saw instead the growth of its membership (300,000 in 1906, 400,000 in 1908) and of its extreme militancy. In addition, his government was forced, month after month, strike after strike, to contend with a hostile Socialist deputation. Jaurès, as neither Guesde nor Vaillant would have denied, led the party's campaign. His spirit was never more insurgent, nor his attacks more comprehensive.

When had French socialism known his like? He spoke to the humble poor who, while they drew from him comfort and wisdom, felt close to this man, so simple in his habits. But he spoke equally to writers and savants, whose social conscience he roused and whose admiration he earned. Aesthetes there were, living for art alone or for pure experience, who could easily ignore Jaurès or even scorn him; yet Jules Renard found him "the equal of the greatest," while even Marcel Proust thought him "wonderfully gifted for thought, action, and oratory." [23] As a prose stylist, even though he might be repetitive or too effusive, Jaurès ranked among the masters of the language. Yet the source of his artistry was not so much technical virtuosity; others in the Chamber had that. Rather it was his deep sensitivity, the integrity of his concern, which directed his acts and his words. "Literature," Whitman once remarked (in *Democratic Vistas*), "has never recognized the people and, whatever may be said, does not today. . . . I know of nothing more rare . . . than a reverent appreciation of the People, of their measureless wealth of latent power and capacity, their vast, artistic contrasts of lights and shades." But in Jaurès Whitman would have found that "rare, cosmical, artist-mind, lit with the Infinite," who "alone confronts man's manifold and oceanic qualities."

II

What will the future be like, when the billions now thrown away in war preparations are spent on useful production to increase the well-being of the people, on the construction of healthful and airy houses for workers, on improving the means of transportation, on reclaiming the land through great irrigation and drainage works? The fever of imperialism has become a sickness. It is the affliction of a badly organized society which cannot utilize its energies and productive forces at home. The only way of curing the disease is to create a new and just society.[24]

So Jaurès wrote in the spring of 1907. For the rest of that year and during those that followed, he devoted unflagging attention to what he considered the futility of French expansion and its provocation to war. On the government's policy in Morocco, he wrote and spoke endlessly, and with an understanding of imperialism that deepened with time.

Conflict over Morocco had been only temporarily resolved at Algeciras. Stéphen Pichon, Radical Senator and intimate of Clemenceau, presided at the Quai d'Orsay, but the permanent officials of the Foreign Office, schooled in expansion by Delcassé, dominated its policy.[25] Alongside the diplomats stood the colonialists in and out of Parliament, all of them anxious to establish the French imperium over Morocco by exploiting the ambiguities of the Algeciras settlement. In the mandate to maintain order, which the powers assigned to France, they found a ready-made pretext for expansion. The rule of Sultan Abd-el-Aziz was undeniably inept, and over the unhappy land of Morocco spread a reign of disorder. As the country moved toward the brink of chaos, it was gripped by yet another challenge, the beginnings of native nationalism. In such conditions life grew increasingly insecure for European settlers, enough so at least to justify French occupation.

Early in 1907 began a series of events which served the expansionists well. On March 19, Dr. Mauchamp, chief of the medical dispensary at Marrakech, was assassinated by Arab brigands, and in the already troubled area of eastern Morocco a great fear spread among the French residents. Receiving no promise of satisfactory reparations from the embattled Sultan, the French government ordered a contingent of troops, then stationed around Oran under Lyautey's command, to occupy the Oudjda, the entire eastern district of Morocco. On March 26, Foreign Minister Pichon justified the occupation before the Chamber, explaining, to the satisfaction of the majority, that the government's policy was guided by no other purpose than the maintenance of order in eastern Morocco.

An uneasy Jaurès, however, aired his skepticism in the public press.[26] Despite Pichon's professions of innocence, he saw in unilateral occupation another step toward the ultimate goal of a protectorate. In the Oudjda, he predicted, there would be friction, then clashes, then the occupation of Marrakech, and finally the march on Fez. But the French could never take Morocco without seriously disrupting international relations. If France persisted along her course, the peace of Europe would be squeezed hard in the vise of Franco-German tension.

His warnings were promptly forgotten, but his predictions were almost as quickly confirmed. On the last day of July, 1907, a band of Moslems in Casablanca, affronted by the plan of a French company to run a railroad across the old Arab cemetery of the city, furiously attacked the European workers, leaving four Frenchmen among the eight dead. The native *caid* who ruled the district proceeded at once to the restoration of order, but he was already too late. To the Comte de Saint-Aulaire, chargé d'affaires in Morocco, the Casablanca incident was a perfect pretext for further occupation. Without clearance from Paris, he called the French cruiser *Galilée*, then anchored at Tangier, to the port of Casablanca. On August 1, the *Galilée* arrived, touching off Moslem riots against Jews and Europeans. Within a week other cruisers arrived and a force of 4500 landed, under the command of General Drude. Not a single echo of Clemenceau's former anticolonialism was heard above the gunfire. General Drude's troops, carrying their campaign far beyond the limits of Casablanca, scored a complete success. And a cheap one, for the entire cost of the expedition was charged up to an already tottering Sultanate.

Again it was Jaurès who punctuated the air with protest.[27] Nothing was so important, he felt, as a strong rein on the government, but the Parliament was now in recess. Speaking for his party, he demanded that Fallières convoke an extraordinary session at once, lest decisions of grave consequences be made without full debate. Again it was a Franco-German rupture that haunted him. Chancellor Bülow, to be sure, had informed the French Ambassador that France was within her rights in restoring order at Casablanca, but he might very well balk at an intervention that carried beyond that city. Despite that danger, the deputies were not called back from their holidays, and the French expansionists continued to fish in troubled Moroccan waters.

By August a fratricidal civil war broke across Morocco when Moulay Hafid, brother of Abd-el-Aziz, raised the standard of revolt against the ineptitude of the Sultan and the imperialism of the French. In the months that followed, the country sank to the nadir of disorder. Moulay Hafid, established as Sultan in Marrakech, won support from Berlin and, if rumor is to be believed, funds from the German metallurgical firm of Mannesmann. Abd-el-Aziz, whose weakness endeared him to French colonialists, had the backing of Paris. On December 28, at the behest of the colonialists, the slow-moving General Drude was withdrawn from his command in the Chaouya, the hinterland of Casablanca, and replaced by the more daring General D'Amade. "Quite obviously," wrote a sarcastic Jaurès, "we must offer the command to a general who acts with speed and muscle."[28] Thus, by the year's end, France had the pretext, the troops, and the commander the imperialists wanted. But on January 24, 1908, Jaurès interpellated the government on its Moroccan policy, and denounced it before all of France.[29]

The worst that can be said of a nation's foreign policy — and it was his essential accusation against the French line in Morocco — is that it is futile on the one hand and immoral on the other. To support Abd-el-Aziz, Jaurès asserted, was to back the wrong horse. What greater imbecility could the Foreign Office commit than to pour out aid to a certain loser? But worse than that, the unilateral operations of France in Morocco, on such a scale as to destroy the Act of Algeciras, could only lead to crisis in Europe and Moslem xenophobia in Morocco. Long before the restiveness of native peoples came to disturb the complacency of French parliaments, Jaurès understood the inevitability of the colonial revolution. Such prescience came naturally to one who believed that all men shared the ideals of justice and freedom. What he urged upon his colleagues was recognition of Moroccan nationalism before the most fanatical among the Moslems converted it into something bitter and anti-Western. "In the Arab lands, the protest movement is divided into two separate tendencies. There are the fanatics, who would use fire and steel to sever every last contact with European and Christian civilization, and there are the modernists . . . who realize that the Arab world can never be developed unless it commits itself to freedom, brotherhood and peace." French policy, charged Jaurès, was strengthening the hand of the fanatics while undermining the position of the enlightened nationalists. Before the European opportunity vanished, before all hope of permanent friendship with the Arabs evaporated, France had to end her interference in the civil war and abandon her dreams of conquest.

The aging Ribot followed Jaurès to the rostrum to urge "prudence but never withdrawal."[30] His confused formulation revealed some disturbed second thoughts about imperialism among the conservatives. But Delcassé, returning to the forum for the first time since his resignation as Foreign Minister, evinced no such doubt. For him, French policy in Morocco had been, from the very start, unassailably correct, and only a sudden failure of nerve had led the Rouvier ministry to accept the Algeciras Conference. In interpreting the Act of Algeciras, he assured his colleagues that the present position of France — her occupation of eastern Morocco and the district around Casablanca — was completely legitimate. In the course of the debate, however, which continued through January 28, the majority displayed a marked hesitancy, not about the wisdom of occupying Morocco, but about taking sides in the civil war. Before that mood the government yielded, so that when it won a vote of confidence, it was on its clearly stated promise to base all future actions in North Africa on the terms formulated at Algeciras. But to Jaurès and his friends who voted against the ministry, Pichon's assurances were empty so long as French troops remained in Morocco, poised for action.

Their suspicions were amply confirmed by French moves, which were neither neutral nor cautious. While the Bank of France extended a loan to the discredited Abd-el-Aziz, French troops under General D'Amade brought the entire Chaouya under their control. A tireless Jaurès, between anger and fear, balked at every new move.[31] The colonialist press showered its abuse upon him, accusing him of "mistakes, exaggerations, and absurd interpretations."[32] Long since toughened against such attacks, Jaurès continued to inveigh against a policy which he termed "reckless and barbaric."[33] To the effectiveness of his campaign André Tardieu, the proexpansionist foreign policy expert of Le Temps, paid high tribute when he wrote that the ministry had moved cautiously in Morocco because it feared "Jaurès and the Socialist opposition."[34] But whether they could do more than delay the inevitable was dubious.

As the civil war progressed, the position of Abd-el-Aziz deteriorated. By September, 1908, Moulay Hafid was the undisputed Sultan of Morocco, but though France had no alternative except to recognize the new ruler, she threatened to undermine his power by demanding extensive reparations for the Casablanca incident. Calculated to weaken Moulay Hafid, the French demand, like the extensive occupation of Moroccan territory, conformed to the spirit of the secret treaties rather than of the Act of Algeciras. It was part of a policy which, pursued further, would certainly create tension between France and Germany.[35]

On January 18, 1909, when Parliament had reconvened, Jaurès questioned the government on its intention in North Africa. The point of departure in his speech of January 18 was an unpublished report, drawn up by General Lyautey, which presumably charted the final occupation of Morocco. Jaurès demanded that the government publish the document, and then either repudiate or support it. From that beginning, he went on to develop those themes which were already the familiar materials of his campaign against imperialism. With hard fact and logic, he denounced the occupation of Moroccan territory as a violation of international agreements; and with his abundant optimism, he foresaw, if France should withdraw militarily, an efflorescence of friendship with the Arabs on the one hand and the Germans on the other.

When Pichon replied, he made hardly a single concession to the Socialists. While France might withdraw from Casablanca when practicable, he declared, she would never court disorder on the Algerian frontier by abandoning eastern Morocco. In fact, by his vagueness about French aims and by his refusal to publish the Lyautey report, Pichon implied aims considerably larger than border defense. Yet he spoke in rather measured words, realizing no doubt that there were even non-Socialists among the deputies, who, as Jaurès noted, "are uneasy about the extent of our actions in Morocco."[36] By his soft-toned generalities the Foreign Minister survived quite easily, winning a vote of confidence for the government's policy, 380 to 98. Jaurès was no doubt discouraged by the government's lack of candor, and deeply suspicious of its plans, but he still counted on public opinion as though it were a great force for peace, to restrain the expansionists: "Europe would be wrong to expect the worst. . . . The ministry will ultimately be restrained by the popular sentiment for peace."[37]

Through a dramatic turn of events in February, 1909, the effervescence of the colonialists was, in fact, temporarily flattened, but not so much by the weight of public opinion as by the influence of certain policy-makers who felt that an agreement with Berlin over Morocco was possible. The Clemenceau line on Germany was inflexible, based as it was on the conviction that a Franco-German war was virtually inevitable. The ruling German groups, according to the view of the Premier and his supporters, were Junkers and militarists who craved land and glory more than commercial advantages and who were prepared to do battle for them. Others in the government, Joseph Caillaux especially, viewed Germany as a nation dominated by great capitalists whose major concern was an outlet for their goods and capital. To an adept in international finance like Caillaux, the relief of Franco-German tension hinged on a reasonable division of colonial spoils.

Under pressure from this group and from French financial circles, the government undertook secret negotiations with Germany late in 1908. Accepting as their assumptions French political preponderance and a Franco-German economic partnership, Paris and Berlin concluded an agreement early in 1909.[38] By this agreement France promised to share the wealth of Morocco with German capitalists, while Germany recognized the "special political influence of France in maintaining order and internal peace." In the moderate and conservative French dailies, the agreement was strongly (and understandably) applauded. As the colonial interests viewed it, the accord removed the last barrier to a protectorate. And this for the not-too-exorbitant price of forming Franco-German economic consortia.

For very different reasons and with strong reservations, Jaurès also welcomed the agreement. The prospect of powerful capitalistic combinations, controlling the wealth of Morocco and exploiting its people, was certainly an ugly one. "German and French capitalists," he wrote "have formed a trust to dominate the country. Krupp and Schneider "have buried the hatchet. . . . These two packs of wolves, only yesterday gnashing their teeth at one another, want to celebrate their new friendship by lunging wildly at Morocco."[39] Yet Jaurès' overriding consideration was peace. Whether it was possible that collaboration among profit-seeking firms would result in anything but renewed friction; whether it was at all logical that French political ambition would stop short of a protectorate; whether it was conceivable that capitalist ventures would conform to the socialist image of a civilizing mission — these were questions which he either avoided or answered weakly. For the moment, he could only celebrate the *modus vivendi* between France and Germany; and however fragile the goods, he gladly bought them.

As Jaurès viewed them, these were times of great urgency. A ministry grown indifferent to human needs, a parliamentary majority devoid of ideals — of what follies were they not capable? They played fast and loose with the rights of workers; they toyed with the freedom of the Moroccan masses; and like the other governments of Europe, they gambled frivolously with peace among peoples. Jaurès had fought for the rights of the workers and campaigned relentlessly against colonialism, but in neither case with much success. On the issue of peace, however, if socialism were to have a future, he could neither compromise nor fail.

III

Once the door was pushed open, the home of the great Jaurès stood revealed in all of its essential mediocrity. The vestibule was devoid of charm. A small metal umbrella stand, a few racks where Jaurès hung his hat and his overcoat (its sleeves so badly rumpled, its pockets hopelessly bulging), and his wife left her coat. In the dining room you saw a large mantlepiece decorated with flowers displayed under glass covers. . . . There were also family portraits in faded, plush frames: Mlle Jaurès in the long dress of her first Communion smiled up at the angels. . . . On the other side of the Louis-Philippe clock, Jaurès' little son, decked out in a sailor suit, smiled like a happy child. Yet it was common in those days to read in the newspapers that Jaurès lived in luxury and opulence, that his heavy peasant's boots trampled across rugs as thick as grass.

To reach his study, you had to go to a sort of attic. I climbed the staircase, startled by the poorness, the drabness, and, one must admit, the ugliness of the surroundings. The place smelled of old papers and mice. The wall itself had to serve as a bannister. His door was the color of burned chestnut. I knocked lightly, and Jaurès' strong, gentle voice bade me enter. . . . His desk was a sort of large board on two trestles. His books lined the shelves along the walls, but many more had fallen to the floor. And as they lay spread around, an intellectual spiderweb was spun, Renan's spirit tied to that of Anatole France, Tertullian's pious, morbid philosophy to Spinoza's full-bodied pantheism.[40]

Such were some first impressions of the Jaurès household on Blanche Vogt, a young woman who served as an editorial assistant at *La Revue de l'enseignement primaire et primaire supérieure*. From 1906 on, Jaurès regularly contributed the first-page article to that bimonthly review for schoolteachers. Pushed and pulled by so many obligations, he occasionally forgot to post his article, and it was then that Mme Vogt came personally to collect it. Her description of Jaurès' ordinary surroundings reveals the essential drabness, the essential propriety of the ménage.

The same Blanche Vogt has supplied two stories which illustrate further how strongly conventional, like those of a bourgeois professor, were the personal habits of Jaurès. Accompanying her to the streetcar one day, Jaurès discovered that he had absentmindedly forgotten his money. When she offered to share her change with him, he refused and with no little embarrassment. Rather than borrow money from a woman, improper by bourgeois standards, he explained his predicament to the ticket-taker, who laughingly let him through.

On another occasion, Jaurès revealed his belief in sexual propriety, even to the point of counseling emotional repression. A strong bond of love had bound one of his socialist collaborators, unhappily married but the father of three children, and a responsive, devoted young woman. The affair infuriated the wounded wife, who one night broke up a public meeting where her husband was the chief speaker by denouncing his infidelity before five hundred startled listeners. Hearing of the public scandal, Jaurès was greatly upset. Not only did he resist any infidelity in his own married life, but he worried lest the party be tainted through the unconventional behavior of its leaders. He arranged a meeting, in the garden of the Musée de Cluny, with the sweetheart in the case. Though gentle in his tone, he urged her to break off the affair in words which she later reported to her good friend Mme. Vogt. "In the lives of individuals as of nations," Jaurès told the girl, "there is a time of judgment when we must pay for our weaknesses, when we are punished for our immoralities. . . . For good reason, the leaders of the party must avoid either scandal or calumny. You must wait. In two or three years, you will know your emotions better." When she protested that such a sacrifice would be unbearable, he replied with revealing spontaneity: "You have no real rights! Girls who are minors don't know how to decide for themselves!" Again she protested, this time about the power of love. Rejecting her romantic definition, he told her that "love is home, children, an escape after days full of public strife."[41]

The stories reveal a Jaurès conventional in private life, opposed to personal license. Quite obviously, his attitudes reflected the endowment of his family background and the conviction of so many leaders in the Second International that bohemianism was nothing but aimless and antisocial individualism. But to understand this personal conformism better one would do well to consider it in relation to the demands of public service. In a pregnant passage, Luther once implied the need for personal repression in those who would devote themselves to thought and action: "The carnal man, though he may work well, has no taste for it, always having the contrary desire." In Jaurès carnality was tightly confined. His relations with Louise lacked the passion which, for example, united Marcel Sembat and his wife, the artist Georgette Agritte.[42] Not for an instant would Jaurès have denied Louise his affection or burdened her with his infidelity; in matters of the household he was dutiful. But by economizing on his emotions at home, he could expend them elsewhere — on his Socialist idealism, the artistry of his politics, his love of humanity. One biographer of Nehru has written that "the masses acted on him like a tonic, that while he poured into them his energy and mental ferment, they gave him in return renewed strength and sustenance, sinew, fiber, and muscle."[43] It is the Antaean tradition, the way of those who pour great reserves of energy into their public purposes, to emerge resuscitated from this fusion with their source.

In his fugitive hours at home, Jaurès read widely and with rare concentration; he wrote about the problems of the day and the wider ones of history. But especially was he absorbed, in the years after 1905, with the biggest questions, those of war and of peace. For in the five years that separated the ministries of Clemenceau and Caillaux, the danger of a European conflict grew constantly greater.

Particularly in the Balkans, where Russia and Austria-Hungary matched aggressive ambitions, international tensions mounted. A palace revolution in Serbia in 1903 had launched the pro-Russian Karageorgevitch dynasty and its dream of a united South Slav kingdom. In Vienna that prospect seemed dismal at best; for it promised not only to upset the stability of the Dual Monarchy, whose inhabitants included a considerable Slav minority, but also to forge an instrument of Russian domination over the Balkans. Austria thus turned her attention to the fate of Bosnia and Herzegovina, those South Slav provinces adjacent to Serbia, which, though nominally part of the Turkish Empire, had been virtual protectorates of Austria since 1878. As Serbia eyed the provinces hungrily, certain leaders in Vienna proposed to thwart Belgrade's ambitions by converting the Dual Monarchy into a Triple Monarchy, including a third Slav State alongside Austria and Hungary. The plan, which had the solid backing of Archduke Francis Ferdinand, the heir to a throne still held by the doddering Francis Joseph, laid the basis for the aggressive diplomacy of the wily Count Aehrenthal, since 1906 Vienna's Foreign Minister.

Threatened equally by Serbian ambitions and Young Turk nationalism, Austria decided upon the definitive annexation of Bosnia and Herzegovina, but Aehrenthal realized that he would have first to deal with Russia. Thus, at the chateau of Buchlau in beautiful Moravia, he engaged the Russian Foreign Minister Isvolsky in fateful conversations on September 15, 1908. While assuring Isvolsky verbally that Austria would not oppose the opening of the Straits to Russian warships, Aehrenthal tricked him into support for Vienna's annexation of the two Slavic provinces. After that, Austria moved with dispatch, and on October 6, 1908, Bosnia and Herzegovina were annexed. But when Russia sought support for her control of the Straits, she succeeded neither in Vienna nor in any other European capital. Thus, in the current of 1909, Austria was triumphant, Russia frustrated, and Serbia embittered. The Balkan pot was almost at the boil.

Was it then too late? Could the forces of war be bridled in such a

Europe? In a hundred forms, these questions haunted Jaurès, and as crisis bred crisis, his optimism was strained to its limits. What visions must not have crossed his mind, of flesh torn and blood spilt, all in the name of French revenge, or British naval supremacy, or Russia's drive to the Straits! Of the decision-makers in France, he and his party harbored few illusions. They saw in the highest echelons men who, they felt, were either bent on war or resigned to it: steel manufacturers who acted through the powerful Comité des forges; chauvinists who followed the Action française;[44] Russian bondholders who feared for their investments; the Clemenceau ministry, which was destroying Radicalism with its conservatism and chauvinism.

Yet his radical Enlightenment faith sustained Jaurès. The instruments of peaceful negotiation were always at hand; if, in the States of Europe, the influence of the masses were organized for peace, if that influence were then turned upon the governments, the chances of war would be sharply reduced. Their tasks, as Jaurès and his friends saw them, were commitment and coördination — to commit the French working-class movement to effective tactics for peace and to coördinate that strategy with the collective efforts of the Second International.

In November, 1906, Jaurès traveled south from Paris to Limoges, where the S.F.I.O. was to hold its third annual congress. For more than a year, as the first Moroccan crisis had unfolded, France had rumbled with threats of war and counterthreats of antipatriotism. While Delcassé pushed France close to the abyss, the most vociferous syndicalists renounced, in the name of the workers, all loyalty to the nation.[45] Thus, as they gathered at Limoges, the Socialists undertook not only to map their strategy against war but also to define the terms of their patriotism.

This congress, like those that would follow, amply demonstrated that if the Socialist Party was now unified, it was not without sharply conflicting factions. On questions of war and patriotism the eclectic realism of Jaurès clashed with the heroics of Hervé and the dogmatics of Guesde. Hervé opened the debate with a speech which carried antipatriotism to its most uncompromising limits: "For the poor, nations are not loving mothers; they are harsh stepmothers. . . . Our nation can only be our class."[46] Exhorting the Socialists to oppose every war, whether offensive or defensive, he presented a resolution, in the name of the Federation of the Yonne, which proposed, in the event of conflict, a revolutionary military strike against the whole social system. Guesde sniffed and thought he smelled anarchists. Hervé and his friends were preaching futile and romantic insurrection, rasped the Marxist sexagenarian. There was no short-cut to revolution; only at the moment of ripeness, when the contradictions of capitalism were in full play, would the system collapse.

Guesde inveighed equally against what he considered the futility of special tactics against war and imperialism. These evils, he insisted in his version of Marxism, inhered in the present social system, and only the advent of Socialism would finally extirpate them. In line with this thinking, he presented a resolution for the Federation of the Nord, which subordinated the specific struggle against war to the larger effort against capitalism itself.

Guesde's orthodoxy was nothing new to Jaurès; for years he had considered it a caricature of a genuinely profound Marxism. He realized, furthermore, that he could cope with it within the party. But Hervé's thrust was something else again. By espousing an irrational, uncompromising antipatriotism, the bespectacled schoolteacher had become not only a hero to a small group of party insurgents, but also a useful ally of certain intellectuals, most of them linked to the S.F.I.O., who were seeking to overhaul both the theory and practice of socialism. They clustered around a throne occupied by the bearded Norman patriarch, Georges Sorel;[47] in their critique of Marxism they cited Pareto, Croce, and Bergson; and they found in Lagardelle's *Mouvement socialiste* their chief literary outlet. They had no formal ties with Hervé, nor did they consider him a profound or serious thinker. But in his denunciation of parliamentary politics and in the very violence of his antipatriotism, he advertised in the Socialist forum some of the ideas which they were elaborating in their theoretical writings.

They were self-conscious intellectuals who denounced intellectualism; self-styled syndicalists who led no strikes;[48] extreme antimilitarists who glorified the purity of violence. It was the "disappearance in bourgeois society of all grandeur and idealism"[49] which drove them into an endless quest for the sources of renewed social energy. They did not find them in politics, where compromise and collaboration were the norms, but in revolutionary syndicalism which, through the myth of the general strike, roused the workers to heroic action. Their doctrine was a meeting ground for Proudhon and Nietzsche; it was the working class as the hero of society.[50]

When Jaurès rose to address the delegates at Limoges, he felt acutely the responsibility of guiding the party safely beyond the ultrafatalism of Guesde and the ultraromanticism of Hervé, while at the same time enlisting them, the most revolutionary Socialists, in the party's campaign against war. At his side in this effort, his comrade, mentor, and rock of support, was Vaillant, whose roots in both Blanquism and Marxism enabled him, better than anyone else, to win over the disciples of both Guesde and Hervé. It was Vaillant, in fact, who presented the resolution for the Federation of the Seine, which both he and Jaurès supported.

That motion, while it affirmed that the proletariat would defend the nation from unprovoked attacks, committed the Socialist Party to "parliamentary action, public agitation, popular protest meetings, even the general strike and insurrection" in order to prevent wars of aggression.

So often had Jaurès reviewed the issues of the debate — the stake of the workers in the nation, the qualitative difference between wars of defense and offense, the need for both political pressure and strike action on behalf of peace — that he now offered little that was new. His eloquence, however, and his sense of urgency were undiminished. "We can't just sit and wait for a catastrophe," he cried impatiently. "We can't just say: all will be well as soon as we have five million socialist voters. . . . What if the storm threatens before that? Should we make no effort to prevent it?" In the final analysis, it was the "reformist-idealist" Jaurès, advocating every kind of socialist action, who was more the revolutionary than Guesde, the keeper of the law, or Hervé, the doctrinaire of the strike.

Though accusing both Guesdists and Hervéists of distorted vision, Jaurès had no intention of consigning them to the dustbin of history. He strove rather for a convergence of viewpoints which, while throwing brighter light on the causes and prevention of war, would satisfy its variety of revolutionaries. The resolution of the Federation of the Seine, which combined the Marxist analysis of war and the syndicalist tactics of the general strike into a single eclectic formula, thus won Jaurès' support. And when the Congress finally voted on the competing motions, the majority followed his lead. The resolutions of the Yonne and the Nord garnered only thirty-one and ninety-eight votes respectively, while the motion of the Seine carried the day with 153.

The action of the Socialists at Limoges did not settle once and for all the question of their tactics against war. Less than a year later, in August, 1907, the S.F.I.O. convened at Nancy where the issues of patriotism and internationalism, war and peace, again dominated the debates. Once more, as the Socialists tried to set their thoughts in order before the forthcoming Congress of the Second International, the challenge of Hervé, the acrid criticism of Guesde, the persuasive replies of Vaillant and Jaurès rang through their meeting hall. The arguments, grown wearisome through repetition, were the same, and so were the results. At Nancy, as at Limoges, the majority supported the resolution which had originated with the Federation of the Seine.[51]

In taking these steps against war, the Socialists felt they were manifesting both courage and will. "The greatness of socialism," Vaillant had once written, "must lie in its ability to act on its premises. . . . In our struggle against war, we must not hesitate; we must, from now on, commit ourselves to a program."[52] Yet the program was full of ambiguities which not even the expository skill of Jaurès could talk away. Could the Socialists distinguish, as the majority claimed and Hervé denied between offensive and defensive wars? Suppose, for example, that Germany, desperate for markets to support a burgeoning industrialism, attacked France in her colonies. Were Socialists then to take up arms in the name of national defense? Or again, could public protests, or parliamentary efforts, or even the general strike forestall wars which Socialists believed to be inherent in capitalism? And if so, was it enough merely to list tactics without charting a detailed course of action? Critics, armed with the facts of later history, have been harsh on the prewar Socialists, accusing them of confusion in thought and failure in nerve. Yet seen from the perspective of those years their resolve was powerful enough to encourage the pacifists and to disturb their opponents.

It was Jaurès who came to symbolize the Socialist resolve for peace. From one end of France to the other, he traveled, a propagandist for peace, a patriot, an internationalist, a voice of conscience. To some, whether sincere nationalists or untamed chauvinists, he seemed dangerous, even treasonable.[53] For that reputation, carved out of a thousand bitter editorials, he would pay dearly one day. But nothing slowed him down, not danger, not exhaustion:

Toulouse, Lille, Montpellier, Roanne, Montluçon, Dijon, Nimes, Bordeaux, Guise, Reims, Roubaix, Avignon, Marseille, Carmaux, Toulon, Lyon — at every railroad station in France, it seemed, Jaurès descended from a train at one time or another, suitcase in hand, the great salesman of peace. In the smallest villages of France, in the greatest capitals of Europe, he came to symbolize Socialism, and in these years especially, its struggle against war. . . . He loved the popular masses who overflowed the provincial amphitheatres, their intense silence broken only by their heavy, emotional breathing.[54]

Just two days after the Congress of Nancy, Jaurès traveled to Stuttgart for the seventh meeting of the Second International and the first since the historic gathering at Amsterdam. For the tarnais it was a thrilling first visit to Würtemberg, the home of so much of the German civilization he admired. "More than any of the rest of us," Vandervelde later recalled, "he was overjoyed at traveling through a part of Germany whose thinkers had been so great an influence on him. One evening as we were returning to Stuttgart, we passed through Tübingen. The night was black as pitch, and a thunderstorm broke over the streets." But Jaurès left his party and, with a kind of reverence, wandered around the university, where young intellectuals had once cheered the French Revolution.[55]

At Stuttgart on August 16 hundreds of Socialist delegates from over a score of countries gathered in a flower-bedecked hall and chanted in unison the words "Eine feste Burg ist unser Bund." But when the singing was over the bickering began. From the start of the debate, it was evident that on the crucial question of how to prevent war the Socialists of the world were not of one mind.[56] The delegates were confronted, in fact, with four competing resolutions. Hervé presented one, which proposed to commit the International to antipatriotism, the military strike, and insurrection in the face of war. In his version of Marxist orthodoxy, Guesde presented a resolution which treated militarism and war as functions of capitalism. Vaillant and Jaurès, defending the majority resolution of the S.F.I.O., admitted no such impotence against war as Guesde's motion implied; instead they called on the working-class organizations of all nations to apply consistent pressure for peace both in Parliament and on the street. The fourth resolution, offered by Bebel for German Social Democracy, was formalistic and breathed little real radicalism. Uneasy about the general strike, hostile to talk of popular insurrection, the Social Democrats demonstrated how, under the influence of the reformist trade unions, they were relegating the revolution to Kautsky's rhetoric. Robert Michels, whose streak of anarchosyndicalism made him a brilliant critic of German Socialism, wrote of its spirit in stinging terms: "In truth, as far as militarism and patriotism are concerned, the attitude of the German Socialists is far from audacious. We have already demonstrated that in these pages. . . . The fear of losing their voters and their status is the *loi suprême* of Social Democracy."[57]

Faced with such a variety of proposals, the delegates turned the debate into a formless wrangle. The task of weaving together the various viewpoints was turned over finally to a special committee of notables, which, of course, included Jaurès. Pooling their considerable intellectual and dialectical resources, the members of the committee produced an unduly long resolution which included concessions to everyone except the doctrinaire antipatriots. With the Marxists, it considered war an inevitable consequence of production crises under capitalism; yet it formulated, as though no contradiction were involved, a program of action to prevent war or, if it eventually broke out, to turn it into revolution.

The resolution listed all the proposals which had been, for some time, the common currency of the Socialist movement: the parliamentary struggle against armaments; the replacement of standing armies with popular militias; the coördination of efforts by the working classes of rival nations; the recourse to courts of arbitration; and the insistent demand for disarmament. But if, read the resolution, nations should be brought to the brink of war even after all of these efforts, "the working classes and their parliamentary representatives . . . must do everything to prevents its outbreak by whatever means seem most effective to them." In deference to the Social Democrats, the insurrectionary strike was not mentioned, but neither was it specifically condemned. The final paragraph, in fact, reflected the thoughts of two determined revolutionaries, Rosa Luxemburg and Lenin, who had been moved and instructed by the lessons of the Russian Revolution of 1905: "Should war break out, despite all of this, it is the duty of the Socialist parties to intercede for its speedy end, and to strive with all their power to make use of the violent economic and political crises brought about by war to rouse the people, and thereby to hasten the abolition of capitalist class rule."[58]

Four resolutions had thus become one; it was Socialist alchemy at its best. The Congress accepted the eclectic resolution with an outburst of enthusiasm, and, when Hervé leaped atop a table to shout his approval, unanimous support became certain. Cool heads might have pondered the compromises within the resolution and the vastness of its obligations; but fervent hearts did not, and the delegates approved with their emotions what their reason might well have questioned.[59]

When Jaurès returned from Stuttgart, he was certainly hopeful, but hardly so sanguine about the powers of words that he believed a resolution, a work of compromise at that, could itself preserve the peace. Almost a decade later, Bernstein recalled a private conversation with Jaurès in one of Stuttgart's parks, which reveals something of his inner thoughts about such resolutions: "Jaurès was trying to win me over to his viewpoint on the general strike. All my objections concerned its impracticality, but he kept coming back to the *moral* effect of such a commitment." And Bernstein, admitting the limited vision of the Social Democrats, added reflectively: "Sometimes our lack of imagination can lead us to serious mistakes." Jaurès believed in the power of the ideal and the force of moral conviction; by any practical calculation, the action approved at Stuttgart might seem impossible; but if the idealism of the masses were roused and their hope stirred, then it might prove both practical and successful.

Once back in Paris, Jaurès sought quickly to spread the gospel of Stuttgart. On September 7, the S.F.I.O. sponsored a public rally at the Tivoli-Vauxhall, where he could explain to the public the results of the recent Congress. From every working-class district of Paris, men and women poured into the Place de la République, and from there into the sweltering Tivoli-Vauxhall. Exhausted after the recent International Congress, hampered by both the poor acoustics and the unbearable heat, Jaurès began slowly and without precise bearings. But at a certain point he took off, his voice and spirit ascending together. At the heart of his speech lay the conviction that the choice between war and peace was still an open one, that throughout France there were millions of non-socialists who might follow where the workers led:

At this very moment, there are wild adventurers, aggressive journalists, grasping bankers, and capitalists who are plotting a profitable expedition to seize Morocco. But while this scum of capitalism floats toward the Moroccan shore, there are millions of men in the middle class itself, especially among the petty bourgeoisie and the democratic peasantry, who, though they aren't yet Socialists, oppose the expenditure of men and money for futile and bloody adventures. But all these aspirations and wills are uncoördinated, dispersed. . . . Ah! How powerful they could become if they were brought together in a centralized drive for peace! . . . It is you, the workers, the wage-earners of the city, who can, who must spearhead the drive![60]

Without the will to peace, Jaurès felt, the proposals of the International could be nothing but bombast; with it, the future remained plastic. At the Tivoli-Vauxhall, if one can judge from the frenetic applause, he had braced his listeners for the coming hour of decision.

Beneath his public optimism, however, one senses in Jaurès a troubled spirit. His campaign for peace rested on premises which invited debate if not outright skepticism. In proposing French disarmament, he was assuming a Germany willing and able to live at peace with the world. Yet the basic facts of German political economy brought that premise into question. To support a burgeoning population; to supply a highly integrated industrial system; to guarantee the profits of Berlin's powerful banking houses, Germany seemed almost driven to imperialism and armaments. "Overproduction, the lack of markets, unemployment — these were like the sword of Damocles hanging over Germany's industrial complex."[61] Against this economic challenge, what chance had the political parties even if, like Social Democracy, they professed their pacifism?[62]

Jaurès worried about the problem, confronted it, and tried to reason it away. The economic and naval rivalry of Germany and England, he felt, was the central one of contemporary capitalism. Yet between the imperative of expansion and the recourse to war, he drew a distinction, based on an analysis of the capitalist mind. It was unlikely, he argued, that the owning classes of either country would risk plant and equipment, the sources of their wealth, in a destructive war. And especially since such a war could only benefit American capitalists, who would exploit the opportunity "to increase their markets and to spread their influence over the entire globe."[63]

But this recourse to logic hardly dispelled Jaurès' uneasiness. Anglo-German rivalry, he realized, could precipitate war, and France, as the ally of England, might be threatened from the east. To deny that possibility was to flout reality; but to admit it openly was to play into the hands of militarists and nationalists who were already calling for a larger army and more destructive weapons. Like most Socialists, Jaurès was caught between the conflicting demands of peace and patriotism. To resolve the dilemma, he became his country's leading spokesman for a radical military reorganization; inspired by the example of the French Revolution and supported by the teachings of the Second International, he proposed the replacement of standing armies which could be used in offensive wars, by popular militias which could guarantee the defense of the realm.

Unlike many other Socialist schemes, this one seemed, especially in a time of international tension, hopelessly utopian. Could armed militias actually defend the nation against modern armies? Without a convincing answer, the military proposals of the Socialists had no chance of either support or success. Jaurès alone among the leaders of the International wrestled seriously with the question. Badly overworked but never at rest, he applied himself to a detailed analysis of military organization; to answer the critics and persuade the public, he proposed to prove both the inadequacy of standing armies and the effectiveness of popular militias. From the inception of his study to its conclusion, three years elapsed; then, in 1911, he published with Jules Rouff a book almost 700 pages long, richly detailed, original, and suggestive. It was *L'Armée nouvelle*, a work unique in the literature of socialism.[64]

The best of reformers have camped squarely on enemy terrain. Was it not Voltaire who became a master of biblical exegesis? So Jaurès invaded the field of military theory and emerged an expert. To stimulate his thinking, to open new lines of thought and to set old ones in order, he had the assistance of a young army officer, Captain Henry Gérard, whose theories were advanced and heterodox. Their relationship began with a chance dinner meeting in 1907 and flowered through many a long conversation over the ensuing years. Gérard brought to Jaurès' attention a wide range of military writings; and it was the philosopher who predicted for the captain the terrible consequences of modern war:

One evening, on the Place du Trocadéro, under the tall trees of the Avenue Henri-Martin, Jaurès described to Gérard what the world would suffer in a major war: the cannon-fire and the bombs; entire nations decimated; millions of soldiers strewn in mud and blood; millions of corpses. . . . Years later, on the battlefield of Roye, the sky was aflame, the shells were bursting everywhere, the earth was shaking, men were falling around Commandant Gérard. Then a friend saw him gaze fixedly into space. "What are you thinking about?" "I feel as though this is all familiar to me. . . . Jaurès prophesied this hell, this total annihilation."[65]

At the core of *L'Armée nouvelle* was a tough-minded realism, which neither Jaurès' poetic expression nor his ardent hope concealed. He postulated the threat of war from Germany, analyzed the requirements of defense, criticized the thinking of the War Office, and sketched the outlines of a new army. To those who charged that because he urged peace with Berlin, he was insensitive to the possibility of a German attack, *L'Armée nouvelle* should have been a definitive answer. It would not be, of course, so long as anti-Socialists felt it politically useful to describe him as pro-German and antipatriotic.

"If war between France and Germany were to break out tomorrow," Jaurès asked, "what form would it take?"[66] To answer that most vital of questions, he searched through the writings of German military theorists and found them committed to the rapid, crushing offensive. With a single campaign they proposed "to overwhelm the enemy, even at terrible cost to their own armies."[67] Should Germany apply that strategy in a war with France, she would send a well-drilled, strongly-massed army across the western frontier to cripple French forces with a single blow. Against such an attack, what chance would France have to resist successfully? None at all, argued Jaurès, if she depended upon her smaller frontline army. But if she were to base her resistance on the *nation armée*, a mass army of trained reserves, then she might delay the offensive and eventually defeat the enemy. At her frontiers France could concentrate an advanced army, drawn from the reserves of the eastern departments, which would slow down the German offensive until the rest of the nation was mobilized: "While the enemy advanced, millions of citizen-soldiers would be formed into a massive fighting force. In the opening stages of the war, France would probably have to yield part of her territory. Her first-line forces, conscripted from the reserves of the frontier . . . would be only an advanced guard, retreating as slowly as possible, fighting to hold its ground, but not engaging in a decisive battle. Meantime, the national energies would be converted into an irresistible defensive force."[68] Yet neither the army chiefs of France nor her leading politicians reckoned seriously with reserves as the basis of national resistance. Rather than arm the masses, they put their faith in the professional standing army; rather than prepare the defense of the nation, they nourished dreams of conquest. It was tradition that bound the chiefs who ruled "the inner sanctum of the rue Saint-Dominique"; it was social conservatism that guided the "pseudodemocrats" of the ministry. Together they accounted for a military system that was both inconsistent and inept: "It is logical that France should have so confusing a military organization. It reflects a social system which oscillates between democracy and oligarchy, between imperialism and peace. Thus, in the organization of her army, republican France assigns a larger role to reserves than does monarchial Germany; but she treats those reserves contemptuously, as though they were inferior, even suspect."[69]

Such thinking, asserted Jaurès, betrayed not only a contempt for democracy but also an ignorance of military realities. Was the standing army based on a two-year training period for a minority demonstrably superior to a universal reserve force? The experience of history belied it: "In reading the bold and imaginative writings of Maurice de Saxe on this question, or the reflections of General Morand on the chief lessons of the Revolutionary and Napoleonic wars, or the interpretations by recent theorists of the Boer and Russo-Japanese Wars, I find almost unanimous condemnation of long, formalistic, and routine military training."[70] To cope with the potential threat of a German invasion, the army chiefs had no idea more effective than to keep conscripts in barracks for two years, where the dull routine sapped their morale. What a difference, exclaimed Jaurès, between the generals of the rue Saint-Dominique and those French Revolutionary commanders whose trust in the people had saved the First Republic!

In recent years, he discovered through his research, the thinking of the military chiefs had been challenged within the stygian world of the army itself. A group of "young Turks," military theorists drawn from the officer corps, had countered official ideas with new and bolder theories. The writings of the late Captain Gilbert and those of General Langlois were the basic scripture of the new school, which, according to Jaurès, now influenced "almost all officers who think and write on military problems."[71] Unlike the traditionalists, these new theorists embraced the idea of the armed nation, but not for purposes of defense. They found their inspiration in the grandiose designs of Napoleon rather than the experience of the French Revolution. And like Bonaparte, they proposed to rouse the patriotic energies of the masses not for defense of the homeland but for a showdown with the enemy.

Yet the ultimate fate of Napoleon, Jaurès wrote, was convincing proof that the mass offensive fails before mass resistance:

Captain Gilbert and his French disciples have not approached Napoleon as objectively or honestly as Clausewitz, the German theorist they most admire. They claim that Clausewitz contradicted himself because he concluded, after having analyzed the remarkable results of Napoleonic offensives, that defensive warfare was superior. . . . But he had seen with his own eyes the downfall of Napoleon before the massive Russian defense. In the same way, Spain demonstrated how the power of the people, when they are fighting for their independence, can cope with the most brilliant offensive.[72]

Against the main currents of French military thinking, Jaurès posed the Socialist plan for a new army.[73] Borrowing heavily from the French experience of 1793 and the Swiss system of militias, he proposed a universal reserve army, inseparable from the living body of the nation, to replace the isolated professional army.[74] The military force, as he conceived it, would be recruited and trained locally, its officers drawn from rank-and-file civilians, its troops physically hardy and morally dedicated, No special military caste would then threaten the peace and progress of France; no spiritual wall would then separate everyday life and the defense of the soil; no intellectual line would then isolate the study of war from the larger body of learning. The working classes, as in '93, would neither fear nor despise the army; no longer would they suffer its violence against their strikes; no longer would they be forced to die on foreign battlefields in its far-flung expeditions. The *armée nouvelle* would serve no narrow ruling class, but would become an army of and by the people.

Could such radical proposals win a wide audience? Or were they only blueprints for an ideal socialist society? Jaurès did, in fact, consider *L'Armée nouvelle* as the first in a series of volumes describing the institutional framework of an eventual socialist France. At the same time, he believed that under the democratic Republic his plan could serve as a guide for the evolution of the military system. "For my part," he promised, "I will work with might and main for a gradual reformation."[75] True to his commitment, he deposited in the Chamber, on November 14, 1910, a long bill which embodied in its eighteen articles his main thoughts on the new army. But that measure never even reached the floor for discussion. Instead, Jaurès found himself, soon afterwards, fighting to retain the two-year army law against the opposition of politicians and generals who were clamoring for three-year military service.

He had counted too much on the force of his argument and on the collaboration of the non-Socialist Left. With but a few exceptions, he failed to persuade army officers, party leaders, or newspaper editors of a point of view which they ridiculed as a naïve fantasy. Nor was there full acceptance of the militia scheme even among the Socialists of Europe. It was Max Schippel, a Revisionist intellectual of German Social Democracy, who wrote sarcastically: "You can't put a cannon in the bed of every former gunner and give each old sea dog a little warship to put in the farmyard trough or wash tub."[76]

That Jaurès' theories failed of acceptance made them no less provocative. Indeed, when France was finally invaded in 1914, the German offensive was stalemated less by the Napoleonic tactics of Foch than by the defensive weight of the French nation. World War I "justified the confidence which Jaurès placed in the nation," General Messimy declared in 1919.[77] Since then, in Russia, in Spain, in China, and in the France of the Resistance, the armed people have demonstrated their strength.[78]

By the irony of history and the alchemy of politics, Jaurès' concern for defense was called treason, his love of homeland antipatriotism. Hervé was no problem for the ultranationalists; his views were crude, simpleminded. But Jaurès — here was the danger. The very passion of his patriotism lent weight to his denunciation of French aggressions. How better to discredit him, reckoned his enemies, than to propound the myth of the "betrayer Jaurès"? Their success was far from complete; but ultimately it was enough.

IV

We are living through times when parties and their leaders lack the courage to face problems squarely. When some of us see our goals clearly and propose the means to achieve them, they laugh at our integrity and call it naïveté. . . . What this Parliament has lacked from the very beginning is a clear sense of purpose.[79]

In a generation which has been witness to the collapse of two French republics, this description of *malaise* is familiar enough. Yet it was written not of 1939 or of 1958, but of the decade before World War I when, according to mellow tradition, the Third Republic was sound and its leaders outstanding. But the politics of drift, Jaurès realized, had already set in. As the bourgeois parties of the Left meandered toward the Center, as Clemenceau and Briand made daily amends for their youthful militancy, a mist of boredom and cynicism settled over the public spirit. From Francis de Pressensé, one of the noblest Dreyfusards, came a cry of frustration: "The politicians who vaulted into public office as Dreyfusards promised a thorough and immediate renovation of France. They have held power, enjoyed the support of the majority, . . . and utterly failed to alleviate social injustices."[80] Pressensé expressed the anguish of all who had believed, on the morrow of the Affair, that the triumph of social democracy was irrevocable. Like their descendants in the Resistance, they counted too much on the permanency of coalitions and too little on the inconstancy of politicians.

As Jaurès viewed it, the debility of French democracy threatened consequences more serious than a mere passing conservatism. For if the proletariat felt defeatist and discouraged about democratic politics, then the fissiparous tendencies of the working-class movement — inflexible Marxism and revolutionary syndicalism — might become its mainstream. Worshiping the general strike or the laws of history as their liberating gods, the workers might retreat into a political fetishism which would rob the movement of its creativity and complexity.[81] But precisely because the times were difficult, Jaurès reckoned, the Extreme Left had need of an iron will and flexible tactics. Now more than ever, the working-class movement had to vary its efforts, expand them, intensify them. In the Socialist Party, therefore, Jaurès became the chief spokesman for a rapprochement with syndicalism and even a *modus vivendi* with Radicalism.

A decade of intense political activity had followed the Congress of London of 1896, but the attitude of the leading Socialists and syndicalists toward the relationship of their movements remained strikingly constant. Within the C.G.T. all factions, except the Marxists of the Nord, rejected formal and organic ties with the Socialist Party. The revolutionaries, who had attacked the bloc as a deception, were more scornful than ever; the reformists, who controlled the largest unions, though not the executive committee of the C.G.T., considered political neutrality the only safeguard for internal trade union harmony. "While we do not reject politics," the reformist Keufer had written after the Congress of London, "we must warn the workers of the dangers for their union of political commitments."[82] The revolutionaries banked on economic action to topple capitalism, and the reformists expected it to improve the conditions of life. Both factions, for their own ends, shared the common distrust of a political liaison.

Within the ranks of Socialism, Guesde and his followers remained the staunchest partisans of a tight alliance between the S.F.I.O. and the C.G.T., which, they hoped, would subordinate syndicalism to the party. At the opposite pole were the Hervéists who, harboring a deep suspicion of politics, like the Allemanists a decade earlier, proposed a sharp separation of the two. Between the extremes stood Vaillant and Jaurès. The old Blanquist had taken a position in London which, viewed in perspective, did credit to his political wisdom. In siding then with those who refused to pledge their allegiance to political action, he had understood their motives as neutralist and not anarchist. Over the next decade, though he was himself immersed in political socialism, he demonstrated, this erstwhile Communard, his appreciation for direct economic action. His constancy was tonic to Jaurès. As the currents of conservatism and militarism deepened, he became more convinced than ever that victory for the working classes depended on the effective partnership of syndicalism and Socialism. Who but the Socialists, acting through parliamentary channels, could restrain a repressive government? Who but the syndicalists, demonstrating through the general strike, could organize mass pressure for peace and reform?

Such were the moods and attitudes of the Extreme Left when the C.G.T. convened at Amiens in October, 1906, to debate the issue of collaboration between syndicalism and Socialism. After three tense days of discussion, the delegates overwhelmingly approved a charter which guaranteed the political neutrality of the unions.[83] The small band of C.G.T. Marxists, concentrated in the textile industry of the Nord and led by the Guesdist Renard, pressed for a formal alliance between the unions and the S.F.I.O. But both reformists and revolutionaries, each group for its own reasons, joined forces to defeat that proposal. What, then, did the charter signify? According to Pierre Monatte, who expressed the viewpoint of the militant anarchosyndicalists, it represented "the culmination of the struggle against Millerandism."[84] But in fact, the charter probably reflected not so much a clear programmatic line as an organizational necessity. "In the C.G.T.," the reformist Coupat had argued at Amiens, "there are workers of many political positions. There are even some who are Catholic. Do we want to force them out of our movement?"[85] To have imposed a rigid party alignment on so diversified a body of trade unionists would seriously have threatened its unity.

But what of Socialism, did the Charter of Amiens boil down to a rejection of it by the syndicalists? Such was the conclusion happily drawn in the anti-Socialist press; but that interpretation was far wide of the mark. Though the charter prescribed neutrality, it in no wise precluded informal ties between the unions and the party for causes both espoused. Nor could it have been otherwise. Among the rank and file of the C.G.T., the majority, one can safely assume, supported Socialist candidates, while a significant number were members of both the C.G.T. and the S.F.I.O. There were reformists, like Keufer, who never repudiated the system of private property, and revolutionaries, who mixed their Socialism with anarchism. But the majority occupied a middle ground where antipathy toward Socialist politics carried little weight. Louis Niel, that long-winded alumnus of the Bourse du travail at Montpellier, reflected the views of the centrists when he said: "There are several ways to emancipate the workers. Syndicalism is one of them, but by no means does it exclude others."[86] Such tolerance was the stuff of partnership. But if the Socialists were to treat the Charter of Amiens contemptuously, or if they were to repudiate the general strike, they would assuredly alienate the C.G.T.

In the opening days of November, 1906, the S.F.I.O. convened at Limoges, and there the Socialists took their stand on the Charter of Amiens. During a year of strikes, they had extended unstinting support to the C.G.T. Though extremism on the general strike and on antipatriotism conflicted with their political praxis, they concentrated their fire on the adversaries of the workers and not on their national union. But at Limoges, the Socialists were confronted with a syndicalist *fait accompli*, and the future of their relations with syndicalism hinged on the nature of their response.

Like every other significant issue of tactics or principle, this one revealed the main factional divisions within the S.F.I.O. Hervé and his faithful, who found in the charter a rejection of political reformism, welcomed its declaration of political independence and warned the Socialists against meddling with the unions. At the other extreme, Guesde attacked the syndicalism of 1906, as though it were but a latter-day version of an earlier anarchism: "Must I recall to you the teachings of the International at Paris in 1889, at Brussels in 1891, at London in 1896, at Paris again in 1900? In each of these Congresses we recognized the insufficiency of economic action in the struggle to liberate the workers."[87]

Guesde's intention could hardly have been obscure. For twenty-five years he had conceived of the unions as a recruiting ground for the Socialist Party, and nothing of later C.G.T. history had changed his mind. As always, Guesde arrived at a Socialist Congress with a strong core of support. The Federation of the Nord, a Marxist bastion built by the pioneers of the P.O.F., assured him a disciplined bloc of supporters;[88] beside them there might very well stand others who, though they were not themselves Marxists, feared for the future of the working-class movement if the excesses of syndicalism should drive bourgeois republicans to extreme measures of repression.

Neither Hervé's enthusiastic support nor Guesde's scornful rejection constituted a realistic attitude toward the Charter of Amiens. What the party needed, if it were to maintain its unity and intensify its pressure on capitalism, was a policy of collaboration with an independent syndicalism. Toward that end Jaurès and Vaillant applied their talent and prestige. In their essential goals, Jaurès argued, the S.F.I.O. and the C.G.T. were so closely allied that their struggle was bound to be a common one: "The unions, I am happy to say, have set their sights higher than simple collective bargaining. Their ultimate objective, like ours, is the reorganization of the property system."[89] If the workers walked two separate roads, one economic and the other political, their direction was the same. What could serve them better, Jaurès asked, than that their struggle against capitalism should spread, coherently and simultaneously, into both the factory and the Parliament?

For his Federation of the Nord Guesde placed before the Congress a resolution which, in essence, subordinated the trade unions to the purposes of the party. Jaurès countered with a resolution, drawn up by the Federation of the Tarn, which foresaw the "voluntary coöperation between two independent organizations" in order to "eliminate whatever misunderstandings have arisen between the C.G.T. and the Socialist Party." It took the strong lead of Jaurès and the lingering insurrectionary spirit of the old Blanquists and Allemanists to block the resolution of the Guesdists. The final vote proved surprisingly close, and only by a margin of eighteen did the motion of the Tarn become the policy of the party.[90]

If the decision at Limoges was more the handiwork of Jaurès than of any other, so was its implementation. To the C.G.T. and its leaders, even the most bombastic among them, he extended a Socialist olive branch. How little it mattered to him that he had been so often and so unjustly attacked in the syndicalist press! He now opened the pages of *L'Humanité* to all manner of syndicalists, so that the revolutionary analyses of Griffuelhes and Pouget found place beside the mild prescriptions of reformist Socialists; and to the consternation of anti-Socialist editors, Jaurès repeatedly defended, though with his oft-stated reservations, the use of the general strike.[91]

The doctrinal quarrel between the revolutionary syndicalists and the parliamentary Socialists, like their temperamental differences, never, of course, disappeared. Griffuelhes, after all, had led the C.G.T. not because he was an original thinker or even much of an organizer (he was neither), but because he represented, in a form pure and unalloyed, the revolution.[92] The world Fernand and Maurice Pelloutier had described in 1900 in *La Vie ouvrière en France*, a proletarian universe without light or hope, was the world he knew; to destroy and then transform it, Griffuelhes insisted, no halfhearted measures, neither the collective bargaining of the C.G.T. conservatives nor the reforms of the Socialists, would do, but only a revolution, total and violent.

Yet in the years immediately preceding the war, the areas of agreement between the C.G.T. and S.F.I.O. widened until the two organizations, one political and the other basically economic, approximated a united working-class movement. And why this significant development? First, because Jaurès led a crusade against imperialism and war so impassioned that not even the most militant anarchosyndicalist could have questioned his integrity. And then, because the C.G.T., caught in the throes of an internal crisis, finally forced Griffuelhes out of office and, behind its consistently revolutionary rhetoric, assumed a more flexible and coöperative tactical position.

The reformists, leaders for the most part of the largest unions, had hoped for years to wrest control of the C.G.T. from the hands of the revolutionaries. Against Griffuelhes, their campaign was relentless and, according to Dolléans, actively encouraged by the government; by his appeal to violence, they charged, and especially by his contempt for reforms, he had signally failed to organize the majority of French workers.[93] Scornful of formal democracy, Griffuelhes, of course, brushed aside the statistical argument. "The French worker," Georges Lefranc, that astute syndicalist historian, once noted, "joins his union with flaming enthusiasm; but when the going gets tough, he drops out."[94] Griffuelhes operated from a similar premise. The revolution, the mission of the C.G.T., depended not on *une majorité de moutons* but on *les minorités agissantes*.

When Griffuelhes finally fell from grace, however, he was brought down not by the cogency of reformist arguments but by a serious division among the revolutionaries. Impatient and intolerant, he managed to antagonize his friends and thus to swell the ranks of his enemies. Finally, on February 2, 1909, thwarted by a coalition of reformists and dissident revolutionaries, Griffuelhes resigned as Secretary General after almost seven heroic years of service. In Louis Niel, his successor, the moderates had a man of their own choosing, but his patent incompetence, particularly evident during the strike of postal workers in May, quickly proved his undoing. Thus, in July, 1909, the extensive powers of the Secretary General passed into the hands of Léon Jouhaux, a militant young anarchosyndicalist. But though Jouhaux passed for a disciple of Griffuelhes, he was flexible, patient, ambitious, and ultimately acceptable to the reformists.

In the future, when the world war had destroyed the morale of both the C.G.T. and the S.F.I.O., new schisms, deep and inevitable, would shatter the unity between and within these organizations. But as the twentieth century passed into its second turbulent decade, their old quarrels, though still reflected in the revolutionary syndicalist press, began to fade into the background. Behind the policy of collaboration lay especially the danger of war and chauvinism; at its heart was the spirit of Jaurès, its prime mover and central symbol.

The era of Clemenceau and Briand, which forced the S.F.I.O. to reconstruct its relations with syndicalism, raised afresh the question of the party's attitude toward Radicalism. At first glance, it appears that there was no question at all. The bitter exchanges between Socialists and Radicals, their sharp division over labor unrest and foreign policy, their evident estrangement after Amsterdam — all led to the incontrovertible conclusion that the tactics of the bloc were forever dead and buried. "The Radicals," Guesde charged at the start of their hegemony, "will lead France down the same road of bankruptcy as the republicans of the Second Empire."[95] It took but a few months of Clemenceau's dominion before Lucien Herr defined a Radical as "a conservative who doesn't go to mass."[96]

Socialist disillusion waxed as Radical purpose waned. On the morrow of the 1906 elections and in the flush of their victory, the effervescent Radicals proclaimed for France a glorious new era of peaceful progress.

In their prognostication they proved as weak as in their will. Weeks of inaction yielded months of aimlessness until even the Radicals were forced to admit the hard truths that their party lacked discipline and their program clarity. At Lille in 1906, J.-L. Bonnet, president of the Radical and Radical-Socialist Federation of the Seine, bemoaned the organizational chaos of a party which, after five years, had still to create Radical Federations for several departments. What manner of party was it, asked critics both within Radicalism and outside it, which exerted no central control over the choice of its candidates and imposed no doctrinal discipline over its deputies?[97] Years later, Daniel Halvéy answered the question with characteristic acuity: "There are hundreds of Radicals, but radicalism is a mere word, empty of meaning."[98]

Yet organization was less the problem of Radicalism than program. In an age of sharpening industrial strife, the Radical creed, a hodge-podge of clichés about anticlericalism and individualism, seemed as little relevant as the spinning wheel in a modern factory. Throughout 1906, Ferdinand Buisson, a Radical of broad culture and high idealism, urged his party to come to grips with the problems of an industrial society. A Protestant by birth and an academician by profession, Buisson stood in the French Chamber for the monopoly of secular education and the rights of the underprivileged. High-strung and frail, his thick beard shielding a withered, drawn face, he was nervous, generally agitated, worrying about his party, seeking to set its course aright. Among so many careless, Buisson was one who cared. Even before the elections of 1906 he had quoted in the Radical Party daily an observation of Tocqueville's, which he offered as a maxim for his colleagues: "It is a contradiction that the people should be at once sovereign and downtrodden."[99] Against the antics of the Sarrien ministry, he urged unswerving dedication to social reforms; against the drift to the Center, he called for collaboration with the Socialists.

But Buisson, like Mendès-France after him, commanded respect rather than support. Even when success crowned their political efforts, the Radicals showed little of the militancy for which he hoped. Hardly had the Radical dominion begun when he predicted its failure: "A Radicalism in which the socialist leaven has been eliminated will soon cease to be radical. It will become nothing but opportunism."[100] However direct, his words failed to exorcise from the Radical spirit the demon of anti-Socialism. The dream of collectivism, Maujan railed in an important policy speech at Joinville-le-Pont, "is a hopeless mirage."[101] But when Radicals chose thus to ridicule Socialism as utopian, they managed to obscure their essential timidity on questions of property. For the real test of their commitment lay in their willingness to collaborate with the Socialists on behalf of reforms — the income tax, social security, even nationalization of natural monopolies — which were the basic stock in the programs of both parties.

The Radicals dug profitably into the nationalistic emotions of the times and came up with an excuse for their moderation. They hammered away at the antipatriotism of Hervé, made it the central issue of political debate, and built it into a barrier against collaboration with the Socialists. Ignoring a spate of evidence which demonstrated that the S.F.I.O. rejected doctrinal antipatriotism, Radical politicians and editors treated Hervé as though his words were fiat in the party. On September 20, 1907, *L'Écho de Paris* published a letter from Senator Delpech, vice president of the Radical and Radical-Socialist Party Committee, who proposed to banish Socialists from the community of loyal republicans. A few weeks later, when over a thousand Radical delegates gathered at Nancy for their annual congress, they agreed that never would they support a Socialist who had not publicly repudiated Hervé.

For most Radicals, there was no better *raison d'etre* than political success. If their party was a shambles and their program a conundrum, their victory, at least, was real. Guardians of petty property and small-town patriotism, they were little inclined to risk the rewards of office for so insubstantial a commodity as social justice. "The Radical Party," prescribed the first-term deputy Ajam, "will win in France only if it opposes Socialism."[102] To deputies who planned for reëlection and dreamed of ministerial office, that advice seemed sound. Under Clemenceau, as under Sarrien, they clung to the phraseology of the Left, but they shuffled toward the shelter of the Center.

The disenchantment of the Socialists was unrelieved. "The Right," Vaillant asserted before the Chamber, "begins for us much further Left than you would think."[103] In many a stinging article Jaurès reiterated that viewpoint. If there were moderates in the Socialist Party who dreamed of reviving the Left bloc on any terms, they were little comforted by his words. And yet Jaurès treated the issue of Socialist relations with Radicalism as an open one, worthy of careful analysis and constant reappraisal. So undogmatic was his approach that he was suspect to certain Marxists who operated within a more rigid framework of ideas. Thus, in a letter to Kautsky, Rappoport complained that despite the dictum of Amsterdam, Jaurès aimed to reconstitute the bloc.[104]

Rappoport, in fact, was not wholly off the mark. Though Jaurès proposed nothing so formal as a revival of the bloc, he continued to explore the merits of temporary alliances, both electoral and parliamentary, with the Radical Party. His motives took root in a tough-minded realism about Socialist politics, for he understood that while the rhetoric of the S.F.I.O. was steadfastly revolutionary, its concrete program was (and would remain) reformist.[105] It was a development which neither disturbed nor surprised Jaurès, who equated revolution in a democratic society with an unyielding will to reform.[106] But what chance had the Socialist deputies, so long as they remained a minority, to implement even a single part of their program without the help of the bourgeois Left? "If we preach reforms but shun the help of others, we will play into the hands of the reactionaries."[107] Only on the plinth of political alliances could the Socialists erect a monument to progress.

On the essential quality of Radicalism Jaurès rendered a judgment no less severe than that of other militants in his party; for two decades he had watched the Radicals oscillate between triviality and self-interest until his eyes were weary. "It is only when one comes to balance the books," remarks a heroine in Mauriac's *Frontenac Mystery*, "that he realizes how much a social conscience costs." The Radicals, Jaurès felt, were forever "balancing the books" to the detriment of their social conscience. One might thus have expected him to generalize, as did Hervé or Guesde, that the Radicals were all of a breed, birds of the bourgeois flock, no better than the moderates and no different.

Yet precisely because Jaurès scrutinized their record and debated with their leaders, he arrived at a less facile, more realistic conclusion — that Radicalism in the era of Clemenceau was critically and significantly divided:

There is the democratic Radical Party, whose leaders are Pelletan and Buisson; there is the conservative Radical Party, of which M. Maujan is the chief trumpeter. The first, though it falls short of collectivism and lacks real understanding of economic evolution, wants to maintain contact with the working class, to ally against the conservatives, to limit the power of the financial oligarchies, and to lessen the burdens on the proletariat by substantial social legislation. The second, out of its blind hostility to Socialism, edges toward the conservative parties. The defection of these pseudo-Radicals has inflicted some real defeats on the Socialists.[108]

This analysis was strongly supported by the facts. After only half a dozen years of organized life, the party already seethed with internal dissension. The greatest challenge to the tenuous unity of the Radical Party was the Clemenceau ministry, which, because its personnel was Radical and its policies conservative, threw the party into confusion and finally split it. Its Executive Committee, swayed by the progressive views of Pelletan, Buisson, and Berteaux, repeatedly debated resolutions of censure against the ministry for its antilabor measures. "The government," Pelletan charged in the course of one such debate, "has become the tool of Ribot's Center."[109] At times the censure proposals were defeated or modified, but on May 12, 1909, the Executive Committee passed a resolution so hostile to the government that Clemenceau was, in effect, read out of the party.[110]

In the Chamber, on the other hand, the majority of the party's deputies, shepherded by Lafferre and Maujan, lent Clemenceau their support. "The Radicals play a very strange game," commented an exasperated Jaurès. "The Executive Committee denounces the government's methods, while their deputies approve them by an overwhelming majority."[111] Yet it was that very ambivalence, he reckoned, which injected uncertainty into the future of Radicalism and gave Socialists cause to hope. He learned, at times from private sources, of the struggle for control of the party's tactics and program. In the fall of 1907 Jaurès had lashed out at Radical spokesmen who, he charged, were leveling their attacks not at the conservatives to the Right but at the Socialists to the Left.[112] Among those he mentioned was Buisson, who immediately dispatched a letter of protest. "You have been the victim of a grossly unjust campaign of calumny," Buisson wrote to Jaurès, "but I feel pained that you should even think me capable of stooping to such despicable tactics. . . . In *Le Radical*, I have persistently fought the opportunism of men like De Lanessan, who are trying to undermine the party's reforming mission."[113] Persuaded that Buisson was a man of sincere and progressive convictions, Jaurès replied at once with a note of apology.[114]

Hopeful that the ferment might yield results beneficial to the S.F.I.O., Jaurès intervened publicly in Radical affairs. To those whom *Le Temps* wrote off (May 22, 1908) as "the incorrigible apostles of the bloc," he offered warm encouragement; against those who proclaimed that they would never form alliances with Socialists, he directed sharp-edged criticism.[115] In the final analysis, his praise and his criticism had little influence in the higher councils of the Radical Party; nor did his closest allies, Pelletan and Buisson, come to control the movement. But neither his campaign nor theirs was futile. As so often happens in the morphology of political parties, Radicalism, pulled toward both the Socialists and the moderates, came uneasily to rest between these two poles. At successive party congresses (Nancy in 1907, Toulouse in 1908, Nantes in 1909), the Radicals, as though repeating dogma, attacked and rejected Socialism, while in almost the same breath they insisted upon the limits of private property and the rights of the working class.[116] Lacking theoretical substance, the Radical Party became a set of reform proposals pasted onto an electoral machine.

In searching out the paths to Socialism, however, Jaurès remained the hopeful explorer. Since the Radicals repeatedly affirmed their program of reforms and admitted the possibility of electoral collaboration, he proposed to his party flexible and realistic tactics. The Socialists, he pointed out, would suffer no loss of principle if they joined with Radicals to push through certain long-awaited reforms; nor would they damage their cause if they united behind the strongest progressive candidate on the second ballot. Rather they would ensure the largest possible Socialist influence in the Chamber. His case was a convincing one, and at two Party Congresses (Saint-Étienne in 1909 and Saint-Quentin in 1911) the Socialists adopted tactics which, if they prescribed nothing so disciplined as the Left bloc, conspicuously modified the spirit of Amsterdam.

For their efforts at collaboration, the Socialists were to reap only small rewards. When they pressed for reforms, they discovered, more often than not, that the Radical commitment was only political flummery; and when they proposed electoral alliances, they were met with the kind of suspicion which Lafferre, then President of the Radical-Socialist Executive Committee, expressed before the elections of 1910: "The Socialists know that their only chance of conspicuous success lies in persuading Radicals, whom they have reviled for years, to bury their grievances and bless the benefits their detractors can bestow on them."[117]

Yet the tactics were not futile. If coöperation between the parties of the Parliamentary Left was sporadic, it did lead to a reform or two and, in the elections of 1910 and 1914, it assured an expanding Socialist influence.

V

As the summer began to bloom in 1909, Jaurès thought more than fleetingly of Bessoulet and the joys of the country. But the duties of party leadership kept him in Paris and at the center of a mounting political crisis. After almost three hectic years of tenure, the Clemenceau ministry was sagging at its foundations, and, on June 25, Jaurès launched an attack against it.

In powerful accents, he reeled off his accusations of repression and conservatism. But his critique was no mere rhetorical exercise; rather it was an analysis, sensitive and troubled, of the cynicism and irrationalism which had worked their way into the public spirit of France. The philosopher's sixth sense was at work that day; when he described the virulent nationalism of the time and the intellectual apathy, when he warned that these currents would widen as faith in democracy weakened, he was forecasting, more than he could possibly have known, the shape of things to come. The demise of two republics within the next fifty years would one day justify the fears he now put to words:[118]

The recourse to violence by the ministry and its failure to reform society have produced a public lassitude, a muffled grumbling, an undercurrent of discontent, which we republicans can ill afford to ignore. We already have signs of what the people may do after so many crushing disappointments. For the first time in several years, the extremist reactionary parties, those which have always plotted against the Republic, have won a new lease on life.

Jaurès was hardly exaggerating. The Dreyfusard movement had disintegrated; the idealism it had engendered was gone, and what was left were opportunism, cynicism, and disorder. In their disillusion, men (especially young men) turned to the prophets of order, certainty, and self-styled heroism. Against the backdrop of an uncertain Republic, Maurras launched his *L'Action française* as a daily in 1908, while his monarchist supporters, carrying high the banners of traditionalism, Catholicism, and nationalism, clustered together in the Camelots du Roi. To the bourgeois students of the Left Bank, critical of Socialism and disillusioned with republicanism, *L'Action française* offered soul-stirring absolutes. These young Camelots du Roi began to emulate their nationalistic predecessors of the previous decade. Outside the classroom of the Sorbonne's Charles Andler, who lectured sympathetically about the history of German thought, they shrieked their patriotic slogans; at the Panthéon, on June 4, 1908, they rioted against the reburial of Zola in the national shrine.

What disturbed Jaurès most deeply was not the lunatic-fringe mob, but the currents of thought which served as intellectual reinforcement for the cults of force, faith, and futility. Bergson's intuitionist philosophy and Sorel's appeal to pure violence were tonic to those who were contemptuous of reason, democracy, and weakness. The creed of *l'art pour l'art*, while it attracted some men of honest dedication, encouraged young artists "to strike affected poses of indifference and insolent disdain." As an intellectual steeped in that humanistic tradition which proclaimed man to be the measure and society the material of art, Jaurès deplored the flight from reality: "From the origin of the human race the greatest geniuses have had two gifts: sensitivity to all of life, to its every tremor and its infinite traits; and the ability to reveal it through works of art, those creations of deep inner vision. . . . So it was from Homer to Goethe, from Goethe to Wagner."

What irritated Jaurès was callousness, the unconcern of the rich for the poor, the indifference of the specially talented toward the masses:

"The pleasures of life, which both dazzle and dull the rich, blind them to the untold miseries of daily existence. As their boats, bedecked with flags, glide merrily over the living hell of society, they know nothing of the unhappiness and disaster hidden below. And if, now and then, the damned rise up from the depths of hell to seize hold of the passing boat, the happy and privileged few, scandalized by this audacity, shout out their curses!" The irrationalism, the cynicism, the moral bankruptcy — all of them, cried a wrathful Jaurès, were the corollaries of Clemenceau's betrayal.

The interpellation, while it failed to topple the ministry, destroyed its moral credit. When Clemenceau answered on July 12, he seemed weary, almost bored. In lieu of defending his record, he turned his attack against the C.G.T. and the S.F.I.O. So unconvincing was his effort that when he called for a vote of confidence on July 15, an unusually large number of Radicals abstained. The Premier managed, however, to rally enough of his majority so that once more, though for the last time, he survived. Five days later, on July 20, 1909, the tottering ministry fell. The Joshua, as it turned out, was not Jaurès but Delcassé. Goaded into one of his infrequent speeches by revelations of incompetence in the Ministry of the Navy, Delcassé subjected Clemenceau's long political record to a bitter review. Almost twenty years after Tonkin, Ferry was avenged by his colonialist heir!

Jaurès and his friends listened as Delcassé berated Clemenceau for his earlier opposition to imperialism, while in his riposte the Premier taunted the former Foreign Minister with his failure to prepare the French army for a showdown at Fashoda and then at Tangier. "Clemenceau has thus revealed," wrote a bitter Jaurès, "that if France had been stronger, she would have fought England at Fashoda and Germany at Tangier."[119] The ministry had lasted too long and antagonized too many. In the battle of chauvinists, the Chamber sided with Delcassé. Deserted by many Radicals and a sprinkling of moderates, Clemenceau failed (212 to 196) to win a vote of confidence, and his government, the third longest in the history of the Republic, finally collapsed.

To form a new ministry, President Fallières called on an ever eager Briand, next to Clemenceau the strongest prop of the discredited government. The ministry which Briand formed was, if anything, more Centrist than its predecessor. Though half the ministers had served in the previous Cabinet, the others included Jean Dupuy, influential publisher of Le petit Parisien, at Commerce, and Georges Cochery, inveterate opponent of the income tax, at Finance in place of Caillaux. Three of the key ministers — Briand, Viviani, and Millerand — still called themselves socialists, but to Jaurès their presence merely demonstrated the poverty of Radical leadership. "Sailing onto the high seas from their islet of independent socialism," he observed, "three navigators have captured the disorganized Radical squadron and raised their own flag."[120]

On July 27, 1909, Briand revealed his ministerial program in a speech of tired generalities and timeless promises. Were there moderates who feared that Briand, the favorite of Gaston Calmette's *Figaro*, still nourished revolutionary ideas? Aristide eased their minds: "A new man has been born in me, a man who will adapt himself to his new position." What was opportunism to some came as reassurance to most, and Briand won his vote of confidence, 306 to 46. The Socialists abstained, except for eighteen Guesdists who voted against the ministry. In defending the tactics of abstention, Jaurès wrote: "We had to deprive the government of any excuse for saying, should it resume the policy of repression, that we forced it to consort with the Right."[121] Thus, at forty-seven, Briand had found room at the top. Cynical and subtle, he won the power he had craved, and the years to come would be shaped by his intention of keeping it.

At Périgueux on October 12, 1909, Briand outlined his political ambition.[122] He would be Premier of all the French; his government would guarantee a reign of peace. To the past he consigned the great struggles for a secular Republic; to the present he assigned the tasks of uniting the classes and restoring stability. "This man . . . loved peace and served it all his life," Suarez wrote in praise of his hero.[123] Jaurès thought otherwise. In an article entitled "Impossible Equilibrium," he attacked "this plan to draw all Frenchmen into one immense party."[124] Such politics would end all politics; "the entire nation would become the clientèle of the ministry." The idea of a national party appealed to men who would convert the electorate "into an amorphous mass, voiceless and inert in a time of corruption and conservatism." In the days of Boulanger, Jaurès had fought it; in the years of De Gaulle he would have resisted it. He was of no mind to succumb now to the wiles of Briand.

No fluttering veil of words about harmony and peace could conceal the realities of social caste and economic concentration. *La Guerre sociale*, Hervé's weekly, described in detail (July 20–26, 1910) the holdings of a banking consortium, which "with billions in deposits and thousands of branches almost controls the wealth of France." And *L'Humanité* (August 19, 24, 25, September 13, 14, 1910) charted meticulously the rise of living costs for the working classes since 1900. In such circumstances, Jaurès asked rhetorically, what was the "national party" but a deception, the last term in the deterioration of a democracy? He strove for nothing so much as a new human community, peaceful and productive. Jaurès' goal was not conflict but harmony, the reintegration into a single nation and around common purposes of all its citizens. "The proletariat must not destroy the nation," he had cried at the Congress of Nancy in 1907; "it must socialize it." But Briand's "national party," like Poincaré's "patriotic front" which followed, wasn't even good medieval corporatism. It was a blanket thrown across a hopelessly divided society.

Against Briand's "social peace" and the Chamber's seeming acquiescence, the Socialists intensified their opposition; carrying into battle not only his powerful oratory but also his expert knowledge of the parliamentary game, Jaurès was both the spokesman of the campaign and its tactician. One would underestimate him, Paul Painlevé wrote many years later, if he thought of Jaurès only as the maker of great speeches; having served with him in the Chamber between 1910 and 1914, Painlevé remembered especially "the Jaurès fully involved in those daily battles which are the very life of the Chamber; the Jaurès of the committees and the corridors; the Jaurès who broke up one little intrigue after another, sometimes by invoking the rules, sometimes by exploding with indignation."[125]

But to what end the campaign? Had the Socialists a precise sense of ends and means, or were they, from habit or inclination, only obstructionists? At the Congress of Toulouse in October, 1908, when they had themselves posed the question, Jaurès had drafted a statement of purpose, which became, probably more than any other document, the creed of the prewar S.F.I.O.[126] It read in part:

Precisely because it is a party of revolution, precisely because it has not paused in its continuous campaign against capitalist and bourgeois property, it is the most active party of reforms, . . . the only party which can turn every reform into the starting point for more far-reaching, more extensive conquests. . . . The evolution of the economy has already paved the way for the transformation of capitalist property. . . . A great effort to educate and organize the proletariat must accompany this economic evolution. . . . Like all exploited classes over the course of history, the proletariat, as a final recourse, may appeal to insurrection; but it doesn't confuse those vast collective movements . . . with futile skirmishes against the full power of the bourgeois State. Its effort, essentially, is a constant and rational one to conquer political power; against all parties of the bourgeoisie and their programs — whether reactionary, incoherent, or partial — it sets its clear collectivist and communist will.

The resolution of Toulouse, which warmed the hearts neither of committed insurrectionists nor of *blocards*, managed to preserve the unity of the party and to establish its lines of action.[127] Thus, though the

times were uncongenial, Jaurès and his friends campaigned not only
to frustrate Briand's grand design, but also to infiltrate French society
with the laws and institutions of the social Republic.

VI

By the end of 1909, social progress, the promise of the morrow in 1906,
seemed a fast-fading hope. But in the opening months of 1910, the deputies finally turned their attention to the long-promised measure to provide retirement pensions for workers. Eighteen years before, in 1891,
such a proposal had first been introduced in the Chamber; but by
masterful delaying tactics, its opponents had consistently sidetracked
pension legislation, and only now, near the end of a disappointing legislative session did the deputies prepare for a final decision.[128]
    The moment for laying this cornerstone of social security was a
propitious one. The adoption of compulsory retirement pensions in
England, Belgium, and Germany had set a standard of progress which
France could not easily ignore. Furthermore, at the approaching general
elections, the deputies would have to justify themselves before their
constituents, the majority of whom had expressed a preference for reforms by their vote of 1906. Encouraged by the prospect of success,
Jaurès joined with other Socialists and Radical-Socialists in sponsoring
the measure and in guiding it through the Chamber. Though far from
perfect, the law, he felt, could be further revised and improved. Of
central importance was the confirmation of a principle — that the community owed to every aged and fatigued worker a minimum measure
of support.
    Among many employers and the most conservative of deputies, op-
position was especially bitter. Almost as hostile, however, was the reaction within the revolutionary wings of the C.G.T. and the S.F.I.O.,
where the prospect of passing the pension law activated a strong if latent
contempt for reforms. In their public statements, revolutionary syndicalists, Guesdists, and Hervéists attacked not the principle of workers'
pensions but the terms of this particular proposal. They opposed especially the provisions for a contribution by workers and for administration of the entire pension fund by the State.[129]
    Within the S.F.I.O., the opposition clustered around Guesde, La-
fargue, and Hervé, who, ever suspicious of propping up capitalism,
interpreted the pension law as a cruel piece of deception. When Guesde
thought he might support the measure and then, if it passed into law,
work to improve it, Lafargue rallied his old comrade to immediate opposition. "I think it would serve Socialism far better," he wrote sternly,

"if you introduced and supported a measure of your own, if you fought the present proposal with the motto: No tax on the workers! No capital fund!"[130] Against the insurrection of the Guesdists and the Hervéists, Jaurès, with Vaillant at his side, once again led the fight for reforms. The controversy, which grew heated in the public press, boiled over at the Socialist Congress of Nîmes in February, 1910. The scenes at Nîmes were reminiscent of a hundred other meetings when, despite the obvious Socialist commitment to democracy, the merits of reformism and revolution were heatedly debated.

On the side of the antireformists were the most caustic tongues — Rappoport, Lafargue, Hervé. In the absence of the ailing Guesde, Lafargue was spokesman for the Marxists, and his arguments against the pension law were wildly cheered by the strong delegation from the Nord. He scored the proposal to exact contributions from overburdened workers; he ridiculed the advanced eligibility age of sixty-five; but his sharpest attack he reserved for the provision to turn control of the pension fund over to the State. What would stop the government, he demanded, from using the money for militarism and imperialism? "Stealing from the workers," he cried, "is the main occupation of the capitalists. It stands to reason that a capitalistic government will also indulge in theft."[131]

But it was Hervé more than Lafargue who revealed the subsurface of bitterness within the unified Socialist Party when he excoriated reformism and its philosopher Jaurès: "Jaurès is Millerand, he is Viviani, he is Briand! His probity is greater than theirs but his tactics are the same. . . . Though we are now fifty strong in Parliament, we are indistinguishable from good Radical-Socialists."[132] It was the plaint of the nondeputy against the privileged of Parliament; it was the envy in a smaller man of the fame of a greater one;[133] but it was also a sharp thrust to the heart of reformism. For unless one could prove that reforms paved the way to collectivism, then precious little separated the Socialists, on domestic issues at least, from Pelletan and Buisson.

In a defense of the pension law the delegates heard a lucid exposition from Renaudel and learned arguments from Vaillant. But everyone awaited Jaurès, who formed his oration around the classic theme of socialism and democracy. "When Socialists speak of the 'bourgeois State,'" he wrote in L'Armée nouvelle, "as if the working class had no part in it, their thinking is much too rigid. There never has been a pure and simple class State, a perfect instrument for every caprice and desire of the dominant class. There never has been a society, even the most brutish, totally subservient to the whim of a single class. . . . The contemporary democratic State is not a homogeneous bloc forged of only one metal. It represents less a single class than the actual relationship of classes."[134]

At Nîmes, Jaurès repeated the same argument. He spoke of democracy as the key to Socialist influence within the capitalist State; of social reforms as the elixir of working-class strength; of cumulative gains as the building blocks of the Socialist house. But once the theorizing was over, the humanism began. Painfully aware that workers were forced to live without dignity and face age without security, he was shocked by doctrinaire opposition to the pension law. Full of emotion, he spoke of the 120 million francs which would be paid at once to needy workers over sixty-five, and of the rural poor, who would enjoy some protection for the first time. By what standard of morality could Socialists betray the humble? Of genuine principle Jaurès was the staunchest advocate, but not of self-righteousness, hair-splitting, mannerism. While he spoke, he was interrupted and heckled until he felt a kind of futility in the debate. At one point, Lafargue cut him off with these words: "Between two thieves — the capitalist-thief and the State-thief, you prefer the latter!" An exasperated Jaurès turned his back on the rebuke: "I am too tired to answer. The Congress will decide."[135]

And so it was. When the delegates voted, they followed the lead of Jaurès and Vaillant. The majority agreed that Socialist deputies should support the pension law, while announcing to the Chamber their intention of working for progressive revisions. But though 193 voted for that proposition, there were 156, mainly Guesdists and Hervéists, who opposed it and, in defiance of party discipline, continued to attack it publicly. Thus when the measure approached a final vote in the Chamber, it was Guesde himself who rose to denounce it.

Article Two of the proposed law, which imposed a levy on workers' wages for the pension fund, was the provision that guaranteed the support of a republican majority. Yet it was precisely this article which Guesde attacked. "When I first embraced socialism," rasped the Marxist chief, "I promised the workers that it would eliminate the robbery of their just rewards by the capitalists: and I assured them that until the day of victory, socialists would help them increase their share of what they produced. . . . Now, for the first time, I would have to confess to them that I voted to decrease their wages. No! I will never do that!"[136]

When Jaurès rose to reply, already a man past fifty and renowned throughout Europe, he might have ridiculed Guesde and his dogmatism. But that was not his way. For the dedicated Guesde he had a lingering regard and to party unity he was irrevocably commited. "To stand here and oppose the man who has been our leader affords me no joy," he confessed. But Article Two, he insisted, was defensible, not only because it was the basis on which a majority could be mustered but also because, in the long run, the workers would regain their contribution. When Article Two was put to the vote, it passed overwhelmingly, 486 to 30; and two days later, on April 1, 1910, the law was approved in its entirety with only four dissenting votes. Among the Socialists, Guesde remained adamant and opposed, but the rest stood more or less solidly behind Jaurès.

In voting for a program of workers' pensions, Parliament took one more step toward establishing a system of social security. But Jaurès attributed to the reform a significance far wider than that. The pension law, he wrote, "signals the increasing influence of the Socialist Party. It is our victory. Only our presence and our pressure forced republicans, who scorn our ideal of social justice, to take another step toward it. When the ocean swells, it uproots even the deeply embedded weeds and stones and shells."[137] These words, as the future would reveal, were better poetry than history. The pension law itself did not provide adequate payments; nor did it usher in a great era of reforms inspired by Socialism. Once again, Jaurès was exaggerating both the importance of certain reforms and the influence of his party. But in the current of 1910, when Socialism seemed everywhere on the rise, it is not so surprising that he should have been carried away. Across Europe the Socialist parties counted a steadily increasing number of members and voters; in France, the S.F.I.O., which reached a widening public through its four dailies, its score of weeklies, its three serious reviews, flew its flag over two hundred city halls and seated more than fifty deputies in the Chamber.[138] Nothing was more human, in an age grown bleak with conservatism and nationalism, than that Jaurès should seize upon these data to predict an increasing Socialist influence. Without that image of the future, he could scarcely have continued.

VII

Reforms were the exception in Briand's France and not the rule. As the nation prepared for the general elections of 1910, the conservative drift of French politics became increasingly clear. Both the reactionary Right and the Radical Left were gliding toward the Center, so that the moderates of the Alliance démocratique, erstwhile Opportunists and Progressists, again set the norm for French politics. For this convergence at the point of retrenchment, several factors were responsible. Rightists like the wily Jacques Piou understood that moderate republicans were reliable allies in the quest for social order; Radicals who chose to defy the dicta of their own party found among the Centrists a community of anti-Socialist interest; and finally Briand, from his crucial platform above the republican majority, strove to erase the lines that had traditionally separated the non-Socialist parties.

On April 10 at Saint-Chamond in the Loire, the Premier, in the course of an important policy speech, spoke these revealing words: "I will not write across the door of the Republic: entry is forbidden for some."[139] It was Briand's invitation to a new kind of party, excluding none but extremists and erasing all sharp doctrinal lines. With such a party in mind, the Premier and his friends organized the Comité de la rue de Valois, in which certain moderates and Radicals united around a program of "consolidation and appeasement." But on the Extreme Right, where some monarchists were taking heart again, and on the Extreme Left, where the Socialists and most of the Radical-Socialists demanded a full program of reforms, the spirit of partisanship remained intact. As their recent congresses indicated, neither Socialists nor Radical-Socialists were disinclined to strike electoral alliances, which were certain, despite conspicuous defections among the Radicals, to be of importance.

For Jaurès the election campaign came as a heavy burden. Running as he did from a semirural constituency in the Tarn, he was forced, in the midst of endless parliamentary and journalistic duties, to climb the village hills again and to tramp the city streets in order to ensure his victory. Early in the campaign, his old friend Calvignac, still Socialist mayor of Carmaux, warned Jaurès that his enemies — the Solages clan, the priests, the conservative editors — were more determined than ever to retire him from politics. Though the Marquis de Solages was not himself a candidate, extensive financial resources were put at the disposal of the conservative Falgueyrettes. The valley of the Tarn once again echoed with bitter epithets: Jaurès the Antichrist, Jaurès the Antipatriot, Jaurès the Communist! The conservative effort was all the more powerful because the Radicals ran a candidate of their own in the second electoral district of Albi, diverting support which the *tarnais* might otherwise have won. The first ballot, on April 24, was thus inconclusive, and Jaurès was forced to meet Falgueyrettes in the runoff of May 8.

Now he returned to his district where he walked among his people, listened to them, bantered with them, shared their confidences. Not a bit of it was patronizing; not a note of it was false. Franz Toussaint, poet and critic who followed him around, has left a description of this tour among the *carmausins*:

Good-natured and cheerful, Jaurès circulated from café to café. He talked with both supporters and opponents, mainly about their work in the fields, or about their personal problems, or about events of local interest. In one street, we saw a campaign manager for Falgueyrettes seated in front of his house. Jaurès knew that the daughter of this good man had just given birth. "Dubosc!" he called out. "I am very happy. I understand that your Louise is doing very well. I'm sending her some chocolates this evening, but don't say they're from me." Dubosc sat speechless and astonished.[140]

When, on April 28, the Radical and Radical-Socialist Federation of the Tarn agreed to support Jaurès in the runoff, his victory was assured. Late in the evening of May 8, Calvignac burst into the modest living room of the *carmausin* Barthe, where Jaurès sat conversing, and announced the good news. Socialism had scored over conservatism, 6445 to 5843. Jaurès then hurried to the City Hall where, in a few moving words, he paid tribute to those who had gathered to honor him: "Citizens, those laurels you are planting along the road of liberty will take root and become mighty trees!"[141]

In the nation as a whole, the election revealed shifts toward both the extreme Left and the moderate Center. For the first time, the Socialists polled more than a million votes (1,106,000) and increased their deputation in the Chamber from fifty-four to seventy-six. The Independent Socialists also added a deputy, returning to the Chamber thirty strong. On the other hand, the moderates of the Center (Progressists and Left Republicans) returned 153 deputies, an increase of eleven, while the Radicals and Radical-Socialists, capturing 252 seats, and the reactionaries, holding eighty-eight, suffered losses of seventeen and eight respectively. In 1906 the Radicals and Independent Socialists together enjoyed an absolute majority; but in 1910, if the majority were not formed with the help of the Socialists, it would be composed of Radicals and moderates. Frenchmen had again voted Left; and again the prospects seemed bright for the Center.

On June 28, 1910, almost three weeks after his ministerial declaration, Briand won an overwhelming vote of confidence.[142] In the debate that preceded the final tally, no one spoke more enthusiastically for Briand's new order than Édouard Aynard, long a powerful figure among the Progressists, who thus acknowledged the Premier's high standing in the political Center. In the new Parliament the deputies would be "more responsive than ever to special interests and to the pressure of the great press. Those heroic times, when great ideas were in conflict, faded away. We had crossed into the 'Republic of Pals.'"[143]

The sky was leaden with clouds of conservatism when Briand resumed power; less than five months later, at the time of the great railroad strike of 1910, the clouds burst, driving Jaurès and his friends into bitter opposition to the ministry.

VIII

"On none of the railroads," *L'Humanité* reported in July, "do workers earn more than 1300 francs a year, even after fifteen and twenty years of service. . . . This past year, the gross income of the companies was 1,702,375,276 francs and their profit 746,703,582 francs."[144] Among French workers, the railwaymen had suffered more than most. While their wages had risen only slightly over a thirty-year period, they were forced to cope with constantly increasing living costs. Such were the conditions which led the two major railway unions, the Syndicat national des chemins de fer and the Fédération des mécaniciens et chauffeurs, to demand of the companies a minimum wage of 1825 francs and strict enforcement of the six-day week. The companies, however, in spite of their eminently favorable economic position, refused to bargain on the basis of these terms or even to discuss them. Thus, the Syndicat national, though one of the least revolutionary unions in the C.G.T., decided on July 17 to prepare for a general strike of railwaymen.[145]

The reaction from the government and from the leading Paris dailies was immediate and hostile. The railwaymen, they insisted in chorus, could not claim the same freedom to strike which other workers enjoyed. "Communications, national defense, the food supply, and business would all be threatened by a sudden tieup of the railroads," wrote Suarez in summarizing Briand's position.[146] "A strike of railwaymen," *Le Temps* asserted on July 2, "would be, as M. Barthou has said, a 'national crime.'" The Socialists and the syndicalists however, who had publicized the economic plight of the railwaymen, insisted just as vehemently that the right to strike belonged to all workers. It seemed clear by the fall of 1910 that a railroad strike would sharpen class lines, divide the Chamber, and demonstrate that France was indeed two nations.

In October the workers crossed the Rubicon. The strike began against the Compagnie du Nord, which, since May of that year, had eliminated overtime work without providing any compensatory wage increase. On October 8, the company finally made an offer, agreeing to increase to five francs a day the wages of those who earned less than that, but offering nothing to the rest. The unions found the offer completely unsatisfactory, and on October 10, at 1 A.M., they announced a strike against the Compagnie du Nord. Just a day later, they called for a general strike against all railroad lines, including those operated by the State.

The response of management was defiant, as expected, and the Compagnie du Nord dismissed several labor leaders, including Taffin, president of the Fédération des mécaniciens. Bitterness erupted from the strike like water from a geyser. To management's intransigence labor responded with collective courage and individual acts of sabotage. But the sabotage proved costly to the workers, for it provided all the pretext the government needed to intervene and tip the scales against the strikers.

Hardly had the strike begun when Briand, who had once drawn a blueprint for the general strike, mapped plans to crush it. Late on the night of October 11, before an emergency Cabinet meeting at the Ministry of the Interior, he proposed to break the strike by conscripting the railwaymen into the army, thus placing them under direct governmental command. So extreme was the plan that the Premier met opposition from Millerand, Viviani, and Barthou, all of whom feared the political consequences of such a move. Briand stood firm, however, and on October 12, he issued the decree conscripting the railwaymen of the five major lines for a period of twenty-one days.[147]

Once committed to his act of strike-breaking, Briand yielded not an inch. Ignoring the concrete issues in dispute, he denounced the aims of syndicalism as sabotage and revolution; charging that the railroad strike threatened to cripple the defenses of France, he explained his decision as a commandment of his patriotic conscience. The major Paris dailies showered their praise on Briand and echoed his words. "The only issue," asserted *Le Temps* on October 16, "is between anarchy and law." But the spokesmen of Socialism, Jaurès chief among them, accepted no such explanations. The intervention of the government, they charged, was but its latest, most far-reaching attempt to cripple the labor movement. On the night of October 14, before an overflow crowd of workers at the Salle du Manège in the rue Saint Paul, Jaurès brought down on the heads of self-styled patriots his monumental wrath: "What patriots they are, these masters of ours! . . . They say that we Socialists profane the nation; but when they confound the selfish interests of the railroad companies with those of the entire nation, they make a mockery of patriotism."[148]

But the strikers' will and the Socialists' sympathy were futile weapons against Briand's heavy artillery. Faced with court-martials as army deserters, the workers capitulated on October 17, while management and the ministry celebrated a patriotic victory. Jaurès warned, however, that the issue was not yet closed: "The ministers are mistaken if they think they're finished with the railwaymen."[149] For if the strikers were silenced, the Socialist deputies were not. Within a week, when Parliament reconvened, they interpellated the government on its role in the recent strike.

From October 25 to October 30, Briand faced a parade of unfriendly Socialist critics — the ex-railroader Jean Colly, the scholarly Albert

Thomas, the blunt Jean Bouveri — all of whom taunted the Premier with reminders of his revolutionary past. On October 29, Jaurès rose to address the Chamber. Reviewing the serious economic plight of the railwaymen, he located the cause of the strike in the refusal of management to bargain and of the government to mediate. In suppressing the strike, he charged, the ministry had stripped the workers of their most effective weapon against the companies. But at the culmination of his oration, he spoke movingly of betrayal and disillusion, of the workers' bitter realization that their present enemies were the very men who once had shaped their dreams. Wheeling round to Briand, Millerand, and Viviani, he scored them directly:

I remember (and perhaps you have forgotten now that you are men of power) — I remember the great popular meetings we addressed together. I recall old workers, gone today, rough-hewn men near the end of their lives, who wondered if it had not all been futile. And I recall young men, adolescents of fourteen, fifteen, and sixteen, their eyes ablaze with a new faith as they listened to our program. . . . Today they are men of thirty or thirty-five, and when they read in their papers that it is you — Millerand, Viviani, and Briand — who are denying them the right to strike, they must be asking themselves if life isn't, after all, a bad dream! [150]

When Jaurès returned to his seat, he was cheered not only by his Socialist comrades but by many on the Radical Left. His speech had been no mere quixotic gesture, but an indictment powerful enough to jeopardize the life of the ministry. Briand, however, did not lose his *sang-froid*. In replying to the Socialist interpellations, he relied heavily on patriotic themes. The right to strike, he asserted, "must yield before the right of the society to live." The government could not suffer the sabotage of the C.G.T. and its will to revolution which threatened to paralyze France and expose her to foreign invasion.

As he spoke, Briand drew applause from all sectors of the House except the Extreme Left. It was evident that even certain Radical-Socialists, though they were sincere friends of labor, recoiled before the danger of national weakness during a prolonged railroad strike. Sensing his strong hold over the Chamber, Briand suddenly grew careless and uttered words that smacked strongly of dictatorship: "If the government had not found some law by which it could have protected France and remained master of her frontiers, if it had not been able to control the railroads, which are an essential part of our national defense, it would have acted illegally." For a moment the deputies sat in tense silence, while the full impact of these startling words sank into their consciousness. Then bedlam broke loose in a scene later described by Jules Romains: "At these words, the whole Socialist group and a whole crowd of Radicals had jumped up, shouting and yelling, shaking their fists, standing on their chairs, leaving their seats and crowding down in front of the tribune. . . . Cruppi had screamed; Jaurès, red in the face, had wielded his Olympian thunders; Jules Guesde, with the air of a prosecutor under the Terror, had announced that he would move an impeachment."[151]

Above shouts of "Resign! Resign!" an unruffled, tenacious Briand tried to explain away his rash words: though he had always worked within the law, he was merely pointing out that in certain national emergencies he, like Danton before him, might act beyond the law. Against an uproar that would not subside, the Premier talked on until eight in the evening. Then, the deputies, agitated and confused, decided to adjourn the debate until the following day; by his own admission, Briand wanted only to "go home and eat."[152] On October 30, in an atmosphere of calm, the Premier won back most of his support. When Raynaud, a Radical deputy from the Charente, moved that the Chamber "approve the actions of the government in safeguarding vital national interests," the resolution passed easily, 329 to 183. Though the Socialists opposed him unanimously, Briand won support from reactionaries, moderates, Radicals, and half the Radical-Socialists.

From the October crisis, the first great test for the Parliament of 1910, Jaurès and his friends learned several sad political lessons. It proved that the Right and Center, as the vulgar Léon Daudet wrote, "looked upon Briand as their savior, the most venal, deceptive personality yet spawned in the dung of the Republic."[153] But it demonstrated further that when the issue was one of social conflict, the Radicals and many Radical-Socialists likewise supported the Premier. Without new leadership and clear direction, Radicalism seemed certain to lose all political bearings. And finally, it revealed that on crucial issues, neither the S.F.I.O. nor the C.G.T., separately or together, had the decisive influence which Jaurès was wont to claim. Despite their protests and interpellations, a major strike had been broken and without great difficulty. The main chance for the Socialists remained the defection of the Radicals from the governmental majority.

On November 2, only three days after his great victory in the Chamber, Briand resigned. His intention was not to relinquish power but rather to strengthen it by shuffling his ministry. President Fallières reinvested him with office, and on November 3 he formed a government in which ministers like Viviani and Millerand gave way to pliant Radicals and Radical-Socialists. When Jaurès examined the ministerial list, letting his eye wander across the names of Klotz, Faure, Puesch, and Raynaud, he could only decry "the incredible triumph of mediocrity."[154]

If Briand's aim was to attract indecisive Radical-Socialists into his camp, he was not conspicuously successful. When the Chamber accorded him a vote of confidence on November 8, his margin had been cut from the substantial 146 of October 30 to an unimpressive eighty-seven. Deserted by the staunchest Catholics, who could not abide the inclusion of well-known Masons in the government, Briand now lost many Radical-Socialists who determined to resist his tactics of domestication. Over the next three months, the ministry reeled under a barrage of interpellations, sometimes from the Socialists, more often from the Radical-Socialists. They pounced on one issue after another — the refusal of the railroad companies to rehire dismissed strikers, the reappearance of the teaching congregations, the murky financial maneuvers in the Congo — and accused the government of complacency or compliance.

Something new was thus astir in French politics, a protest against the nihilistic conservatism of *briandisme*. It came mainly, as Jaurès had hoped, from the camp of Radicalism, where the search for strong leadership and clear issues became increasingly determined. The key figure in that search was the ambitious Caillaux, who, in a dynamic speech at Lille on January 8, assumed leadership of the anti-Briand forces and pumped life into the dying creed of Radicalism. The Premier knew that without the Radicals his days were numbered, and on February 27, though he hadn't suffered a single adverse note, he resigned from office. It was a bloodless victory for Caillaux, and, momentarily, a defeat for Briand's national moderate party.

When Jaurès linked the demise of Briand to the defeat of the railwaymen, he was well off the mark; but when he predicted a time of clearer political definition, his reasoning was sound.[155] For in selecting a new Premier, Fallières had perforce to choose among the leaders of the anti-Briand Left. But the President could and did pass over Caillaux and Maurice Berteaux, outstanding candidates among the Radical-Socialists, calling finally on a colorless Senator from the Gironde, Ernest Monis, to form a government. In selecting his ministers, however, Monis beckoned to the *vedettes* of Radical-Socialism, and on March 2, 1911, he formed a government which included Caillaux, Berteaux, Jean Cruppi, and Paul-Boncour. More than any other ministry since 1905, this one mirrored the spirit of the bloc, and it seemed properly symbolic that several of its members made an immediate pilgrimage to the home of "le petit père" Combes.

On March 6, when Monis won his vote of confidence, the Socialists abstained. If they were hopeful of a new turn in French politics, they remained cautious, even skeptical. Monis was, after all, a member of the Alliance démocratique; and his ministry included their old antagonist Delcassé, while its moving spirits were Caillaux and Berteaux, who had shifted their ambitions from the world of high finance to that of politics.[156] In his ministerial declaration, Monis had come out for the income tax, electoral reform, and the improvement of primary education. But the Socialists wondered, and for good reason, whether the Radicals, so divided on principle and diverse in background, could really practice what Monis now preached.[157] For the time being, their soundest policy seemed watchful waiting.

For fifteen weeks the ministry rattled along without conspicuous zeal or a single major accomplishment. On June 23, time ran out for Monis, who fell from office over a minor question of military organization, and Caillaux finally donned the mantle of Premier. Though the new ministry won a clear vote of confidence, the Socialists this time sided with the opposition. For when Caillaux took a strong line against sabotage by public employees, as he did in his ministerial declaration; when, in practical effect, he turned his back on efforts to force the private railway companies to rehire the *cheminots* dismissed during the recent strike, he seemed even less the Radical than Monis.[158] Undoubtedly, Caillaux was trying, and with considerable success, to conciliate all factions within Radicalism. But his compromises gave Jaurès and his friends little to cheer about. As yet, they had no substantial reason to welcome the reign of Caillaux.

IX

Years of insurgency these were, years of thunder and lightning, of protest and proclamation. Yet the harvest Jaurès reaped seemed small, the personal fatigue he suffered great. Was his protest then a hollow cry, his life a futile gesture? Nourished early on German philosophy, he was later sustained by the teachings of Kant. "Is not a righteous man still supported," the wise man of Königsberg asked rhetorically, "by the consciousness of having upheld and done honor to mankind in his own person, even in the greatest misfortunes of life, which he might have avoided if he could only have disregarded his duty?" Jaurès, one feels, was so supported.

And what was that duty? To effect the humanistic, the socialist revolution, to organize a community free of social and moral distortions. In February of 1911, Jaurès traveled to Toulouse to lecture on Tolstoy, his moral genius and ideological failures. In the course of that celebrated oration, he defined the revolution and its deepest consequences:

In our narrow, confined existence, we tend to forget the essence of life. . . . All of us, whatever our occupation or class, are equally guilty: the employer is lost in the running of his business; the workers, sunk in the abyss of their misery, raise their heads only to cry in protest; we, the politicians, are lost in daily battles and corridor intrigues. All of us forget that before everything else, we are men, ephemeral beings lost in the immense universe, so full of terrors. We are inclined to neglect the search for the real meaning of life, to ignore the real goals — serenity of the spirit and sublimity of the heart. . . . To reach them — that is the revolution.[159]

However impressionistic, the phrases Jaurès used were no mere rhetoric but a call to revolution, social in substance and psychological in consequences, which should free men from bondage to their misery. Some fifteen years earlier, when he wrote with searing indignation of the moral corrosion in contemporary society, he revealed his Balzacian contempt for "capitalist man" and by converse his vision (conviction mingled with hope) of "socialist man." Hostile critics had often charged that a socialist order would be cultural desert, where the luxuries and pleasures which rendered life joyous would disappear. But Jaurès replied:

Yes, when capitalism will have yielded to socialism, many of our vile and hideous forms of luxury will indeed disappear. First, the luxury which Diderot so forcefully calls *le luxe de misère*, that of the poor or near-poor, who try to deceive others or themselves by cheap and pitiful display; the luxury of sickness and debility, that of stomachs ruined by the dissoluteness of parasitical living; the luxury of idleness, that of bourgeois ladies, whose frivolous upbringing has made them useless and incapable of any creative activity; the luxury of vanity, which plays havoc in a society where money is the universal standard; the luxury of deceit and intrigue, that of shady financiers luring their victims, of quack doctors playing up to wealthy patients, of countless others in our cheating society; and finally, the supreme luxury of class, the luxury of domination, haughtiness, power, the luxury of our ruling class.[160]

Jaurès worked to expand his movement, to organize its pressure on the State, to effect the great social transformation. Yet the results were meager; the opposition was formidable; the means seemed inadequate to the end. The resiliency of Jaurès, his capacity to pass on from sore discouragement to renewed affirmation, found its source in conviction, the belief that Socialism not only would but also — and it was the greater support — should triumph. Writing about the British Labor Party, R. H. Tawney once defined the essentials for the strength of any Socialist movement: "Onions can be eaten leaf by leaf, but you cannot skin a live tiger paw by paw; vivisection is its trade, and it does the skinning first. If the Labour Party is to tackle its job with some hope of success, it must mobilise behind it a body of conviction as resolute and informed as the opposition in front of it." That resolution Jaurès had; it sustained him and strengthened his party.

13

The Last Crusade
for Peace, 1911-1914

I

Whenever summer arrived, Jaurès grew impatient in Paris,
and his thoughts then drifted to the Tarn. In Paris he lived at the front
of the political battle, but at Bessoulet he could reflect, relax, and, what
was most important, converse with friends and neighbors — workers and
peasants, teachers and students: "Whenever neighbors dropped in on
Jaurès at Bessoulet, they might find him in shirtsleeves and straw hat.
At once he would ask: 'You will have something to eat with us?' Then,
he would bring in some ham and good wine. He would speak of wines,
of the heavens, and of the earth. To those who asked him about that
'future' for which he was sacrificing all of his present, he would say:
'We will accomplish something worthwhile!' "[1]

In the summer of 1911, however, Jaurès returned to Bessoulet for
reasons other than relaxation. He was spending a few days with his
family before setting sail for South America within a matter of weeks.
There, for the three fall months, he would lecture in Brazil, Uruguay,
and Argentina on the ideals and history of Socialism. When he received
the invitation from an Argentinian delegate to the Congress of Copenhagen in 1910, Jaurès had accepted enthusiastically. The prospect of new

lands and peoples excited him, as did the fee of 100,000 francs, which would help to convert *L'Humanité* into a six-page daily. He welcomed especially the chance to preach peace and Socialism among distant Latin Americans as he had among neighboring Europeans. But all was not happy anticipation that July; for while Jaurès prepared his departure, the rivalry over Morocco again exploded into a full-scale European crisis.

The Franco-German Agreement of 1909, as time proved, had solved nothing in Morocco. To French policy-makers, whether in the ministry or in Parliament, "political prodominance" ultimately meant a protectorate, an interpretation shared, on the basis of secret treaties, by Italy, Spain, and England. As early as November 22, 1909, when Morocco was under debate in the Chamber, the expansionist temper of both ministers and deputies was clearly apparent. In an effort to remove a *casus belli*, Jaurès had risen to demand immediate evacuation of French troops from the Chaouia, the hinterland of Casablanca, and the Oudjda, the frontier district of the east. But when Stéphen Pichon, Foreign Minister under both Clemenceau and Briand, defended the occupation as the sole guarantee of internal order, he won an overwhelming vote of support. All the while, the German expansionists, oscillating between anger and frustration, waited watchfully. The economic rewards they had anticipated under the 1909 Agreement failed to materialize, and they were of no mind, these convinced imperialists beyond the Rhine, to bury their claims without a whimper.

The beginning of the Monis ministry in March, 1911, coincided with the outbreak of fresh disturbances in Morocco. Resentful of French occupation, certain tribes struck out at both the authority of Moulay Hafid and the pretensions of the European settlers. In the subsequent disorders, the French, whose presence had touched them off, found an excuse for more extensive occupation. Within this circle of cause and effect, Moroccan independence was to be finally destroyed.

By the end of April, the rioting around Fez had become so serious that the Sultan requested French assistance in restoring order. Without consulting Parliament, then in Easter recess, the government immediately answered the Sultan's call. On April 26, despite the gravity of its commitment, the ministry ordered General Moinier to move his 25,000 men from Casablanca to Fez. Four weeks later, French troops occupied Fez, and the flame of Moroccan independence flickered low. Spain then reacted by occupying that northern zone which she claimed as her preserve under the secret accord of 1904. Paris, still unwilling to admit that the occupation of Fez violated the Act of Algeciras, filed a strong protest with Madrid; but Spain's blunt interpretation, whatever the protestation of Paris, tore the mask of ambiguity from French policy.

These dangerous events worried Jaurès and made him indignant. When he interpellated Foreign Minister Cruppi on June 16, he reminded the Chamber that every new aggression in Morocco had carried France another step away from the Act of Algeciras and toward final conquest:

A few years ago, when we began our occupation of the Chaouia, . . . I said: you will not stop there, but you will be driven, by evidence of internal disorder and by the ambition of our generals, to continue your aggressions. I said to M. Clemenceau: "You will go to Fez." And he replied: "Why not to Mecca?" Gentlemen, I don't know whether we will go to Mecca, but we are in Fez. And I charge that since the accession of the new Sultan, our policy has been one long trangression of the treaty of Algeciras.[2]

These latest moves, Jaurès warned, would provoke both a virulent anti-French nationalism among the Arabs and a policy of retaliation by the Germans. To safeguard the peace of Europe and the independence of the Sultan, the French had to withdraw their troops from Moroccan soil.

Once he had finished, only the Socialists applauded, while the majority, Caillaux included, reserved their support for Cruppi. In assuring the House that the government's policy, while it aimed to forward French interest, did not violate the Act of Algeciras, the Foreign Minister, in Tardieu's words, "demolished the fantastic arguments of M. Jaurès."[3] But in less than two weeks, when Berlin dived into troubled Moroccan waters, the predictions of Jaurès seemed considerably less fantastic than the assurances of Cruppi.

The German Chancellorship had passed in 1909 from the brilliant Bülow to the unimaginative Theobald von Bethmann-Hollweg, who permitted the conduct of German diplomacy to fall largely into the hands of Alfred von Kiderlen-Waechter, the able but gruff Secretary of State for Foreign Affairs. Successful diplomacy, in the guidebook of Kiderlen, depended on cold nerve and effective force, and in his approach to the Moroccan question he supplied both of these ingredients. In April, Jules Cambon, the French Ambassador to Berlin, sought to persuade German authorities that France, despite her drive to Fez, had no intention of altering the status of Morocco. While acknowledging both the French mandate to restore order and the assurances of Cambon, Kiderlen ominously noted that "events are sometimes more powerful than we assume."[4]

Thus, though Berlin appeared calm on the surface, Kiderlen outlined a plan for German retaliation, which won the strong support of disgruntled imperialists. In a memorandum of May 3, he proposed the German occupation of Agadir and Mogador, ports on Morocco's west coast. Berlin could justify so provocative a move in phrases already coined by France; since her nationals had important commercial interests in these western ports, Germany was obliged to protect their life and property. Behind this smokescreen of national interest, of course, Kiderlen's object was a game of blackmail. Once lodged in western Morocco, Germany would agree to evacuate it only if France, sacrificing part of her far-flung Empire, offered territorial compensation. When Kiderlen's heavy-handed proposal won the Kaiser's support, the stage was set for the second Moroccan crisis.

Despite Cruppi's public self-assurance, the Monis ministry was not of one mind on the consequences of the Fez expedition. A few ministers, led by Caillaux, argued that Germany would never agree to a French protectorate over Morocco unless she received some adequate compensation. To document their contention they pointed to the bellicosity of the German press and the enigmatic language of Kiderlen. Thus, in order to forestall a crisis, Caillaux went behind the Premier's back and, through the agency of certain international bankers, initiated discussions with Berlin on the question of compensation.[5] The negotiations finally pointed to a possible partition of the French Congo, but Kiderlen, pretending only mild interest, suddenly broke off the discussions in mid-June and departed for an extended holiday at Kissingen. Ambassador Cambon followed him there, and in an interview of June 21 reopened the strange negotiations. Though the cagey Kiderlen remained vague, he indicated that Germany would bargain when he said to Cambon: "Go to Paris and come back with something concrete."

By the time Cambon arrived in Paris, the Monis ministry had given way to a government headed by Caillaux. The new Foreign Minister was Justin de Selves, Senator and ex-Prefect, who had parlayed family ties with Freycinet into a political career. Bureaucratic and unimaginative, De Selves was hardly the man to engage in a subtle diplomatic dialectic with the Germans. But Caillaux was, and Cambon was about to return to Germany when Kiderlen abandoned conversation for a *coup de force*. On July 1, at noon, the German Ambassador to France, Baron de Schoen, appeared at the Quai d'Orsay and informed De Selves that the Imperial Government was sending a warship to Agadir in order to protect the life and property of German nationals. At that very moment, in fact, the gunboat *Panther* was already anchored in the waters of Agadir, a symbol of Berlin's muscular diplomacy. French nationalists, who craved the reduction of Germany even more than the conquest of Morocco, seized upon the news to demand the long-awaited showdown of force. For the second time in half a dozen years, France and Germany seemed ready to unsheath their swords for war.

When the story of Agadir broke, Parliament was in recess, but an agitated Jaurès took to the pages of *L'Humanité* to demand "an immediate termination of our imperialistic policy" in Morocco.[6] In the nationalistic mood of 1911, however, his arguments carried little weight outside working-class circles; elsewhere his appeal for peace was drowned out in a patriotic cacophony. In the tense summer of Agadir, the triumph of diplomacy over war depended less on the influence of Socialism than on the policy of Caillaux. While De Selves and Delcassé's bureaucrats at the Quai d'Orsay balked at negotiations with Berlin, the Premier went over the head of his own Foreign Minister and resumed discussions with Germany. Neither pacifism nor anticolonialism directed Caillaux's efforts, but rather the conviction that France could finally win Morocco through the time-tested method of bargaining.

All was secret, all was uncertain as the days of July ticked away. At Bessoulet, a worried Jaurès read the newspapers, sent off daily articles, and with considerable hesitation readied himself for his mission to South America. By the sharpest twist of irony, he would advocate in distant lands a peace seriously threatened at home.

II

In the last weeks of July, 1911, Jaurès traveled through Spain and into Portugal, excited, curious, fascinated by the topography and color of the Iberian landscape.[7] On July 20, he arrived at Lisbon, capital of the newly established Portuguese Republic, where the government and the republican press welcomed him effusively. Upon entering the Portuguese Chamber of Deputies, he was greeted with cries of: *Viva Jaurès! Viva la Republica Francesa!*

Through frequent letters, he shared both his experiences and feelings with his family. To young Louis he wrote with fatherly affection: "I am sending you a small packet of stamps. Some day they will be valuable since, as you can see, they are royal stamps, across which the new government has printed the word Republic."[8] And to Louise, he wrote: "I think of you and Louis constantly. Write me at once, so that when I arrive at Rio I will have news of you."[9]

On July 24, he boarded the *Aragon* and began a seventeen-day voyage across the Atlantic, during which he studied the Portuguese language and practiced his Spanish by reading *Don Quijote*. When the ship finally anchored in the beautiful harbor of Rio on August 9, a delegation of Socialists and journalists awaited Jaurès, greeted him warmly, and escorted him to a flower-bedecked room in the International Hotel. After two whirlwind weeks of lecturing in Brazil, he traveled on to Uruguay, arriving at Montevideo on September 4. Though the local landowners, capitalists, and clergy opposed his visit bitterly, he delivered six lectures to large and appreciative audiences. In Argentina, however, where the Socialist movement was strongest, he made his greatest impact. In Buenos Aires he spoke eight times, and in each of his orations, he demonstrated a sure grasp of Latin American conditions. "He did not come to us with effusive Latin hymns," wrote Juan Justo, the leader of the Argentinian Socialist Party. "He showed his interest in our changing societies by his knowledge of our writers and by his intrepid analysis of our key local issues."[10]

What he could not discover in books, Jaurès sought to learn from first-hand experience. In a matter of weeks, he spoke to the youth of Argentina, visited poverty-stricken peasants, traveled through enormous landed estates, met with and encouraged the Socialists. As his visit drew to an end, Antonio Tomasso, Secretary of the Argentinian Socialist Party, spoke of "the enormous debt we owe him for his magnificent effort on our behalf."[11]

On October 9, Jaurès boarded the *Amazone* for the return voyage, which ended three weeks later when he debarked at Bordeaux. His trip had sharpened his sense of history and strengthened his belief in progress. When he walked among the young Socialists of Latin America, he could foresee the coming of a time, not too far distant, when under-developed, near-feudal countries would destroy colonialism and abolish the poverty it imposed. Even as he sailed back to France, the insurgents of China had overturned the decrepit monarchy of the Manchus and established a republic. The throttle of history was open wide, and the signs portended a world free of its timeless misery. But only—and it was the concern that consumed Jaurès—only if the peace were saved.

III

While Jaurès traveled through South America, the Agadir crisis carried Europe to the brink of war. By his *coup de force*, Kiderlen thought to exact blackmail from France; though he was willing, given the clear military superiority of Germany, to insinuate a readiness for war, he banked heavily on the triumph of diplomacy.[12] Caillaux understood his game and negotiated. In sweltering July days, when temperatures and tempers flared, it was no easy matter to bargain. On July 16, Kiderlen informed an astonished Cambon that the French cost for a Moroccan protectorate would be nothing less than the cession of the entire Congo to Germany. At the same time, London publicly intervened in the crisis to strengthen the hand of De Selves and the anti-Caillaux clique at the Quai d'Orsay. Lloyd George, the flamboyant Welshman who was then Chancellor of the Exchequer, spoke for Asquith's Liberal government when he asserted that England, however pacific at heart, preferred war to a humiliating peace. While England might thereby have precipitated a war, she actually forced Germany to adopt a more moderate position. Thus, though the negotiations went on for weeks and then months, they culminated, in November, 1911, in a treaty to divide the African spoils.

Throughout the crisis, the Socialists and trade unionists on both sides of the Rhine released a flood of propaganda in the cause of peace. At impressive rallies and in countless proclamations, French and German Socialists warned their respective governments that they stood united behind the antiwar resolutions of Stuttgart and Copenhagen. On July 28, delegates of the C.G.T. traveled to Berlin and there, at the height of the crisis, clasped hands with German workers in a stirring show of solidarity. Out of such demonstrations the S.F.I.O. and the C.G.T. created the image of a working-class movement, both internationalist and pacifist, which dominated the thoughts of the nationalists. Yet the evidence hardly supports the contention of Socialist and syndicalist spokesmen that their opposition to war turned the tide for peace; for in the resolution of the second Moroccan crisis the more decisive influence was the will of Caillaux.

Unshaken by the sharp winds of French nationalism, the Premier never relinquished the reins of diplomacy. Through the offices of his private representative Fondère, he made clear to the Germans that his government would barter part of the Congo for a French protectorate over Morocco. With so concrete a basis for bargaining, Cambon and Kiderlen began serious talks, which finally resulted in the Franco-German Convention of November 4. After two crises and seven years of friction, Germany now relinquished her claims to Morocco, while France ceded to her some 265,000 square kilometers of territory lying between the Cameroons and the Belgian Congo.

In settling the Moroccan crisis peacefully, Caillaux set himself against a current of anti-German chauvinism which infected the republican Center as well as the nationalistic Right, which spread from the small towns of Radicalism to the student quarters of Paris. "The German fife has rallied France," exclaimed Paul Deschanel at the height of the crisis, and his words found their echo in the ministerial pronouncements of Delcassé and Klotz.[13] Thus, when Caillaux finally resolved the conflict by treaty, he laid himself open to criticism that was bitter and unsparing. In the eyes of conservatives, he was already the sinner of the income tax; now he was the criminal of the Congo Treaty. But Caillaux held his ground. It was a striking performance which suggested that Radicalism had found a leader of fortitude, and Socialism an important ally.[14]

Born to wealth and distinction, the monocled, impeccably attired Caillaux seemed the least likely champion of the people. One wonders, in fact, why he bothered with politics at all. Briand rose from obscurity through political power, but Caillaux, when he descended to the hurly-burly of daily politics, risked an already gratifying private life. It was probably ambition that charted his course, and a heady sense of his natural superiority. Once settled into public life, he emerged, through his advocacy of the income tax, as a man of the Left; but little in his political posture suggested a Socialist in financier's clothing. His interest in fiscal reform reflected the financial technician who hoped to lend order to a chaotic tax structure, rather than a social radical who resented its inequalities. As for his advocacy of peace in 1911, it had its roots less in lofty idealism than in a kind of hard-headed realism. While Jaurès stood on the high ground of anti-imperialism, Caillaux consistently supported the Moroccan adventure. In ruling out war during the Agadir crisis, Caillaux was guided by his conviction that France was militarily unprepared. In the midst of the crisis, he asked General Joffre whether the French army, as it stood, had a seventy per cent chance of success in a war with Germany. The Chief of Staff thought not. "Very well," the Premier then declared. "We will negotiate."[15]

So wide was the gap between the realistic technician Caillaux and the visionary Socialist Jaurès that their relationship could never be one of intimate collaboration. For Caillaux, at heart an ardent capitalist, the goal of political action was hardly to transform the social system but rather to preserve it by rationalizing its functions. Through diplomacy and bargaining, he would avoid those wars which were the breeding ground of revolution; through cautious concessions, he would relieve the tensions that had developed between the classes. Yet against the unyielding conservatism and the ultranationalism of the immediate prewar years, Caillaux and Jaurès were gradually drawn together in an alliance of convenience. For Caillaux, though more essentially conservative than radical, had — and it was rare in republican ranks — the courage of his strong convictions. In an age when ambitious men of humble origin bent to the material advantages offered in conservative circles, Caillaux was peculiarly immune to such seduction; "he would remain indifferent to the attractions of money and social position, the joys of which he had already exhausted in his youth."[16] Thus, like Ferry before him or Combes, he took seriously his commitment to certain basic reforms; and like Rouvier, he could withstand the insistent demands of the nationalists and negotiate, even with Germany. The Socialists, Jaurès felt, still had to depend on those bourgeois republicans who could carry through partial reforms and preserve the peace. Thus, when Caillaux pressed for the income tax and an international *détente*, rousing the furious opposition not only of reactionaries but of moderates too, he earned the support, albeit critical, of Jaurès and his friends.

The ink was hardly dry on the Congo treaty when Jaurès returned to the political wars; but the agreement had already stirred opposition on both sides of the Rhine. In Germany, the arch-imperialists, uncompromising over Berlin's abandonment of Morocco, forced the resignation of Colonial Minister Lindquist; and in France, Clemenceau expressed a widespread reaction to Caillaux's diplomacy when he denounced "that piece of paper [the Congo Treaty] negotiated under the threat of Adagir."[17] "Is there anyone sufficiently naïve to see in it a pledge of an enduring peace?" asked the old Jacobin Pelletan.[18] The question was purely rhetorical. Who could proclaim, while the backwaters of nationalism rose like a turbulent tide, that peace had been definitively secured? But to Jaurès, who threw behind it the weight of his party, the Congo Treaty had at least temporarily checked the forces of war: "For the time being, we have resolved the crisis in Franco-German relations."[19]

But what Jaurès really defended was the principle of peaceful negotiations and not the particular terms of the Congo Treaty which paved the way for the Moroccan protectorate. He had warned over and again that French expansion into North Africa would start another dangerous round of European imperialism. In the midst of the Agadir crisis, an ambitious Italy confirmed that fear when, late in September, 1911, Rome declared war on Turkey and undertook the conquest of Tripolitania.[20] As the world was confronted with yet another war, a wrathful Jaurès traced its source directly back to French imperialism: "Spurred on by the secret treaties, those bleak monuments of immorality created by our Moroccan policy, Italy has swooped down on Tripolitania in a wholly unjustified act of violence. . . . Now, the ambitious little Balkan States are ready and anxious to seek their fortunes. . . . And in the final analysis, the victims of all this imperialism are the people: the cost of living soars; social reforms are shelved; national budgets sag under the weight of military expenditure."[21]

Thus, when the Chamber began its historic debate on the Franco-German Convention, Jaurès and his Socialist friends approached the treaty with mixed emotions. They felt impelled, as both Sembat and Vaillant pointed out, to support any settlement which eased Franco-German tension; but they remained deeply disturbed by its invitation to expansion.

Nor were the Socialists alone in their reservations. In every other sector of the Chamber, there were deputies who criticized Caillaux's diplomacy, though for very different reasons. To the archcolonialists,

426 | YEARS OF PASSION

the partition of the French Congo seemed inadmissible; to the ultra-patriots, the relaxation of Franco-German tension appeared, at best, inopportune; and even from the ranks of his own party, Caillaux could count on nothing like solid support. For though their interest was always greater in domestic than in foreign and colonial affairs, the Radicals consistently supported the expansion of the French Empire, as their votes during the penetration of Morocco demonstrated. Out of a budgetary concern, they might criticize the high cost of imperialism; but pride in empire was sufficiently strong both among Radical deputies and editors so that the loss of Congo territory might easily appear a national calamity. Add to that the patriotic fervor of many Radicals, especially those from the departments of the eastern frontier, who considered any deal with Germany a betrayal of Alsace-Lorraine, and the depth of Caillaux's difficulties within his party becomes apparent.[22]

Yet despite strong attacks on the treaty, especially from deputies of the Right and Center, the majority finally responded to the hard realism of Millerand and Deschanel — that whatever its shortcomings, the Franco-German Convention guaranteed that Morocco would fall safely within the orbit of French influence. Only toward the end of the six-day debate did Jaurès rise, grave yet hopeful, to offer his support for a treaty which, he asserted, proved the possibility of Franco-German peace.[23] When the vote was finally cast, the Chamber approved the Congo Convention, 393 to 36. But the 165 abstentions or absences, mainly from the Right and Center, augured ill for Caillaux, who, if he had cleared the last road to Morocco, had committed the sin of dealing with Germany. Some three weeks later, as should have been anticipated, he suffered political defeat at the hands of the Senate.

Caillaux, in fact, baited his own trap. Testifying on January 9, 1912, before the special Senate committee reviewing his diplomacy, he rashly denied that he had ever carried on negotiations except through official channels. Clemenceau pounced on this assertion like a tiger discovering meat. Turning to De Selves, he asked sarcastically: "Does the Foreign Minister confirm the Premier's statement?" De Selves, trembling and almost incoherent, refused to verify Caillaux's words. By his silence, he destroyed the moral credit of his chief; and by his resignation the next day, he destroyed the ministry. Deserted by part of his own party, Caillaux tried fruitlessly to reshuffle his government; but he was finally forced, on January 11, to offer his resignation to President Fallières. Two days later, nationalists, moderates, and Right-wing Radicals nailed down their victory over Caillaux, for on January 13, the patriot of Lorraine, Raymond Poincaré, formed a ministry which ushered back into office both Briand and Millerand. Less than a week later, a cynical

Senate, plucking the fruits of imperialism ripened by Caillaux's diplomacy, approved the Congo Convention.

Jaurès could not help but express his regrets over the fall of Caillaux: "I don't share the prejudices against him of certain of my friends. His intentions were good; he knew how to confront a difficult situation; and he rendered his country a great service. Yet I find something in his approach to politics which is obscure, tortuous, secretive, and it bothers me deeply."[24] But if Caillaux was less than the ideal collaborator, Jaurès felt, he was preferable by far to Poincaré and his *équipe*.

With the advent of the new ministry began the last and decisive act in the drama of Morocco. By March 30, 1912, the government successfully imposed on the Sultan the treaty which converted his lands into a French protectorate. But hardly had Moulay-Hafid signed away his people's independence when, as Jaurès had predicted, rebellion broke out in Fez. For three days fighting raged in the capital as angry tribal leaders organized a futile resistance to their invaders. Though effectively repressed, the uprising was a portent of difficulties to come.

On June 28, the government finally presented the protectorate treaty to the Chamber where, it was expected, debate would be perfunctory and approval swift. Yet even at that final moment, when the conclusion was foregone, Jaurès spoke again — to warn this time of the Arab nationalism soon to explode. "I have come to urge that the Chamber reject this protectorate treaty," he began, "and that the ministry negotiate a new convention with the Sultan, one which will recognize the rights and independence of Morocco."[25] His purpose in a cause so clearly lost was to awaken slumbering colleagues to the force of native nationalism:

All of those peoples, who have seemed inert . . . and sunk deep in an eternal sleep, are now awakening, demanding their rights, flexing their muscles. The races of Africa and Asia, the peoples of Japan, China, and India, now linked to the rest of the world through railroads, are stirring. . . . And in our own North Africa, we are witnessing another awakening, which it would be catastrophic for us to ignore or disdain. . . . Never were the circumstances more unfavorable for imposing a treaty of this sort!

Jaurès spoke in vain that day. Louis Barthou, who presided over the Foreign Affairs Committee, replied in the accents of colonialism and, according to Russian Ambassador Isvolsky, "completely demolished the arguments of M. Jaurès."[26] When Poincaré then assured the House that General Lyautey, the French Resident in Morocco, would pacify the country quickly and without extensive reinforcements, a favorable vote became a certainty. On July 1, the Chamber approved the protectorate treaty, and ten days later the Senate did the same. The majority now considered the Moroccan issue settled; Jaurès was among the few who realized it was not.

Standing amid the rubble of his Moroccan campaign, the *tarnais* was like a soldier in defeat. He surveyed the consequences which, he believed, had flowed from the North African adventure: the seizure of Bosnia and Herzegovina, which had upset Austro-Russian equilibrium in the Balkans; the Italian invasion of Tripolitania, which already had churned up the ambitions of Serbia; and worst of all, the increasing tension between France and Germany. But defeats — and how many had Jaurès not suffered? — were the spur to effort, not resignation, and he braced himself for an uncertain future in Poincaré's France.

IV

To the self-styled patriots and social conservatives of 1912, Poincaré was cut to the measure of French needs. In a time of international tension and social disorder, they pictured him as iron-willed and incorruptible. His hostile critics, however, described Poincaré very differently; to them he was a dangerous politician, reactionary and chauvinistic, "He appeared neither good-humored nor frank," wrote Caillaux's friend Paix-Séailles, "he was not of a sensitive nature."[27] Journalists of the Left digging into Poincaré's past, found no shortage of evidence to support their case against him. Out of his association with the Saint-Gobain Chemical Trust,[28] his unyielding opposition to the income tax, his long ambivalence during the Dreyfus Affair, his drum-beating references to Alsace-Lorraine, they created their own legend of a Poincaré who, in every waking hour, served the forces of reaction and war.

The reality conformed neither to the glowing description of his supporters nor to the black one of his enemies. Poincaré's conservatism was real enough; on that score he had changed little since his rise to prominence during the heyday of Progressism. If he accepted the debates of bourgeois parties and the exchange of offices among their leaders as the basis of democratic politics, he detested the Socialists, whom he viewed as a mortal threat to the equilibrium of the political community. When they proposed collectivism, he answered, as Guizot had more than half a century before, that if the worker would but save his money, he could become a property-holder. When they appealed to class consciousness, he called for the patriotic community. "If the Republic is badly governed," he had declared at Remiremont in August, 1895, "it is because it has been weakened by partisan strife. Patriotism can unite us; it can abolish our differences with an outburst of good will."[29] Nor was Poincaré's bitterness toward Germany a myth; a proud Lorrainer, he nourished the idea of revenge as naturally as he breathed. Yet on close examination, Poincaré's record seems less categorical than his critics admitted. A lawyer by training and inclination, he tended more toward caution than boldness; and at certain crucial moments in 1912 and 1913 during the Balkan Wars, he even threw his support behind the diplomacy of peace.

Yet Poincaré *did* emerge as the central figure of France's prewar nationalistic renaissance, and for this his deep suspicion of Germany's warlike intentions was responsible. Naturally fearful of Berlin's purposes, he was encouraged in his extreme distrust by close friends like Maurice Paléologue, the chief political strategist at the Quai d'Orsay, for whom war with Germany was almost an axiom.[30] Thus, though he harbored no love of conflict for its own sake, Poincaré yielded to his patriotic conscience and sought to prepare France for a war which he naïvely thought would be short but glorious.

In forming a government, Poincaré hoped to assemble a "great ministry" of strong personalities, united on the objectives of social peace and military strength. For France it would mean a new nationalism, for the Socialists an old struggle against the government. And only if they rallied the Radicals to their side could the Socialists hope to influence the course of affairs. But when Poincaré, on January 16, presented to the Chamber a ministerial list which included, besides Briand and Millerand, five Radicals and three Radical-Socialists, it was evident that Jaurès and his party would receive scant help from the confused ranks of the non-Socialist Left.[31]

Enjoying solid parliamentary support, Poincaré was able to ignore all discussion of social and fiscal reform while he concentrated almost exclusively on questions of national security. In his preparation for an eventual showdown with Germany, he worked, often behind a cloud of diplomatic secrecy, to tighten French alliances with Russia and England. Especially did he direct his efforts toward St. Petersburg, since Franco-Russian relations had recently grown less intimate. At the time of the Bosnian crisis, France had not rallied to the Russian cause against Austria; and Russia, in her turn, had offered France little comfort during the Agadir crisis. But by 1912, important forces were at work to draw Paris and St. Petersburg tightly together: the reinvigoration of Russian ambitions, the influence of Isvolsky over the Quai d'Orsay, and Poincaré's willingness, almost at any cost, to strengthen Franco-Russian friendship.

From her Far Eastern defeats of 1905 to her diplomatic humiliation in 1908, Russia's dreams of expansion faded, and in the struggle around the Tsar between Pan-Slavist extremists and cautious moderates, the imperialists were temporarily checked. By 1912, however, as the conservative *Correspondant* pointed out, the expansionists were again in control of Russian policy.[32] St. Petersburg's goals remained, as before, control of the Straits and domination of the Balkan peninsula; and the instrument of that policy was the Balkan League, an unholy alliance of Serbia, Bulgaria, Greece, and Montenegro, created, then protected by Russia.

Eastern Europe specialized in little birds of prey, minor powers whose chance for greatness hinged on Turkish disintegration. Serbia, Bulgaria, and Greece all coveted Macedonia, but Belgrade dreamed of even more — a great South Slav state, including Bosnia and Herzegovina, and even the Slavic divisions of the Dual Empire. In such untamed aspirations, Russia found leverage for her drive into the Balkans. Under her guidance, a Serbo-Bulgarian treaty was signed on March 13, 1912, which foresaw war against Turkey and the subsequent partition of Macedonia; less than three months later, when Greece and Montenegro joined the Pact, the Balkan League was a reality.[33]

It was a dangerous and secret game that St. Petersburg was playing, one that could well touch off a general European war. If the Balkan League defeated Turkey, and Serbia created a South Slav state, Austria was bound to intervene with Germany at her side. Realizing that she could run the risk of war only if she could count on the unqualified support of France, Russia played hard upon the anti-German sentiments of the Poincaré ministry, while her agents stepped up their efforts to bribe the French press into line. The chief actor in that Russian diplomatic game was the former Foreign Minister, now Ambassador to Paris, Alexander Isvolsky. He was of that vainglorious breed who would risk a world to avenge his own hurt. Outsmarted at Buchlau and subsequently removed as Foreign Minister, he dedicated his life, its every conspiratorial moment, to revenge against the Central Powers. In Paris he worked tirelessly to persuade policy-makers of the congruity between Russia's Balkan designs and the national interest of France.

Not every Frenchman of influence fell into Isvolsky's net, and he came to regard these dissenters, Caillaux and Jaurès especially, as his bitter enemies. "Recognizing the danger of his intrigue," Caillaux later revealed, "I tried, though in vain, to warn Poincaré."[34] Jaurès was even more explicit in his denunciation of the Russian Ambassador: "The workers and the peasants of France must never fertilize the fields of battle merely to serve the Tsar's ambitions and Isvolsky's vanity."[35] But with others, men in key policy roles, Isvolsky fared very well. An almost daily visitor at the Quai d'Orsay, he established the friendliest of contacts with Paléologue, a snobbish intimate of Russian aristocratic circles. But the most important of Isvolsky's French friends was Poincaré himself who, from the start of his ministry, assured the Russian Ambassador "of his strong resolve . . . to coördinate France's foreign policy with Russia's."[36]

Isvolsky's maneuvers, Poincaré's assurances, the hustle and bustle of the Quai d'Orsay—all were curtained off from the French public by a veil of generalizations about national interest. But Jaurès, exercising intuition when he was deprived of facts, realized that French policy was becoming uncritically pro-Russian, and warned publicly of the danger:

The plain truth is that Russia has her own policy, which she pursues without even consulting us. Of her secret parleys with Austria on Bosnia and Herzegovina she failed to inform us; of her talks with Germany at Potsdam she said not a word; of her agreement with Italy on Turkey and the Straits she told us nothing. . . . Thus, she has negotiated behind our back with every one of the Triple Alliance Powers. No one can blame Russia for looking after her own interests, but we don't have to support her to the detriment of our interests and independence.[37]

Warnings of this sort, though they should have appealed to patriotic sentiment, failed to impress the majority of deputies. Such, indeed, was the mood of the Chamber that on the death of Brisson, the Radical who had so long presided over the House, the majority opted for Deschanel as his successor. Assured the support of the Parliament, Poincaré felt free to carry his pro-Russian foreign policy to its limits. Thus, in mid-June, the French public learned that the Premier intended to visit Russia personally during the coming summer. "He will see the Tsar and all the high-ranking officials," *L'Écho de Paris* elatedly reported on June 12. Six weeks later, Poincaré and his party set sail for Russia, and on August 9, they were enthusiastically welcomed at Kronstadt. From the first moment of Poincaré's arrival, the Russian authorities appealed to his expansive egotism. Happily ignoring President Fallières and the republican tradition, the Premier comported himself as though he were the French version of Tsar; the Russians, if they laughed privately, publicly encouraged his lovely dream. So Poincaré dined with Nicholas, reviewed military parades, and accepted toasts in the name of France. Could anyone persuade him, even for a moment, that Russia was not the best of all possible allies?

The diplomatic mission had a more serious purpose, however, than to polish the Premier's vanity. Poincaré and the diplomats of the Quai d'Orsay, who had been advised of the Serbo-Bulgar treaty only in April, would now learn the exact nature of Russian commitments to the Balkan League, while the Russian expansionists would try to extract from the Premier a definite pledge of support in the event of war. When Poincaré learned the precise terms of the Balkan treaties, he realized, contrary to the interpretation which Isvolsky had offered him, that they constituted a pact of war. Would France then lend her support to Balkan enterprises, so remote from her own interests? An unwavering Poincaré assured Premier Sazonov that his country would honor to the letter all her treaty commitments under the Franco-Russian Alliance. Sazonov then agreed that Russia would hasten construction of rail communications to the German border, while Poincaré promised to work for a rapid increase of French military strength. The die was thus fatefully cast, and as the ceremonial vodka flowed, the peace of Europe ebbed away.

Back in France, the Premier and his close collaborators set themselves to the task of adjusting public opinion to the probability of war. On October 27, 1912, in an important policy speech at Nantes, Poincaré declared that "France must act like a nation which does not seek war but does not fear it."[38] While the Premier spoke on center stage, others acted in the wings. French bankers arranged, for both Bulgaria and Russia, substantial loans which were essential for their war preparations. And in Parliament, influential political leaders, well briefed by the ministry, were organizing the campaign to lengthen the term of military service from two years to three.[39] None of this buildup for war escaped Jaurès who, without respite through the fall of 1912, denounced the grim frivolity of involvement in the Balkans. Let war once begin, he cried, and it would spread like a plague into "the most terrible holocaust since the Thirty Years' War."[40]

But nothing, not even the last-minute caution of Russia, could now restrain the ambitions of the Balkan states. By October 15, Montenegro, Serbia, Bulgaria, and Greece, throwing the switch which ultimately would darken all of Europe, declared war on Turkey. Their success against the Porte was startlingly swift, and within two weeks the Serbs had reached Durazzo, the Greeks Salonika, and the Bulgars were threatening Constantinople. "If Greeks, Bulgars, and Serbs don't turn against each other in the heart of Byzantium," Jaurès predicted, "it will be a miracle greater than all the miracles in the history of warfare."[41] For the war-minded nationalists of France, who looked upon the victories of French-trained Greeks over German-trained Turks as a sign of France's military superiority, these were days of exhilarating anticipation. But not for Jaurès and his friends, who read in the events yet another text on the madness of imperialism.

By November, the swift turn of events threatened to convert the Balkan conflict into a European war. Serbia laid claim to Albania, and Austria, the integrity of her Empire at stake, began to mobilize. If Russia moved to support Serbia, the long-awaited showdown between St. Petersburg and Vienna would certainly follow. At the last minute — and mainly because the Russians felt themselves still unprepared for a war — the great powers localized the Balkan conflict and arranged for a settlement. Responding to an appeal from a badly beaten Turkey, the six major powers sent representatives to London where, by the first week of December, they persuaded the belligerents to accept an armistice and undertake peace negotiations.[42] For the time being, and at least until the Russians rearmed, a general war would be averted.

Through all the months of crisis, what had been the role of Europe's Socialists? Were they, as Jaurès had optimistically expected after Stuttgart, capable of enforcing peace? Until 1912, though they had demonstrated actively against successive wars of imperialism, they had been unable, even in a single instance, to prevent aggression. But in the critical days of the Balkan War, when the fate of so many hung on the whim of a few, the leaders of European Socialism decided upon a great display of solidarity which, they hoped, would prevent the generalization of the war. So it was that late in November some 555 delegates from twenty-three Socialist parties gathered at Basle for an emergency congress. In their optimism, they considered the demonstration a decisive force for peace; in reality, they were meeting together for the last time before the winds of war blew their hopes into oblivion. The International, for all their professions of loyalty, was still only an article of faith and an office in Brussels.

V

On Sunday, November 24, the representatives of world Socialism marched through the streets of Basle until they reached the great cathedral where they held the second session of their congress. The public display of solidarity was impressive, and it fed an optimism of which the converse was despair. Especially was that true of Jaurès, whose belief in Socialist action was rooted not in näiveté but in fervent hope. When he mounted the pulpit of the cathedral, he delivered a speech more moving than any other in the literature of the Second International, to inspirit his friends with the courage of their convictions. The church bells were ringing in his ears, and to their music he set his words: "I think of the motto which Schiller inscribed at the head of his beautiful 'Song of the Bell.' *Vivos voco*: I call on the living to resist the monster which would ravage the land. *Mortuos plango*: I weep for the countless dead, now buried in the east, whose rotting stench fills us with remorse. *Fulgora frango*: I will harness the thunderbolts of war now breaking across the skies."[43] And with strains of Beethoven's "Hymn to Peace" still floating through the air, he concluded his oration on a high note of prophecy:

"We will leave this hall committed to the salvation of peace and civilization."

The next day, he introduced the resolution against war which the International Socialist Bureau had framed; while it outlined no specific plan of action, the motion clearly emphasized, according to Jaurès, "our readiness for any sacrifice."[44] A parade of speakers—Victor Adler, Keir Hardie, Hugo Haase, Clara Zetkin, Vaillant—lent the resolution their enthusiastic support, and it was voted unanimously. When Jaurès returned to France he seemed convinced, as he wrote, that "our declaration is no empty threat but rather the expression of our revolutionary will ... against war." Years later, however, the work of Basle was judged more realistically by that fiery Russian Socialist, Angelica Balabanoff: "In the speeches made by the great masters of European Socialism in the Cathedral at Basle, one detected a sense of duty, a passionate desire to cope with danger, rather than a conviction of success."[45] For at Basle, as at Stuttgart and Copenhagen, the leaders of the Second International hid their doctrinal doubts and their tactical weaknesses behind a cloud of good intentions. Could Socialists and pacifists really rein in the forces of war? Would Socialist parties, almost everywhere reformist, turn revolutionary in their struggle against war?

Did Jaurès wrestle with these questions? More than that, he was haunted by them, and those who have recognized in him only the incurable optimist, lacking a sense of the tragic, have badly misunderstood his complexity. With the Marxists, he considered imperialism the deepest root of war; and better by far than the Marxists, he understood, from the days of the Affair on, the force of nationalism as a source of war. "It is the policy of imperialism," he wrote in *La Revue de l'enseignement primaire et primaire supérieure* (November 24, 1912) in the very days of Basle,

which has so skillfully and treacherously roused the racism and the vanity of whole populations. It is this *patriotisme d'affaires*, so dangerous because it is deceptive, which has united traditional, atavistic instincts and the subtlest modern financial intrigues.

Beyond that, capitalism is anarchic. Despite its effort to regulate and organize itself, it has failed to eliminate wild competition among its groups. . . . And finally, because capitalism has rendered the human mass inert and insecure, . . . it has reduced it to seeking emotional gratification in the drumbeating of chauvinism, in the fever-pitch of raging warfare. At such a low level have human energies been kept by an oligarchy which has reserved for itself all the higher rewards of life!

War, Jaurès realized, was a greater likelihood than peace, and the constancy of Socialists was not so certain as their resolutions implied. At

Basle, he sought out Camille Huysmans, Secretary of the International Socialist Bureau; his words to the Belgian Socialist were both realistic and prescient: "We must think of every eventuality. Your special position is of the greatest importance. If war breaks out, we don't know what effect such an event may have on those who now seem to be the strongest internationalists. *Whatever happens*, you must never leave your post; you must maintain the ties between the working classes of the belligerent countries."[46]

But the die was not yet cast; nothing was so important as to create an atmosphere of peace. Publicly, Jaurès suppressed his doubts and denounced fatalism. To the government, he repeated over and again his warnings of Socialist action; to a France "reactionary, militaristic, convinced that war was inevitable,"[47] he expressed his faith in the International. The root of that faith was his conviction that German Social Democracy, despite signs of hesitancy, had the will and resources to influence the policies of the Imperial government. In the German elections of 1912, when the Social Democrats won an astonishing four and a half million votes and 110 Reichstag seats, he found striking evidence for that belief. "The victory of the German Socialists," *L'Humanité* announced on March 31, "signifies the universal will for peace and the certainty of keeping it." When Philip Scheidemann, Secretary of the Central Committee of Social Democracy, addressed a great rally at the Salle Wagram in Paris, he assured his French comrades that the elections "mean the death of German nationalism."[48] Scheidemann returned to Paris in November, and before a wildly enthusiastic crowd, affirmed the Social Democratic will to peace: "We don't want war! Against all who seek to drive us to such bestiality, we will rise up with unbreakable courage!"[49] Jaurès was reassured, hopeful. And when the Social Democrats demonstrated actively against German involvement in the Balkan Wars, he heaped his praise upon them for their strong resolve.[50]

Thus, though Jaurès harbored doubts about German Socialism, they never cropped to the surface; instead his strong public confidence became standard fare within the S.F.I.O., the essential prop of its belief in a Franco-German *rapprochement*. When anti-Socialist critics questioned the internationalism of the German Socialists, the leaders of the S.F.I.O. dismissed the criticisms as bourgeois propaganda. But late in 1912, when a bitter attack against Social Democracy originated within the S.F.I.O. itself, it could hardly be ignored. Leveled by Charles Andler, a brilliant Socialist academician, it challenged the entire tactical position of Jaurès.

Professor of German literature at the Sorbonne and a specialist on Nietzsche, Andler had an extensive first-hand knowledge of Germany.

Through his travels east of the Rhine, he had become convinced that a strong current of chauvinism originated not only in bourgeois and military circles but in the Social Democratic Party as well. After wide reading in the German Socialist press, he concluded that the assumptions of the S.F.I.O. and especially of Jaurès were either ill-informed or deceptive. "The leaders of French Socialism," he wrote to his anarchist friend James Guillaume, "know very well that among the four million who voted for Social Democracy, there are hardly a million real Socialists. To the other three million, who are simply discontented democrats, imperialism has great appeal."[51]

Convinced that he had to jolt his party into a reappraisal of Social Democracy, Andler summed up his findings on "Imperial Socialism in Contemporary Germany" in two articles (November 10 and December 10, 1912) which he published in *L'Action nationale*.[52] He charged, in brief, that a small but influential group of Socialist theorists were overtly imperialistic. One of them, Gerhard Hildebrand, was so vociferously colonialist that he had been expelled from the party at its Congress of Chemnitz in 1912. Others, however, remained — Max Schippel, Ludwig Quessel, Dr. Südekum — who were quite as nationalistic as Hildebrand. Perhaps his most damaging evidence, however, was a quotation from the revered Bebel who, according to Andler, had said before the Congress of Jena in 1911: "The order of the day is not to disarm, but to increase armaments." The implication was both clear and shocking — that among the top leaders of Social Democracy, nationalism also held sway.

For three months, Andler's articles drew no comment from Jaurès, though they were enthusiastically quoted in the anti-Socialist press. His detractors equated his silence with capitulation. When he finally answered, Jaurès explained the delay differently: "Yes! The days passed because they were completely consumed with the unending struggle against the three-year military law, against the blind folly of armaments, against the rising tide of nationalism, to which Andler has now contributed."[53] In his counterattack, Jaurès concentrated almost exclusively on Andler's use of Bebel's words. Quoting from the official transcript of proceedings at the Congress of Jena, he charged that several words had been deleted from Bebel's statement, which completely altered its meaning.[54] Of the bulk of Andler's evidence, however, Jaurès said nothing.

On the face of it, he offered a weak reply. Though Andler had certainly overstated his case, he deserved a more careful hearing than Jaurès accorded him. Yet this reaction is hardly incomprehensible. Fighting daily and without respite against the three-year law, Jaurès could ill afford the time for a proper debate with Andler, nor could he muster very much generosity toward an antagonist who, he felt, had recklessly supplied the war-minded press with ammunition. But at bottom, Jaurès was convinced that Andler's evidence was inflated out of all proportion and his case essentially worthless. After years of close association with the leading German Socialists, he was of no mind to alter his view of Social Democracy on the basis of random writings by minor theorists. The record of German Socialism — its opposition to expanded armaments and imperialism, its insistence on friendship with England and France — struck him as clearly definitive. "Social Democracy has always believed that one of its chief parliamentary duties is to struggle against militarism, which burdens the people and frustrates their free development."[55] So the German Socialists declared at Mannheim in 1906, and at every Congress after that they had proclaimed their opposition to the forces of war. Their demonstrations against imperialism at the height of the Agadir crisis dominated his memory. Soon, in May of 1913, delegations of French and German Socialist deputies would meet at Berne, where they would promise to work in their respective Parliaments for a reduction of armaments and the arbitration of international disputes. The record, long and continuing, was Jaurès' unspoken answer to Professor Andler.

But beneath all of Andler's smoke, there *was* fire.[56] Between the lines of its public record, Social Democracy had written a history of evasion and timidity which should not have escaped Jaurès. Puffed up with prestige and sated with jobs, its leaders became familiars of the old society and strangers to revolution. While French Socialists, their insurrectionary tradition welded securely onto the movement, seriously debated the views of the Hervéists, their German comrades scornfully swept aside Karl Liebknecht's antimilitarism and Rosa Luxemburg's appeal to revolution.[57] By 1913, when the old heroes of Social Democracy were dead and the bureaucrats — David or Noske — dominated the leadership, the party even supported the government's military expansion. Yet Jaurès never publicly doubted the "four million courageous Germans" who "will shape the destinies of the world."[58]

"The aberration of Jaurès and our Socialists," Paléologue recorded in his diary (March 3, 1913), "reminds me of Bossuet's words: 'The worst defect of the mind is to believe things because one wants them that way and not because one has actually seen them.'"[59] Though Paléologue spoke as one who found nothing but evil in Germany, his harsh judgment on his enemies was hardly baseless. Yet, it was 1913, and each major political event in France augured the disintegration of the Left and the victory of militarism. At every turn — from Poincaré's election to the Presidency in January to the fall of Barthou in December — Jaurès was to lead his party against nationalism triumphant until, by the end of the year, the tide seemed to turn slightly. At all points, it was his belief in the

International and his trust of German Socialism which lent force to his efforts.

VI

The good-natured Fallières was probably the only politician in France who remained calm as the expiration date (January 18, 1913) of his Presidential term approached. Among the rest, the impending event either stimulated ambition or generated concern over the direction of the Republic. For though the Presidency was partly a ceremonial office, it could become, at a time of crisis and in strong hands, a center of very real influence.

Whatever else the Republic lacked, it suffered no shortage of ambitious politicians, and in the months that preceded the Presidential election, the names of Bourgeois, Ribot, Clemenceau, and Delcassé were all casually mentioned. By the end of 1912, however, the undisputed frontrunner was Poincaré, whose campaign was handled, in the corridors and over dinner tables, by the astute Briand. The inspiration of the Poincaré-Briand alliance was nationalistic, its spirit conservative, its program militaristic. It threatened everyone and everything on the Left. Since the Left still dominated the Chamber, in numbers if not in spirit, the Radicals and Radical-Socialists might have thwarted Poincaré's ambitions with a strong, attractive candidate of their own. But no more unified than they had been for a decade, they finally settled on a candidate, Jules Pams, whose only virtue was his obscurity.

A millionaire manufacturer of cigarette paper, Pams was then Minister of Agriculture in the Poincaré ministry. How could the Socialists, who had hoped for a clear choice, go down the line for so mediocre a candidate? "In these difficult times," exploded Jaurès, "how can the Radicals offer France and the Republic a man who has never revealed, either in opposition or in office, either in debate or in action, any real measure of ability? . . . So confused is Radicalism and so badly divided that it can no longer close ranks behind a man of real ability."[60] Bitterly opposed to Poincaré and unable to support Pams, the Socialists ran Vaillant as their own candidate.

When the two Houses of Parliament met in joint session on January 17 to choose Fallières' successor, the ineffectiveness of his opposition played into Poincarè's hands. A politician of proven competence, he scored a clear-cut victory over Pams on only the second ballot. The election of Poincaré to the highest office of the Republic, as the elated conservative press was quick to point out, carried the nationalist revival to a pinnacle. "It is not the victory of a man or a party," declared *Le Journal* on January 18. "It is the victory of the national idea." Isvolsky confirmed that judgment in his wire to the Russian Foreign Office on January 18: "I have just had a long conversation with Poincaré, who told me that as President he would have great influence over French foreign policy, which he would use to ensure the closest ties with Russia."[61] Even the monarchist *Action française* interpreted the election as the victory of the Right over the Left, and accorded the new President its grudging approval.

The Presidential election was but a preface to a series of political events which threatened to immobilize the Left. By January 24, the kingmaker Briand once again assumed office as Premier, presiding over a nondescript ministry of dissident Radicals and former Progressists. Less than a month later, when Poincaré was officially installed as President, he established the mood of his reign with a strong speech before Parliament: "It is impossible for a nation to live in peace," he asserted there, "unless it is always ready for war."[62]

Briand, as it happened, held office for less than two months. He resigned on March 18 when the Senate rejected his proposal for a new election law, but his successor, Louis Barthou, formed a ministry little different from Briand's in composition or in spirit. Even in traits of personality, Barthou bore a striking resemblance to Briand; both were flexible, ambitious, and earthy, though Barthou was less the master of his character than his predecessor. "He is vulgar from head to toe, morally as well as physically," observed Caillaux.[63]

Son of a blacksmith who had worked his way into a clerk's job with the Chemins de fer du Midi, Barthou sprang from that careerist petty bourgeoisie whose cleverest sons found their opportunity for success in the Republic. Barthou, in fact, was to serve continuously in the parliaments of France from his first election in 1889 until his assassination in 1934. His ideas were the unexceptional ones of moderate republicanism. "I am a republican," he had proudly written in *L'Indépendent des Basses-Pyrénées* on September 15, 1889. "In my view, the Republic is the only government which can guarantee order and freedom." Anticlerical, antisocialist, colonialist, and patriotic (he could thus support the Russian alliance against Germany both before and after the Bolshevik Revolution), Barthou defended the capitalist Republic against all its critics, whether monarchists, Catholics, collectivists, or pacifists. Thus, he rallied to the Dreyfusard cause, broke with those Progressists, like Méline, who leaned toward the Church and the army, and help organize the Alliance démocratique. But when the Socialists and revolutionary syndicalists preached class war, Barthou appealed, as he did in *L'Indépendent des Basses-Pyrénées* on December 6, 1911, to "national unity and the glories of the French Revolution." A clever conservative, he supported the mild-

440 | YEARS OF PASSION

est social reforms and actively promoted the *syndicats jaunes*, which were essentially company unions. Like Waldeck-Rousseau, Millerand, and Briand, Barthou was willing to protect "liberal society" with a slight dose of corporatism.

In 1913, as heir to the policies of Poincaré and Briand, Barthou concentrated the energies of his ministry on a single measure, the three-year law, the most important symbol of the new nationalism and the preparation for war. Introduced into the Chamber under Briand on March 6, the three-year proposal seemed, on the surface at least, the French response to German rearmament. Only a month before, Germany had taken measures to increase the number of troops in the Imperial Army to 850,-000, a formidable force against which France could field an active army of only 480,000. Tardieu summed up the sense of danger which gripped France when he wrote: "There is only one point to make: we must act!"[64]

But from the moment of its introduction, the three-year law created a schism in French politics deeper than any since the days of the Affair. "They are militarists and reactionaries who are demanding the three-year military service," the C.G.T. charged in a manifesto of February 13. "The pretext is the increase of her army by Germany, though the latter has already invoked the revival of French chauvinism as her excuse. The governments of both countries want to increase the number of barracks troops and the amount of military expenditures, which weigh so heavily on the workers. And why? . . . Is it not to ensure that on each side of the frontier the chauvinistic and militaristic spirit will increase?"[65] When the husks of bitter suspicion were cut away, the C.G.T. propaganda remained a solid kernel of truth. For as both its friends and enemies realized, the three-year law was more than a measure of preparedness; it was the rallying point of the new nationalism which, since Agadir especially, had infected the public spirit.

Nationalism now influenced the thoughts and program not only of discredited monarchists but also of moderate and conservative republicans. Sweeping well beyond its traditional fiefs in the Catholic west and the anti-German east, the new nationalism permeated Paris, its republican hinterland and departments, often Radical strongholds, of the Massif Central. Among the middle classes — the *haute bourgeoisie* obsessed with fears of the Left and the *petite bourgeoisie* frustrated by insecurity — it found its most fervent converts. In its appeal to grandeur and its glorification of solidarity, nationalism galvanized fast-waning energies and subdued free-floating fears.

No single issue so effectively welded the nationalists together as the three-year law, which, as Aulard was to write in *La Dépêche de Toulouse* (August 19, 1913), had become "an article of faith." To some — Millerand, Doumer, Étienne—it was a way of expressing their close connections with the armaments industry; for while the campaign to remilitarize proceeded on center stage, the munitions-makers, the steel producers, and the shipbuilders, as Jaurès and his friends knew well enough were operating behind the scenes.[66] To others, long tainted with antirepublicanism, it was the road to political respectability. But for most, the three-year law was the political issue of a time without politics; it was the obfuscation of class conflict, the eradication of party lines. Monarchists and moderates, conservatives and Radicals (at least those from nationalistic districts)—all of them rallied round the flag and spoke again of French greatness and national destiny.

There was no ambiguity in the reaction of Socialists and syndicalists, who dug in for a struggle, however protracted, against the three-year law. No sooner had Étienne laid the measure before the Chamber when Vaillant denounced it as "a criminal act" and Jaurès as "a crime against the Republic."[67] It was an explosion of opposition which never subsided; at the heart of the campaign, its greatest voice and most active pen was Jaurès. Relentless in his efforts, never signaling retreat, he waged daily battle, indeed until death, against the three-year law and the powerful coalition behind it.

In his flood of words against the proposal, Jaurès never denied the central importance of national defense; much of his criticism, in fact, was rooted in his belief that the extra year of service, while it would overburden conscripts and provoke German countermeasures, could not possibly increase the military strength of France. "The three-year law will add nothing to the strength of the French army," he wrote early in his campaign. "I intend to demonstrate, on the contrary, that it can only weaken it."[68] In counless articles and speeches, so well-informed that General Gamelin, who exchanged views with him on the three-year law, was struck by "his perfect mastery of military theory,"[69] he criticized the heavy expenditure of three hundred million francs simply to house barracks troops for an extra year. The army stood to gain neither in speed nor in quality; the only valid counterpoise to German superiority, Jaurès insisted, lay in the armed nation, the power of the reserves. Such were the thoughts which became the program of the S.F.I.O. When the party convened at Brest between March 23 and 27, 1913, the delegates resolved to fight unremittingly "*against* the three-year law and *for* Franco-German collaboration, international arbitration, and a national militia."[70]

By the time the Socialists launched their peace campaign, the atmosphere was thick with chauvinism. In Paris especially, where the lower strata of the bourgeoisie provided the shock troops of nationalism, Socialist meetings were invaded and their orators threatened. Wherever he spoke, Jaurès was a favorite target of the young hoodlums of the Came-lots du Roi; at Nice, on March 8, his voice was buried beneath their bar-rage of anti-German epithets. To silence him became the commandment of patriotism. "France is speaking, so keep quiet, Mr. Jaurès!" screamed *L'Écho de Paris*.[71] "In time of war," Péguy wrote in April, 1913, "there is only one policy — the policy of the National Convention. That means Jaurès in a cart and a drum-roll to drown out his powerful voice."[72] The voice was not stilled, not yet at least. On May 25, as the Chamber neared its debate, Jaurès spoke of peace before a huge open-air meeting at the Pré-Saint-Gervais. Though organized in only two days, the rally drew an enthusiastic crowd of 150,000. It was the high point of the mass move-ment led by the S.F.I.O. before 1914.

In the Chamber, Jaurès realized, the Socialist effort was doomed with-out substantial help from the Radicals. But on this issue, as on so many others, Radicalism was a house divided. "There are nationalistic Radi-cals," Jaurès pointed out, "like the editors of *La France* or the group around M. Doumer, who are strongly for the three-year law. And there are some Radical-Socialists who are clearly against it."[73]

Since Socialist hopes thus rode with the Radical-Socialist faction, Jaurès sought out its leader, Caillaux, and during one fruitful evening at the home of Paix-Séailles the two men met to map a common strategy. "We struck an accord," Caillaux later recalled, "which dealt largely with the problems immediately ahead of us, but which looked to the future also. We agreed that we would make a major effort against the three-year law. . . . And if we were beaten, we would concentrate on demand-ing the income tax to finance the extra year of military service."[74]

The Chamber debate, which began in earnest on June 2, continued with uninterrupted intensity for almost seven weeks. The coalition of the Right and Center, spearheaded by Minister of War Étienne, consti-tuted a solid front of support for the three-year law; the Socialists, led by the inexhaustible Jaurès, assailed it afresh each day; only the Radicals, oscillating between their principles of the Left and sentiments of the Cen-ter, wavered, wandered, and split. Beyond the halls of Parliament, the C.G.T. and the S.F.I.O. organized demonstrations so menacing to the authorities that Barthou threatened to curb the trade union movement.[75]

All of the opposition, even Caillaux's dramatic, eleventh-hour interven-tion, finally proved insufficient. When the debate ended on July 19, the deputies approved the full text of the three-year law, 358 to 204. The re-sult turned on Radical ambivalence; of the Radical-Socialists, eighty-six voted against the law, but forty-seven supported it; of the Radicals nineteen followed Caillaux, but eighty-five filed behind Barthou. In the Upper House, where the debate was considerably less animated, the

Senators voted the three-year law on August 7, and among its supporters were Bourgeois, Monis, and Doumergue, who passed for giants in the land of Radicalism.

No documents have survived which reveal Jaurès' inner feelings once France submitted to this militarization. One can only imagine the sore discouragement, the bottomless fatigue which must have squeezed his spirit like giant pincers. In public, however, his mood was ruddy with anticipation of the next phase, the struggle to rally the forces of peace and repeal the three-year law. If Barthou fell from office and Caillaux recast Radicalism in his image, if the Socialists campaigned fiercely and the next general elections brought them success, France might reverse in 1914 the course she had pursued the year before.

Jaurès rode his hopes; yet he realized that the French public was caught, as never before, between apathy and irrationalism. "I believe we are now experiencing a moral renaissance in France. . . . It is the love of energy, the quest for a full and active life."[76] So declared Bergson, whose teaching had stimulated the mysticism, vitalism, and patriotism which had taken hold of university youth. "Renan, Tolstoy, and Anatole France are no longer our masters," asserted Desiré Ferry, scion of a famous republican family and president in 1913 of the Union des Étudiants républicains.[77] "Their most powerful belief is patriotism," concluded Henri Massis and Alfred de Tarde (who wrote under the nom de plume Agathon) in their selective but highly influential survey of the attitudes of educated French youth.[78] "At Polytechnique and Normale, where the antimilitarists and the disciples of Jaurès were once so numerous, and even at the Sorbonne, where the faculty is still dominated by internationalists, there are few disciples of humanistic doctrines."[79]

The authors exaggerated, but their case was not without substance. Never, not even at the height of the Affair, had Jaurès thrown himself against stronger winds of resistance. But he neither paused nor yielded; as the war spirit neared a crest, he carried his humanistic message directly to the students of the Latin Quarter. On January 22, 1914, at the Salle des Sociétés Savantes in the rue Danton, the Socialists sponsored a meeting to honor their comrade Francis de Pressensé, who had died two days before. Here, before students and workers, Jaurès spoke of Pressensé and true heroism: "What he accumulated in the solitude of his study, what he gleaned from the wisdom of the past, he did not absorb for its own sake. Nor did his wide knowledge lead him, in the manner of our reactionary dillettantes, to scorn for the masses and isolation from them."[80] Like the sixteenth-century humanist and the eighteenth-century *philosophe*, he placed his learning at the disposal of mankind. In such a life, intoned Jaurès, and not in mindless vitalism lay the road to heroism. "Today your are told: act, always act! But what is action without thought? It is the barbarism born of inertia. You are told: brush aside the party of peace; it saps your courage! But I tell you that to stand for peace today is to wage the most heroic of battles. . . . Defy those who warn you against what they call 'systems'! Defy those who urge you to abandon your intelligence for instinct and intuition!"

Jaurès' appeal was direct and fervid. But in the atmosphere of Paris it evaporated like a cry in the wind. Only a week later, Déroulède died at Nice, and on February 3, the burial of this prince of nationalists occasioned a tumultuous demonstration in Paris: "More than 100,000 persons . . . lined the streets from the Gare de Lyon to the Church of Saint Augustine, to pay tribute to the patriot who had just died. . . . A number of political personalities were there: MM Briand, Barthou, Leygues, and Millerand."[81] Thus was interred the man who spent his life preaching the war of revenge.

But though the climate of opinion surrounded governmental policy, it did not create it. Effective decision, whether for war or for peace, remained the province of a political élite; in the final analysis, the course of Radicalism and the results of the general elections in 1914 could bestow success or failure of the Socialist effort.

VII

In October, 1913, the delegates of Radicalism assembled at Pau and broke out of their lethargy. In a mood of urgency, they adopted new rules for the party, voted a Left-wing program, and elected Caillaux their president.[82] Faced with the disintegration of Radicalism under the ministries of Briand, Poincaré, and Barthou, the delegates capitulated to their insurgent Left; by the time they left Pau, they were on record *for* immediate fiscal reform and *against* the three-year law. As the general elections approached, the Radical Party declared its independence of the Center and beckoned to the Extreme Left. "To realize our program," admitted Louis Malvy, Radical-Socialist deputy from the Lot, "we must join with every democratic force. . . . Otherwise, the great power of the monied interests will dominate completely."[83]

To some critics, conservative and Socialist alike, the Radical strategy was born rather of self-interest than of insurgency. The aged Guesde, for example, warned his party against Radical trickery: "The elections are approaching, and I can understand very well why intelligent Radicals — and there are some — are so concerned over the discredit which has fallen on their party . . . that they want the Socialist Party . . . as an ally. . . . If we played their game, wouldn't we be guilty of betrayal and stupidity?"[84] Once again, however, it was Jaurès who proposed a more flexible policy. Guesde, he felt, would unwisely confine Socialist action; and others, perhaps less sincere and certainly more ambitious, would revive the bloc. Jaurès counseled neither isolation nor submission: "We cannot commit ourselves unalterably for or against alliances on the Left. We must accept those *ententes* which can help us."[85] As on so many other questions, Jaurès would carry the majority of Socialists with him on this one.

Within only a matter of weeks, the collaboration of the resuscitated Radical Party and the S.F.I.O. proved fruitful. Late in November, Barthou went before the Chamber and proposed a large loan to implement the three-year law, rather than new taxes. Though both Jaurès and Caillaux opposed the government vigorously, the Premier, by the close vote of 291 to 270, won support for his financial orthodoxy. The next day, however, when Barthou proposed, at the behest of interested bankers, that the new bonds be exempted from all future taxation, both Socialists and Radical-Socialists rose in rebellion and threw the *gascon* from office. From the Left and the Extreme Left came enthusiastic shouts of *A bas les trois ans!* For the deepest consequences of Barthou's defeat were political and not fiscal; it promised the end of conservative ministries and nationalistic policies. Or so Jaurès thought. "Yesterday's second of December," he elatedly wrote, "makes amends for the other one."[86]

Though Caillaux had spearheaded the drive against Barthou, Poincaré refused to call on the man who threatened both the income tax and the repeal of the three-year law. He went first to Ribot and then to Jean Dupuy, as though the coalition of Socialists and Radical-Socialists might melt away, but neither of these moderates could form a government. Finally, Poincaré called on Gaston Doumergue, the jovial Senator from the Gard, to form a government. In settling for Doumergue, the President managed to choose a Radical-Socialist who not only voted for the three-year law but considered war inevitable.

On December 11, when Doumergue unveiled his Radical-Socialist ministry, which included Caillaux at Finance, the Chamber rocked with protests from the Right and Center. In reality, the ministerial declaration was more discouraging to Socialists than to conservatives; for when he spoke of the three-year law, Doumergue rejected the dictum of Pau and asserted: "We intend to apply the law faithfully." Before this latest example of Radical ambivalence, the Socialists protested vigorously. "What an impression of weakness and cowardice Doumergue gave," wrote Jaurès.[87] Unwilling, however, to join with the Right against a ministry committed to the income tax, the Socialists abstained on the vote of confidence. Doumergue then drew sufficient votes from the Center to ensure his success.

In the months that followed, though the Socialists lent the government their uneasy support, they found little to cheer them. While Caillaux introduced both the income tax and the capital levy, the Socialists insisted that these reforms would be illusory without a reduction in military expenditures. "The expenses for the army and navy will absorb everything," complained Jaurès. "The new revenues raised by fiscal reforms will disappear like tracks in the sand."[88] But with every passing week, it became abundantly clear that the Doumergue government would support the remilitarization of France. "Despite outward appearances, this ministry will act no differently from its predecessors," Briand confided to his friend Msgr. de Lacroix, Director of the École des Hautes Études. "To survive, it will have to borrow their program, especially the three-year law."[89] In writing to the Russian Foreign Office on February 27, Isvolsky happily reported the same conclusion.[90] If the Socialists were restrained in their criticism, it was because they considered the Doumergue government the lesser of two evils.

If they erred, as in the long run they did, their mistake was natural. Though the opening months of 1914 were a period of circular debate and evident fatigue, they were at least free of that frenetic preparation for war which had exhausted the Socialists under Poincaré and Barthou. While Isvolsky denied that any essential difference separated this government from its predecessors, Baron Guillaume, Belgian ambassador at Paris, thought otherwise: "I feel certain that Europe would profit most from the policies of M. Caillaux, the Radicals, and the Radical-Socialists. As I have already told you, MM. Poincaré, Delcassé, Millerand, and their friends have created and pushed the current policies of nationalism, militarism, and chauvinism. . . . I see in them the greatest threat to the peace of Europe today."[91] When the Socialists lent support to the ministry, tacit but evident enough, they worked from similar premises. For as the all-important elections of 1914 drew near, they felt that they had no viable alternative, if they were to rein in the forces of war, but to cast their lot with the Radicals.

In the waning days of 1913, the *vedettes* of the new nationalism were already organizing in dead seriousness for the coming elections. On December 27, an array of influential politicians, united less by party labels than by a resurgent conservatism, met in the offices of Jean Dupuy's *Petit Parisien* to chart their course to victory. Embattled alumni of Progressism, Radicalism, and even Socialism, they rallied round Briand, who veiled their antilabor, nationalistic aspirations behind a cloud of balmy sentiments: "The country has had enough of violent politics. We want a fresh-smelling house. We want reforms, but with a smile."[92] No spokesman of the new nationalism (and the old conservatism) was missing, save only President Poincaré; the prospect of a Jaurès-Caillaux coalition had finally catalyzed French politics into a sharply defined Left and Right.[93]

Early in January, these leaders met again, this time to found the Fédération des gauches, a political party "in the tradition . . . of Gambetta, Ferry, and Waldeck-Rousseau." In its name and especially in its program, the Fédération des gauches erected something of a progressive façade. By its strong profession of secularism and its tepid advocacy of fiscal reform, the party squatted on familiar liberal terrain; but by its unswerving allegiance to private property and the three-year law, the Fédération des gauches revealed, no less clearly than Girondism in 1793 or moderate republicanism in 1848, that its liberalism was a barricade against radical social change.

With the emergence of the Fédération, the Socialists faced the most serious conservative challenge since the days of the Affair. Thus, in the last week of January, when they convened at Amiens for their annual Congress, their thoughts centered on the question of tactics for the impending elections of April and May. Their problem, even more obviously than in years past, was one of means rather than ends. For when they calculated the strength of the working-class movement and translated it into votes, they faced the hard reality that the S.F.I.O. alone could win no majority for peace.

"It is a crass misunderstanding of working class politics," an English Socialist has recently observed, "to suppose that one necessarily votes for a proletarian party if one was born in a proletarian position."[94] Who better than Jaurès could testify to the truth of that observation? "The real business of Socialists," William Morris once wrote, "is to impress on the workers the fact that they are a class, whereas they ought to be a Society." For long years, Jaurès and his friends clung to that ideal, but the results, even by 1914, remained inconclusive. For neither in the unity of its organization nor in the clarity of its thought did the French working class approximate the classic proletariat of Marxist textbooks.[95]

Over the prospects of the S.F.I.O., the persistent disunity of the working class cast a grey shadow of gloom. "We are still a nation of small farms and peasants," Sembat bluntly admitted. "That is the key to our impotence."[96] This dogged tenacity of the peasantry, its reluctance to yield before the logic of industrialism, created for the Socialists an almost insuperable obstacle at the outset of every election. To overcome it, they went to the village, intensified their efforts, and even managed, in the elections of 1914, to conquer certain Radical strongholds of the departments of central and southern France.[97] Yet the source of their strength remained the urban proletariat, and so long as an appreciable number of workers escaped the Socialist net, the S.F.I.O. could count on no clear-cut victory. "The French working class," Jaurès sadly concluded a fortnight before his death, "has been unable to group its forces, to develop that overwhelming power which alone can tip the scales in favor of peace."[98]

Where, then, could the S.F.I.O. turn but to the Radical Left in its search for electoral strength? To the argument that Socialism and Radicalism were essentially incompatible, few Socialists would have ventured a refutation. Not while Radicals like Klotz, Paul Morel, Guist'hau, Beranger, Jean Dupuy, and Pichon waved nationalistic colors from the front ranks of the Fédération des gauches; not while the Doumergue ministry treated the three-year law as sacred and the income tax as a political game. "No one in our party would even advocate a formal pact with a bourgeois party," asserted Jaurès before the delegates at Amiens.[99] Yet so cold and hard were the facts of French political life that the Socialists could scarcely retreat behind a wall of doctrinal purity. So long as the reactionaries and conservatives threatened to inundate the working-class movement in a flood of imperialism and militarism, they had either to resign themselves to failure or to approach Caillaux and his followers as electoral allies.

Between January 25 and 28, the delegates of the S.F.I.O. assembled at Amiens to raise again the eternal question of tactics; the arguments were by now familiar enough and the passions they roused automatic. The Marxist Bracke, Guesde's trusted lieutenant, denounced any and all collaboration with the Radicals, while Jaurès impressed upon the Congress the urgency of electing deputies, whether Socialist or not, who would cast their votes for peace. The debate, in fact, was more rhetorical than real. "We have a real stake in the existence of a strong, disciplined Radical Party," Lavigne admitted in a letter to a fellow Marxist.[100] Even the most devout Guesdists, though publicly they denied it, privately felt that Caillaux's Radical-Socialism was less risky than Briand's Fédération des gauches. Thus, when the Socialists finally adopted a resolution, they came down solidly behind the tactics of collaboration: "On the first ballot, the Socialist Party will run its own candidate in every electoral district, who will champion the full program of socialism. On the second ballot, it will throw its support behind every effort against militarism. . . . It will rally behind candidates of other parties, who are determined to carry on the struggle against war, chauvinism, and the military-clerical coalition."[101] When the Socialists left Amiens, reasonably united and certainly hopeful, their thoughts of success were considerably more than idle fancy.

Among conservatives, however, the prospect of a Caillaux-Jaurès alliance generated first fear and then a sense of recklessness. To discredit the coalition and destroy it, they needed a pressure point, a center of vulnerability, and they found it in the bizarre career of Caillaux. Across the front page of *Le Figaro*, editor Gaston Calmette, who reflected the views of his friends Briand and Barthou, launched a bitter, well-planned campaign against the Minister of Finance. Warming up slowly, Calmette first repeated the rather musty charge that Caillaux, through his secret negotiations with Berlin, had betrayed France during the second Moroccan crisis. But by the turn of the year, *Le Figaro's* resourceful editor, desperately afraid that his campaign would be stalled, appealed to the sensational. Caillaux, he now charged, was linked to the most intricate chain of corruption in prewar France, the notorious affair of M. Rochette.

Stendhal might have invented the Rochette scandal; Balzac would certainly have relished it; but it took Jaurès to judge it. The rise of Rochette, swindler extraordinary, was possible only in the age of material ambition and easy ethics; his fall was possible only in a society of powerful capitalists and client politicians. A young man in a hurry, a *garçon du café* with an eye to the main chance, Rochette found in fraudulent speculation the key to easy success. Buying up titles to defunct companies and inventing names for nonexistent ones, he sold worthless stock and pocketed large profits. By 1907 he "lived on intimate terms with Senators, dined with ministers, and raced around France in his two automobiles."[102] But when Rochette, who was amusing so long as he operated in the demimonde of financial fantasy, sought to penetrate the upper world of capitalism, he met the concerted opposition of his well-established competitors. When Rochette first tried to win the concession for the Compagnie générale des omnibus, which had been for years the province of Eugène Étienne, he made enemies of both that veteran colonialist and his financial ally, Maurice Rouvier. When Rochette went even further and vied for control of the influential *Petit Journal* with Charles Prevet — industrialist, financier, and former Senator — he ran into a solid wall of opposition. Determined to destroy this interloper once and for all, his competitors arranged for one Pichereau to register with the government an official complaint, charging Rochette with fraud and swindle. Though the government had previously ignored similar charges, Minister of Justice Briand now accommodated the Étienne-Prevet group and ordered Rochette's arrest on March 20, 1908.

Until 1910, the strange circumstances surrounding the arrest escaped the full glare of publicity. But on July 11 of that year, when Jaurès interpellated the Briand ministry, he subjected the whole scandal to a devastating analysis. What was this Rochette Affair, he cried, but a savage death struggle in the capitalist jungle? "The financial and political high command . . . apprehensively, resentfully watched the rise of this inter-loper, this ambush-fighter, who dared to demand the rank of general."[103] In relating the details of this struggle among titans, Jaurès built the facts into an indictment of a social system built upon privilege, influence, and dishonor.

When Briand replied for the government, he was evasive enough to win a vote of confidence from the Chamber and a vote of appreciation from the moderate press.[104] Yet so disturbing were the Socialist allega-tions, so resounding in the public ear, that the Chamber approved the appointment of a committee, under the chairmanship of Jaurès, to estab-lish the facts in the Rochette Affair. Almost two years later, in March, 1912, the Committee of Inquiry rendered a comprehensive report, but the Chamber, unmoved by the evidence of political impropriety, refused to censure the guilty office-holders. Jaurès, between anger and despair, could only cry out: "Are we still living under the Republic? How will we ever pull ourselves out of the abyss?"[105]

The malefactors thus escaped, and the hullaballoo over the scandal faded into an inaudible whisper. But in 1914, at the height of Calmette's campaign against Caillaux, the Rochette Affair became once again a burning political issue. On March 10, Le Figaro bluntly charged, though without documentary proof, that Caillaux had "broken the law on be-half of Rochette." The basis for Calmette's allegation was the mysterious Fabre report, a memorandum written on March 31, 1911, by the Attorney General of the Paris Court of Appeals, which accused both the Premier and the Minister of Finance, Monis and Caillaux respectively, of forcing him to postpone Rochette's trial for several months.[106] But Calmette had never actually seen the Fabre document, which was then in Barthou's possession,[107] nor could Le Figaro reproduce its contents. Without that evidence, the case against Caillaux threatened to collapse before an im-patient, skeptical public. Agitated, almost desperate, Calmette sank to the lowest level of journalism to keep his campaign alive. On March 13, he published a private letter written by Caillaux on July 5, 1901, to his second wife (then his mistress), which revealed his insincerity on the income tax issue during his tenure of office under Waldeck-Rousseau.[108] Calmette's temerity in printing extracts from a personal letter shocked the second Mme Caillaux, who feared that Mme Gueydan (the first Mme Caillaux) might have turned over to Calmette even more personal letters. Determined to silence Calmette once and for all, she forced her way into his office on the evening of March 17, leveled a revolver at him, fired six shots, and killed him.

The assassination of Calmette threw government, public, and press into nervous convulsions. On March 18, Caillaux resigned, while his enemies, anxious to reap their electoral advantages, launched a bitter attack against him in the Chamber. Over and again, they accused him of complicity in the Rochette Affair, while his defenders challenged them to produce the crucial Fabre document. At the height of the tense debate, Barthou went before the House, drew the document from his pocket, and read it word for word. Here, then, was the proof that Monis and Caillaux had used their high offices to tamper with the administration of justice. For the Right and Center, it was a moment of triumph, for the Radical Left, despite the rebuttal of Doumergue and Monis, a very real setback. By the end of the debate, the Chamber voted to organize a second Committee of Inquiry, again under the presidency of Jaurès, to plumb the depths of the Rochette Affair.

For thirty grueling committee hearings, Jaurès resisted the efforts of both the Radical-Socialists, who hoped to whitewash their leaders, and the *briandistes*, who aimed to destroy them. Under his steady hand, the Committee finally wrote a report which, though it recommended no legal action, criticized Monis and Caillaux for their improper intervention on behalf of Rochette. When the recommendations reached the Chamber on April 2, the anti-Caillaux faction exploded with indignation, accusing Jaurès and the committee of shielding the Radical-Socialists from punishment under the law. Replying for the Socialists, however, Sembat denounced the hypocrisy of these most recent converts to public morality: "If Caillaux had supported any other policy as Minister of Finance, if he had only abandoned the income tax, he would never have suffered these moralistic attacks."[109] The real issue of the debate, the Socialists concluded, was not public probity but social progress, and they joined with the Radicals to turn back the attacks from the Right and Center. By the end of the bitter session, the Chamber, following where the Jaurès Committee had led, condemned "the excessive power of wealth over public officials and of public officials over the administration of justice."

In one sense, as *Le Progrès* pointed out, the conservatives had scored a victory; for by diverting the course of public debate, they had forestalled action on the income tax before the legislative session ended on April 4. Yet despite that defeat, the Left emerged from the debate little bloodied and certainly unbowed. As Jaurès and his friends prepared for the final and decisive phase of the 1914 electoral campaign, they still hewed to the tactical line of Amiens.

When he had set his party's course and fulfilled its parliamentary mission, a weary Jaurès faced up to the problem of his own election. In a Europe caught between cynicism and hysteria, he had become hero to millions; but by the irony of politics, he was forced once again, even as

late as 1914, to fight for his own parliamentary seat. Wealth and clericalism were still on the side of Solages, and though the Marquis no longer
stood for office himself, he was as determined as ever to purge France of
the Socialist menace. And in the current electoral campaign, his tactics
seemed more effective than ever before. Passing over the reactionary clerical candidate, Falgueyrettes, Solages now threw his support to the Radical Maurice Rigaud who, if he failed to impress voters with his mediocre
talents, could at least confuse them by his family ties to Louise Jaurès:
"The threat was all the more serious to Jean since the handsome Maurice
said to the electors: 'Vote for me rather than for Jaurès. It really makes
no difference since we're cousins.'" — The Mining Company urged its
workers to vote for the 'cousin.' The Marquis said privately: 'We'll use
Rigaud like a dirty broom to sweep Socialism away.'"[110]

So Jaurès went home. Hardly a day now passed that he did not suffer
a severe headache or throbbing pains in his throat. Yet he made his way
through village and town, talking about the danger of war and the
last desperate chance for peace. When the air was clear of organized
hate, his listeners greeted him warmly and cheered his words; but where
the propaganda of his enemies had prepared the way, they stood silent,
even hostile. "Everyone knows that Jaurès stands for Germany!" ranted
Maurras, and dozens of less talented journalists echoed his accusations,
spreading suspicion and even hatred among the credulous. Did Jaurès
feel that his life was in danger? He hardly doubted it. "Day after day,"
he cried in the Chamber on July 4, 1913, "you gentlemen of the Right
and your supporters agitate for our assassination." Now, at Pampelonne,
where he met his friend Malfitte, he spoke of the threatening letters he
received from irate nationalists.

Yet Jaurès stayed his course. From those early days, when he joined
the strikers of Carmaux, he had been, in the literal sense, a popular
leader, not only speaking from the heights but mingling with the crowd
in one demonstration after another. Writing years later, Victor Serge remembered him that way — at the head of some 500,000 protesting, in
October, 1909, the execution of Francisco Ferrer; leading a great demonstration, one tense evening in 1910, against the execution of the young
worker Liabeuf.[111] Danger had become part of his way of life; and sympathy, even for those who threatened him, was the mark of his humanism. Certainly, he told Malfitte, he might soon be killed. "Yet I could
pardon my murderer. The real guilt would belong to those who armed
him."[112]

When Frenchmen finally voted on April 26, they proved that nationalism, for all its emotional appeal, was not invincible. For though the
first results were still inconclusive, they presaged a defeat for the Right

and Center if the parties of the Left observed their alliance on the second ballot. In the Tarn, Jaurès failed to win an outright majority against his two opponents, but when the Radicals backed him in the runoff, he scored an impressive victory over Falgueyrettes, 6801 to 4847. The national results were no less bright for the Socialist Party. Capturing an unprecedented 1,400,000 votes, 300,000 more than in 1910, the S.F.I.O. won 103 seats in the Chamber. Since the Unified Radicals returned 136 deputies, including Caillaux, and the Independent Socialists thirty, the antimilitarist coalition controlled at least 269 of the 603 seats in the new Chamber. And of the 102 deputies who ran as uncommitted Radicals or Left Republicans, at least thirty or forty were likely to face Left on key political issues.[113] Suspicious, skeptical, and sober, the French masses had refused to follow where Briand and Barthou led; they had heard the thunder of nationalism and the appeals of conservatism, but they voted for the Left.

The Socialist victory, the greatest in the party's history, belonged first and last to Jaurès. In the ranks of Socialism marched *révolutionnaires* and *révoltés*, Marxists and syndicalists, workers and intellectuals, idealistic students and battle-scarred militants. Nothing held them together so much as the generous, all-embracing spirit of Jaurès.[114] "Rien ne l'enfermait," wrote Romain Rolland, "mais il enfermait tout en lui."[115] So he came to embody the movement, to discipline and inspire it.

"Nature de flamme," observed Rappoport, "il communiquait son feu intérieur à l'action monotone de la vie quotidienne."[116]

But the flame was his. The premises of the party had been too long reformist; its other leaders were too often sectarian or ambitious; its time of testing would come too soon. The events of 1914 and 1920 would undo Jaurès' work. But his gifts to the S.F.I.O. — unity, reason, moral fervor, and a revolutionary will — were also his endowment to every future working class movement.

VIII

Along the entire route of French politics, from the conservative Right to the Radical Left, journalists and politicians admitted the Socialist success. "The progress of revolutionary Socialism among the villagers is a significant and frightening development," *L'Echo de Paris* moaned on May 1. Voters by the thousands had swung over from Radicalism to Socialism, declared General Percin, "because the Socialist Party has a program and the Radical Party has none."[117] The drift toward Socialism was thus clear, but what of its immediate significance? Would Jaurès become, as his bitterest enemies feared, the arbiter of French politics? Would conservatism yield to reform and militarism to peace? The answers hinged on the behavior of the Radicals who, despite their resolve at Pau, still seemed plagued by indecision. "The party is bicephalous," quipped *La Lanterne*. "One head is Radical, another Radical-Socialist. . . . Thus, in fact, there are Radical-Socialists and Radical anti-Socialists."[118]

But Jaurès succumbed to neither cynicism nor despair. For in Caillaux he recognized a leader vigorous enough to discipline his party and commit it to peace and reform. "The ablest man we now have in France is Caillaux," Jaurès remarked to the German liberal Conrad Haussmann. "More than ability, he has will, character, and a sense of decision. That is why his enemies despise him."[119] One afternoon, soon after Parliament reconvened in June, Jaurès and Caillaux met in the corridor outside the Chamber and conversed candidly about the immediate future. "As soon as possible," Caillaux insisted, "we must form a strong Leftist ministry which will press for a policy of European peace. . . . But it is only possible if the Socialist Party offers its unqualified support. I mean by that collaboration not only in Parliament but also in the ministry. I would never assume power as Premier, for example, unless you entered the Cabinet as Minister of Foreign Affairs." The proposal was breathtaking. Never before had a bourgeois leader proposed to entrust the Foreign Office to a "traitorous" Socialist. Jaurès pledged his support. The dictum of Amsterdam, he reminded Caillaux, still governed the tactics of the Second International, but "in the present crisis, my party must not founder on the rocks of scholasticism."[120]

On June 2, when the new Chamber was but a day old, Doumergue capitulated before the strong Jaurès-Caillaux faction and submitted his resignation. A staunch supporter of the three-year law and the Russian Alliance,[121] he preferred to withdraw rather than to curry favor from the antinationalist Left. Doumergue's resignation, the most fruitful act of his ministry, roused the hopes of the new Leftist majority and their supporters in the country. But President Poincaré, determined at all costs to protect the three-year law, called upon René Viviani, that flighty exile from Socialism, to form a new ministry. For though Viviani had not originally supported the military law, he convinced Poincaré that, if he were Premier, he would enforce it. But Viviani, distrusted both on the Left and on the Right, stumbled through two frustrating days of negotiations to form a ministry and finally had to admit defeat.

With an astonishing disregard for the popular will, the President then called forth the aged Ribot, whose platform of property and patriotism had remained unchanged over the passing decade. Shocked and then angered, the Socialists and most Radicals united against Poincaré's attempted coup. On June 12, when Ribot presented to the Chamber a ministry dominated by Delcassé and Bourgeois, the parties of the Left united against "this humiliation of the republican party."[122] Millerand, Briand, Barthou, and Klotz all rose during the debate to praise Ribot, but the Leftists had come to bury him and by a clear majority, 306 to 262, they did.

In half retreat, Poincaré turned once again to Viviani, who managed to put together by June 14 a wholly undistinguished Radical-Socialist ministry. Without Caillaux, the proposed government lacked real ability or clear direction; nor was there any indication that its majority would support repeal of the three-year law. "In my view," Isvolsky perceptively wrote of Viviani, "he is of the same stripe as Briand, Millerand, and other ex-doctrinaires who have become reasonable through the experience of power."[123] In his ministerial declaration, Viviani confirmed Isvolsky's impression, for while he played to the Leftists on the income tax, he offered them scant hope on the three-year law. But the Radicals, unwilling to prolong the political crisis already in its third week, went over to Viviani on June 17, and his ministry was confirmed. Only weeks before, a strong Leftist ministry had seemed imminent; now, quite suddenly, that prospect faded and passed.

The war fever of the major powers, however, did not. As July approached, Poincaré and Viviani made ready for a visit to St. Petersburg, where they would pledge fealty to the Franco-Russian Alliance and plan revenge against the Central Powers. And what of Jaurès, as prospect of peace faded? His once-ruddy complexion was now ashen, his once-indestructible energy bent to fatigue. But his faith, that impassioned, unshakable belief in the destiny of man, suffused his spirit and galvanized his will.

Late in June, when the French countryside had burst into bloom, Jaurès took the advice of his comrades at L'Humanité and escaped from Paris for a day. With Landrieu and Renaudel, he rode out to L'Isle-Adam where, in fresh and peaceful surroundings, he enjoyed Blanche Vogt's warm hospitality. The air had never seemed so fresh, nor food so delicious. For a few brief hours, he forgot the problems of the Chamber and the pressures of his newspaper. While they dined, he spoke of Anatole France and recited from Vergil. But in the end he returned to the overriding issue, the only issue — peace. German military preparations, Landrieu thought, would surely drive Europe to war. Jaurès vehemently disagreed: "War, I believe, is impossible!"[124]

Was it naïveté that afflicted him or sheer blindness? Neither really. But it was the optimism born of pessimism, the loud clear cry of affirmation to muffle his own whispers of doubt.

IX

"During the last years of his life," Enjalran explained in his letter to Lévy-Bruhl, "Jaurès thought deeply about the largest problems of man and society. I sensed that his whole philosophy was evolving, that he was going through a kind of crisis, the outcome of which we can never know. In the main, his thoughts bore much more than before the marks of pessimism and positivism, though the optimism and idealism of his youth generally triumphed. . . . The riddle of the world seemed so much more difficult to solve, so much more painful to unravel than it had once seemed."[125]

Enjalran's observations confirm what other documents imply — that Jaurès' socialism was constantly evolving, that under the impact of imperialism and impending war, he was questioning his views on the State, on democracy, on revolution. What could have produced his undercurrent of pessimism if not his growing doubt that moral idealism and democratic action could stem the tide of war? And if capitalism bred imperialism and imperialism war, was there another solution than to destroy the system root and branch and to create a new community? One hardly knows, as Enjalran has written, where such speculations might have led Jaurès. Certain it is, however, that he had traveled long and far from the days of the Left bloc.

"In the first part of his career," Jean Zyromski has recently observed, "Jaurès was under the influence of bourgeois idealism, but he very quickly shucked off that influence, and his life was then a continuous ascension toward Marxism. . . . The years from 1905 until his death in 1914 unquestionably testify to this."[126] Though rendered by a veteran of the French working-class movement, this judgment is oversimplified and colored by special party pleading. In his career, Jaurès followed a course which took him, in four major phases, from republican idealism to a socialism based on both idealism and materialism. And there he stood. But in the decade after Amsterdam, when he had left the bloc behind and embarked on his incomparable campaign against war and imperialism, that synthesis became tighter and more complex.

In his last phase, sometime after 1904, Jaurès wrote a long essay, undated and substantially unpublished until 1960, which catches him whole.[127] He wrote there of the religious spirit — the universal human aspiration for unity and harmony — and its frustration under capitalism. *Dieu est mort!*

We can say that today there is no religion, and, in the truest sense, there is no community. Traditional Christianity is dying, philosophically, scientifically, and politically. . . . History never knew the total Fall of Man, which necessitates the intervention of a tyrannical God in order to restore him. . . . Rather the entire universe suffered the Fall, in the sense that the unity of God was shattered into innumerable competitive and egoistic centers.[128]

Dieu revivra! But the spirit will live again in the Socialist movement and in its ultimate victory:

If we thought that man was now permanently evil and the human conscience powerless, we would despair of love, and we would abandon the great hope of Socialism. On the contrary, we note with joy countless examples of human nobility, and we conclude from them that the conscience of man, who has known how to conceive the ideal of justice, will not long accept an economic regime which daily negates that ideal. But we do not believe that the moral conscience of humanity, unaided by the pressure of external forces, is as yet strong enough to effect fundamental social changes. Accompanying every moral revolution in history, there has been a material revolution, an uprising of oppressed peoples. . . . The moral nobility of the French Revolution would not have been possible without the revolt of the suffering peasantry. And today, in spite of the human capacity for good, Socialism will triumph only because all the victims of the social order are uniting to overthrow it. . . . Socialism, then, can be defined thus: a moral revolution expressed through a material revolution.[129]

Jaurès' idealism and the optimism it bred remained powerful, undeniable; nor could it have been otherwise. As the crisis of 1914 reached its crest, he could scarcely silence his appeal or abandon his crusade. He continued to hope, as he had for a lifetime, that even in the bourgeois State, the people, ethically roused, could act and would be heard; he continued to believe that the ideal of justice, translated into the vision of a new society, would galvanize the popular will to Socialism. But one senses also in Jaurès a revolutionary urgency, a conviction that the time had come to find the breaking-point in the old society and to establish the new — by legal means and extralegal, by political action and direct economic action, by democracy and mass demonstration. Had Jaurès experienced the war and its aftermath — the Russian Revolution, the disintegration of Western Socialism, the success of fascism — he might have evolved beyond those premises which, in the heyday of the parliamentary Republic, seemed so sound, to a unique brand of Western Socialism which none of his successors could ever devise.

14

Assassination
July, 1914

I

On June 28, 1914, in the Bosnian city of Sarajevo, a terrorist's bullet struck down an archduke and crippled the hopes of mankind.

Behind the assassination of Francis Ferdinand lay the determination of Serbian nationalists, regardless of cost or consequence, to create a South Slav state at the expense of the Austrian Empire. The most reckless among them organized the secret, terroristic Black Hand Society, which enjoyed strong support from the Serbian officer corps. In an atmosphere heavy with conspiracy, the terrorists of the Black Hand hatched a plot to assassinate Francis Ferdinand, whose efforts to create a South Slav state within the orbit of the Habsburg monarchy seemed the most serious threat to Serbian nationalism. When they learned that the archduke planned to observe Austrian military maneuvers in Bosnia late in June, they charted their nihilistic path to freedom. The murder assignment fell to Tchabrinovitch and Prinzip, two Austrian Serbs then living in Belgrade, who slipped across the frontier into Bosnia under the sympathetic eyes of the Serbian border guard. On June 28, as Francis Ferdinand and his wife rode through the streets of Sarajevo, the assassins awaited them. Tchabrinovitch missed his mark with a grenade; but Prinzip leveled his pistol and felled the royal couple.

The assassination touched off yet another European crisis. In Vienna, both the Chief of Staff, Conrad von Hötzendorf, and the Foreign Minister, Count Berchtold, clamored for immediate war against Serbia, but the conciliatory influence of Count Tisza, the Hungarian Premier, temporarily checked their success. Confused by conflicting advice, the aged Francis Joseph solicited counsel from Berlin. Germany had heretofore sought to restrain Austria's ambitions, but now it was different. Convinced that her own rearmament program was already a success while Russia's was not, Germany felt ready and able to back her ambitious ally. Thus, when the Kaiser received the Austrian Ambassador at Potsdam on July 5, he promised that Germany would back a strong Austrian policy of retaliation against Serbia. The "blank check," as history has come to know Berlin's commitment, ensured the victory of Vienna's military clique.

While the German bloc planned its policy of revenge and glory, the governments of the other major powers remained strangely unresponsive. Were they finally, after so many years of tension, inured to crises? No doubt they were, and especially before they had even an inkling of Berlin's most recent commitment to Vienna. But even later, when it was evident that Austria aimed to humble Serbia, they seemed unmoved, even fatuous, as though war might be a boon and its results a blessing. Whether in Paris, St. Petersburg, London, or Rome, the decision-makers had dwelt too long upon the gains, territorial and commercial, which might accrue from a defeat of the German bloc.

Jaurès was apprehensive in these uncertain days, but certainly not fatalistic. Some time between July 2 and 5, he composed for a foreign periodical a long article on the ways to peace; originally unpublished because the magazine collapsed before he sent it off, the manuscript, found among his papers after his death, appeared several months later (the first two days of October) in *L'Humanité*. The grim frivolity of power politics, the free play of imperialism and militarism — preyed on his mind and gnawed at his optimism. Yet he could not believe, after two Moroccan crises and two Balkan wars, that the latest Austro-Serb imbroglio would finally shatter the peace. No, war was not inevitable, he insisted, if — and here his hopes seemed detached from the realities — the governments of Europe, responsive to the popular will, worked to eliminate the causes of world tension. First, he wrote in outlining a program of peace, those peoples who had lost their independence through conquest must again enjoy the fruits of freedom; second, "Europe can and must send her products over the world without destroying the autonomy of other countries and subjugating their populations"; finally — and it was a point of view that brought him close to Caillaux — the capitalistic groups of Europe must engage in peaceful coöperation, each willing to share rather than to dominate the markets of the world. One day, and not far distant, Socialism would extirpate the roots of greed and discontent in the world; until then, though capitalism bore within itself the seeds of war and colonialism, it could regulate and restrain itself. It was possible, Jaurès felt; men could still influence the course of affairs. But it would not be easy, and if the effort failed, the social system and its leaders would stand condemned. In the meantime, in the present crisis, all the forces for peace, the Socialists at their head, had to raise their voices loud; and in France and Germany especially, they had to exert pressure on their governments to exercise a moderating influence upon Russia and Austria.

Toward that end, Jaurès appeared briefly before the Chamber on July 7. The government had requested 400,000 francs in order to send Poincaré and Viviani on a special mission to Russia, but its explanations of the proposed trip were vague and, as far as the Socialists were concerned, suspicious. What kind of commitments would the President and the Premier make in St. Petersburg? Would they force the Russians to restrain the Serbs in the present crisis, or would they promise them full French support against the Austrians? Since the government shed no light on these crucial questions, the Socialists opposed the request for funds.

The hour had grown late when Jaurès rose to defend his party's position. Acquiescence was passing for debate and patriotism for policy; but Jaurès would not be silenced. "We find it inadmissible," he cried, "that France should become involved in wild Balkan adventures because of treaties of which she knows neither the text, nor the sense, nor the limits, nor the consequences." If the democratic revolution had succeeded in Russia, if a representative Duma had been running the affairs of that unhappy land, the Franco-Russian Alliance might have served the legitimate defensive needs of both countries. "But when the Tsarist counter-revolution . . . executed or imprisoned those brave Russians who tried to keep the basic freedoms they had heroically won, France lost her only guarantee that the treaty . . . would serve just ends."[1]

In the Chamber, those words fell on deaf ears. Only the Socialists refused funds for the St. Petersburg mission, and on July 16 Poincaré and Viviani embarked for Russia aboard the battleship *France*. But the parliamentary rebuff failed to silence Jaurès and his friends. Nor did the roar of nationalism drive them to cover. On July 14, the Socialists assembled in Paris for their annual Congress where, before government and public alike, they would reaffirm their unyielding opposition to war.

The weight of their responsibility fell heavily upon the conscience of the delegates. Could they really unleash a revolutionary strike against war? Would they risk ostracism and even repression? And if so, would the workers follow them? Frail but impassioned, the sixty-nine-year-old Guesde warned the Congress against the "nostrum" of the general strike. But his argument was now less anti-anarchist than anti-German; for if the general strike succeeded in France and not in Germany, he warned as did the anti-Socialist press, then the nation would lie helpless before its enemy. At his side, paradoxically enough, stood Hervé, the *enfant terrible* of the revolutionary Left, who now insisted that the patriotic workers would never respond to the call of the general strike. Thus, at the moment of crisis, the Marxist and the syndicalist, both of them fore-shadowing their wartime nationalism, repudiated a lifetime of inter-nationalism.

But not Jaurès; his was the opposite route. "We have often agreed," he reminded the Congress, "that the general strike is one way of in-fluencing and warning our rulers." Not a strike of French workers alone, he explained, which could paralyze France before an invader, but a coördinated proletarian effort in every belligerent country. "Thus, if France were exposed to the aggressions of German imperialism, Ger-many would be similarly threatened by Russia." Jaurès' intervention proved decisive. Emboldened by his courage, the Socialists agreed to use every means at their disposal, including the general strike, to prevent a European war.

But what did it really mean? "The war," the insurgent Alfred Rosmer wrote in *La Vie ouvrière* on April 30, 1919, "was the great test. It cre-ated a new division. On the one side, the betrayers of Socialism, the weaklings, those who, when faced with revolution, turned out to be only simple democrats. On the other side, the revolutionaries." In re-trospect, one can sense the division well before that. If Guesde weakened, if Sembat had so far retreated from his Blanquist origins as to flirt with Maurras and *L'Action française,* what could one expect of those, how-ever sincere, who had never been more than mild reformers? In its politics and in its bargaining, in its very success, the party had sacrificed its passion, and a movement without passion belongs less to the future than to the past. It was not a matter of reforms; who could really doubt their worth? But it *was* a question of attitude. "A Socialist," one critic has written, "should be in a perpetual state of insurrection; not neces-sarily out of the injustice he personally suffers, but because of the evils that society tolerates and sanctions."[2] Jaurès, one feels, was such an insurrectionary; and so too were many good militants, but not the majority.

In conservative and nationalistic circles, the S.F.I.O. resolution touched off a bitter campaign against the Socialists. *Le Temps* on July 18 denounced their "treason against the homeland," while Daudet of *L'Action française* hinted openly at the assassination of the "Prussian Jaurès."[3] Unabashed and patient, Jaurès used the pages of *L'Humanité* on July 18 to set the Socialist position straight: "The general strike will never be unilateral. . . . No matter what our enemies say, there is no contradiction between the maximum effort for peace and, if we should be invaded, the maximum effort for national independence." The explanation was clear and unequivocal. Yet what chance had this logic against the atavistic surge of nationalism? In the final, fateful week of July, while European diplomacy foundered on rocks of ambition, miscalculation, and sheer inertia, the "bastard internationalism of the Labour and Socialist movement collapsed like a house of cards."[4] Perhaps Jaurès suspected that it would be so. But not for a single minute did he lose hope or betray his compact with humanity.

II

At 6 P.M. on July 23, the Austrian Ambassador to Belgrade handed the Serbian government an ultimatum which led to the great war of 1914. After almost four weeks of ominous silence, Vienna bluntly accused Belgrade of complicity in the crime of Sarajevo and demanded immediate suppression of the anti-Austrian movement in Serbia. The ten demands in the ultimatum,[5] to which Belgrade was asked to comply within forty-eight hours, were so harsh that Sazonov, when he first learned of them early on July 24, could only gasp: "C'est la guerre européenne!"

Affronted and ambitious, Serbia was spoiling for the inevitable showdown with Austria, but she could hardly hew to a strong line without the promise of Russian help. From St. Petersburg, however, where Sazonov and the Council of Ministers realized that the long-range Russian military reorganization was still incomplete, Belgrade received only counsels of caution. Yet European diplomacy, so long rooted in false pride and overconfidence, was unequal to the task of averting war. Berlin, which had approved the Austrian ultimatum before it was sent, would openly encourage the pretensions of Vienna; Paris, Poincaré had affirmed in St. Petersburg on July 21, would stand behind the Franco-Russian Alliance; and London, which had vigorously restrained Berlin during the Agadir affair, would heighten the present crisis by deliberate hesitancy.[6]

On July 25, barely within Vienna's time limit, Serbia answered the Austrian ultimatum. In her moderate reply, she agreed to comply with all the demands, except that of Austrian collaboration in the Sarajevo investigation. Yet Belgrade's capitulation was insufficient for Vienna. Since Serbia had not accepted the ultimatum unconditionally, Austria recalled her ambassador the same evening and prepared her declaration of war. Thus, over the destiny of the South Slav nation, the peoples of the civilized world were suddenly threatened with death and destruction.

As the crisis deepened, Socialist and trade union leaders across Europe rallied the working classes to resistance to war. In Germany, the Executive Committee of the Social Democratic Party addressed the workers in a proclamation that rang with revolutionary fervor: "The ruling classes, who in peacetime oppress you, despise you, exploit you, want to use you as cannon-fodder. Everywhere the cry must ring in the despots' ears: 'We want no war! Down with war! Long live international brotherhood!'"[7] In France, the high command of the C.G.T. unleashed a bitter attack on the merchants of war and exhorted the proletariat to demonstrate for peace. But the most memorable words of the hour came from Jaurès.

On July 25, the day Austrians rejected the Serbian reply, he was in Vaise, near Lyons, where he was scheduled to make a campaign speech for Marius Moutet, the Socialist candidate in a special by-election. But when Jaurès stood before the overflow crowd that sultry evening, he was thinking of matters weightier than a local election. Without a moment's hesitation, without even a word of adornment, he spoke at once of the European crisis:[8]

Citizens, the note which Austria has sent to Serbia is full of threats; and if Austria invades Slavic territory, if the Austrians attack the Serbs, . . . we can foresee Russia's entry into the war; and if Russia intervenes, Austria, confronted by two enemies, will invoke her treaty of alliance with Germany; and Germany has informed the powers through her ambassadors that she will come to the aid of Austria. . . . But then, it is not only the Austro-German Alliance which will come into play, but also the secret treaty between Russia and France.

Vienna's military clique was not alone responsible for unhinging the peace of Europe: "The imperialism of France, the crude ambition of Austria, the devious policy of Russia — they have all contributed to this horrible state of affairs." By inculpating the ruling class of every major power, Jaurès was calling on the European masses everywhere to act upon their governments, lest a universal war destroy their future: "Think of what that disaster would mean for Europe. . . . What a massacre, what destruction, what barbarism! That is why I still fervently hope, even as the black clouds thicken, what we can prevent the catastrophe. ... The proletariat must rally all of its vast forces. The workers of France, England, Germany, and Italy, those countless thousands of men and women, must unite. Their hearts must beat as one to prevent this horrible disaster!"

The speech was Jaurès' last on French soil. The road from Castres to Vaise had been a long one. Prophet, utopian, revolutionary, he had brought his thundering wrath down on a whole society. He stood now fully exposed to the ridicule of the realists and the hatred of the ultra-patriots. But he had long since calculated the cost of courage and accepted it: "A day may come when we will be assassinated, perhaps by someone we are trying to help. But after all, what does that matter? We don't have to be protected by praise and honor against the convolutions of life and the upheavals of history. We must remain faithful to our ideal, serve the cause of justice, create a future for men abandoned by society."[9]

III

On July 28, Austria declared war on Serbia. For two days, the leaders of the great States had twisted and turned, searching for a magical policy to save the peace while satisfying their ambitions. They finally yielded, however, not to their belated apprehension but to their conception of national power. By July 29, the question before Europe was whether the powers could localize the Austro-Serb war and prevent it from spreading. If neither Russia nor France mobilized, then Germany might force Austria to mediate her differences with Serbia; but if they continued their military preparations, Germany would certainly intervene at the side of her ally. Yet when night fell on July 29, the Tsar had authorized partial mobilization, while Poincaré and Grey had pledged their allegiance to the Triple Entente. Trapped by suspicion, fear, and pride, the diplomats seemed to accept the inevitable.

Jaurès returned to Paris close to exhaustion; yet he summoned up energy enough to direct the Socialist effort for peace. On July 28, before word of the Austrian attack on Serbia reached Paris, he drew up, in the name of the Permanent Administrative Committee of the S.F.I.O., a strongly worded manifesto calling on the French and German governments to restrain their respective allies. When he learned the following day of Austria's "unjustifiable declaration of war," Jaurès warned the great powers against rash policies which could turn a local conflict into a general war.[10] Like the legatee of European civilization, he spoke up for the peoples of all nations, weary and discouraged before "this relapse into barbarism. ... For a moment, we ask ourselves if life is worth the trouble, if man, incapable of either accepting his animal nature or transcending it, is not eternally destined for suffering. But then, in spite of everything, we must rally to the forces for good, the forces for progress, which are our only barriers against the flood of barbarism."[11]

Yet words alone, even stirring words, could hardly stem the tide of war. Thus, on July 29, Jaurès left for Brussels, where the delegates to the Bureau of the International would assess the European situation and coördinate their plans of action. The prospect that Socialist leaders of every country could meet at such a time to unite against war inspired in him a hope that never really died. At Brussels, the delegates met in the new wing of the Maison du Peuple where, despite the bitter antagonisms among their respective governments, they greeted each other as comrades. "I can still see it, and I will remember it all my life," recalled Vandervelde a year later. "Haase threw his arms around Jaurès' shoulders, confirming by this gesture the alliance against war."[12]

But if Jaurès and his comrades had faced up to the harsh truth, if they had not been so befogged by their own past professions, they might have admitted the near-helplessness of the Second International before the present crisis. Even when Victor Adler, aging and ill, confessed to his colleagues at the Bureau that Vienna's war against Belgrade had wide support and that Austrian Socialists could do almost nothing to end it, they seemed not to listen. Instead, they gave their rapt attention to Hugo Haase, who promised that the German Social Democrats would oppose Berlin's intervention, even if Russia were to enter the war against Austria. But though Haase was party chairman, he could now speak only for a minority. The overwhelming majority, as the events of August 4 would prove, were ready to join the disciplined ranks of German patriots. A decade earlier, in his great philippic against Bebel, Jaurès had foreseen the failure of German Social Democracy, but now, in the hour of crisis, he could hardly admit his own analysis.

The leaders of the International could and did sponsor antiwar street rallies; they could and did issue fiery proclamations. But it was all too little and too late. Despite the resolutions of Stuttgart and Copenhagen, they had neither extirpated the nationalism within their separate movements nor prepared the military strikes that might have shaped State policies. The weapons they displayed at Brussels were little more than noble sentiments and endless goodwill. Yet they could neither confess their impotence nor even believe it. So they continued to inveigh against war until the roar of guns silenced their voices.

That evening, the International sponsored a great mass-meeting at the Cirque Royale, where thousands of Belgian workers and intellectuals assembled to hear words of comfort and purpose: "When at last the long-awaited delegates appeared at the entrance, the whole audience rose to a man, with a wild roar of joyous, friendly, triumphant acclamation. And spontaneously, unheralded, the 'Internationale' broke from every throat, drowning the volleys of applause."[13]

From the opening address of Vandervelde through the speeches of Haase, Keir Hardie, Rubanovich, and Morgari, the hall rang with denunciation of imperialism, professions of international solidarity, and enthusiastic shouts from the audience. At the climax, Jaurès rose to speak. All that day he had suffered from a dreadful headache, which affected his step but not his spirit. "His head sagged between his burly shoulders," Martin du Gard has written, "and his hair, matted with sweat, hung in wisps over his low forehead. When, after slowly climbing the steps, he took his stand solidly, composedly, facing his audience, he brought to mind a stocky giant straining forward, bent-backed, his feet deeply planted in the soil, to stem the onrush of some catastrophic landslide. 'Citizens!' A clarion call. By some prodigy of nature, which recurred whenever he mounted a platform, Jaurès' voice suddenly drowned the fitful clamor of the crowd and a religious hush ensued; the stillness of a forest before the storm breaks."[14]

His analysis was not new, nor particularly well organized. But when he attacked the vanity of diplomacy and offered his prayer for peace, he "induced in the serried mass of listeners a high tension current, causing it to vibrate at the speaker's will, to thrill like a harp in the wind with anger or fraternity, hope or indignation."[15] Above all, it was hope that he sought to instill: "For us, the French Socialists, the task is simple. We don't have to force a policy of peace on our government. It already practices it. I have never hesitated to invite the bitter hatred of the chauvinists by my relentless, unhesitating campaign for a Franco-German understanding; but I can say that now the French government wants peace and is working to save it."

A startling passage, and without private documents it remains difficult to interpret. At its face value, it expresses faith in the peaceful intentions or at least the caution of the Poincaré-Viviani government. Like the C.G.T. manifesto of July 28, which threw the blame for the crisis on Austria and seemed to exonerate France of guilt, these words were soon enough seized upon by the government to rally the masses behind the war effort. Undoubtedly, Jaurès hoped fervently that the war could be localized, and his confidence in the French government may have been far more an article of faith than a rational belief. Certainly it conformed neither to his attacks of the past nor to his accusations of the next forty-eight hours, when it was a social system and its chiefs that he so bitterly condemned, not any particular nation. Yet these words, though he may have intended by them to shore up the courage of his comrades from many countries, compounded the confusion of the critical hour that approached.

But at the climax of his oration, Jaurès stood, without a syllable of equivocation, squarely on revolutionary terrain. For if all the governments of Europe were to falter and if the peace were violated, then, he cried, the working classes would rise up to turn war into revolution:

When typhus finishes the work begun by bullets, disillusioned men will turn on their rulers, whether German, French, Russian, or Italian, and demand their explanation for all those corpses. And then, the unchained Revolution will cry out to them: "Begone, and ask pardon of God and men!" But if we avoid the storm, then I hope that the masses will not forget and will say: "We must prevent this specter from rising out of its grave every six months to terrify the world." Men of all countries, we must reach our goal of peace and justice!

So Jaurès finished his last public oration.

IV

The following morning — it was July 30 — the members of the International Socialist Bureau met once more, signed a manifesto against war, and left for home. With an hour to spare before his train was scheduled to leave, Jaurès rushed over to the Museum of Art to look at the Flemish paintings of the Northern Renaissance. Before these great masterpieces, he was lost in thoughts of art and beauty, of the human achievement which inspired his lifelong effort.

Along with his Socialist comrades — Vaillant, Guesde, Sembat and his wife, and Jean Longuet — Jaurès finally boarded the train for Paris. What were his thoughts, how deep his hopes and fears in that hour of crisis? One can never know; but Longuet, who later described the journey back from Brussels in *Le Populaire du centre* (August 3, 1916), sensed his sadness, his terrible fatigue:

All those fortunate enough to know Jaurès personally had always been struck by his good humor, inspirited by his inexhaustible vitality and his universal curiosity; but now, it seemed to us, he was deeply worried, sad, already full of grief brought on by his clear vision of the horrible catastrophe which was about to overtake mankind. . . . As the train from Brussels rolled on, he fell asleep, worn out from emotional strain; as we looked at his wonderful face, so full of expression, we were suddenly overcome with a feeling, Mme Sembat and I — later we learned we had had the same impression — that he was dead. I froze with fright. How often I had thought to myself: "What would we do if we lost him, how could our party live and grow without his incomparable genius?"

Early that evening, the little group of Socialists arrived at the Gare de l'Est. Jaurès was still hopeful that Paris, Berlin, and London could and would localize the Austro-Serb war. But he had only to buy a newspaper and read the latest news before his confidence crumbled. Russia, he learned, had mobilized twenty-three divisions, and the threat of German retaliation hung over Europe.

The situation was, in fact, more serious than that. Confronted with Berlin's demands that St. Petersburg halt all military preparations, Sazonov and the Russian military chiefs opted for war. Arguing that peace was impossible and honor at stake, they persuaded a vacillating Tsar to approve full mobilization, and by six in the evening that fateful order went out over the far-flung Russian empire. In Berlin, the moderates of the Wilhelmstrasse already faced the opposition of Moltke and the military extremists. The Russian decision to mobilize was bound to strengthen the hand of the German General Staff and to destroy, once and for all, the basis for mediation.

In Paris, Poincaré and Viviani were concerned more with the preparations for war than with its prevention. At a dark, early hour on July 30, sometime between 2 and 3 A.M., a triumphant Isvolsky handed Viviani a telegram from Sazonov, which proclaimed the imminence of war. After consulting Poincaré, the Premier sent a telegram to Paléologue, the French Ambassador to St. Petersburg, reaffirming loyalty to the Russian Alliance, but urging caution, lest Russia "offer Germany a pretext for a total or partial mobilization of her forces."[16] The design of French policy thus became clear; though France accepted the inevitability of war, she hoped for a German initiative which would then throw responsibility squarely upon Berlin. Isvolsky was reaping his rewards after long years of wild sowing.

Nonetheless, Viviani's instructions might have served to deter St. Petersburg from full mobilization, except for the initiative of Paléologue. On July 28, he had already assured Sazonov of France's unswerving support; now, on July 30, when the Russian Foreign Minister disclosed to Paléologue the Tsar's order for general mobilization, the Ambassador, far from discouraging the plan, stressed Viviani's profession of loyalty to the Alliance.[17] Not until the morning of July 31, when it was already too late for effective French pressure, did Paléologue inform Paris of the Russian decision for full mobilization.

The French Cabinet meanwhile met in the early morning hours of July 30 to take those military measures which would ready France for war. On the urgent advice of the War Minister, the government ordered a sharp increase in the number of frontier troops; but to avoid incidents which might touch off a war, they were to advance no further than a line ten kilometers from the frontier. Was this, then, a sign of genuine restraint? "It would be a mistake to regard it mainly as a proof of Poincaré's love of peace," S. B. Fay has concluded. "Rather it was a measure primarily calculated to win British approval and military support, and to minimize the fact that France was taking an important military measure preparatory to war."[18]

An anxious Jaurès, still weary from his long Belgian trip, rushed first to the offices of *L'Humanité* and then to the crowded corridors of the Palais Bourbon where, amid the scorn of the nationalists and the jubilation of the militarists, he organized his party's pressure for peace. At eight that evening, he led a Socialist delegation into Viviani's office to demand of the Premier a precise explanation of French policy. When Jaurès pleaded that France should make no move that would provoke German retaliation, Viviani confidentially revealed the government's decision to hold its frontier troops ten kilometers from the border. Reassured on that point, Jaurès asked whether the ministry intended to round up those labor and Socialist leaders whose names filled the police file known as *Carnet B*. Once again, Viviani appeased his former comrades, assuring them that he contemplated no such move. The Premier's tone was sincere and convincing, but in his information he had been far from candid. Of the firm pledge to St. Petersburg he said nothing; nor did he reveal that orders had already gone out to the police to break up antiwar demonstrations anywhere on the streets of Paris.[19] When Jaurès left Viviani's office, his suspicions and anxiety lingered on, but so did his hopes.

The evening had disappeared; it was already night. Jaurès dined hastily with a few friends at the Coq d'Or, a restaurant far too gay for his mood. By midnight, he returned to his offices at *L'Humanité* where he composed, quickly but thoughtfully, his lead article for the next day. *Sang-froid nécessaire* he called it, a plea for "nerves of steel, firm, clear, and calm reason."[20] The night was oppressively hot, and when Jaurès left *L'Humanité* with Landrieu, Poisson, and Amédée Dunois, he suggested that they refresh themselves with a drink at the Café du Croissant.

While they sat drinking, a young man with a beard and a flowing tie paced back and forth outside the Croissant. It was Raoul Villain who, with the darkest of intentions, was stalking Jaurès. Born in Reims in 1885, the son of a local court clerk, Villain had lived a random existence, distinguished by neither success nor security. Moody and confused, he had once sought solace in Marc Sangnier's Christian democracy and then in the Ligue des jeunes amis de l'Alsace-Lorraine. Among the ultrapatriots who imbibed the doctrines of Maurras and the Action française, Villain learned to worship the nation and to hate Jaurès. In his suffering, he formulated a plan of action which would lend meaning to his barren existence. He would assassinate the traitor Jaurès. So it was that the pale, half-demented young man stood, on the night of July 30, outside the offices of *L'Humanité*. When Jaurès and his friends emerged, he followed them to the Croissant and took his place outside the café. His goal was clear, but his will, on this particular night, weakened. The time ticked away, and so did Villain's opportunity.

It was already past 1 A.M. when Jaurès suddenly realized he had missed the last métro. He left the café with his companions and walked to the main boulevard, where Landrieu hailed a taxi. Still carrying his battered suitcase, Jaurès entered the cab, while Landrieu shouted to the driver: 8, impasse de la Tour. When he arrived home, a weary soldier back from his wars, he found a light still burning. For though the self-centered Louise had left Paris for Bessoulet, Madeleine had stayed behind to comfort her father on his return from Brussels. Jaurès was delighted; the next night, he promised his daughter, they would dine together at home.

V

On July 31, a seasonably warm Friday, Jaurès rose early. At breakfast, he surveyed the morning newspapers, which had blazoned across their front pages the story of the enveloping crisis. Around 9 A.M. his lifelong friend Lévy-Bruhl dropped by, and for the better part of the forenoon, the two men talked about the imminence of war. Lévy-Bruhl was deeply worried, but Jaurès insisted that the avenue to peace still lay open: "I am going to the Chamber to see the ministers, to find out whether France and England together can't start up negotiations again."[21] Yet even as they conversed, Europe took the final plunge toward war. At 8 A.M. Vienna responded to Russian preparations by ordering the general mobilization of Austrian troops. At 1 P.M., under heavy pressure from the General Staff, Berlin ominously proclaimed *drohende Kriegsgefahr*, the "threatening danger of war."[22]

By mid-afternoon, Jaurès was at the Palais Bourbon where he spent the rest of the day. In the corridors of the Chamber, he bitterly attacked Tsarist foreign policy; nor did he spare its French accomplices. "Are we going to unleash a world war," he exploded before a group of journalists, "because Isvolsky is still furious over Aehrenthal's deception in the Bosnian affair?"[23] When Louis Malvy, the Minister of the Interior, entered the Palais Bourbon, Jaurès detained him and pleaded for a firm restraining hand over St. Petersburg: "It's no longer sufficient to talk gently to the Russians. We must tell them in no uncertain terms that if a war should break out, they would run considerably less risk than the French."[24] Malvy seemed neither to understand nor to care. "Superficial, dull, and indifferent, . . . he listened only half-attentively to the Socialist leader's demands."[25]

In the early evening, the news spread through the halls of the Palais Bourbon that Germany had proclaimed her *drohende Kriegsgefahr*. With several of his Socialist colleagues, Jaurès, shaken and feverish, called on Viviani once again, but the Premier could not receive them. For at 7 P.M. Baron Schoen, the German Ambassador to France, came to the Quai d'Orsay and informed Viviani that Berlin was serving an ultimatum on St. Petersburg to suspend mobilization within twelve hours or face a declaration of war. Schoen then demanded that within eighteen hours France declare whether or not she would remain neutral in the event of a Russo-German War. Viviani, who had already consulted Poincaré, put the Ambassador off with a noncommittal answer.

Unable to see the Premier, Jaurès, accompanied by Cachin, Longuet, and Bedouce, carried the Socialist case to Abel Ferry, the Under Secretary of State for Foreign Affairs. Neither ministers nor deputies, even the most conservative among them, could afford to ignore Jaurès; more than any other Socialist in the parliaments of Europe, he was a moral and political force, hated by some, feared by more, but almost universally respected.[26] When Ferry received the Socialist delegates, he offered them little comfort and less information; but he revealed something of the government's anxiety when he asked what the Socialists would do if events took another turn for the worse. Without hesitation, Jaurès replied: "We will clear our party of any guilt; to the very end, we will continue to struggle against war." To which Ferry answered prophetically: "No, you won't be able to continue. You will be assassinated on the nearest streetcorner." As the Socialists were leaving, the Under Secretary, who couldn't bear to compound Jaurès' suffering, pulled Bedouce aside and told him the bitter truth: "Everything is finished. There is nothing left to do."[27] If Jaurès didn't hear Ferry, he undoubtedly divined his meaning. "He looked as though he had been hit with a sledge hammer; all that day, his friends had seen him weighed down by the impending tragedy. But at this moment, his moral suffering seemed to be transformed into genuine physical suffering."[28]

It was after 8 P.M. when Jaurès returned to the offices of *L'Humanité* at 142 rue Montmartre. His gait was heavy and his face deeply lined, but when he spoke, he betrayed neither resignation nor despair: "Tonight I'm going to write a new *J'Accuse!* I will expose everyone responsible for this crisis."[29] He would reveal the government's ineptitude, Russia's militarism, Isvolsky's influence; he would identify all the malefactors of Poincaré's France. Like Zola before him, Jaurès would appeal to the public to turn the tide of history.

It was already near 9 P.M., and the Socialist journalists decided to adjourn for dinner before composing the August 1 issue. Someone proposed the Coq d'Or, but Jaurès suggested rather the Croissant, a café popular with journalists, which was closer and generally more sedate. On that sultry July night, however, the café was fairly crowded, and the Socialists had to share a table next to the windows which opened onto the street. Flanked by Landrieu and Renaudel, Jaurès occupied a bench with his back to the rue Montmartre, while Dubreuilh sat on a chair facing him. Others drifted in—Daniel Renoult, Maurice Bertre, Marius Viple, Ernest Poisson, Longuet—and clustered around the table. To provide some privacy for the group, a waiter placed a low screen between the bench and the street. As they dined, they all conversed, seriously and animatedly, but their center of attention, their Vergilian guide was Jaurès.

On the sidewalk in front of the Croissant, a young man stared fixedly at the Socialist group. It was Villain, who had returned to fulfil his mission. Carrying a pistol in one pocket and, aesthete that he was, two typed pages of Maeterlinck's *Blue Bird* in another, he was determined, once and for all, to assassinate Jaurès. For a moment, Daniel Renault noticed Villain and caught his steady stare, but the young man quickly disappeared. Jaurès and his friends had just finished their light dinner when René Dolié, a journalist for *Le Bonnet rouge* came over from the next table and handed Landrieu a photograph of his little girl. With a smile, Jaurès asked to see the picture; he looked at it admiringly and complimented the proud father. It was 9:40 P.M.

Suddenly the screen was pulled aside from the street. For an instant, Villain, a revolver cocked in his hand, stood motionless. Then, in rapid succession, he fired two shots, and Jaurès, bleeding and unconscious, slumped to the left. The café became a scene of shock and confusion. Renaudel leaped toward the street, and with the heavy blow of a bottle, felled the assassin; Bertre and Landrieu stretched Jaurès out on the bench and opened his shirt; others ran outside in desperate search of a doctor; Compère-Morel, who had heard the shots from the offices of *L'Humanité*, burst into the café, his eyes blind with tears. Like an uncontrolled flame, the news spread through the street until the rue Montmartre was an inferno of grief. The doctor finally arrived, pushed his way into the café, and examined Jaurès. It was too late. Within minutes, the doctor pronounced him dead.

Every man, Trotsky once wrote, dies his own death. "Lafargue, an Epicurean disguised as a Stoic, lived his seventy years in an atmosphere of peace, then decided it was enough, and committed suicide. Jaurès, athlete of the Idea, fell on the fighting field while struggling against the worst scourge of mankind — war."[30]

JULY, 1914 ASSASSINATION | 473

VI

"My heart is breaking," wept Anatole France. "My grief is smothering me."[31] "The blow was crushing for old Vaillant," Amédée Dunois recalled. "I knew when I saw him that he couldn't live much longer."[32] In his apartment on the rue Singer, the ailing Guesde "fell, numb and stupified, across his bed."[33] At *L'Humanité*, young and old alike wept unashamedly: "Not one among us — oh! we beg you to believe us — would have hesitated to give his own life for that of Jaurès. We are crushed. Our eyes burn with tears. Our father! Our teacher!"[34] "In Jaurès," proclaimed the Central Committee of the C.G.T., "the most farsighted, the most impassioned defender of humanity has perished."[35]

From Poincaré, President of the Republic, Louise received a letter of sympathy: "Jaurès was often my adversary. But I admired his talent and his character. At an hour when national unity is more necessary than ever, I must convey to you the respect I had for him." From Viviani, the people of France heard official words of appreciation: "M. Jaurès, the great orator who honored the French tribune, has been treacherously assassinated. He . . . struggled for noble causes."[36]

Yet peace, the greatest of those causes, died with him. Even as men eulogized Jaurès and praised his purposes, they rallied, almost without exception, to the standards of war. By August 4, the day the notables of France assembled for his funeral, the first total war of the twentieth century began.[37] Everywhere, save only in Russia and Serbia, the Socialist and labor movements submitted to the appeal for national unity. With the speed of light, the ideal of international brotherhood crumbled before resurgent tribalism.

And what of Jaurès? Would he have resisted war to the bitter end? Rappoport believed so. Hoping to fortify the weak forces of peace, the old Marxist recalled in the *Berner Tagwacht* (July 31, 1915) Jaurès' mood and attitude on the last day of his life. During these crucial hours, Rappoport insisted, he uttered not a single word which implied any course other than continuous opposition to war. But Renaudel and all those Socialists who rallied to the national effort repudiated Rappoport's interpretation. Jaurès, Renaudel insisted, would not have hesitated a minute to defend the homeland against an unprovoked German invasion.[38] Thus, both the internationalists and the patriots attempted to justify their position with authority from beyond the grave. The controversy, of course, can never be resolved. But in a fruitful insight, G. D. H. Cole offered probably the best key to speculation:

It has often been said that Jaurès, had he lived, would have rallied to the cause of national defense against Germany, as Guesde and Vaillant both actually did. This view is probably correct; but it is also probably the case that he would have shown greater wisdom than they did in working for a negotiated peace. His chance for this could have come only later, after Germany had failed to achieve a rapid victory. But it would have come; and in the situation after 1916 his presence might have made a real difference.[39]

VII

More than a decade after his assassination, on November 23, 1924, Jaurès' remains were transferred from his native Tarn to the Panthéon, the mausoleum of the nation's heroes. "He has an excellent claim to this honor," intoned Premier Édouard Herriot on that occasion. "No one ever had a nobler conception of France and the Republic."[40] Ten years dead, Jaurès may have seemed no longer a threat to the established order, and republicans of all parties were now willing to do him homage.[41] For his incomparable talents, declared Herriot, had embellished the public life of France and glorified the Third Republic.

But such republican sentimentality obscures rather than defines the essential greatness of Jaurès. To cast him as the leader of a loyal opposition or merely a social reformer is to misunderstand or to mock him.

Jaurès was an uncompromising Socialist who strove for the total transformation of his society; a humanist in the grand tradition, who denounced war and defended an awakening mankind; an impassioned tribune who roused the conscience of men and charted their course to Socialism.[42]

He had the integrity to be partisan, the courage to be revolutionary, the humanism to be tolerant, and the wisdom to evolve. He was, as Romain Rolland once wrote, "a whole man, harmonious and free."[43]

What richer legacy to this age of confusion and upheaval?

Le courage, c'est de chercher la vérité et de le dire; c'est de ne pas subir la loi du mensonge triomphant qui passe et de ne pas faire écho de notre âme, de notre bouche et de nos mains aux applaudissements imbéciles et aux huées fanatiques. *Discours à la jeunesse*, 1903

Les souffles qui viennent de l'Orient comme de l'Occident, des colères du proletariat d'Occident comme de la mysticité orientale de Tolstoï, tous ces souffles se mêlent en un tourbillon de tempête, autour de la vieille société pourrie et rongée comme le tronc creux d'un vieux chêne malade. Préparez donc une société nouvelle et plus juste! *Discours sur Tolstoï*, 1911

Et nous, nous disons aujourd'hui que l'affirmation de la paix est le plus grand des combats. *Discours prononcé aux obsèques de Francis de Pressensé*, 1914

REFERENCE
MATTER

Appendix I

THE UNPUBLISHED MEMOIRS OF
CHARLES RAPPOPORT AS A SOURCE
FOR THE LIFE OF JAURÈS

After I had completed the manuscript of this book, I turned up a document, the unpublished *Mémoirs* of Charles Rappoport (1865–1941), which is of unusual interest to historians of European Socialism. Like Jaurès, Rappoport was a Socialist with a rich philosophical and literary background, who became a brilliant journalist of the extreme Left. A Russian by origin, he participated in the revolutionary movement against the Tsarist government until he fled to Paris in 1888. During the next decade, he lived first in Germany and then in Switzerland, studying philosophy and working actively among Russian revolutionary refugees. He returned to Paris in 1898 where he soon began to participate in the French socialist movement. An idealist strongly influenced by Peter Lavrov, he was attracted to Jaurès at the height of the Dreyfus Affair. On the issue of ministerial participation, however, he broke with the party of Jaurès, embraced Marxism wholeheartedly, and identified himself with the Guesdists until 1914. Bitterly opposed to World War I and disillusioned by the ineffectiveness of the Second International in preventing it, Rappoport rallied to the cause of the Russian Revolution and in 1920 was one of the important founders of the French Communist Party. As a result of the Russian purge trials, he broke with the Communist Party in 1938 and in the last years of his life became an outspoken critic of Stalin.

Rappoport wrote his memoirs between November, 1939, and January, 1940,

477

at St. Cirq Lapopie in the Lot, a little over a year before he died. The memoirs remained in the hands of his family until his daughter, Dr. Fanny Vogein-Rappoport, deposited them in the Manuscript Division of the Bibliothèque Nationale in 1959. The manuscript has not been catalogued and is available only with special permission. Through the generosity of Dr. Vogein-Rappoport, I was able to read this important document. A typewritten manuscript of 333 pages, the memoirs contain fascinating insights into the personalities and activities of outstanding figures of Russian, German, Swiss, and French Socialism and Communism. Though they do not alter any of my basic interpretations of the French movement, they are full of interesting facts and character sketches. I have thought it useful, therefore, to present a few of the most significant passages. The numbers in parentheses follow the pagination of the manuscript.

The Dreyfus Affair

When Rappoport arrived in Paris in 1898, the Affair was at its height. He confesses that at first he did not understand its full implications, but eventually he agreed with Jaurès that it was a revolutionary movement:

"At the start, I must confess, I shared the views of the Guesdists and Blanquists, though I had no contact with the Marxist leader or his friend Vaillant. I even refused to sign a petition, brought to me by a Professor Mauss, in favor of Émile Zola. But I soon came to understand that the Dreyfus Affair involved far more than justice for a single individual, that the fate of freedom and democracy for the entire nation was at stake in this stupendous drama." (p. 89)

"The French State was almost completely secularized. The Republic became republican, albeit bourgois republican." (p. 92)

Jaures, Guesde, and Vaillant

Rappoport knew all three of these leaders very well, and in pages 98–107 he sketches excellent portraits of them:

"Jules Guesde and Jean Jaurès, two men, two worlds, two psychologies, two personalities, two philosophies. Implacable struggle and the spirit of conciliation. Analysis and synthesis. Harshness and generosity. Sectarianism and flexibility." (p. 99)

"There are three kinds of orators. Some prefer to appeal to the emotions. They use their fiery eloquence to rouse the emotional sympathy of their listeners. Others try to persuade us by the force of their reason, by the power of facts and figures. Finally, there are orators who win us over by the beauty of their delivery and the magnificence of their language. Jaurès combined all of these techniques. He was the perfect, the complete orator. Even when he improvised, he spoke only of subjects he had studied extensively. He appealed at once to our reason, to our emotions, and to our ear." (p. 101)

"In my dedication to socialism and the revolution, I was unfair to Jaurès. I overlooked the positive results of his reformist efforts, which came to fruition only later. I didn't give sufficient credit to his socialist idealism, which never failed to glorify socialism (though this was not the case with so many of his disciples)." (p. 153–54)

THE DOCTRINAL AND TACTICAL WEAKNESSES OF GUESDISM

Though Rappoport ranged himself with the French Marxists in the S.F.I.O. and was a bitter opponent of reformism, he criticizes Guesde for his simplified version of Marxism:

"On the question of syndicalism, as on so many other questions, the fault didn't lie with Karl Marx, who recognized the historic role of an independent trade union movement. In the First International, he respected that independence; by seeking the friendship of the English trade unions, which were certainly not socialist, he strengthened the socialist cause. I advised my friend and leader Jules Guesde against trying to subordinate the unions to the party, but I was crying in the desert." (p. 166)

"As the danger of war grew greater, Jaurès and Vaillant, who were more astute about international politics than Jules Guesde and less dogmatic, considered the struggle against war and militarism of the greatest importance. Jules Guesde, on the other hand, used to exclaim: 'No *anti!*' (antimilitarism, anti-alcoholism, etc.) 'Anticapitalism is enough.'" (p. 167)

THE ATTITUDE OF GUESDE TOWARD JAURES

After the party was unified, Rappoport was close to Guesde. He became a leading contributor to *Le Socialisme*, the weekly of the Guesdist faction. He was in a good position, therefore, to study Guesde's reaction to the leadership of Jaurès in the S.F.I.O.:

"As I have already noted, Jules Guesde remained inflexible. A bluntly honest man, he didn't conceal his surprise at the success of Jaurès who, because of his immense talent and noble character, had won the respect of the general public and the deepest admiration of the working class. To be absolutely candid, Jules Guesde didn't like Jaurès. Their personalities were too dissimilar; so were their ways of living and their types of action. Jaurès lived like a respectable bourgeois, while Jules Guesde, like Karl Marx, was often in terrible economic straits. His was the life of the proletarian intellectual with all of its privations, great and small. 'Jaurès is going too far,' Jules Guesde said to me one day. 'We must oppose what he is doing and saying,' he once said to his friends, then meeting at the offices of *Le Socialisme* (3, rue de la Roquette). I don't remember the specific reason for the outburst. 'Jaurès is too complicated,' he said on another occasion, this great simplifier and clarifier of truths in the fashion of the 18th century." (pp. 178–79)

GUESDE'S ATTITUDE IN THE FINAL DAYS BEFORE WAR

In the two years before the World War, Rappoport grew closer to Jaurès. Unlike the Guesdists, he felt that the struggle against war and militarism was the most important duty for the S.F.I.O. Toward that end, he founded in November, 1912, a review, *Contre la Guerre*, which was published only eleven times. Guesde's attitude was different. Though Rappoport discusses it in his Memoirs, he goes into greater detail in an article, "Mes Souvenirs de guerre à la guerre," which he wrote for his own Communist periodical, *La Revue marxiste*, No. 7 (August-September, 1929), pp. 12–30. His story about Guesde's attitude right before the meeting of Second International leaders at Brussels on July 29 is particularly revealing:

"On the way to Brussels, Jules Guesde, Édouard Vaillant, Marcel Sembat, his wife, Jean Longuet, and I were all together in a first-class car. We were engaged in a spirited, varied, excellent conversation, almost cheerful. Huddled in a corner, Jules Guesde remained unsociably silent during most of the trip. A few minutes before our train arrived at the Brussels station, he exploded: 'I don't understand your fear of war. War is the mother of revolution.' No one breathed a word. The answer was, of course, obvious. It was true, provided that one married the daughter, as Lenin died, and not the mother, as Jules Guesde and the leaders of the Second International did." (p. 23)

Appendix II

THE FUTURE
OF JAURÈS RESEARCH

The publication of Marcelle Auclair's well-received biography in 1954 and of numerous excellent studies in 1959–60, the centenary year, marked the beginning of a new period in Jaurès research. Instead of superficial or tendentious books, one can now anticipate an increasing number of serious historical works, based on widely scattered printed and manuscript sources. A number of excellent French scholars already have works in progress which will immeasurably increase our knowledge of the life and thought of Jaurès; among them are: Jean Bruhat, *L'Anticolonialisme en France*; Michel Launay, *Jaurès et le XVIIIᵉ siècle;* Pierre Rimbert, *L'Évolution idéologique de Jaurès*; Rolande Trempé, *Le Mouvement ouvrier à Carmaux;* and Claude Willard, *Le Guesdisme* [later published as *Les Guesdistes,* Paris, Editions Sociales, 1965]. Furthermore, one can hopefully look forward to critical editions of certain important Jaurès documents; a good start in that direction has already been made by Launay in *La Question religieuse et le socialisme* and by Madeleine Rebérioux in her *Textes choisis. Tome Iᵉʳ. Contre la Guerre et la politique coloniale.*

Fortunately, this research will be stimulated by an organization of French scholars, the *Société d'Études Jaurèsiennes,* founded on November 14, 1959, under the Presidency of Ernest Labrousse, Professor of History in the Sorbonne and president of the Institut Français d'Histoire Sociale. In the first issue of the *Bulletin de la Société d'Études Jaurèsiennes* (June, 1960), Mme Rebérioux, a vice president of the organization, outlined the kinds of projects the Société hopes to undertake or encourage. First, its members will search for and collect most of the Jaurès documents, both published and unpublished, which have thus far eluded

481

historians. To indicate the possible scope of this search, Mme Rebérioux suggested the following kinds of documents:

UNPUBLISHED MANUSCRIPTS

Personal Jaurès correspondence, especially letters in the possession of families in Albi, Castres, and Toulouse; documents concerning Jaurès in the archives, however incomplete, of the early socialist parties, the S.F.I.O., certain unions (especially the miners, the glass workers, and the railroad workers), and the newspapers to which he regularly contributed; documents concerning Jaurès in the police archives of Paris, the Seine, the Tarn, the Nord, and the Haute-Garonne; the *comptes rendus manuscrits* of the Toulouse municipal council for the years 1889–92; the unpublished minutes of the parliamentary committees on which Jaurès served; the documents in the Foreign Ministry Archives relating to the speeches and activities of Jaurès abroad; and the documents relating to Jaurès in the archives of the Bureau Socialiste International in Brussels and of the foreign Socialist parties. Many of these investigations will undoubtedly yield little, but others will almost as certainly turn up some revealing documents.

PUBLISHED DOCUMENTS

A thorough search of local newspapers for articles by Jaurès and reports of his speeches; a search through those reviews for which Jaurès wrote only occasionally; publication of collected writings and speeches on certain specific subjects, such as democracy, socialist unity, religion, and education.

Then the Société will sponsor an extensive program of interviews with contemporaries of Jaurès or their descendants, who can throw some light on his many activities.

To these excellent proposals, I would add a few others. It would be fruitful to study the writings of Jaurès' teachers, especially in the École Normale, in order to evaluate the intellectual and political influences on him during his school years. It would be equally profitable to analyze his formal philosophical works, his early socialist writings, and the books in his library with great care in order to determine precisely the sources of his evolving thought. Of the greatest importance are rigorously scientific studies of the French socialist movement, department by department, especially for the years between 1880 and 1893 and then for the years between 1905 and 1914. Finally, along the research lines that I am now following, scholars can profitably devote themselves to a detailed history of Socialism, syndicalism, and, after 1920, Communism in the decade following the death of Jaurès in order to evaluate his ideological and tactical legacy.

Jaurès was the greatest of modern French Socialists. It will take time and much research before scholars can compile a complete record of his vast political and intellectual activity. But the collective effort it will require will prove worthwhile. For Jaurès, who helped to create the past, addressed himself likewise to the future.

Notes

CHAPTER 1

1 Roger Martin du Gard, *Summer 1914* (New York, 1941), p. 548.
2 Marcelle Auclair, *La Vie de Jean Jaurès* (Paris, 1954), p. 13. (Unless otherwise indicated, all translations from French works are by the author.)
3 *Ibid.*, p. 23. See also Louis Soulé, *La Vie de Jaurès* (Paris, 1921), pp. 7–8.
4 Auclair, *Jaurès*, p. 25.
5 The family also maintained a flat in Castres where Jaurès spent a great deal of time. La Fédial, it might be noted, was bought in February, 1854, for ten thousand francs by Adélaïde Jaurès from her dowry of twelve thousand. The other two thousand was used for the building of the four-room house and the barn.
6 Charles Rappoport, *Jean Jaurès* (Paris, 1915), p. 6.
7 Quoted in Auclair, *Jaurès*, pp. 25–26.
8 Quoted in Rappoport, *Jaurès*, p. 15.
9 L. Lévy-Bruhl, *Jean Jaurès: esquisse biographique* (Paris, 1924), p. 16. See also Félicien Challaye, *Jaurès* (Paris, n.d.), p. 12.
10 J. Hampden Jackson, *Jean Jaurès* (London, 1942), p. 159.
11 Quoted, *ibid.*, pp. 158–59.
12 For the Languedoc setting, see Paul Desanges and L. Mériga, *Vie de Jaurès* (Paris, 1924), p. 22; F. Pignatel, *Jaurès par ses contemporains* (Paris, 1925), p. 22; Challaye, *Jaurès*, pp. 9–10; Auclair, *Jaurès*, p. 26.
13 *Journal officiel de la Chambre des Députés*, April 21, 1905.
14 Ludovic Valatx, *Monographie sur le mouvement de la population dans le département du Tarn de 1801 à 1911* (Albi, 1917), pp. 191–201. The author cites the following statistics: the urban population stood at 38,762 in 1820 and 77,772 in 1911; but the total population of the department in 1911 was 324,094.

15 P. B. Gheusi, *Cinquante Ans de Paris. Mémoires d'un témoin, 1889–1938* (Paris, 1939), I, 10.
16 Valatx, *La Population du Tarn*, pp. 40–41.
17 Harold Weinstein, *Jean Jaurès: A Study of Patriotism in the French Socialist Movement* (New York, 1936), p. 33.
18 Valatx, *La Population du Tarn*, pp. 20–36.
19 *Ibid.*, pp. 60–63.
20 Lévy-Bruhl, *Jaurès*, p. 8. See also A. Zévaès, *Jean Jaurès* (Paris, 1951), p. 12.
21 Auclair, *Jaurès*, p. 22.
22 *Ibid.*, p. 23.
23 Quoted in Soulé, *Jaurès*, p. 13.
24 *Ibid.*, pp. 12, 14.
25 *Ibid.*, pp. 16–17; also Auclair, *Jaurès*, p. 32.
26 *Ibid.*, p. 30. The Vercingetorix episode appears most fully in Gustave Téry, *Jaurès* (Paris, 1915), pp. 224–27.
27 Gheusi, *Cinquante ans*, pp. 2–3.
28 Challaye, *Jaurès*, p. 13.
29 Jean Jaurès, *La Guerre franco-allemande* (Paris, 1908), *passim*.
30 Auclair, *Jaurès*, p. 27.
31 Gheusi, *Cinquante ans*, p. 6.
32 Auclair, *Jaurès*, p. 47. Eight of the letters, which Jaurès wrote to M. Jean Julien between 1878 and 1886, have recently been published by Elizabeth Poulain: "Huit lettres de jeunesse de Jean Jaurès," in *Revue d'Histoire Économique et Sociale*, Vol. XXXVIII (1960), No. 1, 41–53. The original manuscripts are in the Musée Jaurès in Castres. Though not a great deal is known about M. Julien, one can ascertain from the content of these letters that he was a cultured man since he asked Jaurès to locate a number of scholarly books for him in Paris. It also seems evident that he was a staunch republican since Jaurès expressed to him republican sympathies he might have concealed from certain monarchist relatives.
33 On the rationalist atmosphere, see Jacques Chastenet, *Histoire de la troisième République* (Paris, 1952–55), II, 21–22.
34 Quoted in Jackson, *Jaurès*, p. 19.
35 Zévaès, *Jaurès*, p. 276.
36 Challaye, *Jaurès*, p. 19.
37 Auclair, *Jaurès*, p. 32.
38 *Ibid.*, p. 34.
39 *Ibid.*, pp. 37–38. Later, when Jaurès was already in public life, he was able, in a very tangible way, to repay Deltour by serving as a benevolent sponsor for other worthy students. Michel Launay, who has made some significant discoveries of unpublished manuscripts by or about Jaurès, recently located and published a long letter from M. Enjalran, a teacher of philosophy at the lycée of Albi before and after World War I, to Lucien Lévy-Bruhl, distinguished anthropologist and close friend of Jaurès. Written sometime between 1915 and 1917, it contains important recollections by Enjalran, who saw Jaurés frequently in and around Albi, which were useful to Lévy-Bruhl who was then preparing a biographical essay on Jaurès for the Association des anciens élèves de l'École normale supérieure. The letter, one of two previously unpublished documents, has been published by M. Launay in a small volume: Jean Jaurès, *La Question religieuse et le socialisme*, Paris, 1960. In his letter,

Enjalran reveals that in 1886, when he was only ten, he first met Jaurès, who was then a friend of his parents. In the years that followed, he met him often, and Jaurès played an important part first in promoting Enjalran's career and later in clarifying the major points of philosophy: "He treated me with the greatest affection, as was his natural habit. He helped me get a scholarship at the lycée of Albi and later to Louis-le-Grand." *Ibid.*, p. 13. Deltour's letter to Dubief is quoted in Henriette Psichari-Renan, "Jaurès lycéen," *L'Éducation nationale*, February 1, 1951.

40 *Le Journal de Genève*, August 2, 1915.

41 Jean Jaurès, *Oeuvres*, 9 vols. (Paris, 1931–39), VIII, 207.

42 Jean Jaurès, *Les Origines du socialisme allemand* (Paris, 1960), p. 32.

43 Frédéric Lefèvre, "Une Heure avec Monseigneur Baudrillart," *Les Nouvelles Littéraires*, June 1, 1935.

44 Quoted in Soulé, *Jaurès*, p. 25.

45 A. J. Ladd, *École Normale Supérieure; An Historical Sketch* (Grand Forks, N.D., 1907), p. 3.

46 Quoted in Jackson, *Jaurés*, p. 10.

47 For the details of Bergson's life, see Ben-Ami Scharfstein, *Roots of Bergson's Philosophy*, New York, 1943. That Jaurès made friendly overtures to Bergson seems probable. When Lucien Lévy-Bruhl published his biographical sketch of Jaurès in 1924, he appended sixteen letters from Jaurès to Charles Salomon (*Jaurès*, pp. 131–85). In one of them, dated September 17, 1881, Jaurès wrote: "Do you know Bergson's address in London? I don't know how I forgot to ask it, and I want to know how he is and what he is doing."

48 André Cresson, *Bergson: sa vie, son oeuvre* (Paris, 1941), pp. 3–4.

49 Auclair, *Jaurès*, p. 53.

50 *L'Humanité*, March 13, 1905. Jaurès wrote this article as an indignant answer to the Antidreyfusard reactionaries who were claiming Fustel de Coulanges as one of their forerunners. Charles Maurras, Paul Bourget, and Maurice Barrès were not without evidence, however, in claiming kinship to Fustel de Coulanges, who, despite the apparent objectivity of his historical work, was consistently antiliberal, anti-German, and patriotic. For the best discussion of the links between Fustel de Coulanges and the later ultranationalists, see Claude Digeon, *La Crise allemande et la pensée française* (Paris, 1959), p. 239–52, 437–38. Jaurès was quite right, however, in stressing the historical integrity of Fustel de Coulanges and in refuting claims about his religious spirit. Thus, Digeon has written: "In fact, he was agnostic and his only great passion was for historical truth." *Ibid.*, p. 235.

51 Quoted in Edmund Wilson, *To the Finland Station* (New York, 1940), p. 8.

52 See, for example, his speech in Chambre des Députés, *Journal officiel*, November 18, 1909. See also the discussion in Maurice Boitel, *Les Idées libérales dans le socialisme de Jean Jaurès* (Paris, 1921), pp. 38–39.

53 Quoted in Auclair, *Jaurès*, pp. 61–62.

54 Jaurès, *Oeuvres*, IV, 305.

55 Auclair, *Jaurès*, pp. 49–50.

56 Quoted by Paul Deschanel, *Gambetta* (Paris, 1919), p. 31.

57 Jaurès, *Oeuvres*, III, 224.

58 *Le Figaro*, March 20, 1895.

59 On this theme see John Plamenatz, *The Revolutionary Movement in France, 1815–1871*, London, 1952.

60 Chastenet, *La troisième République*, II, 56–57.
61 Auclair, *Jaurès*, p. 58.
62 *Le Figaro*, March 20, 1895. About was a novelist popular under the Second Empire who, by insisting on his anticlericalism, was trying to demonstrate his support of the new Third Republic.
63 Samuel Bernstein, *The Beginnings of Marxian Socialism in France* (New York, 1933), pp. 57–98. For an understanding of Guesde in the years between 1867 and 1882, see Jules Guesde, *Textes Choisis*, Paris, 1959, which has an excellent introduction by Claude Willard.
64 Aaron Noland, *The Founding of the French Socialist Party* (Cambridge, Mass., 1956), pp. 6–20.
65 Quoted in Zévaès, *Jaurès*, p. 25.
66 Maurice Dommanget, *Édouard Vaillant* (Paris, 1956), pp. 18–86.
67 Ladd, *École Normale*, p. 43.
68 Jaurès at La Fèdial to Salomon in Paris, September 17, 1881. Lévy-Bruhl, *Jaurès*, p. 150.
69 Quoted in Auclair, *Jaurès*, pp. 83–84. The last is a free, idiomatic translation of the following: "Un bon tiens vaut mieux que deux tu l'auras." Fifteen years later, in a reflection on the bourgeois family, he wrote rather bitterly: "Marriage is based on an association of material interest." Jaurès, *Oeuvres*, VI, 90.
70 The unpublished *Cours de philosophie*, written down by Louis Rascol, who was a student of Jaurès', in 1882–83, is now deposited in the Collège Technique at Albi. Michel Launay has published significant extracts from it in *Europe*, No. 354–55 (October–November, 1958), pp. 125–39.
71 Quoted in Georges Bourgin and Pierre Rimbert, "La Pensée de Jaurès en 1881–83," *La Revue socialiste*, No. 79 (July, 1954), p. 130.
72 Quoted in Auclair, *Jaurès*, pp. 79–80. Thomas, born in Castres in 1814, was a man of letters who first entered the Chamber of Deputies in 1881 when he was already sixty–seven. He died, in fact, in 1884.
73 Jaurès expressed his great sorrow over the death of his father in a letter, written at La Fédial on June 11, 1882, to his friend Salomon, who was then studying classical literature in Rome. Lévy-Bruhl, *Jaurès*, pp. 164–65.
74 Jaurès at Albi to Salomon in Rome, November 19, 1882, *ibid.*, pp. 172–75.
75 Toulouse did not achieve the status of a university for another decade.
76 From a speech by Perroud, July 30, 1897, quoted in Louis Rascol, *Claude-Marie Perroud* (Paris, 1941), p. 161.
77 Quoted, *ibid.*, p. 153.
78 Auclair, *Jaurès*, p. 92.
79 Quoted, *ibid.*, pp. 93–94.
80 Gheusi, *Cinquante ans*, pp. 10–11.
81 Soulé, *Jaurès*, p. 47.
82 Quoted in Jackson, *Jaurès*, p. 28.
83 Jaurès, *Oeuvres*, III, 318.
84 Harry Alport, *Émile Durkheim and His Sociology* (New York, 1939), p. 18.
85 Jean Jaurès, "Compliment à Fustel de Coulanges, directeur de l'École Normale Supérieure," *Europe*, No. 354–55 (October–November, 1958), pp. 123–24. Jaurès was asked to deliver this speech because he was the *cacique*, the student who had placed first in the entrance examination for the École Normale. The manuscript was found in the school library and published first

in 1958. Though Jaurès' first speech, it bears many signs of his mature style.
86 Auclair, *Jaurès*, pp. 106–8.
87 Jean Jaurès, *Alliance française. Association nationale pour la propagation française dans les colonies et l'étranger*, Albi, 1884.
88 Excerpts from the campaign speech are in Soulé, *Jaurès*, pp. 49–57.
89 Auclair, *Jaurès*, p. 111.
90 Quoted in Soulé, *Jaurès*, pp. 55–56.
91 Gheusi, *Cinquante Ans*, p. 12.

CHAPTER 2

1 Jaurès, *La Guerre franco-allemande*, p. 25.
2 *Ibid.*, p. 94.
3 Quoted in Charles Seignobos, *L'Évolution de la troisième République* (Paris, 1921), p. 53.
4 E. Beau de Loménie, *Les Responsabilités des dynasties bourgeoises* (Paris, 1943–54), II, 37.
5 Quoted in Chastenet, *La troisième République*, II, 55.
6 Maurice Reclus, *Jules Ferry* (Paris, 1947), p. 342.
7 Chastenet, *La troisième République*, II, 76.
8 Quoted, *ibid.*, p. 103.
9 Joseph Reinach, *La Politique opportuniste* (Paris, 1890), p. 294.
10 From February 4, 1879, to November 14, 1881; January 30 to August 7, 1882; February 21 to November 20, 1883.
11 Reclus, *Ferry*, p. 175. The Syllabus of Errors (December 8, 1864), was a sharp denunciation by Pope Pius IX of science, rationalism, and progress. It was a warning to Catholics to reject these elements of modern civilization.
12 On the emergence of the bourgeois dynasties, see Beau de Loménie, *Dynasties bourgeoises*, I, *passim*.
13 *Ibid.*, II, 51. On the connections of Gambetta with the aristocracy, see Ludovic Halévy, *Trois dîners avec Gambetta*, Paris, 1929.
14 Quoted in Émile Labarthe, *Gambetta et ses amis* (Paris, 1938), p. 115.
15 A. Dansette, *Histoire des Présidents de la République* (Paris, 1953), p. 127.
16 Those who later came to hate Jaurès, the militant socialist, looked back and pictured him in unflattering, even harsh terms. Yves Guyot, the journalist who devoted his life to an extended battle against what he called "the socialist tyranny," described him thus: "In 1885 we saw arrive in the Chamber a rather short man, one shoulder pitched higher than the other, badly dressed, his hair and beard a yellowish color as nondescript as the coat of d'Artagnan's horse, hobbling, uneasy, always prying, interfering in all the groups, his begging eye shutting before every direct stare with a compulsive tic; it was said that he was called Jaurès." Yves Guyot, *La Comédie socialiste* (Paris, 1897), p. 144.
17 *La petite République*, April 15, 1894.
18 Jean Jaurès, *Discours parlementaires* (Paris, 1904), p. 20. The long introductory essay by Jaurès is called "Le Socialisme et le radicalisme en 1885."
19 *Ibid.*, p. 13–14.
20 *Ibid.*, p. 16.
21 *Ibid.*, p. 3.
22 See, for example, the unflattering review of the book in *Le Journal des débats*, May 12, 1904.

23 Jaurès, *Discours parlementaires*, pp. 28–29.
24 *Ibid.*, p. 33.
25 *Ibid.*, p. 21.
26 *Ibid.*, p. 22.
27 *Ibid.*, pp. 42–43. Léon Blum reported that in 1914, shortly before his assassination, Jaurès still defended his preference for Ferry over Clemenceau. "I came rather to dislike Ferry," he said to Blum, "but if the choice were put to me again, I would choose him over Clemenceau." *Le Populaire du centre*, August 2, 1920.
28 Chambre des Députés, *Journal officiel*, February 11, 1886. What Jaurès failed to understand in these youthful years was the terrible impact upon the poor or the near-poor — the urban workers, the small peasants, the petty bourgeoisie — of the economic crisis in France between 1882 and 1887. That depression forms the background for explosive strikes like those at Carmaux (1883), Anzin (1884), and especially Decazeville (1886). In fact, it was misery and insecurity which later enabled Boulanger to impress the working classes. Had Jaurès understood the depression and its consequences, he might have understood better the violence of the strike.
29 Jaurès, *Discours parlementaires*, p. 176.
30 *Ibid.*, pp. 176–77.
31 Noland, *French Socialist Party*, p. 10.
32 Jaurès, *Discours parlementaires*, p. 175.
33 *Ibid.*, p. 177.
34 L. Lévy-Bruhl, *Quelques pages sur Jean Jaurès* (Paris, 1916), p. 18.
35 Rappoport, *Jaurès*, p. 202.
36 Quoted in Soulé, *Jaurès*, p. 61.
37 For a list of his conservative votes, see Guyot, *La Comédie socialiste*, p. 145.
38 Quoted in Soulé, *Jaurès*, p. 62.
39 May 7, 1887.
40 *La Dépêche de Toulouse*, August 6, 1887.
41 October 23, 1886.
42 Quoted in Léo Larguier, *Le Citoyen Jaurès* (Paris, 1932), p. 48.
43 *La Dépêche de Toulouse*, March 19, 1887.
44 Chambre des Députés, *Journal officiel*, June 17, 1887.
45 *Ibid.*, July 1, 1887.
46 *Ibid.*, May 24, 1889.
47 Comité central des houillères de France, *Documents relatifs à la grève des mineurs de 1902* (Paris, 1903), p. 17.
48 Jaurès, *Discours parlementaires*, pp. 217–18.
49 For the debate on this issue, see *ibid.*, pp. 265–69.
50 Chambre des Députés, *Journal officiel*, May 26, 1886.
51 Chastenet, *La troisième République*, II, 344–45.
52 *La Dépêche de Toulouse*, June 10, 1888.
53 *Ibid.*, February 19, 1888.
54 7ᵉ Congrès National du Parti Socialiste, tenu à Nîmes, 1910, *Compte rendu sténographique*, p. 370.
55 Quoted in A. Dansette, *Le Boulangisme* (Paris, 1946), p. 145.
56 *Ibid.*, pp. 144–59.
57 *Ibid.*, pp. 30–40.
58 A. Zévaès, *Henri Rochefort, le pamphlétaire* (Paris, 1946), pp. 189–208.

59 Dansette, *Le Boulangisme*, pp. 72–76.
60 *Ibid.*, pp. 86–90.
61 *La Dépêche de Toulouse*, May 28, 1887.
62 *Ibid.*
63 *Ibid.*, June 4, June 25, July 16, September 17, September 24, 1887.
64 *Ibid.*, June 25, 1887.
65 *Ibid.*, April 1, 1888.
66 *Ibid.*, May 13, 1888.
67 *Ibid.*, August 12 and 26, 1888.
68 *Ibid.*, September 2, 1888.
69 Numa Gilly, *Mes Dossiers* (Paris, 1889), p. xxxiv.
70 Henri de Rochefort, *Les Aventures de ma vie* (Paris, 1896–98), V, 149–51.
71 *La Dépêche de Toulouse*, December 23, 1888.
72 *Ibid.*, February 3, 1889.
73 Chambre des Députés, *Journal officiel*, February 11, 1889.
74 Quoted in Chastenet, *La troisième République*, II, 212–13.
75 Chambre des Députés, *Journal officiel*, July 13, 1889.
76 *Ibid.*
77 Dansette, *Le Boulangisme*, p. 371.
78 A. Zévaès, *Au Temps du Boulangisme* (Paris, 1930), p. 243.
79 *La Dépêche de Toulouse*, July 14, 1889.
80 See letters of Engels of June 6 and 12, 1888, in "Extraits inèdits de la correspondance Engels-Lafargue," *La Pensée*, No. 61 (May-June, 1955), pp. 2, 14.
81 *Ibid.*, p. 18.
82 For the position of Vaillant, leader of the Blanquists, see Dommanget, *Vaillant*, p. 93, and *Le Cri de peuple*, January 3, 1889.
83 A. Zèvaés, *Le Scandale du Panama* (Paris, 1931), pp. 18–24.
84 *Ibid.*, pp. 34–35.
85 *La Dépêche de Toulouse*, November 21, 1892.
86 Chambre des Députés, *Journal officiel*, December 14, 1888.
87 *Ibid.*, July 6, 1897. See also his comments on Panama in *L'Humanité*, June 16, 1904.
88 Quoted in Auclair, *Jaurès*, pp. 151–52.
89 Jackson, *Jaurès*, p. 29.
90 Auclair, *Jaurès*, p. 168.
91 *Ibid.*, p. 169.
92 Quoted in Soulé, *Jaurès*, p. 109.
93 *Ibid.*, pp. 110–11.
94 *La Dépêche de Toulouse*, August 2, 1889. Jaurès thus learned firsthand — and it was a lesson that helped push him toward socialism — that unequal economic power endangered political democracy. In Spain and Italy, as historians have pointed out, political democracy was almost a farce during these years; but even in France, employers and landed aristocrats could apply strong pressure on poor workers and peasants so that elections might be anything but free. Louis Oscar Frossard, the socialist who was to become one of the founders of the French Communist Party and then one of its earliest defectors, wrote thus of elections in the 1890's in his native Haut-Rhin: "The secret ballot boxes simply did not exist. The boss accompanied the worker to the ballot box. And if, despite these precautions, the election results were

still unfavorable, the worker was sure that he would be out of a job the next day." *De Jaurès à Lèon Blum* (Paris, 1943), p. 17.
95 *Le Dépêche de Toulouse*, August 11, 1889.
96 *Ibid.*, September 17, 1890.
97 Quoted in Soulé, *Jaurès*, p. 112.

CHAPTER 3

1 Quoted in Soulé, *Jaurès*, p. 126.
2 Quoted in Auclair, *Jaurès*, p. 175.
3 Among them were Hauriou, later dean of the Law Faculty of Toulouse; Delbos, later professor at the Sorbonne; Émile Mâle, later art historian at the University of Paris; Audouin, later professor at the University of Poitiers; Benoît, later rector of the University of Montpellier; etc.
4 Quoted in Soulé, *Jaurès*, p. 116.
5 *Le Populaire*, March 8, 1931.
6 Charles Andler, *Vie de Lucien Herr* (Paris, 1932), p. 95.
7 *La Dépêche de Toulouse*, February 25, 1890.
8 Léo Figuères, "Sur la position de Jaurès et du jaurèssisme dans le mouvement ouvrier français d'avant 1914," *Cahiers du communisme* (January-February, 1956), p. 416.
9 *La Dépêche de Toulouse*, August 1, 1892. Jaurès came to know extremely well the writings of earlier French socialist theorists. His articles and speeches abound with references to St. Simon, Fourier, Blanqui, and Proudhon. But he was not a disciple of any one of them. Rather Jaurès appreciated them as great forerunners of contemporary socialism who contributed to the movement many penetrating insights and a fervent socialist spirit. In their concrete proposals for social reorganization, these earlier French socialists differed radically; but in their common rejection of liberalism, in their desire, as St. Simon put it, "améliorer le sort de la classe la plus nombreuse et la plus pauvre," and in their appeal to human dignity, justice, and fraternity, they created something of a common socialist tradition, essentially idealistic and collectivist. It was the French school of socialism, whose variety and unity have been so well described in Armand Cuvillier, *Hommes et idéologies de 1840*, Paris, 1956.

With all due respect for their pioneering efforts, Jaurès did not spare his criticism when he considered them confused, impractical, or shortsighted. Of Proudhon, for example, who proposed to eliminate exploitation without suppressing private property, Jaurès wrote: "The work of Proudhon is full of hesitations and contradictions; one finds in it a strange mixture of reaction and revolution." (*La petite République*, September 7, 1901.) But insofar as these early socialists considered socialism the natural culmination of the French Revolution, insofar as they appealed to the ideal of justice and fervently denounced the selfishness of capitalism; insofar as they envisioned a new community based on the fraternity and dignity of men, Jaurès drew inspiration and confirmation from them. So it was that he attempted, as he would say in his Latin thesis in 1892, to reconcile "dialectical socialism ... with moral socialism, German socialism with French." Jaurès, *Socialisme allemand*, p. 150.
10 Quoted in Soulé, *Jaurès*, p. 129.

11 *Ibid.*, p. 133.
12 *Ibid.*, p. 138. This sign of "clericalism" in Jaurès was resurrected by his violent foe, Urbain Gohier, a decade later. See *L'Aurore*, October 23, 1901.
13 Soulé, *Jaurès*, p. 141.
14 *Ibid.*, pp. 148–53.
15 Beau de Loménie, *Dynasties bourgeoises*, II, 206–7.
16 *Ibid.*, p. 215.
17 *La Dépêche de Toulouse*, March 10 and 17, 1889.
18 *Ibid.*, May 28, 1890.
19 Chastenet, *La troisième République*, II, 260.
20 Beau de Loménie, *Dynasties bourgeoises*, II, 224.
21 Quoted in Chastenet, *La troisième République*, II, 262.
22 Quoted in D. W. Brogan, *France Under the Republic* (New York, 1940), p. 26.
23 *La Dépêche de Toulouse*, January 7, 1892.
24 *Ibid.*, October 29, 1887.
25 *Ibid.*, January 7, 1892.
26 *Ibid.*, October 6, 1889; August 21, 1890; July 4, 1892.
27 *Ibid.*, January 7, 1892.
28 *Ibid.*, August 21 and December 17, 1891; July 4, 1892.
29 *Ibid.*, January 28, 1892.
30 *Ibid.*, March 12, 1891.
31 *Ibid.*, June 3, 1891; June 21 and April 27, 1892.
32 *Ibid.*, October 1, 1891.
33 *Ibid.*, March 30, 1892.
34 Andler, *Lucien Herr*, p. 113.
35 The best study of the Fourmies episode is by Claude Willard: *La Fusillade de Fourmies*, Paris, 1957. This excellent monograph, based on original sources, is better than the two older studies: Édouard Drumont, *Le Secret de Fourmies*, Paris, 1892; and A. Zévaès, *La Fusillade de Fourmies*, Paris, 1936.
   In the letters exchanged by Engels and Paul and Laura Lafargue, one can find important evidence of the furor created in working class circles by the events at Fourmies and their importance in the growth of the Parti ouvier français in the Nord. See Friedrich Engels, and Paul and Laura Lafargue, *Correspondance (1868–1895)* (Paris, 1955–59), III, 38–130.
36 Quoted in Willard, *Fourmies*, p. 60.
37 *La Dépêche de Toulouse*, May 7, 1890.
38 *Ibid.*, May 7, 1891.
39 Zévaès, *Fourmies*, p. 40.
40 The actions of the government emboldened rather than intimidated the workers of the Nord. Despite financial and political obstacles, the textile workers of Fourmies formed a union which, by the end of June, had some 3500 members. Then, in the fall of 1891, Lafargue, though imprisoned, ran for the vacant Chamber seat in the first district of Lille. In thirty-eight days Marxist leaders made thirty-four speeches in the district. On November 8, Lafargue, Marx's son-in-law, was elected to the Chamber of Deputies and released from prison.
41 *La Dépêche de Toulouse*, July 15, 1891.
42 *Ibid.*, October 14, 1891. See also February 19, 1890.
43 By 1890, the following socialist groups existed: 1) the Parti ouvrier français,

founded by Guesde and sometimes called the Guesdists; 2) the Comité révolutionnaire central, founded by Édouard Vaillant in 1881 and sometimes called the Blanquists; 3) the Fédération des travailleurs socialistes de France, founded by Paul Brousse and sometimes called the Broussists or the Possibilists; 4) the Parti ouvrier socialiste révolutionnaire, founded in 1890 after a split within the Possibilists, sometimes called the Allemanists; 5), 6), and 7) three groups originating in the Société d'économie sociale, founded by Benoît Malon in 1885, from which the Independent Socialists partially derived.

On these groups one can consult the following: A. Zévaès, *Les Guesdistes*, Paris, 1911; Charles de Costa, *Les Blanquistes*, Paris, 1912; S. Humbert, *Les Possibilistes*, Paris, 1911; M. Charnay, *Les Allemanistes*, Paris, 1912; Albert Orry, *Les Socialistes indépendents*, Paris, 1911. Unfortunately, these slight books are not serious histories; rather they are chronological accounts which explain little about the geographical background and nothing about the socioeconomic roots of these factions. Indeed, the available histories of French socialism under the Third Republic are in general superficial, lacking in substantial information about the social and economic conditions which encouraged or inhibited the movement. Badly needed are serious local and departmental histories of the working-class movement, based on the mass of local socialist and labor newspapers, on the documentary evidence of local archives, and on the economic data for local areas. Only with such histories will a real synthesis of socialist history be possible. Lacking the time and the resources to make such investigations, I have depended largely on the available monographs, fully aware that some day, when the history of French socialism has been more meaningfully presented, future biographers of Jaurès will write of his life with deeper understanding than is now possible.

44 *The Economic Development of France and Germany, 1815–1914* (Cambridge, 1923), p. 240.
45 Mermeix, *Le Syndicalisme contre le socialisme* (Paris, 1907), p. 118. On the life of Guesde, see A. Compère-Morel, *Jules Guesde*, Paris, 1937.
46 Louis Lévy, *Comment ils sont devenus socialistes* (Paris, 1932), pp. 122–24.

CHAPTER 4

1 Quoted in Challaye, *Jaurès*, pp. 76–77.
2 J. Benrubi, *Les Sources et les courants de la philosophie contemporaine en France* (Paris, 1933), II, 545.
3 Jaurès, *Oeuvres*, VI, 8–10.
4 See Challaye, *Jaurès*, pp. 102–3, for a letter from Lachelier to Jaurès, April 24, 1892, in which the former recognizes the link between them.
5 Jean Jaurès, *De la Réalité du monde sensible* (Paris, 1891), pp. 42–43. The citations are to the first edition. A second printing appeared unchanged in 1902; a third comprises Volume 8 of the *Oeuvres*.
6 *Ibid.*, p. 7.
7 *Ibid.*, p. 9.
8 *Ibid.*, p. 39.
9 *Ibid.*, p. 315.
10 *Ibid.*, p. 163
11 *Ibid.*, p. 48. He held, as before, to the eternity of matter (*ibid.*, p. 110).

12 *Ibid.*, p. 92.
13 *La Dépêche de Toulouse*, January 1, 1891.
14 Jaurès, *De la Réalité*, p. 154.
15 Jaurés, *Oeuvres*, VI, 144.
16 *Ibid.*, p. 146.
17 *Ibid.*, pp. 148–49.
18 Jean Jaurès, "Le Théâtre sociale," *Revue d'art dramatique* (1900), pp. 1072–76.
19 *La Dépêche de Toulouse*, January 1, 1891.
20 Jaurès, *Oeuvres*, VI, 147.
21 Jaurès, *De la Réalité*, p. 2.
22 Jaurès, *Oeuvres*, III, 152.
23 *Ibid.*, VI, 151.
24 3ᵉ Congrès National du Parti Socialiste, tenu à Limoges, 1906, *Compte rendu analytique*, p. 174.
25 Quoted in Challaye, *Jaurès*, pp. 121–23.
26 Jaurès, *Oeuvres*, III, 264.
27 Jean Jaurès, *Les Origines du socialisme allemand*, Paris, 1960. This is the latest printing of the thesis, and it includes a perceptive introduction by the Marxist critic, Lucien Goldmann.

The thesis was almost a *cause célèbre* at the Sorbonne. It was an audacious decision to invade that rarefied academic community with a thesis on contemporary socialism. Before Jaurès' public defense of the thesis, Gabriel Séailles, professor of philosophy, told his students: "Don't miss the debate on Friday. It will center on the question of socialism, and the candidate, they say, is as eloquent as Gambetta." Quoted in Zévaès, *Jaurès*, p. 51.

The jury before which Jaurès successfully defended his thesis on February 5, 1892, was composed of Émile Boutroux, Paul Janet, Charles Waddington, and Gabriel Séailles.
28 For drawing quotations out of context, and for attributing to certain thinkers a socialist content, unwarranted by the general direction of their work, Jaurès has been criticized by both hostile and friendly critics. The antisocialist Maurice Lair accused him of so denaturing the texts that German thought "becomes unrecognizable." *Jaurès et l'Allemagne* (Paris, 1935), p. 10. The Marxist critic, Lucien Goldmann, has written: "he [Jaurès] manages to reinterpret certain passages, certain ideas in the light of his own bias, as though saying to us: the thinker whom I am studying, though he actually wrote this way, nonetheless anticipates socialist thought. . . . From a Marxist point of view, this is all pretty dubious. Tying values tightly to concrete conditions, concerned with an over-all, total view, Marxist thought does not separate, whether in the study of history or in the analysis of some thinker, what is 'good' from what is 'bad.'" Goldmann goes on to justify the work of Jaurès on its own terms, as an essay posing important problems of socialist theory: "The reading of an essay has its own laws. If one read Nietzsche's book on the origin of tragedy for precise, objective information on the birth of Greek tragedy or Malraux's works on art for a history of painting and sculpture, he would miss what is important in them." Jaurès, *Socialisme allemand*, pp. 18–19.
29 Jaurès, *Socialisme allemand*, p. 45.
30 *Ibid.*, pp. 48, 50.

31 *Ibid.*, pp. 51, 59, 61, 63.
32 *Ibid.*, p. 65
33 *Ibid.*, pp. 77, 111–12, 130.
34 *Ibid.*, p. 141.
35 *Ibid.*, p. 101.
36 *Ibid.*, p. 137.
37 *Ibid.*, p. 145.
38 *Ibid.*, p. 147.
39 *Ibid.*, p. 150. Jaurès was convinced, as he wrote on many occasions, that the socialist revolution had to spring from a movement of the masses, who were not mere agents of history but active, volitional men and women striving for a just society. He wrote, for example: "The revolution cannot succeed except by the general, almost unanimous will of all. In the interest of all, it should be prepared and accepted by almost all; for there comes a time when the force of an overwhelming majority discourages the last resistance of the ruling class." Jaurès, *Oeuvres*, VI, 329 .
   Jaurès would certainly have agreed with the formulation of E. P. Thompson, the talented English socialist, who recently wrote in an article called "Revolution": "A revolution does not 'happen'; it must be *made* by men's actions and choices. During a period of exceptional fluidity and heightened political awareness, institutions may be built or re-moulded which become 'set' for many years. A revolution which is botched or muddled into will entail consequences which reach far into the future." *New Left Review*, No. 3 (May-June, 1960), p. 7.
40 Jaurès, *Socialisme allemand*, pp. 150–51. In his attempt to harmonize materialism and idealism, Jaurès at one time found links between Marx and Malon, and another time between Marx and Michelet. See Jaurès, *Oeuvres*, III, 272; and *La petite République*, July 16, 1898.
41 Jaurès, *Oeuvres*, III, 267.
42 *La Dépêche de Toulouse*, December 11, 1893.
43 As a Communard, the Blanquist Vaillant made some serious educational efforts. See Dommanget, *Vaillant*, pp. 47–48.
44 Hubert Bourgin, *De Jaurès à Léon Blum, l'École normale et la politique* (Paris, 1938), p. 192.
45 *Ibid.*, p. 193.
46 Jean Jaurès, *Discours prononcé à la distribution solennelle des prix du lycée, 3 août, 1883* (Albi, n.d.), p. 6.
47 Bertrand Russell, *Selected Papers* (New York, 1927), p. 171.
48 Jean Jaurès, *Discours prononcé par M. Jean Jaurès à la distribution solennelle des prix. Lycée d'Albi, 31 juillet 1888* (Albi, n.d.), p. 5.
49 Jaurès, *Oeuvres*, III, 307.
50 Jean Jaurès, *Discours à la jeunesse* (Lille, 1926), p. 17. This speech originally delivered in 1903, has been reprinted many times.
51 Note how closely Jaurès' viewpoint coincides with the conclusions in Alan Spitzer, *The Revolutionary Theories of Louis Blanqui.* New York, 1957.
52 Jaurès, *Oeuvres*, III, 420.
53 *Ibid.*, p. 274. On this theme, see Maximilien Rubel, *Karl Marx, essai de biographie intellectuelle* (Paris, 1957), pp. 190–205.
54 On this theme, see Reinhard Bendix, *Social Science and the Distrust of Reason* (Berkeley, 1951), p. 12.

55 Charles Van Duzer, *Contribution of the Ideologues to French Revolutionary Thought* (Baltimore, 1935), p. 196. For a most interesting view of the *philosophes* as radical reformers see the first chapter of Judith Shklar, *After Utopia. The Decline of Political Faith*, Princeton, 1957.

56 Jaurès, *Oeuvres*, VI, 146.

57 Jean Jaurès, *Histoire socialiste de la Révolution française* (Paris, n.d.), I & II, 32. This is the original Rouff edition. Hereafter, the first two volumes will be referred to as I–II, and the last two as III–IV.

58 Van Duzer, *French Revolutionary Thought*, p. 97.

59 Jaurès, *Histoire socialiste*, I–II, 1116.

60 *Ibid.*, p. 1142.

61 Jaurès, *Oeuvres*, VI, 404.

62 Ian Cumming, *Helvétius* (London, 1955), p. 141.

63 Jaurès, *Discours au lycée, 1883*, p. 7.

64 *Ibid.*, p. 15.

65 Chambre des Députés, *Journal officiel*, March 3, 1904.

66 Émile Levasseur, *Questions ouvrières et industrielles en France sous la III⁰ République* (Paris, 1907), p. 203.

67 For the details of these laws see *ibid.*, pp. 203–5; E. Acomb, *The French Laic Laws* (New York, 1941), pp. 163–78; G. Weill, *Histoire de l'enseignement secondaire* (Paris, 1920), pp. 169–94.

68 Quoted in Albert Thomas, *La Liberté de l'enseignement en France de 1789 à nos jours* (Paris, 1911), p. 96.

69 Émile Bourgeois, *La Liberté d'enseignement: histoire et doctrine* (Paris, 1902), pp. 39–40.

70 Bourgeois presented with considerable alarm the figures on the rising number of Church schools from the time of the Falloux Law of 1850. *Ibid.*, p. 143.

71 *La Dépêche de Toulouse*, August 21, 1890.

72 *La petite République*, April 1, 1894.

73 *La Dépêche de Toulouse*, August 23, 1892.

74 Chambre des Députés, *Journal officiel*, December 1, 1888.

75 *Ibid.*, March 18, 1893.

76 *La petite République*, April 1, 1894.

77 *L'Enquête sur l'enseignement secondaire. Procès verbaux des dépositions présentés par M. Ribot, Président de la Commission de l'Enseignement* (Paris, 1899), p. 219.

78 *La Dépêche de Toulouse*, August, 7, 1890.

79 *Ibid.*, June 26, 1890.

80 *Ibid.*, June 4, 1890.

81 *Ibid.*, February 17, 1892.

82 Jean Jaurès, "Les Idées politiques et sociales de Jean-Jacques Rousseau," *Revue de metaphysique et de la morale* (May, 1912), p. 381. This is a reprint of a speech originally given in 1889.

83 *Le Journal de Genève*, August 2, 1915.

84 Lavrov also developed a system built on both idealism and materialism. Few of his works have been translated from the Russian. See, however, his *Quelques survivances dans les temps modernes*, Paris, 1896. For an excellent analysis of Lavrov's socialism, see the long essay by Charles Rappoport, who was once his disciple: *La Philosophie social de Pierre Lavroff*, Paris, 1900. That Jaurés knew of Lavrov and his ideas is evident from a letter he sent

to Rappoport on August 26, 1901, after reading the essay. Published in the preface to the third edition of Rappoport's *Jean Jaurès* (Paris, 1925), the letter says in part: "I find your Lavrov extremely interesting and important."

CHAPTER 5

1 See especially Jean Montreuil, *Histoire du mouvement ouvrier en France*, Paris, 1946; and Levasseur, *Questions ouvrières*. On the development of labor agitation in Carmaux, See Rolande Trempé, "Les Premières Luttes des mineurs de Carmaux," *Cahiers internationaux* (January, 1955), pp. 49-66.

2 A. Coste, *Les Bénéfices comparés du travail et de capital dans l'accroissement de la richesse depuis 50 ans* (Paris, 1897), pp. 13-14.

3 In 1861, the daily pay for the miner averaged 2 francs 57; by 1905 it stood at 4 francs 53. Montreuil, *Mouvement ouvrier*, p. 233.

4 On the causes and frequency of economic crises in France, see Jean Lescure, *Des Crises périodiques et générales de surproduction*, Paris, 1938.

5 Levasseur, *Questions ouvrières*, pp. 656-60.

6 A. Marchal, *L'Action ouvrière et la transformation du régime capitaliste* (Paris, 1943), p. 33.

7 Daniel Halévy, *Essais sur le mouvement ouvrier en France*, Paris, 1901. Halévy cited evidence of many antilabor devices used in the 1890's: the imposition in some areas of the compulsory *livret*; the burning of union cards in the presence of the working force; the circulation among employers of blacklists of "agitators."

8 See Beau de Loménie, *Dynasties bourgeoises*, and also his contribution in J. Boudet, ed., *Le Monde des affaires en France*, Paris, 1952.

9 Eugène Fournière, *Ouvriers et patrons* (Paris, 1905), p. 47.

10 *La Dépêche de Toulouse*, May 20, 1888.

11 *Ibid.*, May 27, 1888.

12 *Ibid.* See also August 27, 1890, and January 4, 1891.

13 *Ibid.*, October 14, 1888.

14 *Ibid.*, November 18, 1888.

15 *Ibid.*, October 29, 1890.

16 *Ibid.*

17 *Ibid.*, December 17, 1890.

18 Louis Calmels, *De Carmaux médiéval à Monestiès-Combefa et au Néo-Carmausin* (Rodez, 1932), pp. 70-82.

19 A. Zévaès, *Les Mines et la nation* (Paris, n.d.), pp. 51-57.

20 Auclair, *Jaurès*, p. 214. See also Trempé, "Les mineurs de Carmaux," pp. 59-61.

21 The company's point of view is most succinctly expressed by A. Gibon, *La Grève de Carmaux*, Paris, 1893. The workers' position is stated in a letter (September 28, 1892) by one August Galonnier, imprisoned after the invasion of Humblot's house, to the Minister of the Interior. Archives Nationales, BB[18] 1887, Dos. 883 A92.

22 See Reille's statement in *Le Temps*, August 19, 1892.

23 *Ibid.*, August 22, 1892.

24 *Ibid.*, August 26, 1892.

25 *La Dépêche de Toulouse*, August 29, 1892.

26 *Ibid.* Much the same point of view was expressed by the Radical Camille Pelletan in *La Justice,* September 8 and 11, 1892.
27 *La Dépêche de Toulouse,* September 6, 1892.
28 *Ibid.,* September 19, 1892.
29 *Ibid.,* October 4, 1892.
30 *Ibid.,* October 11, 1892. See *Le Temps,* October 15, 1892, for reasons why neither the law of 1810 nor that of 1838 could be applied.
31 See *Le Temps,* October 11 and 18, 1892.
32 *Ibid.,* October 19, 1892.
33 Auclair, *Jaurès,* pp. 219–20. See also Chapter 6.
34 Chambre des Députés, *Journal officiel,* October 18, 1892.
35 *La Dépêche de Toulouse,* October 24, 1892.
36 Gibon, *La Grève de Carmaux,* p. 34. Note Jules Guesde's hostile reaction in *Le Socialiste,* October 31–November 6, 1892.
37 *La Dépêche de Toulouse,* November 8, 1892. The attitude of Solages toward these events can be seen in his letter of resignation carried in *La Justice,* October 15, 1892.
38 Quoted in Auclair, *Jaurès,* p. 225.
39 *Le Journal,* January 20, 1893.
40 *La Dépêche de Toulouse,* February 14, 1893.
41 *Ibid.,* April 3, 1893; see also March 13, 1893.
42 *Le Gaulois,* May 2, 1893.
43 *Le Temps,* May 4, 1893.
44 *La Dépêche de Toulouse,* May 8, 1893.
45 Years later that interpretation was confirmed by the Prefect of Police. See E. Raynaud, *Souvenirs de police* (Paris, 1926), p. 35.
46 Jaurès, *Discours parlementaires,* p. 444.
47 *La Dépêche de Toulouse,* May 23, 1893.
48 *La petite République,* July 7, 1893.
49 Of the thirty-seven socialists, twenty were Independents, six Guesdists, five Allemanists, four Blanquists, and two Possibilists. There were also a dozen Radical-Socialists and former Boulangists who identified themselves with socialism.
50 Quoted in Auclair, *Jaurès,* p. 231.
51 There are, unfortunately, very few detailed local and regional socialist histories from which one could form a clear picture of the sources of French socialism in the 1880's and early 1890's. Two good studies, however, comprise an entire issue of *L'Actualité de l'Histoire,* Nos. 20–21, December, 1957: G. Thomas, "*Le Socialisme et le syndicalisme dans l'Indre des origines à 1920–22*"; and Pierre Cousteix, "Le Mouvement ouvrier limousin de 1870 à 1939."
52 Quoted in Auclair, *Jaurès,* p. 234.
53 Quoted in Zévaès, *Jaurès,* p. 75. On this spirit of unity, see the comments of *Le Temps,* March 14 and April 29, 1893. Recalling the spirit among the socialist deputies in 1893 after an interval of twenty years, remembering mainly their close collaboration in the Chamber between 1893 and 1898, Jaurès underestimated the tensions and rivalries that were still very much a part of the socialist movement. The third volume of the *Correspondence* of Engels and the Lafargues, which was published only in 1959, is a particularly

rich source of information on the inner history of the French socialist move-ment between 1891 and 1895. These letters reveal that behind the outward display of unity and fraternity, the struggle for control of the socialist move-ment went on. They establish several interesting facts, which should be noted: 1) The bitter struggles among the socialist factions in the 1880's (Marxists against Possibilists, Allemanists against Broussists, anti-Boulangist Blan-quists against pro-Boulangist Blanquists, revolutionaries against reformists, centralists against decentralists, collectivists against cooperators) left a legacy of distrust within the movement in the 1890's. See, for example, the letters of Laura Lafargue to Engels, April 9, 1891, and of Engels to Paul Lafargue, June 2, 1894. *Ibid.*, pp. 35, 361. 2) The collaboration among the parliamen-tary socialists proved to be very effective, but it was also uneasy and often opportunistic. Each faction hoped to win the entire movement over to its principles. 3) Though they early recognized the great drawing power of Jaurès in the movement, the Marxist leaders suspected him and Millerand of trying to convert French socialism to reformism. See especially Paul Lafargue to Engels, February 23, 1893, Laura Lafargue to Engels, March 6, 1893, and Engels to Laura Lafargue, March 14, 1893. *Ibid.*, pp. 254, 266, 270. When Jaurès first emerged on the national scene, Engels was especially suspicious of him. He questioned Jaurès' understanding of economic and social matters, and he warned the French Marxists against letting Jaurès steal the spotlight in the Chamber. See Engels to Laura Lafargue, December 19, 1893, and Engels to Paul Lafargue, March 6, 1894. *Ibid.*, pp. 346, 353–54. These were the understandable reactions of men who had waged a dangerous war to establish a revolutionary socialist movement and to keep its principles pure. As the legislative session wore on, however, the Marxists became more en-thusiastic about parliamentary political action and more convinced of Jaurès great value to the movement. Thus, in one of his last letters to Paul Lafargue, Januaray 22, 1895, Engels wrote: "Jaurès, in fact, though he is developing a little slowly, seems completely honorable." *Ibid.*, pp. 394–95.

54 Quoted in Auclair, *Jaurès*, p. 233.
55 *La Dépêche de Toulouse*, September 25, 1893.
56 See Chapter 9 for his views on agricultural organization.
57 *La Dépêche de Toulouse*, November 7, 1893.
58 *Ibid.*, November 14, 1893.
59 The following quotations are from the debate, published in Chambre des Députés, *Journal officiel*, November 21, 1893.
60 Quoted in Auclair, *Jaurès*, p. 239–40.
61 Quoted in Jaurès, *Oeuvres*, VI, 20.
62 Jean Jaurès and Paul Lafargue, *Idéalisme et matérialisme dans la conception de l'histoire* (Paris, 1895), p. 3. No formal verdict, it should be noted, followed this debate.
63 *Ibid.*, p. 9.
64 *Ibid.*, p. 27.
65 *Ibid.*, p. 24.
66 *Ibid.*, p. 26.
67 *Ibid.*, p. 28.
68 *Ibid.*, p. 34.
69 Lafargue's assumption that the concept of a just society, as developed by Jaurès, was akin to ideas of fair distribution is essentially false. Writing some

time later, Jaurès categorically rejected the goal of equal shares for all: "The idea of an equal division of all goods among all citizens is crude, absurd, and untenable." Jaurès, *Oeuvres*, VI, 400. On many occasions he wrote of the communist society as a new community, rooted in new institutions and producing a culture of its own.

CHAPTER 6

1 Dupuy, installed on April 4, 1893, was replaced by Casimir-Périer on December 3; this ministry fell on May 22, 1894, and was replaced a week later by another Dupuy ministry; Dupuy lasted until January 27, 1895, when Ribot was called to power; Ribot was replaced in November, 1895, by the all-Radical ministry of Léon Bourgeois.
2 *La Dépêche de Toulouse*, June 5, 1894.
3 Quoted in Auclair, *Jaurès*, pp. 232–33.
4 *La Dépêche de Toulouse*, April 3, 1894.
5 *Ibid.*, April 10, 1894.
6 Quoted in Auclair, *Jaurès*, p. 255.
7 Proudhon, in *Idée général de la Révolution au XIXe siècle*, quoted by Jean Maitron, *Histoire du mouvement anarchiste en France (1880–1914)*, (Paris, 1951), p. 30. Like every social movement, French anarchism was more complex than any generalizations about it suggest. Thus, in his definitive history of the movement, Maitron identifies several groups or sects, each of which had its own approach to the meaning and method of anarchism: the *syndicalistes*; the *illégalistes*; the *propagandistes par le fait*; the *anarchistes individualistes*; the *coöpératistes*; the *propagandistes par la parole*; the *philosophes*. Yet, as the text which follows indicates, a given brand of anarchism would dominate at a certain time, and though not all anarchists adhered to it, it would come to color the entire movement.
8 According to other versions, Dupuy either uttered those words fifteen minutes later, when the deputies were coming out from under their desks, or did not speak them at all until the Secretary General, M. Pierre, had said them first. Auclair, *Jaurès*, p. 244.
9 Francis de Pressensé, *Les Lois scélérates de 1893–94* (Paris, 1894), p. 10.
10 *Le Temps*, December 14 and 18, 1893.
11 *Ibid.*, December 17, 1893. On the role of the Prefects as opponents of radical political activity, see Louis Andrieux, *A Travers la République*, Paris, 1926; Louis Lépine, *Mes Souvenirs*, Paris, 1929; and Brian Chapman, *The Prefects and Provincial France*, London, 1955.
12 Quoted in Maitron, *Le Mouvement anarchiste*, p. 217.
13 *La Révolte*, July 1–7, 1892. This was the paper of Jean Grave, shoemaker and printer, who became a leading anarchist publicist.
14 *La petite République*, January 14 and February 6, 1894.
15 *Ibid.*, December 31, 1893.
16 *Le Temps*, July 9 and August 18, 1894.
17 The three laws on freedom of the press and of assembly, passed on December 12 and 15, 1893, and July 26, 1894, were grouped together by the socialists as the *lois scélérates*. For the full texts of these laws, see Pressensé, *Les Lois scélérates*, pp. 55–62.
18 Jaurès, *Discours parlementaires*, p. 595.

19 Years later, Prefect of Police Andrieux admitted that the bomb thrown in the Chamber had been manufactured in a police laboratory. Auclair, *Jaurès*, p. 245. Other corroborative evidence of the use of *agents provocateurs* among the anarchists is set forth in a letter of February 23, 1892, from the Radical deputy Goblet to Senator Ranc. Arthur Ranc, *Souvenirs-Correspondance* (Paris, 1913), p. 399.

20 *La Dépêche de Toulouse*, March 12, 1894.

21 Jaurès, *Discours parlementaires*, pp. 599–600.

22 *La Dépêche de Toulouse*, July 24, 1894.

23 See, for example, *Le Matin*, July 9, 1894.

24 *La petite République*, February 20, 1896.

25 Jaurès, *Discours parlementaires*, p. 655.

26 *Ibid.*, pp. 661–65. Later in the year Jaurès intervened again in a case that was not very different from that of Marty. It involved a twenty-nine-year-old teacher, Mirman, who had been elected to the Chamber as a Radical-Socialist. A strong opponent of the Dupuy ministry, he was ordered by General Mercier, then Minister of War, to report for military induction on November 16, since he had left teaching before doing his army service. The Chamber approved the action, though it was bitterly attacked by Jaurès (Chambre des Députés, *Journal officiel*, October 30, 1894). Jaurès' stand was roundly condemned in the nonsocialist press, which now supported the principle of equality in military service. *Le Temps*, November 1, 1894; *Le Matin*, October 31, 1894.

27 Jaurès, *Discours parlementaires*, p. 667. A teacher and scholar, whether in philosophy or history, Jaurès manifested both his spirit of inquiry and his socialist convictions. That, at least, is the judgment of scholars and academicians who knew his work well. Consider the remarks of Camille Bloch, the renowned archivist and historian of the French Revolution, who, along with other noted academicians, sat, almost a decade later, on the Commission de recherche et de publication de documents de l'histoire économique, over which Jaurès presided: "As presiding officer, he was never pedantic or pompous. He was friendly and kind; if he led us, it was not because of his position, but because of his purely intellectual prowess. . . . He was impartial, not because he presided, but because he was filled with the spirit of curiosity and scientific inquiry." *L'Humanité*, July 31, 1915.

28 Francisque Sarcey, "La Politique à l'école et au lycée," *La Revue bleue* (June 20, 1894), p. 810.

29 Jean Jaurès, *Action socialiste* (Paris, 1899), p. 239. Jaurès' reply, which appeared in *La Revue bleue* on July 7, 1894, was reprinted in this collection.

30 See *La Dépêche de Toulouse*, August 22 and September 3, 1894, for other articles on academic freedom.

31 Chambre des Députés, *Journal officiel*, July 10, 1894.

32 *Ibid.*, July 12, 1894. Jaurès again pressed for the income tax in a long speech toward the end of the year. *Ibid.*, December 1, 1894.

33 See, for example, the attack by Clemenceau in *La Justice*, July 11, 1894.

34 Quoted in Noland, *French Socialist Party*, p. 45.

35 *La Dépêche de Toulouse*, July 24, 1894.

36 Chambre des Députés, *Journal officiel*, July 25, 1894.

37 *La Dépêche de Toulouse*, July 31, 1894.

38 *Le Chambard*, September 29, 1894.

39 Jules Renard, *Journal* (Paris, 1927), p. 745.

40 Jaurès' long address was printed in *La petite République*, November 8, 1894. The proceedings of the entire trial were reprinted in Jean Jaurès, *Le Procès de Chambard*, Paris, 1895. The quotations which follow are from the *compte rendu* in *La petite République*.

41 For a strikingly similar review of the Périer family history, see Beau de Loménie, *Dynasties bourgeoises*, I, *passim*.

42 See the reaction of *Le Matin*, November 8, 1894.

43 Guy Chapman, *The Dreyfus Case* (London, 1955), p. 80.

44 The *bordereau* was a letter containing a list of documents which the author intended to hand over to the Germans. It was unsigned, and reached the Statistical Section of the French War Office in the last week of September, 1894, through an agent in the German Embassy.

45 Jaurès, *Discours parlementaires*, p. 866.

46 *Ibid.*, p. 872.

47 Chapman, *Dreyfus Case*, p. 97.

48 *La Dépêche de Toulouse*, December 26, 1894. The same theme was repeated a week later in the same paper, January 1, 1895.

49 Nicholas Halasz, *Captain Dreyfus* (New York, 1955), pp. 59, 101.

50 Quoted in Auclair, *Jaurès*, p. 261.

51 Chapman, *Dreyfus Case*, p. 35.

52 According to agreements in 1883, the government had guaranteed interest on the railway stock of private companies. The ministry now claimed that the terminal date for this provision was 1914; the proponents of the companies said it was 1956. The Conseil d'État found in favor of the companies, Barthou and Poincaré resigned, and Dupuy, seeking a vote of confidence in the Chamber, did not receive it.

53 Quoted in Chapman, *Dreyfus Case*, p. 108.

54 *La petite République*, January 21, 1895.

55 Chambre des Députés, *Journal officiel*, February 11, 1895.

56 Jaurès, *Socialisme allemand*, p. 62.

57 *La petite République*, June 30, 1903.

58 Jaurès, *Oeuvres*, III, 306. Between March, 1895, and May, 1896, Jaurès wrote a series of long articles for *La Revue socialiste*, which not only embodied his views on freedom and socialism but also described, in greater detail than anywhere else, the probable institutions of a collective society. These important articles are included in the third volume of the *Oeuvres*. For a generous though lengthy analysis of Jaurès' collectivism by an antisocialist academician, see Maurice Bourguin, *Les Systèmes socialistes et l'évolution économique* (Paris, 1904), pp. 28-40.

59 Jaurès, *Oeuvres*, III, 312. Jaurès illustrated his charge that in the struggle between capital and labor, public officials were generally on the side of management: "Some time after Fourmies, I witnessed a bitter strike which threw a large city into a frenzy. The poor streetcar workers, who put in a sixteen-hour day for fifty sous, struck; riots followed. What excitement among the authorities, who feared a possible revolution! What gentleness with the strikers! What precautions! . . . And then this offer was made to the workers by the Attorney General: "Keep cool, my good friends; we will see that you get some satisfaction; we will forget this morning's disturbances; go back to work, and we will prove our good intentions." Two weeks later, when

the strike was not only over but forgotten, almost all the strikers were haled into police court; they were sentenced for the most insignificant infractions; and the severity of their sentences went far beyond what the law prescribed." *Ibid.*, pp. 322–24.

60 *Ibid.*, p. 301. In answering the predictions of bureaucracy under socialism, Jaurès sketched the following theory: Every society requires an administration. The real issue is whether the bureaucracy is good or bad. Under capitalism, it is bad, a threat to freedom, because it serves the interests of the rich against the poor; because its officials are arrogant and expect subservience; because the masses, lacking education, security, and self-confidence, submit to this arrogance. Under socialism, when men enjoy freedom and dignity through education and economic security, the bureaucracy, working in the interest of the entire nation, would serve and not dominate. *Ibid.*, p. 325.

61 There was surprisingly little discussion in these years of the precise form a socialist society might take. The Marxists especially argued that since it was impossible to anticipate the specific needs and problems of the future, such speculation was essentially utopian. Jaurès, of course, demurred. He thought it vitally important not only to answer the criticisms of antisocialists but also to discuss in advance the technical and institutional problems that socialists would confront. Not to do so, he felt, was to risk complete unpreparedness and to leave the future to chance: "One can only submit to blind chance if he ignores human reason which, by its constant curiosity, helps to light our way." *Ibid.*, p. 296.

62 Thus, Jaurès criticized those who went no further than to advocate welfare legislation, "moderates tainted with a kind of 'socialism,' and Radicals." In the main, he wrote, "they want to uphold rather than transform the present system of property." He criticized also the advocates of State capitalism: "When the present State becomes the owner, it opposes labor demands like any other employer: it too is a capitalist, a bourgeois, an exploiter." *Ibid.*, pp. 297, 331.

63 *Ibid.*, p. 338.

64 *Ibid.*, pp. 346–48.

65 Jaurès raised many points about the functions of a collectivist economy and made concrete proposals; thus, he described the workings of the central planing commission, the local labor councils, the pricing and wage systems, and the raising and expenditure of the investment fund. *Ibid.*, pp. 349–80.

66 *Ibid.*, p. 408.

CHAPTER 7

1 *La Dépêche de Toulouse*, February 27 and 28, 1893; *La petite République*, October 8, 1893; Chambre des Députés, *Journal officiel*, July 7, 1894.

2 Léon de Seilhac, *Une Enquête sociale. La Grève de Carmaux et la verrerie d'Albi* (Paris, 1897), pp. 7–37. For an excellent analysis of the political battle between the socialist workers and the companies of Carmaux, see Rolande Trempé, "L'Échec électoral de Jaurès à Carmaux (1898)," *Cahiers internationaux* (February, 1958), pp. 47–64, on which the following several paragraphs are based.

3 *Le Temps*, August 9, 1895. In trying to forestall the strike and arrange a

settlement acceptable to the workers, Jaurès was acting in accord with a principle he shared with other leading socialists. Paul Lafargue expressed it clearly in a letter of May 21, 1891, to Engels: "What is most deplorable is the readiness of workers to go out on strike suddenly without considering how they will eat within a few days. A strike which fails leads to their disorganization and discouragement for a long time." Engels and Lafargue, *Correspondance*, III, 57. Once a strike began, Jaurès supported it firmly. But in his opposition to "revolutionary romanticism," in his many discussions with syndicalists on the general strike, he spoke in much the same way as Lafargue did in his letter to Engels.

4 Quoted in Seilhac, *La Grève de Carmaux*, p. 85.

5 *La Dépêche de Toulouse*, August 14, 1895.

6 Jaurès' speech was reprinted, *ibid.*, September 2, 1895.

7 *La petite République*, August 8, 1895.

8 *Le Temps*, August 8, 9, 21, 23, 1895; *Le Matin*, August 3, 1895; *Le Figaro*, August 27, 1895; and *Le Journal des débats*, August 31, 1895.

9 *La Dépêche de Toulouse*, September 4 and 11, 1895. Even so conservative a critic as Lucien Millevoye could write in *La Patrie*, September 9, 1895: "This incident, which will be discussed in all labor centers, will certainly have the effect of giving Jaurès and his friends more moral force and authority." The author discovered at the Musée Social in Paris, in a dossier on the Carmaux strike, a revealing letter, dated November 22, 1895, containing a full explanation of Sirven's resignation. It was unsigned, but a comparison of the writing with Sirven's autograph, as well as the internal evidence of the letter, leads to the conclusion that Sirven wrote it. In it, the writer especially makes the point that Rességuier goaded the union into the strike to get rid of surplus inventory.

10 The entire speech is reprinted in *La Dépêche de Toulouse*, September 16, 1895.

11 *La petite République*, October 4, 1895.

12 Auclair, *Jaurès*, pp. 274–75.

13 Archives Nationales, BB[18] 2010, Dos. 2244 A95.

14 *Ibid.*, BB[18] 1999, Dos. 1215 A95.

15 *La Lanterne*, October 17, 1895.

16 *L'Autorité*, October 25, 1895.

17 *La Dépêche de Toulouse*, October 6, 1895.

18 *La petite République*, October 20, 1895.

19 See the articles of Francis Charmes in *Le Télégramme*, September 7 and 8, 1895. See also *La Revue des deux mondes*, August 9, 1895.

20 Seilhac, *La Grève de Carmaux*, pp. 99–103.

21 *Ibid.*, pp. 107–9.

22 *La petite République*, October 8, 1895.

23 Jules Cornély in *Le Matin*, October 13, 1895.

24 Chambre des Députés, *Journal officiel*, October 24, 1895.

25 *Ibid.*, October 25, 1895.

26 Note Rochefort's insinuation, in *L'Intransigeant*, October 27, 1895, that there was some sort of complicity between Leygues and Rességuier.

27 Chambre des Députés, *Journal officiel*, October 26, 1895.

28 *La Dépêche de Toulouse*, October 27, 1895.

29 *Le Temps*, October 26, 1895.

30 *La Presse libre*, October 26, 1895.

31 *La République française,* October 27, 1895.
32 *Le Temps,* November 24, 1895.
33 *Le Parti ouvrier,* December 13 and 14, 1895.
34 The idea is generally attributed to Rochefort. Such is Seilhac's claim; see *La Grève de Carmaux,* pp. 111-12. But Rochefort's biographer says simply that the idea was in the air. Zévaès, *Rochefort,* p. 218
35 A. Lugan, *La Verrerie ouvrière d'Albi* (Paris, 1922), p. 3.
36 Note *Le Temps,* December 30, 1895.
37 *La petite République,* March 21, 1896.
38 *Ibid.,* July 3, 1897.
39 Quoted in Auclair, *Jaurès,* p. 290.
40 *Ibid.,* p. 293.
41 *La petite République,* October 27, 1896.
42 Quoted in Auclair, *Jaurès,* p. 297.
43 *Ibid.,* p. 296.
44 *La petite République,* October 28, 1896.
45 *Ibid.,* October 29, 1896. The Méline ministry had been formed when Léon Bourgeois resigned in April, 1896.
46 *Le Matin,* November 6, 1896.
47 Chambre des Députés, *Journal officiel,* November 5, 1896.
48 Quoted in Trempé, "L'Échec de Jaurès," p. 54.
49 *Ibid.,* pp. 56–57. Mlle Trempé has made excellent use of local police archives.
50 See Sébastien Faure in *Le Libertaire,* December 24, 1896. The moderate press made much of this internal dispute. See *Le Temps,* December 23, 1896.
51 Chambre des Députés, *Journal officiel,* May 10, 1907.
52 Jaurès, *Oeuvres,* III, 305.
53 *Ibid.,* p. 310.
54 *Ibid.,* p. 305.
55 *Le Matin,* April 8, 1907.

CHAPTER 8

1 Urbain Gohier, the journalist who was to travel a strange route from monarchism to antipatriotism to ultranationalism, was pushed toward Radicalism by Ribot, during whose ministry, he wrote, "money dominate[d] politics." *Contre l'Argent* (Paris, 1896), p. 16.
2 Georges Suarez, *Briand, sa vie, son oeuvre* (Paris, 1938), II, 97-98.
3 Quoted in Chapman, *Dreyfus Case,* p. 114.
4 A. Milhaud, *Histoire du radicalisme* (Paris, 1951), p. 104.
5 Chambre des Députés, *Journal officiel,* November 4, 1895. A classic expression of the standard Radical program can be found in Pelletan's article in *La Justice,* September 17, 1892.
6 For the efforts of Jules Guesde on behalf of social reform measures, see his collected interventions in *Quatre Ans des luttes sociales à la Chambre, 1893-98* (Paris, 1901), *passim.* See also the discussion of the change from revolutionary to reformist doctrine in French Marxism and Blanquism in Noland, *French Socialist Party,* pp. 51-60.
7 *La petite République,* November 16, 1895.
8 The political theorist Maurice Duverger has aptly summed up the problems of alliance between socialist and nonsocialist parties: "In the long run it seems

that the alliance is finally dominated by the most moderate party; the extremist is compelled on the parliamentary level to support a certain number of measures in contradiction with its own dynamics." *Political Parties* (London, 1954), p. 346.

9 *L'Humanité*, September 2, 1909.

10 Note the following corroborative description of French society toward the end of the nineteenth century, in Jean Labasse, *Hommes de droit. Hommes de gauche* (Paris, 1947), pp. 46–47: "The numerical and qualitative importance of the working class, politically and economically, was not what it was later to become. But there were other popular forces — the artisans, small merchants, and peasants, together with the bourgeoisie of the liberal professions — who advocated a democratic philosophy, Leftist in spirit."

In describing his early life in the village of Foussemagne in the Haut-Rhin, Frossard documents this point very well. For his father, though a skilled artisan, had a hard life, which linked him closely to the poor peasants and the workers of the community. In general, their outlook was Leftist though not specifically socialist: "Between the years 1890 and 1900, my father was an artisan who, like all others of his class, had difficulty in making ends meet. He worked very hard as a harness-maker. Rising at dawn and even before dawn, he was still working at nightfall by the glimmer of a kerosene lamp. . . . During the long winter evenings, his workshop became the meeting place for the villagers. There, the workers from the tile factory met the peasants. . . . In that quasi-familial atmosphere, the peasant spoke of his hard life. On his ten or twelve hectares of land, usually highly mortgaged, he couldn't eke out much of a living. . . . The life of the worker was no better. At the tile factory, he put in ten or twelve hours of work a day. He lived on credit from the grocer and at the end of the year he was burdened with debts he couldn't pay off. Nothing safeguarded him against sickness, accidents, unemployment. When old age came, he was forced to depend on his children, who were as poor as he." Frossard, *De Jaurès à Blum*, pp. 15–17.

11 Suarez, *Briand*, I, 420.

12 His social attitudes can be found in the collected addresses of this period. See Georges Clemenceau, *La Mêlée sociale*, Paris, 1895.

13 This speech is reprinted in *La Dépêche de Toulouse*, May 11, 1891. Jaurès' reaction can be found, *ibid.*, May 14, 1891.

14 On Pelletan's role in Carmaux, see Tony Révillon, *Camille Pelletan, 1846–1915* (Paris, 1930), pp. 106–9. It should be added that Jaurès took the same optimistic view of the growing social consciousness of René Goblet, who had been Premier briefly in 1887. See *La Dépêche de Toulouse*, December 3, 1891. In fact, when Goblet died in 1905, Jaurès wrote an appreciative obituary in which he noted that "in spite of his repugnance for socialism, which he understood badly, he was guided by the idea of democracy to an alliance with the socialist party." *L'Humanité*, September 17, 1905.

15 *La Dépêche de Toulouse*, June 25 and July 8, 1891.

16 This distinction was made very clearly by Jaurès himself when he sought to to spell out for Clemenceau the formative and shaping influence of ideals in history: "It is Proudhon, the favorite theorist of our contemporary syndicalists, who said that if the Roman plebeians remained plebeians, without becoming a class, it is because they lacked an idea; it is because that idea did not come until later, in the decaying Roman world, in the form of the Christian affirma-

tion proclaiming the equal dignity of all human beings; that equal dignity, transposed from the supernatural to the social order, having become the affirmation of everyone in the modern theory of rights, has been the foundation of all claims to justice by the proletariat." Chambre des Députés, *Journal officiel*, June 25, 1909.

17 *Le Dépêche de Toulouse*, May 11, 1892. "We believe that capitalism will and should end. . . . The Radicals, on the other hand, . . . wish only to introduce correctives."

18 *La petite République*, September 2, 1893. Clemenceau reciprocated in 1906 even after the two men had so bitterly clashed in Chamber debates over the 1906 strikes. When some Radicals proposed to Clemenceau, then Minister of the Interior, that he urge the Prefect of the Tarn to work against Jaurès, he replied: "Do you think there are too many worthy men in the Chamber?" Quoted in Zévaès, *Jaurès*, p. 197.

19 *La Dépêche de Toulouse*, October 16, 1893.

20 Jaurès, *Oeuvres*, VI, 298.

21 Chambre des Députés, *Journal officiel*, November 14, 1895.

22 *La petite République*, November 16, 1895.

23 Jean Allemane, *Notre Programme* (Paris, 1895), p. 6.

24 Chambre des Députés, *Journal officiel*, January 22, 1896.

25 *Ibid.*, March 20, 1896. Gérault-Richard had entered the Chamber from jail on February 2, 1895, after the Ribot ministry had granted amnesty for certain political crimes, including offenses of the press.

26 *Ibid.*, March 23, 1896.

27 In 1955, 50,000 francs would equal 9,000,000, or something over $25,000.

28 See, for example, *Le Temps*, November 20, 1895; March 26 and 28, 1896. Léon Bourgeois answered some of the key criticisms in a speech at Lyon on January 13, 1896, reprinted in *La Lanterne*, January 14, 1896.

29 The following quotations are from Jaurès' Chamber speech. Chambre des Députés, *Journal officiel*, March 22, 1896.

30 Quoted in *La petite République*, March 25, 1896.

31 *Ibid.*, March 28, 1896.

32 *Ibid.*, April 13, 1896.

33 *Ibid.*, April 18, 1896.

34 *Le Matin*, April 21, 1896.

35 Quoted in Chastenet, *La troisième République*, III, 91.

36 *La Dépêche de Toulouse*, April 21, 1896.

37 *La petite République*, April 24, 1896. Years later, the Left-Wing newspaper *Le Bonnet rouge*, referring back to the resignation, said of Bourgeois (June 11, 1914): ". . . he made the only forceful decision of his career; he capitulated."

38 Chambre des Députés, *Journal officiel*, April 24, 1896.

39 The speeches at the Tivoli Vauxhall meeting are reproduced in *Le petite République*, April 26, 1896.

40 Henri Turot. *Ibid.*, April 30, 1896.

41 *Ibid.*, May 1, 1896.

42 *Ibid.*, May 2, 1896.

43 *Le Matin*, June 29, 1896.

44 *La petite République*, October 23, 1897.

45 *Ibid.*, October 16, 1897. Radical Senator Ranc won approval from Jaurès when he urged a Radical agreement with socialists whenever there was a

danger that "a clerical conservative might win." *L'Éclair*, April 14, 1897.

46 Jean Jaurès, "Le Socialisme français," *Cosmopolis*, IX (January, 1898), 129-30.

47 The socialists gained control of the municipal councils in 150 cities and towns. In addition, they won the mayor's office in Lille, Roubaix, Bordeaux, Carmaux, Dijon, Roanne, Toulon, Limoges, Sens, Marseilles, Commentry, and Montluçon.

48 The full text of Millerand's speech is reprinted in Alexandre Millerand, *Le Socialisme reformiste français* (Paris, 1903), pp. 19-35.

49 Dommanget, *Vaillant*, pp. 200-8.

50 At its fourteenth Congress, the Parti ouvrier français, meeting between July 21 and 24, 1896, declared itself "partisan of the largest possible union." It went on to declare that no one could be considered socialist, however, who did not believe in collective property. Léon Blum, *Les Congrès ouvriers et socialistes français* (Paris, 1901), p. 158.

51 The Congress of London of 1896 was the fourth meeting of the Second International. After the founding of the Congress in Paris in 1889, it convened again in Brussels in 1891 and in Zurich in 1893.

52 On the distinction between these two kinds of unions, see Colette Chambelland, *Le Syndicalisme ouvrier français* (Paris, 1956), pp. 20-21.

53 On the growth of syndicalist hostility to socialist politics, see E. Dolléans, *Histoire du mouvement ouvrier* (Paris, 1939), II, 23-24; Robert Goetz-Girey, *La Pensée syndicale française* (Paris, 1948), pp. 32-38.

54 Joseph Schumpeter thus described the appeal of syndicalism: "Beholding, as the whole nation did, the sorry spectacle of political inefficiency, incompetence, and frivolity, . . . they [the workers] placed no trust in the state. . . . And to those who had overcome their bourgeois propensities, syndicalism was much more attractive than any of the available species of straight socialism, the sponsors of which bade fair to reproduce on a smaller scale the games of the bourgeois parties." *Capitalism, Socialism, and Democracy* (New York, 1942), p. 339.

55 Pelloutier's thought is well expressed in his work, published after his death, *Histoire des bourses du travail*, Paris, 1902. Filling a serious gap in syndicalist history, James Butler has written a dissertation on the life of Pelloutier, and the author is indebted to him for certain insights. That unpublished dissertation, "Pelloutier and the Rise of French Syndicalism," is in the Ohio State University Library.

56 Though there is considerable dispute over whether Pelloutier was formally an anarchist, the anarchists claimed that he was and had declared it in 1900. *Les Temps nouveaux*, April 13-17, 1906.

57 *Le Socialiste*, October 16, 1892.

58 12ᵉ Congrès national du Parti ouvrier français, tenu à Nantes du 14 au 16 septembre 1894, *Compte rendu* (Nantes, 1894), pp. 16-17. *Le Temps* sarcastically suggested that the Guesdists were hushing up talk of general strikes now that they were in Parliament. Suarez, *Briand*, I, 204.

59 Jaurès described his position and motives at Nantes in a speech, years later, on February 10, 1900. *Oeuvres*, VI, 136.

60 The syndicalist movement is thus very complex. It was split in at least three ways, between anarchists and socialists; reformists and revolutionaries; extremist leadership and less extreme rank and file. The reformist unions, like the Fédération du livre, headed by Keufer, were especially articulate in the

C.G.T. The C.G.T. in general always contained a strong current not only of reformism but also of support for political socialism. See these debates of the C.G.T.: 10ᵉ Congrès national corporatif, tenu à Rennes, 26 septembre á l octobre, 1898, *Compte rendu analytique* (Rennes, 1898), pp. 128-57; 11ᵉ Congrès national corporatif, tenu à Paris, 10-14 septembre 1900, *Compte rendu analytique* (Paris, 1900), pp. 114-17; 126-28.

61 From 1889 on, the socialists of the Second International had sought to purge anarchists from their midst, and in the process they attacked all syndicalist elements. In the 1891 Congress of Brussels and in the 1893 Congress of Zurich the majority of delegates had sought to eliminate those who denied the validity of political action. At the conclusion of the Zurich Congress a resolution had been adopted, making only those trade unions and socialist parties eligible for membership in the Second International, which recognized "the necessity of political action." Introduced by the German Marxist leader Bebel, the resolution was strongly supported by the Guesdists but opposed by the Allemanists and the syndicalists.

62 *La petite République*, July 15, 1896.

63 A. Hamon, *Le Socialisme et le congrès de Londres* (Paris, 1897), pp. 85-87. Note the comment of the fiery Dutch socialist-syndicalist, Domela Nieuwenhuis, veteran of many frays with the political Marxists: "If one excludes from socialism people like Kropotkin, Reclus, Cepriani, Louise Michel, and Malatesta, he becomes ridiculous. Who, after all, has the right to monopolize socialism?" *Le Socialisme en danger* (Paris, 1897), p. 255.

64 The connections of anarchists in the union movement were spelled out in detail and for hostile purposes by the foreign affairs editorialist for *Le Temps*, André Tardieu. He listed the anarchists at various key meetings, including the Congress of London. See André Tardieu, "La Campagne contre la patrie," *La Revue des deux mondes*, XVI (July 1, 1913), 80-105.

65 At the Musée de l'Histoire at Montreuil, there is a collection of *feuilles*, the note sheets on which Jaurès copied passages from books he read. That museum also houses the bulk of his library, and certain notebooks and *fiches* in which he compiled notes for his books and speeches. On one of the *feuilles* Jaurès had copied a passage from the Belgian poet and philosopher Maeterlinck, which particularly impressed him. It read: "Nevertheless, it would be interesting to calculate, since we achieve good only through evil, if the evils of a sudden, radical, and bloody revolution cancel out the evils that hang on in the process of slow evolution. . . . We gladly forget that the hangmen of perpetual misery are less blatant, less colorful, but infinitely more numerous and cruel than those of the bloodiest revolutions." It was the kind of thought that made Jaurès, though a reformist, sympathetic to revolutionaries.

66 International Socialist Workers and Trade Union Congress, *Report of Proceedings* (London, 1896), pp. 1-2.

67 One of the very few carefully documented and informative biographies of a syndicalist is Jean Maitron, *Le Syndicalisme révolutionnaire: Paul Delesalle*, Paris, 1952. It is interesting to note that Bouillon actually sided with the anarchists at the Congress but later made his way into the Radical Party.

68 Les Révolutionnaires au Congrès de Londres, *Conférences anarchistes* (Paris, 1896), p. 10.

69 Jaurès repeated that accusation in *La petite République*, July 31, 1896. See

also *Le Matin*, July 31, 1896, where Jaurès challenged the delegation of a well known anarchist like Tortelier.

70 For the resolution were many small, fairly insignificant delegations, dominated by the Marxist parties of their countries. Thus, among national groups that voted *for* were the delegations from Australia, Bohemia, Bulgaria, Denmark, Hungary, Poland, Portugal, Romania, Spain, Switzerland, and the U.S.A. The major groups in support came from Belgium, Great Britain (by the split vote of 223 to 104), and especially Germany. Against were France (57 to 56) and the Netherlands (9 to 5). Italy, hopelessly divided, abstained.

71 Vaillant, with his insurrectionary Blanquist background, always had a strong sympathy for syndicalist fervor and on various occasions supported the general strike against the strong opposition of Guesde. Dommanget, *Vaillant*, pp. 176–78.

72 *Proceedings of the Congress of London (1896)*, p. 32.

73 International Socialist and Trade Union Congress, *Illustrated Report of the Proceedings of the Workers' Congress* (London, 1896), p. 23.

74 *Proceedings of the Congress of London (1896)*, p. 46.

75 *La petite République*, August 9, 1896.

76 Eugène Guérard, *Le Congrès de Londres* (Paris, 1896), p. 31.

77 *Le Libertaire*, August 8–14, 1896. Note similar criticism by the Allemanists in *Le Parti ouvrier*, August 16, 1896. The Congress of London was also attended by George Bernard Shaw, who wrote after the meetings about the contradictions of political Marxists, especially the German Social Democrats, who spoke revolution while practicing the most obvious reformism. Of Liebknecht he said that he "covers every compromise by a declaration that the Social Democrats never compromise." Quoted in James Joll, *The Second International* (London, 1955), p. 76.

78 Charles Péguy, *Oeuvres Compètes, 1876–1914* (Paris, 1916–50), XII, 54.

79 Unpublished manuscript letter in La Musée Sociale, Paris. Zévaès, the socialist historian who was both spectator and participant in the Latin Quarter during the early 1890's, reports an amusing incident about a young anarchist publicist, Mecislas Goldberg, who, after the Congress of London, wrote a critical letter to Jaurès and received a sixteen-page reply. Jaurès tried even to reconcile so marginal a young man to a collaboration with socialism. A. Zévaès, *Sur L'Écran politique, ombres et silhouettes* (Paris, 1928), p. 50.

80 Dolléans, *Le Mouvement ouvrier*, II, 46.

CHAPTER 9

1 Péguy, *Oeuvres*, XII, 34.

2 Chambre des Députés, *Journal officiel*, July 3, 1897.

3 Barthou, Minister of the Interior and the most articulate spokesman for the ministry, stated the conservative case for the government in his celebrated Bayonne speech. See his *Discours prononcé à Bayonne, 30 octobre 1897*, Paris, 1897. Méline's friend and biographer, Lachapelle, likewise singled out maintenance of social order against the Left as the chief aim of the ministry. G. Lachapelle, *Le Ministère Méline* (Paris, 1928), p. 34.

In recalling the political history of his native Haut-Rhin during his youth, Frossard indicated the kind of great capitalist support that Méline had enjoyed: "The local ironmasters had wrested political control of the area from the republicans. The head of the great dynasty, Armand Viellard, son of Senator Viellard-Migeon and nephew of Count Migeon, represented the district in the Chamber. His son-in-law, the Viscount Salignac-Fénélon, won the seat at Lure over the incumbent Caudrey, son of a martyred Communard, after passing around gifts of sausages, lard, and wine. The all-powerful *maison* Viellard assigned the Senatorial seat to the *maison* Japy of Beaucourt; it was General Japy who thus succeeded Dr. Fréry. M. Armand Viellard headed the Compagnie de l'Est. Did one want to find a job for a relative on the railroad? Then he had to look up M. Viellard and say the right word. M. Viellard, of course, belonged to the faithful majority of M. Méline." Frossard, *De Jaurès à Blum*, pp. 20–21.

4 *La Matin*, May 12, 1896. For his comments in the same vein, see *La Lanterne*, August 15, 1896, and *La petite République*, October 9, 1897.

5 Quoted in Chapman, *Dreyfus Case*, p. 115.

6 The rural population, which had constituted 67.6 percent of the total in 1876, fell to 57.9 percent in 1906. M. Augé-Laribé, *L'Évolution de la France agricole* (Paris, 1912), p. 174.

7 The Midi, a center of grape culture, was a special distress area after 1870 because of the appearance of the phylloxera, a dreaded plant insect. The material loss brought on by the phylloxera between 1878 and 1893 was estimated at about twenty-two billion francs. See M. Augé-Laribé, *Le Problème agraire du socialisme* (Paris, 1907), pp. 89–91.

8 M. Augé-Laribé, *Petite ou grande Propriété?* (Montpellier, 1902), pp. 122–25.

9 *La petite République*, January 7, 1893.

10 For a discussion of the popular view of the peasants, see H. Goldberg, "The Myth of the French Peasant," *The American Journal of Economics and Sociology*, XIII (July, 1954), 363–79.

11 *La Dépêche de Toulouse*, January 18, 1893.

12 *Souvenirs d'un militant* (Paris, 1939), p. 160.

13 A letter of August 23, 1879, quoted in Zévaès, *Jaurès*, p. 23. Many of the passages from books, which Jaurès extracted and copied, referred to rural beauty or the joys of nature. He drew such passages, for example, from Leonardo and Rousseau. Unpublished manuscripts in the Musée de l'Histoire, Montreuil.

14 *La Dépêche de Toulouse*, September 9, 1897.

15 Fernand Pignatel, *Jaurès*, p. 8. The Tarn afforded Jaurès an excellent opportunity to study a wide variety of rural types and conditions. The 1892 Inquiry into agricultural statistics revealed the following facts about the department: (a) of the 50,305 farm persons, 34,132 were listed as proprietors when 12,772 tenants, sharecroppers, and day laborers, who owned insignificant holdings, were included; 16,173 were listed as completely without land; (b) there was sharp inequality in the size of holdings: 29,566 cultivators had holdings of less than one hectare, totaling 17,600 hectares; at the other end, only 1444 cultivators had very large holdings, covering 203,600 hectares. Conditions of this sort in the Tarn provided, of course, the most direct data for Jaurès. The statistics cited can be found in Ministère de l'Agricole, *Statistique agricole de la France. Résultats généraux de l'enquête décennale de 1892*, Paris, 1897.

16 Jaurès made extensive analyses of the rural situation in *La Dépêche de Tou-*

louse, January 20, February 5, June 18, September 3 and 10, 1887; April 8 and August 5, 1888; and July 7, 1889.

17 In the 1892 statistical survey the number of proprietors, even counting non-owners who possessed a garden plot, came to 50.83 percent of the rural population.

18 Jaurès, *Discours parlementaires*, p. 654.

19 *La Dépêche de Toulouse*, January 22, 1891.

20 *Ibid.*, August 1, 1892.

21 *La petite République*, July 31, 1901.

22 *La Dépêche de Toulouse*, July 26, 1892.

23 These reforms included minimum wages for landless agricultural workers; social security for the sick and aged, established through a tax on large land-owners; cheap credit, coöperatives, low freight rates, and technical education for small landowners; and equitable leases for *fermiers* and *métayers*. Paul Lafargue, *Programme agricole du parti ouvrier français* (Lille, 1897), pp. 1–4.

24 *La Dépêche de Toulouse*, April 28, 1893.

25 *Ibid.*, January 13, 1893.

26 See, for example, *Le Temps*, July 29, 1893.

27 *Ibid.*, October 10, 1893.

28 Especially the editorials of October 5 and 28, 1893. See Jaurès' answer to *Le Temps* in *La Dépêche de Toulouse*, October 30, 1893.

29 *Ibid.*, October 23, 1893. The views on rural collectivism that follow are drawn from this article.

30 Jaurès even foresaw the sporadic hiring of farm workers on a greatly re-duced scale but for an indefinite future: "In return for these great reforms, the nation will ask of them [the small peasants] only one thing — that when by chance and on rare occasions they hire a few farm workers, they pay them a decent wage, one determined by the government."

31 For example, Jaurès spoke frequently for the socialist group on tariff ques-tions. Thus, early in 1894, when the Tariff Commission, headed by Méline, was proposing to raise duties again on foreign, especially Russian wheat, Jaurès introduced a counterproposal, co-sponsored by Millerand, Viviani, Sembat, and Vaillant, to create a State monopoly over the import of foreign wheat and flour. Thus, said, Jaurès, private grain speculators who cornered the market to raise prices artificially would be eliminated, while the amount of foreign grain admitted would be commensurate both with cheap prices and the survival of French agriculture. It was a position equally distant from doctrinaire protectionism and free trade. Chambre des Députés, *Journal of-ficiel*, January 16, 1894. By a vote of 481 to 52 the proposal was defeated. *Ibid.*, January 20, 1894. For a harsh criticism of the essential unreality of Jaurès' proposal, see Engels' letter to Lafargue, March 6, 1894, *Correspondance*, III, 353–55.

32 Quoted in Zévaès, *Sur L'Écran politique*, p. 250.

33 *La Dépêche de Toulouse*, April 24, 1894.

34 The most recent French printing is F. Engels, "La Question paysanne en France et en Allemagne," *Cahiers du communisme*, XXXI (November, 1955), pp. 1467–88. All the quotations from Engels that follow are from this version.

35 A great number of books and articles constitute the basic documents in the debate opened by Engels. The fiery Dutch socialist, Domela Nieuwenhuis,

was a sharp critic of the reformist program (*Le Socialisme en danger*, pp. 80–82). The leading German Marxist theorist, Karl Kautsky, sided essentially with Engels in his *La Politique agraire du parti socialiste* (Paris, 1903), although he made his case equivocal by tacking a program of reforms onto his deterministic doctrine. The same equivocation marked the position of the Belgian Vandervelde in "Le Socialisme et la transformation capitaliste de l'agriculture," *La Revue socialiste*, XXXI (June, 1901), 641–61. The Italian Gatti, coming from a country with a large peasant class, was less inflexible than Engels in *Le Socialisme et l'agriculture*, Paris, 1901.

36 *Le Parti ouvrier*, February 16–23 and September 21–28, 1895. The same sort of criticism came also from the ranks of revolutionary syndicalism. See Georges Sorel in his preface to Pelloutier, *Bourses du travail*, pp. 14–15.

37 Bonnier to Guesde, June 22, 1896. Guesde Archives, International Institute for Social History, Amsterdam. This Institute possesses the finest collection of unedited manuscripts on the history of the Second International. The Guesde and Kautsky Archives are particularly rich. There are occasional Jaurès pieces scattered in several collections, but unfortunately Jaurès Archives do not exist there.

This is explained to a great extent by the comment of Pierre Renaudel to Louise Kautsky: "As to Jaurès, after his death Landrieu and I found hardly any papers or correspondence. Jaurès committed a great deal to his memory. Further, he was too consumed by daily tasks to devote himself to organizing his papers." Letter of January 20, 1925. Kautsky Archives, Amsterdam.

38 Note, for example, a letter Guesde received, November 15, 1897, from the P.O.F. in the Pyrénées-Orientales, stating that the "moral servitude in which most agricultural workers live prevents us from establishing sections of the party in all rural towns." Guesde Archives, Amsterdam.

For an excellent discussion of the Marxist dilemma on the peasant problem, see Carl Landauer, "The Guesdists and the Small Farmer: the Early Erosion of French Marxism," *International Review of Social History*, VI (Part 2, 1961), 212–25.

39 *Proceedings of the Congress of London* (1896), p. 26. The final report read thus: "The conditions of land tenure and the division of classes among the rural population in different countries are too various for it to be possible to formulate a program binding on the labor parties of all countries."

40 Péguy, *Oeuvres*, XI, 59–60.

41 Quoted in L. and V. Thonet, "Jaurès et Léon XIII," *Europe*, No. 354–55 (October-November, 1958), p. 108.

42 Jean Jaurès, "La Politique de réaction du ministère Méline," *Almanach de la question sociale*, 1897, p. 194.

43 Robert Guilloux, "Le Style imagé de Jaurès," *Europe*, No. 354–55 (October-November, 1958), pp. 47–48. See also B. Voirin, "L'Art de l'image chez Jaurès orateur," *L'Actualité de l'histoire*, No. 17 (December, 1956), pp. 32–44.

44 Paul-Boncour, who knew him well, writes in his memoirs that Viviani was as tormented over the right word and inflection as Flaubert. J. Paul-Boncour, *Entre deux Guerres* (Paris, 1945), p. 174.

45 Leon Trotsky, "Jean Jaurès," *Bulletin Communiste*, No. 47 (November 22, 1923), p. 847.

46 Quoted in Michael Launay, "L'Éloquence de Jaurès," *Europe*, No. 354–55 (October-November, 1958), p. 25. This article was based on an interview

between Launay and Bracke in 1955, when the old socialist was ninety-four. Bracke also recalled that Guesde, introducing Jaurès once at a meeting, said, half-marveling, half-exasperated: "La parole est à la parole."

47 Chambre des Députés, *Journal officiel*, June 19, 1897. All the quotations that follow immediately are from the speech of that day.

48 Marcel Cachin, the Communist deputy who had been an ardent Guesdist at the start of the cetury, once told a revealing story of Jaurès' capacity for delivering a long speech under the worst conditions. It was at the time when the parties of Guesde and Jaurès were in bitter debate, before the Congress of Amsterdam in 1904. Cachin reported: "Once, at Béziers, Jaurès was to make a speech and Guesde assigned me the job of answering him. It was a scorching day. The heat beat down mercilessly; yet he spoke for an hour. When my turn came — and I had a strong voice then — I could speak no more than ten minutes, so dehydrating and torrid was the air." Quoted in Launay, "L'Éloquence de Jaurès," p. 36.

49 Jaurès once reported in the following fashion an instructive colloquy between Léon Say, spokesman for industrial interests wanting low agricultural prices, and Méline: "M. Léon Say, having one day said to M. Méline: 'Protectionism is the socialism of the rich,' M. Méline, visibly ruffled, replied: 'Free trade is the anarchism of millionaires.' That amused the socialist gallery." Jaurès, *Histoire socialiste*, I–II, 135. For Jaurès it was interesting proof of the anarchy of French capitalism, oscillating between intervention and laissez faire, depending on the strength of organized interests.

50 Chambre des Députés, *Journal officiel*, June 26, 1897. All quotations that follow immediately are from the speech of that day.

51 It was when the conservative critic and author Jules Lemaître heard Jaurès make this speech that he was moved to write: "As far as I can judge on a single performance, M. Jaurès is a born orator — with the imagination of a poet." But he went on to criticize the dangerous implications in the words of socialist dreamers: "They are led to believe that the generosity of their dreams entitles them to run the risk of terrible public catastrophes for the hazardous establishment of a social order they can't even define precisely." *Les Contemporains* (Paris, 1899), VII, 131–32.

52 Chambre des Députés, *Journal officiel*, July 3, 1897. All quotations that follow immediately are from the speech of that day.

53 The speech is reported in *Le Temps*, July 6, 1897.

54 *Le Journal des débats*, July 5, 1897.

55 *La petite République*, July 6, 1897.

56 Lemaître, *Les Contemporains*, p. 136.

57 Paul Leroy-Beaulieu, *Les Citations de M. Jaurès et la véracite des socialistes* (Paris, 1897), p. 1.

58 *Ibid.*, pp. 7–8.

59 *La petite République*, July 31, 1897. Note that Jaurès' anti-Semitic enemy, Édouard Drumont, used the issue of false citations to try to discredit Jaurès in the Dreyfus period. *La libre Parole*, February 16, 1898.

60 Jaurès at Albi to Salomon at Reims, March 11, 1883. Lévy-Bruhl, *Jaurès*, p. 177.

61 *Le Dépêche de Toulouse*, February 12, 1887.

62 This is a point of view, always a component of Jaurès' political outlook, which E. H. Carr has identified with the utopian approach to international relations:

"Both Rousseau and Kant argued that, since wars were waged by princes in their interest and not in that of their peoples, there would be no wars under a republican form of government. In this sense, they anticipated the view that public opinion, if allowed to make itself effective, would suffice to prevent war. In the nineteenth century, this view won widespread approval in Western Europe." *The Twenty Years' Crisis* (London, 1951), p. 25.

63 *La Dépêche de Toulouse*, October 22, 1887.

64 *Ibid.*, June 11, 1887. See also February 12, 1888, on the need to make sacrifices for military preparedness.

65 Gambetta, though he had led the patriotic war against Prussia in 1870, came gradually to stand for a peaceful accommodation on the question of Alsace and Lorraine. See G. P. Gooch, *Studies in Diplomacy and Statecraft* (London, 1942), p. 15.

66 See, for example, *Le Socialisme*, March 13, 1886; August 20 and October 15, 1887.

67 There is a valuable commentary on Marxist thinking between 1885 and 1914 in the work of a leading contemporary Marxist, Henri Lefebvre. He writes in *La Pensée de Lénine* (Paris, 1957), p. 22: "Marx died in 1884. He left his work unfinished. One can't stress this fact too much. Marx's successors were left facing realities which he couldn't have begun to analyze." Then, as Lefebvre indicates, little was done among orthodox Marxists to extend and deepen the doctrine.

68 The value of a combination of causal analysis and moral appeal is suggested by Carr: "All healthy human action, and therefore all healthy thought, must establish a balance between utopia and reality, between free will and determinism." *Twenty Years' Crisis*, p. 11.

69 Quoted in Launay, "L'Éloquence de Jaurès," p. 28.

70 *La Dépêche de Toulouse*, January 9, 1890.

71 *Ibid.*, July 2, 1890.

72 On the history of the Franco-Russian Alliance, see W. L. Langer, *The Franco-Russian Alliance, 1890–94*, Cambridge, Mass., 1929; Georges Michon, *L'Alliance franco-russe*, Paris, 1928; V. Khvostvov and I. Mintz, *Histoire de la diplomatie* (Paris, n.d.), II, 88–116.

73 Jaurès wrote early against an entangling alliance that might commit France to Russia's Balkan aims. *La Dépêche de Toulouse*, February 26, 1887.

74 Between 1888 and 1890, six large loans to Russia had been subscribed to by French bankers.

75 The Reinsurance Treaty had not been renewed by the Kaiser, and though the French, not knowing of the original treaty, could not know of its subsequent collapse, the change in Russian mood was evident.

76 *La Dépêche de Toulouse*, August 6, 1891.

77 *Le Prolétaire*, August 22, 1891.

78 *Le Socialiste*, June 10, 1891.

79 Quoted in Michon, *L'Alliance franco-russe*, p. 53. The terms which eventually became the secret Franco-Russian Alliance were as follows: 1) If Russia were attacked by Germany, or by Austria with the help of Germany, France would help her militarily; if France were attacked by Germany, or by Italy with the help of Germany, Russia would help her militarily. 2) France would provide 1,300,000 men against Germany, and Russia 700,000 to 800,000 men. 3) The

two powers would make no separate peace. 4) The treaty was to be strictly secret.

80 Quoted in Khvostvov and Mintz, *La diplomatie*, p. 116.
81 For the changed position of the P.O.F. on *la patrie*, see *Le Socialiste*, May 27, June 10 and 17, September 9, 1893.
82 *La Dépêche de Toulouse*, January 3, 1893.
83 *La petite République*, October 15, 1893. See also October 29, 1893.
84 Quoted in Michon, *L'Alliance franco-russe*, p. 76.
85 *La petite République*, September 23, 1894.
86 Chambre des Députés, *Journal officiel*, March 7, 1895. All quotations that follow immediately are from this speech.
87 Unpublished letter from Duc-Quercy to Guesde, July, 1896. Guesde Archives, Amsterdam.
88 Étienne's procolonial writings and speeches have been collected in two volumes, *Son Oeuvre: coloniale, algérienne, et politique, 1881–1906*, Paris, n.d. Hanotaux expressed his position in *Le Partage de l'Afrique*, Paris, 1909.
89 *La petite République*, May 17, 1896. For examples of his criticism of corrupt colonial practices, see Chambre des Députés, *Journal officiel*, March 2 and December 24, 1895. For his acceptance of the conquest of Madagascar, *La Dépêche de Toulouse*, April 1, 1896. Thus, at this point, Jaurès was not nearly so vigorous a critic of colonialism as Vigné d'Octon and Gustave Rouanet, who boldly attacked the conquest of Madagascar, or Turot and Goullé, his collaborators at *La petite République*, who exposed the human misery imposed by French rule in Algeria and Indo-China.
90 Quoted in E. P. Thompson, *William Morris* (London, 1955), pp. 724–25.
91 Alexander III had died in November, 1894, and been succeeded by Nicholas II,
92 Article 61 of the Treaty of Berlin imposed upon Turkey the obligation to institute reforms in the condition of the Armenians and the Kurds.
93 The Cretan rebellion of 1896 was led by men who sought annexation to Greece. On June 28 the Sultan had nominally accepted Russian proposals for reform in the administration of Crete in order to maintain as much of the status quo as possible.
94 *La petite République*, August 14, 1896. See also, September 1, 1896. Jaurès showed here a keen understanding of fundamental changes developing in Russia. The young Lenin also noted them, the next year, in his *Development of Capitalism in Russia*. For pertinent data on these changes, see the material cited in Lefebvre, *Lénine*, pp. 43–49.
95 *La petite République*, October 4, 1896.
96 Quoted in Chastenet, *La troisième République*, III, 102.
97 *La petite République*, October 11, 1896. Lafargue for the P.O.F. expressed sharp criticism also of the Tsar's visit. *Le Socialiste*, November 29, 1896.
98 Chambre des Députés, *Journal officiel*, November 3, 1896. The quotations which follow immediately are from this debate.
99 Quoted in Chastenet, *La troisième République*, III, 362.
100 Chambre des Députés, *Journal officiel*, March 15, 1897. The quotations that follow are from the same debate.
101 The charge that the Franco-Russian Alliance was a weapon of the Méline ministry against French democracy was made often by Jaurès, but reached a high point when he and his fellow socialists accused the ministry of planning

to dissolve the Chamber. Jaurès made the charge in an article for *Le Matin*, which that newspaper refused to publish. It marked the end of his occasional pieces in *Le Matin*. He printed the article in *La petite République*, September 14, 1897.

102 Jaurès said in the Chamber of Deputies on July 3, 1897: "Our political impotence will last for some years still, and if there are men, who, to fight on our side, need immediate victory, let them go elsewhere."

103 Jaurès, "Le Socialisme français," p. 124.

104 Compare the comment of the Tharauds, friends and biographers of Péguy, in explaining the lifelong love of that poet for the Jews: "At the lycée and at the École we always lived with our Jewish comrades in the same intimacy as with our Christian comrades." Jérôme and Jean Tharaud, *Notre Cher Péguy* (Paris, 1926), p. 134.

105 The debate is summarized by Zévaès, who took notes at the meeting. See his "L'Affaire Dreyfus. Quelques souvenirs personnels," *La nouvelle Revue*, CXXXI (January 1, 1936), 17–19.

Lafargue was just as emphatic in denouncing anti-Semitism. See his article of September 11, 1892, in *Le Socialiste*.

106 *La Dépêche de Toulouse*, June 2, 1892.

107 In the period of his socialist transition, Jaurès had referred to the role of Jewish financiers in the fall of the Gambetta ministry, the collapse of the Union générale, the expansion into Tunisia, and the Panama scandal, that "enormous and unfinished swindle." *Ibid.*, February 5, 1890.

108 The theme of anti-Semitism in socialist literature has been most fully explored in E. Silberner, *Western Socialism and the Jewish Question*, Jerusalem, 1955. This work is in Hebrew, but pertinent portions of it have appeared in English: "Charles Fourier on the Jewish Question," *Jewish Social Studies*, VIII (October, 1946), 245–66; "Proudhon's Judeophobia," *Historica Judaica*, X (April, 1948), 61–80. Fourier was moved to a dislike of the Jews by his hostility to commerce and urban life. Proudhon reflected the peasant or petty bourgeois mentality in his xenophobic hostility to Jews as aliens and his suspicion of their alleged power in finance, press, and politics. He inspired through his imagery the anti-Semitism of Chirac, Malon, and Sorel.

109 *La Dépêche de Toulouse*, June 2, 1892.

110 2e Congrès international ouvrier socialiste, tenu à Bruxelles, 1891, *Rapport* (Brussels, 1891), p. 41.

111 Until the time of the Dreyfus Affair, Jaurès was actually in the good graces of certain anti-Semites who, because they attacked Jewish capitalism, fancied themselves "socialists." Drumont, Rochefort, and Barrès liked in Jaurès a socialism which they chose to believe was native, provincial, French, and untainted by German-Jewish Marxism. Note Drumont's support of Jaurès at the time of the Carmaux glass strike and in his great peasant interpellation. *La libre Parole*, October 30, 1896, and July 6, 1897.

112 There are two comprehensive studies of the history of the Algerian Jews: Claude Martin, *Les Israélites algégiens de 1830 à 1902*, Paris, 1938; and Michel Ansky, *Les Juifs de l'Algérie du décret de Crémieux à libération*, Paris, 1950. Adolphe Crémieux, author of the decree of October 24, 1870, passed by Gambetta's Government of National Defense, was a distinguished French lawyer of wide social contacts.

113 On the existence of a large, poverty-striken Jewish proletariat in Algeria, see

Louis Durieu, "Le Prolétariat juif en Algérie," *La Revue socialiste*, XXIX (May, 1899), 513–53.

114 As typical of the propaganda by French settlers, note the writings of F. Gourgeot, a former interpreter for the army in Algeria, who spent his retirement warning against the moral and economic domination of the Jews: *La Domination juive en Algérie*, Alger, 1894; and *Les Sept Plaies de l'Algérie*, Alger, 1891.

115 *La Dépêche de Toulouse*, May 8, 1895.

116 *Ibid.*, May 1, 1895.

117 Joseph Caillaux, *Mes Mémoires* (Paris, 1942–47), II, 131. In the Chamber on May 25, 1895, one deputy, Théodore Denis of the Landes, proposed that the Jews be moved to the Center, away from the frontier, where treason would be less dangerous.

118 Reported by Goblet in *La Dépêche de Toulouse*, November 30, 1898.

119 Péguy, quoted in Daniel Halévy, *Péguy and Les Cahiers de la Quinzaine* (New York, 1947), p. 141.

120 On behalf of the socialists, Zévaès dismissed Lazare's pamphlet, calling it a piece of sensationalism. *La petite République*, November 10, 1896. One of the few socialists to call for a reappraisal of the Dreyfus conviction was Maurice Charney of the Allemanists. See *Le Parti ouvrier*, January 7, 1895.

121 Picquart uncovered by March, 1896, the so-called *petit bleu*, a letter on thin blue paper, addressed to Esterhazy from someone signed "C," probably the mistress of Colonel von Schwartzkoppen, military attaché of the German Embassy in Paris.

122 Quoted in Chapman, *Dreyfus Case*, pp. 120–21.

123 These are the words Picquart reported at the Rennes trial in 1899. Quoted, *ibid.*, p. 129.

124 Léon Blum, *Souvenirs sur l'Affaire* (Paris, 1935), p. 25.

125 *L'Aurore* had been founded by Ernest Vaughan, a close associate of Rochefort at *l'Intransigeant*, who could not accept the latter's Antidreyfusard views. Among the contributors to *L'Aurore* were Urbain Gohier, Octave Mirbeau, Bernard Lazare, and Gustave Geffroy. The course of Rochefort's career, meanwhile, took a strange turn, carrying him from near-socialism to ultranationalism. Both of these tendencies were, of course, evident in his earlier and never-forgotten Boulangism.

126 Quoted in Jean Ratinaud, *Clemenceau ou la colère et la gloire* (Paris, 1958), p. 119.

127 Quoted in George Wormser, *La République de Clemenceau* (Paris, 1961), p. 187. Wormser, who has written a very well-informed, if completely sympathetic, biography of Clemenceau, suggests that he was influenced also by his sympathy for the steadfast Mathieu Dreyfus, whom he called "ce brave homme sans détours." *Ibid.*, p. 185. Arthur Meyer, the editor of the reactionary *Gaulois*, stressed the opportunism of Clemenceau's stand. He reported an alleged conversation about the Affair, in which Clemenceau said: "I still don't know what it's really about. But I can see in it a fine weapon in the hands of the parties." Arthur Meyer, *Ce que mes yeux ont vu* (Paris, 1911), p. 137.

128 Blum, *Souvenirs*, p. 17.

129 Quoted in Auclair, *Jaurès*, p. 303.

130 Jaurès referred here to a secret dossier on Dreyfus, which Du Paty had given

to the military judges; Demange, the lawyer for the accused, assumed that the *bordereau* was the only evidence and had thus no chance to refute the other material.

131 *La petite République*, November 27, 1897.

132 Chambre des Députés, *Journal officiel*, December 4, 1897. Reinach has written a stirring, though one-sided, account of this session. See Joseph Reinach, *Histoire de l'Affaire Dreyfus* (Paris, 1901–8), III, 141–44. "Imagine! The legend of the Syndicate, invented by the Jesuits, was ratified by the republicans!"

133 *La Dépêche de Toulouse*, December 8, 1897.

134 *La petite République*, December 11, 1897.

135 Louis Leblois, *L'Affaire Dreyfus* (Paris, 1929), p. 67.

136 *Le Temps*, January 5, 1898.

137 Andler, *Lucien Herr*, p. 118. For a good summary of the sources of Péguy's socialism — the influence upon him of the wheelwright Boitier, for example, or of his early renunciation of Catholicism — see Basil Guy, "Notes on Péguy the Socialist," *French Studies*, XV (January, 1961), 12–30.

138 Halévy, *Péguy*, p. 18.

139 Tharaud and Tharaud, *Péguy*, pp. 99–100.

140 Péguy, *Oeuvres*, XII, 35–36. Reinach puts it this way: "The little socialist group, united and active till then, stopped in order not to split. Jaurès hesitated still to repudiate his old error publicly. . . . But his heart, his reason, his eloquence had chosen." *L'Affaire Dreyfus*, III, 33.

141 *La Dépêche de Toulouse*, January 15, 1898.

142 *La petite République*, June 4, 1901.

143 Quoted in Jaurès, *Oeuvres*, VI, 197.

144 Blum, *L'Affaire*, p. 128.

145 On the regrouping of the Right, see the interesting discussion in René Rémond, *La Droite en France* (Paris, 1954), pp. 150–56. He notes perceptively: "Nationalism has no theory, hardly a program. It has powerful sympathies and ambitions; it is instinctive, passionate, easily roused to fury."

146 "At Brest," notes André Siegfried, "until 1898 moderates and Radicals always coöperated to check a candidate of the Right; it was no longer so, beginning with 1898. With the Dreyfus Affair, the moderates joined the Right." *Ibid.*, p. 157. And Reinach says of his own moderate party: "The liberal bourgeoisie of the period before the Falloux Law would have been the first to fight for such a cause. . . . But men like Dufaure, Léon Say, and Jules Lemoinne had left no heirs." *L'Affaire Dreyfus*, III, 74.

147 Andler, *Lucien Herr*, p. 120.

148 Jaurès, *Oeuvres*, VI, 197.

149 For a penetrating analysis of the impact of the Dreyfus Affair on French intellectuals, see Victor Brombert, "Toward a Portrait of the French Intellectual," *Partisan Review*, XXVII (Summer, 1960), 480–502. Among the intellectual groups formed to support Dreyfus was the Groupe des étudiants collectivistes, whose leading members (Hubert Lagardelle and Jean Longuet, law students, Philippe Landrieu, a student of agriculture, Louis Révelin, a lawyer, and Marcel Mauss, a young philosopher) were to play roles of some importance in the socialist movement. They founded a new socialist review, *Le Mouvement Socialiste*. Though Marxist in orientation, they soon fell out with the Guesdists because of their independent line.

150 The manifesto was published in *La petite République*, January 20, 1898.
151 Chambre des Députés, *Journal officiel*, January 22, 1898. The quotations that follow immediately are from the same debate.
152 Reinach, *L'Affair Dreyfus*, III, 330; 313.
153 Quoted in Jaurès, *Oeuvres*, VI, 198.
154 *La petite République*, February 14, 1898. The quotations that follow immediately are from the transcript that appeared in the newspaper.
155 See the telegram of congratulations from the Calais federation of the P.O.F., *ibid.*, February 15, 1898.
156 Zola never served his prison term. He appealed, lost again in July, and was persuaded to flee to England. Picquart was dismissed from the army on February 16.
157 Chambre des Députés, *Journal officiel*, February 19, 1898. According to Téry, Jaurès had actually become a lover of the Jews, who allegedly said: "I recognize so well his [the Jew's] excellent qualities that I regret not being one." Téry, *Jaurès*, p. 133.
158 Lafargue to Guesde, May 5, 1897. Guesde Archives, Amsterdam.
159 The figures on election expenses have been produced by Rolande Trempé, who has had access to the papers of the Marquis de Solages. Mlle Trempé has broken down the figure into the following expenditures: newspapers, 4,974 francs (57,639 free copies distributed); brochures, 1,157 francs; posters and handbills, 963 francs; incidental expenses, 1,181 francs; but the largest amount, over 10,000 francs, for free drinks. See her article "Jaurès et Carmaux," p. 69.
160 *La Dépêche de Toulouse*, May 11, 1898.
161 Auclair, *Jaurès*, p. 324.
162 *La Croix* had been founded in 1883 as a daily newspaper by the Augustine Fathers of the Assumption. The Assumptionists, expressing there a violent hostility to the Republic, represented the most notable example of clerical intransigence.
163 *La Dépêche de Toulouse*, January 12, 1901. It is important to note that Jaurès and Guesde were in accord during the elections. The P.O.F. made a sharp denunciation of anti-Semitism and also issued a strong manifesto in favor of the election of Jaurès.
164 *La petite République*, May 10, 1898.
165 There is a revealing collection of anti-Guesde handbills and brochures in the 1898 file of the Guesde Archives, Amsterdam.
166 *La petite République*, May 13, 1898.
167 Blum, *L'Affaire*, pp. 121–22.

CHAPTER 10

1 Blum, *L'Affaire*, p. 80; and Zévaès, "L'Affaire Dreyfus," pp. 99–100.
2 *L'Intransigeant*, June 1, 5, 9, 1898.
3 *Ibid.*, June 10, 1898.
4 *La petite République*, June 14, 1898. In an interesting letter to Bernstein, written sometime after World War I, Albert Thomas referred to Jaurès' financial plight: "Despite his important place in the French political world, Jaurès constantly had trouble making ends meet." Thomas to Bernstein, n.d. Bernstein Archives, Amsterdam.

5 Tharaud and Tharaud, *Péguy*, p. 98.
6 Francis Jourdain, "En ce Temps là," *Europe*, No. 354–55 (October-November, 1958), pp. 14–15.
7 *La petite République*, June 7, 1898.
8 The quotations are from the report of the meeting, *ibid.*, June 9, 1898.
9 Lafargue to Guesde, June 11, 1898. Guesde Archives, Amsterdam.
10 *La petite République*, July 7, 1898.
11 *La Lanterne*, July 8, 1898.
12 Quoted in Blum, *L'Affaire*, p. 150.
13 *La libre Parole*, August 11, 1898.
14 *Le Socialiste*, July 24, 1898. The Blanquists issued a similar manifesto. See Noland, *French Socialist Party*, p. 70. Note Rochefort's support of Guesde's neutralism in *L'Intransigeant*, July 31, 1898.
15 *La petite République*, August 10, 1898.
16 *Ibid.*, August 28, 1898.
17 *Ibid.*, September 20, 1898.
18 Quoted in Chapman, *Dreyfus Case*, p. 228.
19 October 7, 1898.
20 They were members of the League of the Rights of Man, founded soon after the Zola trial. The League enrolled a good number of men from the university, but also men like Guyot from *Le Siècle* and Francis de Pressensé, the foreign policy expert of *Le Temps*. Pressensé was one of the very few who made the trip all the way to socialism and remained there.
21 Within the C.G.T. the collapse of the railway strike produced an inquiry, as a result of which Lagailse was accused of ineptitude and even betrayal. He was removed as Secretary, and the ensuing reorganization paved the way for the leadership of Victor Griffuelhes.
    The anarchist Émile Pouget, soon to become editor of the C.G.T. weekly, *La Voix du peuple*, later described an alleged attempt by *La petite République* to discredit the strike: "It was the time of the Dreyfus Affair, and it was considered necessary to discourage any diversion from this Affair, such as a strike. To achieve that result, it published a piece, saying that agents of the Duc d'Orléans were among the workers, pushing the strike." According to Pouget, the accusation discredited such strike leaders as Guérard of the Federation of Railway Workers. Given the atmosphere of the time, it is comprehensible that *La petite République* passed on a rumor that may have been in wide circulation. Pouget's contention that the socialists around that paper wanted no diversion from the Affair is certainly true. Pouget's words are quoted in Pierre Monatte, *Trois Scissions syndicales* (Paris, 1958), p. 101.
22 Dureau to Guesde, November 7, 1898. Guesde Archives, Amsterdam.
23 Zévaès, "L'Affaire Dreyfus," p. 204.
24 BN. N.A.F. 24274 (88–90).
25 *La petite République*, November 5, 1898.
26 *Ibid.*, November 9, 1898.
27 *Ibid.*, November 17, 1898. For other analyses of the dangers of imperialism in the Far East especially, see *ibid.*, July 27, 1898; October 8, 31, 1899; December 3, 1899; March 4, 1900. See his cogent remarks on the Boxer Rebellion, *ibid.*, August 5, 1900.
28 Jaurès was alluding here to Barrès' first book, *Sous l'Oeil des barbares* (1887), in which the author declared war on organized authorities (*les barbares*) for

suppressing the self (*moi*). Consult the discussion of Barrès' thought in Pierre de Boisdeffre, *Métamorphose de la littérature* (Paris, 1953), I, 27–99.

29 *La petite République*, January 7, 1899. For a comprehensive discussion of antiliberal, anti-German views among the Antidreyfusard intellectuals, see Digeon, *La Crise allemande*, pp. 301–16, 399–450.

30 Albert Thibaudet, *Histoire de la littérature français* (Paris, 1936), p. 407.

31 Quoted in Chapman, *Dreyfus Case*, p. 252. Essentially the same sentiment was expressed in a letter late in 1898 from Dupuy to Poincaré. Cautioning Poincaré against wrecking the Progressist movement by speaking out on the Affair (even after Henry's suicide), Dupuy wrote: "Don't do it! You could only lose. You have no right to jeopardize your friends." Quoted in Pierre Miquel, *Poincaré* (Paris, 1961), p. 166.

32 Quoted in Chastenet, *La troisième République*, III, 162.

33 *La petite République*, February 23, 1899.

34 The speech is recorded, *ibid.*, May 15, 1899.

35 Eventually Christiani was tried and sentenced to a four-year prison term for his actions at Auteuil.

36 *La petite République*, June 15, 1899. Vaillant led the socialist attack on Dupuy in the Chamber session of June 12. He accused the Premier of leaving the President unprotected on June 4, while flooding Longchamps with police on June 11 when the Dreyfusards demonstrated there. That speech was decisive in Dupuy's fall.

37 *Ibid.*, June 16, 1899.

38 Jaurès, *Oeuvres*, IV, 295–96. One contemporary historian has corroborated his judgment with this comment on the nationalist groups: "They wanted to react against the anarchy which, they felt, flowed from the proclamation of the Rights of Man." Rémond, *La Droite*, p. 171.

Symptomatic of the vitality of nationalism was the founding of *Action française*, a weekly review launched by Maurras on June 20, 1899. It was monarchist and intensely nationalistic.

39 Poincaré revealed the details of this visit in a speech at Nancy on May 12, 1901. See *Le petit Sou*, May 14, 1901, for a long summary of that speech. Millerand was, in fact, a personal friend of Poincaré, and though they were now separated by the issue of socialism, they would, in later years, collaborate closely in the nationalist cause.

40 Suarez, *Briand*, I, 256.

41 *Le Matin*, February 6, 1911. *Le Matin* published during the winter of 1911 large extracts from the private papers of Waldeck-Rousseau, which were passed on to the newspaper by the ex-Premier's confidant, Henry Leyret. See also Paul-Boncour, *Entre deux Guerres*, p. 96.

42 Paul-Boncour, *Entre deux Guerres*, p. 98.

43 The influence of Waldeck-Rousseau was such that Raymond Lavigne of the P.O.F. Federation in the Gironde could write to Guesde: "Following the lead of Waldeck-Rousseau, all conservatives, whatever their political connections, are united on the crucial issue of anticollectivism." Lavigne to Guesde, July 29, 1897. Guesde Archives, Amsterdam.

44 In the Guesde Archives for the year 1898, one can find Jaurès' article, much underlined, which Guesde had saved.

45 *La petite République*, April 20, 1901. It was in this article that Jaurès revealed the details of his conversations with Millerand.

Jaurès had never met Waldeck-Rousseau personally. In the course of this first attempt to form a ministry, he was contacted by Waldeck's emissary, Joseph Reinach, who impressed on Jaurès Gallifet's importance in restoring law and order in the army command.

A personal meeting with Waldeck-Rousseau was arranged after the ministry was finally established. Jaurès went to see the new Premier, accompanied by Gérault-Richard and Paul-Boncour. See Paul-Boncour, *Entre deux Guerres*, pp. 94–95.

46 Poincaré, in a letter to Waldeck-Rousseau written the evening of June 20, complained of a Radical and socialist plot to seize control of the ministry. *Le Matin*, February 8, 1912.

47 *La petite République*, June 23, 1899.

48 Almost four years later, at the socialist Congress of Bordeaux in April, 1903, Millerand gave his version of this June 21 meeting. See Congrès socialiste de Bordeaux, tenu les 12, 13, et 14 avril, 1903, *Dix discours* (Paris, 1903), p. 44.

49 2ᵉ congrès général des organisations socialistes français, tenu à Paris du 28 au 30 septembre, 1900, *Compte rendu sténographique* (Paris, 1901), p. 229.

50 Delcassé remained at Foreign Affairs; the Progressist Leygues was at Education; the colonial expert De Lanessan went to the Ministry of the Navy; a newcomer, Caillaux, son of a conservative capitalist, was named Minister of Finance; Jean Dupuy was at Agriculture, and the Radical Monis at Justice.

51 *Le petit Sou*, April 26, 1901. This article is Vaillant's version of the events of June. Fourteen years later, the socialist Gustave Hervé concluded that without Gallifet in the picture, all socialists, with the exception of some Guesdists, would have accepted Millerand's accession to office. *La Guerre sociale*, June 25–July 1, 1913.

52 Bonnier to Guesde, June 23, 1899. Guesde Archives, Amsterdam.

53 The details of the meeting between Herr and Jaurès are in Andler, *Lucien Herr*, pp. 149–50.

54 *La petite République*, June 24, 1899. *Le Temps*, on the same day expressed its opposition to the inclusion of Millerand because of the danger of socialism.

55 Suarez, *Briand*, I, 259.

56 *Le Matin*, February 10, 1911.

57 High in the councils of the Alliance démocratique (as it became known) were Adolphe Carnot, brother of the ex-President of the Republic; Christophle, recently governor of the Crédit foncier; Rouvier; Étienne; Aynard, and his son-in-law Jonnart; Poincaré; and Barthou. The latter became the most vocal spokesman for the group. The Alliance had strong connections with influential newspapers — *Le petit Journal, Le Matin, Le petit Parisien*, and *Le Temps*.

58 *La Dépêche de Toulouse*, June 29, 1899. Briand asked rhetorically: "From their position to that of Millerand, how much distance is there?" Quoted in Suarez, *Briand*, I, 260.

59 Lavigne to Guesde, July 11, 1899. Guesde Archives, Amsterdam.

60 The terminology of the conflict is therefore confusing. While Millerand held office (1899–1902), the contending factions were often referred to as Ministerialists and Antiministerialists. But other contrasting terms were at times used interchangeably: reformists and revolutionaries; collaborationists and anticollaborationists.

61 The position of the Independents was fairly clear: most were followers of

Millerand; beyond that, Jaurès' stand had been decisive. The Possibilists were moderates and reformists, following the lead of Paul Brousse, who declared in *La petite République* (August 7, 1899) that when the country was in danger every means of defense had to be used to safeguard it. The Allemanists, though hostile to the idea of Millerand's holding office, were nonetheless worried by threats from the Right. See Allemane's article in *Le Journal du peuple*, June 29, 1899.

62 *La petite République*, July 17, 1899.
63 Lavigne to Guesde, July 16, 1899. Guesde Archives, Amsterdam. Lavigne's prediction was, in fact, correct. The intransigence of the P.O.F. leaders led several of the party cells (in the Ardennes, the Bouches-du-Rhône, the Côte d'Or, the Ain, the Doubs, and the Seine-et-Oise) to become autonomous socialist clubs; several others became affiliated with the Independents. See Orry, *Les Socialistes indépendents*, pp. 44–46.
64 Lafargue to Guesde, August 8, 1899. Guesde Archives, Amsterdam.
65 *Le Populaire*, January 29, 1940.
66 The first letter of the series from Liebknecht to Guesde is dated July 27, 1899.
67 Liebknecht to Guesde, November 1, 1899. Guesde Archives, Amsterdam. The position of international socialist leaders was not, however, uniformly favorable to the Guesdists. In order to ascertain the views of foreign socialist leaders, Jaurès had opened the pages of *La petite République* to some of them. Between September 14 and November 19, 1899, the paper carried the replies of Van Kol, Auguste Bebel, Émile Vandervelde, George Plekhanov, Pablo Iglésias, Andrea Costa, Enrico Ferri, Karl Kautsky, Louis Bertrand, Wilhelm Liebknecht, Eduard Bernstein, Léon Defuisseaux, Peter Lavrov, H. M. Hyndman, Sibvald Olsen, Henry Quelch, Antonio Labriola, Tom Mann, Keir Hardie, Herman Greulich, Robert Blatchford, Georg von Vollmar, and Troelstra to these two questions: 1) Can the socialist working class, without abandoning the principle of the class struggle, take sides in the conflicts among various bourgeois factions, whether to save political liberty or, as in the Dreyfus Affair, to defend humanity? 2) To what degree can the socialist working class share in bourgeois power? Does the principle of the class struggle absolutely and in all cases forbid ministerial participation? All of them gave an unqualified "yes" as the answer to the first question, and several included high praise for Jaurès in the Dreyfus Affair. The responses, even from the leading Marxists, were thus different from the one the Guesdists were giving. On the second question, the answers were much less categorical. A few, like the German Revisionist Bernstein and the Belgian and Dutch reformists openly approved Millerandism; a few others, like the Spaniard Iglésias, the German Liebknecht, and the Russian Lavrov said flatly that it was contrary to sound socialist principles. The majority believed that it was impossible to set down a hard-and-fast line; while in general ministerialism was a violation of the principle of the class struggle, it might be permitted under exceptional circumstances. Most of the replies, however, criticized Millerand for entering the Ministry without the permission of the entire French movement.

In France, both the Ministerialists and the Antiministerialists tried to use these replies to buttress their case. See, for example, the article of Lafargue in *Le Petit Sou*, September 17, 1900, and the article of G. Lévy, a supporter of

Jaurès, in *L'Éclaireur de l'Ain*, March 27, 1900. Both sides exaggerated; but certainly Jaurès could expect that before any international congress, his prestige would be high and his tactics would find supporters.

68 *La Dépêche de Toulouse*, August 21, 1899.

69 *Ibid.*, September 1, 1899.

70 Quoted in Chastenet, *La troisième République*, III, 171.

71 *La Dépêche de Toulouse*, September 14, 1899.

72 Quoted in Georges Suarez, *Soixante Années d'histoire française* (Paris, 1932), II, 43.

73 When Dreyfus was released he issued a statement which read in part: "The government of the Republic has returned me to freedom. But that means nothing to me without honor. From today on, I will continue to seek reparation for the frightful judicial crime." *Ibid.*, p. 48. These words were written for Dreyfus by Jaurès, sitting at Millerand's desk in the Ministry of Commerce.

74 Dolléans, *Le Mouvement ouvrier*, II, 52.

75 The debates of the Congress are found in Congrès général des organisations socialistes français, tenu à Paris du 3 au 8 décembre 1899, *Compte rendu sténographique officiel* (hereafter cited as *Congrès général de 1899*).

76 Suarez, *Briand*, I, 266-67.

77 *Congrès général de 1899*, p. 60. The quotations which follow are from Jaurès' intervention, *ibid.*, pp. 60-63.

78 The resolution for which Jaurès spoke read: "The Congress declares that the proletariat must apply itself, above all, to the conquest, in the Commune, the Department, and the State, of that part of public power directly dependent on election. It warns the working class against illusions born of the participation of a socialist in a bourgeois ministry; an action necessarily limited and dominated by both the general laws of the capitalist system and the interests of the bourgeois class, which will yield only on the total political and economic expropriation. The Congress recognizes at the same time that there are cases where the participation of a socialist in bourgeois power can be viewed favorably, especially when a serious crisis threatens the political freedoms which are essential for the proletarian movement. . . . The Congress declares, however, that in order that this participation keep a class character and remain connected with the general action of the organized proletariat, a socialist can share power only with the formal assent of the party, for a purpose and under conditions determined by the party."

79 See the brilliant summary discussion of the confusion and unreality that characterized the notion of revolution in the Second International in G. D. H. Cole, *The Second International*, London, 1956. Even as recently as 1958, Maurice Duverger noted perpetuation of the same confusion: "The Marxist Left remains attached to the old revolutionary formulas: fall of the bourgeois State, dictatorship of the proletariat, eventuality of communism. Will it realize that these formulas are no longer applicable to modern industrial societies? And that the proletariat is no longer revolutionary in the traditional sense of the word?" *Demain, la République* (Paris, 1958), p. 147.

80 Fernand Pelloutier, *Congrès général du parti socialiste français* (Paris, 1900), p. 40. It is interesting to note that Pelloutier, who is generally harsh with all reformists, always has kind words for his old friend Briand.

81 Suarez, *Briand*, I, 279.

82 Pelloutier, *Congrès général*, p. 42.

83 *Congrès général de 1899*, pp. 242, 243.
84 Pelloutier, *Congrès général*, p. 55. The record of this scene is in *Congrès général de 1899*, pp. 275–81.
85 Among those who voted for the Guesde amendment, ironically enough, were four future ministers: Sembat, J. L. Breton, Blum, and — Guesde.
86 Later in December the important General Committee was constituted. Composed of forty-eight members, including Jaurès, Guesde, Lafargue, Vaillant, Brousse, Allemane, Briand, Zévaès, and Viviani, the Committee contained fifteen Guesdists, eight Blanquists, six Independents, four Allemanists, three Possibilists, and twelve from affiliated organizations. More than half the members were antiministerial in outlook.
87 *Le Dépêche de Toulouse*, December 13, 1899.
88 Lavigne to Guesde, December 15, 1899. Guesde Archives, Amsterdam.
89 Pelloutier to Delesalle, n.d. Pelloutier Manuscripts, Institut Français d'Histoire Sociale, Paris.
90 On the futile attempts of the General Committee to lay down a socialist line to the parliamentary group, see Noland, *French Socialist Party*, pp. 115–23. The clash came over the insistence of the General Committee that the socialist deputies condemn the Waldeck-Rousseau ministry for its conduct in the strike of Chalon-sur-Saône in the spring of 1900. The Ministerialists refused to jeopardize the ministry, and on June 15, 1900, voted against a hostile order of the day.
91 On the Bernstein controversy, see Cole, *Second International*, pp. 249–96; Carl Schorske, *German Social Democracy, 1905–17* (Cambridge, Mass., 1955); and Peter Gay, *The Dilemma of Democratic Socialism*, New York, 1954.
92 The speech appears in Jaurès, *Oeuvres*, VI, 120–40.
93 *La Dépêche de Toulouse*, January 2, 1901.
94 The report of the incident appears in a newspaper clipping of an open letter from Lavigne to Jaurès, dated March 29, 1900, on behalf of the P.O.F. Federation of the Gironde. Guesde Archives, Amsterdam.
95 *La Dépêche de Toulouse*, March 9, 1900.
96 *La petite République*, March 11, 1900.
97 *Le Socialiste*, March 6, 1900. See also the interview with Guesde in *Le Temps*, April 12, 1900. For a discussion of the whole dispute, see Charles Bouglé, "Le Socialisme et l'enseignement populaire," *Annales de la Jeunesse laïque* (January, 1903), pp. 241–45.
98 To put his proposals into effect, Millerand decreed on August 10, 1899, that: 1) a day off each week was required for workers in industries doing business with the State; and 2) the Conseil supérieur du travail, founded in 1891, was to be reorganized and revitalized. On March 30, 1900, he pushed through the highly controversial Millerand-Colliard Law, which ordered a uniform ten-and-a-half-hour day for men, women, and children by 1902, and a ten-hour day by 1904. This roused great opposition on the Left, where it was judged a setback from the Law of November 2, 1892, which had fixed the working day for women and children at ten hours. Millerand's contention was that it had not been applied, nor could it be until hours were uniform for men, women, and children. His critics asked why, then, he did not set the uniform working day at ten hours. In November, 1900, he proposed machinery for compulsory arbitration of labor disputes.
On the work of Millerand as Minister of Commerce, see the favorable ac-

count of his friend and assistant Aimé Lavy: *L'Oeuvre de Millerand, un ministre socialiste, 1889–1902,* Paris, 1902. For a sharply critical evaluation, see Charles Verècque, *Trois Années de participation socialiste à un gouvernement bourgeois,* Paris, 1904.

99 *Le Temps,* June 24, 1900.

100 This was a reflection of Griffeulhes in his speech before the C.G.T. Congress of Amiens in 1906. Jaurès, nonetheless, tried to maintain friendly contacts with both the Fédération des bourses and the C.G.T., urging them both to take part in the coming September Congress of socialists, while endorsing the general strike as one of many valid working-class techniques. See *La petite République,* August 26, and 30, September 1, 1900.

101 For his defense of the Millerand-Colliard Law, see *ibid.,* December 23 and 26, 1900.

102 Jean Jaurès, "La Réglementation des grèves et l'arbitage obligatoire," *La Revue socialiste,* XXXIII (May, 1901), 531. On the history of French corporatist doctrines, see Matthew Elbow, *French Corporative Theories, 1789–1948,* New York, 1953. One can find confirmation of the idea that Millerand had corporatist ideas in this observation by Georges Sorel: "The organized workers have shown considerable opposition to Millerand's plans for enforced social solidarity. Millerand, in fact, seems to be completely converted to Social Catholic ideas." *L'Avenir socialiste* (Paris, 1901), p. viii.

103 Note this judgment of Édouard Dolléans in his *Histoire du travail* (Paris, 1943), p. 181: "For some time, the structure of industrial capitalism ceased to be governed by individual competition."

104 *Ibid.,* p. 185.

105 Jaurès, "La Réglementation des grèves," pp. 531–32.

106 *La petite République,* June 26, 1900.

107 For the movement toward industrial and commercial concentration, see Dolléans, *Histoire du travail,* pp. 224–31, and *Le Monde des affaires* (Paris, 1952), *passim.*

108 Note this observation of Dolléans, in *Histoire du travail,* p. 215: "During the period from the Waldeck-Rousseau ministry to the intervention of M. Briand in the railroad strike of 1910, the government tried to arbitrate in social conflicts, but it lacked the strength."

109 Jaures, "La Réglementation des grèves," p. 537. This position of Jaurès' conflicted sharply with that of the Marxist fundamentalists, who argued that although capitalism grew up within the cadre of feudalism and finally replaced it, socialist institutions could not develop under capitalism. In his article "Revolution," E. P. Thompson has commented upon this "crippling fallacy of the fundamentalist" in a way which Jaurès could only have applauded: "From this conceptual inhibition, many consequences flow. From this, the sterility of the usual Fabian-Marxist debate between 'reformism' and 'revolution,' which has scarcely advanced since the days of Hyndman and Shaw. From this, the caricaturing of social advances as 'bribes' to buy off revolution, and the attribution of supreme cunning to the capitalist system, which by a superb Marxist logic is able to anticipate and deflect every assault by the working class. From this also, the hypocritical attitude which concedes the need to struggle for reforms, not for the sake of reform but for the educative value of the struggle. Hence, finally, the alienation of many humane people who detect in the doctrinaire revolutionary an absence of warm response to the needs of living people and a disposition to anticipate the coming of depression or hard-

ship with impatience. . . . The countervailing powers are there, and the equilibrium (which is an equilibrium *within capitalism*) is precarious. It could be tipped back towards authoritarianism. But it could also be heaved *forward*, by popular pressures of great intensity, to the point where the powers of democracy cease to be countervailing and become the active dynamic of society in their own right. This is revolution."

110 Cf. the discussion of effective socialist tactics in Lefebvre, *Lénine*, pp. 32–33.

111 The proposed Law on Associations would require the regular clergy to seek authorization for their congregations or suffer dissolution. At stake, of course, was the control of education, the central issue between Church and State since the clerical interests had begun, early in the nineteenth century, their successful assault on the Napoleonic university. Since many of the religious congregations maintained schools, it would be a blow to Church control over the young if the teaching orders were dissolved. As finally reported out of committee, authorization had to be granted by Parliament.

The resignation of Gallifet must be placed within the context of continued Antidreyfusard activities. In May, 1900, for example, the nationalists and clerical Right won a majority in the Paris municipal elections. Gallifet, embittered by continued insubordination in the Statistical Section and savage nationalist attacks in the Chamber, resigned on May 28. For Jaurès' support of the Law on Associations and the early moves of André, see *La petite République*, January 18, March 17, June 2 and 16, 1900.

112 *Ibid.*, July 17, 1900.

113 Lafargue to Guesde, August 12, 1900. Guesde Archives, Amsterdam. Édouard Anseele, the Belgian socialist, was one of the founders of the Parti ouvrier belge; Victor Adler was the leader of Austrian socialism.

114 Jaurès, *Oeuvres*, VI, 199–200.

115 The translation used here is from Cole, *Second International*, p. 40.

116 *La petite République*, September 27, 1900.

117 For the transcript of the day's debate, see *ibid.*, September 28, 1900.

118 Suarez, *Briand*, I, 305.

119 Jean Bertrand Bracke, *Leur congrès à la salle Wagram* (Paris, 1901), p. 6.

120 An extensive account of Briand's role appears in Suarez, *Briand*, I, 305–13, from which the following quotations are drawn.

121 2° congrès général des organisations socialistes françaises, tenu à Paris du 28 au 30 septembre 1900, *Compte rendu sténographique officiel* (Paris, 1901), p. 254.

122 The debate is reprinted in Jaurès, *Oeuvres*, VI, 189–217.

123 *La petite République*, January 23, 1901.

124 *Ibid.*, February 28, 1901.

125 Chambre des Députés, *Journal officiel*, January 21, 1901.

126 *Ibid.*, March 11, 1901. Pelletan made a tremendous attack against all congregations; among the charges he brought against the Jesuits was the accusation that they ran houses of prostitution in Shanghai. Clemenceau was equally outspoken. See *Le Bloc*, February 5, 1901.

127 *La petite République*, January 23, 1901.

128 *Ibid.*, January 20 and February 6, 1901. The law on Associations did, in fact, eke out a majority in both Houses, becoming law on June 28, 1901.

129 For the Guesdists' position, see Lafargue's article in *Le petit Sou*, February 13, 1901.

130 *La petite République*, April 4, 1901.

131 3ᵉ congrès général des organisations socialistes, tenu à Lyon, du 26 au 28 mai, 1901, *Compte rendu sténographique* (Paris, 1901), p. 252. On a few occasions, as though to placate its Blanquist members, the Parti socialiste française did protest against certain actions by the government. Thus, in a manifesto signed by such men as Blum, Briand, Gérault-Richard, Jaurès, Longuet, and Renaudel, the Parti socialiste français strongly objected to the dissolution of the Cercle socialiste italien at Nice and the expulsion from France of several of its members. *L'Éclaireur de l'Ain,* April 14, 1901.

132 *La petite République,* May 4, 1901. The same phrase was used by Dolléans in assigning reasons for the low level of membership in the C.G.T. Dolléans, *Le Mouvement ouvrier,* II, 46. By 1906, it may be pointed out, the C.G.T., its leaders hewing to the revolutionary line, had organized only 300,000 of the 5,700,000 wage-earners in industry and commerce.

133 The organized miners' movement was highly confused, and in that confusion, Jaurès' persuasiveness was effective. In the Nord, the leadership was generally Guesdist, revolutionary but not syndicalist; in the Saône-et-Loire, the syndicalists had a strong grip; in the Tarn, the leaders were closely associated with Jaurès; and Cotte himself tended toward reformism.

134 Rappoport to Kautsky, n.d. Kautsky Archives, Amsterdam.

135 On August 15, 1901, the Antiministerial groups (Guesdists, Blanquists, and the autonomous Federations of Deux-Sèvres, Vendée, Doubs, Haute-Saône, Haut-Rhin, Seine-et-Oise, and Yonne) worked out a program of unity for a new party, the Parti socialiste de France.

The others (Independents, Allemanists, Possibilists, and several autonomous Federations) remained the Parti socialiste française. In January, 1902, however, this party was again split when the Allemanists and the autonomous Federations of the Ain, Loir-et-Cher, Jura, and Var withdrew over failure of the General Committee to discipline Millerand for taking part in the 1901 reception for Tsar Nicholas II. See Noland, *French Socialist Party,* pp. 138-44.

136 Jaurès, *Oeuvres,* VI, 227.

137 Bonnier to Guesde, April 30, 1901. Guesde Archives, Amsterdam. See the same attitude expressed by Lafargue in *Le petit Sou,* July 29, 1901.

138 *L'Aurore,* July 23, 1901.

139 Auclair, *Jaurès,* p. 398.

140 Suarez, *Briand,* I, 337.

141 *La petite République,* October 12, 1901.

142 *L'Aurore,* October 12, 13, and 14, 1901.

143 *La petite République,* October 16, 1901.

144 *Ibid.,* October 20, 1901.

145 *Ibid.,* April 23, 1901.

146 In his library, preserved in the museum at Montreuil, one finds a large collection of general and specialized works on the French Revolution, many heavily annotated.

147 Blum, *Oeuvres,* I, 154, 156.

148 From Aulard's critique in *La Revue de la Révolution française,* reprinted in *La petite République,* October 17, 1902. In response to the review, Jaurès wrote a very modest letter to Aulard, appreciative of the changes and corrections suggested. Quoted in Georges Belloni, *Aulard historien de la Révolution française* (Paris, 1949), p. 45. The work and career of Jaurès led the Radical Aulard to declare: "In my view, the greatest of all socialists was

Jaurès." *Ibid.*, p. 120. In 1903, Jaurès was chairman of a commission meeting at the Sorbonne to plan extensive publication of economic documents; of this meeting Hubert Bourgin observed: "In his long speech on the economic history of the Revolution, a subject he approached as archivist and historian, Jaurès manifested a largeness of view, a passionate curiosity, a wisdom, which made the work of professionals like Aulard and his school appear shallow and poverty-stricken." *De Jaurès à Blum*, p. 197.

Note also the tribute which Georges Lefebvre, the dean of recent French Revolutionary historians, paid to Jaurès as historian: "I follow no other master but Jaurès." Quoted in Albert Soboul, "Georges Lefebvre, historien de la Révolution française, 1874–1959," *Annales historiques de la Révolution française*, No. 159 (January-March, 1960), p. 3.

149 Jaurès to Bernstein, January 27, 1901. Bernstein Archives, Amsterdam. In regard to the French Revolution itself, Jaurès believed that Marx viewed it too narrowly as a purely bourgeois movement. See *Revue de l'enseignement primaire et primaire supérieure*, August 23, 1908.

In his long chapter on German thought during the Revolution, Jaurès sharply criticized Mehring's book on Lessing for being much too narrow in its economic interpretation. Mehring struck back in an article attacking what he considered the vague pluralism in the historical method of Jaurès. See Franz Mehring, "Jaurès historien," *Le Mouvement socialiste*, No. 119 (May 1, 1903), pp. 43–63.

150 Jaurès, *Histoire socialiste*, I-II, 8. Jaurès had already posed this dualism in an article in *La petite République*, July 10, 1898, in which he had sought to reconcile Marx and Michelet.

151 Jaurès, *Histoire socialiste*, III-IV, 734–35.

152 *Ibid.*, I-II, 134.

153 *La Dépêche de Toulouse*, January 1, 1904.

154 Jaurès, *Histoire socialiste*, III-IV, 115, 174.

155 *Ibid.*, pp. 1458, 1464.

156 *Ibid.*, p. 1074.

157 *Ibid.*, p. 1036.

158 *Ibid.*, p. 158. There was a very long section, running more than a hundred pages, analyzing the social and political thought of all the key figures in the Convention. *Ibid.*, pp. 1465 ff.

159 *Ibid.*, pp. 244, 248.

160 *Ibid.*, p. 1631.

161 *Ibid.*, p. 169.

162 Quoted in H. Stuart Hughes, *Consciousness and Society* (New York, 1958) p. 77.

163 Jaurès, *Histoire socialiste*, I-II, 684.

164 *Ibid.*, III-IV, 52.

165 *Ibid.*, pp. 1823–24. From his intensive study of the French Revolution, Jaurès drew both facts and inspiration for a series of articles on peaceful social change, which appeared originally in September and October, 1901, in *La petite République*; they were reprinted in Jaurès, *Oeuvres*, VI, 363–425. The immediate purpose of these articles was to analyze the programmatic assumptions of the newly founded Radical Party, which promised to protect and preserve a regime of individual private property. Beyond that, however, they were an answer to Jaurès revolutionary critics who denied that the socialist revolution

could be made peacefully and legally within the cadre of the bourgeois State.

Jaurès thus made three essential points: 1) the organization of property, which always reflected social and economic evolution, changed constantly over the course of history, and individual private property was no more sacred or eternal than feudal property expropriated by the bourgeois revolutions. In fact, the growth of large, anonymous corporations had already worked such changes that individual property-holders, in the sense that the Radicals thought of them, were gradually becoming extinct.

2) Though the French Revolution had indeed enthroned the bourgeoisie, it established the precedents and principles, since codified in the bourgeois legal system, for limiting and even expropriating individual property in the interest of the community: "Through all its great spokesmen, Mirabeau as well as Robespierre, through its great lawyers, Dupont de Nemours as well as Tronchet, the Revolution forcefully asserts that property is a social phenomenon, that it derives from society, that it does not and cannot exist outside of society; that society, in its own interest and in the interest of freedom, has given it an individual form; but that individuals, holding it only by the approval of society, should be regulated in the use of their property by the conditions that society imposes upon them." *Ibid.*, p. 396. Thus, in many articles of the French civil code (Jaurès quoted and commented upon Articles 537, 544, 629–35, 644, 655, 664, 682, which imposed certain limitations on the free use and disposal of private property; and Articles 731, 920–22, 929, 930, 1048–50, which imposed on the testator the obligation of equal division of his estate) he demonstrated that regulation was built into the bourgeois legal system. But even more, the Revolution proclaimed the right of and established the precedent for legal expropriation of property. When the Declaration of the Rights of Man declared that no one could be deprived of his property, except by law and with just compensation in advance, "bourgeois society . . . laid down the principle of legal expropriation in the public interest." *Ibid.*, p. 403.

3) The instrument for the peaceful revolution has already been forged by the bourgeoisie. When the socialists gain a legal majority, they can use it to transform capitalist property into socialist property: "Today, public utility demands the general expropriation of the capitalist class for the benefit of the entire community. . . . By using articles of the bourgeois code, the lawyers of the social revolution will be able to pass from the bourgeois legal order to the communist legal order." *Ibid.*, p. 408.

These articles, which attempt a theory of social change, reflect strongly the issues of the day. Locked in struggle with the revolutionaries and committed to the tactics of democratic concentration, Jaurès was considerably more sanguine about the legal transfer of power than he had been in the 1890's or would be again after 1905. At no time would he consider violence essential to the revolution; he was, in fact, a brilliant critic of revolutionary romanticism, whether of the Blanquist, Marxist, or syndicalist variety. (See, for example, his analysis of the general strike and the only conditions for its success: *Ibid.*, pp. 331–38.) At other times, however, when he approached the state and its supporting institutions as essentially class-dominated, he showed a greater understanding of the massive pressure necessary to dislodge and replace not only a certain property order but also its cultural base.

166 Hughes, *Consciousness and Society*, p. 340.

167 A brief summary of these lectures appears in *La petite République*, February 26 and 28, 1902.

168 The article is reprinted in Blum, *Oeuvres*, I, 493-507, from which the following quotations are taken.

169 The Parti socialiste français, in its Congress of Tours in March, 1902, adopted a comprehensive reform program, drafted largely by Jaurès. The delegates approved a resolution in conformity with the dictum of the Paris Congress of the Second International, however, in which it was stated that from the start of the next legislature no socialist could participate in a ministry without party approval.

170 Chastenet, *La troisième République*, III, 216.

171 Between June 21 and 23, 1901, the Radicals and Radical-Socialists had formally organized a political party, which proved particularly strong in the small-town milieux of the Massif Central and the Midi. Pelletan wrote the program, which became the Radical platform for 1902, and it expressed strong reformist goals: separation of Church and State, reduction of the term of military service, a progressive income tax, workers' pensions, nationalization of public utilities and national monopolies. It also expressed devotion to individual property. On that score, see criticism by Jaurès in *La petite République*, June 25, 1901.

On the founding and structure of the Radical Party, see Albert Milhaud, *Histoire du radicalisme*, Paris, 1951; Pierre Andréani, "La Formation du parti radical-socialiste," *Revue politique et parlementaire*, No. 614, January, 1952; P. Avril, "Les Origines du radicalisme," *Les Cahiers de la République*, No. 3, 1956.

172 Téry, *Jaurès*, p. 37.

173 *La petite République*, May 14, 1902. The socialists had shown increasing strength in the elections, making them a force to reckon with. They had polled 900,000 votes against 800,000 in 1898; they had won forty-eight seats against forty-two in 1898. Only twelve of the forty-eight belonged to the Guesdist-Blanquist wing of the movement. Among those elected for the first time was Briand.

174 Quoted in Suarez, *Briand*, I, 385.

CHAPTER 11

1 For his own statement of his beliefs, see Émile Combes, *Mon Ministère* (Paris, 1956), pp. 32-35. Note the following from a leading historian of religion: "Combes, the heretic, remained a churchman, dreaming of a national cult whose Savoyard vicars he would name. But the faith of this priest-in-reverse gave rise to a vindictive tenacity against the Roman cult from which he had departed." Adrien Dansette, *Histoire religieuse de la France contemporaine sous la troisiéme République* (Paris, 1951), II, 302.

2 See Combes, *Mon Ministère*, pp. 24-25. In this passage Combes explains that he chose Rouvier to quiet the fears of moderate republicans as he pursued his anticlerical program.

3 *Le Journal des débats*, June 9, 1902.

4 Daniel Halévy, *La République des comités* (Paris, 1934), p. 36.

5 Chambre des Députés, *Journal officiel*, June 13, 1902. The quotations immediately following are from the same speech.

6 The four groups of the majority were: the Union démocratique (the old Progressists of the Alliance démocratique), the Radicals, the Radical-Socialists, and the governmental socialists. The bloc supplied about 370 votes.

The Union socialiste révolutionnaire, the parliamentary group of the twelve Antiministerial socialists (Allard, Bouveri, Chauvière, Constans, Coutant, Dejeante, Delory, Dufour, Sembat, Thivrier, Vaillant, and Walter) shunned the bloc and the Délégation des gauches. The thirty-six members of the Union socialiste, however, included such prominent socialists as Breton, Briand, Gérault-Richard, Jaurès, Millerand, Pressensé and Rouanet.

7 There were twenty-six members of the Délégation des gauches, including five socialists (Breton, Briand, Colliard, Jaurès, and Pressensé).

8 Suarez, *Briand*, I, 397.

9 Combes, *Mon Ministère*, p. 279.

10 According to *Le Temps* (January 15, 1903), this election signified "the humbling of the bloc before the orders of the authoritarian, collectivist group."

11 *La petite République*, July 3, 1902. In order to perfect the machinery of democracy, Jaurès always favored clearly defined issues and well-organized parties. Thus, though he had attacked the program of the new Radical Party in 1901, he supported the decision of the Radicals to organize formally and to stand on a written platform: "With organized parties, issues are clearly defined and questions clearly posed. Thus, the socialists and Radicals will be able to debate the social question more effectively." *L'Éclaireur de l'Ain*, June 30, 1901.

12 *Le Socialiste*, July 13-20, 1902.

13 Quoted in *Le Temps*, September 26, 1902.

14 Louis Dubreuilh, "Après le Congrès de Reims," *Le Mouvement socialiste*, No. 130 (November 15, 1903), p. 386. In practice, the antigovernmental socialists, while voting against the ministry on budgetary matters, voted for it on questions of confidence, whenever it seemed threatened by a coalition of Right and Center. Thus, for the revolutionaries, the ministry was the lesser of two evils, and the sin of Jaurès and his friends, as Dubreuilh implied, was not temporary collaboration, but the intimate and apparently permanent tie established.

A dozen years later, one might point out in passing, Dubreuilh was to write very differently. With France engaged in the great European war, he then hailed democracy no less enthusiastically than Jaurès had so often done. See, for example, *L'Humanité*, March 8, 1915. Almost ten years of growth by the S.F.I.O., when he served as party secretary, had evidently tempered his earlier *blanquisme*.

15 See Gustave Hervé's perceptive review of C.G.T. history, written after he had dropped his own affection for the general strike. *La Guerre sociale*, September 10-17, 1913.

16 *15ᵉ Congrès national corporatif de la Confédération général du travail* (Paris, 1906), p. 167. The French labor movement had bent in several doctrinal directions, and, in principle, there was little common ground between the revolutionary political theories of the Guesdist labor leaders of the Nord, the syndicalism of an ex-Blanquist like Griffuelhes, or the pure anarchism of Delesalle. But in the period of the bloc, they were thrown together in their opposition to the bourgeois State. For the moment, those who believed in the powerful workers' State and those who believed in no State at all linked arms and tried to smother the reformist tendencies of large unions like those of the printers and even the miners.

17 Dansette, *Histoire religieuse,* II, 304.

18 *Ibid.,* p. 312. For the opposition of Waldeck-Rousseau, see his speech in *Journal officiel du Sénat,* June 27, 1903. There he condemned the procedure of lumping the fifty-four authorizations, into a single bill.

 See *Le Temps,* August 1, 1902, for a letter from Gabriel Monod of the École Normale, dissociating himself from the anticlerical campaign and denouncing both State and Church monopolies in teaching as the "two intolerances."

19 Jaurès, *Histoire socialiste,* III–IV, 251.

20 Chambre des Députés, *Journal officiel,* March 4, 1904. A sharp Catholic reply to Jaurès was delivered on March 4 by Denys Cochin, who accused him of deciding, by his own judgment, who had the right to teach.

21 Note the succinct explanation of André's reasoning given by Chapman, *Dreyfus Case,* p. 335. "André thus felt fortified in accepting the principle, provided the strength of the army was maintained at 575,000. Under the Law of 1889, the annual contingent was larger than could be incorporated, and there had been dispensations from service in certain categories. Under the new scheme there would be a deficiency in numbers. It was therefore proposed to fill the gap by the suppression of dispensations and by an increase in the numbers of reëngaged N.C.O's and privates. At last, said the Left, the great democratic principle of equality of sacrifice will be realized."

22 It was Jaurès, in the Chamber session of July 8, 1902, who proposed that an income tax be introduced for discussion by the Minister of Finance. Passed 503 to 10, this carefully worded resolution committed those who voted for it only to a discussion of an income tax.

23 Quoted in Félicien Challaye, *Péguy socialiste* (Paris, 1954), p. 124.

24 *Ibid.,* pp. 125–26.

25 Péguy, *Oeuvres,* XII, 42–43, 68. Forty years later, François Mauriac seemed to capture the essence of Péguy's reaction, as well as the dilemma confronting Jaurès: "It is certain that this idealist was a flexible political bargainer, and even rather crafty. Which is what Péguy never forgave him. The *mystique* in him gave way to politics as soon as the religious question was in play, that is, at every turn; for the history of the Republic, at the start of the century, was fully involved in the unfortunate clash between a Right which compromised the cause of religion by tying it to a bitter social conservatism and a hideous anti-Semitism, and an irresponsible Left which profited from the depth of this confusion." *Le Figaro,* August 6, 1946.

26 From Péguy's *Notre Jeunesse,* quoted in Hughes, *Consciousness and Society,* p. 353.

27 *L'Humanité,* June 12, 1912.

28 Jaurès, *Oeuvres,* III, 80.

29 The text was published in the Italian paper *Avanti* and reproduced in *La petite République,* September 23, 1902.

30 Caillaux, *Mes Mémoires,* I, 153.

31 Quoted in Chastenet, *La troisième République,* III, 256.

32 See the revealing documents on these bribes, published from the secret Russian archives by the Bolsheviks: Arthur Raffalovitch, *L'abominable Vénalité de la presse,* Paris, 1931.

33 *La petite République,* March 26, 1902.

34 Pelletan, in particular, traveling to Corsica and Tunisia as Minister of the Navy, made intemperate remarks. At Ajaccio, on September 13, he warned

Italy against aggression. At Bizerte, on September 17, he spoke of "German barbarism and brutal force." See *Le Figaro*, September 14 and 18, 1902.

35 September 16, 1902. See also *Le Temps*, September 24 and 27, 1902, for a similar position.

36 The following summary and quotations are from the articles in *La petite République*, September 18, 20, and 23, 1902.

37 Jaurès was influenced in his belief that contact between the two Alliance systems was already taking place by the overt signs between 1900 and 1902 of Franco-Italian friendship. See his articles, *ibid.*, April 6 and 11, 1901. What he did not know were the secret terms of the agreements between the two countries, which conformed to Delcassé's colonial and anti-German designs. Lengthy negotiations between Barrère and the Italian Foreign Minister (first Visconti-Venosta and later Prinetti) ended in an accord in December, 1900, in which France consented to Italy's free hand in Morocco. Though secret, the accord was followed by public signs of friendship. After Italy had renewed the Triple Alliance in 1902, there was an exchange of letters (June 28, 1902) whereby she assured France that she was not committed to support of German aggression against France. If France attacked Germany, under "direct provocation," Italy would remain neutral.

38 *Le Journal des débats*, September 20, 1902.

39 *La petite République*, September 30, 1902.

40 Quoted in *Le Journal des débats*, May 29, 1903. At the same time, the energetic Lyautey was given a military command in Algeria.

41 *La petite République*, September 24, 1902.

42 At the Amsterdam Congress of the Second International in 1904, when Jaurès was defending his support of the Combes ministry, he claimed, with what must be considered exaggeration, that the socialists had helped to bring about the French *entente* with Italy and England. 6ᵉ congrès socialiste international, tenu à Amsterdam du 14 au 20 août 1904, *Compte rendu analytique* (Brussels, 1904), p. 189.

43 Chambre des Députés, *Journal officiel*, January 23, 1903. The quotations which follow are from the same speech.

44 *Le Temps*, January 25, 1903.

45 The speech, reprinted many times, appeared in its entirety in *La petite République*, August 2, 1903, from which the following extracts are drawn.

46 Jean Longuet's career in the French socialist movement has an element of tragedy about it. Enjoying "prestige by birth," he might have become a very important leader. In fact, he seems to have craved such a role. But though he was a man of honesty and good intentions, he was neither a forceful personality nor a particularly creative thinker. The high point of his career came toward the end of World War I as leader of the so-called *minoritaires* in the S.F.I.O. His career declined, however, after the schism at Tours in 1920.

47 Longuet to Kautsky, March 31, 1902. Kautsky Archives, Amsterdam. Longuet, who apparently knew very little German, usually wrote in French; occasionally, fancying himself an expert in the English language, he wrote in what usually proved to be unidiomatic English. Indication will be made in the footnotes whenever Longuet wrote in English, and his mistakes will be reproduced.

48 Longuet to Kautsky, March 27, 1903. Kautsky Archives, Amsterdam. The Left-wing case against Millerand rested, to a great extent, on his recent voting

record in the Chamber. In January, 1903, he had voted *for* the Ministry of the Interior's budget of secret funds, used in part for *agents provocateurs; for* the Minister of War's prosecution of certain syndicalist leaders for antimilitarist propaganda; *against* socialist proposals to abolish the religious budget and to break relations with the Vatican.

49 Pierre Renaudel, "Le 'Cas Millerand' et le Congrès de Bordeaux," *Le Mouvement socialiste,* Nos. 116, 117 (March 15 and April 1, 1903), p. 485. A corpulent, good-natured socialist from the Var, Renaudel would later, in the years after 1914, become a stalwart of the socialist Right.

50 Quoted in Suarez, *Briand,* I, 357.

51 *La petite République,* November 30, 1901.

52 The major speeches of the Congress are reproduced in Congrès socialiste de Bordeaux, tenu les 12, 13, et 14 avril 1903, *Dix discours,* Paris, 1903.

53 Longuet to Kautsky, May 26, 1903. Kautsky Archives, Amsterdam. (Written in English.) In an article for *Le Mouvement socialiste* Longuet listed the federations now in the hands of the Left and predicted that several more would soon pass to the Left-wingers, thus giving them control of the party. Jean Longuet, "Après la Grâce de Millerand," *Le Mouvement socialiste,* No. 121 (June 1, 1903), p. 182. Thus, in another letter to Kautsky, Longuet predicted that when the Left triumphed in the Parti socialiste français, the Marxists and Blanquists could return and unity would be realized (September 28, 1903. Kautsky Archives, Amsterdam). Hubert Lagardelle, however, writing on behalf of the Parti socialiste de France, voiced suspicion of these Left-wingers. He criticized them for attacking only the excesses of reformism and not the method itself. "La Comédie de Bordeaux," *Le Mouvement socialiste,* No. 118 (April 15, 1903), pp. 625–29. However, Longuet was in a sense correct. The growth of the Left in the Parti socialiste français made it much easier to achieve unity after the Congress of Amsterdam in 1904.

54 Quoted in Cole, *Second International,* I, 48. The text of the Dresden resolution and a detailed analysis of it can be found in Edgard Milhaud, *La Tactique socialiste et les décisions des congrès internationaux* (Paris, 1905), I, 16–44.

55 *La petite République,* January 3, 1903. Jaurès' private feelings were indicated in letters which he wrote to Albert Thomas early in 1903. These letters, part of the private collection held by Mme Thomas at Garchy in the Nièvre, have been summarized and in part quoted by B. W. Schaper in his recently pubblished *Albert Thomas: Trente ans de réformisme social,* Paris, 1960.

Thomas, a *normalien* whose socialism owed a great deal to the influence of Lucien Herr, was only twenty-five in 1903; he had been traveling in Germany for some months when he became involved in a newspaper controversy in the pages of *Vorwärts.* That socialist daily had published a strong attack on *millerandisme,* which Thomas, a lifelong admirer of Millerand, answered. The controversy brought him two letters from Jaurès.

The German socialists, Jaurès complained in the first letter, had developed the faultiest of tactics; for though they had rejected alliances with bourgeois progressives, they hadn't assaulted the system so vigorously as to rouse the working class from its inertia. Thus, they could succeed neither in reform nor revolution. If it came to a showdown, if universal suffrage in Germany could be saved only by the tactics his own French party had adopted, the Germans would be more likely to split hairs than to wage an effective fight. In his second letter to Thomas, dated January 16, 1903, Jaurès noted how little understanding the German socialists had of the struggle French socialists were waging against reactionaries and conservatives. He specifically asked Thomas to send him German socialist newspapers and reviews.

56 Jean Fréville, *Né du Feu* (Paris, 1960), pp. 31–32. Fréville writes with a Communist bias. But Chastenet does not, and here is his judgment on the social conditions of the period: "The margin of security hardly expanded, and if a certain number of working class families were able to put some money into savings, the majority scarcely made ends meet." *La troisième République*, III, 338.

57 *La petite République*, July 26, 1903. For a reply by Leroy-Beaulieu, see *Le Journal des débats*, August 9, 1904.

58 At the Congress of Amsterdam in 1904, Jaurès emphasized this point in his defense of the bloc: "I don't pretend that the government is collaborating with strikers or encouraging their attacks on property; but I do say that when its instructions are obeyed, it permits strikes to develop freely." *6e congrès socialiste international (1904)*, p. 188. Despite attacks by the C.G.T. and the Parti socialiste de France on labor repression under Combes, there is evidence of a conciliatory attitude toward labor by the Premier and his Prefects, who often arranged arbitration. See, for example, Combes, *Mon Ministère*, pp. 56–57, and his speech in Chambre des Députés, *Journal officiel*, February 5, 1904. On labor questions Jaurès' influence on Combes was considerable.

59 On Jaurès' approval of attempts at labor arbitration, see his interesting interview on the subject in Jules Huret, *Les Grèves* (Paris, 1902), pp. 149–54. On the idea of the Combes ministry supporting a kind of labor code, see Albert Thomas' article in *L'Humanité*, May 24, 1904.

60 The speeches at Armentières (October 24), Caudry (October 25), and Cateau-Cambrésis (November 1) are reproduced in Jean Jaurès, "Les Grèves d'Armentières," *La Revue socialiste*, XXXVIII (November, 1903), 578–602, 605–11.

61 Chambre des Députés, *Journal officiel*, November 7, 1903.

62 *Le Journal des débats*, November 9, 1903.

63 *La petite République*, November 17, 1903. See *L'Humanité*, April 22, 1904, for an analysis of the resumption of the textile strike. The issue of wages remained a plaguing one, and management consistently refused arbitration.

64 *Le Figaro*, August 6, 1946. Jean Guéhenno has also told the story, *ibid.*, January 19, 1955.

In a passage of his recollections, Frossard recounted how, as a mere boy, he was pushed toward socialism by Jaurès' speeches: "It was a speech of Jaurès' which revealed the Promised Land to me. . . . In the rich imagery of his orations I discovered that socialism held out to me the key to their happiness." At the École Normale of Belfort, where Frossard was then a student, "the *garçon de cuisine*, who was my accomplice, would bring me *L'Humanité* every day. I would hide Jaurès' speeches in my locker, and, moreover, I just about knew them by heart." Frossard, *De Jaurès à Blum*, pp. 24, 28.

Marcelle Capy, who during World War I contributed to the pacifist *Hommes du jour*, also has recalled her passage to socialism after listening to Jaurès. See *Germinal*, July 28, 1944.

65 *La Dépêche de Toulouse*, January 21, 1904.

66 On June 11, 1903, the Chamber appointed a commission of thirty-three members, under the presidency of Buisson and including Baron Amédée Reille,

Vaillant, Dejeante, and Briand, to consider revision or abolition of the Concordat with the Vatican. By the end of the year, a project for abolition of the Concordat had been agreed upon in the Commission. The measure eventually brought forth for discussion was not vindictive in tone or procedure. Though it meant the end of ties between the State and Church, as established in the Concordat, it left Catholicism free to function as a religion, each congregation forming a civil society, authorized under the 1901 Law on Associations, and retaining the wealth and property of the Church.

Under the Concordat originally agreed upon by Bonaparte and Pope Pius VII, the government named the bishops while the Pope instituted them canonically. The government paid the priests and took care of the upkeep of Church buildings.

67 Even on issues like disarmament, the standard fare of socialism, Millerand was now voting with the bourgeois Center. See, for example, Chambre des Députés, *Journal officiel*, November 23, 1903. That day Millerand supported the government in opposition to Gustave Hubbard's proposal for French support of international disarmament.

68 *La petite République*, January 21, 1904.

69 Longuet to Kautsky, March 26, 1904. Kautsky Archives, Amsterdam. (Written in English.)

70 Jean Jaurès, "Discours au Congrès de Saint-Étienne," *La Revue socialiste*, XXXIX (April, 1904), 348, 350.

71 A new central committee was created, the National Council, composed of the old Interfederal Committee and the party deputies. Meeting at the start of each legislative session, the National Council was to lay down a general line of policy. But since Ministerialists constituted a majority on the new National Council, the deputies were able to set their own course without interference.

72 For Millerand's attack and Jaurès' reply, see Chamber des Députés, *Journal officiel*, March 8 and 17, 1904.

Note this comment of Combes': "Revealing his impatient ambition, Millerand had put himself at the head of the opposition." *Mon Ministère*, p. 166.

73 *La Dépêche de Toulouse*, February 12, 1904.

74 Jaurès, *Oeuvres*, II, 101–2; 99.

75 Auclair, *Jaurès*, p. 408.

76 Jules Renard, *Journal* (Paris, 1927), p. 608.

77 Dansette, *Histoire religieuse*, II, 318.

78 Combes revealed that as a result of this public revelation, he was able to convince at least one of his undecided ministers (Chaumié, Minister of Education) that separation was a desirable course of action. *Mon Ministère*, p. 197.

79 Jaurès' speech is printed in *L'Humanité*, May 29, 1904.

80 *Ibid.*, July 3, 1904.

81 Halévy, *Péguy*, pp. 295–96.

82 *Europe*, No. 354–55 (October-November, 1958), p. 142.

83 From an interview with Vincent Auriol. See Lévy, *Comment Ils sont devenus socialistes*, p. 80. Cachin later became a leader of the French Communist Party, Auriol the Socialist President of the Fourth Republic.

84 Interview of Bracke by Michel Launay, *Europe*, No. 354–55 (October-November, 1958), p. 26. Bracke's real name was A.-M. Desrousseaux.

85 In a letter to Kautsky, Longuet wrote: "I was overjoyed at the striking victory

our friends scored at Dresden, and I hope that the crushing of Revisionism in Germany will help us greatly over here in defeating French Ministerialism." September 28, 1903. Kautsky Archives, Amsterdam. Since Longuet went on to complain that Kautsky and his friends drew their inspiration about French socialism almost exclusively from Marxists like Guesde and Lafargue, one can assume that the Social Democrats were at least skeptical of these Left-wingers who chose to remain in the reformist party. Yet it is certainly conceivable that Longuet's information helped persuade the German Marxists that even a strong attack on reformism by the Second International would not destroy any chance for unity in the French socialist movement.

86 Thus, though Jaurès opted for the bloc at the Congress of Saint-Étienne, he identified himself neither with the Left-wingers nor with such outspoken reformist deputies as Jean Augagneur, the mayor of Lyon, Gustave Rouanet, or Gabriel Deville. Unfortunately, since Jaurès had ceased to contribute to *La petite République* in 1904 and *L'Humanité* did not appear until mid-April, it is difficult to follow the evolution of his thought at this time. However, as though in a warning to the Rightists in the party, he came out strongly in *L'Humanité* (June 13, 1904) against "Millerand's reactionary social and political policies." One can assume that by the summer of 1904 he was much closer to the Left-wingers, who, after all, did not deny the principle of reformism, than to the rightist deputies.

87 Jaurès, *Discours parlementaires*, p. 63.

88 In the Reichstag elections of 1903, the Social Democrats won eighty-one seats, an increase over their previous fifty-six.

89 See Cole, *Second International*, p. 49.

90 Vandervelde, *Souvenirs d'un militant*, p. 153.

91 *Ibid.*, p. 154.

92 *L'Humanité*, August 19, 1904.

93 The quotations that follow are from the Congress debates, *6ᵉ congrès socialiste international (1904)*, pp. 67-83.

94 *Ibid.*, pp. 84-93.

95 *Le Journal des débats*, August 20, 1904. Engels, it should be pointed out, who had been very much more than Bebel a "Pope of socialism," had made certain remarks in his letters which were similar to Jaurès' arguments. In a letter to Laura Lafargue on October 14, 1892, he had written of the value of the French revolutionary tradition: "The Continental movement, to be victorious, must be neither all French nor all German, but *franco-allemand*. If the Germans taught the French how to use the suffrage and how to organize strongly, the French will have to penetrate the Germans with that revolutionary spirit which the history of a century has made traditional with them. The time has passed forever when one nation can claim to lead all the rest." Engels and Lafargue, *Correspondence*, III, 218. In another letter to Laura Lafargue, January 19, 1895, he had expressed his enthusiasm for the parliamentary tradition: "Anyhow our 50 French socialist members are in luck. In less than 18 months they have upset three ministries and one president. That shows what a socialist minority can do in a parliament which like the French or English is really the supreme power in the country. A similar power our men in Germany can get by a revolution only." *Ibid.*, p. 391. No such remarks were mentioned by the French or German Marxists at Amsterdam.

96 *Ibid.*, August 22, 1904.

97 Téry, *Jaurès*, p. 113.

98 *La Dépêche de Toulouse*, October 3, 1904. See also *L'Humanité*, August 29, 1904, where Jaurès ridiculed the ban on voting the budgets of a friendly government by pointing out that the Blanquist Marcel Sembat had for some years been reporter for the Budget Commission on Post Office, Telegraph, and Telephone. G. D. H. Cole (*Second International*, III, 59) wrote that reformism could not be eliminated in the International: "What Amsterdam did bring was more unity, not more discipline."

99 *La petite République*, November 2, 1904.

100 Rappoport to Kautsky, September 27, 1904. Kautsky Archives, Amsterdam.

101 Quoted in Dommanget, *Vaillant*, p. 212.

102 Trotsky, "Jaurès," p. 847.

103 Vandervelde, *Souvenirs d'un militant*, p. 157.

104 Combes, *Mon Ministère*, p. 228.

105 Combes states that personal ambitions were mainly responsible for a cabal against him. Especially does he accuse Clemenceau, who attacked him with increasing ferocity in the latter half of 1904. Combes wrote thus: "Finally, a cabal was raised against me by Clemenceau, who judged the moment right for reversing my ministry in order to form a government of his own, or at least to find some place in the next ministry. Since that day when he slammed the door of my office behind him because his secretary had not obtained the post he sought, his paper had made war on me." *Ibid.*, p. 251.

106 Promotions in the army had been regulated by Soult's Law of 1832, whereby all promotions through the rank of major were made on straight seniority; beyond that level, they were made by the Classification Commission of the corps commanders. This led to favoritism toward those of conservative views.

107 Chambre des Députés, *Journal officiel*, October 28, 1904.

108 Combes, *Mon Ministère*, pp. 244-45.

109 Chambre des Députés, *Journal officiel*, November 4, 1904. The quotations that follow are from this intervention.

110 *La Dépêche de Toulouse*, December 28, 1904.

111 Quoted in Zévaès, *Jaurès*, p. 214.

112 Quoted in Auclair, *Jaurès*, p. 455.

113 *Le Journal des débats*, December 8, 1904.

114 For Jaurès' criticism of the Doumer election, see *L'Humanité*, January 11, 1905.

115 Chambre des Députés, *Journal officiel*, January 14, 1905. This analysis by Jaurès is corroborated in detail by a later critic, Beau de Loménie, *Dynasties bourgeoises*, II, 352-53.

116 *La troisième République*, III, 276.

117 *L'Humanitè*, January 23, 1905.

118 Quoted in Suarez, *Briand*, II, 18-19.

119 Chambre des Députés, *Journal officiel*, May 24, 1905.

120 Briand was influenced by Monsignor Fuzet, who expressed concern about Church property. Jaurès actually drafted Article Four, but consulted on the text with the Catholic deputy Denys Cochin. See Dansette, *Histoire religieuse*, II, 347-48.

121 Chambre des Députés, *Journal officiel*, April 21, 1905.

122 *Le Revue de l'enseignement primaire et primaire supérieure*, March 1, 1908.

The hope that Jaurès held out for Loisy's modernism was too optimistic. In 1903, Cardinal Richard, Archbishop of Paris, and several other high prelates banned Loisy's books in their dioceses. Rome acted after the accession of Pope Pius X, and his books were placed on the Index. By 1908. Loisy had been excommunicated. On the great regret Jaurès felt over Loisy's expulsion from the Church, see Enjalran's letter to Lévy-Bruhl in Jaurès, *La Question religieuse*, p. 19.

123 *L'Humanité*, July 4, 1905. The application of the new law went less smoothly than Jaurès and Briand had hoped. Part of the hostile Catholic reaction of 1906 came as a result of the encyclical *Vehementur nos*, which condemned the Law of Separation. For the rest, it came over the application of Article Three, which provided for inventories of all Church property by State officials. Catholics, agitated by rumors of confiscation and by the propaganda of young nationalists and monarchists stimulated by Maurras' *Action française*, clashed with these officials at the churches.

124 Chambre des Députés, *Journal officiel*, February 23, 1906.

125 In *L'Humanité*, September 10, 1905, he listed the following immediate socialist objectives: the eight-hour day; social security; the progressive income tax; nationalization of the railroads, mines, insurance companies, refineries, and distilleries; legalization of picketing; public works.

126 In practice, this meant that the party deputies would refuse to vote funds for military or colonial expeditions; in fact, they would withhold support for the budget as a whole.

127 For Briand's speech, see *L'Humanité*, March 27, 1905.

128 For Jaurès' speech, see *ibid.*, March 30, 1905.

129 Quoted in Suarez, *Briand*, II, 34–35. See also Charles Péguy, *L'Esprit de système*, Paris, 1953, in which Péguy accused Jaurès of blindly following the dictates of Kautsky. This *cahier* was originally prepared for publication in 1905, but it was withdrawn by Péguy in favor of his more strongly worded *Notre Patrie*.

130 Its organization was marked out as follows in the Party Charter: a) the basic units were the local groups; all the local groups of the same commune formed the sections; all the sections of the same department formed the federations. The federations, administered by federal committees, were to maintain a kind of discipline over their rank-and-file members and also over their candidates for public office. b) An annual national congress, delegates to which were chosen by the federation in proportion to the number of their paying members, was to set the general party line. A national council, composed of representatives of both the federations and the parliamentary group, and a permanent administrative committee, elected by the congress, were to guide the party between annual congress meetings. Thus, the party rested, as the revolutionaries had wanted it to, on the principle of centralization. Yet the federations had enough autonomy and the deputies enough freedom to provide a counterbalance of decentralization. As for goals, the Party Charter, proclaiming the S.F.I.O. a working-class party, separate and distinct from all bourgeois parties, organized for the conquest of the State and the transition of capitalism to communism, was a loud echo of the dictum of Amsterdam.

131 The moderate socialists, who now broke away from the S.F.I.O., styled themselves Independents once again. At a congress in March-April, 1907, they

reconstituted the Parti socialiste français, which later became the Parti républican socialiste, as a strictly reformist movement. In fact, it never had any real success. Several well-known Independents — Briand, Millerand, and Viviani especially — demonstrated less and less interest in socialism, and it was probably more of a gain than a loss for the S.F.I.O. that such men were not part of it.

132 The Independents, who bolted after Rouen, were bitter towards Jaurès for seemingly abandoning the reformist position he had for years espoused by persuading the Parti socialiste français to accept the Pact of Union. Thus, J.-L. Breton wrote some years later of the Rouen Congress: "The reformists could still have resisted and the Congress would have been spared the shameful capitulation which the revolutionaries insisted upon. If Jaurès had wished it, if he had made the slightest effort in that direction, he would easily have carried the majority of the Congress with him. But completely hypnotized by his vision of unity, which he wanted to realize at any price, he abandoned his friends and renounced the policy he had defended with so much fervor." J.-L. Breton, L'Unité socialiste (Paris, 1912), p. 51. But when, at the Congress of Toulouse in 1908, the S.F.I.O. backed the effort for social reforms and for increased parliamentary strength, it was evident that neither Jaurès nor the party had abandoned reformism; on the other hand, unlike Breton and his friends, Jaurès never denied the possibility of revolution.

133 L'Humanité, April 28, 1905.

134 Bonnier to Guesde, February 24, 1906. Guesde Archives, Amsterdam.

135 Quoted in M. Prélot, L'Évolution politique du socialisme français, 1789-1934 (Paris, 1939), p. 177.

136 On the history of French expansion into Morocco, see especially Eugene Anderson, The First Moroccan Crisis, Chicago, 1930; Ima Barlow, The Agadir Crisis, Chapel Hill, 1940; Paul Cambon, Correspondence, Paris, 1940; Charles Porter, The Career of Théophile Delcassé, Philadelphia, 1936; Melvin Knight, Morocco as a French Economic Venture, New York, 1937.

137 On Lyautey's thought, see H. Lyautey, Paroles d'action, Paris, 1927.

138 Le Temps, March 15, 1903.

139 Quoted in Auclair, Jaurès, p. 489.

140 La Dépêche de Toulouse, September 19, 1903.

141 La petite République, October 6, 1903.

142 La Dépêche de Toulouse, March 4, 1904.

143 To follow this line of separation, see La petite République, September 25, 1903, and Chamber des Députés, Journal officiel, November 20, 1903. See also Combes, Mon Ministère, pp. 216-18, for his blanket approval of Delcassé's foreign policy.

144 La Dépêche de Toulouse, September 23, 1903; La petite République, September 23, 1903.

145 Camille Sabatier, "La Pénétration pacifique et le Maroc," La Revue politique et parlementaire, XXXIX (January 10, 1904), 27.

146 Combes, Mon Ministère, p. 217.

147 The resolution on colonialism at Amsterdam, moved by Van Kol of Holland, actually combined two ideas: first, opposition to all imperialist ventures and credits for them; second, support of measures to improve the lot of peoples in the colonies. All this represented an attempt to prevent further expansion, while improving existing conditions. Yet Marxist analysis held that both

expansion and exploitation were inevitable. *Le Temps*, August 23, 1904, brought up these contradictions.

148 Chambre des Députés, *Journal officiel*, November 10, 1904.
149 *Ibid.*, April 19, 1905.
150 Maurice Paléologue, *Un grand Tournant de la politique mondiale, 1904–6* (Paris, 1931), p. 307.
151 The assurances were given in a note handed to Delcassé on April 25 by Sir Francis Bertie, the British Ambassador to France, and in an exchange of letters between Cambon and Lansdowne on May 25.
152 In January, 1905, the Russians surrendered Port Arthur to the Japanese; in March, the Russian army under General Kouropotkin was crushed by the Japanese at the entrance to the Sea of Japan. In January, 1905, the burdens of war on Russian workers and peasants caused riots and strikes. Beginning with Father Gapon's unarmed demonstration in St. Petersburg on January 9, the first Russian Revolution led to a great general strike in October and the granting of a Duma by the Tsar.
153 *L'Humanisté*, January 25, 1905.
154 *Ibid.*, June 10, 1905. The Revolution of 1905, which promised for a time to breach the wall of Russian autocracy, aroused tremendous enthusiasm in all sectors of the French working-class movement, whether socialist, syndicalist, or anarchist. To the extreme Left, it represented several things: the beginning of the end for the privileged classes of Russia; the transformation of the Franco-Russian Alliance into a peaceful, defensive instrument; positive proof that a spontaneous mass uprising was possible; evidence, particularly valuable for the anarchosynicalists, of political decentralization. No one wrote more hopefully of this Russian revolution than Jaurès, who had long considered Tsarist imperialism a terrible danger to the peace of Europe. See, for example, *ibid.*, January 24 and 30, February 6, March 4, June 8, 1905; January 20, May 23 and 28, October 5, 1906. Nor did anyone recognize more clearly than Jaurès that a) a Russian revolution, relentlessly opposed by the ruling classes, would be driven, and understandably so, to excesses; and that b) the divisions among the Left-wing Russian parties could only weaken the revolutionary cause. These insights, a dozen years before another Russian revolution proved them correct, were incorporated in an essay by Jaurès, deposited in the Institut Français d'Histoire Sociale among certain manuscript papers of Eugène Fournière, and recently published in the Institut's journal, *L'Actualité de l'histoire*, No. 25, October-November-December, 1958. In that essay, Jaurès wrote in part: "If the Tsarist regime persists in its bitter and criminal resistance, it will bear full responsibility for the atrocities that will accompany the liberating revolution. In the drama that is now unfolding, one of the greatest in history, the Russian socialist parties will only weaken themselves unless they unite. Scholastic quarrels and meaningless rivalries should be swept aside; the greatness of the events demands a greatness of spirit." Though undated, the essay was probably composed late in 1905.
155 Quoted in Khvostov and Mintz, *La Diplomatie*, p. 184.
156 *L'Humanité*, June 5, 7, 16, 27, 1905.
157 *Ibid.*, March 4, 1906.
158 Jaurès, *Oeuvres*, II, 244–45.
159 *L'Humanité*, January 21, 1906. This is from a speech at the Grand Orient on

January 19, presided over by Anatole France. The quotations that follow are from the same speech.

160 Jaurès, *Oeuvres*, II, 246.

161 *La Dépêche de Toulouse*, June 21, 1905.

162 *L'Humanité*, June 24, 1905.

163 *Ibid.*, June 22, 1905.

164 *Ibid.*, April 3, 1906.

165 Quoted in Challaye, *Péguy socialiste*, p. 292. Such nationalistic sentiments grew increasingly louder and more widespread in the years leading up to World War I, reflecting not only the spirit of revenge for the defeat of 1870–71, but also the generalized French fear and shame before German economic superiority. French readers were constantly confronted with an array of startling statistics on Germany's economic growth, especially in the production of coal, iron, steel, and chemicals. Her imports and exports increased from 5¾ billion marks in 1872 to 21 billion marks in 1903; her exports alone increased from 4 billions in 1890 to 11 billions in 1913. Such data, accompanied by appropriate gloom and alarm, were reproduced in a spate of topical books, such as: G. Blondel, *L'Essor industriel et commercial du peuple allemand*, Paris, 1898; M. Lair, *L'Impérialisme allemand*, Paris, 1902; F. Delaisi, *La Force allemande*, Paris, 1905; H. Lichtenberger, *Allemagne moderne*, Paris, 1907; A. Barre, *La Menace allemande*, Paris, 1908; L. Hubert, *L'Effort allemand*, Paris, 1911. Confronted by the brute facts of German superiority in commerce, finance, and technology, many Frenchmen reacted in an irrational, chauvinistic manner.

166 Quoted in Goetz-Girey, *La Pensée syndicale*, p. 48. It should be pointed out that the reformists in the C.G.T., led by Keufer, opposed this antipatriotism, though their influence was a minority one in the annual congresses.

167 It is significant that at the international trade union congresses of Dublin (1903) and Amsterdam (1905), the French proposals on antimilitarism were rejected.

168 The debate is printed in *L'Humanité*, May 29, 1905. Hervé's later attacks were so strenuous that he and twenty-six of his followers were brought to trial for treason in December, 1905. He was convicted and sentenced to four years' imprisonment. After serving six months, however, he was released. For Jaurès' objection to his conviction, see *ibid.*, May 28, 1906. Jaurès' decision to answer Hervé publicly at this time, it should be noted, rested in large part on his realization that Hervé's influence had rather suddenly spread. Up to 1905, Hervé had found almost no audience except among schoolteachers. But on April 26, 1905, he addressed a large crowd at the Tivoli Vauxhall and right afterwards addressed several large meetings in the provinces.

169 Combes, *Mon Ministère*, p. 229.

170 For Jaurès' comments approving the action of the National Council, see *L'Humanité*, March 22, 1906.

171 *Ibid.*, April 22, 1906.

172 *Le Temps*, April 3, 1906.

173 In preparation for running their own class candidates, the Socialist Party adopted a comprehensive program: proportional representation; election of judges; free education at all levels; the progressive income tax; the weekly day off for workers; the eight-hour day; social security; nationalization of

railroads, mines, the Bank of France, the insurance companies, and refineries; unionization rights for State employees, militias instead of permanent standing armies.

174 The incident was reported by Jaurès. Chambre des Députés, *Journal officiel*, July 2, 1906.

175 *Ibid.*, June 12 and 14, 1906. These speeches are the source of the quotations that follow.

176 *Le Radical*, June 15, 1906.

177 Chambre des Députés, *Journal officiel*, June 18 and 19, 1906.

178 Quoted in Auclair, *Jaurès*, p. 507.

179 *Le Revue de l'enseignment primaire et primaire supérieure*, June 24, 1906.

180 *Ibid.*

181 Chambre des Députés, *Journal officiel*, June 19, 1906.

182 Maurice Barrès, *Mes Cahiers* (Paris, 1932), V, p. 35.

183 June 19, 1906. See also *Le Temps, Le Journal des débats, Le Radical*, June 20, 1906.

184 Barrès, *Mes Cahiers*, V, 161.

185 Trotsky, "Jaurès," p. 849.

CHAPTER 12

1 From the preface to Georges Bonnafous, *Histoire politique de la troisième République* (Paris, 1956), p. ix. A detailed record of the strikes of 1905 appears in Paul Delesalle, "Les Grèves en 1905," *Le Mouvement socialiste* (October, 1906), pp. 154–64.

2 Bonnefous, *Histoire politique*, p. xii.

3 The ministry which Clemenceau presented to the Chamber on November 5 contained seven Radicals, two Independent Socialists (Briand and Viviani), and two moderates (Barthou and Thomson). General Picquart, a symbol of the Dreyfusard movement, became Minister of War.

4 Wythe Williams, *The Tiger of France* (New York, 1949), p. 101.

5 Quoted in Ratinaud, *Clemenceau*, p. 140. For Clemenceau's heavy debt to Darwin, see his long philosophical reflections in *In the Evening of my Thought*, New York, 1929.

6 Clemenceau, *Evening of my Thought*, I, 54.

7 Quoted in Williams, *Tiger of France*, pp. 273–74.

8 *Ibid.*, p. 102.

9 Quoted in John Scott, *Republican Ideas and the Liberal Tradition in France, 1870–1914* (New York, 1951), p. 150.

10 *L'Humanité*, November 6, 1906.

11 For Jaurès' interpellation against this action, see Chambre des Députés, *Journal officiel*, March 11, 1907.

12 Quoted in Dolléans, *Le Mouvement ouvrier*, II, 143. See also M. T. Laurin, "Le Syndicalisme et les instituteurs," *Le Mouvement socialiste* (April, 1904), pp. 297–321. For the most comprehensive study of the history of unionism among teachers, see Max Ferre's *Histoire du mouvement syndicaliste révolutionnaire chez les instituteurs (Des origines à 1922)*, Paris, 1955. Ferre stresses the point that the bitter opposition of moderates and conservatives to those teachers who wanted to join the C.G.T. was strongly influenced by their feeling that these teachers were openly anti-conservative in their classrooms.

Marius Nègre, according to the author, was "one of the most heroic and magnificent figures in the movement for teachers' unions." *Ibid.*, 109.

13 Chambre des Députés, *Journal officiel*, June 25, 1909.

14 For Jaurès' views on the "neutrality" of teachers, see his article in *Revue de l'enseignement primaire et primaire supérieure*, October 25, 1908.

15 Jean Jaurès, Introduction to B. Malon, *La Morale sociale* (Paris, 1895), pp. iv–v.

16 Chambre des Députés, *Journal officiel*, May 10, 1907. The quotations that follow are from this intervention.

17 *Ibid.*, May 11, 1907.

18 *Ibid.*, May 13, 1907.

19 Quoted in Suarez, *Briand*, II, 190.

20 Chambre des Députés, *Journal officiel*, May 13, 1907.

21 For the Midi crisis, see Bonnefous, *Histoire politique*, pp. 68–75. For Jaurès' intervention against Clemenceau's policies in the Midi, see Chambre des Députés, *Journal officiel*, June 28, 1907.

22 Dolléans *Le Mouvement ouvrier*, II, 145.

23 Thus one finds hardly a reference to Jaurès in Gide's *Journals*; and in the letters that passed between those two young writers, Jacques Rivière and Henri Alain-Fournier, the few remarks are tinged with scorn. Early in 1907, Rivière witnessed a debate between Clemenceau and Jaurès; of this he wrote to Alain-Fournier (January 26): "Clemenceau came on to the scene with self-assurance and forcefulness. He is admirable. The rest, even Jaurès, turned the session into a joke. They are people without real style." His young friend then wrote on February 1: "Clemenceau. I like him in his position, his little position. He is strong. Strength. But Jaurès; *un concierge.*" Jacques Rivière and Henri Alain-Fournier, *Correspondence* (Paris, 1926), II, 25, 33.

The reference by Renard is from a letter to A. M. Vadez, dated September 20, 1906, which was published in Jules Renard, *Correspondance (1864–1910)* (Paris, n.d.), p. 344. The reference by Proust is from one of the occasional pieces he wrote for *Le Figaro* under the name Horatio; this one, which appeared on January 4, 1904, was reproduced in Marcel Proust, *Chroniques* (Paris, 1936), pp. 51–52.

24 *La Dépêche de Toulouse*, April 4, 1907. In his sustained attack on militarism and colonialism, Jaurès frequently emphasized what he considered the wastefulness and irrationality of French capitalism. The weaknesses of the French economy — its low rate of growth, technological backwardness, high prices, and inadequate mass purchasing power — he linked to the waste of resources, in military preparations especially, and to the flight of capital from domestic and foreign markets.

In this analysis, Jaurès was close to the mark. Later economists have likewise attributed French economic backwardness to waste and fruitless foreign investment. See especially the authoritative work of Harry D. White, *The French International Accounts, 1880–1913*, Cambridge, Mass., 1933. According to White, one-third of all French savings between 1880 and 1913 was invested outside France. Thus, on the one hand, the interest rate on available capital rose at home, inhibiting much-needed public improvements and industrial expansion, and, on the other hand, French savings were drained off into risky and useless foreign enterprises. As White pointed out, the great French banks, enjoying handsome promoters' profits, pushed the sale of foreign bonds, even spreading about false accounts of their prospects and bribing newspapers to publish these accounts.

When he criticized the waste of resources and the flight of capital, Jaurès had few illusions that rational planning and useful production would develop under capitalism. These, he felt, would be the economic characteristics of a socialist society. For ultimately, the present decision-makers would balk at both the redistribution of income necessary to guarantee large-scale expansion at home and nonprofit State expenditures for public works.

25 Jacques Chastenet, *Jours inquiets et jours sanglants* (Paris, 1957), p. 46. This is the fourth volume of Chastenet's *Histoire de la troisième République*, and will hereafter be cited as such. On the later history of the Moroccan problem, consult, in addition to the works previously mentioned, Joseph Caillaux, *Agadir: ma politique extérieure*, Paris, 1919; and André Tardieu, *Le Mystère d'Agadir*, Paris, 1912.

It should be noted, of course, that Pichon was thoroughly committed to the French colonial venture in North Africa. He had served for a time as Resident Minister in Tunisia during the Combes ministry. In that capacity, he helped one Basilio Couitéas, whose wife was related to Pichon, to obtain a huge concession of some 38,000 hectares of Tunisian land.

26 Jaurès' four articles on the Oudjda occupation are in his *Oeuvres*, V, 89–96.

27 See *L'Humanité*, September 4, 5, 6, 7, 11, 24, and November 14, 1907.

28 *Ibid.*, December 30, 1907.

29 For the debate, see Chambre des Députés, *Journal officiel*, January 24, 1908.

30 The proëxpansionist *Temps* criticized Ribot for his hesitant stand (January 26, 1908).

31 See Chambre Des Députés, *Journal officiel*, February 10 and 19, March 27, June 19, July 7, 1908; *La Dépêche de Toulouse*, February 19 and 26, March 6, April 30, May 29, June 4, and 25, 1908; *L'Humanité*, April 16 and 21, July 5 and 17, August 25, 26, 27, 1908.

32 *Le Temps*, February 26, 1908.

33 *La Dépêche de Toulouse*, March 27, 1908.

34 Tardieu, *Agadir*, p. 129.

35 Incidents between France and Germany were becoming serious again in Morocco. Especially touchy was the issue of the Casablanca deserters. In September, 1908, the German Consul Lüderitz attempted to help six deserters from the French Foreign Legion, three of whom were German, to escape from Casablanca. They were, however, arrested by the French. The issue was finally arbitrated (May 22, 1909) at the International Court of the Hague in favor of the French.

36 *L'Humanité*, January 27, 1909.

37 *La Dépêche de Toulouse*, January 24, 1909.

38 For the text of the agreement, see *Documents diplomatiques. Affaires du Maroc* (Paris, 1901–12), V, 1–6. On the consequences of the agreement, consult especially Caillaux, *Agadir*; Tardieu, *Agadir*; and Maurice Viollette, *La N'Goko-Sangha*, Paris, 1924.

39 *L'Humanité*, February 11, 1909. In the years between Amsterdam and World War I, as this quotation indicates, Jaurès was keenly aware of both the extent and the processes of colonial exploitation. In the press and in the Chamber, he analyzed and exposed many shocking cases of rapacity and chicanery in the colonies.

In 1911, for example, a fierce public debate took place round the charge, made first by the League of the Rights of Man, that privileged *colons*, recipients of special political favors, had received concessions of more than 800,000 hectares of Tunisian land. Conservative deputies, like Émile Driant, as well as certain Radicals, like François Thalamas, tried to defend the Tunisian concessions, but Jaurès, well supplied with data by Tunisian socialists, particularly Joachim Dorel, bitterly denounced the rapacity of imperialism: "Above all, it is time to protect the native populations. In Tunisia, as in Algeria, the Congo, and Morocco, thousands of colonial pirates have grown rich through pillage. The Moroccan loans and monopolies, the violent expropriation of the Algerian Kabyles, the vast Congolese concessions, the huge Tunisian estates — they are so many claws which rapacious imperialism has dug into the flesh of its victims." *Ibid.*, May 4, 1911. In the Chamber, Jaurès proposed a committee to study the question of the Tunisian concession, but his proposal was beaten in the vote of February 1, 1912, 408 to 104.

He led the same kind of fight against the unsuccessful attempt by Tardieu to win for the N'Goko-Sangha Company, in which he was interested, an indemnity of 12,675,000 francs for alleged damages in the Congo through German interference. See Jaurès' interventions in Chambre des Députés, *Journal officiel*, April 6, 1911, and April 8, 1912.

40 Blanche Vogt, "Un Jaurès inconnu," *Les Oeuvres libres*, CXL (Paris, 1933), 300-1.

41 *Ibid.*, pp. 331-36.

42 Mme Vogt tells the story of a dinner held in honor of Anatole France and attended by Jaurès, Sembat, and other leading Socialists. In the midst of a serious discussion about war and peace, Sembat abruptly left to keep an appointment with his wife. This startled Jaurès. *Ibid.*, p. 323.

43 Frank Moraes, *Jawaharlal Nehru* (New York, 1956), p. 69.

44 Action française was a royalist movement, but its strength derived from its newspaper of that name, which became a daily on March 1, 1908, and was dominated by the ultranationalism of Charles Maurras, Léon Daudet, and Henri Vaugeois.

45 The results of an extensive investigation of the attitudes of trade union leaders toward patriotism and militarism, carried in the pages of *Le Mouvement socialiste*, revealed a strong antipatriotism and a preference for the military general strike. Only a few, like the reformist Keufer, were in the minority. See *Le Mouvement socialiste* (August 1 and 15, 1905), pp. 433-71; (September 1 and 15, 1905), pp. 36-72; (October 1 and 15, 1905), pp. 202-32; (November 1 and 15, 1905), pp. 320-38.

46 3e Congrès national du parti socialiste, section française de l'internationale ouvrière, 3e Congrès national, tenu à Limoges les 1, 2, 3, 4, novembre 1906, *Compte rendu* (Paris n.d.), p. 214.

Frossard, who attended several socialist congresses before World War I, wrote as follows about the internal factions: "If one analyzed the origin of the leading party militants after unification, he would notice that most of them were out of the school of Guesde." Prominent Independents there were, as well as Allemanists, Blanquists, Possibilists, and Hervéists. But because of their more effective organization, the Guesdists had delegations and important spokesmen not only from the Nord, where they were strongest, but also from many other departments: the Oise (Compère-Morel), the Allier

(Paul Constans), the Gard (Hubert-Rouger), the Seine (Marcel Cachin), the Dordogne, the Isère, the Haute-Vienne. Within the Unified Party, the Guesdists retained a good bit of their partisan spirit. "Bracke was the great public speaker for the Guesdists, Gustave Delory their tactician at the Congresses." Frossard, *De Jaurès à Blum*, pp. 129, 131. It was quite evidently the great personal force of Jaurès and his effective alliance with Vaillant which helped him to set the party's course.

47 There is now an extensive literature on Sorel. See Richard Humphrey, *Georges Sorel: Prophet without Honor* (Cambridge, Mass., 1951; James Meisel, *The Genesis of Georges Sorel*, Ann Arbor, 1951; and Hughes, *Consciousness and Society*, pp. 161–83. Of Sorel's works, consult especially *Reflections on Violence*, Glencoe, Ill., 1950; and *Les Illusions du progrès*, Paris, 1908.

48 The leaders of the C.G.T. had virtually no contact with Sorel and his disciples. When Maxine Leroy asked Victor Griffuelhes whether he read Sorel's writings, the C.G.T. chief replied: "I read Alexander Dumas." Dolléans, *Le Mouvement ouvrier*, II, 127.

49 Hubert Lagardelle, "L'Évolution du prolétariat français," *Le Mouvement socialiste* (October 1, 1906), p. 151.

50 The interest of the syndicalist-minded intellectuals in Nietzsche is worth investigating. See, for example, E. Gystrow, "Neitzsche et son temps," *ibid.* (October 1 and 15, 1909), pp. 194–206.

51 For the debates of the Nancy Congress, see *4ᵉ Congrès national du parti socialiste*, section français de l'internationale ouvrière, tenu à Nancy les 11, 12, 13, et 14 août 1907, *Compte rendu*, Paris, n.d.

52 *Le Socialiste*, February 14 and 21, 1904.

53 A revealing description of the ultrapatriotism among certain upper bourgeois families of this period is provided by the novelist and philosopher Simone de Beauvoir, who has written of her father: "Without actually being affiliated with L'Action française, he had many friends among the *Camelots du roi*, and he admired Maurras and Daudet. He would not hear any criticism of the nationalist movement in politics." *Memoirs of a Dutiful Daughter* (Cleveland, Ohio, 1959), p. 38.

54 Auclair, *Jaurès*, pp. 542–43.

55 Vandervelde, *Souvenirs d'un militant*, pp. 166–67.

56 For the debates at Stuttgart, see 7ᵉ congrès socialiste international, tenu à Stuttgart du 16 au 24 août 1907, *Compte rendu analytique*, Brussels, 1908.

57 Robert Michels, "Les Socialistes allemands et la guerre," *Le Mouvement socialiste* (February 15, 1906), p. 139. Michels, who reported frequently on German developments for Lagardelle's journal, had a varied background: German on the paternal side, French on the maternal side, and Italian by choice. He wrote an influential book on party structures: *Les Partis politiques*, Paris, 1914.

On the failure of the German trade unions to join with the C.G.T. in a show of labor solidarity at the time of the first Moroccan crisis, see Griffuelhes' article in *La Voix du peuple*, February 11, 1906.

The influence of the trade union movement in shaping the conservatism of German Socialism was well illustrated in 1906 when the issue of the mass strike was debated at that year's Party Congress. The leaders of the party yielded to union pressure in refusing full approval for the strike. See Edmond

Vermeil, *L'Allemagne contemporaine* (Paris, 1952), I, 98–99.

58 Quoted from Joll, *Second International*, p. 198.

59 Two years later, when the International met in Copenhagen, the delegates reaffirmed the stand taken at Stuttgart. It is important to note, however, that the Germans succeeded in voting down Kier Hardie's proposal for a general strike. For the debates at Copenhagen, see 8e congrès international, tenu à Copenhague du 28 août à 3 septembre 1910, *Compte rendu analytique*, Gand, 1911.

60 The Bernstein conversation was originally discussed in an article in the *Yidischer Kämpfer* of New York, May 18, 1917. The Tivoli-Vauxhall speech is published in Jaurès, *Oeuvres*, V, 123–42.

61 Vermeil, *L'Allemagne*, I, 74.

62 At best, the Reichstag had limited influence under the German constitution. Though elected by universal suffrage, it suffered from the absence of real ministerial responsibility. The Chancellor ultimately held office on the suffrance of the emperor. *Ibid.*, pp. 183–217.

63 Chambre des Députés, *Journal officiel*, November 18, 1909.

64 There are three main editions of this book. The original appeared in 1911; it was reprinted by *L'Humanité* in 1915; it appeared again as Volume IV of the *Oeuvres*. The quotations below are all from the 1915 edition.

65 Quoted in Auclair, *Jaurès*, pp. 538–39.

66 Jean Jaurès, *L'Armée nouvelle* (Paris, 1915), p. 109.

67 *Ibid.*, p. 111.

68 *Ibid.*, p. 118.

69 *Ibid.*, p. 49.

70 *Ibid.*, p. 24.

71 *Ibid.*, p. 59. The two most important books by Captain Gilbert were: *Essais de critique militaire* (1890) and *Sept études militaires* (1892).

72 Jaurès, *L'Armée nouvelle*, pp. 101–2.

73 For the technical details of his plan, see *ibid.*, pp. 146–340.

74 In his plan for universal training, Jaurès proposed to begin instruction in the adolescent years, between the ages of ten and twenty, in the form of physical education under the guidance of officers, schoolteachers, and doctors of the area. At the age of twenty-one, every Frenchman would be conscripted for six months of barracks training, again in the local area, where the techniques of warfare would be taught. During the next thirteen years, between the ages of twenty-one and thirty-four, Frenchmen would be part of the active militia army, attending brief exercises eight times during that period. From the ages of thirty-four to forty-five, they would remain part of the reserves. In the eastern departments, where the invasion might most likely come, they would keep their arms at home. Only one-third of the officers would be professional, and they would be recruited from the unions, coöperatives, and educational institutions, and trained not in military schools, but in the six most important universities. Their training would not be narrowly technical, but broad and humanistic. Two-thirds of the officers would be civilians, their duties discharged in their local areas.

75 Jaurès, *L'Armée nouvelle*, p. 544.

76 Quoted in Joll, *Second International*, p. 111.

77 *Le Procès de l'assassin de Jaurès* (Paris, n.d.), p. 131. For similar judgments, see the comments of General Percin in Pignatel, *Jaurès*, pp. 123–24, and André

Hauriou, "Jaurès et le problème de l'armée," *Cahiers internationaux* (July–August, 1959), p. 70.

78 On Trotsky's deep appreciation of Jaurès as a military thinker, see Isaac Deutscher, *The Prophet Armed* (New York, 1954), pp. 477–80. Note the similarities between the views of Jaurès and those of Mao tse-tung in the latter's *Oeuvres choisis* (Paris, 1955), I, 211–300.

79 *Revue de l'enseignement primaire et primaire supérieure,* December 15, 1907.

80 Quoted in Georges Michon, *La Préparation à la guerre* (Paris, 1935), p. 55. This quotation is from Pressensé's speech before the League of the Rights of Man in 1910.

81 Compare this recent criticism by an outstanding Marxist philosopher: "The absence of a concrete political and economic program, and more than that, the curious resistance to the idea of a program give rise to political alienation — to political fetishism." Henri Lefebvre, *La Somme et le reste* (Paris, 1959), I, 288.

82 *Typographie française,* September 15, 1896.

83 The Charter of Amiens contained two main points: 1) that members of the C.G.T. were free as individuals to join any party; 2) but that the C.G.T. itself and its constituent groups were to avoid alliances "with parties and sects."

84 Monatte, *Trois Scissions syndicales,* p. 114.

85 Quoted in Dolléans, *Le Mouvement ouvrier,* II, 135–36.

86 15ᵉ Congrès national corporatif de la C.G.T., *Compte rendu sténographique* (Paris, 1907), p. 143.

87 *Parti socialiste, 3ᵉ congrès national* (1906), p. 192.

88 According to Article 13 of the party rules, the departmental Federations were entitled to one delegate for the first hundred dues-paying members and one additional delegate for every two hundred members beyond that. The Federation of the Nord, which inherited the discipline and machinery of the P.O.F., had more members and thus more delegates than any other.

89 *Parti socialiste, 3ᵉ congrès national* (1906), p. 166.

90 The same sort of decision was repeated a year later, in August, 1907, at the Congress of Nancy. As late as February, 1912, at the Congress of Lyon, the issue was still being debated, and again Jaurès defended the autonomy of the C.G.T. The Guesdists' attacks against the anarchosyndicalist leadership of the C.G.T. continued unabated in 1907 and 1908. In *Le Socialisme,* the weekly newspaper of the Guesdist faction, one can find a flood of anti-C.G.T. articles. The Guesdists were, however, somewhat appeased by the statement of party aims drawn up by Jaurès and adopted at the Congress of Toulouse in 1908, which specifically condemned sudden uprisings against the bourgeois state.

91 For the debate between Jaurès and the Radical Albert Sarraut, in which Jaurès defended the general strike, see *La Dépêche de Toulouse,* September 4, 10, 15, 16, 23, 1908.

92 Lucien Roux, *Le Syndicalisme* (Paris, 1961), p. 17.

93 See Dolléans, *Le Mouvement ouvrier,* II, 147–53. In their numerical charge, the reformists were correct. In fact, even among the organized workers, the majority were not enrolled in the C.G.T. Thus, in 1908, of 977,350 organized workers, only some 400,000 belonged to the C.G.T. The moderates also accused Griffuelhes of needlessly spreading fear among the bourgeoisie and inviting governmental repression. Again, there was some substance in the

argument. The historian Lavisse, for example, revealed to Drumont in 1909 that he considered a syndicalist revolution almost inevitable. See Eugen Weber's very useful monograph, *The Nationalist Revival in France, 1905-14* (Berkeley, 1959), p. 41.

94 Quoted in Roux, *Le Syndicalisme*, pp. 10-11.

95 From a speech by Guesde at Saint-Mandé on June 4, 1906. Quoted in *Le Radical*, June 5, 1906.

96 Quoted in Georges Tétard, *Essais sur Jean Jaurès* (Colombes, 1959), p. 13. Note also the comment of Beau de Loménie, *Dynasties bourgeoises*, II, 394: "More and more, only the anticlerical logomachy and Masonic attacks serve as a Radical program."

97 The Executive Committee of the Radical and Radical-Socialist Party did not begin to wrestle with real problems of organization until 1906, and it was not until 1913 that real party rules were adopted. See G. Fabius de Champville, *Le Comité exécutif du parti radical et radical-socialiste de 1897 à 1907* (Paris, 1908), pp. 28-39.

98 Quoted in Weber, *Nationalist Revival*, p. 39.

99 *Le Radical*, April 3, 1906.

100 *Ibid.*, July 3, 1906.

101 *Ibid.*, June 19, 1906.

102 *Le Siècle*, September 22, 1907.

103 Quoted in Weber, *Nationalist Revival*, p. 39.

104 Rappoport to Kautsky, May 16, 1907. Kautsky Archives, Amsterdam.

105 The reform objectives of the party remained fairly standard between 1906 and 1914: the eight-hour day; the progressive income tax; comprehensive social security; the nationalization of monopolies; and a system of proportional representation.

106 At the Toulouse Congress of the S.F.I.O. in October, 1908, Jaurès declared: "Precisely because we are a party of revolution, we are the most deeply reformist party, the only one which can give response to the demands of the workers, and make each conquest a point of departure for further conquests." Quoted in Paul Louis, *Histoire du socialisme en France* (Paris, 1925), p. 302.

107 *L'Humanité*, July 3, 1909.

108 *La Revue de l'enseignement primaire et primaire supérieure*, June 7, 1908. See also *La Dépêche de Toulouse*, April 1 and 15, 1908. For confirmation of this analysis, though with a considerably different tone, see *Le Temps*, March 3, 1908.

109 *Le Matin*, June 27, 1907.

110 *Le Radical*, May 13, 1909. For the story of the instructive debate before the Party Executive on May 12, 1907, when censure was proposed by Chauvin and opposed by Maujan, see *ibid.*, May 12, 1909. Two months later, Maujan was rewarded with a post in the Clemenceau ministry.

111 *L'Humanité*, May 15, 1909.

112 *Ibid.*, October 2 and 5, 1907.

113 B.N. NAF 24328 (64-70).

114 *Ibid.* (71-72).

115 *La Dépêche de Toulouse*, May 15, 1908. This article was part of a long exchange between Jaurès and A. Huc, the Radical editor of *La Dépêche*. See *ibid.*, May 13, 15, 21, 1908.

116 For the text of the Radical program adopted at Nancy and a summary of the debates at Toulouse and Nantes, see Claude Nicolet, *Le Radicalisme* (Paris 1958), pp. 48–56. See also the revealing commentary on the Nantes program in *Le Radical*, October 11, 1909.

117 *Ibid.*, August 31, 1909.

118 Chambre des Députés, *Journal officiel*, June 25 and July 2, 1909. The quotations that follow are from the debate of those two days.

119 *L'Humanité*, July 21, 1909.

120 Quoted in Halévy, *La République des comités*, pp. 99–100.

121 *L'Humanité*, July 28, 1909. Holding that Socialists had to oppose every bourgeois government, the Marxists sharply criticized the Socialists who abstained. See Bracke's article in *Le Socialisme*, November 6, 1909. In the same issue, see the long report of the debates before the National Council of the S.F.I.O., where Jaurès clashed with the Marxists on this tactical question.

122 Most of his interesting speech at Périgueux is reproduced in Suarez, *Briand*, II, 242–43.

123 *Ibid.*, p. 241.

124 *L'Humanité*, October 12, 1909.

125 Paul Painlevé, *Paroles et écrits* (Paris, 1936), p. 465. Bracke also wrote of Jaurès in the corridors, of his "sly good humor when he took a colleague by the arm to ask him what would go on the next day." *L'Humanité*, August 1, 1915.

126 The resolution was unanimously adopted, with only J.-L. Breton, who urged a return to the bloc, abstaining. One can find the full text of the resolution in Hubert Rouger, *La France socialiste* (Paris, 1912), pp. 202–4.

127 In successive party congresses, the Socialists passed resolutions which, taken together, constituted their program of political action; they were pledged, in part, to fight for agrarian reforms (Saint-Étienne, 1909), workers' pensions (Nîmes, 1910), vigorous coöperatives (Paris, 1910), repurchase of the railroads (Saint-Quentin, 1911), public ownership of municipal services (Saint-Quentin, 1911), proportional representation (Limoges, 1906; Saint-Quentin, 1911; Lyon, 1912), defense of the secular school (Saint-Quentin, 1911), women's suffrage (Limoges, 1906; Lyon, 1912), the end of religious intolerance (Lyon, 1912). These resolutions were generally passed by overwhelming majorities, but only after some strenuous opposition. That opposition was inspired mainly by antireformist Guesdists, antiparliamentary Hervéists, or out-and-out *blocards*; their proposals were usually decisively defeated, and the party, led by Jaurès and Vaillant, followed a course which was represented as both reformist and distinctively Socialist.

This was reflected in the action of the Socialist deputies in the Chamber, who, on the one hand, refused to vote the military and colonial budgets, but on the other hand introduced and pressed for, generally unsuccessfully, countless reform measures. Rouger listed well over one hundred such measures between 1905 and 1912, of which four were adopted. *Ibid.*, pp. 314–25.

One issue, the control and direction of *L'Humanité*, illustrates particularly well that factional divisions persisted in the S.F.I.O. Under the leadership of Jaurès, and especially after *L'Humanité* became a six-page daily in 1913, it was the best-written, most brilliant Socialist paper in the world. But from its founding, Jaurès was constantly beset with both economic and ideological problems. The original capital invested in *L'Humanité* by private individuals proved to be insufficient so long as sales lagged. By 1906, when the paper was losing 13,000 francs a month, Jaurès sought fresh capital. Refusing to accept the offers of certain financiers, who insisted as part of the bargain that the paper end its campaign against loans to Russia, he turned first to the German Social Democratic Party for help; on October 16, 1906, Bebel turned over 25,000 francs to Jaurès. Then, before a meeting at the Manège Saint-Paul, Jaurès appealed to the S.F.I.O. to buy new shares and become the effective owner of *L'Humanité*. The Party responded, as did certain trade unions and coöperatives; their representatives were then added to the Board of Directors. At the Socialist Congress of Paris in 1910, Lafargue announced that the Party had finally bought Rosnoblet's shares to become the effective owner of the daily. As the sales increased, the paper finally became solvent.

All during the prewar years, however, Jaurès was criticized on ideological grounds by both Guesdists and Hervéists. The Guesdists resented any line but their own in the paper. Thus, at the Congress of Nancy in 1907, Compère-Morel attacked the policy of opening columns in *L'Humanité* to revolutionary syndicalists like Griffuelhes and Pouget. That was a policy Jaurès continued to defend on the grounds of freedom of expression and collaboration with the trade union movement. He also pointed out that of the seven regular political writers for *L'Humanité*, five (Lafargue, Dubreuilh, Allard, Bracke, and Sembat) had belonged to the *Parti socialiste de France*. The Guesdist attacks became particularly bitter in 1911 when *L'Humanité* looked more kindly on the Monis Ministry than on the former Briand Ministry. See especially *Le Socialisme*, April 15, 1911. For the Hervéists, Francis Delaisi made the unsubstantiated charge that the paper's line was being set by certain Jewish stockholders. See *La Guerre sociale*, August 31 and October 5, 1910. From these two factions, though they were hostile to each other, came a concerted attack on the direction of *L'Humanité* at the Congress of Saint-Quentin in 1911. Thus, a small but vocal minority sought to wrest control of *L'Humanité* from Jaurès. Rappoport, who made the strongest criticisms, resorted to Delaisi's anti-semitic charges, though he himself was a Jew. The majority, however, shouted Rappoport down, and even the Marxists disowned him. Jaurès, who alone summed up in his eclectic position all the views in the party, easily weathered the storm. After the Congress of Saint-Quentin, criticisms of the paper were much less frequent. And, in fact, with both Marxists and Hervéists writing for it, it was a genuinely free Socialist forum.

128 The Commission on Social Security produced a text which the Chamber approved on February 24, 1906. By its main provisions, compulsory pensions were to be introduced for most workers of sixty or over; the minimum pension was to be 360 francs a year, raised by a levy of two percent of workers' wages, two percent contributed by employers, and an additional sum to meet the minimum pension paid by the State. The money thus levied was to be paid into a National Fund. Covered under the measure were not only urban workers but also sharecroppers, farm tenants, and small proprietors. The Senate Commission, however, changed the age of beneficiaries to sixty-five. In the Senate, the measure was approved on March 22, 1910, after almost five months of sporadic debate.

129 For Hervé's opposition, see *La Guerre sociale*, January 5–11, 1910. The opposition of the C.G.T. extremists is summed up by A. Luquet in *L'Humanité*, January 3, 1910, and in *La Voix du peuple*, January 2, 1910. In 1908, further-

more, a Senate Commission sought the opinion of the trade unions on the pension proposal. Only 349 unions supported it, while 751 were opposed. The figures do not, however, indicate the number of workers represented by each faction; the very large unions tended to be reformist. However, the C.G.T. was definitely on record against the measure.

130 Lafargue to Guesde, January 5, 1910. Guesde Archives, Amsterdam. The Marxist arguments against the pension law are summarized in articles by Lafargue and Bracke in *L'Humanité*, January 8 and 9, 1910.

131 7ᵉ Congrès national du Parti socialiste, section française de l'internationale ouvrière, tenu à Nîmes les 6, 7, 8, et 9 février 1910, *Compte rendu sténographique* (Paris, 1910), p. 294.

132 *Ibid.*, pp. 141, 132.

133 Note the edge of bitterness in Hervé's comment in *La Guerre sociale*, January 6–12, 1909, when he said of Jaurès' popularity that "even the Guesdists are in his lap."

Guesde himself was no doubt angered by Jaurès' commanding position in the S.F.I.O. Yet he remained a good party man. When the orthodox Marxist weekly *Le Socialisme* reprinted an attack on Jaurès from *Le Temps*, Guesde wrote furiously to the editor: "We may fight within the party, but we do not indulge in character assassination. . . . Above all, we do not dig in the bourgeois press and borrow attacks on our comrades." Guesde to *Le Socialisme*, September 16, 1911. Guesde Archives, Amsterdam.

134 Jaurès, *L'Armée nouvelle*, pp. 432–35.

135 7ᵉ *Congrès national* (1910), p. 388.

136 Chambre des Députés, *Journal officiel*, March 30, 1910. The split between the S.F.I.O. majority and the Guesdists over reforms was almost as bitter on the subject of the nationalization of the railroads. The issue was raised especially after the railroad strike of 1910, when Socialists demanded nationalization of the private lines. But how? The Guesdists strenuously opposed any indemnity to the owners. The majority, led by Jaurès and Vaillant, were willing to repurchase as a way of getting the railroads into public hands. The most moderate elements of the S.F.I.O., like Édgar Milhaud, Albert Thomas, and Alexandre Varenne, especially favored this variation of the old Possibilist *socialisme municipal*. The issue was debated at the Congress of Saint-Quentin (April, 1911), but it was not resolved. The motion adopted merely approved the general principle of nationalization of monopolies.

137 *L'Humanité*, April 1, 1910.

138 It should be pointed out that though the Socialist deputies introduced, between 1906 and 1914, some 150 measures, most were only changes in existing laws and only four Socialist proposals were voted into law. For a list of these measures, see Rouger, *La France socialiste*, pp. 314–25.

139 Quoted in Chastenet, *La troisième République*, IV, 73.

140 Franz Toussaint, *Jaurès intime* (Toulouse, 1952), pp. 51–52. In his recollections of Jaurès among the people of the Tarn, Léon Jouhaux wrote: "Let me recall one beautiful summer day when we both got on the little coach running between Albi and Cognac, in order to go to the mines. It was crowded with peasants returning from market. Utterly unaffected, with complete simplicity, Jaurès spoke to them in the local patois. With his jokes and good humor, he made everyone laugh. . . . Who can really describe his warmth and his joy?" *L'Humanité*, August 2, 1915.

141 Quoted in Toussaint, *Jaurès*, p. 64.
142 The 404 supporting votes were those of 362 Radical-Socialists, Radicals, and moderates (Left Republicans and Progressists, the old core of the Alliance démocratique), plus forty-two members of the Action libérale (the Catholic group of Jacques Piou) and the reactionary Right. The 121 opposing votes included seventy-four Socialists, thirty-five Rightists, and twelve Radical-Socialists.
143 Chastenet, *La troisième République*, IV, 74. The phrase, *La République des camarades*, was coined by the journalist Robert de Jouvenel in a book of that title published in 1913.
144 July 22, 1910. For detailed figures on the wages of railwaymen, see *ibid.*, September 27, 1910.
145 Pierre Semard wrote in his brief, polemical history of the railroad workers' movement: "The Syndicat national des chemins de fer, which belonged to the C.G.T. before 1914, was among the most reformist unions of the times. It especially favored parliamentary action." *Histoire de la Fédération des cheminots* (Paris, 1934), p. 10.
146 Suarez, *Briand*, II, 277.
147 The conscription of transportation personnel was technically legal, having been ordered under Article 230, Section 5, of a law of June 9, 1837.
148 *L'Humanité*, October 15, 1910.
149 *Ibid.*, October 19, 1910.
150 Chambre des Députés, *Journal officiel*, October 29, 1910. Briand's reply which follows comes from the debate of the same day.
151 Jules Romains, *The Earth Trembles* (New York, 1936), p. 43.
152 Quoted in Suarez, *Briand*, II, 291.
153 *L'Action française*, November 1, 1910.
154 *L'Humanité*, November 3, 1910.
155 *Ibid.*, February 26, 1911.
156 Caillaux was president of the Board of Directors of the Crédit foncier égyptien and the Crédit foncier argentin, which brought him into close contact with international financiers. On these financial connections, see the detailed article by André Morizet, *ibid.*, July 11, 1911. Berteaux was an important and wealthy stockbroker. His ambition was cut short, however, when he was killed in an accident on May 21, 1911. A plane crashed at the airport of Issy-les-Moulineaux, killing Berteaux and injuring Monis, both of whom were among the spectators at the airfield.
157 Béranger, in fact, who grew increasingly nationalistic and conservative within the ranks of Radicalism, quickly launched a campaign against the Left-wing tendencies of the ministry. See *L'Action*, March 2, 3, 7, 8, 10, 1911. In stressing the incoherence of Radicalism, *L'Humanité* pointed out on February 20, 1911, that Marc Raty, one of the owners of *Le Radical*, was a member of the Comité des forges.
158 For Caillaux's ministerial declaration, the interpellations that followed, and Caillaux's responses, see Chambre des Députés, *Journal officiel*, June 30, 1911. Note that in the Chamber session of April 14, both Monis and Charles Dumont, his Minister of Public Works, asked for and received a mandate from the deputies to try to force the railroad companies to rehire the *cheminots*. Dumont even threatened nationalization of the lines. Caillaux's position was thus a distinct retreat.

159 Jean Jaurès, "Léon Tolstoi," *La Revue socialiste*, No. 315 (March, 1911), p. 209.
160 Jaurès, *Oeuvres*, III, 380–81.

CHAPTER 13

1 Auclair, *Jaurès*, p. 582.
2 Chambre des Députés, *Journal officiel*, June 16, 1911.
3 *Le Temps*, June 18, 1911.
4 Quoted in Khvostov and Mintz, *La diplomatie*, p. 218.
5 Caillaux's key agents were the financiers Lenoir, Fondère, and Spitzer, all of whom had ties with German finance.
6 *L'Humanité*, July 2, 1911.
7 Jaurès' observations on his trip were recorded in a series of letters to his wife and son, published in 1933. See Jean Jaurès, "Lettres," *Europe*, XV (February 15, 1933), 153–73.
8 July 23, 1911. *Ibid.*, p. 161.
9 July 24, 1911. *Ibid.*, p. 162.
10 Quoted in Auclair, *Jaurès*, p. 571. In fact, the entire South American journey was like an intellectual feast for Jaurès. He concerned himself not only with contemporary conditions but with the largest historical and sociological problems. His enthusiasm right before his trip was summed up by Enjalran in his letter to Levy-Bruhl: "The primitive history of pre-Columbian America, of the old empires destroyed by the Spaniards, . . . of the subsequent mixture of the races — all of that, he felt, would be a springboard for expressing his ideas on many subjects, especially on the collaboration of different races in a common effort, on the conditions for coöperation among peoples in the future, and finally, I think, on that immanent Providence in history, which was at the center of his religious thought." Jaurès, *La Question religieuse*, p. 15. This indicates both his extraordinary intellectual curiosity and his determination, especially when war was threatening, to use his knowledge to point the way to the unity of mankind.
11 Quoted in *L'Humanité*, October 14, 1911.
12 In the larger arrangement of German diplomacy, Kiderlen, who was sympathetic neither to Austria nor to Turkey, actually hoped for a *modus vivendi* with the Triple Alliance. Thus, his death in 1912 returned German diplomacy to a more pro-Austrian and pro-Turkish orientation.
13 Deschanel's comment is from *Le Temps*, September 17, 1911. Quoted by Weber, *Nationalist Revival*, p. 98.
14 There is unfortunately no substantial biography of Caillaux. See, however, his *Mes Mémoires*; A. Fabre-Luce, *Caillaux*, Paris, 1933; and E. Roche, *Caillaux que j'ai connu*, Paris, 1949.
15 Quoted in Fabre-Luce, *Caillaux*, p. 64. Joffre had been named Chief of Staff on July 28 as part of the preparations for a possible war.
16 Charles Paix-Séailles, *Jaurès et Caillaux* (Paris, n.d.), p. 43.
17 Quoted in Fabre-Luce, *Caillaux*, p. 65.
18 *Le Matin*, December 18, 1911. Quoted in Weber, *Nationalist Revival*, p. 98.
19 *L'Humanité*, November 4, 1911. See also *ibid.*, November 14 and 25, 1911.
20 Italy was supported by France on the basis of the secret clauses in the Treaty of 1900 and by Russia on the basis of the Treaty of Racconigi of October, 1909.

21 *La Dépêche de Toulouse,* November 6, 1911.
22 On the expansionist position of the Radicals in the years before World War I, note the observations of J. C. Cairns in "Politics and Foreign Policy: The French Parliament, 1911–14," *The Canadian Historical Review,* XXXIV (September, 1953), 250–52. For an example of a particularly virulent kind of colonialism by a leading Radical, see Maurice Ajam, *Problèmes algériennes,* Paris, 1913.

There are many examples of the budgetary consciousness of Radicals on colonial questions. See, for example, *Le Siècle,* January 24, 1906; *Le Radical,* August 4, 1907; January 24, 1908; March 9 and 15, 1911.

At their eleventh Party Congress in October, the Radicals adopted a resolution critical of the Congo Treaty. And when the vote on the treaty was finally cast, the deputies of the frontier departments did, in fact, abstain.
23 Chambre des Députés, *Journal officiel,* December 19 and 20, 1911.
24 Quoted in Paix-Séailles, *Jaurès et Caillaux,* p. 59.
25 Chambre des Députés, *Journal officiel,* June 28, 1912.
26 *Un Livre noir. Diplomatie d'avant-guerre d'après les documents des archives russes* (Paris, 1923), I, 287. Isvolsky to the Foreign Office, July 4, 1912.
27 Paix-Séailles, *Jaurès et Caillaux,* p. 76. For other hostile views of Poincaré, see two books by Gouttenoire de Toury: *Poincaré a-t-il voulu la guerre?* Paris, 1920; and *Jaurès et le parti de la guerre,* Paris, 1922.
28 On Poincaré's corporation connections, see Francis Delaisi's article in *La Bataille syndicaliste,* July 7, 1912.
29 Quoted in Miquel, *Poincaré,* p. 141. Miquel's book, though it is uncritical, is the most complete and best-documented biography of Poincaré. A shorter account can be found in Jacques Chastenet, *Raymond Poincaré,* Paris, 1948. For Poincaré's own version of his career, see his memoirs, *Au Service de la France,* Paris, 1926–33. Clemenceau, who disliked Poincaré as self-righteous, cautious, and heavily conservative, said of him once: "No character — Poincaré? He has the worst one I've ever encountered." Quoted in Wormser, *Clemenceau,* p. 283.
30 This is well illustrated throughout Paléologue's private *Journal, 1913–14,* Paris, 1947.
31 Despite Poincaré's ministerial declaration, which stressed social order and military preparations, only one Radical, Thalmas, voted against him, and only four, including Pelletan, abstained. For Radicals, who underestimated Poincaré's strength, his ministry seemed to guarantee Radical predominance. See *Le Radical,* January 15, 1912. For others, frightened by the German menace, Poincaré seemed to guarantee France's frontiers. See *Le Siècle,* January 17, 1912.
32 *Le Correspondant,* July 25, 1912.
33 For the terms of these agreements, see Ministère des Affaires Étrangères, *Les Affaires Balkaniques, 1912–14* (Paris, 1922), I, 111–16. The first secret article of the Serbo-Bulgar Treaty was the crucial one. It signified that when Serbia and Bulgaria found the opportune moment, they would attack Turkey. They would, however, first consult Russia. Through that consultation, Russia held something of a restraining hand over her Balkan allies.
34 Caillaux, *Mémoires,* III, 20.
35 *La Dépêche de Toulouse,* October 16, 1912.
36 *Un Livre noir,* I, 185. Isvolsky to Foreign Office, January 2/15, 1912.

37 *L'Humanité*, May 21, 1912.

38 *Le Temps*, October 28, 1912.

39 In a conversation with Caillaux in 1916, Jacques Piou revealed that Albert de Mun had urged the parliamentary Right to support Poincaré for the Presidency of the Republic because he would, on the basis of his commitments at St. Petersburg, ensure passage of the three-year military service. Caillaux, *Mes Mémoires*, III, 24.

40 *La Dépêche de Toulouse*, October 16, 1912.

41 *Ibid.*, November 4, 1912.

42 The negotiations were tortuous at best and finally broke down on February 3, 1913, when the Turks, unwilling to cede Adrianople to the Bulgars, resumed the first Balkan War. Again, the concern of Austria and Russia, the two most interested great powers, was decisive in producing an armistice. Austria was concerned about the aggrandizement of Serbia, Russia about the pretensions of Bulgaria. On April 16, the six great powers forced resumption of peace talks in London, and on May 30, a settlement of the first Balkan War was reached. Macedonia and Crete were divided among the Balkan allies, while Albania was made an independent state. Within a few weeks, a second Balkan War began when Bulgaria, desiring more than she had received, went to war against Serbia, Greece, and this time Rumania and Turkey. Her defeat was swift, and the Treaty of Bucharest (August 10) brought that conflict to an end.

43 "Compte-rendu analytique du Congrès international extraordinaire, tenu à Bâle les 24 et 25 novembre 1912," *Bulletin périodique du Bureau Socialiste International*, No. 10 (Brussels, 1912), p. 6.

44 *Ibid.*, p. 12. The entire resolution is reprinted, *ibid.*, pp. 9-12.

45 Quoted in Milorad Drachkovitch, *Les Socialismes français et allemand et la problème de la guerre* (Geneva, 1933), p. 343.

46 The authority for this conversation is Huysmans himself. It was reported in *Le Populaire du centre*, March 26, 1916, and was confirmed by Kautsky in *Vorwärts*, July 3, 1916. It played, of course, an important part in the movement by the so-called *minoritaires* of French and German Socialism during the war, who wanted to reëstablish ties among Socialists and thus to press for peace. That many felt Jaurès would have led in that effort was revealed in a letter from Romain Rolland to Jean Longuet, published in *Le Populaire du centre* on August 3, 1916: "Always the same sigh: 'If Jaurès had lived!' Always the same unspoken conviction: 'If he had lived, he alone could have stopped this misery.'"

47 Weber, *Nationalist Revival*, p. 105.

48 For the speeches at the Franco-German Socialist rally on March 30, see *L'Humanité*, March 31, 1912.

49 Quoted in Drachkovitch, *Les Socialismes*, p. 126.

50 *L'Humanité*, November 10, 1912.

51 Reprinted in James Guillaume, "La Citation falsifiée," *La Vie ouvrière*, No. 84 (March 20, 1913), p. 363.

52 The original articles were reprinted almost at once in three installments in Guillaume's *La Vie ouvrière*. See Charles Andler, "Le Socialisme impérialiste," and "L'Allemagne contemporaine," *ibid.*, No. 81, February 5; No. 82, February 20; No. 83, March 5, 1913.

53 *L'Humanité*, March 31, 1913.

54 *Ibid.*, March 4, 1913. Andler had quoted Bebel as saying: "The order of the day is not to disarm." According to the official transcript, he actually said: "The order of the day *for bourgeois Europe* is not to disarm."

55 Quoted in Drachkovitch, *Les Socialismes*, p. 269.

56 See the objective approval of Andler's articles by the Swiss Socialist Fritz Brubacher, in "Le Socialisme impérialiste et les ouvriers allemands," *La Vie ouvrière*, No. 86 (April 20, 1913), pp. 449–54. Several details about Andler and his charges should be mentioned in order to understand the resentment they roused among Socialists, especially the Marxists. Charles Rappoport, for example, assailed Andler as "that new Faust, an unknown in the world of organized Socialism, who has manufactured his own kind of Social-Democracy in his mysterious laboratory." *Contre la Guerre*, March 5, 1913. Andler was suspect not only because he challenged the Socialist position on Social-Democracy, but also because he was himself an anti-Marxist, consistently critical of the German influence in the S.F.I.O. Furthermore, though his articles would have received scant attention in the obscure *L'Action Nationale*, they were reprinted by Alfred Rosmer and Pierre Monatte in the syndicalist review, *La Vie Ouvrière*. For Rosmer's reasons, see his "Première lettre aux abonnés de *La Vie Ouvrière*," in *Les Cahiers du Travail*, No. 2, March 2, 1921, pp. 20–21.

57 At the Congress of Jena in 1911, Rosa Luxemburg was sharply attacked for her public criticisms of the German Socialist Party over its failure to undertake immediately a large-scale anti-imperialist campaign at the time of the Agadir Crisis. See Drachkovitch, *Les Socialismes*, pp. 278–81.

58 Chambre des Députés, *Journal officiel*, June 17, 1913.

59 Paléologue, *Un grand Tournant*, pp. 65–66. Jaurès, of course, was not alone in rejecting Andler's argument. Most of the leaders of the S.F.I.O., who were on friendly terms with the leading Social Democrats, took the same position. Thus, in a letter to Kautsky, Jean Longuet wrote: "I have been asked by our *Commission Administrative* to write a popular pamphlet on 'the German Socialists and Militarism,' a very necessary weapon for our propagandist now, with exceitement going on and after Andler's stupid article in the *Action Nationale*, against whom Grumbach has written such a witty answer in last week's *Neue Zeit*." Longuet to Kautsky, February 19, 1913. Kautsky Archives, Amsterdam. (Written in English.)

60 *L'Humanité*, January 17, 1913, and *Revue de l'enseignement primaire et primaire supérieure*, February 2, 1913.

61 *Un Livre noir*, II, 14.

62 Quoted in Bonnafous, *Histoire politique*, p. 325.

63 Caillaux, *Mes Mémoires*, III, 54–55.

64 *Le Temps*, February 15, 1913.

65 Quoted in Dolléans, *Le Mouvement ouvrier*, II, 208.

66 There were two especially powerful pressure groups among the producers of war materials: The Syndicat des constructeurs de navires, which included such influential spokesmen as Charles Roux and André Lebon (Méline's Ministers of Colonies), and the Syndicat des fabricants et constructeurs de matériel de guerre, a trust of some thirty-five companies, including Schneider's Société du Creusot, Aynard's Compagnie des forges de Saint-Étienne, and Prevet's Société de Montbard-Aulnoye. These groups were analyzed in an article by A. Mairey, a Socialist lycée professor and a friend of Jaurès, in

Le Populaire du centre, April 26, 1914. There is a striking similarity between the remilitarization and the colonial pressure groups. See the description of the colonial bloc in Henri Brunschwig, *Mythes et réalités de l'impérialisme colonial français, 1871–1914* (Paris, 1960), pp. 111–39.

67 Chambre des Députés, *Journal officiel*, March 6, 1913.

68 *L'Humanité*, March 25, 1913. See also *ibid.*, February 20 and 25, 1913.

69 Unpublished letter from General Gamelin to Lucien Lévy-Bruhl, August 25, 1924. Musée Jaurès, Castres. For an excellent description of the hard, daily, untiring work of Jaurès in the Chamber Committee of the Army during the three-year-law debate, see Painlevé, *Paroles et écrits*, pp. 465–68.

70 For the text of the resolution, see Paul Louis, *Histoire du socialisme en France* (Paris, 1925), pp. 309–10.

71 March 9, 1913. For Léon Daudet's unrestrained approval of the Nice incident, see *L'Action française*, March 14, 1913.

72 Charles Péguy, *La République: notre royaume de France* (Paris, 1946), p. 314. The increasing fury of Péguy's attacks led to a decisive break between the editor of the *Cahiers de la quinzaine* and some of his friends and collaborators. Thus, Eugène Fournière, Socialist philosopher and teacher, wrote to Péguy on February 24, 1913: "Obviously, Péguy, too many things now separate us; I can no longer remain a friend of either you or your *Cahiers*. Your recent invective against Jaurès . . . is so excessive that I have no patience left. I don't want to discuss it with you; I wouldn't know how. But I simply want to tell you that what you are doing is an offense to the intelligence, ours as well as yours." This manuscript letter is among the Fournière papers at the Institut Français d'Histoire Sociale in Paris; it was recently published in *L'Actualité de l'histoire*, No. 25, October-November-December, 1958.

73 *Revue de l'enseignement primaire et primaire supérieure*, May 11, 1913.

74 Caillaux, *Mes Mémoires*, III, 61.

75 For Jaurès' response to Barthou on this threat to the unions, see Chambre des Députés, *Journal officiel*, July 4, 1913. Jaurès was almost howled down by the Right and Center, but managed to finish.

76 Henri Bergson in an interview with *Le Gaulois littéraire*, June 15, 1912.

77 *Le Matin*, March 17, 1913.

78 Agathon (pseud. Henri Massis and Alfred de Tarde), *Les jeunes Gens d'aujourd'hui* (Paris, 1912), p. 22. The book won one of the *prix* Montyon of the Académie française.

79 *Ibid.*, p. 28. See also Étienne Rey, *Renaissance de l'orgueil française*, Paris, 1912; and Agathon, *L'Esprit de la nouvelle Sorbonne*, Paris, 1911.

80 The oration on Pressensé was published in *L'Humanité*, January 23, 1914. Pressensé's was the third death in two weeks among men Jaurès admired. Eugène Fournière, the jewelry worker who became a learned professor, died on January 4; General Picquart, the Dreyfusard hero, died on January 18.

81 *Le Matin*, February 4, 1914.

82 The Radical and Radical-Socialist Party adopted rules at Pau to assure unity and discipline. Henceforth, all deputies or political candidates who claimed the Party label had first to receive approval from the Executive Committee in the rue de Valois. In the Chamber, the party representatives were required to submit, on all important issues, to the position of two-thirds of their parliamentary group. Though this action did not eliminate many Radical interlopers, it helped discipline the party.

83 *La Dépêche de Toulouse,* October 20, 1913.
84 *L'Humanité,* November 3, 1913.
85 *La Dépêche de Toulouse,* October 19, 1913. The most outright spokesman of
ministerial participation in the S.F.I.O. was probably Albert Thomas, of
whom one of his contemporaries said in 1913: "He even dreams of a ministerial post; he dreams of it while wide awake, for he is never afraid to tell
what he's dreaming about. One can well believe that this broker's son has
dreamed of throwing his party into a real fix." Quoted in Schaper, *Albert
Thomas,* p. 97. Though Jaurès publicly opposed Guesde's position, he never
suspected either his integrity or his dedication to Socialism. With the others
who espoused a revived millerandism he had a greater problem; some of
them, he knew, looked upon the party only as an instrument for a career.
When Paul Faure wrote in *Le Populaire du centre,* May 14, 1914, that he
could accept temporary election alliances but not ministerialism, he reflected
a majority viewpoint which Jaurès continually put into words. Charles Rappoport, an astringent but generally reliable witness, reported that when
Thomas espoused ministerial participation in 1913, Jaurès was "greatly dis-
pleased." *La Révolution mondiale* (Paris, 1921), p. 77. Of another moderate,
Alexandre Varenne, deputy from the Puy-de-Dôme, Jaurès said that "he
thinks only of Varenne." *Ibid.,* p. 103.
86 *L'Humanité,* December 3, 1913.
87 *Ibid.,* December 12, 1913.
88 *Ibid.,* January 16, 1914.
89 The conversation took place on February 10, 1914. Quoted in Suarez, *Briand,*
II, 464.
90 *Un Livre noir,* II, 245.
91 Dispatch from Guillaume to the Belgian Foreign Office, January 16, 1914.
Quoted in Alfred Rosmer, *Le Mouvement ouvrier pendant la guerre* (Paris,
1936), p. 73.
92 Quoted in Suarez, *Briand,* II, 458.
93 According to a recognized authority on French elections, the alliance of
Caillaux and Jaurès "brought the Center and Right together so that they
represented a single political tendency, just as after 1899 the Center had
actually disappeared and fused with the Right." François Goguel, *Géographie
des élections françaises* (Paris, 1951), p. 40.
94 Raymond Williams, "Class and Voting in Britain," *Monthly Review,* II
(January, 1960), 328. On the imperfect correlation between voting preference
and class position in France, see J.-D. Reynaud and Alain Touraine, "La
Représentation politique du monde ouvrier," in Duverger, *Partis politiques
et classes sociales,* pp. 31–48.
95 The C.G.T. had enrolled in its ranks by 1912 no more than five percent of
the industrial labor force; by 1914, less than sixty percent of the 1,026,302
workers who belonged to the unions had also joined the C.G.T. Short of
working capital but long on internal controversy, the C.G.T. had frightened
off some workers, ignored others, and galvanized only a minority to militant
class action. For a detailed analysis of the figures on labor organization in
the years before 1914, see Drachkovitch, *Les Socialismes,* pp. 149–51. See the
incisive analysis of C.G.T. weaknesses in Michel Collinet, *Esprit du syndicalisme* (Paris, 1951), pp. 149–70.
96 Marcel Sembat, *Faites un roi, sinon faites la paix* (Paris, 1913), p. 70.

97 Goguel, *Élections françaises*, pp. 64–65. The need to win rural votes was so pressing for the S.F.I.O. that the party devoted most of the Congress of Saint-Étienne (April, 1909) to improving its approach to the peasants. The party there adopted the long report of Compère-Morel.

98 *L'Humanité*, July 19, 1914.

99 *Ibid.*, January 28, 1914.

100 Letter to Dazet, March 6, 1914. Guesde Archives, Amsterdam.

101 For the full text of the resolution, see *L'Humanité*, January 29, 1914.

On Jaurès especially, the demands of this all-important election campaign would be almost crushing. Yet two weeks after the Congress of Amiens, he was in Toulouse to deliver an address before an overflowing crowd at the Théâtre des Variétés on February 13; the subject was "The Social Ideas of 19th-Century Novelists." Though the speech was never published, Louis Braud wrote a detailed account of it in *La Dépêche de Toulouse*, February 13, 1914. After touching on the ideas of Tolstoy, Goethe, Dickens, and Disraeli, Jaurès concentrated on the thought of Balzac, George Sand, Flaubert, and Zola — French novelists whom he praised for their depth of human understanding and the courage of their criticism of bourgeois society. His concluding words, which in essence differentiated true patriotism from chauvinism, called the people of France to the mission entrusted to them by these writers: "George Sand said: 'Humanity will soar to the heights!' We should remember this magnificent affirmation and work to make it true; we must conceive of patriotism as the impassioned will to strengthen and develop the peculiar genius of our race."

102 *La Guerre sociale*, July 13–19, 1910.

103 Chambre des Députés, *Journal officiel*, July 11, 1910. For Jaurès' earlier views on the Rochette Affair, see *L'Humanité*, March 28, 1908; April 1 and 10, 1909.

104 *Le Temps*, July 13, 1910.

105 *L'Humanité*, March 21, 1912. For the debate, see Chambre des Députés, *Journal officiel*, March 20, 1912.

106 For the text of the Fabre document, see Maurice Barrès, *Dans Le Cloaque* (Paris, 1914), pp. 4–5.

107 In 1913, Fabre had given the document to Briand, who was then Premier. When Briand fell from office, he passed it to his successor Barthou, who simply took it with him when he left office.

108 The letter contained the comment by Caillaux, who was then Minister of Finance, that he had "crushed the income tax, even while seeming to defend it." The letter had been turned over to Calmette by Mme Gueydan, Caillaux's first wife, who was bitter toward both Caillaux and his former mistress.

109 Chambre des Députés, *Journal officiel*, April 2, 1914.

110 Auclair, *Jaurès*, p. 604.

111 Victor Serge, *Mémoires d'un révolutionnaire, 1901–41* (Paris, 1951), pp. 34–37. Ferrer was a Spanish humanist, executed by the Spanish government on the charge of fomenting a popular uprising. Liabeuf was a twenty-year-old worker who claimed to have been falsely charged and imprisoned as a procurer. On his release, he wounded four policemen, for which he was executed.

112 Quoted in Auclair, *Jaurès*, p. 605. Vincent Auriol rather well described Jaurès' reaction to a hostile crowd: "He had a serene kind of courage, even when directly faced with violent attacks. Once, in 1908 at Toulouse, his face was

full of kindness and sympathy when he had to push through a howling gang and drunks, who hurled threats at him while the police just looked on. He overcame them by the very intrepidity of his attitude." *Le Populaire du centre*, July 30, 1916.

113 The results for the Right and Center were approximately as follows: Fédération républicaine and Républicains progressistes, 54; Action libérale, 34; Droite, 26; Indépendants, 16.

114 For an interesting discussion of the difference between *révolutionnaires* and *révoltés* in the Socialist movement, see J. Martin's article in *Le Populaire de Paris*, February 6, 1921. Around Hervé's *Guerre sociale*, for example, a group of *révoltés* — Eugène Merle, Almereyda, Louis Perceau, Victor Méric — had gathered. Méric has noted how generously Jaurès suffered their *boutades*. See his *Coulisses et tréteaux* (Paris, 1931), p. 150.

115 *Le Journal de Genève*, August 2, 1915.

116 *Le Journal du peuple*, July 31, 1920.

117 Quoted in Weber, *Nationalist Revival*, p. 138. Percin was the unsuccessful Radical candidate at Neuilly-Boulogne.

118 *Ibid.*, p. 139.

119 Quoted in Paix-Séailles, *Jaurès et Caillaux*, p. 134. In a penetrating essay on Jaurès, which constitutes the introduction to her recent collection of Jaurès' writings on war and colonialism, Mme Madeleine Rebérioux offers this explanation of the friendliness of Jaurès toward Caillaux: "Jaurès came to distinguish between two tendencies in contemporary capitalism: an unyielding tendency toward chauvinism, manifested especially in colonial conquests, and a tendency toward organization and internationalism, centered in the *haute banque*, which, in certain circumstances and under popular pressure, could serve the cause of peace. A man like Caillaux, he felt, was the French spokesman of that position. " Jean Jaurès, *Textes choisis. Introduction et notes par Madeleine Rebérioux* (Paris, 1960), p. 33. She goes on to criticize Jaurès for not realizing that Caillaux's position would inevitably break down before the contradictions of capitalism.

Actually, Jaurès never spelled out his views in such categorical terms; but there is no doubt that he distinguished among groups, even though they might represent the same class, and that he based some of his hope for peace on the internationalism of capitalists, especially bankers.

120 Quoted in Paix-Séailles, *Jaurès et Caillaux*, pp. 139–40.

121 Note Isvolsky's comment in a letter to Sazonov, May 21, 1914, when Doumergue's resignation was first in the rumor stage: ". . . we will have nothing to rejoice about if M. Doumergue withdraws, since he has shown no less solicitude for our interests than his predecessors." *Un Livre noir*, II, 268.

122 Jaurès in *L'Humanité*, June 12, 1914.

123 Isvolsky to Sazonov, June 3, 1914. *Un Livre noir*, II, 272.

124 Auclair, *Jaurès*, p. 608.

125 Jaurès, *La Question religieuse*, pp. 20–21. Launay, who prepared the letter for publication, has pointed out that Enjalran undoubtedly meant Marxism when he wrote positivism. In short, Marxist determinism had come to modify, more than ever before, his idealistic faith in human free will. Certainly, Jaurès was always an open, strong critic of positivism, and in a late essay on Socialism and religion he attacked the positivistic cult unsparingly: "If today's so-called liberal bourgeoisie, if, for example, the doctors and lawyers

have so little understanding of the social problem, it is because positivism has made them lose the metaphysical sense — the sense of justice and democracy." *Ibid.*, p. 44.

Enjalran lists in his letter a great number of key writers and thinkers in Western civilization whom Jaurès read or reread extensively in the last years of his life, seeking clues to the great riddles he faced: Homer, Dante, Rousseau, Pascal, Tolstoy, Shakespeare, Cardinal Newman, Hume.

126 Jean Zyromski, "La Scission de Tours (1920)," *Cahiers internationaux*, No. 14 (September-October, 1960), p. 54. Zyromski, who joined the S.F.I.O. in 1912, broke with it during Blum's leadership and is now a member of the French Communist Party. His views on Jaurès are less distorted, however, than those of certain contemporary Socialists who picture him as a social reformer plain and simple.

127 This is the second of the two documents which Launay has presented in Jaurès, *La Question religieuse*, pp. 29–59. A manuscript of twenty-three typed pages, it was probably composed at Bessoulet and made its way into the hands of Enjalran.

128 *Ibid.*, pp. 31, 38. In a striking passage, Jaurès exposed what he considered the deception of hiding "the odious evils" of capitalism behind a veil of Christian piety: "Capitalism is covered over in this society with Christian kindness and generosity, like a foul-smelling factory in a sweet-smelling forest. It depends on the direction of the wind whether one detects the nauseating odors of the factory or the sweet perfumes of the forest." *Ibid.*, p. 29. Jaurès followed this section with a lengthy critique of Christian postulates.

129 *Ibid.*, pp. 30–31.

CHAPTER 14

1 Chambre des Députés, *Journal officiel*, July 7, 1914.

2 Paul Golay, *Le Socialisme qui meurt et le socialisme qui doit renaître* (Lausanne, 1915), pp. 20–21.

The debates of the Congress of Paris are reprinted in *L'Humanité*, July 15, 16, and 17, 1914.

Once the war came, Guesde would become Minister without Portfolio in the coalition ministry. Hervé would convert *La Guerre sociale* into *La Victoire*, a strongly nationalistic sheet. Of Hervé, Frossard wrote in retrospect: "On careful reflection, one could see that his rabid antipatriotism did not express his true nature, that at heart . . . he was always a petty bourgeois democrat and a chauvinistic Frenchman." *De Jaurès à Blum*, p. 161.

Hervé, of course, would soon have history on his side. When war came, the most unyielding antipatriots were unable to act. Some simply turned into ardent patriots; others were afraid. Péricat, a C.G.T. militant, wrote rather pathetically later: "Though I believed neither in frontiers nor in nations, I lacked the force of character not to serve. I admit it; I was afraid." Quoted in Dolléans, *Le Mouvement ouvrier*, II, 221.

Guesde's wartime patriotism strikes one at first as less consistent than that of Vaillant, an old *blanquiste* Communard. But then, the Marxist party was itself inconsistent on the question. Though class and not national allegiance was its basic teaching, the P.O.F. had declared at its Congress in 1893: "If France is attacked, she will have no more ardent defenders than the socialists of the Parti ouvrier."

3 Quoted in Auclair, *Jaurès*, p. 617. For Maurras' bitter attacks, see *L'Action française*, July 18 anad 23, 1914.

4 G. D. H. Cole, quoted in Anne Fremantle, *The Little Band of Prophets* (New York, 1959), p. 217.

5 These included suppression of anti-Austrian publications and organizations (especially the Black Hand), the supervision of education, the removal of anti-Austrian officers and officials, and Austro-Serb collaboration in investigating the Sarajevo plot.

6 On the outbreak of war in 1914, see the following: G. P. Gooch, *Before the War*, New York, 1936; Luigi Albertini, *Origins of the War of 1914*, New York, 1953–57; S. B. Fay, *The Origins of the World War*, 2nd ed., New York, 1941; and B. E. Schmitt, *The Coming of the War, 1914*, New York, 1930.

7 Published in *Vorwärts*, July 25, 1914. Quoted in Joll, *Second International*, p. 160.

8 The speech is reproduced in its entirety in Rosmer, *Le Mouvement ouvrier*, pp. 485–90, from which the following quotations are drawn. Marius Moutet, it might be pointed out, won the special by-election. He served as a Socialist deputy from 1914 to 1942, specializing in problems of colonial reform.

9 Chambre des Députés, *Journal officiel*, October 25, 1895.

10 *L'Humanité*, July 29, 1914.

11 *La Dépêche de Toulouse*, July 30, 1914.

12 *L'Humanité*, July 31, 1915.

13 Martin du Gard, *Summer 1914*, p. 438.

14 *Ibid.*, p. 439.

15 *Ibid.*, p. 440. The speech is reproduced in *L'Humanité*, July 30, 1914.

16 The telegram is reconstructed by Fay, *Origins of the War*, II, 484.

17 On Paléologue's role, see *ibid.*, pp. 443–46, 471–79.

18 *Ibid.*, pp. 491–92.

19 The day before, a mass C.G.T. rally against war had been prohibited by the government. Rosmer, *Le Mouvement ouvrier*, pp. 106–9. Some time during the day of July 30, Jaurès conferred with a delegation of C.G.T. leaders to map a common Socialist-syndicalist strategy against war. The exact circumstances are obscure, but Alphonse Merrheim, Secretary of the Fédération des métaux, mentioned the meeting some four years later in a speech at a C.G.T. congress. See 19ᵉ Congrès national corporatif, tenu à Paris, du 15 au 18 juillet 1918, *Compte rendu des travaux* (Paris, 1919), p. 197.

20 *L'Humanité*, July 31 ,1914.

21 *Le Procès de l'assassin de Jaurès* (Paris, n.d.), p. 62.

22 Fay gives the meaning of *drohende Kriegsgefahr* as follows: "This proclamation set in motion a number of precautionary measures preparatory to actual mobilization." *Origin of the War*, II, 523.

23 Quoted in Auclair, *Jaurès*, p. 642.

24 *L'Humanité*, August 1, 1914.

25 Zévaès, *Jaurès*, p. 251.

26 To understand something of Jaurès unique role in French political life, one should keep in mind that Socialists were still treated rather patronizingly or scornfully by most other deputies. On this subject, Rappoport once wrote: "The Parliament is a very special kind of world, run by bourgeois deputies who set all of its rules. No one much listens to Socialist speakers, except those few, Jaurès especially, who command attention by their outstanding ability. . .

In the corridors, the Socialist intruder has to prove to his skeptical colleagues that he has some culture at least and is not a 'barbarian.' If these *Messieurs* should greet him with a condescending familiarity, he may be flattered and won over." Charles Rappoport, "Communisme et parlementarisme," *La Revue communiste*, No. 7 (September, 1920), p. 80. It meant something then that Jaurès never had to insist upon his culture and could easily resist the flattery of others.

27 *Le Procès de l'assassin de Jaurès*, p. 392.

28 Auclair, *Jaurès*, p. 645.

29 *Le Procès de l'assassin de Jaurès*, p. 391.

30 Trotsky, "Jaurès," p. 849.

31 *L'Humanité*, August 2, 1914. Barrès who, despite the bitter resentment of his Action française friends, retained a lifelong admiration for Jaurès, wrote a letter of genuine sympathy to Madeleine, which was published in *L'Écho de Paris*, August 1, 1914. And in his *Cahiers*, Barrès was moved to write that Jaurès was "for all his faults, a noble man, yes, a great man! Adieu, Jaurès, whom I would have wanted, had it been possible, to love more freely." Quoted in Tétard, *Jaurès*, p. 41.

With Péguy, however, it was different. His attacks on Jaurès had become so frenetic that Zévaès, who in 1919 was the lawyer for Villain, believed the assassin to have been more influenced by Péguy than by *L'Action française*. Zévaès, *Jaurès*, pp. 304–5. Yet on the very day of his assassination, Jaurès carried in his pocket a copy of Péguy's recent article on Bergson, and he spoke of it sympathetically to Léon Brérard. But what was Péguy's reaction to the news of the assassination? "The next day, Péguy greeted the news with what Halévy described as 'a shout of savage exultation.' And Romain Rolland, Péguy's fervent friend, could not help asking very sadly: 'Who was the more Christian of the two?'" Tétard, *Jaurès*, p. 39.

32 *Le Populaire*, January 29, 1940.

33 *L'Humanité*, August 1, 1914.

34 *Ibid.*

35 Quoted in Rosmer, *Le Mouvement ouvrier*, p. 113.

36 *L'Humanité*, August 1, 1914. Poincaré, of course, was concerned with integrating the working-class movement into the Union sacrée. In the Poincaré household, if one can believe the word of Victor Margueritte, the presence of Jaurès was hardly a cause for joy. He attributed to Mme Poincaré these words spoken shortly before the war: "What we should have are a good war and the suppression of Jaurès." Victor Margueritte, *Aristide Briand* (Paris, 1932), pp. 136–37.

37 Germany declared war on Russia on August 1 and on France on August 3. On August 4, England declared war on Germany for violation of Belgian neutrality.

38 Rappoport's position is reproduced in a short pamphlet, *Défense légitime contre une attaque brusquée de Renaudel*, Paris, 1915. Renaudel's attack on Rappoport appeared in *L'Humanité*, August 20, 1915. To a great extent the debate centered around the question whether or not, as Rappoport reported in the *Berner Tagwacht* (July 31, 1915), Jaurès actually said to Abel Ferry: "We will continue our campaign against war." This, of course, could have implied action, even strike action, in case of war. Renaudel, who was witness to the conversation with Ferry, did not mention it in his article in *L'Humanité*,

August 2, 1914; then, he categorically denied it in his response to Rappoport. But Marcel Cachin and Jean Longuet, both of whom were with Jaurès during his interview with Ferry, confirmed it, the former *Ibid.*, August 1, 1914, the latter in the *Labour Leader*, September 9, 1915. Essential confirmation, however, has come from Abel Ferry himself, who wrote in his private notebook, recently published: "He [Jaurès] had come to see me with a delegation three hours earlier, and here are the notes I took while he spoke: 'You are victims of Isvolsky and of Russian intrigue; we will denounce you, harebrained ministers, even if we should be shot.'" *Les Carnets secrets d'Abel Ferry, 1914–18* (Paris, 1958), pp. 26–27.

Two other reports of comments by Jaurès in the last days before the war, both of them unconfirmed by other sources, indicate that he would have considered the French government less guilty than the German when war came. Roubanovitch reported as follows a conversation between Jaurès and the German Socialists at Brussels on July 29: "At around six in the evening, during the meeting of the International Socialist Bureau, Jaurès, turning to Comrades Kautsky and Haase, asked them the following question: 'Are you absolutely sure, as you have just said in your analysis of the situation, that your government and your emperor especially, knew nothing of the Austrian ultimatum to Serbia?' Haase replied: 'I am absolutely convinced that our government has had no part in that quarrel.' Jaurès shook his head and expressed his doubts. Among other facts, he cited the case of an influential German journalist who, when leaving Paris a few days before, had said quite openly that within a few days 'one would hear a resounding blow on our Kaiser's table.'" *Le Populaire du centre*, October 21, 1914.

Bedouce, who saw him frequently during those last days, reported that Jaurès, from the time he returned from Brussels, was in daily touch with the French government. First, he was assured by M. Bienvenu-Martin, the acting Foreign Minister during Viviani's absence, that France would work with England to mediate the conflict. Then, after his interview with Viviani, when the Premier had not only reiterated the government's agreement with British mediation proposals but had also said that French troops would be pulled back from the frontier, Jaurès seemed satisfied that his government was doing what it could. On leaving Viviani's office, he reportedly turned to Bedouce and said: "You know, Bedouce, if we were in their place, I don't know what more we could do now to assure peace." *Ibid.*, August 3, 1915.

39 Cole, *Second International*, II, 94. Cole's judgment certainly coincides with the attitude of those Socialists who supported the war at the start but who, as it dragged on at frightful cost, demanded some sort of peace settlement long before the official heads of the S.F.I.O. were willing to support it. He would have acted, they felt, on the dictum of Stuttgart of 1907: "In case war should nonetheless break out, they [the working class and its representatives] are obliged to intervene in order to bring it promptly to a halt." See, for example, Alvarez' article in *Le Populaire du centre*, February 9, 1915.

Even if he had rallied to the national cause, would Jaurès, once the spokesman of Ministerialism, have accepted a government post? Again there is no definite answer, despite the assumption of many commentators. One might well ponder the implication of a statement Jaurès made ten years earlier in the midst of the debates at Amsterdam. Under discussion was the resolution Kautsky had composed at the Congress of Paris of 1900, which foresaw ministerial participation only under exceptional circumstances, by which, he explained, he meant a threat of invasion. At Amsterdam, Jaurès answered Kautsky in these words: "When I heard citizen Kautsky say that he could conceive of the possibility of socialist participation in the government in case of a threat to the nation, I asked myself whether Ministerialism would become orthodox only to support nationalism and whether it was legitimate to abandon the class struggle only in order to defend a homeland run and exploited by the bourgeoisie. I asked myself if political liberty, individual freedom, the right of association were not of more essential interest to socialists than *la patrie*. I feel, in certain circumstances, that I could not follow our comrade to the limits of his nationalistic Ministerialism."

40 *L'Humanité*, November 24, 1924.

41 In the immediate aftermath of the war, Jaurès was still the victim of nationalistic antagonism. Thus, on March 29, 1919, Raoul Villain, who had been imprisoned during the war years while awaiting trial, was acquitted. The chief calculations of the jury were probably anti-Socialism and the acquittal of Mme Caillaux right before the war.

Villain nonetheless suffered a violent end. Unable to find regular employment in the years after his release, and then picked up by the police for passing counterfeit money, he finally drifted to Spain. In Minorca, after the civil war had begun in 1936, he was killed by republican soldiers.

42 Such was the theme stressed by Camille Huysmans, the representative of the Second International, who declared at Jaurès' funeral: "For us, for ten million organized workers across the world, . . . he was more than the Word. He was Conscience itself." *L'Humanité*, August 5, 1914.

43 *Le Journal de Genève*, August 2, 1915.

Bibliography

UNPUBLISHED MANUSCRIPTS

The unpublished Jaurès correspondence is relatively small. As far as one can gather, Jaurès wrote few long, reflective letters. So crowded was his schedule that he simply had no time for extensive correspondence. Essentially, he expressed himself through his published articles, which occasionally struck the personal note of letters. Nonetheless, the search for manuscripts proved to be far from fruitless. The archives and libraries listed below possess collections of unpublished papers which shed some light on the life of Jaurès and the history of French Socialism.

International Institute for Social History (Amsterdam). The Institute possesses an excellent collection of unpublished letters written or received by several important leaders of the Second International. The Guesde Archives, which are particularly useful, contain hundreds of letters which Guesde received between 1892 and 1914 from such leading Marxists as Lafargue, Lavigne, Bracke, Liebknecht, and Rappoport. The Kautsky Archives contain revealing letters to Kautsky from Jean Longuet, Vaillant, and Rappoport. In the Bernstein Archives, there is one very important letter from Jaurès and an interesting one from Albert Thomas.

Bibliothèque Nationale (Paris). In the manuscript collection of the BN, there are some fifty letters to or from Jaurès. The group of sixteen from Jaurès to Charles Salomon, written between 1880 and 1914, has been published by Lévy-Bruhl or Auclair (see below — Published Correspondence). Those still unpublished are as follows: NAF 24328 (64–72); 24274 (84–92); 24520 (427–29); 24497 (47–50); 13191 (174–180, 185–86).

Institut Français d'Histoire Sociale (Paris). The *Institut* has three of Jaurès letters, written in 1904, about the founding of *L'Humanité*, and a number of drafts for *La Dépêche de Toulouse* articles. Among the Eugène Fournière papers, there is an unpublished essay by Jaurès on the Russian Revolution of 1905. In the papers of both Fournière and Paul Delesalle there are letters with references to Jaurès.

Musée de l'Histoire (Montreuil). This museum possesses not only part of Jaurès' library but also certain unpublished *fiches* and *carnets*. These are notes on his extensive reading, outlines for speeches, and drafts of articles and books.

Musée Jaurès (Castres). The museum has acquired some eighty letters by Jaurès. Though most of them are trivial, certain others are of historical interest: nine letters to Jean Julien, written between 1878 and 1886; four letters to J.-B. Calvignac, the socialist mayor of Carmaux; and one to Aulard, written in 1902 and concerning Jaurès' history of the French Revolution. The museum has a smaller number of letters about Jaurès.

Musée Social (Paris). This library contains a few manuscripts of some interest: an unsigned letter probably written by Sirven, vice-president of the Carmaux glass works at the time of the 1895 strike; a few Pelloutier letters in a collection of newspaper clippings about that syndicalist leader.

Archives Nationales (Paris). Two documents related to the glass strike of 1895 are of interest: BB^{18} 2010; Dos. 2244 A95 and BB^{18} 1999; Dos. 1215 A95.

PUBLISHED WRITINGS AND
SPEECHES OF JAURÈS

The articles and speeches of Jaurès comprise a source of almost endless riches for the biographer. So much did he write and so often did he speak that his published words constitute a detailed record of his political and intellectual evolution, a catalogue of major and minor European issues before 1914, and a gallery of portraits of his leading contemporaries.

By their very volume, however, and their appearance in widely scattered newspapers and journals, these published writings present a major challenge to the biographer. Some fifteen years after Jaurès' death, a *comité de publication* was organized by certain of his friends to sponsor the publication of his *Complete Works*. To M. Max Bonnafous fell the task of collecting, organizing, and editing these writings. On May 11, 1931, the first volume of the *Oeuvres de Jean Jaurès* appeared, but in his preface, M. Bonnafous announced that his edition would contain only selected writings of Jaurès. His explanation was as follows: "When we decided to publish the works of Jean Jaurès, we had no very clear idea of the magnitude of such a publishing venture. We knew that the sum of his works was very large; we discovered that it was enormous. At the end of a few months of work, we realized that to publish his complete works would require 80 or 90 octavo volumes of some 400 pages each." Instead of such an enormous edition, Bonnafous promised about thirty volumes, containing the most important and representative books, articles, and speeches. Unfortunately, World War II interrupted publication of the Bonnafous edition, and only nine volumes of the projected thirty ever appeared.

For the sake of all those interested in Jaurès, and especially of his future biographers, one can only hope that a more definitive edition of his writings, including all of the known unpublished correspondence, will one day appear. At present, one must search widely to track down Jaurès' writings. The following references, however, should provide the key to that search.

Books

De la Réalité du monde sensible. Paris, Félix Alcan, 1891. A second edition, revised and corrected, was published by Alcan in 1902. This edition was republished by Bonnafous as Volume VIII of the *Oeuvres.* Paris, Rieder, 1937.

De Primis socialismi germanici lineamentis apud Lutherum, Kant, Fichte, et Hegel. Toulouse, A. Chauvin et fils, 1891. This Latin thesis was translated into French by Adrien Veber for the *Revue socialiste* (June, July, August, 1892). This translation then appeared in book form as *Les Origines du socialisme allemand.* Paris, Écrivains Réunis, 1927. It was included by Bonnafous in Volume III of the *Oeuvres.* Paris, Rieder, 1931, 49–111. It has recently been republished with a useful preface by Lucien Goldmann. Paris, François Maspero, 1960.

Histoire socialiste (1789–1900), ed. Jean Jaurès. 13 Vols., Paris, Jules Rouff, 1901–8. Jaurès himself wrote Volumes I through IV, called collectively *L'Histoire socialiste de la Révolution française: La Constituante* (1901), *La Législative* (1901), *La Convention* (2 Vols., 1902). He also wrote the first part of Volume XI, *La Guerre franco-allemande (1870–71)* (1908) and a summary essay at the end of volume XII, entitled "Le Bilan social du XIXe siècle" (1908). The four long volumes on the French Revolution were later republished in a much more attractive edition by Albert Mathiez: *Histoire socialiste de la Révolution française.* 8 Vols., Paris, Éditions de la librairie de *L'Humanité,* 1922–24.

L'Organisation socialiste de la France. L'Armée nouvelle. Paris, Jules Rouff, 1911. A second edition of *L'Armée nouvelle* included a preface by L. Lévy-Bruhl. Paris, Éditions de la librairie de *L'Humanité,* 1915. It was published a third time as Volume IV of the *Oeuvres.* Paris, Rieder, 1932.

Newspaper and Periodical Articles

Newspapers and periodicals in which articles by Jaurès appeared regularly:
La Dépêche de Toulouse (1887–1914). The dates refer to the years during which he contributed.
La petite République (1893–1904)
L'Humanité (1904–14)
La Revue de l'enseignement primaire et primaire supérieure (1905–14)

Newspapers and periodicals in which articles by Jaurès appeared occasionally:

La Lanterne	*La Revue socialiste*
Le Matin	*La Revue de Paris*
Cosmopolis	*Le Mouvement socialiste*
Le Bulletin de la Ligue des droits de l'homme	

Collections of newspaper and periodical articles:
Les Preuves. Paris, *La petite République,* 1898. This is a collection of the articles on the Dreyfus Affair which Jaurès wrote for *La petite République* in 1898.
Études socialistes. Paris, Ollendorff, 1902. This is a collection of articles on socialist

theory which first appeared in *La petite République*. An abridged English version, translated by Mildred Minturn, appeared as *Studies in Socialism*. London, Independent Labour Party, 1906. These articles were republished by Bonnafous as part of Volume VI of the *Oeuvres*. Paris, Rieder, 1933.

MISCELLANEOUS ESSAYS

"Duchâtel à François Iᵉʳ: 'discours français' pour le Concours général, année 1878, par M.-J.-J.-A. Jaurès," in *Recueil de discours français. Extraits des Annales des concours généraux, période de 1831 à 1897.* (Paris, Delalain frères, 1879), pp. 376–81. This essay, written by Jaurès while a student at Sainte-Barbe, was thus his first publication.

"Socialisme et radicalisme in 1885." This is an extremely important essay of 178 pages, which Jaurès wrote as the introduction to a collection of his *Discours parlementaires*, ed. Edmond Claris. Paris, Édouard Cornély, 1904.

"La Question religieuse et le socialisme." This is the title given to a previously un-published essay which has recently been edited and published by Michel Launay: *La Question religieuse et le socialisme*. Paris, Les Éditions de Minuit, 1959. The first part of this volume contains a letter, written during World War I, from Enjalran to Lévy-Bruhl, which discusses Jaurès' thought in the late years of his life.

PREFACES

A list of Jaurès' prefaces to books, fourteen in number, has been compiled by Georges Tétard in his *Essais sur Jean Jaurès* (Colombes, Centre d'apprentissage d'imprimerie, 1959), pp. 195–98.

PARLIAMENTARY SPEECHES

Journal officiel de la Chambre des Députés, 1886–89, 1893–98, 1902–14. This is the essential source. Maurice Boitel, in his *Les Idées libérales dans le socialisme de Jaurès* (Paris, L'Émancipatrice, 1921), pp. 191–200, compiled a very useful list of 380 major speeches. He included the dates and subjects of the speeches.

Discours parlementaires, ed. Edmond Claris. Paris, Édouard Cornély, 1904. This is an excellent edition of the speeches Jaurès delivered in the Chambers of Deputies between October, 1886, and December, 1894.

Because of their great value in the spread of socialist doctrine, Jaurès' most im-portant orations were sometimes published as separate pamphlets which might run to sixty or seventy pages in length. The citations below refer only to the first such publication, though some of the speeches were published one or more addi-tional times; indication is given, however, if the speech appears also in the *Oeuvres*.

Le Socialisme à la Chambre. Lille, Imprimerie ouvrière, 1893. Speech of Novem-ber 21, 1893. Also in *Oeuvres*, III, 225–41.

L'Instruction publique. Paris, Godfroy, 1896. Speeches of June 21, 1894, and February 11, 1895.

Patriotisme et l'internationalisme. Paris, Bureau du *Socialiste*, n.d. Speech of April 8, 1895. This pamphlet contains also a manifesto of the Parti ouvrier français.

La Grève de Carmaux. Paris, Bibliothèque du Parti ouvrier français, 1895. Speech of November 24 and 25, 1895.

Socialisme et paysans. Paris. *Petite République,* 1897. Speech of June 19 and 26, and July 3, 1897.

L'Internationalisme à la Chambre. Paris, Librairie du Parti socialiste, 1906. Speech delivered December 8 and 15, 1905. Also in *Oeuvres,* II, 411–53.

Replique à Clemenceau. Paris, Éditions de *L'Humanité,* 1906. Speech of June 12, 14, 15, and 18, 1906.

La Grève des électriciens. Paris, V. Lecoffre, n.d. Speeches delivered by Jaurès, Clemenceau, and Biétry on March 11, 1907.

Discours prononcé par le citoyen Jaurès dans le discussion du projet de loi sur l'impôt sur le revenu. Paris, *L'Humanité,* 1908. Speech of February 27 and 28, 1908.

Le Parti socialiste et la crise postale. Paris, *L'Humanité,* n.d. Speech of May 13, 1909.

Pour la Laïque. Paris, *L'Humanité,* 1910. Speech of January 21 and 24, 1910.

L'Accord franco-allemand. La Protestation du droit. Pour la Paix contre la guerre. Paris, *L'Humanité,* n.d. Speech of December 19 and 20, 1911. Also in *Oeuvres,* VII, 394–434.

Contre les trois Ans. Paris, *L'Humanité,* 1913. Speech of June 17 and 18, 1913.

Contre l'Emprunt et le déficit. Paris, *L'Humanité,* 1913. Speech of November 27, 1913.

Non-parliamentary Speeches

Since Jaurès did not write out his speeches, but delivered them from brief notes, many of them have probably been lost to history. A very thorough search of the provincial socialist press might recover at least summaries of some of those. His most important speeches, however, especially those in Paris and other major cities, were usually published in the socialist dailies or journals from stenographic notes. A good number of these speeches were republished as separate pamphlets. The citations below refer to the first such publication.

Speeches on socialist theory and action:

Idéalisme et matérialisme dans la conception de l'histoire. Paris, Imprimerie spéciale, 1895. Also in *Oeuvres,* VI, 225–41. This is the debate with Paul Lafargue.

Les deux Méthodes. Lille, Imprimerie de P. Legrange, 1900. Also in *Oeuvres,* VI, 187–219. This is the debate with Jules Guesde.

Bernstein et l'évolution de la méthode socialiste. Paris, Librairie populaire, 1926. Also in *Oeuvres,* VI, 117–40.

Conférence du citoyen Jean Jaurès, au grand théâtre de Nîmes, 4 février 1910. Nîmes, Imprimerie Coöpérative *L'Ouvrier,* 1910.

Jean Jaurès et les causes de la guerre. Paris, Comité pour la reprise des relations internationales, n.d. Jaurès delivered this speech at Vaise on July 25, 1914. Also in *Oeuvres*, IX, 382–86.

Speeches before socialist congresses: The debates of the French socialist congresses, both before and after unity in 1905, and of the International Socialist Congresses, comprise an essential source of information on the history of French socialism. Especially from 1899 on, Jaurès played a very active part in these congresses, and in the reports of the debates one can find some of his most important statements on socialist theory and practice. A comprehensive list of these reports appears in Aaron Noland's *The Founding of the French Socialist Party, 1893–1905.* (Cambridge, Mass., Harvard University Press, 1956), 211–14. They are also conveniently listed in Jack Alden Clarke's "French Socialist Congresses, 1876–1914," *Journal of Modern History*, XXXI, (1959), 124–29.

Speeches on education, literature, and philosophy:

Discours prononcé à la distribution solennelle des prix du lycée d'Albi, le 3 août 1883. Albi, Imprimerie de Pezous, n.d.

Discours prononcé par M. Jean Jaurès à la distribution solennelle des prix, le 31 juillet 1888. Albi, Imprimerie de Pezous, n.d.

Les Idées politiques et sociales de Jean-Jacques Rousseau. Paris, A. Colin, 1912. This was originally a lecture Jaurès delivered at Toulouse on December 19, 1889. It was published as an extract from the May, 1912, issue of the *Revue de métaphysique et de morale*.

L'Art et le socialisme. Paris, Le Théâtre civique, 1900. Also in *Oeuvres*, VI, 143–57.

Deux Discours sur Tolstoï. Paris, L'Emancipatrice, 1911. This pamphlet contains Anatole France's speech on Tolstoy, delivered at the Sorbonne on March 12, 1911, as well as Jaurès' speech delivered in Toulouse on February 10, 1911.

Miscellaneous Speeches:

"Compliment à Fustel de Coulanges, directeur de l'École Normale Supérieure," *Europe*, No. 354–55 (October–November, 1958), pp. 121–25. As the *cacique,* the student who had scored highest in the entrance examinations, Jaurès delivered for his class the 1881 address to the head of the École Normale. Though only recently published, it was nonetheless Jaurès' first public oration.

"Extraits du cours de philosophie," *Europe*, No. 354–55 (October–November, 1958), pp. 126–39. The lectures on philosophy, which Jaures delivered at the *lycée* of Albi in 1882–83, were preserved in two notebooks by one of his students, Louis Rascol. These notebooks are now in the *Collège Technique Louis Rascol.* From them, Michel Launay published these significant portions.

Alliance française. Association nationale pour la propagation française dans les colonies et à l'étranger. Conférence de M. Jean Jaurès, Maître de Conférences à la Faculté des Lettres de Toulouse. Albi, Imprimerie de Pezous, n.d.

Le Procès du "Chambard," plaidorie de Jean Jaurès. Paris, Bureau du *Chambard,* 1895.

Conferencias. Prologo de Juan B. Justo. Buenos Aires, Vanguardia, 1911. This is a collection of speeches which Jaurès delivered in South America in 1911. They were published in Spanish, and only two of them have appeared in French: one, under the title "Civilization et socialisme" in Henri Barbusse's journal *Clarté*, No. 40 (July 31, 1923), 333–36; another, on French military organization, in *Europe*, No. 354–55 (October–November, 1958), pp. 98–106.

COLLECTIONS OF PUBLISHED ARTICLES AND SPEECHES

Action socialiste. Le socialisme et l'enseignement; le socialisme et les peuples. Paris, G. Bellais, 1899. This is a collection of certain parliamentary speeches as well as articles from *La Dépêche de Toulouse* and *La petite République*; one article is from *La Revue bleue*. Péguy was primarily responsible for the publication, as he was for the *Études socialistes*.

Anthologies published since the death of Jaurès:
Desanges, Paul and Mériga, Luc. *Pages choisies*. Paris, Rieder, 1922.
———. *Pages choisies*. 2ᵉ série. Paris, Rieder, 1928.
Vandervelde, Émile. *Jaurès*. Paris, F. Alcan, 1929.
Crastre, F. *Les plus beaux Discours de Jaurès*. Paris, Éditions du Centaure, 1931.
Lévy, Louis. *Anthologie de Jean Jaurès*. Paris, Calmann-Lévy, 1946.
Bourgin, Georges. *Jaurès*. Monaco, Éditions Hemmera, 1952.
Rebérioux, Madeleine. *Textes choisis. Tome Iᵉʳ. Contre la Guerre et la politique coloniale*. Paris, Éditions Sociales, 1959. This is a work of solid research, containing not only an excellent fifty-page introduction but also several little-known articles and speeches.

PUBLISHED CORRESPONDENCE

The few letters of Jaurès which have thus far been published in full or in part appear in the following:
Lévy-Bruhl, L. *Jean Jaurès, esquisse biographique. Nouvelle édition suivie de lettres inédites*. Paris, Rieder, 1924. Sixteen letters from Jaurès to Charles Salomon, based on manuscripts in the Bibliothèque Nationale, are appended on pages 131–85.
"Lettres inédites," *La nouvelle Revue*, LXXV (January 1, 1925), 3–10. Only one of these several letters is by Jaurès; the others are by Anatole France. They were all addressed to Dr. Loris-Mélicof, an Armenian patriot, and expressed sympathy for the Armenian cause.
"Lettres inédites," *Europe*, No. 122 (February 15, 1933), pp. 153–73. Of these thirteen letters published by Bonnafous, nine were written by Jaurès to his wife and son during his trip to South America in the summer of 1911. Three are letters of sympathy to his brother Louis, commanding officer of the battleship *Liberté* when it was destroyed by an explosion. One was written to his *vénéré maître* Henri Weil on his ninetieth birthday.
"Huit lettres de jeunesse de Jean Jaurès," *Revue d'Histoire Économique et Sociale*, Vol. XXXVIII (1960), No. 1, 41–53. These eight leters, carefully annotated by Elizabeth Poulain, were written by Jaurès to Jean Julien between February 24, 1878, and March 5, 1886. They are part of the manuscript collection at the *Musée*

Jaurès; their most important passages had already been quoted by Mme Auclair.
Auclair, Marcelle. *La Vie de Jean Jaurès, ou la France d'avant 1914.* Paris, Éditions de Seuil, 1954. Mme Auclair quoted those passages from the Jaurès-Salomon group, which Lévy-Bruhl had left out. She also quoted from the Jaurès-Julien correspondence at the *Musée Jaurès.*
Schaper, B. W. *Albert Thomas trente ans de réformisme social.* Paris, Presses Universitaires de France, n.d. On pages 31 and 32, two letters, written by Jaurès early in 1903 to Albert Thomas, are summarized and quoted. They express Jaurès' attitudes at the time toward the German Marxists.

Three other Jaurès letters have been published: 1) In *L'Humanité*, February 9, 1922, Albert Mathiez published a letter of appreciation, dated February 4, 1904, which Jaurès sent to him after he had reviewed the first half of the *Histoire socialiste de la Révolution française* in *La Revue critique.* 2) In the Preface to the third edition of his *Jean Jaurès. L'Homme, le penseur, le socialiste* (Paris, Marcel Rivière, 1925), Charles Rappoport included a letter he had received from Jaurès in 1901. 3) In his *Aulard, historien de la Révolution française* (Paris: Presses Universitaires de France, 1949), Georges Belloni included on page 45 the letter Aulard received from Jaurès after he had reviewed Jaurès' history.

COLLECTED WORKS

Oeuvres de Jean Jaurès. Textes rassemblés, présentes et annotés par Max Bonnafous. 9 vols., Paris, Rieder, 1931–39. The Bonnafous collection has certain serious shortcomings. It contains few speeches by Jaurès, and the articles it includes deal almost exclusively with foreign policy, imperialism, and socialist theory. There is very little on strikes, the peasant problem, or domestic politics. Yet the *Oeuvres* are an important contribution to Jaurès studies and a monument to their editor. For in these nine handsome volumes some of the best writings of Jaurès have been made easily available to scholars and general readers.

BIOGRAPHIES AND OTHER
STUDIES OF JAURÈS

BOOKS AND SIGNIFICANT PERIODICAL ARTICLES

Auclair, Marcelle. *La Vie de Jaurès, ou la France d'avant 1914.* Paris, Éditions du Seuil, 1954. Though it is not a serious history of either French Socialism or the Third Republic, this moving book, better than any other biography, brings alive the personality of Jaurès.
Auriol, Vincent. *Souvenirs sur Jean Jaurès.* Paris, Éditions de la Liberté, 1945.
Blum, Léon. *Jean Jaurès. Conférence donné le 16 février 1933 au théâtre des Ambassadeurs.* Paris, Librairie Populaire, 1933.
Boitel, Maurice. *Les Idées libérales dans le socialisme de Jaurès.* Paris, L'Émancipatrice, 1921.
Bruhat, Jean. "Jean Jaurès devant le problème colonial," in *Cahiers internationaux*, No. 94 (March, 1958), pp. 43–62.
Challaye, Félicien. *Jaurès.* Paris, Mellottée, n.d. Written for a series on *Les Philoso-*

phes, this is the most detailed study of Jaurès as a philosopher.

Desanges, Paul and Mériga, Luc. *Vie de Jean Jaurès*. Paris, G. Crès, 1924.

Feuillard, Jean. *Jaurès, homme d'aujourd'hui*. Périgueux, P. Fanlac, 1950.

Figuères, Léo. "La Pensée et l'action politiques de Jaurès," *Cahiers du communisme* (April, 1956), pp. 413–35.

———. "Sur la Position de Jaurès et du jaurèssisme dans le mouvement ouvrier français d'avant 1914," *Cahiers du communisme* (January–February, 1956), pp. 76–93.

Gaumont, Jean. *Au Confluent de deux grandes idées. Jaurès coopérateur*. Paris, Fédération Nationale des Coopérateurs de Consommation, 1959.

Gouttenoire de Toury, F. *Jaurès et le parti de la guerre*. Paris, Rieder, 1922.

Jackson, J. Hampden. *Jean Jaurès*. London, 1942.

Klement, J., *Jaurès réformiste*. Paris, Bureau d'Éditions, 1937.

Lair, Maurice. *Jaurès et l'Allemagne*. Paris, Perrin, 1935.

Larguier, Léo. *Le Citoyen Jaurès*. Paris, Éditions des Partiques, 1932.

Lévy-Bruhl, L. *Jean Jaurès, esquisse biographique. Nouvelle édition suivie de lettres inédites*. Paris, Rieder, 1923.

———. *Quelques pages sur Jean Jaurès*. Paris, Librairie de *L'Humanité*, 1916.

Méric, Victor. *Coulisses et tréteaux. A travers la jungle politique et littéraire*. Paris, Librairie Valois, 1931.

Paix-Séailles, Charles. *Jaurès et Caillaux*. Paris, Figuière, 1920.

Pease, Margaret. *Jean Jaurès*. London, 1916.

Rappoport, Charles. *Jean Jaurès, l'homme, le penseur, le socialiste*. Paris, L'Emancipatrice, 1915. Written soon after the assassination, this book still ranks as one of the best studies of Jaurès' thought.

Shao, Ho-Ting. *La Pensée de Jaurès, sa théorie de la Révolution*. Paris, L. Rodstein, 1932.

Soulé, Louis. *La Vie de Jaurès (1859–92)*. Paris, Floréal, 1921.

Tétard, Georges. *Essais sur Jean Jaurès*. Colombes, Centre d'apprentissage d'imprimerie, 1959. This book includes a very fine annotated bibliography.

Téry, Gustave. *Jaurès*. Paris, *Oeuvre*, 1915.

Toussaint, Franz. *Jaurès intime*. Toulouse, Privat, 1952.

Trempé, Rolande. "L'Échec électoral de Jaurès à Carmaux, 1898, *Cahiers internationaux*, No. 93 (February, 1958), pp. 47–64.

———. "Les premières Luttes des mineurs de Carmaux," *Cahiers internationaux*, No. 62 (January, 1955), pp. 49–66. These articles, based on original research are among the few very solid historical contributions to Jaurès studies.

Trotsky, Leon. "Jean Jaurès," *Bulletin Communiste*, No. 47 (November 22, 1923), pp. 845–49.

Vogt, Blanche. "Un Jaurès inconnu," *Les Oeuvres libres*, CXL (1933), 295–336.

Weinstein, Harold. *Jean Jaurès, a Study of Patriotism in the French Socialist Movement*. New York, Columbia University Press, 1936.

Zévaès, Alexandre. *Un Apôtre du rapprochement franco-allemand*. Paris, Aux Armes de France, 1941.

———. *Jean Jaurès*. Paris, La Clé d'Or, 1951.

———. "Jules Guesde et Jean Jaurès," *Revue de Paris*, No. 13 (July 1, 1936), pp.

79–112. An indefatigable historian of French Socialism, Zévaès was often rather superficial. When he wrote, as in this article, on the basis of his own observations within the movement, he offered many valuable insights.

Jaurès par ses contemporains. Ouvrage précédé d'une introduction par F. Pignatel. Paris, Étienne Chiron, 1925.

Le Procès de l'assassin de Jaurès. Paris, Éditions de *L'Humanité*, 1920.

NEWSPAPER ARTICLES

Countless articles about Jaurès have appeared in the Socialist, Communist, and syndicalist press. Some of them, written by friends and observers, contain valuable bits of information about the personality, thoughts, or impact of Jaurès. Those listed below are a few of the most useful:

Auriol, Vincent, in *Le Populaire du centre*, July 30, 1916.
Bernstein, Eduard, in *Le Journal du peuple*, July 8, 1917.
Blum, Léon, in *L'Humanité*, July 31, 1915.
France, Anatole, in *L'Humanité*, March 24, 1919.
Frossard, L.-O., in *Paris-Soir*, August 1, 1925.
Jouhaux, Léon, in *L'Humanité*, August 2, 1915.
Mauriac, François, in *Le Figaro*, August 6, 1946.
Paul-Boncour, Joseph, in *L'Humanité*, July 31, 1919.
Rouanet, Gustave, in *L'Humanité*, May 21 and 22, 1916.
Téry, Gustave, in *L'Oeuvre*, June 3, 1923.
Valière, Sabinus, in *Le Populaire du centre*, July 31, 1916.
Vandervelde, Émile, in *L'Humanité*, July 31, 1915.

SPECIAL JAURES ISSUES OF PERIODICALS

Revue de l'enseignement primaire et primaire supérieure, November 23, 1924.
Les Hommes du Jour, August, 1935.
Actualité de l'Histoire, No. 17, December, 1956.
Europe, No. 354–55, October-November, 1958.
Revue d'Histoire Économique et Sociale, Vol. XXXVIII (1960), No. 1.

NEWSPAPER SOURCES FOR FRENCH AND SOCIALIST HISTORY, 1885–1914

The newspaper resources for the study of the political and social history of the Third Republic are rich and valuable. In addition to those dailies, already cited above, for which Jaurès wrote, those listed below, ranging from the extreme monarchist Right to the extreme syndicalist Left, proved helpful. The dates in parentheses indicate the years of publication:

L'Action (1903–32)
L'Action française (1908–40)
L'Aurore (1897–1914)
La Bataille syndicaliste (1911–20)
Le Bonnet rouge (1913–17)
L'Écho de Paris (1884–1938)

L'Éclaireur de l'Ain (1894–1933)
Le Figaro (1854–1942)
Le Gaulois (1868–1929)
La Guerre sociale (1906–15)
L'Intransigeant (1880–1940)
Le Journal des débats (1800–1939)

Le Libertaire (1895–1914)
La libre Parole (1892–1924)
Le Parti ouvrier (1888–1914)
Le Populaire du centre (1905–34)
Le Radical (1881–1928)

Le Socialisme (1907–12)
Le Socialiste (1885–1913)
Le Temps (1861–1942)
La Voix du peuple (1900–14)

A SELECTED LIST
OF USEFUL BOOKS

For a much more complete bibliography, the reader is advised to consult the notes.

Andler, Charles. *Vie de Lucien Herr (1864–1926)*. Paris, Rieder, 1932.

Beau de Loménie, E. *Les Responsabilités des dynasties bourgeoises*. 3 Vols., Paris, Denoël, 1943–54. Volume II covers the period from 1876 to 1914.

Bernstein, Samuel. *The Beginnings of Marxian Socialism in France*. New York, Social Science Studies, 1933.

Blum, Léon. *Souvenirs sur l'Affaire*. Paris, Gallimard, 1935.

Bonnafous, Georges. *Histoire politique de la troisième République*. 2 Vols., Paris, Presses Universitaires de France, 1956–58. The first volume covers the years 1906–14.

Brogan, Denis W. *France Under the Republic*. New York, Harper and Bros., 1940.

Byrnes, Robert F. *Antisemitism in Modern France*. New Brunswick, New Jersey, Rutgers University Press, 1950.

Caillaux, Joseph. *Mes Mémoires*. 3 Vols., Paris, Plon, 1942–47.

Chapman, Guy. *The Dreyfus Case, a Reassessment*. London, R. Hart-Davis, 1955.

Chastenet, Jacques. *Histoire de la troisième République*. 4 Vols., Paris, Hachette, 1952–57. This work is still in progress, but these four volumes cover the period from 1870 to 1918.

Cole, G. D. H. *The Second International, 1889–1914*. 2 Vols., London, Macmillan, 1956. These volumes are the third and fourth of a series entitled *A History of Socialist Thought*.

Combes, Émile. *Mon Ministère. Mémoires, 1902–5*. Paris, Plon, 1956.

Compère-Morel, Adéodat. *Jules Guesde, le socialisme fait homme, 1845–1922*. Paris, A. Quillet, 1937.

Dansette, Adrien. *Le Boulangisme*. Paris, A. Fayard, 1946.

———. *Histoire des Présidents de la République*. Paris, Amiot-Dumont, 1953.

———. *Histoire religieuse de la France sous la troisième République*. Paris, Flammarion, 1951.

Digeon, Claude. *La Crise allemande et la pensée française (1870-1914)*. Paris, Presses Universitaires de France, 1959.

Dolléans, Édouard. *Histoire du mouvement ouvrier*. 3 Vols., Paris, A. Colin, 1936–53. Volume II covers the period 1871 to 1936.

Dommanget, Maurice. *Édouard Vaillant, un grand socialiste, 1840–1915*. Paris, La Table Ronde, 1956.

Engels, Friedrich, and Lafargue, Paul and Laura. *Correspondance (1868–1895)*. 3 Vols., Paris, Éditions Sociales, 1955–59. Volume III, which includes the letters for the years 1891 to 1895, is especially valuable.

Girardet, Raoul. *La Société militaire dans la France contemporaine, 1815-1939.* Paris, Plon, 1953.

Halévy, Daniel. *La République des comités, essai d'histoire contemporaine.* Paris, B. Grasset, 1934.

Joll, James. *The Second International, 1889-1914.* London, Weidenfeld and Nicolson, 1955.

Langer, William. *The Diplomacy of Imperialism, 1890-1902.* 2 Vols., New York, Knopf, 1935.

Lecanuet, le R. P. *L'Église sous la troisième République. Les Signes avant-coureurs de la séparation.* Paris, F. Alcan, 1930.

Levasseur, Émile. *Questions ouvrières et industrielles en France sous la IIIe République.* Paris, A. Rousseau, 1907.

Maitron, Jean. *Histoire du mouvement anarchiste en France (1880-1941).* Paris, Société Universitaire d'éditions et de librairie, 1951.

Miquel, Pierre. *Poincaré.* Paris, A. Fayard, 1961.

Noland, Aaron. *The Founding of the French Socialist Party, 1893-1905.* Cambridge, Mass., Harvard University Press, 1956.

Paléologue, Maurice. *Journal, 1913-14.* Paris, Plon, 1947.

Prélot, Marcel. *L'Évolution politique du socialisme français, 1789-1934.* Paris, Édition Spes, 1939.

Reinach, Joseph. *Histoire de l'Affaire Dreyfus.* 7 Vols., Éditions de la *Revue blanche,* 1901-11

Rémond, René. *La Droite en France de 1815 à nos jours.* Paris, Aubier, 1954.

Rouger, Hubert. *La France socialiste.* Paris, A. Quillet, 1912. This is the third volume of a series, *Encyclopédie socialiste, syndicale, et coöpérative de l'internationale ouvrière,* edited by Compère-Morel.

Scott, John. *Republican Ideas and the Liberal Tradition in France, 1870-1914.* New York, Columbia University Press, 1951.

Seignobos, Charles. *L'Évolution de la troisième République.* Paris, Hachette, 1921. This is Volume VIII of the *Histoire de France contemporaine,* ed. Ernest Lavisse.

Suarez, Georges. *Briand, sa vie, son oeuvre. Avec son journal et de nombreux documents inédites.* 6 Vols., Paris, Plon, 1938-52. Volumes I and II cover the years 1862 to 1914.

Weber, Eugen. *The Nationalist Revival in France, 1905-14.* Berkeley, University of California Press, 1959.

Wormser, Georges. *La République de Clemenceau.* Paris, Presses Universitaires de France, 1961.

Zévaès, Alexandre. *Sur l'Écran politique. Ombres et silhouettes. Notes, mémoirs et souvenirs.* Paris, Dubois et Bauer, 1928.

Index

Jaurès, Jean (*cont.*):
and the elections of 1910, 408; role of in the railroad workers' strike (1910), 411–13; and his trip to South America, 417–18, 421–22, 556; and his relations with Caillaux, 424–25, 442, 443, 445, 454; against militarism and nationalism (1913), 441–44; and the Rochette Affair, 449–51; and the elections of 1914, 451–53; on Socialist tactics, 457, 494, 529–30, 540; and his final efforts for peace (1914), 459–61, 463–72; influence of the earlier French socialist position on, 490; views on protectionism, 511, 513
Jaurès, Jules, 4, 5, 25, 486
Jaurès, Louis (brother of Jean), 5, 575
Jaurès, Louis (son of Jean), 236, 243–44, 281, 283, 375, 421
Jaurès, Louise Bois, 26, 42, 44, 107, 281, 236, 320, 421, 470, 473
Jaurès, Madeleine, 61, 236, 281, 282, 283, 375, 424, 470
Joffre, Joseph, 424, 556
Joindy (Allemandist), 263
Jonnart, Charles, 60, 123
Jouhaux, Léon, 4, 394, 554
Jourdain, Francis, 237
Jourde, Antoine, 221
Jouvenal, Henry de, 320
Judet, Ernest, 67, 216
Julia, Édouard, 339
Julien, Jean, 11, 18, 484
Justo, Juan, 442

Katayama, Sen, 324
Kautsky, Karl, 186, 266, 275, 280, 308, 309, 311, 324, 325, 326, 329, 396, 512, 567–68
Keufer, Auguste, 271, 390, 391, 547
Kiderlen-Waechter, Alfred von, 419, 420, 422, 423, 556
Klotz, Louis-Lucien, 423, 448, 455
Krantz, Camille, 247

Lachelier, Jules, 78
Lacroix, Monsignor de, 446
Lafargue, Paul, 55, 72, 73–74, 112–15, 228, 238, 257, 270, 274, 276, 290, 404–5, 406, 472, 491, 503, 554

Lafferre, Louis, 398
Lagailse (labor leader), 242, 520
Lagardelle, Hubert, 309, 379, 518
Laguerre, Georges, 50
Laisant, Charles, 50
Lamarzelle, Gustave de, 37
Lamouère (schoolteacher in Toulome), 281
Landrieu, Philippe, 455, 469, 470, 472, 518
Landrin, Émile, 280
Lanessan, Jean de, 398
Lansdowne, Marquis of, 343
La Porte, Amédée de, 271, 280
Lasies, Joseph, 306
Lasserre, Joseph, 126–27
Laur, Francis, 50
Laurent (Prefect of the Tarn), 102
Lavergne, Bernard, 110
Lavigerie, Cardinal, 67
Lavigne, Raymond, 71, 256, 257, 265, 291, 448, 521
Lavrov, Peter, 92, 477, 495–96
Lavy, Aimé, 143, 221
Lazare, Bernard, 213, 214, 215, 297
Lebas, Jean-Baptiste, 109
Leblois, Louis, 216, 218, 219
Lebret, Georges, 246
Lefebvre, Georges, 529
Lemaître, Jules, 193, 246, 247, 513
Lenin, Vladimir Ulyanov, 383
Lenoir (Caillaux agent), 556
Leo XIII, Pope, 66, 67, 69–70, 72, 187, 320
Lépine, Louis, 317
Leroy-Beaulieu, Paul, 105, 160, 191, 193–94, 203, 313
Lesseps, Ferdinand de, 56
Lévy-Bruhl, Lucien, 8, 210, 217, 319, 456, 470, 484
Leygues, Georges, 123–24, 144–45, 251, 353, 444
Liabeuf (executed worker), 452, 562
Liebknecht, Karl, 437
Liebknecht, Wilhelm, 199, 259, 263
Lindquist, von (German diplomat), 425
Lloyd George, David, 422–23
Lockroy, Édouard, 220
Loisy, Alfred, 337, 540